Maggie

...From Indiana to Montana
A Pioneer Woman's Story

Myrna Shafer Carpita

Maggie
.... from Indiana to Montana
A Pioneer Woman's Story
by Myrna Shafer Carpita

Copyright © 2016 by Myrna Shafer Carpita

Copyright © All rights reserved. No part of this book may be reproduced in any form by any means wthout the express permission of the author. This includes reprints, excerpts, photocopying, recording or any future means of reproducing text.

If you would like to do any of the above, please seek permission first by contacting the publisher at: Pioneer Publishing, 4605 Argenta Rd., Dillon, Montana 59725, or at http://bookpub16@gmail.com

ISBN Number: 978-0-9976114-0-3

Library of Congress Control Number: 2016959618

Published by
Pioneer Publishing
4605 Argenta Rd.
Dillon, Montana 59725

Printed in the United States

Cover design: Providence Prairie Home Productions, PO Box 687, Dillon MT 59725

Cover Photo: Maggie Ellen Halbert taken in 1892 or 1893 by A. J. Dusseau Portraits, N.E. Cor. Main St. and Broadway, Butte, Montana

Lanes of Yesterday

I'd like to travel down the lanes -- the lanes
    of yesterday --
With long, green hedges winding, and crab
    trees' fragrant spray.
I'd like a stake-and-rider fence with vine-
    hung sagging rail
Where tangled grasses and wild flowers
    conceal a nesting quail;
A meadow lark's sweet aria, a catbird's
    variant call,
Blue space and sunny silence, and time to
    love it all,
I'd want wild roses nodding, each slow,
    meandering way,
Along the dear forgotten lanes -- the lanes of
    yesterday.
I'd like the old-time carriages with teams of
    dappled gray.
Of course, the towns they'd take us to would
    seem quite far away.
But oh, the dip of dallying road to rustic
    bridge and pool,
Where padded water lilies lay in shadows
    long and cool.
Well kept and white the highways gleam,
    where motors speed today,
But in my heart I love the lanes -- the lanes
    of yesterday.

Martha Bell Tumey

From Maggie's Scrap Book

**Dedicated to all of my family -
Past, present and future**

Table of Contents

Chapter   **Page**

	Lanes of Yesterday	
	Preface	
	Acknowledgements	
	About the Author	
I	The Shirleys and The Halberts	1
II	Susan and Enos	9
III	Gold Rush	11
IV	Starting Over	20
V	Prosperity	22
VI	The Civil War	23
VII	Rebuilding	52
VIII	The Move to Kansas	60
IX	Kansas	65
X	Montana's Early Settlers	95
XI	Dewey Flat's New School Teacher	120
XII	Maggie and Horace	157
XIII	Off to New Brunswick	195
XIV	The Donovan Place	196
XV	Lavon	206
XVI	New Home in Oregon	213
XVII	Back to Lavon	216
XVIII	Tough Times	232
XIX	Home and Garden	242
XX	Life Goes On	258
XXI	Shattered	277
XXII	Lay It In God's Hand	284
	Epilog	287
	Appendix A—Maggie's Spelling	290
	Appendix B—Location Maps	292
	Appendix C—Photograph List	293
	Appendix D—Recipes and Poems	294
	Appendix E—Family Trees	295
	Selected References	301
	Index	303

Preface

Maggie received a letter written September 11, 1936 from her niece, Arta, asking, "Aunt Maggie would you do something for me? Get a 5¢ tablet or note book and as you recall incidents—stories—descriptions—expressions—crisis—frictions—conflicts—experiences—all things that makes up a life, will you write them down and then send them to me?" And write she did!

Maggie's writings are as she wrote them, with an occasional word addition for ease of reading. All of Maggie's writings or other information and writings are typed in the regular fonts. Anything I have personally added as additional information or explanation is italicized.

Maggie left her family and future generations a very wonderful legacy in her writings. She saw, she listened, she remembered, and most importantly, she wrote. In these writings you will find spellings that are incorrect or spelled differently than we do today. Some of this is the influence of the older ways and some is the influence of the Midwest speech mannerisms. I have left them as they were written as they reflect the speech patterns that Maggie apparently had.

> A list of Maggie's spelling, her spelling short cuts and the translation of these spellings may be found in Appendix A, page 290.

Maggie did and saw many things in her 79 years of life. She, as a child, and throughout her life, heard family stories, observed life's comings and goings and experienced history in the making the same as we all do. She saw vast changes in our society, experienced the building of the frontier, from Indiana to Kansas and Montana, and lived through the many changes in technology and life. She understood that things would not remain the same and the old ways and times needed to be remembered.

As our lives progress we are busy and the day to day things that happen to us seem mundane. We cast them off like old clothing and do not seem to understand that in the future things will not be done in the same way as now. Future generations may try to understand how the past generations lived, how they survived their struggles and celebrated the joys of life. They may want to know how their ancestor's lives affected who and what they are. Maggie understood the importance of the changes that were going on during her lifetime and thank God she took the time and made the effort to write these memories down on paper for generations to come.

Maggie, I believe, lived life as it was given to her and did the best under the circumstances as she understood and believed them to be. She was a woman ahead of her time in many ways. She had more education than most women of the time and believed in education. Maggie also had an adventurous spirit that led her west and on to a new life with some twists that she never expected. She made many new friends, met and married her husband, and raised her family. She looked to the future, worked very hard in the present, and remembered the past. She took initiative in matters at hand, dealt with life as it came and after her passing we, her descendants, are doing the same. Maggie left us a great legacy in her writings and memories. She also instilled this love of memories and history in her children and thus the grandchildren, great grandchildren and hopefully future generations.

Sample of Maggie (Halbert) Hand's Writing

Acknowledgments

Without the love of memories being passed from Maggie to her children and grandchildren this book would not be possible. There are many people responsible for this book. Her oldest son, John, my grandfather, would tell me many stories of times past, and how things were. Oh, how I wish I had been older and truly understood what he was telling me. He did some writing. I cherish those writings and memories shared.

Then there was Aunt Thelma (Hand) Kalsta. Thelma clipped, saved and wrote. We spent many hours going over family and area history. I stayed at Thelma's many times; we visited, and reviewed. She told many stories, and shared her diaries, photos and memories.

Aunt Susan Hand and I spent many hours together. I also stayed overnight many times, visiting and enjoying so many memories. Susan kept Maggie's writings which she in turn gave to me with the hope they would be shared with others. Susan also shared photos, clippings and scrapbooks. She also shared Maggie's and Nettie's diaries.

Uncle Rock Hand had many stories and allowed me to visit with him, ask questions and review his many personal records and allowed use of his writings and photos from his photo albums.

Many others, my mother, Louise (Hand) Shafer; my Aunt Shirley (Hand) Groff; my cousins, Gunnar Kalsta, and his wife Elaine, Virginia (Hand) Johnson, Roger Hand and cousins in Kansas, all contributed to the wonderful memories. They all allowed me to review and use records, old letters, photos and most of all their memories. My thanks to cousin Michelle Olsen and Phil Padget for their many hours spent on this document, to cousin Janice Hand for her proofing and sharp eye for errors, and again to Janice Hand and Rick Sanders for helping with the final layout ideas. Thanks to cousin Brent Conklin and friend, Alex Morrill, for their computer expertise and cousin Verna Hand for her able assistance. Thanks to Frank Odaz for his computer savvy and assistance and Patty Odaz for her patience and help and to Krista DeGroot for her cover design and literary review. To my husband, Jim, who encouraged, dealt with my absences, and gave up his share of the computer, my love and most sincere thanks. There are many other people who have helped with suggestions and supported in many ways. To all who assisted, in any manner, thank you.

In all of this I found great love of family, past and present, and a wonderful sense of humor that has passed down through the generations. To all who contributed, encouraged and supported me - thank you! - Myrna

About the Author

The great granddaughter of Maggie (Halbert) Hand, the author, was two years old when Maggie passed away. Although she does not remember her great grandmother she connected with Maggie through her writings. Myrna noted that "transcribing Maggie's 800 hand written pages was like having a wonderful visit with her."

Born into a mining and ranching family that lived in the small town of Argenta, Montana, as a child Myrna was raised by her parents with grandparents, aunts, uncles and cousins living nearby. As such there were multitudes of stories about everyday happenings, and stories about the past. She took an early interest in the story telling around her particularly those of her grandfather, John, Maggie's oldest child. He spoke of the past and the people in his life as a young man. She listened and tried to understand all that he told her. With Maggie's writings there came a clarity to John's stories and a deeper understanding of family and area histories.

The author has lived in various parts of the United States, including near where Maggie was born. As a result of living in the Illinois and Indiana area she came to understand the area dialects the upshot of which was being able to recognize the Midwest dialect in Maggie's writings and spellings.

As the clan historian she has been given extensive family records allowing her to conduct genealogy research, interviews and family and area history exploration. She has published family genealogy books on several family lines and has other extensive family and historical records.

After living in various parts of the United States Myrna and her husband Jim returned to Montana in 2002 and now live on part of what was the John and Ida Hand ranch at Argenta.

Maggie

...From Indiana to Montana
A Pioneer Woman's Story

Chapter I

The Shirleys and The Halberts

****

The Shirleys

The Shirleys came to this country in 1700, settled in Virginia, coming from Holland and later went to Pennsylvania. Then from there we hear of them in the Blue River, Ohio area and from there they came to our settlement in Orange County. They bot land and in time passed land on for every child. Three of Henry's children chose to move on to new land in Illinois - Harriet, Garrett and Margaret. Henry bot them land and saw them all comfortably located. Each of his children inherited alike, 3 cows, 11 sheep, a good saddle horse, geese and chickens, a sow and pigs. The girls all had woven their bedding at home and had for years been adding to their supply of coverlids, sheets and pillow slips, towels, every day dress goods, winter flannel and lindsey as they had helped their mother keep up her household supplies.

> Taken from the Genealogy of Valentine Shirley and Related Families by Henry Shirley Rothrock, copyright 1983. He states: Record of Henry Shirley's will shows that "Bequests of land in Orange Co. (T2N-R1W) to Susanna Shirley, 160 acres in Section 9" and "Additional bequests to Susan Shirley - 1 horse, 2 cows, 4 sheep, 1 bed and furniture or their value in money (states Susan received $200.00 in lieu of the livestock), will being probated January 4, 1848, Book 3, p. 140." Also shows that "170 acres were sold to Susan Shirley's husband Enos Halbert" in Orange County a few months following this. [*It should be noted here that Susan Shirley and Enos Halbert were "married January 16, 1848", a month after Henry's death December 22, 1847. - mc*]

Mother [*Catherine*] Shirley, like all good house wives of the time, always had something in the loom to be woven and worked at it between other house hold duties. One time a neighbor was sick and she was called away. She had a coverlid partly done. Susan, my mother, then a young girl, whom had woven only on plain pieces, tho was willing to weave on the 4 harness [*loom*], if only her mother would let her. Now that her mother was gone she would try the coverlid. When her mother came back in a few days the coverlid was done, out, sewed together and hemmed. After that she wove many.

The Shirleys were thrifty people, tended their land well and owned good horses, cattle, sheep, hogs, geese, and chickens. Grandpa Shirley tanned his own leather and made shoes and boots for his household. He also made rope out of hemp. Mother remembered this well. He also made his own furniture from the native timber. He made most all his children their furniture, feather beds fitted with dovetail corners, and gave them enuf of groceries and meats to last till they could get more and shoes. My mother [*Susan Shirley*], I know, appreciated her father's gifts. Mother, too was a good cobbler. On Saturday the children's shoes she repaired for the next week wear.

Shirley Family Tree Ancestor Chart may be found in the Appendix E, page 295.

Grandpa Shirley

Grandpa [*Henry*] Shirley died December 22, 1847. He had lived in this settlement since the first settler came. He had known all there, up and down, tho he lived to himself and family as much as one could in those early days. Buying more land, fencing, clearing, building a good house for his family and good barns for his stock, ever improving.

In early day the settlement minister had such a large circuit to serve that their meetings were held on a Thursday at the chapel. Grandfather Shirley was a very devout Methodist and the minister's wife and family often came there [*to the Shirley home*] while the meeting was in progress. This causing an extra commotion in the household, cooking and preparing for the minister's folks and then the cleaning up and putting the house to rights afterward, often lasted till the next Thursday.

The women, being a driven slave to the religion, they never had any money for themselves as all money had to go in the collection box. Once Grandfather Shirley gave Susan (when a child) 10 cents to throw in the collection box on Thursday. She had wanted a hair ribbon (so long what 10 cents would buy) that she failed to throw the 10 cents in that meeting Thursday. The first time she got a show at town she bot that said ribbon. When Grandfather saw it, he asked where she got the money to buy it with and leaked out that that was the 10 cents she should have thrown in to the collection box the last meeting. Then the Devil was to pay. (I would not have my reader think he was a bad man, far from it. Tho he was over balanced in dealing with the women folks.)

One day in Indiana when Grandmother Shirley came over to our house and everybody was sewing, Annie, [*my older sister,*] set down beside her grandmother, everyone was making ruffles and in those day ruffles had to be scratched to be made fine and uniform, each gathered in its place. Annie gathered up the edge of grandmothers silk apron and began scraping up a ruffle. We all loved to sew and imitate our elders in everything they did.

Almost invariably each farm home was built near a good spring which was plentiful in this country. As time went on grandfather built on to his house and made a very nice home. In the meantime his oldest son, George, married a little girl of 16 years [*Elizabeth Wilson, b. 2-6-1822, married 9-13-1838*] from over near Orangeville and brot her home, so another house for him was built on the other side of the big orchard and near [*the spring*], so they could use water out of the same spring.

When Grandfather Shirley died George and family moved into the big two story house and kept grandma Shirley as long as she lived. [*Grandma Shirley was Catherine Wyman, b. 5-29-1790, N.C., d. 10-8-1872*] George seen to it then that Susan nor any of the others of the family got anything. Think as he was want to say "I see that Enos Halberts don't get any more land to trade off."

Uncle George then kept it all. In the meantime he had three boys, [*actually 4 boys, a Samuel Albert Shirley was b. 4-22-1849 and d. 3-15-1854,* Will or William [*William Crawford Shirley b. 8-31-1839*], Henry [*Henry Wilson Shirley, b. 5-15-1842*], and Lee [*LeRoy O'Blenis Shirley, b. 9-20-1845*] and Lizzie or Elizabeth, [*Maria Lavinia Elizabeth Shirley, b. 5-5-1857, d. 8-1931, married Nathan McPherson 2-13-1879*] much younger than the boys. William the oldest went to the war when it was most over. Then his father gave him some land his mother had inherited from her folks down west of Orangeville. Henry was educated for a doctor after war and became the best in south most Indiana. He married Emma Pitcher and from their union was born three children.

Lee studied for a minister tho never practiced and later changed to a farmer after the old folks bot him our old home place. [*Married a Mary Emily Campbell*].

Lizzie, being the only girl some younger, was looked down on by the boys so she was kept at home to learn all the household arts. This she learned well while the boys were up to Bloomington going to school, spending the life blood of Uncle George and Aunt Betsy like pouring soap suds in to a sink hole.

Uncle George, with a little hired help, farmed and made the money while Aunt Betsy and Lizzie ran the house by gleaning all the by products of the barn yard, making butter, raising the poultry, geese, chickens, sell fryers, hens, geese and feathers. Selling all this to the peddler for the up keep of the house, preparing the yarn and weaving the cloth for wearing material and linen for the household.

Lizzie was a "stay at home", had no brothers or sisters to chum with. Her education was at the Gulf schoolhouse and at Shoals, staying with her brother and wife. Henry would have permitted her to teach but a teaching job was looked down on by her folks and she never taught. Aunt Betsy never took her any place as she, Aunt Betsy, thot it was her place to stay home and look after things so Uncle George took her to fairs and picnics and she, by this influence, was always shy.

After the boys were married and settled a sharper from French Lick heard of this wealthy Shirley girl and proceeded to throw a trap to catch her much to the protest of the father, mother and boys. She listened to this sharper story and in a few weeks he [*Nathan McPherson*] had won her over with his alluring stories of an easier life that he would give her. They were married and he took her to St. Mary's, Kansas on a farm where he was boss. There he set her down in a heavy cooking job for the company, which in time, along with raising a family, all but wore her life away. He was the foreman for Dave Mulrany. When he passed on she went to live with her daughter in P.H. and to be near her sons. She is gone now. One son is in Long Beach, David McPherson. Her daughter inherited the haughty disposition of her father and never was good or kind to her mother. She gave them the best education she could.

The Halberts

Just how this name started or when in Wales would be hard to tell. Tho I have heard the name means battle ax. One Halbert in Virginia, he can trace his stock to a way back in 1000. The first authentic date we have of our particular line was noted as a calvary man in Virginia in the Continental Army in 1774. This William Halbert was our ancestor and we can trace down his linage

Halbert Family Tree Ancestor Chart may be found in Appendix E, page 296

to my father, Enos Halbert. Enos was born in Indiana, 1825, Orange County, grew to manhood in what was a wilderness. Later his father moved to Illinois, then back to Indiana. Like many of that day the country was new and it was hard to decide which state was the best.

William Halbert was a native of Virginia. Excerpts from an **Anderson, (S.C.) Independent** newspaper article, **"William Halbert: An Unsung Legend," by Rita Horton McDavid, dated April 10, 1971** relates, "William's life had not been an easy life. His own hands had cleared wilderness acres, pushed a plow and shot wild game for food. Fear had been a constant companion too, since the French had armed the Indians, when he was a boy of ten, and incited them to attack frontier settlers.

His Mother's people had been long in the Old Dominion tradition [which] says she was seventh in descent from Pochantas; his Grandfather Halbert had immigrated thence from Wales.

William Halbert was a lieutenant in "Light-horse Harry" Lee's famous Virginia Legion [during the Revolutionary War]. In 1781 he was thirty-six, almost middle-aged for a man of that day.

After the war ended, and several years after the peace Halbert, and many other veterans, received a grant of South Carolina land, in lieu of long overdue payment for his military service to the State.

When Anderson County, [South Carolina] was founded William Halbert had been dead ten years. Though he was the father of thirteen children, and many of his descendants still live in the county, the memory of his accomplishments had already begun to fade. The new county was named for his friend and associate judge on the first court in Pendleton District, Colonel Robert Anderson. Nor has anything in Anderson County ever been named for him. Except among his posterity he is forgotten.

This is strange, for he had held office in Abbeville County before he and Anderson and Gen. Andrew Pickens were commissioned by the legislature to organize "Washington District of Pendleton County". (Washington was one of several circuit court districts which existed for only a few years.) And his life reads like a historical novel.

Halbert's home was near the spot where the Counties of Anderson, Greenville and Abbeville came together. He is buried there, the grave marked as that of a Revolutionary soldier."

****

Copy of the Will of
William Halbert

In the name of God Amen. I William Halbert of Pendleton District being of perfect mind and memory, thanks to God Almighty, calling to mind the mortality of my body knowing that it is appointed for all men once to die, do make and ordain this my last will and testament, that is to say -

I recommend my soul into the hands of Almighty God that gave it, my body I recommend to the earth to be buried in a decent manner at the discretion of my executors nothing doubting but at the general resurrection I shall receive the same by the mighty power of God, and as touching such worldly estate wherewith it has pleased God to bless me with, I demise and dispose of the same in the following manner;

First my lawful debts to be paid.

I also lend unto my beloved wife Elizabeth Halbert, two hundred acres of land including the plantation whereon I now live, also all my household furniture with all my stock of old negroes and other stock of all kinds during her natural life or widowhood, provided she should marry then she to have a childs part, after all my children is toted off with what I allow them to have at their setting out or leaving me. My will and desire is that all my children at their coming of age or marrying shall have as follows:

I do give my son Joel Halbert, the land I bought from Ralph Owens and Llija Owens, that he has now in possession and two negroes, vis Sal and Mose, with other necessaries he has in possession.

I do give my son John Halbert two negroes, viz Gene and Hilly, and other goods he has now in possession.

I do give my son Enos Halbert what land he has in possession including the land I bought from Henry Burdin, one negro, viz Rhode with the other properties.

I do give my son Arthur's children, two hundred acres of land, the tract whereon he died, and fifty of a tract we call Hireth to be divided between his children, viz; Henry Halbert, John Halbert, and Arthur when they come of age.

I do give my son James Halbert, two hundred acres of land joining that where Arthur died and running cross all the tracts, with one young negro viz; Peter and all the other I gave or put in his possession.

I do give my son William Halbert, two hundred and 32 acres of land including the mill on Big Creek and a tract of ninety acres called Datenal, one young negro, horse, briddle and saddle, bed with stock of different kinds to begin.

I do give my son Joshua Halbert, two hundred acres of land joining James cross all tracts and one young negro also thirty acres and the mill shoal on Saluda I purchased from William Acker and at his mother's death to have the plantation she lives on with horse and saddle and bed and furniture and stock of different kinds.

I do give my daughter Martha Grisham two young negroes, with what other property I gave her that she has in possession.

I do give my daughter Susanna Acker two young negroes with what other property I gave in her possession.

I do give to my daughter Frankah Garrison two young negroes with what other property I gave in her possession.

I do give my daughter Elizabeth Berry two young negroes with what other property I gave in her possession.

I do give my daughter Mary Halbert two young negroes, horse, saddle, bed and furniture with stock of different kinds to housekeep with.

I do give my daughter Lucinda Halbert two young negroes, horse, saddle, bed furniture and stock of different kinds, I don't mean more but equal to what the rest of you had.

I do desire that my beloved wife Elizabeth Halbert shall enjoy all my personal estate only what my children take as they become of age provided she does not destroy or deminish it during her natural life or widowhood after her death what is remaining of the estate to be divied among the children, Arthur's children to have a share.

I likewise constitute, ordain and appoint Joel Halbert, John Halbert, Enos Halbert, and John Grisham executors to this my last will and testament, wills, legacies, bequeath and execution by me in any wise before named and bequeathe by rectify confirm this to be my last will and testament in the witness whereof I have herunto set my hand this thirtieth day of July in the year of our Lord, and Savior Jesus Christ one thousand eight hundred and six.

William Halbert
In the presence of William Harper, James Brown, David Brown

The will was proven 1809.

- **From the Susan Hand Collection.**

****

William Halbert's large family divided at his death, some going south of the Mason Dixon Line and our faction of his family, Joel, went north in to Southern Indiana. This was in early times before the Indians were driven out of Indiana. They settled and bot the land where the famous mineral springs, French Lick and West Baden now stand.

French Lick and West Baden was on a creek. These Mineral Springs came out of pools and ran down in to the creek. When Emma was a child she visited the grave yard with our mother and remembers well our mother noting the old dates on the head stones which were leaning and old. This was the grave yard that our forefathers were buried in. Later it was said they had moved it and built on the sight of it the famous Mineral Hotel and grounds. Some French settlers had preceded and owing to the number of springs that oozed out of the earth in places and the deer coming here to lick in the springs it was named French Lick Springs, tho the early day settlers never gave it a thot as to its curative properties.

Taken from the Genealogy of Valentine Shirley and Related Families by Henry Shirley Rothrock, copyright 1983. He states: Joel Halbert [b. 6-13-1769, d. 6-24-1848, buried St. Marys Cemetery, Hancock County, Illinois] and Mary Lindley (or Lindsey) [daughter of John Lindley and Sarah Pyle, b. 9-27-1779, d. 7-22-1839, buried Spring Hill Cemetery, Martins County, Indiana] were married [January 10, 1789 according to Henry Shirley Rothrock or April 20, 1790 according to **Halbert-Holbert History** by Karen R. Moore] in South Carolina."

Find a Grave site states that "Joel Halbert served in the War of 1812 under Gen. Andrew Jackson".

There Joel, along with other new settlers Charles, Bolton, Tolviers, in the wilderness, bot land at $1.50 per acre from the government and prepared to make their homes.

The Genealogy of Valentine Shirley and Related Families by Henry Shirley Rothrock, copyright 1983, states that, "About 1815 Joel and family came to Indiana, entering land in Orange County June 1815, 160 acres, adjacent to the lands entered by Valentine, Henry and Jacob Shirley. Joel was an associate Circuit Judge in 1816. **The History of Martin County, Vol. II by H.G. Holt (1966)** states that Joel Halbert of South Carolina became one of the largest individual land owners in the pre-county period (e.g. before 1820). On May 27, 1815 he entered 582 acres, land called Halbert's Bluff that is the site of the present [*Martin*] county seat, Shoals. Halbert Township was named for him. Later he entered 160 acres east and 563 acres up White River. Joel was a founder of Memphis (now Shoals) and he offered 42 1/2 acres in 1844 for county buildings. In 1820 Joel was proposed for sheriff. He was a school commissioner in 1828. He was recognized as an expert in shodding oxen. As JP he performed marriages in 1830-1831." [*Joel and Mary had twelve children, Seth being the third child. - mc*]

Seth, our lineal heir, grew up here. When the first settler came they built a fort for protection, keeping sentinels and scouts on watch day and night. When in danger the women and children and the sick were hurriedly rushed to the fort for protection and kept there till they were safe to go home and there pick up the threads of life again.

Money was not such an essential thing those day for with the woods full of game one could live for a few weeks. One could go horse back in a few days to other settlements, get a few pounds of corn meal and live till land could be cleared and raise some corn.

The Halberts were easy going people. They lived good in an easy going way. The boys going to Illinois and back. Grandpa Seth always had a horse or two to sell at a good price. When home the boys and father hunted, had some revenue from their furs, arise a good garden, a few acres of corn and by this time farmers were raising some wheat which had to be flailed out but it always brot a good price. There were grist mills that ground wheat and one could afford to have white bread for Sunday breakfast and flour for pie crusts. Newer and better kinds of apples and other fruit had been introduced and were growing and bearing.

Grandpa Seth had a good sympathetic heart. The poorer folks were often helped whether they deserved it or not. Many poor bashful kids of poor families often were sent over for things. They'ed get no farther than the rail fence. There they'ed set on the top rail. Someone of Grandfather's household would have to go out and ask the child what he had been sent for. Then he'd look away in the opposite direction and bashfully tell the mission for which he was sent. Then Grandfather would hunt the butcher knife, go to the smoke house, cut off a big slab of bacon, go out and hang the slab on the saddle horn and Grandfather would tell him he better go on home. Then he'd mount the poor old crow bate of a horse and slowly disappear down and around the trail in the direction of home.

Grandmother [*Frances (Charles) Halbert*] was a good conscientious helpful wife. She had her loom always threaded and a man's suit was often made from the loom. Then her bed and bedding showed her effort in keeping up her house.

> **Mush Scrapple**
> Boil three or four pounds of fresh pork (quite fat) until very tender; then take out the meat and season the water in which it was boiled, and thicken with yellow cornmeal as thick as for hasty pudding, and let it cook a long time to thoroughly cook the meal. Chop the meat tolerably fine, season well, and add it to the mush. When it is cooked, put in a square bread tin to cool. When cold cut in slices and fry until brown.
> **"TESTED RECIPES",**
> **By The Ladies' Aid Society Of The First Baptist Church, Dillon, Montana. Third Edition, Tribune Publishing Company, Dillon, Montana 1913.**

The Odd Fellows and Masons had a lodge room over Hoblets store. Enos (our father) joined both lodges as soon as he was old enuf and was a member in good standing till his death in 1911. Grandfather Seth's family grew up, in turn, and were married. Uncle Joel married Hattie Hadden from Green County and settled there. Ezra and John also married girls in Green County, their wives maiden names were a Jolly and Florance. Enos married Susan Shirley, daughter of Henry Shirley a farmer that had acquired land in our vicinity and by diligently working and saving he and his wife were quite well off. Enos and Susan settled on 80 acres of land her father had given to her and then by the other gifts from her father.

Sarah, the only daughter of Grandfather Seth, married a fellow by the name of Crosgrove and lived in Orleans. Silas at this time was a young lad at home.

When Grandfather Seth's family had grown to man hood and all were married the world yet had not progressed with long bound. Much of the old early days ways of living held sway tho by this time the country was pretty well settled up. There being a family on most every 160 acres, tho some only had 80 acres. Many a family were there to make a home and others were too indolent to make a living and only barely existed.

Those in our immediate settlement were Nathanial Wilson or Uncle Nate, he lived about two miles away. Uncle Jimmie Street, Bruners, Mathers, Aunt Mary Wilson. This old lady, Mary Wilson, came galloping a past our school house at the age of 85 much to the children's delight. She owned fine horses. These foregoing three were distant relations of ours, the Halberts. The Pitcher, Stackhouses, Bonds, Higging and Bolton, J. Cowards, Scott, Tolivers, Huddleson, Noblit and Biuskirk [*were neighbors*]. These last two ran stores at Orangeville. Bryant Coward taught school at the Gulf school house - a place 15 acres in the land that had sunk down taking all trees as they stood. There they would not near reach the level of the surrounding country. There were several of these places clost Emma knew of. Henry Shirley, our Grandfather owned the place joining our place when he gave the land to mother as her share.

When anyone went on a long trek they often parched the corn and ate it like the Indians did before the advent of the stone wheel to grind it on. Corn, being an Indian grain that grew well on new cleared land, was tended jealously. With it and the wild game of deer, possum, coons, squirrels and wild turkey and along with the wild fruits of the region the new settlers diet was complete.

Then later when stone grinding wheels were brot in and harnessed to the water power of that country, corn was ground and more palatable foods could be made. Meal made into mush with the addition of milk made a dish fit for a king. Corn bread, corn dodger, fried mush or mush scrapple, all were early day diets we ate. Most every man in those day were a good hunter, trappers, and traders and a ready market was found on the Ohio River traffic boats going up and down to New Orleans and Pittsburgh in the form of exchange or barter. When the land was sufficiently cleared to raise more corn, the corn too could be sold to trader boats on the river. Then the farmers could have a more varied diet of foods such as molasses, coffee and clothing. The ladies now and then got a new calico for summer and their linsies were laid aside for winter. Then too once in a life time a wife could have a silk dress.

With the coming of the saw mills there was better frame buildings built at all these small towns and thru the country. The school house and church at Wesley Chapel Corner were now of frame buildings.

Seth, Joel's son, spent his early life here and having explored the region far and near bot 160 acres land 7 miles north west of Paoli. Here he built a two room log house, cleared some land and set up his home. He married Francis Charles, raised a large family of Joel, Enos, Azor, Silas, Sarah and another boy, William.

In time the country settled up and each little farmer had acquired saddle horse, teams, a few farm implements, cows, sheep, and hogs from which much of their meat came. Roads yet were very poor, mere trails, and most of their going to towns and grist mills was done on horseback. They took their corn to be ground at the mills horseback, two sacks of corn, one in front and one behind. They would go early and try to get their grist in first, in order to get theirs out early and on their way home. Millers tried to accommodate each patron that came, even if he had to stay up late, as often the families was waiting anxiously for the meal to feed the hungry ones at home. Women often went to see their distant neighbors horse back, taking the smallest child up behind the saddle or on her lap. Most of the near places people walked such as church or school. Orangeville, Orange County was our folks post office after the settlement was safe from Indians and all had settled down to quiet frontier life.

Down thru the Halbert race they were noted horse lovers and always bred the best Morgan and general purpose horses. It was the horse, the oxen, and mule that helped his master tear open the virgin soil all the way till the advent of the gas engine. Horses always demanded a good price from the consul, horse trader or at Evansville where a horse or more could be sold for ready money.

> **Corn Bread**
>
> 2 cups corn meal
> 2 cups sweet milk
> 2 tablespoons flour
> 2 heaping tablespoons sugar
> 2 tablespoons lard
> 2 eggs
> 2 heaping teaspoons baking powder
> 1 large teaspoon salt
>   Have pan heated and bake in hot oven 25 minutes.
>
> **"TESTED RECIPES",**
> **By The Ladies' Aid Society Of**
> **The First Baptist Church,**
> **Dillon, Montana. Third Edition,**
> **Tribune Publishing Company,**
> **Dillon, Montana 1913.**

This southern part of Indiana was very slow to progress. With the food that mother nature provided there was little more to add. There were no rail roads clost and only artery of commerce was the Ohio River 25 miles away. The center was Evansville, Indiana. The schools, if any, were private schools or subscription. The teacher boarding around week at a time with each patron as his turn came. Lodges were few if any at first. Churches or their religion was brot with them and continued here. Every one was intensely religious in his faith and a log meeting house was the first community center set up in any new settlement.

The land was hilly soil. In places clay soil in good bottom land was used for corn land tho some times over flows ruined all crops. The rough hilly parts was covered with heavy timber, hickory, beach, walnut, black and white, oak, sugar maples and poplars of immense size. Then with brushy growth, wild plums, hazel brush, dog wood, persimmons, papas, sassafras. Vines were wild blackberries, currants, raspberries, fox grape, most as good as our tame grapes and other. In the fall young and old would go forth to gather these wild fruits and nuts for the winter use. Crops were mostly corn. Both man and beast could live well on that and the corn fodder made a good roughage for the stock. There was no hay till after land was cleared and then blue grass seemed to be a native. Clover, timothy, red top and white clover, orchard grass had to be sowed for hay. There was only one market, the boot leg still, for corn and in small quantities. Then if one neighbor had plenty and another hadden enuft they were helped thru the winter, tho enuf was always kept for seed and saddle mare.

Chickens were few those days on account of the near timber harboring hawk that prayed on the bunch. Small animals preyed on them such as mink, weasels, coons.

Dogs, hunting dogs, were a needcessity, for without a dog to tree the coons and possums the meat would be scarce. They were an asset to any family and earned their keep. The guns were mostly, in early day, flint lock rifles. Most every man was a good marksman and made their single shot count always bringing down his game or Indian.

Our grandfather Seth was an extra good shot with his flint lock gun. The charge had to be made with gun powder and shot (which they molded at home) and cotton. The flint when properly set off by a spark ignited the small amount of powder in the small pan, set off the charge in the gun thru a small tube leading to that in the gun. This kind of shooting or hunting I call a fine art.

There were very few rodents till after trade with ships, then they came in. Snakes - the most dreaded ones, were the big timber rattler, native to the land, often 10 feet long. The copperhead, a rattler, tho had no rattles, but was a dreaded poison. They often staid around old buildings and brush heaps, were sly and vicious if molested. Water moccasin a poison snake. Then the harmless kind were black snakes and blue racers often 10 to 12 feet, water snakes, green snakes, often found in elder blossoms inhabited the trees and leaves and grass.

Wild life - Deer was quite common and would have been more plentiful had it not been for a vicious panther that inhabited these parts and kept the deer thinned out. They preyed on deer by hiding, laying flat on a tree limb till its pray came along in easy distance to jump on and in the melee cut its throat bringing it to the ground. Panther was feared and hunted by man also as it would attack a man, woman or child. Everyone feared the panther. Life in this early day was no coward or weakling's job. It was an eye for an eye and a tooth for a tooth.

Women often staid alone or with relatives for weeks or months while the husband was away to other settlement on some needed errand. If Indian trouble, all were brot in to the forts. This was their part in early day life and they played their part well.

Gardens - The seed and plants of the early garden were brot from their former homes by some of the families that particularly had a liking to plant life and from the standpoint of various foods to help supply the larder. The protector of seed and plants was generally the wife and mother of the new travelling settler. The flowers were brot to beautify the place and often some were used for teas and medicines. Often choice seeds of peach or plum even apples were hoarded and brot to the new country. As I read about "Johnnie Appleseed" I can vision he was of this period when one would welcome most any seed that would bring in a new variety. It was from the early day wild fruits and some new that our fore mothers gathered and dried our winter fruits in those days. Peaches and plums, apples cut in half, spread on trays, made from slats or edging from the mill made a handy receptacle to dry fruit on. Grapes were dried whole. Persimmons, after frosted, dried on the tree and were welcomed by children.

The country was low, with many swamps, bogs and rivers and with the dense timber growth, it created a hard country, as far as health was concerned. Most every one or some one in each family was subject to chill fever often called malaria. Sometimes the whole family was stricken with it. People so affected would go about their work and on the third day be down in bed with chill and fever for a month in the fall.

The medicines of early days in Southern Indiana was mostly from the herbs that grew wild there. Wild cherry bark for cough and wild hops for run down condition. Hops were boiled down and drank the juice. Sassafras was a spring tonic. Maple sap was used for sweetening. About the only medicine bot in those days was quinine given for chills and fever. Chills and fevers weakened the patient so he often fell prey to some other kind of sickness.

The tobacco the men used was tended carefully by an old man of the family. When ready, cut and dried in the shade to the proper degree, it was then twisted and laid away for use. I preferred sweeter - some good New Orleans molasses were brot home, the tobacco packed in proper size box and molasses added among the layers, some salt, then a board put on and weights till it was properly cured. This was used for chewing. The twist could either be used for the old corn cob pipe or chewing.

Land Clearing & Fencing

This land was heavily timbered when first settler came to this part of Southern Indiana with huge poplar, large beach, white and black walnut, sugar maple that they tapped each March for its sap to make their sugar syrup from, hickory trees and every conceivable undergrowth that would grow in that southern damp Indiana climate. Man in time sawed, chopped and lumbered for what they called civilization. Then man cleared to raise fields of grain and corn till he so upset this pleasing plan of nature, as it were the equilibrium. Then low springs dried up and rivers, slough and pool and to their surprise man had drouth such as never happened before since God set his hand to these fair parts of Southern Indiana.

A Mr. Sam Hix was the miller for Orangeville community where he settled on the river there and served the community far and wide for years. He gave an honest tole to everyone. When children were sent he seen to their need at

Missouri Folding Table Loom
Taken from an advertisement
From the Susan Hand Collection

once, then carefully tied on their sacks of meal and sent them home early. Grist mill were a needcessity and proceeded saw mills, tho they came in clost second. Neither one were an absolute needcesity as the first settler had neither. Their corn was ground between flat stones of suitable size. After grinding or parching they could cook as they desired and with the addition of fats from their wild game they had an appetizing dish. The houses were made of logs. Where nails were needed they used wooden pins. The saplings were split for door jams and smaller ones were split and nailed together on cleats or split poles and a door was made. The windows were curtained with most any thing handy when needed tho some used greased paper if it could be obtained.

It was in these early day that the arts and crafts were needed and used. About the only way for each family to do was make such articles as was needed. Furniture and wearing material, shoes and caps. The finest, best woods grew there in the forest. A step higher than the old slab stool was hickory. With chair, the frame work was made of hickory poles after the bark had been taken off in long withes as possible about 3/4 inch wide. Then withes were taken back and forth over the seat frame with sufficient withes were put on that way. They wove the cross withes in back and forth over the other till the seat was wove in which made a very desirable chair for that day. Beds too were made at home but rope was laced in each way for springs. But they never made a very good bed as they often had to be relaced if they sagged. Tables were made. Then with a table and chairs and beds, the furniture was complete.

Many women of these early days possessed looms. If they did not most any handy man could make one. On these most all the weaving material for the family was made, bedding, linen sheets, towels, table clothes woven in patterns, coverlids or counterpanes many fine 4 harness kinds and even more harness kind, blankets, fine quilts and quiltings for their beds, lindsey for dresses.

Father, [*Enos Halbert*] when a young man went up in to Iowa and took up a homestead where Dubuque now stands. The Indians were so bothersome causing all kinds of depredations that he soon gave it up and went back to his home in Southern Indiana.

Chapter II

Susan and Enos

****

Enos [*Halbert*] was 23 and Susan [*Shirley*] was 20 when they married, tho knew each other for some time. Enos said to her father, "I want that black eyed, curly haired daughter of yours." They had been bashful beaus up till that time. When married they went to housekeeping on a new piece of land her father had given them. The land adjoined the old Halbert homestead in the riverbed in Orange County, the post office being Orangeville. He built a good sized log cabin. With the inheritance her father and mother gave her they were able to go to housekeeping. A cow, sheep, pig, chickens, all their household goods, feather beds, home made linen and cover lids she had previously prepared with her mothers help. Also supplying the yarn and chain to weave them with, towels and sheets were woven. When they got settled she got a loom. With the sheep's wool she bot the cotton warp. Then shirts, dress goods were all made at home for she was well trained in the art of keeping up demands of the house by the loom. When seventeen she wove her first cover lid, the wool spun and died with native barks from the dense forest that covered southern Indiana. The flax she grew. It was twilled then hackled into shape for the spinning wheel. The first was woven into table linen. Then the balance was made into sheets and towels and thread. After the linen was woven it was wet [*and*] laid on the grass to bleach. This process had to be repeated often to whiten, tho often the coarser product was used in the brown state. They were still keeping up the linen for the house when I first could remember and not till we moved to Kansas did our house have cotton sheets. It is true, there was finer cloth on the market all the time but farmers were thrifty and made most of their every day wear.

The Enos and Susan (Shirley) Halbert Descendent Chart may be found in Appendix E, page 297.

For the Indiana Map and general locations, see Appendix B, page 291.

Shortly after Enos married mother, he felt so elated over mother's property that he began doing business with mother's possessions. At that time women were only chattel. Men could trade their property and they dare not say a word. So the first thing he did was to sell the best 80 acres of her land for a stallion that proved to be worthless - putting in the whole summer neglecting the farm, standing this stallion at various stations.

At another time when Susan had $50.00 in cash come in, he took it out of her hand and paid off a note he had given to a man - paid the note! Then on trips when he would come home from standing his stallion he would lay around, play sick so she would have to make an extra effort in getting him extra good foods such as chicken, etc., all the delicacies of the day. If there had been any way, she would have left and gone back to the hard working Shirleys but alas she labored on trying to please.

The relatives and good people at large condemned him bitterly for this careless way of handling her property and I think these hard feelings were always held against him as long as he lived in Indiana and kept her from inheriting any more of Grandfather Shirley's estate when he died as his boys knew their fathers hard knocks and his sterling worth and was determined that Enos Halbert should get no more of the Shirley money to speculate on.

The rift between the Shirley family and Halberts was never healed. Those days when married there were no separations. The man could be as mean as he please and she meekly tried to please and went about carding, spinning, weaving, taking care of the flock in and out doors. With mother diligently tending her flock of sheep, hogs, geese, and chickens and the land they progressed beyond expectation of the relatives.

In a few years Enos and Susan had accumulated a nice little home with cows, sheep and horse enuf to have a nice living. Those days the main room was the kitchen and work house. Looms and wheel were in this room. Made the work handy. Often times the bed was in this room, tho I think in ma's house they had a bedroom upstairs. Living was much more simpler then, tho some what unhandier as the water had to be brot by buckets from a spring. Washing also was done at the spring.

In the summer there was all kinds of vegetables and fruit along with the ever staple diet of corn meal. In the winter corn meal was used in many way. Corn bread twice daily, corn mush at night. Tho in the winter lye hominy was made. A good wholesome dish. Corn meal mush and milk constituted the evening meal. With simple living the house work was lighter. Lived a quite peaceful life. At the end of the week preparation was made to go to church on Sunday,

> **Lye Hominy**
>
> Two quarts of nice white corn brought to the boil, then add one large tablespoon of lye. Cook about fifteen minutes or until corn is all slick, then turn in sink and wash through many waters, then return to stove and when it boils again wash it, continue this way four or five times or until water is clean when boiled. Cook twelve hours, keep covered with water, salt (in eight or ten hours) to taste. Then remove from fire and keep out of doors. This will keep good for a week or more. Serve just as needed by heating in butter or if one has fresh pork warm it where the meat was fried in part of the greese. -Mrs. R. R. Rathborn
> **From "TESTED RECIPES",**
> **By The Ladies' Aid Society Of The First Baptist Church,**
> **Dillon, Montana. Third Edition,**
> **Tribune Publishing Company,**
> **Dillon, Montana 1913.**

where after church they met their neighbors and friends. Often a neighbor or the minister was invited home for dinner which could not be at 12 o'clock, perhaps 1 or 2 o'clock. Then after supper they would go again to church in the evening.

Uncle George, Ma's brother, lived on a farm clost by. They were thrifty people. Uncle and Aunt worked very hard - early till late. Lizzie was grown when I first remember. She was at home and helped her mother till about the time we moved away. Bruners lived on the other side of the school house and church. They raised a big family and their home hummed with the wheels and looms.

Joel Halbert was a cousin. He and wife lived below the school house on a steep hillside. They raised no family but took a boy to raise. She was the tidiest, thrifty woman we ever knew. When a dish or crock was broken it was taken out to a bench in the back yard and mended amediately with white lead. After months of drying in the sun it was as good as new. I have a vivid picture of their home on the side hill.

One rainy day Ma took me up on the horse behind her and she went thru the woods to Joels. I shall never forget the dogwood in bloom in the forest as we went slowly along on the horse. Grandpa Seth Halbert lived clost to our old place, just over the little spring creek. Clost enuf for our children and uncles to be together every day.

Chapter III

Gold Rush

****

Gold was found at Fort Sutter, California in 1848 but it was some time before the fabulous news reached the state of Indiana. It took two years before the settlers all conceived the idea that, too, they might go. So the story poured in mostly by word of mouth from those whom had returned from California. Some were too well satisfied in this quiet peaceful valley to heed the news.

Not so with my father and his two brothers. They must go. Go they must, never stopping to concider what might happen in rushes. There are always too many at the place for all to get gold.

Enos & Susan's first child, Mary Frances Catherine Halbert, born March 25, 1849.

Then men had to have strong wagons made, ox yokes and two wagons, 4 oxen on each wagon and supplies. Money that Grandpa Seth had saved by selling horses, cows, hogs and laid it by, not especially for this trip but to have in case of emergencies. These boys of his knew if they could get him to go they would have good backing and a good outfit to go with.

They finally persuaded Grandfather Seth that he should go too. Joel, Azor, John and Enos, all were able bodied men and they knew they would come back rich, yes rich beyond all calculations of that time. It would be better than staying home and eking out an existence by selling a horse or cow or a few bushels of corn or wheat. They would come back rich. They had heard that gold was still there in abundance. So these stories were told over and over thru Orange County, Green County and so other cousins and neighbors wanted to go. Finally enough joined in, 38 or 40, enuf to make a good big caravan. In those early days one or two wagons never could travel alone on the account of wild, murderous Indians roving the plains. There were no women in this train. All the daughter-in-laws were to go and stay with grandmother Halbert in her home. Uncle Silas [*b. July 31, 1835*] was the only boy or man left and he was supposed to do the field work and helping on the general farm.

So father sold off all the extra animals Susan had. Grandfather and his two other sons did likewise, took horses, wagons and a pair of oxen each. In the spring of '50 they bid farewell to their loved ones and bent their way to the far away west, gold in California. They would come back rich they thot. Mother never thot that, she knew what precious animals they took was gone and she was left poorer. Then when they first began there was nothing to do but tend the stock she had left, plow and sew, raise all the crops she could and raise her baby. Grandma Halbert and Joel's wife were left alone just over the spring creek too. They was more helpless than she. Grandma was too old to work hard and Joel's wife never cared for work. When they worked in the field, Hetty, Joel's wife would hoe a few hills of corn and then lean on her hoe and talk while mother worked away the summer.

The Halberts thot they preferred the ox teams to either mules or horses as the oxen could eat along the way and they would not have to haul their feed, besides their slow gate would take them over the long distances in the end. They were good loggers and never worried or fretted. They took a saddle horse, one to round up the herd on in the mornings. Others in the train took mules and some took horses. After a month out and had left settlements, they would then have to depend on buying their grain at way stations and then they would have to pay high prices for it. Being early in the spring and grass those days was good and luscious everywhere and for a time the stock did well. Each wagon was loaded with provisions such as flour, corn meal, corn, dried fruit, apples and peaches, bacon, salt side meat and hams. This meat was in lard. Salt and other needcessities were packed along with their out door cooking tools, then their clothes and bedding. These wagons, if not sufficiently loaded at first, would have to finish loading at St. Joe as that was the farthest outpost. Here they could get supplies reasonably priced so there they did their final loading.

Before leaving a wagon manager was chosen and every man was expected to obey orders from him. He was a man that had gone over this route before and knew every campsight, creek, river and mountain range. He knew the most likely place the train might be attacked by Indians. When stops were made in the evening cattle and horses and mules were turned out to graze. A herder was sent to watch over them lest some should stray away or be stampeded by Indians. Then at night wagons were formed into a round corral by putting the wagon tongue under the hind end of another wagon and slightly forward continuing all in to a ring. An opening was left at one end. Then cattle, horses and mules were driven in this corral. The wagons then shoved together and the gate was closed. Then one man was left on guard and all went to bed early so as to be up early. Each family cooked his own food and all were expected to be ready at a given hour and all go together. Plans had been laid to meet another train from Albany, Indiana and at Vincennes, making a train of 80 to 100 wagons thereby insuring better protection from the Indians when they reached the plains.

The women took up the load of living and helped make the living day by day. Mother had one child, Mary of about two years. She was no longer a baby and mother was free to work, yes work in the house and out, where ever there was anything to do.

Time dragged on with the ceaseless days of drudgery. From her stock she had left she had a steady increase. The hens gave eggs to sell, then there was the wool she sheared from the sheep's back, for sale. From her corn she got her meal. The apple trees, they set out at first of their farm life, began to bear. She dried apples for sale. Other kinds of small fruit was plentiful in the hills.

Joel's wife had two small children then and enjoyed being unable to work besides had nothing to care for. Grandmother was not able to do much tho she spun. The sheep had to be sheared, cloth made, bedding and wool socks and mitts made, the loom kept busy. The crops had to go in and be tended at the proper time, most all of this had to be done by women as Uncle Silas could not be depended on. The regular chores were done morning and night as well as the house work for six had to be carried on. Mother soon began to feel the burden and knew when she was imposed upon but she dared not leave as all of her stock had been brot here. She had to see to it or loose all.

The Halberts now were going west spending day by day what they had accumulated years before. The women at home, the best they could do would only make a bare living.

The Shirleys were at home working like beavers saving everything they made. Raising corn, wheat, hogs, cattle, and horses. If nothing more to do, they would clear a few acres of land to be put in next year. Rainy days were utilized by making shoes, harness and furniture. Wheat had to be flailed out but sold for good money, corn was used to fatten cattle and hogs. The women kept busy preparing wool for making cloth and bedding. They always had a big apple and peach orchard, dried fruits, small fruits and a good vegetable garden. Beans and peas were the staple food so a large patch of them had to be raised, harvested and hulled for the coming winter for bean soup, beans boiled or baked was the standby. Then cabbage would be eaten in the summer and late fall then holed away in the ground. Most any day one could dig in and get out a head thru the winter. And kraut could be kept and used on thru the winter. Good solid winter apples too could be kept in a hole like the cabbage. Everything that could be kept was saved for the hard, lonely winter ahead. Everyone worked and lived well and saved their money.

Everything went well. The train was crossed laboriously and tediously on a ferry boat at Vincennes and it was the second day before the train were ready to go. The trip on to the Mississippi River thru Illinois was uneventful. There was nothing to worry about and they made fairly good time owing to the spring rains and mud. At St. Louis the train all had to be taken over on a ferry, each man drove his team on to the ferry. When he was placed he tied up his oxen, horses or mules to the ferry railing so all would be quiet going over.

One of father's oxen, near the railing, became unruly and jumped overboard, breaking its neck. They towed it over along side the ferry and cut its throat then hunted a butcher that would buy the meat. After this was over father then had to find another ox for sale, put it in along side the other and the train moved on thru Missouri, crossing the Missouri River at St. Joe, Missouri. At St. Joe every wagon that was not loaded with enuf supplies for the trip was now loaded to the utmost as this was the last town that they could get supplies at a reasonable price, it being out on the edge of civilization. The next town was Atchison, Kansas. This lap of the road was good. When they arrived there they past on.

Every eve if there was any repair work, it was done then. The train was new and they had an abundance of guns and powder. Shot was made at nights or at long stops. Everything that was needed they had and they passed on up the Blue River in Nebraska, ever hoping to spy a buffalo so they could display their skill in hunting. In these trains every able bodied man was expected to take his place along side his team and walk. They must be alert to every thing in case of a surprise or ambush attack. The wagon boss expected this of every man when on the trek. There were to be no laggard. Wagons must not fall behind. In case of this he often road a horse so as to move freely from one end of the train giving orders, lest someone should fall out and lag behind. His job was unceasing and ever watchful as to the good of the train. Each man had his gun or guns, his ammunition so as to be handy at any minute. At St. Joe each man had carefully taken in a supply to last the entire trip.

At Grand Island they took an extra day off to let the teams rest. They never drove on Sundays either as Father always said that both man and beast needed the rest. Then too, his religion forbid it so they always chose a spot where there was both feed and water, where the weeks cooking, washing and bathing could be done and all could take a quiet rest as well as their stock. Sometime if the travelling was too tough they took an extra day but that ever present thot of going goaded them on for they must get over the Sierra Mountains before the deep snow that fall.

Grand Island is peculiarly situated. On going up, one crosses the main south fork of the Platte, a good big river. This had to be crossed at high water this time of the year as there were no bridges anywhere. Travelers were in too big a their strength should be respected and that they have their water and food first for it was by their strength they would reach the goal.

The first thot that worried them was not gold but to find a suitable place for their cattle. So they took them to Grass Valley, so they could set up a place called home, where the cattle could be kept that winter. One could stay with their things, then the others could be free to look the country over, take up a prospect and work. On arriving in California each bunch of this train struck out for themselves.

Winter now was coming on and every one must throw up a shelter from the winter rain and damp cold. Azor would stay with the cabin, cattle and wagons. The supply of food was running low. Someone must go to Sacramento and get flour and other needcessity they had to have. Flour was an exorbitant price and other things in proportion. Their money too was low. There was plenty of game in the hills so they would not suffer for meat. They all talked the situation over. Gold had to be found, but where, with such a motley crowd at ever little town one could not take anybodies word. Enos and Seth went to Sutters Fort to see what would be the show in staking out a claim. The ground for miles around was all taken, no chance there. So they could now part with a team of oxen for some provisions. The sale was eagerly made as well broke oxen were at a premium now. No one had time to break a pair. Everyone was in a rush. Provisions were scarce when such a motley crowd of emigrants arrive. Enos and Seth went back to their newly throwed up shack with the grub minus the oxen. They still had high hopes of getting work, and in staking a claim.

Soon the cold rains came on but the three worked as they had never before, for others. They worked at the sluice, getting timber from the forests, sawing, making sluices, building flumes to sluice the gravel in or anything there was to do. In the mean time, they learned all they could about finding gold. Tho it seemed that every likely place had been taken and being now worked.

The hoard of idle, indolent men around those little mining centers was disgusting, drinking and playing cards with a hurd gurdy house in connection. Man's life in such places was not worth much. To one raised in the quiet frontier, back wood country, he could hardly believe there was such a place in existence like this. Houses were only shacks as no one could tell where the next stampede might lead this crowd. They were here today and gone tomorrow at the next discovery of gold.

When work gave out they now began to prospect on their own. But the best they could do with food so high was only get enuf for supplies that winter. Clothes all had to be patched and boots soled to keep comfortable that winter. One blessed hope in California, spring comes early. The ground a carpet of luscious grasses and flowers to gladden the eye and give hopes for a bright future.

Forty Niners Bill of Fare

The following bill of fare was actually served in a California hotel in the fifties, and is vouched for by many old timers living in this community says the Mining World:

SOUP

Bean, $1   Ox Tail (short), $1.50
Beef, Mexican (prime cut), $1.50
Beef (plain), $1
Beef (tame), from the States $1.50

VEGETABLES

Bakes Beans, plain, $0.75   Greased $1
Two Spuds, fair size, $0.50
Peeled, $0.75

ENTREES

Sauerkraut, $1   Bacon, fried, $1
Bacon, stuffed, $1
Hash, low grade, $0.75   18 carats, $1

GAME

Codfish balls, $0.75
Grizzly, roast $1   Fried, $0.75
Jackass Rabbit, whole $1
Rice Pudding, plain $0.75
Rice Pudding with Molasses, $1
Square Meal, $3, payable in advance.
N.B. - Gold scales at the end of bar

Dillon Examiner, August 28, 1895

This kind of life hunting for gold was hard on Grandfather Seth. So he would let Azor go and he'd stay home. Now that spring had come they delighted in exploring the country and new diggings, learning all the time the ways gold was found and got. This was indeed an odd, laborious way of living. In Indiana there was no hurry unless on the chase for a fox or coon. Here one had to cook, keep house, see after his clothes, if he had any. At home this all was supplied by his wife, no worry or hurry. Yes, this was gold. They would work hard, get as much as they could and go home. Thus they worked on and planned on an early return.

Enos said to his father one night, "You remember those wagons, oxen, mules and horses that was left by the way in Nevada? If we had only staid a few weeks, gathered up everything making trips back and fourth before the snow fall we could have sold them for more than we have made so far and had money to the good. Just look at those traders. They can't get enuf iron to pound in to spades and picks. Every conceivable thing was left and abandoned there for two hundred miles. It is now almost impossible to buy tools." That summer they worked the country around Marysville with only moderate success then they moved on to Auburn tho later moved to Coloma. The summer being hot and dry, many people on the headwaters of the mountain stream all thru these parts polluted all the streams. Then the sanitation of the towns were dreadful. In July typhoid (called mountain fever) broke out in the camp causing many deaths. The sick were taken care of by anyone that felt sympathetic and willing to care for them in their hovel. There were no doctors or nurses nor medicine. Each doctored his patient with herbs and roots. If the patient got well it was mostly owing to his own physical resistance to the fever. Diarrhea was a common complaint. There was no vegetable or no fruits for sale on the market. California had never before saw such an influx of people and were not prepared.

Those that prospected and roamed the hills found wild fruits at times tho not in quantities to bring home. Late August and September was very hot. Many took the fever. Then Azor came down with it. Grandfather Seth was a good herb doctor and he tended Azor faithfully day and night still he could not break the fever on him and he finally sank rapidly, was unconscious for days and refused food. He grew weaker and weaker till he died. Of this two years struggle this was the worst. Enos and Joel mourned their loss so far away from home in a distant country. Grandfather Seth could not write home to mother. No, he would go home and tell her himself.

A big cedar log was brot from the forest and with their broad ax and adze they dug the log out in fashion of a coffin. With a piece of the wagon sheet that had fluttered on the wagon bows they wound it around for a shroud. They lifted him sorrowfully and placed him in the redwood coffin. Then a big redwood slab was used for the lid with cedar pins that held the coffin lid fast. They dug a grave and rocked it up, then gently placed the redwood coffin in. They fashioned this rock wall around and over the coffin to make it safe from burrowing rodents.

It was agreed that Grandfather Seth would go home, yet they had no money. They could sell the two wagons and three yoke of oxen and send him home. He was heart broken now that Azor was gone. He must go home. Hang the gold idea. If it was there in big quantities they had not yet found it. He was sick so they sold wagon and oxen.

> Azor is shown to have died in California in 1850 as in the Valentine Shirley history it states, "Shortly after their marriage (probably in 1849 or early 1850) Enos, his brothers Joel and Azor and his father joined the gold rush to California. There Azor died of fever and the others returned empty handed (according to the **William Fancett diary** this was 1851, not after 3 years)", page 104. [*In various other places in her writings Maggie states they were gone for four years. – mc*]
>
> * * *
>
> The U.S. Census, 1850, El Dorado Co., California shows "Four of them, Seth, Enos, Joel and John were mining on Mathias Creek. John was a cousin, the son of William Halbert. . . .Azor was not named so had died before this, I believe." [*this taken from a letter dated Oct. 29, 1981 from Walter P. Halbert to Susan Hand. – mc*]

Enos and Joel took him to San Francisco - secured him passage on a sail boat with other passengers to New York by way of Cape Horn. He had enuf money on him to see his way safely home. This wind jammer sailed out of the Golden Gate September 20, [*1850*] fully stocked with food and water rigged and manned by competent sailors for a 3 month trip. They expected to restock supplies at some Brazil, South American port and trade their wares, hides and gold for South American or tropical fruits and coffee to take on to New York.

This wind jammer progressed in its southern course without an accident till they entered the Tropic zone of typhoons and tropical rains. To the surprise of the captain, they were caught in a calm and his little bark was unable to get out. They sailed and sailed tho could not get ahead or behind in such a given area of the calm. The sailors worked hard to set the sails in a position to move it out but to no avail. Each day the order came to try and set the sail in such an angle that would move the ship ahead. All to no avail. The ship would swing out and round in the same calm. As time went on they knew if they could not move on all would perish as the good drinking water was low so they set to catching water in sails and saving it. That part of the situation was solved but the food was getting low. Each day the rations were eaten till finally the last scrap of meal and flour was gone. Men had already died and more were sick and dying. What could they do? Just all starve to death leaving a ghost ship to drift out of this calm to the high sea? Could they not do something for the dying men? The only thing that could give a little sustenance was their boots. They gladly parted with them, pair by pair. They were cut in thin strips and boiled. The soup and strips were eagerly devoured, washed down with rain water caught in the sails. At last the last pair of boots had been eaten. There were still a few passengers and sailors alive. What was there but human life left to subsist on? Were they that was left impelled to turn cannibals? They were all weak and hungry. They had met for the last time to face a drastic issue. Would it be cannibalism - to save the lives of a few they had to resort to that? They would wait till tomorrow. God help us to break the calm before they had to kill their older comrade, Grandfather Seth. He was the oldest. He best could afford to go. God forbid! Give him time to pray as he never had before and before the break of day, without the hands of the feeble sailors, the ship broke the calm and they pulled out in to the open ocean making to the nearest Chilean port. They drifted in. The excitement of those famished passengers and sailors could not be measured. Sustenance was brot aboard when the wharf men found they were starving. In a few days all was well, except the shock of a 62 day maroon, some never got over. Part of the load of hides were traded for enough provision to last to Buenos Aires where they would load for New York. With the rigging repaired and a plentiful supply of drinking water on board and a crew of trusty sailors to man the ship all set sail praying for a safe voyage. The horn was rounded in safety, that being a graveyard of many a good ship and cargo and Buenos Aires sighted. A tug drew them safely in to the harbor. Here the hides and gold paid for a load of coffee and fruits which was loaded in time and the good little vessel was pulled out to open seas. There now was no stops to make and nothing to delay them till they were picked up by a pilot and brot safely to the New York harbor. Grandpa Seth bade his comrades a sincere good by. Going to the dry good store, there he bot Grandmother yards enuf for a nice silk dress, black cashmere, a shawl, tassels all around with a silk fringe, a pair of shoes. Then he made his way to the railroad for New Albany on the Ohio River 50 miles from home. Then he came out on horse drawn stage. He wasted no time in getting home where, thank God, he would stay till his dying day.

    He now helped and encouraged Silas to stay home and help - help lighten the load from those poor women's back. The drudgery they had suffered and endured. And Mother, poor woman, it was hard to tell her of Azor's death but now they were together. They could bear the sorrow together.

In a letter dated October 29, 1981 from Walter P. Halbert to Susan Hand was the enclosed letter. It was written May 27, 1851 by Samual Charles to a Mr. William Pickens, Newel Post Office, Anderson District, South Carolina. – mc. This letter states:

This from the Envelope: *Paoli, Ind*
May 30th

Mr. William Pickens
Newel Post Office
Anderson District
South Carolina

Dear friends your letter dated April 4 we have received and was glad to hear that you arrived safe at home and found all the friends well the connection in this part of the country are generally well so far as we have any knowledge of Uncle Seth Halbert got home about the twentieth of March he was well but he made a very long trip of it he left California for home the first of last December he was blown off in a storm which took him forty days to get back again he lived eight days on a pint of Molassis and two hard buiscuit and had to work hard at that he had to help to pull the ship back part of the way with oars none of the boys come back with him he left them all there a digging up the gold they are doing tolerable well if they have their health they will make a good deal of money by fall to come home with if no bad luck. Uncle Seth Halbert brought home some money but how much no person knows that I know of but I guezs some where between five or sic hundred dollars. William and Wilson Charles was well that last we heard of in Californa and a doing tolerable well Stock of evry discription are very high produce is a tolerable fair price bacon is high from 6 1/3 to 8 3/4 live hogs from 2.15 to 3 dollars per hundred lbs grozs money is up tolerable plenty here something uncomin in this country we have had a very dry spring until the fifteenth of this month we had some heavy frosts here the first of the month which has succeeded in killing all the fruit and in fact a good portion of the timber in low places such as the birch a great many of them look like the fall of the year or more singular still killed the tops and the lower branches are yet alive which presents quite a singular appearance for my part I think a good many of them will entirely die. We have no prospects as yet of selling your land and I also think it will be tolerable hard to sell it for cash in hand for there are but very few persons in this country that has got the money to pay cash in hand we would stand a great deal better chance to sell on short time say two and three years credit The Lindley land that lay joining yours has been sold it sold on a credit of one two and three years it went low only eight hundred dollars we have understood by some of the neighbors that a good portion of your lands over flow so it will be tolerable hard to sell Father is going out to see it and Uncle Seth will go along and they will then find out whether it does or not they will also try and do the best they can for you for the chance they have they live a most to far off to visit it often but will see to it according to promise I have nothing more to write at present but remains your affectionate friend till death.

To Wm Pickens   /   Samuel Charles
    (Newel P.O.   (Paoli, Ind.)
    Anderson Dist. S.C.)

Enos and Joel went back to their diggings a sorrowful pair, alone, with no money. They must work hard now and save for their passage home as California was no place for a man so far away from home and family. Joel worked on but Enos thot he'd prospect around and perhaps strike riches. One day he ran in to a place he thot was rich with gold tho having no way to tell. He shoveled in a part of a sack full and started to Sacramento two days away to have it assayed. On his way he ran in to some other fellows that persuaded him to put that sack down and help. So he did. When he came back to his claim he found two ruffians working away. When he told them that was his claim they up and drew their six shooters on him. His life then was not worth much till he was out of range. Then he and Joel worked for wages. On Sundays they would prospect ledges of rocks where seams of free gold could be seen. Here they would dig out $21 to $25 per day with their jack knives.

Here they worked on in this conglomerate congestion of men, both good and bad till in the fourth year since they left home they took a boat from San Francisco to Panama where they took a boat which had been dug and hewed out like a big trough. They were steered by rude paddles - the Shagras River - the Gatun Lake just thru where the Panama Canal is now. When they saw the lay of the country, lakes and rivers, they predicted that some time in the future a canal would be built to connect the Atlantic and Pacific Ocean traffic. In this boat only 10 or 12 heavily armed men could be taken at a time by these native wild men of that country. The river was so densely over grown the oarsmen would have to cut a new road thru this river over hanging with vines each trip thru so thick was the growth there. The native oarsmen cautioned the passengers to not put their hands in the water least a shark should seize his hand thereby capsizing the boat and all drowned. The remainder of the trip was thru dense trail.

The natives were mostly treacherous wild men of the region. Tho with 20 or 30 well armed white men they had no show and never attacked them. "Once when going along a dense path one of the most vicious men I had ever saw appeared. Tho when he took in the situation he disappeared in to the brush and nothing came from his peep in," Enos related.

At the coast the trail ended. A boat that plied the gulf took the party that Enos and Joel were in to New Orleans. There Enos and Joel bot silk for dresses and other articles for their wives and families and bot a ticket on return boat for Evansville, 20 miles from home. The boats those days took lumber and other saleable commodities down the Mississippi River to New Orleans. Before this, having no power to return with, they were sold for junk. Tho of late they were brot back by a mule tread power that had been made quite proficient. At Cairo they took passage on a boat up the Ohio River to Evansville. This was a long ways from home. Tho was too anxious to think of distances and taking their precious pack on their back soon arrived to find their surprised wives and children all at Grandfather Seths.

The families soon all went to their homes for mother was disgusted to think she had staid there laboring for others that would not keep up there trace in the harness. Never again would she live with Joel's wife and Polly. Grandmother and ma got along well but Grandmother was not able to work. Silas was the same, never could be depended on to do any of the chores on time. Enos and Susan moved their stock and dry goods to their own little cabin and life was begun again. Sowing and reaping, she keeping the house in trim, raising chicks and geese. Hackling the flax and spinning it and making it into cloth, towels, table linen and sheets, grain sacks. The wool was washed, spun and dyed for their clothes. Mary, by this time, was ever ready to help.

While living at Grandfathers she had but very little time to weave and keep up her household supplies beside she was worn out. There, with this four years him being away, it seemed as all was lost. Grandfather Shirley, his boys had all prospered and had plenty.

The following is a copy of a letter to Seth Halbert from his sister, Sarah. Walter Halbert sent this to Susan Hand. It is typed as it was written. - mc

South Carolina, July the 3, 1851

Dear brother I received your kind letter dated April 15th was all well and still remain so. I was very glad to hear you had got Safe home to your family A gain. Trips way going of to make fortunes causes A lot of trouble that is the Ways of the World. it has been very dry in many places oats did not get high enoughf to Save many. Wheat is tolerble onety corn is very Scarse In this part of the world this selling from 80 to one dolar pe bushel and very scarce at that The corn crop that is growing ar very Small the Prospect of making a nother crop is very Dim. I hope it will rain yet in time to make sweet potatoes So when you come I can kook A oposom for dinner I want you to come and bring your Wife and as many as you pleas of our relation I Want to See them all if I could. I have Sent to your country but availeth nothing but to spend money the last trip cost me one hundred dollars I can't tell When I can get that much more to spend I am A fraid I shall hav corn to by next year I Want you to come and bring a little gold I am sorry you Was not at home if you had been there I would been better Sattisfide you can spare the time you all hav good land you can come and never mizs the time then you can see our new town at the minreral spring it is on big creek above sideings, rild mill there is three stores one black smith shop one Acadame two boarding houses the rail road runs through the town it begins at bill parsons ould place and has built houses on to the creek and on thizs side for some 2 or 3 miles it will be A great place in A few year to sell eggs and butter I want you to come and See how carlina is improving I think you Would want to sell out and come hear to live Where you could hav darkes to black your shoes and wash your cloths and cach your horse and go to mill and evry thing you Want them to do darkes is very useful they are as good mules and stubborn so I want you to git as much gold as you can and bring it over With you When you come. Sister ruth pummely is Well as far as I know they are gitting rich very fast - his boys is quite smart and his daughters has married Well and is doing well I Want you to giv my best respects to all my friends do my Dear bother and sisters come if you can it won't take you half So long as it did to go to california nor won't see half the furtig you did I Want you to Write to me as soon as you can and let me know When you are A coming So come A long it all goes in your life time May the Lord blezs you all is My Prayer for christs Sake So for you Well to all.

(To) Seth Halbert and his Wife   /   Sarah Welborn
    (Frances)   (Silver Glade, S.C.)
    (Paoli Indiana)   Pendleton District, South Carolina
    (Orange Co)

> For California Map and general locations see Appendix B, page 292.

Chapter IV

Starting Over

****

Grandfather Seth, Joel and Enos were worse off than ever and had to begin at the bottom. What little money they brot home did not go far on a depleted farm. That fall mother got wind fall apples and peaches from neighbors, cut and dried enuf for the winter use with some pigs to kill and occasionally wild meat. Then a cow for fresh milk and butter, a few potatoes and corn, her share, they managed to live good thru the winter. Then the men had come back in time to shock the fodder for roughage for the cows.

A sorrowful return with one left, never to return, in California. With but little money they picked up the broken threads where they left off. The women had kept the home fire burning tho weary of doing the outdoor and indoor work. The depleted stock they had left had increased and they were better off then they thot. Joel and family lived with grandfather till in a few years he had the longing to go back to California. This time to live and make his home. He could see the possibilities of a good easy living there in the hills so he moved. Took up a sheltered place in the foot hills where he could raise cattle. They could graze the year around, could have a small farm to raise grain and fruits on so he settled in California. He and wife lived to be a good old age and his children are scattered thru the state. Two sisters, Polly and Francis followed him to the state.

In those four years they had had bad luck with their sheep. Dogs got in to the bunch at night and killed several each at each attack. A Mr. Abanatha Bolton lived four miles south of Grandfather Seth's place. Grandfather Seth found they had sheep for sale so Grandfather took his youngest son Silas along and went over. So happened when they got there it was about dinner time or would be before they counted out the sheep. They were, of course, invited to dinner. Mrs. Bolton had her daughter Rhoda to run down the chicken and cut it's head off in preparation to cooking it. Silas had an ever watchful eye out and saw the girl run the chicken down.

Seth Halbert
Born May 12, 1795
Pendleton District, South Carolina
From the Susan Hand Collection

Frances (Charles) Halbert
Born November 10, 1799 in Tennessee
From the Susan Hand Collection

This was the starter to a love affair and a very happy married life. The sheep were bot and taken home. Mother got a part of them for her own work to be woven and made in to clothes.

Silas went back to see Rhoda three times at intervals. At last he got up courage enuf to ask the old folks for the girl. "No," the old folks said "we don't have any objections but we think you had better wait a year till you are older," he being 18, she 15 years past. So they proceeded to take matters in their own hands with the help of Mrs. Bolton's hired girl. Rhoda's clothes were put in a small package and hid under a jimpson weed in the 20th panel of the worn fence down the road. Silas was to come at a late hour a certain night. She was there, grabbed

20

her bundle under her arm and sprang from the worn fence on behind him and away they rode down hill on a dirt road, headed to Albany on the Ohio River 55 miles away. They rode out at leisure gate, in order to save the horse, after they got a mile away.

A man owned a hotel built on an island in the middle of the Ohio River and knew a way couples like these could go there and get married. They reached the river about noon the next day. The horse was put in a livery stable, fed and groomed. They were ferried acrost and were married as soon as she could wash her face, comb her hair and put on her wedding dress that was in the package.

They were married now tho had no home to go to. Silas had courted Rhoda Bolton quietly and the girl's mother had never suspected that her daughter was thinking about eloping. The Boltons were staunch old backwoods people. No, he could not take her to Boltons as he did not know them well enuf. He'd had many a jangle with his father Seth. He'd rather quarrel with him than a stranger so he concluded to take her home with him. His mother had not been so well so he thot he would take her there. He knew Rhoda was a good worker. After six months Grandmother died. Rhoda was a good worker and he had found her a place. Then if they moved away Grandfather would be alone. That would never do. Grandfather Seth owned everything and ran the business as long as he lived. Silas had never done much and was contented, as it was, for Grandfather paid the taxes, sold the hogs, raised corn and wheat, kept enuf hogs for their growing family each year and enuf extra for the needy. Their children came along and they were about my mother's and father's children's age. Seldom a day passed that we children were not together, in fact they were our only playmates.

Chapter V

Prosperity

****

Now that father was home fences had to be built and repaired. To do so posts had to be gotten out of the timber, some split for rails. Fences built that way took time and labor and lots of material. Then with the crops to be put in, tended and harvested, this kept a man busy the year round. There was wood for the house to be gotten, corn to be gathered for the winter feed and food. Corn was taken to the mill horse back and one had to stay all day and sometimes was late in getting back, all owing to if his neighbors got his grist in first.

Enos & Susan's second child, Sarah Elizabeth Halbert, born October 18, 1854.

Mother had always insisted that they must plant an orchard. Four years passed by before he could get at it. A plot of ground then north west of the old house was chosen. Mother had saved apple seed, planted them in the nursery bed so she could give them extra attention. So the second year they were carefully planted the proper distance in rows for an orchard. The next spring after they had gotten a good start father went to the neighbors best trees and got grafts for those little trees. When properly done, they, in a few years, grew in to nice trees. The peaches were from good seed mother had saved the year before. Peach trees in most countries will bear the 3rd or 4th year. Apples takes longer. Gooseberries were gotten from the neighbor and planted in two nice rows, then blackberries from the hill and raspberries of common varieties. There were plenty of wild grapes in the woods. Then two long rows of sage. When old enuf the leaves were gathered and dried and always brot a good price from the peddler that came every two weeks. He sold household needcessities and took butter, eggs, sage, feathers and often good hardwood ashes in return.

Enos & Susan's third child Seth Henry Halbert born March 16, 1857.

Father often had the urge to go back to California but never could go. With an increase in family he was obliged to stay clost to the farm. There was Mary, Sarah, Hattie (Cynthia) and Seth. This family of four kept mother very busy seeing to their needs, tho the older ones helped raise the younger ones all the way down. Enos improved the farm, set out trees for a new building place and the new orchard. Mother now needed a new home so he would build one. But the Civil War cloud was hovering over the new country.

Enos & Susan's fourth child, Cynthia Harriet Halbert, born October 8, 1859.

Life on the farm was progressing. The livestock had increased and Enos was making good. One day he went to Paoli to hear a speaker talk about the war then in progress. The speakers were urging men to join the army in most ever settlement. They needed volunteers. After the speaking was over the man called for volunteers. Father was the first one in this community to sign up to go to war, July 1861.

Enos still wanted to go some place and this was a two fold opportunity. He should help to protect his country so he should and did without talking the question over with Susan. Well, it would not last long. She could manage now. The children could help. He joined and went in to training despite her pleading. All she could do was do as she had before.

Chow Chow

To 3 gals. of cabbage, add 1 gal. green tomatoes, 1 dozen onions, 6 pods green peppers, all chopped fine; 1/4 teaspoon each cloves, cinnamon, allspice, mustard, horseradish and salt. Boil enough vinegar to cover, put in jar or crock and keep in cool place.

From "TESTED RECIPES",
By The Ladies' Aid Society Of
The First Baptist Church,
Dillon, Montana. Third Edition, published by the Tribune Publishing Company,
Dillon, Montana 1913.

Chapter VI

The Civil War

****

Mother & Family When Father Is At War
1861-65

When father came back from Paoli that night and told mother of his volunteering she thot she was one of the most abused women that ever lived. They had only begun to live since his California trip. They sold some of the stock but kept four or five cows and the sheep, all they could pasture. From the sheep she would need the wool and the mutton. Also a sow and pigs for meat and a team of horses as they now had four growing children that must have food. This time she would stay on the land and if need be hire a neighbor to do such work as she could not do.

Grandfather's youngest son, Silas, was home this time. Grandfather and Silas managed to get the ground plowed for a crop. There were always men yet left in the country that could be hired to plow and harrow. Corn then was planted by hand and other seeds such as wheat broadcasted. She could tend it with one horse and a single cultivator, then she could hoe it and it could be laid by and later get some one to shock it. She, with the children's help, Mary or Sarah to tend the youngest and take the other two with her. She would haul in the shock and later she would shuck out the corn, putting it in the bin for feed, seed and meal. The stocks made good roughage for the cows and horses. What little flour she used, she would buy. Anyway money was scarce and they could not afford to pay out money when she could hoe the corn. Thus with pork and lard and mutton and her always goodly supply of dried fruit and vegetables stored, they could live, go thru the winter. The summer she never feared for she raised a good garden and with the wild fruit, chicken, geese, butter and milk she would get along fine.

With a larger family there was more clothes needed and hence more weaving to be done. She still had sheep. When the time came to shear she did it. Put the sheep on a bench, tied it's legs, sheared one side and then turned it over and sheared the other. With her wool she could spin and always have some yarn for sale. The balance was made into blankets for her beds. Her corn field grew and was nice. But Grandfather's was poor, for lack of hoeing. Tho when fall came both families had enuf feed for the stock, corn for meal and hominy and enuf for seed for another spring.

The garden seed was saved carefully and hung in packages from the ridge pole out of reach of mice. She brot small wood from the forest such length she could handle and often sawed or chopped long pieces to fit in the fire place. It supplied heat for the big room and ample hearth for the cooking.

To bake corn pone, when mixed, it was placed in a dutch oven. The oven placed on a nice nest of hot coals then some coals put on top of the oven lid. In due time it was done. Another very good corn bread was made by mixing up corn meal with water and salt, make stiff patties by hand and placed in the oven so they did not touch each other and bake till hard. These we children enjoyed between meals when we got hungry. Then with a ham bone when the ham was done, Mother often dropped in corn meal dumplings made like the dodger and boiled in the ham liquor. This ham and dumplings made a good meal.

All the fruits in those days were dried. When there was a surplus they were cut and dried, dried out in the open sun mostly which was a very tedious job. They were put out in the sun on wooden slat trays, brot in at night and out again in the morning till dry. Then put in sacks and hung on the ridge log. Beans, when dry in the fall, was shelled out and put away for winter use. There was black walnuts and butter nuts, hazel nuts in the woods that could be gotten for winter use. Children enjoyed these and enjoyed the outing going on foot for them, packing back sacks just as large as they could trudge along with. In the fall, papaws were good just after a freeze. In the early spring Mother often cooked greens gathered from the garden and hedge rows. Was a mixture of many young tender shoots. I remember well the tall tender poke shoots she would get just a few and cooked in meat liquor with other greens. Was good spring tonic she would say.

Corn Meal Crackers

1 cup yellow cornmeal
1/2 tsp. salt
1/4 cup butter or lard
1/2 cup water or just a bit less
2 eggs

Combine ingredients; drop by tablespoons on oiled cookie sheet, spread to 3 - 4 inch rounds. Bake at 400 until golden. [*Susan thought this to be similar to the corn meal crackers Maggie talks about - mc*]

From the Susan Hand Collection

All summer long there were berries in the woods to be had for the getting. She took the children and went on treks thru the woods for berries. The woods were grand from early spring till late fall. When once one grew up in such surrounding, one never can forget the deep cool woods in Indiana.

If the country called, others would have to go. How would they manage? She was only one of many. She had lived alone before, now she would have to live to take care of the family. All arrangements were made. Father went at once. Spare times, when alone, was given over to tending the field and garden in the summer. In the fall she was busy drying fruit, harvesting garden seeds and roots, pulling the flax, weighing it down in the little spring creek to get the fiber. Then when rotted bringing it out and dry. Then hackle, leaving the outside of the stock or linen lint that then could be stored away for winter spinning.

There were no news papers and very few letters, most all the news came by word of the mouth. She was lucky in a way to be far away of the war torn area. In her girlhood day she had never been a babied child. She was taught to rely on herself at all times. This teaching was now needed. She must be both father and mother.

After the heavy fall work was done the children would help with the light work around the house and Seth could lead the horses to water and count out ears of corn and pick the nubbins for the cows to feed at milking time. When in the house they helped pick the wool apart so as to have it nice and loose for carding. From bark in the forest she dyed the yarns. When woven she turned out beautiful checked flannel, lindsey, and jeans for their clothes. Blankets were woven and cover lids for the beds were all turned out in the winter.

Once Noblet, the store keeper at Orangeville, had stocked up to some nice factory made dress goods. She had wanted the goods. Noblet told her that he'd have to soon mark them up but if she wanted any he would cut off her lengths and lay them back for her and she could pay a little every week till paid for. Now she could have them as she would have eggs and butter to pay on them, so the bargain was made and ere long could take home the goods. Then she and the little girls could have nice store dresses for Sunday. This showed her ambitious to always have plenty as it were, something laid on the shelf or in other word forewarned - always ready.

That first winter she wanted some wheat to send to mill for flour. She knew brother George had plenty so she went to him to buy the grain. Wheat then sold for $2.50 per bushel. But brother George would not sell it for that. He thot that he was accommodating a Halbert when he and a lot of others were staying at home dragging in the money to get rich on. This life mother was living, she had taken on the Halbert name then lived among her own people in spite of their abuse. It would have been better for her if she had lived so far away they could have never seen her. When Enos went to war they could not even lend her a helping hand.

The commissary men would pay a good price for dried fruit if sold in large quantities. Uncle George had fruit going to waste so he got some of the poorer people living near to come and dry his fruit. When drying, it had to be tended night and day. Mother's orchard was not bearing yet. A neighbor up in the hills two miles away had more than he could use so sent word mother could have all she wanted to dry.

She built a drying kiln and two drying slat trays. She built up a good place to build the fire in then covered it with a big flat rock. Then over this she built the kiln of board large enuf to hold the trays. Then a roof over this and a door to close when the trays were in.

Each day thru the hot days of August she'd take an old mare, some sacks and Seth atop of the mare with his legs off on each side like nobs and walk all the way up the hill, pick the apples and come home. Mary had to stay with Sarah and Hattie at home. When mother got back, she would peel and cut till the chores were to do, set her kiln going and cut and tend as long as she could after supper. Then get a little sleep and up often tending the kiln till she drew the fire and could take a little rest. She kept this up till the apple drying season was over. When Uncle George heard from the buyers (he wanting to make amends for his shortcomings), he came over and told her if they could buy in large quantities the buyers would pay bigger price, so she let Uncle George handle her dried apples. The toes sacking she had made the winter before for towels had to be made now into sacks to ship the dried apples in. All went well and she got pay for her dried apples.

In the fall when cold weather came on she often asked Uncle Silas and Grandfather Seth to come over and butcher a hog or mutton. They were always willing to prolong the coming till one day she and a girl, Lavina, 13 now, that staid with Mother when she could not get work, Mother says, "Lavina, I believe you and I can butcher that hog." "Yes," says Lavina.

The water was on scalding hot in no time. Mother sharpened up the butcher knife. When all was ready took an ax, knocked the pig in the head then she and Lavina rolled it over on the back and she stuck it in the proper place to bleed. Scalded it, then cut it open and cleaned it out, saving heart and liver and the entrail fat. When done a gambrel stick was placed in place and a rope tied to the hind stretcher and the rope throwed over a big limb of a tree nearby. Mother lifted on the pig and Lavine pulled on the rope and it was left hanging to let cool over night. Next morning it was let down on some boards and cut up in proper pieces. The lard was saved and the side meat salted down. Head cheese was made. The pigs feet were cleaned, cooked and pickled. A shoulder and a piece of liver was sent to Silas and Grandpa Seth. If Pa came home on furlough, which sometimes he did, he did the butchering for her otherwise after this she and Lavina (if there) did their own butchering, both hog and mutton. Then beside she thot nothing of butchering geese and chickens for table use or to sell to Noblet.

Enos During the Civil War
1861-1865

[*Maggie (Halbert) Hand had written various things she and her sisters had remembered her father, Enos Halbert, talk about regarding his time in the Civil War. The majority of the following information is taken, by Maggie, from the* "**History of the Thirty-Third Indiana Veteran Volunteer Infantry - Four Years of Civil War - From Sept. 16, 1861 to July 21, 1865**" *by John R. McBride, Indianapolis, Wm. B. Bruford, Printer and Binder, 1900. -mc*]. Two years previous to the firing in Ft. Sumpter, the President had tried to avert war. This being the last straw, volunteers were called from the northern states. In almost every town rally days were held and call for volunteers was made. My father responded at the first call in Orleans, Indiana. Company I, his company was organized at Hope, Bartholomew County during July 1861 under the name of "Hope Guard". They went into camp at Camp Morton, July 28, 1861 but were not mustered into service until August 23, 1861. On September 2, 1861, the company was assigned to the Thirty Third Indiana which was mostly made up of farmers tho some from towns and villages - all ignorant to that which they were now engaged in, woefully deficient in the science of war, yet filled with enthusiasm and with the determination to excel in this pending struggle with Honorable John Coburn, a colonel. The supply of guns were inefficient, many trained with stick or clubs till they were called to active duty when guns were supplied.

The men were supplied at once with uniforms and all other articles to complete a soldiers outfit as soon as possible. Many of the guns were old and had been changed from flint lock to percussion cap, which when the load was discharged gave a "Kicking" power. "One end guaranteed six months sickness, the other death."

There were no military experts in the entire organization. It's true, there were some hang overs from the Mexican War but when mixed in with the new recruits, they had nothing over the new enlisted men.

Regiment Ordered to Kentucky

It [*Kentucky*] being a border state bid fair to be the battle ground. The Confederate Army, under Zollicoffer, moved north to Lexington, Kentucky. Troops had to be sent to Kentucky unprepared. The Thirty Third Indiana was probably in better condition than any other in the organization as good material for soldiers as any in the world.

September 29, 1861 they left for the front, amid cheers, waving of hats and handkerchiefs by friends. The Thirty Third was among the first Indiana regiment to enter the state of Kentucky. They were ordered to Camp Dick Robinson, then Lexington and on to Nicholasville, the terminus of the R.R. From here on the army must go on foot, carry a load of about 40 lbs. = 1 Springfield rifle musket, one cartridge gun belt, forty rounds of cartridges, one knapsack and strap, one blanket, one great coat, one poncho, one canteen with water, one haversack with rations, one shirt, pair of drawers, one pair of socks, and incidentals.

After a few days on foot found many discouraged and foot sore and physically exhausted. Officers wisely relieved the men by pressing in to service teams and wagons of farmers along the line of march.

Brigadier General W. L. Sherman took command at Camp Dick Robinson, finding everything in the raw, unorganized, no money, no arms, no transportation. The Thirty Third Indiana was the only regiment having transportation, being supplied with twenty seven wagons and seven loaded with ammunitions.

By Sherman's frantic appeal for more, better supply and men to fill so many posts, he was dubbed "insane". The heads of the army soon found out this all was not to be a "Holiday Affair" as first supposed. However, the promoters of the contest " builded better than they knew". The struggle would be long and with a lasting victory.

By request of Colonel Coburn, the Thirty Third Indiana was sent to Crab Orchard, Kentucky, then on to Camp Coburn.

Battle of Wild Cat

Colonel Garrard was stationed at Camp Wild Cat about twenty two miles south of Crab Orchard. The approach of the enemy under General Zollicoffer made it necessary for Gerrard to call for Colonel Coburn for assistance.

> **From Enos Halbert's Civil War records:** Enos was a Wagoner, Company H from August thru October, 1861 and was listed as a Teamster from November to December.

On the eve of October 20, three regiments of the 33rd Indiana all slept on their arms. In the morning Zollicoffer with four regiments led the attack on the union troops who had quickly took their position. Companies D, I, E and G of the 33rd Indiana were posted on an eminence east of the camp which the enemy was headed for. After two distinct charges, two hours, the enemy were driven from the field. The rebels were poorly equipped with mostly squirrel rifles and scanty clothing.

Colonel Coburn and his regiment deservedly received great praise for their part they took in the engagement. On November 30, 1861 the 33rd Indiana was designated the first regiment of the first division of that army in honor of what it had done.

In camp at London, November 10, orders were issued to build cabins of logs and it looked as the army were building a winter camp, breast works were thrown up and proved it otherwise.

Posting of pickets was more of form, more of educational purposes than anything else until now and orders were very strict. General Schoepf exercised a rigid surveillance but at no time found a flagrant violation of his orders by any of the sentinels on the outposts.

At one time, thinking the pickets were not as vigilant as they should be, he took it upon himself to make a personal investigation. It so happened that the first picket he met was Private James Holley of Company B. Between the two was a creek and a patch of briars and thorns. Holly challenged the General "Who comes there?"

"I am General Schoepf." was the reply.

"I don't care who your are," said Holley. "Get down off that horse, approach and give the countersign," at the same time cocking his gun.

The boys will remember what a noise those old guns made in the stillness of the night. The General was compelled to pass through the briars and wade the creek. He gave the countersign and told Holley that if he would give him the proper directions he guessed he would go back to camp. At this point all sorts of rumors of the advance of the enemy were kept in circulation till it was believed that an attack was immanent at any moment. All the approaches from the south were picketed in force. It was a new departure to many of the men and they engaged in it with most gravity, and the silence, together with the impenetrable gloom of the night seemed rather to increase the solemnity. Should anyone cause a twig to crack or leaf rustle a nervous thrill would shock the sentinels entire system, sounding, as it did to him, loud enuf to awaken the Confederacy. Indeed, one night, one of the soldiers abstained from the use of tobacco, as he said, because he was afraid the enemy would hear him spit! The suspense of the night would only disappear with the approaching dawn; but all this trepidation vanished. In fact, the men got so that they seemed to rather enjoy the excitement incident to the skirmish line and picket post.

From London to Crab Orchard

The Union men of East Tennessee were most untiring and determined in their efforts to be relieved from the dominion of the Confederacy - at once. London was forty miles beyond Crab Orchard. The country was poor, no crops, with winter coming on, it was most impossible to get food from the north, owing to bad road, rivers not bridged and the lack of transportation.

The 33rd Indiana received their orders to make ready at 3 p.m. and it was not til 10 o'clock at night they got orders to move out.

A cold dreary rain began to fall in torrents. The roads soon became most impassable and streams swollen. A most deplorable move - wagons stuck in the mud, mules gave out, and the men lost all respect and command of their superiors. There was no haste. The Thirty-Third Indiana, when the march began, was in the rear of the entire command and consequently the recipient of all stragglers. They reached Rockcastle River in daylight. The ferry equipment was limited, all was confusion.

In the absence of the General in command, Colonel Coburn did everything possible to restore order and to get the Thirty Third Indiana across. Other regiments lost heavily, wagons, munitions, men and teams.

When the Thirty Third Indiana left London one hundred eighty nine were on the sick list. Contrary to Colonel Coburn and Surgeon McPheeters, they were taken out of the hospital, put in open wagons and moved with the army. When they reached Crab Orchard they were 250 sick, some died on the road. There was no organized hospital staff to take care of the sick. Private houses were either given to the army for the sick or taken over. Many loyal people helped feed and shelter the soldiers. In one case a seminary was taken over, the fires were still burning.

The belated wagon trains at last arrived with all kinds of the soldiers, supplies and equipment. Many died. Company I lost three men. School houses, they were forbidden to use for the sick. There were no nurses and few doctors. The sick took care of the sick so the able men could perform their duties in the army. When word filtered out north, women from all walks of life came to nurse and aid in caring for the sick that winter. The large resort at Crab Orchard Springs was filled with the sick and dying.

> **From Enos Halbert's Civil War records:** Enos was promoted to Assistant Wagon Master on December 1, 1861.

Colonel Coburn was stricken with typhoid fever. His wife and Lieutenant Hendrick's wife did excellent work taking care of the management of the hospitals, sick and dying within. By January most all the sick were able to leave the hospitals. The Thirty Third Indiana was ordered to Lexington, Kentucky for winter quarters.

During those trying times there was often jangles and quarrels among the officers that took a strong mind and often a hand to avert greater troubles. Then there was the incorrigible soldier, occasionally one that would not comply or fit in in an army - in such rare cases they were "Drummed out" and ordered never to return - which they complied willingly.

Expedition to Cumberland Gap

During the fall and winter of '61 and '62, tho they had many reverses, they felt they possessed Kentucky. General Grant had captured Fort Henry and Fort Donaldson and they had defeated Zollicoffer at Wild Cat and Mill Springs.

April 11 [*1862*] the Thirty Third moved out of its camp at Lexington for Cumberland Gap. The three months rest had been very beneficial to the Company as now all were well and hearty, ready for the road, fit now to meet any army condition.

Again bad spring rains set in, made moving the army slow and tiresome but they, this time, moved at an easy gate. They encountered bad conditions again at London and Crab Orchard. The country too were impoverished, was hard to get supplies and they had to be brot in 80 to 90 miles, horrible roads.

Carter's brigade had ravished the country so there was not even straw enuf for a bed tick for the sick.

The impoverished country condition was extreme. That the citizens, few as they were, had enuf to live on would have been surprising had it not been that they were very primitive in their habits and mode of living. Grist mills, run by water power, were limited in capacity, not yielding bread stuffs beyond the actual need of the people. Quaint, rude little mills set upon four posts thrust into the ground. A rude constructed dam built of boulders would give a current strong enough to propel a clumsily constructed wheel. These were taken over by the army and experienced (soldiers) millers found they were inadequate - gave poor results. When the cause was looked in to the meager output, one of the boys solemnly stated that the meal was consumed by two squirrels as soon as it was ground!!! However, fresh meat was furnished which had not been tasted for months and the army was threatened with scurvy.

By this attack and securing Cumberland Gap, east Tennessee would fall into the Union's hand, so a desperate effort was made to keep the army there thru bad weather, lack of food or what ever befell them.

Owing to the mountainous character of the country, it was best to secure pack mules as means of transportation. Eight hundred were secured at Louisville and driven thru unloaded (badly as the army needed supplies, an ill started plan). Twenty second of May, the Thirty Third Indiana struck camp, moved up to Rodgers Gap. There not finding enuf level ground to "pitch a tent" or "whip a dog on". They was ordered to return. Many was the ill started plans if all put to the good would have moved the Confederates out. Thus the union officers and men were getting good experience by those blunders.

June 5 [*1862*]. The Thirty Third Indiana moved to the north side of Rodgers Gap, 32 miles. New roads had to be made and cutting out six miles of blockade. After the fallen trees and other debris were removed the Thirty Third, with the army, at sunset, commenced the passage over the mountain. The ascent seemed almost impossible. Everything was left behind, but articles of absolute needcessity and the men put their shoulders to the wagon and artillery to assist them over the mountains. In this work the men of the Thirty Third did a herculean task with cheerfulness and activity. They were in Powell's Valley by morning. The "Promised Land" moving now to feel the enemy. They found it had flour, so they returned with cattle (not confederates) which the army was in need of. Captain Foster, Chief of Artillery, relates the awful task (too long to relate) of how artillery pieces were let down over sidling cliffs varying from 100 to 500 feet with ropes and pulleys, a miss would have caused loss of guns and men's lives. Both men and horses had been upon short rations and forage, it was impossible for feed trains to follow clost upon the troops over such terribly rough roads. "Many of my command have been over the overland route to California and all concede there was nothing to compare with the steep ascents and decents on the route." In a letter from

> **From Enos Halbert's Civil War Records:** Enos was promoted to Wagon Master in June, 1862.

General Morgan to General Buell about this time, in commenting upon the worth of his troops said: "The Thirty Third Indiana commanded by Colonel Coburn is one of the best regiments in my division and in no small degree is this attributed to its Colonel."

In Powell's Valley lives a simple primitive people, shut out from the world, with the speech, manners and ideas that their fathers brot there when they settled, a half century or more before. Little change had occurred since then. Men and women traveled on horseback and their clothing was the product of the farm and the busy looms of the women. They were rich in cattle, hogs, horses, sheep and products of the fields. Having this, there seemed to be very little care for more. The enemy now had left the Gap for Morristown and Chattanooga. Our wagon train did not reach the Gap till the following day leaving the soldiers to sleep on the damp ground in the cold. The enemy had destroyed all their cabins and tents before leaving. Thus terminated a campaign of hard work and thrills, which placed in our possession a stronghold that had been won and lost in many a conflict between the Indians. Daniel Boone and his hardy companions and still later saw the Gap the favorite haunt of noted bandit John G. Murrell and his followers. Some of the descendant of Murrell's gang, however, lived about the Gap at the time it was occupied by the Union forces. Then white men battled for it, with the expense of many lives.

Occupation of Cumberland Gap

Cumberland Gap was recognized as a Gibraltar. It was long recognized and famous as the most accessible route through the great mountain chain of Virginia, Kentucky and Tennessee. It was considered the key to east Tennessee tho ten thousand men would be necessary to hold it.

On the south is a triangular shaped amphitheater not excelled in beauty anywhere, and from the mountain gushed a spring that furnished power for a mill with a grinding capacity of sixty ton of wheat per day. In occupying the gap the demand of the loyal east Tennesseans had been met. That was all! Nor did they rally to their cause further. The Tennessee people wanted their protection while they peaceably stayed home. It seems that the possession of the gap too was over estimated. With privations, losses and hunger, it was far from the position they thot it to be. The first day of the occupation was given over to sightseeing and erecting the flag high up the pinnacle along with the cannons roar.

The Thirty Third Indiana was composed generally of men who possessed a manly independence and despised those forms of military discipline or despotism that deprived them comforts of their camps. So at once they began to pick up clap boards and improve their quarter. Major Garber had the men put in the guard house. They smothered their indignation till this same major would happen to come near. They then would all yell "Clapboard", "Clapboard" and other slang. He was a sensitive man, he was so mortified that he apologized to the boys. Thus matters rested till in 1865 when some of the boys recognized him in North Carolina and reminded him of the clapboard incident.

Troops were now posted around the gap to the best advantage - the Thirty Third near Tazewell Road where they began again to improve their camp, it being in a barren, hot field. The enemy still hovered near. General Morgan realized he needed more men and calvary men. Each time his requests were turned down. The Thirty Third was sent to Virginia Valley with 50 wagons for corn which they brought in. Enemy was watching every move. Buell sent him word to strengthen the Gap so one man could hold it. Morgan replied, "the place could not be held by one regiment, no more than it could be held by one man." Thus things moved on till the enemy began to show increased activities. Then Lieutenant W. P. Craighill and a Corps of Engineers built two forts which entailed a lot of hard labor for 70 days, land cleared of timber, till nothing was left to be done but wait development.

Drills, guard mounts, dress parades and other duties incident to camp life were conducted as tho the enemy was not near. Bands at reveille or tattoo thrilled their vast audience with patriotic music.

Nobody can forget the fifer of the Forty Ninth Indiana Infantry, who ever heard him, Pres Wornell, born and raised in Orleans, Orange County, Indiana. He was host every day in camp and at reveille, tattoo or taps he was divine. There was a thrilling electric power about the notes of his fife. He was conqueror. He fifed many a boy away from home into the army and electrified them with hope and joy in their most adverse conditions, foot sore, over loaded on long hard trails, their loads always became lighter when he began to play.

Bragg's Army Enters Kentucky

On the 10th of August the rebel army commenced to invade Kentucky and seven days later appeared at the Gap and vicinity. The facts were General Morgan's forces were being surrounded. The enemy had captured 175 wagons, 650 mules and horses, which was bringing supplies from Lexington to the Gap. Nothing could be done but hold the Gap and wait for results.

The enemy, under a flag of truce, demanded a surrender. Come and take it if you can was the answer! They finally withdrew from the Gap, tho hovered near, reconnoitering parties reported. The Thirty Third was ordered to build a large bon fire on the heights so if attacked they could light, tho it was not needed. The corn fields within our lines were diminishing, only 30 days rations in sight, horses and mules were dying from starvation. It was evident to all they would have to soon fight, surrender or evacuate.

During the 32 days our men captured 500 officers and men and killed 170 against our loss of 40. Colonel John McCrea as a master of transportation saw that roads were put in fairly good conditions for quick transportation, realized keeping our troops with provisions. After the battle of Perrysville, he was the first man to bring in needed supplies. Previous to the battle of Richmond, Kentucky and before it was known that General Bragg and his army had taken the Blue Grass region, McCrae was urging forward two trains of supplies to the Gap. One of these trains was in charge of Enos Halbert (my father), a regimental wagon master. It was on its way from Danville and was met by the enemy, in the Rockcastle Hills, who captured wagons and supplies. The men managed to escape with the teams. When he saw them coming, he says "Boys, the rebels will get us, get your horses off quick as you can anyway, cut them loose. The quicker the better for they are coming, yes coming and they will get us."

The men (100) under command of Halbert, thirty of whom belonged to the Thirty Third Indiana reported to the command near Richmond and volunteered to go in to the fight. Some of them as artillerists, were given four pieces of artillery, did good work while it lasted. The entire party was captured except Halbert, who narrowly escaped after two horses were shot from under him. He caught a third horse and made his escape. (I can remember father telling this story). He says "Boys, we are goners, yes, sure, but cut the traces and try to save them if you can." He loosed his from the supply wagon, mounted the best one and took the road back in a frantic wild chase, with horses on the run and the rebels coming up after them shooting at the bunch. First horse was shot under him, he grabbed another clost by, by the bridle and swung on. He went down shortly and he grabbed another in the wild chase and down the road saw two men in an old buggy. Thot he now, I am a goner. They must be rebels. As he drew near he swung himself Indian fashion on the opposite side of the horse and leveled his horse pistol at them saying "Shoot, Dam you shoot." The old man sat there paralyzed for fear father would shoot them. He dashed on unhurt. He had left the pursuers far behind. As he drew near to a stream he slackened his pace to give the horse and himself a drink. Report was carried by word of mouth that Enos Halbert was killed. Tho it was only the two horses. A few days afterward he was sent on a furlough home. Then the community became the wiser.

Evacuation of Cumberland Gap

Just three months since they entered it, orders for evacuation came September 16, '62. The Thirty Third and the Ninth Ohio Battery were the first to move out. Under command of Colonel Coburn the Thirty Third was selected as escort to the ammunition train of the entire army. This was post of honor and dangerous. The regiment did not get started till 2 a.m. of the 17th, was graphical described by a writer. "The moon rose over the Pinnacle and the great fort on the east, the train wound down the northern slope of the mountain, slowly and silently, passed under the clouds of mist which covered the valley and disappeared."

Next day a rebel division tried to head off the Union Army headed for the Goose Creek salt work but were defeated and driven off. The army took line of march next day to the Ohio River over a rough country where wagons never went before and the ration began to be scantier than before. Each soldier was stripped down to the least amount of pounds possible to carry and slept out on the ground.

Pack saddles carried the scanty supplies of the people there, to market and grain to mill. Rude bridle paths traversed and these alone formed the medium of communication with the outside world. The supply of rations deminished, farms only yielding small patches of corn, stunted cattle, few "razor backed" hogs, sometimes called "elm-peelers". Succulent pawpaws grew in abundance, and gave some food. Each man had punched his tin plate full of holes, by aid of the bayonet, furnishing a grater for his corn. This mixed with water could be baked into an appetizing "hoe cake".

General Morgan gave strict order to shoot any soldier who attempted to get on to a wagon when empty, even if footsore, should not ride. Nor soldiers should not take corn or any other thing from farmers, even if hungry. These were two orders that could not be enforced. In the face of hunger the members of the Thirty Third had no regard for orders that deprived them for the needcessaries of life.

September 22 took up march in the evening. They camped at Red Bird Creek near a farm house. The boys helped theirselves to the geese and honey hives. By a midnight march Colonel Coburn saved a grist mill at Booneville from flames. When the boys came along the old wheels were rattling merrily to the ears of the hungry.

At Proctor men threw away extra clothing. Roads were bad and the enemy blocked their way. The sick were taken with them despite Morgan's orders to leave them at West Liberty. Food was scarce, even the pawpaws tasted good. The water was scarce and poor from stagnant pools.

Ohio River, October 3, the objective completed, a march of 220 miles in seventeen days with no shelter at night of any kind and exposed to all sorts of weather, a remarkable march up to that period of the war. They had valuable experience, which they profited by later on. "Taking care of themselves." In General Morgan's escape from Cumberland Gap, he saved his little army from starvation and capture and also saved Louisville from the Confederates who chased after Morgan.

On Sunday 5, the Thirty Third Indiana crossed the Ohio in a ferry boat while the band played "Ain't you glad you are out of the wilderness". When we placed our feet on Ohio soil we all reverently exclaimed, "Thank heaven we are again in God's Country." They were given a royal welcome.

October 14 the Thirty Third, Ninth Ohio Battery, all under command of Colonel Coburn were ordered to Covington, Kentucky.

Reorganization of the Army

While at Covington, Kentucky the members of the regiment had ample time to reflect upon the exciting scenes thru which they had just passed. They held only a small part of Kentucky. Their forces were somewhat depleted as well as their courage. They were ragged, dirty and hungry.

Bragg, in his sweep, had gained east Kentucky and almost the whole of the state was in his possession. When the situation became known, Buell collected the scattered Federals and hurled back Bragg so hard that he was driven out of the state never to return. Without the Kentuckians rallying to his support, as he so hoped and counted on at this time, the Federals cause looked all most hopeless.

Bragg occupying Kentucky, together with the disaster that over whelmed Banks in the Shanandoah Valley seven day disaster near Richmond, Virginia - the loss of Kentucky, the Union cause looked gloomy indeed. It was a year of reverses. Loyal people now became aroused. The calls for troops in July and August were promptly filled.

In the reorganization of the army the Thirty Third Indiana was brigaded with the Nineteenth Michigan, Colonel H. C. Gilbert, Twenty Second, Wisconsin, Colonel Wm. L. Utley, and Eighty Fifth Indiana, Colonel John P. Baird, regiments which had just entered the service. All soon became firm friends and remained so until the close of war. Armies passing thru these "Border states", there was always the question of "State rights". Then the question, "How does this affect state rights?", thru fear of giving offense.

When the greater question of Union or Disunion was considered, the paltry submission seemed unaccountable. This was often well illustrated in connection with the use and distinction of property and the use of slaves. On one occasion two regiments with a battery marched to the boarder line, with orders to not cross it. To obey the order, the captain of the battery planted his guns so that the wheels were in Pennsylvania and the muzzles in Maryland. In another incident men were not allowed to cross the state line to get water. These strong ideas, however, were lost in the sorry struggle later on.

Nov. 12th - The evening of the same day found the regiment again at Camp Henderson, near Lexington, Kentucky from which point it had started in the spring to Cumberland Gap, making the entire circuit all ready alluded to in seven months. Later they moved to Danville, Kentucky till ordered in to Tennessee.

While in camp here the ladies of Terre Haute, Indiana presented to the Eighty Fifth Indiana a beautiful regimental flag, made out of the richest silk, the spread eagle and stars being all worked with the needle. John Morgan was in his second raid in Kentucky. About this time, scouting parties were sent out to investigate; found to not be strong. Co."I" was sent to Nicholasville to erect a telegraph line. Trains of foragers were successful here.

The Culinary Department

Cooking was a lost art to many soldiers - was some time before it was learned and many never learned it. In many incidents uncooked or improperly cooked foods were the cause of much sickness. The companies, at first, were divided into messes of about six soldiers to each. The labor to fall equally on all. It was not a great while till this method proved impracticable. Men not knowing the nature of foods, wasted it either one way or the other by over cooking or not cooking enuf - there is always the story about cooking rice. Time and quantity has to be taken into consideration. To become palatable after the first method of cooking was tried out it was decided to let the best cooks handle the job. Then often negro men and women were called into service for a small sum.

The amount of foods were quite enuf if cooked and served judicially. Even the lowly bean was wholesome if cooked right. It took the soldier from the Northern pine woods to teach the "Bean Hole" art of cooking beans.

A hole was dug, a fire built in it, the beans boiled till when taken up in a spoon and your breath blowed on them, the hide would roll up. They then were right to drain. Put in an iron kettle a layer of beans, thin pork, beans and pork, till the kettle was full. All seasoned with salt and pepper and onion if one likes. The coals then was dug out of the pit and the pot set in, covered well to keep the ashes out then the coals pulled in around and over the pot, then cover all with the hot dirt and leave for 8 to 12 hours. When served with bread and coffee made a most delicious meal.

> Now a bean in its primitive state
> Is of plant we have all often met
> And when cooked in the old Army style
> It has charms we can never forget.

Many places their diet could be changed by obtaining vegetables. They were a most agreeable bunch of men and could adapt themselves to most any conditions.

When every man cooked for himself they were more self reliant, having no one to complain to. In many a case, necessarily of ordinary prudence in the use of rations, gave them a fund on hand, representing rations due the men but not drawn. When war closed, this money was often given then to some faithful but unfortunate comrade in loss of leg or arm.

Transportation

As war progressed, means of transportation was one of the most serious problems that confronted those in charge of the war and was not until several years of bitter experience that they made radical changes.

When the Thirty Third Indiana went to the "front", transportation facilities consisted of twenty-seven wagons and often citizen wagons pressed into service. Tents with sticks and poles were bunglesom. If teams failed to arrive there was no rest or sleep. This causing much discontent. Finally after much changing in kinds of tents, each man was given a square of canvas. Each man carried his own personal belonging and cover. When four canvases were placed together it made a shelter for four men. Then wagons were reduced and only supplies and ammunition, forage and provisions were hauled.

Slave Question

As war progressed, the slaves became more bold and defiant. The Union camps were the refuge of many a runaway. The soldiers were not in sympathy with slavery, nor did they have an undying love for the negro. At times tho relations between the slaveholders and soldiers would become very strained with the knowledge of hot pursuit by their masters; and the certainty of punishment, if captured, and with the uncertainty of protection, the sincere friendships of the soldiers, the negro would continue to flock into our camps.

In the fall of 1862, when the regiment was encamped near Nicholasville, Kentucky the question of the policy of the Administration was sharply raised by slave holders of that state as to what was the thing called the "Kentucky Policy". Judge Robertson and others claimed that it was the duty of the military officers to deliver up, on demand, any colored person claimed by his owner who might be found in his camp. The judge, who had been the most distinguished jurist of Kentucky, claimed a runaway slave. The slave was found in the lines of the Twenty Second Wisconsin, commanded by Colonel Utley, which was in Coburn's brigade and Baird's division. He asked Baird and Coburn for an order on Utley to deliver up the slave. They both declined to give it and referred him to Colonel Utley saying that the slave was in Colonel Utley's camp and under his control. Utley refused to deliver up the slave and informed the judge. The slave went with them to Tennessee. Judge Robertson sued Utley in the U. S. Court of Kentucky at once. Utley was served with process and allowed judgment to go by default against him for the value of the slave, contrary to others advice. After the war he returned to his home in Racine, Wisconsin. A suit was brot against him on this judgment and another judgment was reordered against him for the amount with cost and interests and he was compelled to pay it. Afterward Congress passed an act to reimburse Colonel Utley. This was the last slave whose purchase money was paid in the United States and paid out of the National Treasury.

This case did not stop slaves running away and entering the army where there many found employment and congenial company, free from many unreasonable masters.

Brigade Ordered to Tennessee

Before reaching Louisville, slave holders made their threats. They'd take every slave before reaching the river. The Union soldiers "fixed" bayonets and marched to the river.

Orders were given that no slave should go on board. They were enforced to a measure. But there was a suppressed determination to remain, if possible. The servants of Colonel Coburn, Lieutenant Colonel Henderson and Wagon Master Enos Halbert, Mrs. Coburn, quickly grasping the situation, suggested that Coburns and Hendersons servants be hid in the harness and saddle room under the harness and saddles and Halbert's hid under the boiler while the others were sent ashore. The Captain, thinking all had gone ashore, pushed off the shore. One poor slave attempted to swim and follow, but he was only a "Nigger", and was fired on by the slave holders and sank into the river.

Trip to Nashville

The Thirty Third, with the rest of the brigade took passage on a steamer, which was very much crowded, some having to stay on deck in the cold. The fleet reached Ft. Donaldson the morning after the "second battle" at that place. They arrived at Nashville February 7th, then on to Bentwood March 2nd [*1863*].

Situation in Indiana

The political situation at this time in Indiana was in great measure embarrassing to the United State's cause, to both Governor Morton and President Lincoln. The Indiana State Legislature was then in session and hostile to the Union.

The soldiers, not being permitted to vote in the field, gave both branches of the legislature into the hands of their enemies, and but for the wisdom and the strong hand of Governor Morton and some trusted friends, would have seriously damaged the Union cause. Their methods and designs called for amediate action by all interested. The Thirty-Third and Eighty-Fifth Indiana jointly met in convention for that purpose. The meeting was presided over by Colonel Coburn and Colonel Utley of the Twenty-Second Wisconsin.

A series resulted, denouncing the Indiana Legislature for "its manifest intentions to embarrass the general government in prosecuting the war." Also, "We stand ready at the call of the Government to go home and crush out treasonable combinations which defamed the fair name of Indiana and also denounce the authorities for not construing the constitution so as to permit Indiana soldiers to vote in the field, the priceless and unalienable right of self government."

The Battle of Thompson Station, Tennessee
March 4 & 5, '63

While the enemy was near, little was known of its strength. Fighting was brisk the first day. The men were glad of the chance to move out and joking that they would lick the federates at once. In the night two negro boys slipped into camp and warned the officers in charge of the enemy's strength. Coburn and his brigades were ordered out not knowing this. After fighting most of the day he saw that it was useless to fight longer as he was surrounded.

The Surrender

Arms and ammunition were stacked, 1221 men and Colonel Coburn were marched off the battle field and began that terrible trip to Libby Prison. While on the way, they suffered untold misery and starvation and lack of clothing, which the confederates took off their backs. My father, being wagon master in this battle, escaped capture.

Just fifteen days from capture the men entered Libby Prison. Time and space permits me from describing that horrible corral where men were treated worse than cattle. Due to starvation, filth and lack of shelter and water, many died. Coburn and men were released in two weeks. Several died of this treatment. When released, these men were placed in hospitals and cared for. Many weak and starved ones died. Many kind and wealthy ladies helped with foods and clothing where these hospitals were located. Mrs. Polk, (widow of ex-president Polk) assisted in many ways.

From Enos Halbert's Civil War Records: Enos was shown to be on Furlough in Muster Roll dated June 23, 1863.

After the regiments were exchanged, Governor Morton extended a furlough to those, of ten days. They were sent the 18th day to Franklin. Fragments of the regiment at Franklin, with the band, met the returning boys to welcome their return. Friends of Colonel Coburn presented him with a handsome sword.

Advance of the Army

When the army was fit for service they were sent forward to Lexington, Kentucky in the direction of east Tennessee. The enemy was falling back to Knoxville and Chattanooga.

After the Confederates fell back, part of the force at Franklin left via train for Murfreesboro. There rested three days, then marched on to Christiana. That night orders were given to feed five hundred rebel prisoners. At midnight reached Guy's Gap. Here 150 men and same number of negroes were detailed to build a bridge. The country was infested with bushwhackers who objected to the men cutting down the trees. Colonel Hollingsworth gave them to understand that if any of his men were killed he would retort in kind.

Nine were molested, tho the day previous to leaving Guy's Gap a captain and private took some chickens to a house outside of the Pines to have them cooked for lunch the following day. They did not return. After the regiment moved on the following day, Lieutenant Maze, dressed in citizens clothes, with Lieutenant Hollingsworth and about 40 men in hailing distance, went to the house and pretended to the lone woman of the place, that he was on his way to the rebel lines and thru her learned that Dill and Jones had been killed there and to prove it showed him the blood spots. At first he discredited her story. The further proof convinced, where upon he called to his men to round up all negroes and bushwhackers in the neighborhood and had them all taken to Murfreesborough. Later the woman took very ill and sent for the Lieutenants and again told the same story, tho it still remained a mystery thereafter.

The Brigade Guards the Railroad

In the advanced movement, regimental and brigade organizations were shifted back and forth, without any apparent design, to confuse the enemy.

The Thirty Third continued its march to Shelbyville then to the Guy's Gap, and from there to Murfreesboro where it remained until September 6. It then took the train for Tullahoma, from which point it was scattered along the Nashville and Chattanooga railroad as far south as Dechard, Tennessee.

All these detachments rendered good service in keeping open the "Crackerline" from Nashville to Chattanooga and the coal road, which were important to the welfare of Rosecran's army. The enemy would make a dash and attack here and there, derailing cars, burning bridges, tho seldom ever stayed long enuf for an engagement. The road had never been a good one. The spade and shovel changed it very little from the natural rough surface. Some grades were up to 100 foot per mile. The track was made of light inverted U or bridge rail, laid upon cedar stringers, seven inches high. The stringers were gradually replaced with crossties. The iron had been in use for 12 years. Over this single track everything had to be transported for the entire army and necessarily required a very large force to protect and keep in repair.

Company "C" and Company "G" were on detached duty at Cowan Station, a tunnel, on north end of Nashville and Chattanooga railroad. Here, with five partially filled companies of new colored troops, they had charge of the first convalescent camp in rear of Rosecran's Army, with acres of ammunitions of war and at times several hundred partially disabled men from the front, commanded by Captain Day. During the two month stay, the duties were various, receiving and shipping supplies, and disabled men once a week, issuing rations to half starved citizens. It was here the men were first reconciled to the use of colored troops.

To prevent surprise and loss of stores by rebel cavalry and raids by bushwhackers, the picket lines had to be quite extensive and at first the men complained if the colored pickets intruded on our side of the camp, but they were not long in learning that although green in the service and black in color, they made excellent guards and soon our men were asking for shorter guard lines with the colored picket lines extended. Soon they would have been contented if the colored soldiers [were] doing all guard duty.

Being scattered over so much territory it was deemed best to concentrate the regiment of the brigade, and if possible, quell the dissension that invaded that western part of the army. The Thirty Third Indiana was scattered at seven different posts and therefore of little service, except the company at Tracy City.

When the eastern troop were sent, each questioned the valor of the other and a general discontent ensued. Finally Colonel Coburn became justly tired of the condition and in his report of October 9, 1863 at Tullahoma, he wrote in his report, "We will cheerfully do duty anywhere, but would rather be with our friends than distributed over hundred of miles of mountains and plains."

This report was indorsed by General Gordon Granger as follows - "I respectfully request that Colonel Coburn's brigade be relieved and brot to the front. It has an old grudge to settle in the Thompson Station Affair."

The Thirty Third Indiana was ordered to concentrate at Christiana, Tennessee. On November 5, the fourth companies left for Tullahoma, reaching Shelbyville that eve - left Shelbyville on the 6th. After marching 17 miles went in to camp at Christiana. Other companies came by railroad.

On arrival, conflict of authority arose and for a time looked as serious trouble would ensue. However, soon after, a very conciliatory and sensible letter was written by General Slocum to General Coburn covering the matter and requesting all parties to use forbearance and cultivate friendship.

Enos & Susan's fifth child, Emma Susan Halbert, born November 22, 1863.

The bridges at Murfreesborough was guarded. The army went into winter with the men in the best of health. Tho anxious to move foreword, as army life is always tiresome when not on the move. A considerable amount of foraging for supplies for the teams had to be done and sometimes they had to go fifteen to twenty miles from camp for supplies. The country abounded with bushwhackers or guerrillas. One of these foraging parties was out fifteen miles from camp. They stopped at a house where the people of the neighborhood were engaged in a dance. Some of them were bushwhackers and it was not long till a free fight was on hand - a fight to death. Two men were severely injured, two got away unharmed. A bushwhacker was killed, one wounded and another escaped. The boys hastened to camp. The following day a detail of men went to the scene of conflict and found the citizens holding an inquest over the dead guerrilla, who had been pierced by eight bullets. The jury returned a verdict, simple and direct, "He was killed, the community is rid of a nuisance."

From Enos Halbert's Civil War records: From the Field and Staff Muster Roll, November and December 1863 shows Enos absent, sick in Indiana.

Notation shows "battle of Richmond, Ky". as commander of a section of Artillery - promoted Q.M. Sergeant December 2, 1863. Transferred to Non-Commission Staff.

The Regiment Reenlists

The war had now been in progress for more than 2 1/2 years. Billions of dollars had been spent and thousands of noble and loyal lives had been sacrificed on the country's alter.

The close of 1863 showed a marked improvement over the previous year. General Grant had opened the Mississippi River by the capitulation of Pemberton at Vicksburg and the Union Troops under General Meade had won a signal victory over General Lee, on the heights about Gettysburg. These magnificent victories, together with the more recent successes at Lookout Mountain and Missionary Ridge, gave to the soldiers and to the loyal people of the North great hopes of success.

From Enos Halbert's Civil War records: The Detachment Muster-out Roll shows Enos being mustered out on February 14, 1864 in Christiana, Tenn. It shows his clothing account as being last settled August 31, 1863 in the amount of $21.93. His last pay collected is shown to be October 31, 1863.

From Enos Halbert's Civil War records: The Muster-in and Descriptive Roll of Veteran Volunteers shows Enos as enlisting February 16, 1864 and his Muster-in date the same at Christiana, Tenn. Bounty paid $60.00.

At this juncture of the war, reenlistments were called for to strengthen their forces, which disheartened the enemy.

The Governor was anxious for reenlistment. The soldiers had decided to choose their own officers. When that was granted, the ranks were soon filled. Then all were allowed 30 days furlough. Days passed swiftly at home.

The Veterans at Home

The reception of the Thirty Third Indiana veterans by their friends upon reaching home, like that accorded all returning veterans, was most cordial and sincere. The leave of thirty days, however, soon expired. Father was home during this time.

Atlanta Campaign

The spring of 1864 found the Union Army well organized, better than ever before. General Grant, having been placed in command of all the armies, was an improvement over the old plan. The many successes of the Union army that following summer and winter fully justified the new order of things. The

From Enos Halbert's Civil War records: Enos was commissioned to 2nd Lieutenant on April 28, 1864.

Thirty Third Indiana left Indianapolis May 3rd and the 7th [*1864*] camped on Chickamauga battle field and later on Trickum, Georgia in Dogwood Valley.

Each regiment was allowed only one mule and one wagon for transportation purposes and thence desks, valises, papers & [etc.] were left at Chattanooga. Even General Sherman dispensed with his tent and had but one wagon for his entire headquarters, consisting of himself, his aid, staff officers and orderlies.

At Snake Creek, two wagon roads had to be made large enuf to let Sherman's army thru. The Thirty Third served in that capacity of road building. Then, done building, Sherman's mighty army fell thru the gap. The possession of Snake Creek was a blow to the enemy, a mistake in Johnston's orders.

At Rasaca, May 15, Johnston's army took their stand, throwing up breast work and mounted four guns. For two days, Sherman's army attacked the rebels, back and forth in a desperate attempt to take the four gun battery. At the end of the first day when the firing ceased at the battery, the Union men thot the rebels had retreated. Just to test the suspicion, some of the scouting parties placed a hat on the end of a pole and hoisted it above the breast works, whereupon it was riddled to bits. (When a child I heard these stories quite often.) They had not evacuated and was quite alive. The Federals were determined after day and night siege to take the battery and guns. A ditch was dug up under the battery. Ropes were attached to the guns and all were pulled down under withering fire from the enemy. On the morning of May 16 rebels were found to have evacuated their works and retreated across the Conasauga River, destroying the bridges in their rear. This was the only battery captured from the enemy during the Atlanta campaign. In this battle the Thirty Third lost no men, but had 29 wounded. There were constant skirmishing going on all the time.

A pontoon bridge was laid and they crossed Consesauga River. Then crossed Cuosawattie River on a ferry boat. By the enemy it was thot at

Enos Halbert, on horse, during Civil War
This photo was taken near the end of the war
and was reproduced from a daguerreotype.
From the Susan Hand Collection

Cassville a decisive battle would be fought. Johnston said to his men, "We would now turn upon the enemy and give him battle." They made an attempt to advance but withdrew "untenable, being too much exposed to the enfilading fire of the Federals artillery."

Those who were most anxious to fight, now fully realized, as one of the Confederate officers said, "How often is the word of promise held to the ear but broken to hope." Our troops held this possession till 20th May. The 22nd troops were inspected and ordered all useless articles thrown away. March to the Etowah River, reached, bridge being burned. The army was crossed on pontoons. The facility with which a stream could be spanned by a pontoon bridge was marvelous. This work was done under command of Colonel George P. Buell of the Fifty-Eighth Indiana, who commanded the pioneers of the Twentieth Army Corps. A rebel was caught up a tree nearby watching things. He said, "Boys, you can beat us". Someone asked, "Why?" "Because," said he, "anybody who could make bridges out them d---d dog tents could beat us." The pontoon bridge was one of the most valuable auxiliaries of the army.

Battle of New Hope Church

This engagement was brought about by a blunder. It was a surprise to both sides. General Johnston reported their strength as a "much larger force of infantry and artillery" than that of the Federals.

Along with other regiments, the Thirty Third Indiana, with five hundred and fifty muskets and the Nineteenth Michigan, poured a most destructive fire into the ranks of the enemy, silencing their batteries completely and under a galling fire from the artillery. Our troops had no breast works. General Stevenson, in his report says of the losses, "altho protected, our loss was 3 to 4 hundred men, artillery 43 men and 44 horses."

Colonel Coburn says in his report: "Shell, grape shot, canister, railroad spikes and very deadly missile rained upon us. I now know that no regiment could have borne with more unfaltering daring, this fearful cannonading and musketry than did the Thirty Third Indiana that day. Their losses: four men killed, one officer and 48 wounded. The fight did not stop until dark, breast works were thrown up with bayonets, tin plates, and cups, in a short time, a heavy rain set in. The men laying on their arms the rest of the night."

Skirmishers were sent out next morning finding their breast works abandoned, tho found them farther on in a timbered hill ready for battle. Breast works were soon thrown up, tho was exposed to a dreadful firing. Just then General Sherman and Colonel Coburn reached that part of the line and were informed that the shots came from a certain old house. A battery was soon in action and the house demolished, then the sharpshooters disappeared. Next day and night the battle still wore on. The 29th of May the enemy made two early attacks and kept a steady battle all day.

The second of June, breast works were thrown up in an incredibly short time with bayonets, tin cups and plates under the enemy's artillery.

The difficulty of supplying rations to the army increased, being sometimes from two to three days behind and only part of the rations being issued at a time.

On one of these occasions when General Hooker happened to pass the brigades, the men called out, Hardtack, Hardtack! This cry multiplied when Hooker passed, transportation of food stuff was poor. Whereupon Hooker ordered the headquarter wagons unloaded and sent for the food in the rear. Before the day was over the men got additional rations. Ever afterwards he was a favorite with the soldiers.

The men were reasonable, knowing the difficulty in distributing provisions. However, not many calls like this were made.

On the fourth of June, by order of General Butterfield, division commander, two men were detailed from each company to do the cooking, who were excused from all other duty. These [men] were required to carry the camp kettles, and had orders to boil all fresh meat. All cooking apparatus, save coffee pots, frying pan, mess pan or kettle were left at Chattanooga. The result was of the worst kind of health - the commissary consisted of hard bread, salt pork or bacon, fresh beef, sugar and coffee. Little, if any, beans, rice, soup, vinegar but after they reached Marietta, they had supplies of all kinds.

Each succeeding day the troops would advance a few miles and throw up breast works. As soon as line of battle was formed they would intuitively throw up breast works without aid of trench tool, exposed to a steady fire from the enemy and the ever present sharpshooter. So constant was the need of protection, it is no wonder that three hundred miles of rifle pits were constructed during this campaign.

The movements of the troops were made regardless of roads, crossing many streams bridged by rails, and were often waded by them. The woods were filled with a thick undergrowth of jack oak, pine and & [etc.] and portions of the two armies would frequently get uncomfortably near each other and both glad to withdraw without formality.

On June 6th the regiment, with the brigade, moved, going out five miles, took position near Mount Olive Church, in view of Pine Knob on the left and Lost Mountain on the right. Breast works were again thrown up. They remained here till June 15th. They then continued their march, found the enemy had moved on. Literally they were being drove to a new stand of battle. Here they again entrenched right up to within two hundred yards of the enemy, under fire of the musketry and artillery.

The 16th, they remained in camp, strengthening breast works, with a loss of four killed and 24 wounded. The Thirty Third was in the front, lost some men. The 17th, the enemy moved back, the 19th, again they moved. This post was strong and well protected. Heavy rain set in. An impassable stream in front caused the regiment to wait till a rail bridge could be built. Shortly an other river had to be bridged in same way. On June 20th, the Thirty Third moved, shifted positions frequently, then built more works, stayed all night.

Battle of Culp's Farm

The battle lasted for two days, being very severe. After the battle, they went in to camp at Marietta to rest. Almost all the time men were exposed to merciless fire from sharpshooters. From 3rd of June up to and including 22nd, it rained every day.

More skirmishes, with the Union Army drawing them to Culp's Farm, where a brisk engagement ensued - loosing thirty five men. Finally retired and went in to camp. Johnston had thrown up good breast works all thru, in and out this country of Marietta. The Union army was under constant fire from Johnston's sharpshooters. Several men were lost. Colonel Coburn was ordered to be in readiness. At daybreak the "ping, ping" of the sharpshooter's laden messengers were again heard. All thru this campaign rain poured down mercilessly, making living miserable.

Finally threw up protection. This was at a point three miles from Marietta and immediately in front of the works of the enemy which enclosed the town. The country was one vast fort and Johnston had fifty miles of connected trenches with abatis and finished batteries. Sharpshooters continued for two days. About 10 o'clock at night the picket firing almost ceased and Colonel Coburn was notified to hold his brigade in readiness to repulse an attack in case one was made as the enemy's barrage had ceased. At day light, the "ping, ping" of the sharpshooter's laden messengers were again heard.

Battle of Kennesaw Mountain

Orders were not always given or received correctly, in instance of Ward, Colonels Coburn and Butterfield, orders were not delivered, whereby Butterfield was relieved.

The lines of the armies were always in uncomfortable positions, skirmishes constantly kept up, not unlike the grappling of two monster giants. Sherman keeping clost to the enemy.

The country for thirty miles had been stripped of grain and grass, so supplies had to be brought in from the north.

July 1 [*1864*] was spent in cleaning up, received new clothes. July 3, the enemy having evacuated Marietta and Kennesaw Mountain, marching through their strong fortification, many Johnnies were found sleeping in the ditches, probably the "Last Ditch".

Following up, they found the enemy strongly posted on a range of hills. Our men at once threw up breast works under fire from the enemy. This day's work was one of the severest experiences of the campaign. The day being hot and sultry, the men were worn out as half had been on night duty. July 6, the regiment moved southeast course, crossed Nickajack Creek and in some steep ridges and hills went in to camp. From 6th to 17th, the entire corps were encamped near Chattahoochie River. The time was devoted to resting and repairing for a renewed campaign. On the 10th, the enemy evacuated the works in our front and crossed the Chattahoochie River and in the evening the banks of the river marked the skirmish lines of the two armies.

> **From Enos Halbert's Civil War records:**
> **Remarks:** sick, sent to hospital at Vinings Station, Georgia, July 1864.

An armistice was agreed upon by the pickets who became very sociable, visiting each other, trading coffee, tobacco and exchanging newspapers.

One day a Johnnie asked "who commands the army across the river." "General Sherman," was the reply. "Well, he commands ours too," said the Johnnie, "For everytime you are ordered to move, we move too." Another Johnnie said, "You'ns don't fight we'ns fair. You'ns go around and fight we'ns on the end."

On the 17th of July, the regiment with the brigade, crossed the Chattahoochie on pontoons at Pacer Ferry, and by evening of the 19th, the entire army had effected a crossing. The river was about 150 yards wide and was spanned by two pontoon bridges. To make the passage as speedily as possible, the front rank men went to the right and the rear rank men to the left, going about three miles, went in to camp. Up to this time the enemy had been steadily falling back. The Confederate soldiers were becoming more or less discouraged. The authorities at Richmond were impatient. General Joe Johnston had done his very best under the circumstances, but not enuf to meet the demands made upon him and he was succeeded by a dashing and impetuous General Hood, who did more fighting but with no better success.

On the 18th, with some difficulty, the troops crossed Nancy's Creek, then marched to Two Pines Hill. The road narrowed down to one platoon according to the width of the road. Later went in to camp at Buck Head.

The Battle of Kennesaw Mountain was fought 27th of July. A vain attempt was made to dislodge the enemy from this strong hold. General Sherman had two reasons of making the assault. "First, because the two armies had settled down to the conclusion that flanking alone was the game and second, if it had been successful Johnston's center would have been broken and his army pushed back in confusion and with great loss to his bridges on the Chattahoochie." But it was not successful and no more direct assaults were made upon the enemy line by our forces during the rest of the campaign. However, the assault caused the sacrifice of many lives and it is believed by many to have been a grave error of judgment.

Battle of Peach Tree Creek

At about 2 o'clock, orders were given to march at day light; at 10 a.m. they reached and crossed the creek. Skirmishers were sent out to look for the enemy. Private Henry Crist, of Company "I", who had been out near the skirmish line gathering blackberries, discovered what he supposed to be the enemy advancing. He hastily reported to General Coburn, who at once informed General Ward, the division commander, urging him to advance. Ward refused, stating Hooker had ordered him to stay in the valley. Colonel Coburn insisted that unless a forward movement was made quickly the division would be driven into the creek and overwhelmed with disaster. Ward and Colonel Harrison, with first brigade, both moved quickly together and forward. Coburn gave command to his brigade to "Fall in". The enemy was coming. It was important to gain a certain commanding ridge before the enemy did, which could only be done by rapid movement and overcoming great difficulty in having to cross deep ravines and to pass through dense growths of pine and oak.

Upon the advance of the main line of the enemy, the skirmish line of the brigade - the 22nd Wisconsin, was ordered to "Rally upon the reserve", which was done very soon after the second brigade advanced together. In the meantime, the first and second brigade advanced together with the right of the Eighty-fifth Indiana resting on the left of the First brigade and the 33rd Indiana on the left of the 85th, with the 19th Michigan in the rear or second line. These regiments had to cross an intervening ravine or ditch and in doing so were met with a galling fire. The 85th crossed with some difficulty and upon reaching the opposite bank, and being partly protected by it, as the enemy came charging down the rise, poured a continuous and deadly fire into his ranks, who was then only about fifty feet away.

The advance of the Thirty Third was even more difficult and hazardous, especially that of the right wing of the regiment, the left wing being more or less protected by an undergrowth of bushes, though the right of the regiment, while crossing the ditch was exposed to a deadly fire and not being able to return it. It did not waver but, unflinchingly crossed over, reformed its ranks and the united regiment and brigade poured a well directed and effective fire into the ranks of the advancing foe, which checked and for a time dismayed the rebel front.

The enemy at this time was rather forward in position, but when the command "Forward" rang along the Union lines, upon its being reformed with a yell heard above the roar of artillery and din of musketry, the regiments of the brigades intermingled and as one command or organization dashed up the hill and above the enemy from the coveted position the temporary breast works which had previously been erected by the skirmishers of the 22nd Wisconsin. It was a race between the two lines as to which would first reach the top of the ridge, the key to the situation. The position that was necessary to the success of the line that could gain it and hold it.

The position was now gained and held by Ward's Third Division, but by severe fighting and under most adverse circumstances. The enemy fought gallantly, with confidence, for the position they held, sometimes fighting hand to hand. Three or four distinct charges were made, tho was gallantly repulsed. Prisoners and Enfield riflers were captured by the wholesale and several battle flags. The 33rd Indiana captured 92 Johnnies and 150 muskets. The conflict lasted about four hours and was the severest during the campaign.

It was at Peach Creek General Joe Johnston had planned this battle. Due honors are to Colonel Coburn and Harrison in ordering the sudden advance on the enemy, July 20th. The 33rd Indiana went into fight with ten line officers and 380 men. Loss was 20 enlisted men killed and 4 officers and 67 enlisted men wounded.

The battle was altogether successful to the Union, as it established their position on the south side of Peach Tree Creek. Captain William M. Merideth, a gallant officer in the 70th Indiana Infantry said, "What impressed me most at the battle was the conspicuous gallantry of Colonel Coburn. I have always held that he saved the Army of the Cumberland that day and that hadn't not been for his promptness, our brigade would have been surprised and driven into the creek."

Colonel Coburn, the brigade commander, in closing his report of the battle says, "To all the officers and men are due the honor and gratitude earned by heroic valor and enthusiastic devotion to principle and theirs are the laurels of a victory snatched from the trembling balance of the battle which wavered on either hand of our division."

Advance to Atlanta

The two days after the battle at Peach Creek was occupied by burying the dead on both sides, for the Confederates fled toward Atlanta. The Union Army followed leisurely without meeting with any resistance (July 23rd).

On going into camp, the 33rd Indiana was posted in reserve. Details from the regiment for picket duty were now heavy and a constant fire was kept up all along the line. The regiment remained in reserve of brigade until the evening of the 25th, when it occupied the advance line of works built by details from the 33rd and other regiments of the brigade. These works had been completed with so little noise and confusion that even the officers and men of the picket reserve knew nothing of it. On the 27th, four companies were placed in, all lines being subject to the shells of the enemy from 3 to 4 batteries. The death of General McPherson on July 22, necessitated the shifting of command. Howard became his successor, which promotion was claimed by General Hooker. Failing to get it, he was, by his own request, relieved of the command of the 20th corps. Hooker was succeeded by General Slocum, who in turn, upon the reorganization of the army at the close of the campaign, was succeeded by General A. S. Williams, commander of 1st division.

From the 28th of July till the 9th of August, the army was in close proximity to the Confederates and under constant fire. The skirmish lines was under orders to keep up a constant fire, and the expenditure of ammunition was very great. One sharpshooter was especially annoying to the men in camp during the day. The smoke from his musket finally exposed his position in a pit in an open field about a mile away. A cannon was at once placed in position on the front line of the works occupied by the 33rd Indiana and after getting range on the sharpshooter, the regiment was no longer molested by him.

The lines were now drawn so closely about Atlanta that the city became a target for long ranged guns and dropping shells into its limits was a daily recreation, until its downfall three weeks later.

From 40 to 60 men were detailed every day from the regiment for picket duty.

On the 9th there were about 3000 solid shot and shell thrown into the city from a 4 1/2 inch rifled cannon and a 20 pounder sent 4000 more shots into the city of Atlanta. All the time lines were strengthened firing had been kept up constantly and the artillery kept pouring shells into the doomed city, with the exception of three days when the skirmishers mutually agreed to stop shooting. On the 14th, Co. "D" and "I" were detailed to go with a wagon train after roasting ears, but succeeded in getting only enough corn for the horses. On the 24th, fire raged fiercely in Atlanta, artillery still pounding away. To add to the horrors of the siege, fire broke out in the city while the Union Army poured shot shells into the town with long ranged guns. The Third division retired to Chattanooga, strengthening the lines all the way.

Surrender of Atlanta

The defeat of the enemy at Jonesborough destroyed the enemy's hopes of holding Atlanta. September 1, [*1864*] evacuation of the city began.

On the morning of the 2nd, General Coburn, with 900 men and 40 calvary men, in "light marching trim", a days rations and 60 pounds of ammunition, moved in the direction of Atlanta. They advanced without hindrance until they reached the earth works recently abandoned by our men, where a skirmish took place, tho caused no delay.

Colonel Coburn was met in the suburbs of the city by Mr. Calhoun, the mayor, with a committee of citizens bearing a flag of truce. The mayor surrendered the city saying "We only ask for protection for persons and property." Colonel Coburn asked him if there was a part of the army in the city. He replied that there was a force of cavalry commanded by Colonel Ferguson. To this Colonel Coburn said, "You cannot surrender this city unless the cavalry evacuates it. My force is not here to fight citizens or women and children, but the army and I cannot promise any protection to anyone, til the army and soldiers go out." He and troops entered as the calvary left at 11 a.m.

About noon an additional detail was made from the regiment, consisting of Co. "H", "C" and "I" to go to the assistance of the first detail. At night, the rest of the regiment "C", "A", "F" and "D", were ordered to join the regiment and did so on the following day, south and west of the brigade, all under command of Major Miller of the 33rd Indiana. Thus, under Colonel Coburn, were the first Union troops to enter the city of Atlanta. At 4 p.m., the 33rd with the rest of the brigade, went to camp on the east side, formerly the enemy's breast works.

About all the citizens that were left were women and children, who seemed to be delighted to see Union troops, altho having been subjected so long to the merciless range of artillery and musketry.

Houses in the interior of the city were demolished by bursting shells and those on the outskirts were riddled by the constant firing along the skirmish lines. The enemy did not, however, leave till they had ransacked the stores and destroyed the arsenal, foundries, 5 locomotives, 81 cars, 28 car loads of ordnance, 13 heavy guns, carriages and some quartermaster, medical and commissary stores.

General Sherman, having determined to strengthen his position in and about Atlanta, gave orders that the citizens of all classes must leave the city. They demonstrated, and the Confederate military authorities joined them in their protest, but "Old Tecump" was unyielding, and in response to his orders, 98 men, 395 women, 605 children and 70 servants (1168 in all) went southward to join their friends, after being first supplied with 5 days rations. A large number went north on the R.R. and were allowed to move furniture and personal effects.

There was some dispute as to whom the mayor surrendered, but was proven beyond a doubt it was Colonel Coburn. Father was there at the time, under Coburn.

Thus ended one of the most skillful, successful and stupendous campaigns of modern times.

> *Oliver P. Morton*
> *Govenor of the State of*
> *Indiana*
>
> *To all who shall see these Presents, Greetings:*
>
> *Know ye, That reposing special confidence in the patriotism, valor, fidelity and abilities of Enos Halbert, I have appointed and by virtue of the authority vested in me as Governor of the State of Indiana, hereby commission him Captain in the thirty third (33) Regiment, Indiana Volunteer raised under the authority of the President of the United States, and the Laws of Congress, to serve during the period for which said Regiment was called into the Service of the United States (Co. "I") and he will be, Governed, obeyed and respected according to the Rules and Articles governing the Volunteer Armies of the United States. Given under my hand at Indianapolis, In the state of Indiana. This fifth day of October, One thousand Eight Hundred and Sixty Four.*
>
> *Laz Hubler*   *O. P. Morton*
> *Adjutant General of Indiana*   *Governor of Indiana*

Note: This is apparently taken from a certificate that Maggie (Halbert) Hand either had or saw at some time in her life.

The word "Defeat" was not in its vocabulary. The lost, killed and wounded in the 33rd Indiana was 242. The casualties of the 33rd were greater than that of any other single regiment in General Sherman's vast army during the campaign.

Valuable Auxiliaries

The members of quartermasters and commissary departments and engineer corps following in wake of Sherman's army were not only numerous, but also a very necessary adjunct to it. To say that with out them the army could not have advanced may seem strange, but it is true. They were pioneers and was by them that roads and bridges were repaired or built. They were often harassed by sharpshooters from their hidings. The rapidity with which streams were bridged, either by pontoons or wooden structures, was simply marvelous.

The rail road bridge, which spanned the Chattahoochie River more than 1000 feet long and 100 foot high, was made from timbers freshly cut, and was put up and trains were moving over it in four days. When a hit took away some forty foot, it was replaced in 24 hours.

Muster Out of Non Veterans
Reorganization of the Army

Men that had enlisted for three years, the time was up, September 16, 1864. There was some misunderstanding owing to such active campaign records in some instances had been confused. The muster roll finally being completed 19th, September, on that date Captain Beecher mustered out 143 non veterans on the 20th. Colonel John Coburn, Captain E. T. McCrae, Captain Day, Lieutenant Day, Lieutenant Jeff Farr, under the original order; these men and officers were a loss to the regiment and the service, each having seen three years of continuous service and were well fitted for their duties in war.

At the battle of Thompson Station, where from lack of support, General Gilbert was captured and thrown in to prison. He was, however, brevetted Brigadier General March 13, 1865. At the close of the war he was elected to Congress four successive terms. He urged Congress to preserve the records of the Civil War. His efforts brot forth the "Records of Rebellion", also a law for the marking of every Union soldier grave. After his retirement from congressional life, he was U. S. District Judge in the Territory of Montana and afterward practiced law in Indianapolis.

On the 24th of September, Captain James E. Burton of Co. "H" assumed command of the regiment. November 8 gives the new officers, Enos Halbert as Captain of Co. "I" (my father) also the author of the "**History of the 33rd Veteran Volunteer Infantry, Four Years of the Civil War**" by John R. McBride. From September 16, 1861 to July 21, 1865, John R. McBride was Quartermaster Sergeant of the new reorganization of the army.

Colonel John Coburn's Farewell Address
Headquarters of Second Brigade,
Third Division, Twentieth Army Corps.
Atlanta, Georgia, September 20, 1864

Soldiers of the Second Brigade: My terms of service has expired and I am about to be separated from you. We have been associated as a brigade almost two years. We have borne in that time all the burdens and endured all the trials and hardships of war together. This experience has made us friends - such friends as only suffering and toil together can make. In time you have shared an eventful part in the great struggle of the age. In Kentucky, Tennessee, and Georgia you have nobly illustrated the history of your own state of Indiana, Michigan and Wisconsin. That history cannot be written without a record of your calm, patience, disciplined courage and heroic daring. The bloody and desperate battle at Thompson Station and the successful fight at Franklin in Tennessee, gave early proof of your valor, while in past campaigns, Resaca, Carsaville, New Hope Church, Culp's Farm, Peach Tree Creek and Atlanta you have, in the front of the fight, borne straight onward your victorious banners. At Resaca your flags were the first to wave on the enemy's ramparts, at New Hope Church the fury of your onset redeemed the day's disaster, at Peach Tree Creek your charge rivaled the most famous feats of arms in the annals of war and at Atlanta your ranks were the first to climb the works of the enemy and take possession of that renowned city.

The 33rd Indiana at Wild Cat fought the first battle and won the first victory gained by the army of the Cumberland and the united brigade fired the last shot at the flying foe as he fled from his stronghold in Atlanta.

But not alone in the story and fierce fight have you been tried, you have by long marches, by herculean labors upon field work, stayed cheerful obedience, by watching that knew no surprise and by toil that knew no rest or weariness eclipsed the fame of your daring in battle and placed high above the glitter of victorious arms the steady light of your solid virtues.

We have lived together as brethren in great common cause, we part, our hearts glowing with the same patriotic ardor and hereafter when the war is over and the light of home is smiling around you, you will have no prouder memories than those associated with this brigade.

Your comrades in arms are sleeping beneath the clouds of the valley from Ohio to Atlanta, and from Atlanta to Richmond. Faithful, patient, and brave, they have given to their country and God whatever martyrs and heroes can give, and as one by one they fell out from your glorious ranks they have added new testimony to the sacredness of our cause.

My friends and soldiers, farewell.
John Coburn, Colonel
33rd Volunteers, Commanding Brigade

Occupation of Atlanta by the 20th Corps

The enemy remained a safe distance from Atlanta thru September, giving our troops ample time to recuperate and strengthen their position and was kept ready for motion at a moment's notice as the enemy's next move was uncertain. On the 29th the troops began to build better quarters, built out of materials taken from abandoned houses in and about Atlanta.

**Captain Enos Halbert
Civil War
From the Susan Hand Collection**

All the troops, except the 20th corps, were taken from Atlanta on October 3rd. This corps lost no time in strengthening the defenses and 143 men were detailed from the 33rd Indiana to assist in the work. The building of fortifications did not cease until about the 15th.

The persistent attacks of the enemy along the railroad in the rear caused a scarcity of rations and for several days the troops were nearly destitute of meat. But relief came, 2200 cattle, 6000 bushels corn, rations for the animals for 10 days. On the 16th at 5:30 a.m., a foraging party, consisting of one brigade from each of the three Divisions and including the 33rd Indiana of the 20th Corps, a division of cavalry and a battery of artillery, started on a 5 day foraging expedition, having in charge a train of 133 wagons. The 33rd moved out as rear guard for the expedition. At night went in to camp between Yellowstone and South Rivers. On the following day the third brigade, first division and two sections of artillery, were left in charge of about 400 wagons at Flat Shoals, while the remainder of the troops and wagons moved to the left bank of South River in quest of forage. Tho the country was poor, the train was loaded by night fall and other expeditions was sent out with 800 wagons. They were loaded without resistance. The several expeditions secured 6000 bushel of corn, 5 mules and 21 bales of cotton.

On November 6th and 9th the enemy made an unsuccessful attack on Atlanta lasting an hour, leaving in our hands two dead, 2 prisoners, one mortally wounded and 15 to 20 carried away. On the 11th, the regiment had its first battalion drill since the campaign opened in May. The reveille was beaten every morning at 5 a.m. when companies formed in line, stacked arms, ready for attack, which never came. On the 12th, military authorities were engaged in destroying the city by fire.

Jeff Davis sent Hood into Tennessee to draw the Union army out of Georgia. When the race in the direction of Nashville began between Hood's army and the 4th and 23rd Corps, the rest of Sherman's army was being skillfully concentrated in Atlanta and in so doing, the railroad from Chattanooga and Atlanta was destroyed. The army of the Cumberland held Atlanta. The army of Tennessee was grouped at East Point and the army of Ohio held Decatur.

On the 13th, the army was organized and called "Army of Georgia". The 15 and 17th Corps formed the right wing under General Howard and the 14th and 20th left wing under General Slocum. The 20th corps was commanded by General A. S. Williams.

Orders had previously been given to ship all surplus artillery, all baggage not needed, to the sea and all sick, wounded and refugees to Chattanooga. Orders completed by November 11, leaving an aggregate strength of 60,000 infantry, 5500 calvary and artillery reduced to one gun per 1000 men. By the 7th, all sick of the 33rd Indiana was sent north. Thus everything was in readiness on the 14th when troops were ordered to march at 7 a.m. on the 15th, to begin what is known in history and to all the people as "Sherman's March to the Sea".

March to the Sea

General Sherman had a staff of 5 officers to transmit orders to subordinates, besides chief of artillery, to look after that arm of the service; chief quartermaster, to look after transportation; inspector general to see that troops were properly equipped; chief engineer to supervise the building of defense; a medicine director for medical supplies; a chief commissary to provision the army and a chief signal officer, under whose direction messages were sent to and from different parts of the army by codes of signals. They chiefly controlled the destiny of Sherman's army.

The troops were supplied with good wagon trains, loaded with ammunitions and supplies, about 20 days of bread, 40 days of coffee and sugar, salt for 40 days, beef cattle for 40 days and 3 days of forage and grain.

The 33rd Indiana, with the rest of the brigade and divisions, moved out of camp and toward the sea at 9 oclock a.m., November 15, 1864, leaving Atlanta a smoldering mass. Leaving Decatur burning after them, they marched all night and part of the next day, went into camp 8 miles east of Stone Mountain. Houses all along the way mysteriously took fire and lit the way. The army now was cut loose. When supplies were needed they took from the country things that were needed for its progress. Foraging parties were sent out for supplies. The main army passed thru Sheffield by Summer's Mill, crossed Haynes Creek without halting. The march continued, no sleep, nor eats till 18th.

They were now in the heart of the best agriculture region of Georgia. Smokehouses, barns, farms and gardens yielded the necessities of life.

Upon reaching Rutledge Station on the Augusta and Atlantic, the railroad was destroyed in haste. Rail were taken from the ties and placed in alternate layers in a huge pile and set fire to. With claw to twist the bars after being heated, destroyed their future usefulness.

At Madison, all the male population had left. They still lived high off of the fat of the country, but prudent. Orders were issued prohibiting burning of buildings or shooting without the corps commander's orders. About this time Howell Cobb called to Georgians to "rise and defend their home, liberties and, [*etc.*]" As the army progressed, the negro population began to flock to it until it became a serious burden. Men, women and children poured in from every direction. On the 21st, the 33rd passed thru Eatonton, went into camp 1/2 mile from Little River. The road being muddy, teams gave out, and was replaced by drafts off of the country.

Milledgeville

The Georgia legislature had been in session, but left hastily on our approach. After a brief halt, [*the soldiers*] then crossed the Oconee River, halted for a few hours as marching was quite difficult thru swampy country. Combined with a cold fog, darkness came in. Fences were torched, tho could not penetrate the darkness. The army marched on till 3 a.m., then halted till 7 a.m. Could only make a mile an hour. At Buffalo Creek, went into camp for the night, on the farm of the man that burnt the bridge there. For revenge, his house was burned and the Pioneer Corps rebuilt the bridge. After crossing, destroyed [*the bridge*] on 26th. The negroes still continued to flock to the army. Some were used as servants. No persuasion or threats could drive them away. They had to be fed and was treated as humanely as the army could.

When the army left Atlanta, the horses and wagons were reduced to the actual needs of transportation of supplies then on hand. At first foragers went on foot but not long. They became possessed of wagons, carriages, mules and horses to carry all supplies found, none was wasted or was missed by them. On the 28th the 33rd moved before daylight in advance of the corps. At Ogeeche River, the troops were fired in to. A brigade was thrown to the left, the 33rd in the front line of battle till 5 a.m. on the 29th. The bridge being destroyed by the enemy caused a delay. When the pontoon bridge was built, the entire division crossed over, except the 33rd who guarded. Wheeler's Calvary harassed our army on the way - and reported our route in confusion. When in fact, as the army advanced, the enemy scattered like chaff before a wind.

The regiment staid in camp till 6 p.m. of the 30th, crossed the river and the pontoons were taken up. Marched thru swamp before reaching Louisville. After going 1 mile beyond the town, crossed another pontoon bridge and then plunged into another swamp, most serious of the march. Darkness and fog made it impossible to see each other in mud and water waist deep. They were often tumbling over each other and at times was difficult to get out of the deep mud. Those on horseback gave the horse the reign.

The brigade did not get into camp till 1 a.m. December 1. After a brief rest continued till 12 o'clock, went into camp. On the 2nd, the regiment moved in advance of the division without breakfast thru swamps and crossing Baker's Creek where quicksand added to their misery of getting the train over. In the afternoon they struck good road. At 9 p.m., after crossing Buckhead Creek, they went into camp. Reports reached the troops that foragers were being killed. On 26th of November, the Savannah, Georgia Daily News, among other things, said of Sherman's army, "We have reasons to believe they will be seriously bushwhacked and we trust cut to pieces. They are sprawling all over the country and those who are not willing to surrender can be beautifully bushwhacked. Let all the old and young folks turn out and give the rascals a taste of Georgia State sovereignty."

Miller Prison

December 3rd, Brigade was placed in charge of 240 wagons belonging to the calvary. Men guarded four paces apart. Roads were good to the prison, which was built for the Anderson prisoners. It was located 5 miles north of Miller, 80 miles from Savanna, 50 miles from Augusta and until our arrival had contained 6 to 7 thousand prisoners for exchange. The stockade was 800 ft. square, covering nearly 15 acres. It was enclosed with heavy pine logs, about 15 feet high. On top, sentry boxes were about 80 yards apart and 30 ft. from the fence was the "dead line".

Prisoners were turned into this pen in dead of winter without shelter. They, however, improvised some with sod and mud. Eight brick bake ovens were partly constructed. Three men were found dead in a hut and on a board, at the end of a ditch outside, said 650 were buried here. To the southeast two forts were partly constructed and southwest a stockade incomplete.

Mr. John McElroy, who was there as a prisoner, in a book entitled "Andersonville" says in regard to Miller prison: "As November wore away, long continued chilling, searching rains desolated our days and nights. The great cold drops pelted down slowly, dismally and incessantly. Each seemed to beat thru our emaciated frames against the very marrow of our bones and to be battering its way remorselessly into the citadel of life like the cruel drops that fall from the basin of the inquisitors upon the firmly fastened head of the stillness.

The lagging, laden hours were impressibly dreary. Compared with many others we were comfortable, as our hut protected us from the actual beating of the rain upon our bodies, but we were much more miserable than under the sweltering heat of Andersonville, as we lay almost naked upon our beds of pine leaves, shivering in the raw rasping air and looked out over acres of wretches lying dumbly on sodden sand receiving the benumbing drench of the sullen skies, without a groan or a motion. It was enough to kill healthy, vigorous men, active and resolute, with bodies well nourished, and well clothed and with minds vivacious and hopeful, to stand these day and nights long cold drenchings. No one can imagine how fatal it was to boys whose vitality was sapped by long months in Andersonville by coarse, meager, changeless food, by groveling on the bare earth and hopelessness of any improvement of conditions.

Fever, rheumatism, throat and lung diseases and despair now came to complete the work begun by scurvy, dysentery and gangrene in Andersonville. Hundreds, weary of the struggle and of hoping against hope, laid themselves down and yielded to fate. In the six weeks that we were at Miller one man in every ten died. The ghostly pines there sigh over the unnoted graves of 700 boys for whom life's morning closed in the gloomiest shadows. As many as would form a splendid regiment as many as constitute the first born of a populous city, more than three times as many as were slain outright on our side in the bloody battle of Franklin, succumbed to this new hardship. The country for which they died does not even have a record of their names. Blotted out as never had been."

Leaving Miller in the evening, the brigade plunged into an other swamp and continued till 2 a.m., hungry, wore out, went into camp. December 4, crossed Big and Little Home Creek and moved five miles and went into camp.

The 33rd moved in advance of the corps. At 6 a.m. the train was ordered to camp, four day's rations of feed for horses as the abounding country would be swampy and destitute of feed.

However, the foragers were busy. With the aid of the negroes, they located cattle secreted in the swamp. In many instances they learned where needed supplies were hidden. Roads were badly blocked with fallen trees. The 7th the army crossed Turkey Creek. After 15 mile march camped at Springfield. Leaving there they plunged into deep swamps, with the enemy causing trouble. Roads were terrible, quicksand and water engulfed corduroy. Wagons, sunk to the hubs, were scattered along the way and in many instances men had to put their shoulders to the wheel to lift them out. Roads were blocked all the way and the enemy disputed every step of the way. On December 11 the corps reached the vicinity of Savannah. Throwing the line of battle around it meant an early down fall of the city. The batteries of the enemy continued to dispute our position, with very few casualties. Rations became reduced, 1/3 rations of crackers, very little potatoes were issued to each man. The foragers of the 2nd brigade were the first to take possession of some rice mills on the upper end of Hutchinson's Island, whose duty, also, was to guard a battery commanding the river.

The mill was under the direction of Captain Halbert (my father), brigade commissary. When all the rice was hulled and sacked, it was shipped to the army on the mainland where needed. Now the rations consisted of beef, rice and very little salt. The woods were well supplied with "Spanish Moss" which men used for bedding but which had to be abandoned very soon because of its transmitting malarial poison to most all the men who slept on it. (A mistaken belief now as their malarial came from mosquito bites in the swamps they traveled thru.) [*This note made by Maggie*].

December 14, Fort McAllister was captured, 19 cannons, 300 prisoners, thus tightening the army's grip on the city of Savannah. On the 20th the enemy evacuated the city.

Immediately upon the city's downfall and occupancy of it by the Union troops, General Sherman forwarded the following dispatch to President Lincoln: "I beg to present to you, as a Christmas gift, the city of Savannah, with 150 guns, ammunition, and also 25 thousand bales of cotton."

General Sherman said of the campaign: "Not a wagon was lost. The trains were in better condition than when they started: 265 miles of railroad were destroyed - Georgia RR 60 miles from Atlanta to Madison, and 140 miles of the Georgia Central from 10 miles west of Gordon to Savannah and about 50 miles on the Charleston road."

On the 17th the troops received their first mail from the North from home and friends. Brigade inspection took place 18 and 19th of December 1864.

The Army Crosses the Savannah River

The march across the Carolinas was next in order. Rainy season had now set in. Progress was slow. Roads had to be corduroyed. Unusually high water in the rivers submerged the low and swampy banks, making it almost impossible to find a place to lay pontoon. Finally "Sisters Ferry" was chosen. A crossing was finally made, but frequent explosions of torpedoes concealed underwater and drifts subjected the working parties to considerable danger. Men were killed and wounded by these infernal machines. A full month was consumed in getting the army together with the necessary supplies, acrost the river to Hutchinson's Island. It was about 7 miles long, 900 acres devoted to raising rice.

On January 1, 1865, moved to the island, laying pontoons to connect the South Carolina shore. A cold snow storm set, only a few divisions crossed. The 2nd, the 33rd and two more divisions were crossed by the help of the steam boat, Planter. Robert Smalls, the captain of the Planter, was formerly a slave.

[*The story of Robert Smalls is as follows. - mc*] On the night of May 12, 1863, the officers of the boat slept on shore in Charleston, South Carolina, leaving the boat with the crew of 8 colored men. Smalls was the wheel man, virtually the pilot. Under existing conditions colored men were not permitted that title.

He [*Smalls*] had previously considered the idea of escape, decided at once to make his escape - to fail was death. At 3:25 o'clock a.m. of the 13th, the Planter started. Small was thoroughly familiar with the surroundings and the usual salute in the passage of the forts in the vicinity of Charleston. Approaching Fort Sumpter he stood in the pilot house leaning out of the window, with his arms folded across his breast after the manner of Captain Relay, the commander of the boat and head covered with a large straw hat which the Captain usually wore on such occasions. The purpose of the Planter was not discovered until too late. He [*Smalls*] served as pilot on vessels, was in several naval engagements. For many and timely brave acts he was promoted to Captain of the Planter. He afterwards held many positions of trust, having served his district in Congress for years.

After landing, the brigade went in to camp up the river, not knowing the surroundings. About midnight the water rose to 12 inches all over the camp, which conditions had to be endured until day light when they moved to high ground.

On the 4th, the brigade went in to camp about 7 miles from the river in a beautiful grove, passing fortifications said to have been built by the Americans during the siege of Savannah in 1779.

They were truly landmarks of the industry and valor of our revolutionary fathers. Here they fought (1779) to establish a republic of and for the people and here in 1865 we were engaged in its preservation.

The March Across the Carolinas

The troops were highly elated over the fact they were at last in South Carolina, the birthplace of the rebellion. They were determined that this state should experience the full malice that its people had precipitated on the country.

The brigade went in to camp at Hardee's plantation. With what material was at hand they built a comfortable camp. While supplies of all kinds were being received, the men rested in readiness for the order "strike tents". All the time they were heavily guarded, enemy being near. Having driven the Confederates so far, every man in the army was anxious to keep them going. Continuous rains made it impossible for the 3rd division to advance beyond this point. On this very spot, General Lincoln's army, during the Revolutionary War, was "swamped" while on its way to reinforce General Pulaski at Savannah. The 33rd remained at Purysburg guarding stores.

February 1, the 33rd Indiana "struck tents", marched 15 miles, went into camp. The course of the army was often marked by dense columns of smoke. The 2nd joined the brigade at Robertsville, went in to camp near Lawtonville, a 22 mile march.

While crossing a swamp, the enemy contested our way. The interruption was brief, as we marched toward them they fled. Wheeler's calvary was near. On the 6th, another swamp, a mile wide, with fortifications, built by the enemy. With a flank movement they were driven out and our men captured four pieces of artillery.

The "Bummers" captured vast supplies from the surrounding country. "Rain! Swamps." These two elements obstructed more than did the enemy. Foragers or "bummers" were killed on sight.

On the 7th, the 33rd guarded 50 wagons and crossed the Salkahatchie and went in to camp near Bamburg or Lowery's Station.

On the 8th, the 33rd moved back one mile to Patterson's house, picketed till 5 p.m., marched to Graham's Turnout on the R.R. and went in to camp. Abundant supplies were brot in tho two foragers were killed. Next day went thru Blacksville, tearing and destroying the R.R. thoroughly, on the 10th, at Winston destroyed two more miles of track. On the 11th, the brigade left the R. R., moved back to Williston then north to Mill Creek. Crossed then on the South Edisto River at Clark's Mill, remained till Guignard's bridge was rebuilt. The farmers along the way was not able to ascertain our course, found it impossible to hide their stock and provisions, everything was abandoned on the way. The bridge being destroyed, the men had to wade the ice cold river. Then proceeded to Davis' Mills, thence to Orangeburg and Columbia road. After a march of 17 miles, camped on Lexington Road. The rain continued to pour, swamps and creek to cross made travelling miserable. Many places, roads had to be made or repaired.

First View of Columbia

On the 16th of February, crossed Twelve Mile Creek, leaving Lexington, advancing toward Columbia. On the 17th, moved up the Saluda River to Mount Zion. The 18th, found the pontoon bridge insecure - it took the brigade all day crossing the river, went in to camp, three miles from Broad River.

With the expectation of an attack, the army staid in line of battle for two days. Then crossed the river on pontoons, built new road from the river to Columbia and Winnsborough highway, then crossed Little River and went in to camp at Thompson's Post Office. The army now received notice that the campaign would probably last forty days longer, provisions scarce. Not encouraging, but the men quietly accepted the situation. The corps passed thru Winnsborough on the 21st, in review before Generals Slocum and Ward. The town was destitute of male population and all the R.R. buildings and rolling stock were destroyed. Some of the foragers, in their zeal to get ahead of the advanced guard, were dismounted and put afoot. This did not change them. They continued to go where ever they could get supplies, regardless of danger. On the 22nd, the regiment moved early, marched 20 miles over a succession of hills and went in to camp on Rocky Mount, to be ready to cross the Catawba River at a moment. This rapid movement was made to cut Butler's Calvary, reported crossing our lines, which did not show up. The brigade bivouacked till 12 o'clock midnight. At 2 a.m. of the 23rd, descended the mountain to river's edge. The 33rd, with the brigade, was detailed to repair the road, having not been used. It was a very steep hill, 3/4 miles long.

They cut a new road thru a swamp from the head of the pontoon bridge to the main road, 100 yards. Then, having to corduroy it, with numerous other places corduroyed. Because of the scarcity of material they had to carry poles, by man power, a mile to complete the job. The Brigade command said of it: "The exceedingly hard labor was performed during one of the darkest nights of the season without proper tools, without sleep or rest and above all, after having just completed a march of ten miles. The endurance of the men in this instance was heavily taxed and they are deserving of special mention."

Corduroy Road

[*Corduroy roads were commonly constructed through swampy areas by cutting trees and laying them side-by-side across the roadbed to form a road. These may be several layers of logs deep in some areas where the swamp was very deep. By laying the logs side by side you got a "corduroy" look, thus the term corduroy road. - mc*]

Until this time, the army had been travelling north, but now turned east, surprising the enemy in the vicinity of Cheraw. This caused a reduction on the sea coast, and also the evacuation of many important points.

Roads here was in a wretched condition, miles of corduroy had to be repaired, rain continued, some days the army only moved three miles. Three foragers of Co. "I", 33rd Indiana was captured. On the 25th and 26th, due to rain and fog, brigade stayed in camp. The brigade assisted in building corduroy road most all the way to Hanging Rock.

This vicinity was noted for being the center of operations of "Marion and his Merrymen" during the Revolutionary War.

On the 27th, a detachment was sent in search of the Fourteenth Corps. When found, it had not yet crossed the Catawba River because of a sudden raise in the river, loosing 12 pontoons.

The 28th, crossed Hanging Rock. The rain continued to fall, making roads most impassable and did not get in to camp till 11 a.m. The Bummers had been successful in getting forage of all kinds. A negro, as usual, led the way to a place where 6 horses, 23 mules, one wagon, a buggy and other valuables were. When marching into camp the procession looked like an oldtime caravan. From this supply of animals the field and staff officers of the 33rd were fortunate. (The white horse father road in the army was gotten this way).

March 1st, the army crossed Little and Big Lynch Creek going in camp two miles beyond. The regiment was deployed along the wagon train, covering 48 wagons. Also March 2nd, at this point, a mill dam gave away, which delayed camp till midnight.

The 33rd broke camp early, on the 3rd passed thru Chesterfield, South Carolina. Then camped the rest of the day. The regiment was deployed along a train of 50 wagons and 27 ambulances. Moved out early, crossed Deep Bottom Creek. Roads better. Captured some of the enemy, marched on into North Carolina, camped on Grandy's Plantation at 1 o'clock p.m. The Brigade remained in camp, Sunday, 5th, near Great Pedee River, while pontoons were being laid. About this time General Breckinridge was succeeded in command of the Confederate forces by General Joseph E. Johnston.

An occasional loyal family was found in South Carolina. Four officers had escaped from a rebel prison and reached the Union lines. They had taken refuge at the house of a loyal white woman while being pursued. She placed them under a feather bed. When the rebels appeared, she was lying on the bed and feigned sickness. They did not disturb her and the officers escaped. At an other time a private soldier sought protection at the same house. She had him blackened, put in an old suit of clothes, and as a colored servant, he drove the family carriage into the Union lines.

Capture of Cheraw

The roads being now good, Cheraw, was entered without any resistance. The rebels thot the Union Army was headed for Charlotte, North Carolina, so stored a great quantity of ammunitions in Cheraw. Twenty canons, thousands of small arms, commissary stores, 20 ton powder all fell to our hands.

Destroying bridges did not delay the advance of Pioneer Corps as pontoons were laid quickly. On the 8th, the 33rd marched in advance. For a long distance two roads were parallel, and the 14th and 20th corps marched side by side, crossed North Carolina line.

Foragers were successful, securing sweet potatoes. On the 9th, the march was interrupted by continuous rain and swamps. Went in to camp at 10 p.m. On the 10th, a swamp called Lumber Creek was crossed by wading, after which the brigade was deployed along the wagon train. The 33rd Indiana was covering 60 wagons and 20 ambulances. Road being corduroyed made travelling very slow. Foragers were successful in getting feed for the mules and horses, but none for the men. On 11th the corps crossed Rock Fish Creek or swamp on pontoons. The 33rd were engaged in building roads. Finally reached Fayetteville and Rockingham plank road. Along the road were mile post, notched to designate miles. It was said that this was for the benefit of the negro and "Po white trash", who could not read.

At Terry, a steam tug with mail from the north awaited them, the first since February 1st.

Supplies also were received. Sick and wounded men were sent home. Negroes were marched to Wilmington. There was about 25,000 of them whom had joined the army after leaving Savannah. There were some whites, but mostly women and children. One little black fellow stuck to my father waiting on him hand and foot, and begged passionately to go with him.

The 12th being Sunday, they rested. Here a bridge had been destroyed by the enemy.

Private property in Fayetteville was respected by the Union troops. The day was devoted to the troops writing letters, their first opportunity since the march began. The arsenal, that contained great amount of machinery, formally belonged to Harper's Ferry arsenal. That, and all the buildings, were thoroughly destroyed by our army. The 13th, the army passed thru Fayetteville in review before Generals Slocum, Sherman, Williams and Ward, was near midnight, went in to camp. The 33rd Indiana foragers, under command of Leiutenant Henry Jeter of Co. B, were captured this day. The party had crossed Little River for corn, were cut off and surrounded by the enemy. They were confined in a house that stood well off the ground. At night they cut a hole in the floor, letting two escape at intervals. At last the Lieutenant fell asleep before his time and two others were to go. Later they were exchanged.

The 14th remained in camp, all the crippled and broken down mules were disposed of. Troops moved out on 15th at 6 a.m. Marched 14 miles on the Raleigh road. Rain began, crossed Silver Creek, encamped near Taylor's Hole Creek in a heavy rain, in line of battle. The Union army had been very watchful of the enemy's move and even now more so.

Battle of Averasborough

On the 16th, this battle was fought, lasting all day with some losses on the Union side. Tho captured several hundred prisoners, and two 12 pound cannons, which was turned on the fleeing enemy. As the enemy fled the next day, the road was strewn with wagons, and ambulances, which were filled with the enemy's dead, dying and wounded. The retreat was disorderly and demoralizing. The 18th the brigade moved to the rear 2 miles, then crossed Black River, wading in water waist deep. The road passed thru swamps partly corduroyed, movement was very slow. The entire brigade guarded 125 wagons. The head of the train began to camp at 10 p.m. The rear arrived at 5 o'clock in the morning.

Battle of Bentonville

On the 19th, Sunday, the rear of the brigade, altho not getting in till 5 a.m. moved out again at 8 a.m. The brigade was again deployed a long the wagon train. After a few miles march, General Ward received orders from General Williams to "push forward and let the wagon train go to hell," that the 14th corps were being pushed by the enemy.

The battle was on - a surprise. Works were thrown up in 40 minutes on the edge of an open field skirted with a dense woods. For the time engaged the slaughter of the enemy was heavy, 2462; Union 1144. Night closed the contest and the enemy withdrew.

The 20th all was set for another battle, but as the army advanced the enemy withdrew again. With the restoration of General Joe Johnston to the command of the Confederate forces, everyone was convinced that greater effort would be made to crush Sherman's army. On the 21st, the wagon trains were ordered to report to Cox's bridge on the Neuse River and then to Kingston for supplies. Then each officer were to take supplies enuf for 3 days; coffee, hard bread, sugar, meat. They were now on half rations till more was received. Rain continued. On 23rd the brigade advanced 5 miles of Goldsborough. Rebel calvery was reported to be near. Road to Smithfield was strongly guarded.

Matt B. Collins of Co. "I" and others were captured when out foraging by Wheeler's scouts under Captain Shannon. Came near being hung after being robbed. Then, fortunately, the rebel scouts began quarreling among themselves. One was humane and brave enough to denounce such proceedings. Drew his revolver and said "Look here, Captain Shannon, I have seen enough of this kind of work going on and am getting tired of it." Serious trouble was eminent, but taken before General Allen, they were then taken before General Wheeler who ordered them placed with the other prisoners and proceed to Raleigh, thence to Goldborough, where orders were issued to make a more thorough search. "And if any written papers or gold or silver coin or ornaments or weapons of any kind were found on their persons, such articles should be taken from them as lawful prizes and in behalf of the Confederate States of America." Guards were instructed to shoot down any prisoner found concealing anything. This order was only legalizing the robbery, but was amusing since they had previously been robbed of everything. From Goldborough they were taken to Danville and then to Richmond, Virginia and confined in Libby prison. They did not remain long. One day Dick Turner said, "Get out of here, every d__d one of you, we will send you to your own lines." 1800 obeyed the command.

There was such haste and confusion following the announcement and to facilitate the matter a Brigadier General, who was among the prisoners, proposed to take the "parole oath" for the whole of them, which proposition was accepted.

They were then marched to the river and placed on transport, bound for City Point. These were the last prisoners placed in Libby prison by Confederate authorities.

The 24th the brigade marched into Goldsborough and in review past General Sherman and went in to camp north of city on Weldon Railroad.

On the 25th of May, the camp was changed. Lieutenant Thomas and six men captured 40 head of cattle and the brigade was now in possession of a grist mill. The living was much the same as that before "the march to the sea".

On the 9th of April, Major Maze returned from the north with 150 recruits for the 33rd Indiana making 770. On the 10th the brigade moved out toward Smithfield. At Moccasin Creek, a bridge had to be built, they rested till morning. The weather was hot, many was prostrated by the heat. They moved 15 miles, camped at Smithfield.

At 5:30 o'clock a.m. of the 12th, the 33rd moved out in advance of the corps passing thru Smithfield, marched 15 miles, then camped at Swift Creek.

Orders came to assist General Kirkpatrick, as it was feared he had been stopped by the enemy. However, this proved false. They returned to camp, and while there received an official notice of the capture of Richmond - they were delighted with the news.

Absalom Waddle of Co. "B" was this day killed while out foraging. He was the last one of the regiment to be killed by the Confederates. On April 13th the brigade moved out at 5:30 o'clock a.m. and reached Raleigh about 3 p.m. and went in to camp inside the enemy's earthworks near the city.

Surrender of General Joe Johnston

The capture of Richmond, Virginia, by the army under General Grant and his amediate pursuit of General Lee's army, made a change in General Sherman's plans necessary and the swift movement toward and possession of Raleigh was thot to prevent Lee and Johnston from conferring and making new combinations. It was Sherman's intention to continue the pursuit upon reaching Raleigh, but Johnston finding future success hopeless, that Lee had surrendered and Sherman's Army was pressing him hard, on April 14 was the first to suggest a cessation of hostilities, with a view to ultimate surrender.

There was fear of Johnston playing a trick, but Sherman had faith in his personal sincerity, yet every precaution was taken to prevent the escape of the army. The brigade remained in camp till the 25th.

Assassination of President Lincoln

On the 17th of April [1865] the news was given to the army. The 19th was devoted by the troops in giving expression of their grief. A meeting of the 33rd Indiana was called by Colonel Burton to take some action.

Great sorrow was manifest thru out the regiment and army. Major Maze and Adj. McBride was appointed to formulate suitable resolutions.

For nearly two weeks negotiations were pending between Sherman and Johnston without definite results. On the 24th General Sherman issued his ultimatum that "the suspension of hostilities agreed to between us will cease within 48 hours after this is received at your lines." And also demanded the surrender of Johnston's army "on the same terms as were given to General Lee at Appomattox of April 9th, instant, purely and simple."

With the surrender of the armies under Lee and Johnston, the war was now over. Sherman's army had now completed a march, beginning at Chattanooga, accrossed the states of Georgia and South Carolina and now resting at the capital of North Carolina. Without revenge, the army was ready to lay down its arms, as eager as they were to take them up in 1861, when the flag was assailed and the integrity of the Union threatened. Sherman's army was harassed by 30,000 men under General Hardee, Johnston and others all the way. Orders had been issued by the Confederate authorities calling upon the people to destroy all supplies on the line of march, but they could not be enforced.

The citizens were demoralized and Sherman's "Bummers", as well as the army itself, seemed to be every where. Under the

---

A Bible Found

In one of the many camping places, Father noticed the ground was broken. He dug down, found a large box, tho when opened was a writing desk inside, a large bible and etc. This all was shipped home and used for years.

I remember the bible well, with many illustrated pages. We took it to Kansas - after we moved from the farm in to town (Beloit) one day someone was looking thru it. They found two leaves stuck together. Upon prying them apart there was the name and address of the owner. Father got busy and wrote to the address and in due time received an answer asking the bible be sent back, which father did. Tho never had a word in reply. Perhaps the old southern grudge still rankled in them and was not thankful to father for its return. **- From Maggie's writings** circumstances, they probably did the best they could. All kinds of meat and boxes of valuables were often located underground and livestock were hid in deep swamps. Much credit it is due to the sagacity and unwearying activity of the "bummer" but there is some need of praise due the negro. The farm hands, however, rather than the house servant, rarely failed to give whatever information was possible.

All the food for both animals and man were gleaned of the surrounding country they went thru except the sugar, coffee and salt.

The health of the army was good; of 65,000 men, was but a fraction of 2% that needed care and until the battle of Aversborough and Bentonville there was but little use of an ambulance, except to carry supplies.

The Bummer

The term "Bummer", as applied to that class of soldiers who became so distinguished in Sherman's army, is not well understood by a great many. It is not a term of reproach. On the contrary, their operations were most praiseworthy. They did choice work in feeding the army, by sapping the very life of the Confederacy, in depriving it of the very substance upon which it thrived - their livestock and the products of the soil.

A bummer "was a being peculiar unto himself ". He had to be audacious as well as courageous. He had to fathom human nature, diagnose a statement made by citizens and negroes as well, act with discretion, possess unlimited energy and endurance. Sometimes the best "Bummer" was found among those who could not tolerate the camp. The indifferent soldier often made the best "Bummer" in quest of food. Without cruelty he could get the best service out of a packmule and utilize space on a captured wagon or carriage. They knew the success of the army depended upon them in their duty. It was valuable to the army during the march to the sea, as much as any other branch, and was firmly entrenched in the heart and affection of the army.

Foraging off the enemy was war and it was that system of warfare that made the movement of Sherman's army a possibility and a success. Time, nor distance, nor danger, did not deter them. All these were bravely met and overcome. General Sherman referring to the march said: "My men seem to get fat and healthy on parched corn and bacon."

General Slocum said: "I have witnessed, on the campaign, scenes which have given me more exhaulted opinion than I ever before entertained of earnest patriotism, which actuates the soldier of the army. I have repeatedly seen soldiers of my command who were making parched corn supply the place of bread and who were nearly destitute of shoes or a change of clothing go cheerfully to their labor in the swamp of South Carolina working hour after hour in mud and water to bring forward our immense trains, and yet during all these privations and hardships I have never heard from an officer or soldier one word of complaint."

During the time from January 3 till April 15, 1865 there were 107 skirmishes, 8 actions, 2 affairs and 2 battles. Thus, two armies were closely watching each other's movements.

On to Richmond and Washington

The dissolution of the Confederate Army being well established, the "Boys in Blue" looked to the homeward march with satisfaction and pleasure. On April 30th started north. Two corps tried to reach Richmond first, made 20 miles first fore noon, but had to stop to rest the horses. However, both reached Richmond at the same time.

Richmond and Its Prison Pens

Upon reaching Richmond, ample time was given the men to visit the prison pens; Belle Isle, Castle, Thunder and Libby. Just two years before, the 2nd Brigade was enforced inmates of Libby. Now what a mighty change – door open, keepers gone. On the 12th troops resumed their march, passing thru the Chickahominy Swamps, where deadly miasma [(*pollution, miainein, to pollute) poisonous vapor formerly supposed to arise from decomposing animal or vegetable matter, swamps, etc. and infect the air, especially at night: such vapor was once thought to cause malaria*] killed more of the Army of the Potomac than did the enemy's bullets. Thence to Chancellorsville and Spotsylvania Courthouse, where some of the hardest fighting was done. On the morning of the 24th, the corps passed thru Alexandria, acrossed the long bridge, and moved up Maryland Avenue to the Nation's capital building, moving without delay.

The Grand Review

The review of the combined armies of General Grant and Sherman, the East and West at the Nation's Capital, was a glorious climax in the closing scenes of the war! It was a red letter day for the men that had so long, so zealously, so gallantly, defended their country. All together it is said there were 150,000 men in line, extending thirty miles.

Muster Out of Regiments

The war being over, the next thing in order was the swift dissolution of the army.

In June 1865, the regiment took passage in box cars on the Baltimore and Ohio R.R. and arrived at Parkersburg, West Virginia. The following day, they were transported in boats down the Ohio River to Louisville, Kentucky. Remained there till mustered out July 21, 1865 and from there went to Indianapolis, Indiana to dissolve as a military organization for all time to come.

"To All Whom It May Concern"

Know ye, that Enos Halbert of captain of Company ("I") 33rd Regiment of Virginia (Indiana?) veteran.

Volunteers who was enrolled in the 14th day of February one thousand eight hundred and Sixty four to serve three years or during the war is hereby Discharged from service of the United States this 21st day of July 1865 at Lewisville, Kentucky by reasons of G.O. 26 Army _____ July 3rd, 1865. (No objection to his being re-enlisted is known to exist.*)

Said Enos Halbert was born in Orange Co. in the State of Indiana is 40 years of age, 5 ft. 11 1/2 inches high, light complexion, blue eyes, light hair and by occupation when enrolled a Farmer.

Given at Lewisville this 21 day of July 1865.

R. Papst,
Capt. 10th Mich Inft.
Commanding the Reg't.
A.C.M. 2nd Div. 14th A.C.

John P. Wiederana Litent.
Commanding Regt. Ind. Vet. Vols. Inft.

Note: This is apparently taken from a certificate that Maggie (Halbert) Hand either had or saw at some time in her life.

Four years had now nearly elapsed from the date of organization. It is sad to contemplate that all the boys did not return - there were those, however, who did return severely wounded or shattered in health and others still returning who were apparently in the full glow of health. Having closely followed the pursuit of military life, yet they fully recognized their duty as citizens and when the regiment was finally dissolved entered upon their life's work with the same zeal and loyalty to the laws of the country that characterized their military career and at once won the admiration of all law abiding people.

Christian Organizations

Rev. Joseph L. Irwin was the regiment's first chaplain. There were many earnest Christians in the regiment. In 1864, Rev. John McCrea became chaplain at Atlanta. Opportunities to preach was rare - he rendered good service in hospitals, attending the spiritual wants of the sick and wounded.

At Goldsborough, North Carolina, a pulpit and seats were improvised. Many publicly declared to live an upright Christian life. The "Creed and Pledge" were broad and liberal for all religiously inclined to stand upon.

Gambling

Even if it did exist to a very considerable extent, it aught not to be surprising in the absence of the influence which tend to elevate society - the law, the church and the home. Human nature was the same in the army as at home. Some followed the games to the lowest depths of misery, while others indulged mildly and many not at all. Like all games of chance, the winners were generally with the banker. The old ditty was this:

> Some play for gain: to pass time, others play
> for nothing; both play the fool, I say;
> Who gets by play proves loser in the end.

Gold and Greenbacks

The only time the 33rd Indiana was paid in gold was at Crab Orchard, Kentucky, in December 1861. All subsequent payments were made in greenbacks. The private soldier was paid at the rate of $13.00 per month from the beginning of the war until April 30, 1864 when pay was increased to $16.00 per month. This rate continued till the close of the war.

A calculation shows that each private soldier of the 33rd Indiana who served from September 16, 1861 to July 25, 1865, if paid the difference between the value of the greenback dollar and the gold dollar, would be entitled to $203.81+. In this calculation bounties are not concidered. In other words, if they had been paid in gold, they would have received, during that same time, $656.00 instead of $452.18+, the value of the greenback in gold.

This finishes the book, with the exception of queer happenings and anecdotes, which happened thru the campaigns and I don't feel they are really needed here. Would take days to rewrite them.

After a short period of drilling from army duties, Father was taken to the ranks in Kentucky, Cumberlin Gap, Boling Green, Chattanooga, and Look Out Mountain. Many other smaller engagements was with Buell part of the time. From private soldier he gradually held other office till he was made Captain. Also served in the calvary. Once a year when the army was in Kentucky he was allowed to go home on a furlough. Toward the last he was in Sherman's Army and was in that memorable march to the sea, "From Atlanta to the Sea". The flower of the army was taken for this march. This march as we all know, was to cut the south in two, thru the best of the south on their grainery, burning and destroying all property and food in their reach. All entreaty to spare their homes were turned aside. After the army was fed and clothed, the balance, if any, was destroyed. Often the owners burned their buildings rather than have the soldiers or Northerners burn them. One can't blame the south for hating the north. To have ones homes, barns, negro quarters, grainery, all wiped out by an invading army. The hatred must have been great. Old and young all kicked out to rustle for themselves or go find some one other planter that the army had missed on the sides. This devastation went on steadily and surely. My father hated to see those lovely estates laid lo but he was in the army and must obey. So, they went on searching the houses for hidden money and valuables, then ripping open feather beds and stuffed furniture, taking up carpets, rummaging thru drawers till all were thoroughly searched. Then they would take all the food and horse feed needed and then set all on fire, leaving a guard to see it was not put out. Then the main ranks marched on to rummage other homes. The soldiers often suffered exposure, sleeping in damp ground, marching thru swamps, making their corduroy roads as they went. There were enough able bodied men left home to resist. Savanna was reached and Sherman had ordered to march north to split the coast country thru and destroy everything in its wake. Richmond was surly falling, then Sherman would have depleted the south and joined the victorious army in Virginia.

Grant was a far seeing commander in chief. The end came. Father marched in Sherman's army as Captain, thru that memorable parade at Appomattox court house. It was the spring of '65, April, all was over. He had served four long years. Older and tireder than he had ever been on the California Trip. He had gone thru without any accident, tho many hear breds [*breadth*] escapes. At Cumberland Gap he escaped by the fleetness of his horse. He clung on Indian fashion and let the horse go at full speed. Word was sent home of his death. Tho, later word was corrected.

In the dusk of the evening he often sat at the fire place and told these army stories. I so disliked the stories I'd cover up my head and try to forget them. Now I wish I had remembered. When word of Lee's surrender came to Orleans, the town rejoiced and then rejoiced again when the soldiers of that vicinity came home.

It is true one could hire a substitute. That was done when one was able to pay a man to go for him. One man agreed to give his place [*farm*] to a man if he would go for him. The man went, served out the time and came back and took the place. The once owner [*a man by the name of Stackhouse*] had to go west to find a home.

Chapter VII

Rebuilding

****

With the war over, not all came home with able bodies. With the damming influence of four years of war, no man could really be the same again. Tho I think my father one among the many that settled down and went to work on the home place.

We were poor, for mother could do no more than she did. It was impossible to raise a large crop each year tho she did well to keep the stock and the increases. Other neighbors were getting rich selling their stock and grain at war prices while father was away fighting for his and their country. After the farm was brot back to its full production, fences repaired and gullies filled, he turned his attention to a saw mill as lumber was needed in this vicinity as yet the lower Indiana was a forest of choicest woods. First buying 80 acres of heavily timbered land, he sawed this lumber up for sale. Then he hired men to clear and plow the land. The large stumps had to stand and rot out so corn and wheat, barley and rye was about the only crops that could be raised among the stumps. After the stumps were rotted out and burned they planted wheat. He often built a nice sized house on this plot of ground and it then was a good farm in those days and would bring a good price. He logged on in this way several years and made money. Then another girl, Annie, [Lucy Ann] came. With mother's steady planning the bunch was clothed and taught to help in all the phases of home keeping and clothing, weaving and sewing. Then he decided to build a new house and barn north of the edge of the orchard.

Enos & Susan's sixth child, Lucy Ann Halbert born December 7, 1866.

The new house finally was finished, a nice substantial building for those days. On the main floor there was the shed where the girls did the spinning on the big wheels. In fact, that was a workshop, from there the kitchen pantry and a shared bedroom. A real stove graced this kitchen. A stepstove was a great improvement over the fire place. In one corner stood the big wooden loom and the small spinning wheel with a place left for the eating table for now there were 6 children to eat (with mother and father was 8). Off of the kitchen was a large sitting room. Then the parlor joined on to the spare bedroom, making an almost square structure. Then a hall ran the full length of the sitting room and parlor. The outside doors were one at each end. Then on the side of the hall was three bedrooms and a stairway for an upstairs room used as a store room and play room. It also was used for summer bedroom for the girls. There was a small cellar under the kitchen where they went in from the outside which was used for the milk in the summer. Off of the back porch was the carriage shed, ice house and smoke house, where the meat was cured. This house set back off the main road with a lane leading out.

On two sides were large cedar trees, the other side an apple orchard. Acrosst the lane leading to the barn and corral was a large mulberry tree. It grew in clost to the fence so when the mulberries ripened it was handy for the children to climb in to the tree and eat mulberries their fill, then take home more of the luscious black berries for dinner. We moved in to the new house in the fall and the following March I was born.

After the war, people continued to trek west, California and Kansas, Nebraska, in fact to every nook and corner of the west, farmers especially wished to seek new land. Then there were a certain amount of miners and laborers. All were needed to build a new empire. My father had had the urge to go since the close of war. If it had been possible, he would have went then. Mother believed in staying with her home. Then the fearful stories of Indian atrocities committed on families in the far west served to keep him farming for a few years in Indiana. After the new house was built, a home in Indiana for life was planned.

Enos & Susan's seventh child, Maggie Ellen Halbert, born March 17, 1869.

Maggie Ellen Halbert

First saw the light on a farm March 17, 1869, Orangeville, Orange County, Indiana. The youngest of 7 children (Perhaps spoiled) - Mary, Sarah, Seth, Hattie, Emma, Annie (Lucy), Maggie.

I was born in the new house, the others in the old house by the spring creek. Father and Mother planned this house years before as there were a row of nice cedars and other trees planted some distance from the house to make a nice yard. A collection of nice stalactites and other curios were in the yard, so no wonder I like curios. I think most of them came from big caves not far away. I vividly remember the hollow sound when we passed over on the road in places. Then there were big sink holes. At Orangeville a river came out of a big cliff.

Mother and Mary bot my first doll in those days, a china head and they made the body of a heavy cotton cloth (Drill) and legs and arms of goat skin they tanned (an art Mother was quite proficient at). They said when first bot they wrapped it in a breakfast shawl and I learned to walk with it in my arms.

Memories of home and other children - the big house - sitting room, a big stove and bare floor - parlor with a striped rag carpet and furniture, whatnot in corner - and some rooms we were not allowed to enter often. In the kitchen, stove, chair and table and best of all, a big loom. When I grew large enuf, I often crawled up on the seat and tried to weave. I remember the older girls spinning on a big wheel in the shed. Lovely fluffy rolls brot from the woolen mills (don't remember where). How they would walk up and give the wheel a spin or turn and back up to allow the twist to run in the rill and size it with their fingers till it was right and let it run on the spool. All easier than I can explain it. This yarn was used in white blankets and colored for other goods they wove - black and blue check, flannel, a linsely-woolsey cloth, colors and madder red, blue and perhaps a little white. Part wool and cotton for girls dresses, then there was mens pants cloth and suits cloth made. The older girls all helped make the cloth on the loom. If I only could tell you just how it looked.

In the summer we often went over to Uncle Silas's place, about a half a mile away. The older children often drug the little ones along on excursions. One time, I remember, they took us to a clift over looking the river bed where a whirl pool played for us as we looked over the edge by laying flat and some one holding our heel. We had to cross a spring creek to go to uncle's. We were often tempted to linger and wade looking for frogs, snails, etc. Then a mulberry tree clost to a fence was a nice place to visit when the berries were ripe. The barn with some nice horses was a urins [*urinous*] place to go - clost to the house was a buggy shed and smoke house. Over in the field east was a spring but I think we had a cistern at the house.

I remember many a trip along the hedge rows with mother in the spring, hunting greens and various wild herbs that were used. I remember well the poke weed she cut for greens. They came up out of the ground a straight shoot, which she cut. Dock too was used, mustard, horseradish leaves, many more. I can't remember [*everything*].

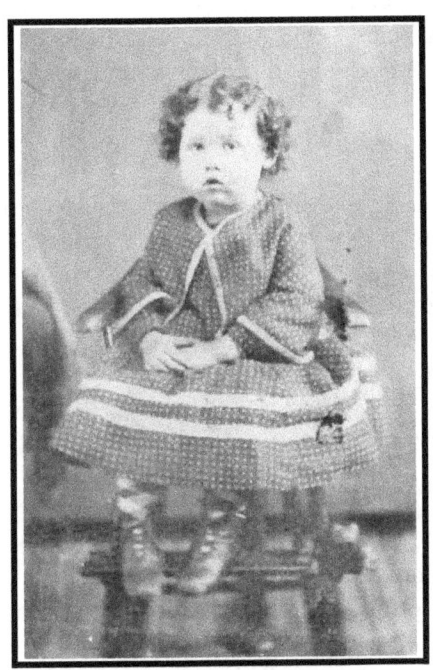

Maggie Ellen Halbert
About 1872
From the Susan Hand Collection

The men always raised a patch of tobacco. The plants were gotten from a neighbor or raised in one corner of a hot bed mother always had made each spring to raise sweet potato sprouts, cabbage and etc. The year I remember, the tobacco patch was back of the smoke house and ice house near by so they could carefully tend the small plants and continue the attention till full grown. This day it was nearly large enuff to pull and dry. When Seth was giving it the last hoeing over, suckering the small patch of tobacco and killing the big tobacco worms, he says to me, "If you will help me I'll make you a cart for your doll." I had carried the doll. At first it was only a china head rapped around with an old breakfast shawl. Then later Mary and Ma made a body and dressed it up quite respectable. It was then Annie and I thot we needed a cart to haul it in.

As soon as he finished the tobacco he cut two round discs out for the two wheels, about 12 inches in diameter. He bored holes in the middle of each wheel, put a connection square sided piece in, whittled down round to fit in the hole in each wheel. He got a wooden box about 6 x 12 x 4 inches, placed it on the axle and nailed a stick on for a tongue. There we, Annie and I, went off happily giving the doll its first ride. Some of the older girls were working in the cellar. Annie and I took the cart down to show them. The head of the doll jutted out a little over the back part of the cart and as we helped it down over the stone steps, the back part of the head hit on the stone step, knocking a three cornered piece out of the head. Such a howl I set up when we saw what we had done and could not be pacified soon, till Sarah said she could fit the piece back with white lead. So it was and is to this day.

Annie was my constant companion and looked out for doll and I. Tho we often got into mischief. Took sticks, put a berry on the end and dipped in the crocks of milk but doing it around to get all the cream. Sarah detected the culprits and that was the last of that game.

Then, as I got bigger, I often rode behind Ma on a horse to go places. One spring she went quite a ways to see a sick boy. Annie and I went along and such a delightful walk. Thru spring flowers, trees and all kinds of lovely shrubs, and again one rainy spring morning thru the woods. White dogwood in bloom, we went over to see cousin Joel. He lived over a mile or two toward Orangeville and such a place to build a house up a steep hill. They were a lovely pair. The school, church and graveyard was about a mile or more a way on a corner of roads. On the way there was Uncle George's and Aunt Betsy's house, a lovely farm house, all their children gone but cousin Lizzie, a nice place to go - thrifty people.

As I was small I only remember going to church a few times, which was all dutch to me, tho songs were the best I thot and learned some tunes very early.

On rainy days our upstairs room was a good place to congregate and play. I learned to sew early, seeing so many older ones sew I wanted to patch. I was told everything was mended. One day a neighbor laughed at me patching, making a patch work quilt. Goods were too precious those days for me to ruin, so I was given old calico dress pieces to begin with. I wanted squares so I got them to tear me pieces and then turned them over and cut the squares (a rude square). Then after a while they gave me better pieces and I began to patch. Mother went to see a woman and baby acrossed the dry riverbed. I went too. I was restless after dinner and they let me look thru her scrap bag and pick some pieces for my quilt, which pleased me. That was a lift for my quilt. The Bruners, were neighbors. We did not go there often. They had looms and remember coverlids and etc. made by several girls in the family. She was the woman Ma referred to when she said it took a lazy mother to have industrious girls.

In the spring the men tapped the maple trees and gathered sweet sap which they guarded with care for children liked it all to well.

The most universal outer wrap that was worn those days was the shawl, both big and little. Everyone had to have a shawl to wear when going out, used as we do coats now. Men had heavier shawls they wore. On the return of the soldiers they bot back both coats and capes. Coats were found to be warmer and snugger and soon the shawls were discarded by the men. The uniform coats were nice, thick, good wool. I can remember the army coats men wore - with big brass buttons (eagles on the buttons). Some were blue and others a blue green broadcloth. Then men wore big double shawls - and shawls were about the only wrap the women wore. There were more expensive shawls of various kinds. Then first the good scraps was pieced into tops for wool comforters. When these nice woolens wore out, past making over for the smaller children, the scraps were saved, cut and sewed into carpet filling. Our parlor carpet was made of wool rags. Worn pieces used this way served a good purpose.

Father was a horse fancier and had good horses. Then we had cows that supplied milk and butter for the home. Sheep supplied meat and wool, which was always needed at the loom, flannels, lovely red and white, red checked flannels for underskirts and shirts. Then too, there was the blue, white, and black checked flannel made in our loom used for the same purpose. Those days the jean pants goods were woven in the loom at home and cut and made in the home. Heavy white muslin was bot and made into everday shirts for men. Their suits were made from gray or blue flannel, fulled and tailored at home. My mother was a handy, skillful seamstress and with the help of the girls every thing was made in the home for every day wear. There were sheer silk goods and lawns on the market which was bot by the yard and made in to nice Sunday dresses.

Religion

There was a Baptist Community east of us, but in those days it was far away and we knew but very little about any one there. In our community all belonged to the Methodist Church, Wesley Chapel, and attended it religiously, as many meetings as was held each Sunday. There was also a very old grave yard at this church. From the time Emma was born she could remember these meetings and almost every family had prayers said each morning and grace before each meal. Each family used the bible once each morning at the morning services and many were tattered and wore tho kept on a table at hand.

Friends and neighbors often discussed this book freely on visiting each other and it seemed to be the law of our settlement. A chapter of the bible was read each morning and each child, in his turn, was required to learn Psalms and recitation. In those days father and mother were religious and kept up their part in the church. Each Sunday some brother and sister invited the minister and his wife home for dinner. Then all would go back to church in the afternoon.

To weave, cut and make the clothes for mother's brood to go to church respectable, was quite an undertaking, not to mention the shoes required to shoe them. Saturday night late found her laying out suits, dresses and shoes for each and seeing that the shoes were polished and good strings in. Then each Sunday morning she arose, all tired out, to tired to go, but she must.

In those days, children went barefoot most all summer and when they had to dress up, it was a punishment to wear shoes. So most of them would take their stockings and shoes on their arm and walk to church, as most everyone did those days. Then on nearing the church, they would sit down on a log, put on the stockings and shoes and go on in to church.

Then after it was out, they would go out to the log, take off the stockings and shoes, put them over their arm and happily go home. This had to be repeated as often as they attended church that day.

A man by the name of Waran depended on day work for a living. Being a little queer, it was hard to secure a job. So father, out of sympathy, often gave him a few days work. Waran was quite religious and attended church faithfully. On Sunday he'd dress all up with a stiff collared white shirt, polish his shoes till they shone, then walk to church. On real hot days he perspired till the collar would wilt and before going in to church he'd take out his red bandana, wipe the old red clay dust off his shoes and then go in up to the amen corner and sit up clost to Mr. Bruner, much to Mr. Bruner's chagrin. Then he'd take out the red kerchief and wipe the sweat off of his face, leaving red clay streaks all over his face from the handkerchief. This would provoke Mr. Bruner so much that he'd forget himself and suck away at his false gold teeth. This all amused the younger generation and they would have something to laugh about all week.

Quarterly meetings were held each third month at the chapel, then the next meeting would be at another chapel in a different settlement and so on.

The church fathers generally came during the week, Thursday, Friday or Saturday, to hold their business meetings. Ministers from other parts came to help transact the business. Each family was expected to board and room their allotted amount of this as long as they staid. After the business was transacted they visited each family and each family was expected to entertain them. Sunday was an extra big day at church. One or two of the new ministers generally took the pulpit for that day. Children were baptized and new members taken in. Last, but not least, these visiting ministers had to have a collection taken up for them besides getting their board and room for a week and also to get Sunday School paper for the children.

Protracted meetings were generally held in the fall or winter and had one or more helpers from within the community. This was to get more joiners to the church. There was preaching at 10 o'clock in the morning, then the ministers went to various members homes, got dinner and supper and visited till evening. Then all went to the night service at the chapel. This continued each day and night for two or three weeks, till the settlement was worn out. (I have my doubts as to the lasting good of those meetings?) After a few weeks of those meetings there were some light headed individuals that let it go to their heads and would break out shouting Hallalugha and sing "When The Roll Was Called Up Yonder, I'll Be There" and other religious songs. This generally could be heard for over a mile away - singing and shouting their favorite songs. These meetings were more of a source of amusement to the young people and rather disturbed the piety of the older members in the dark.

The country yet in places was deeply wooded. People on foot always was afraid of panthers and wild cats. On hearing a noise, we would stop to listen and then Al (Seth) would say, "O come on, it's nothing but Preachers Honk's wife shouting again," for she generally closed each nights meetings a long last by going down the isle shouting Hallalugha. And invariably her veil would catch on the chandeliers, hang, she going on singing and shouting.

Religion, I believe is a good thing for some people in this world. Tho I believe there are some people who could live without it. Where mother had to work so hard, I don't believe she needed religion, for she had it all the way thru to have worked and kept her flock together. Rest was what she needed, Not Religion!

There were men that set theirselves up for ministers of the gospel that made a soft living, with wife and children, off of the poor settler in the name of the Lord. To my opinion hell could never sizzle to hot for such ministers. A broom maker at Simpson professed to be an ordained minister. When asked if he could marry a couple, he did, then two weeks after the wedding it was found out he had no authority at all to marry couples. Then at the chagrin of bride and groom another minister had to be found to marry them.

By the foregoing, one would think my faith in Christianity had long been blasted? No, No, No, for I have known several good ministers that was all right and believe in what they had to tell the people. Reverent Shirtz, Alfred Stackhouse, both had farms, worked week days and preached their faith on Sundays. They set a good example to their people.

Cards - 1870

Cards in our settlement in Indiana were hardly ever heard of, least seen, among the better class of church families. One Sunday after church and Sunday school, Seth and his two cousins, Enos, Jr. and Willie, Uncle Silas's boys' thot the'd explore just another cave. There being many in these parts, thot the'd explore the one south of the chapel. They took torches and explored it thoroughly. In one corner, on a nook shelf, they spied something and on examining it thoroughly they found it contained a pack of damp cards.

Seth brot them home and the girls gathered around to see the queer pictures on them, the first they ever saw. Those days, of course, they took the children's eyes. They were too damp to handle so Seth spread them out to dry under the big sheet iron stove, on the sheet iron the stove stood on. He spread them out good and was drying nicely when father came in and spied the deck, which he gathered up deftly, chucked them in the stove, slamming the stove door with all vengeance, saying, "Don't let me ever see you with cards again," and wound up with a regular lecture on the evil of card playing. Seth was wanting this deck for himself and was jealously guarding them.

Illinois Trip When Emma was 2 1/2 Years Old

Once in the fall of '65, Mother left her three oldest with Aunt Rhoda, and took Emma, then a baby, with her to see her sister, Margaret and brother Garret and their families near Sumner, Illinois.

They went on the train. When riding along a spark from the engine flew back into the open window, lighting on mother, burning a small hole in her black silk apron. When upon, Emma, out of reverence to Mother's silk apron, began to cry and it was some time till she was pacified. Women in those days prided theirselves by having one silk dress and apron of the same material ruffled around to wear when they went visiting.

Emma remembers vividly the visit at Margaret's and with the daughter Etta. Etta was a few years older and insisted on carrying Emma everywhere. Mr. [*Isaac*] Boggs was a farmer and at that time of year had pinned up four young mule colts to wean. Two were black and two buck in color. They would fight and rare and play in this pen, much to Emma and Etta's delight. So, every once in a while Emma would insist that Etta carry her over to the pen and climb up on the door, and hold on for dear life to watch the young mules play. Then between times they'd play in Etta's playhouse where she had old broken and discarded pots and pans and a chair. They would play happily away till they took an other peep at the mules. Tho Etta's twin brothers would slip in and wreck their house. They were sly little fellows. When the girls came back they would run up the outside stairway and hide. When the girls were off their grounds the twins would peep down, keeping this up till their mother found them out. Then all was quiet and they played on.

Emma thot these twins, light haired boys, very queer as the mules, as her brother Seth was older and a dark complexion. Mr. Boggs was Margaret's second man and was of a very crabby, sullen nature. It might have been on account of the times. War was then at its height and he perhaps was worried, owing to financial reverses. The call of draft for more men in the army was then taking able bodied farmers and mechanics. The army of the nation needed more and more men and who knew when his turn might come.

Colery

Colery [*Cholera*] was a very bad scourge that broke out in Indiana and Illinois about 1847 and continued to appear over several years. The doctors at this time did not understand this scourge. Many died of this infection in the middle states. About the only remedy was Calomel [*mercuous chloride, a white, tasteless powder, used as a cathartic, for intestinal worms, etc.-mc*] given in proper doses. Then the patient could not drink water. I remember mother told me how she suffered for water all the time when sick. Many died thru these years of unsanitation.

The Whippoorwill

In the late evening in the deep wood, the Whippoorwill began its wailing and continued till dark. One would cry out whippoorwill and in a few minutes would seem to be the same plaintive sound, Whippoorwill. I often wanted to see the bird and I come to think they were a large bird from their loud heavy voice. On our moving away, we never heard it any more for it does not live in the West.

The old croaking frog was heard, too, each clear evening. From the swamps would come a chorus of voices. There were many kinds of frogs there. The boys often hunted the big frogs for their meat, the hind legs making an excellent dish equal to fried chicken.

Fire flies, too, came in the evening. The girls often caught them in the late evening and took several to their room to see if they would light their room. There were a few mosquitoes at this time. They were not suspected as the malaria fly.

Older people thot the night air gave one the malaria. Our Aunt Betsy so thoroughly believed it came in on the night air that she strictly forbid all of her children to never open a window any higher than an ink bottle. If she found out they did not adhere to her teaching, there would be trouble.

Aunt Betsy was Uncle George's wife. George was mother's brother. Their farm was on the right of the road going to church and school. Their children were older than some of ours. Lizzie, being Hatties or Mary's age. Lizzie was a home loving girl. From the time she was four she began to help Betsy. At five years old when Betsy picked geese she would help. Lizzie, being a girl, was not given an education past the home school. She took hold of the house work like an old woman and when that was done she sewed or wove. Living clost together she was at our house quite often and our girls with her at her home. Betsy was inclined to be fretful. Lizzie never acquired that disposition. Uncle George came to see mother in summer of 1893, in Kansas. He was very old then.

These farmer trips did not lend to father's farm instinct and the wide prairie lured him on. Shortly after the war he talked of the wide prairie country, without a stick or stone, lying open for the taking. This time Mother had her way, said she'd not take her family in to an Indian country. Never the less, these talks came to nothing and he went on clearing land, sawing lumber and selling cleared places. Once when his sister Sarah had the misfortune to loose her barn by fire, he sawed out the dimensions for her another. He took his teams and delivered the lumber ten miles away without pay.

When the war broke out, there were both northern and southern sympathizers. A Mr. Wilshire, living in the South, joined the North. As soon as the war was over, he knew, for the safety for himself and family, he would have to move, so crossed the Ohio River into our country and settled. When Mr. Wilshire come into our settlement, he was living with his third wife. Each wife had children by other former marriages. He had children by former wives. This made five sets of children. Tom and Henry were of the older sets of his children. In all he had seven or eight children to support in his household. Being a great horse fancier, he always had a fine saddle horse. Each morning he'd have one of the boys groom his horse, lead him out to the porch and he'd be dressed up like a lord, mount and then ride to Paoli. He'd lobby around town each day in the court house square, with people coming in from farms, to find out who needed help and place his boys around on paying jobs. Then, in a few weeks, he'd ride to the men that had hired his boys and collect their wages. He managed to keep them all working and never sent them to school. These boys were kept working and were never presentable for lack of clothes. An older girl was kept at home as a slave to wait on him and her and to do the general housework. So when Tom [*Wilshire*] came to us, he had no clothes to speak of and could not read or write. When father got hold of Tom, he cut that part of the old man's revenue out. When the old man came to collect, father told him what he had been doing to his children - just raising up a lot of ill fed and clothed boys and girls, living off their wages, making ignorant serfs of them all, not able to read or write, browbeating them to the level of a slave. Mr. Wilshire brot his family up south of us on a poor farm that would not sprout peas.

Father hired Tom to help Seth take care of the stock while father was away. He was a faithful young man. In the summer Father paid him wages. In the winter Tom helped with the chores and went to school, as his schooling had been neglected. When Tom found a good place he knew it and did not want to leave. He used his money for clothes, as his father had always collected his wages heretofore.

Father often bot horses. He paired them up in to good teams and lead them to Louisville - lead 20 to 30 head at a time - also to Memphis or New Orleans, wherever they could get the best price. The South needed horses now that the war was over and one could take them very cheap on the boats. Father always went with the horses and once or twice took Tom with him.

Mother always found a job for the girls. The orchard had been bearing the finest fruit in the country for years and always walked off with the highest prize at the county fair. Under her watchful care, each girl was busy. The soap suds were saved and the girls took brooms and rags and washed the trunk of each apple tree, in their turn, to keep off the coddling moth. Then the orchard was regularly cultivated, all weeds kept down. We had all the peaches, apples and pears we could use and dry for winter. The girls now did the gathering, paring and drying. Others kept the two long rows of sage picked at the proper time to dry. They often received the proceeds, when sold to the peddler, in the form of new dress goods.

Blackberries from the hill were gathered. On these trips I never could go, as it was too far for my short legs. They often took a lunch and staid till all their buckets were full. If we could not use them all fresh, part was dried for winter use. In the fall, the girls would take buckets and bags and go to the wood and pick hazelnuts, black and white walnuts, hickory nuts, and chestnuts. We always kept a barrel full. All we got over [*what we could use*] was sold to the peddler for things needed in the house. Once, just the fall before we left [*for Kansas*], mother bot a bolt of calico from the proceeds of the nuts. The goods was made in to dresses in Kansas.

When at home, we were encouraged to spend part of the time sewing to help make dresses or make a quilt. Each had their little sewing basket, needle, thimble, thread and shears. When done they were put away with our work in them. Then the next day we'd work again under mother's guidance, setting around her knee. She never joked or cajoled with us, nor petted us much, tho we loved and respected her always. She always taught us useful things and never told a smutty story.

Basketry was an art she had learned from her mother when quite young. She taught all the girls the art of making baskets from willows gathered in the spring when the sap was coming up. They went to the creeks, cut long, one year's growth, and boiled them in an oblong iron kettle that fit on the two front holes of the stove. They were wound around in the boiler, weighted down with a rock till boiling. Then taken out, held with two rags in hand and stripped of the bark by hand, one by one. Could be laid away and when used, soaked in water for a while as she worked.

Sometimes we thot we were abused, as Uncle Silas's girls and boys were allowed to run and play. Aunt Rhoda had so much to do. She did not stop to concider the fact she could not do everything and plodded away bringing all the water from a spring, washing and tending all as far as she could. The balance went undone until her oldest girl later took hold and helped her mother.

Aunt Rhoda, while a good worker, was no general as she should have been in this mob of kids. In a way, Rhoda's wants were taken care of and she did not have to weave or spin. Grandfather Seth still trapped. When he sold his furs he always shod each child and grown folk.

Then Aunt Fanny Bolton had only one child left, a boy to buy for. So she raised geese and chickens and with other products from the farm, bot all the dry goods for this fast increasing family [*of Rhoda's*].

All Aunt Fanny Bolton's boy, Abanatha, craved was a fiddle. To own a fiddle was a sin in those days. He was not a very strong child, so Aunt Fanny bot him a fiddle, but he was always to keep it from his father. So he only played when he knew his father was away up to Indianapolis selling his copper bottom horses. (This was a general purpose horse he raised with all good qualities combined and always sold readily. Coach horses, drivers, and saddle horse always took the premium at the fairs.) Or when Abanatha sneaked out and went to the woods, he had to be dead sure his father was not near. His fiddle was often held as a whip over the boy's head. If he would not do this or that as the mother asked him to do, she'd say, "Now, if you don't do this I'll tell your father you have a fiddle." Shortly after this the boy passed on. Then Aunt Fannie was so lonesome. Rhoda let her have the second girl, Pheoba, to keep. Pheoba proved to be good help for Aunt Fannie. Much to the disgust of the girls at home, she was dressed better than they and there was always a clash between them over Pheoba having better clothes.

Shortly after our house was built, Grandfather Seth built a large house for Silas and Rhoda's ever increasing family. Silas yet was no manager. He would get on a horse and ride away to the Orangeville post office. Grandfather managed the crops, stock, and all Silas did was play around, come and go. Rhoda slaved on and never a helping hand he gave her. She was no woman to complain about any bodies faults, so she slaved on. Had it not been for grandfather's helpful hand and Grandmother Bolton, the load could never have been pulled. Each Sunday afternoon the Boltons loaded up with things Rhoda needed and brot them over, good food, furniture and curtain stuff. They saw that she never wanted for anything.

From the time Mother moved into the new house, the loom and wheel was part of the household machine. It was set up in the corner of the kitchen where it was handy and kept threaded to either jeans for men clothes, flannel for skirts, linsey for beautifully checked dresses, blankets, linen or coverlids.

When Father first began to talk and plan about going to Kansas, four years before we moved, Mother began to plan and weave bolts of material to have if things were not so brilliant as then expected to be. Now there were woolen mills where one could send the wool and have it made into nice long wool bat. This was a great help in preparing the yarns and could then be spun on a big wheel so much quicker than before.

Henry Stackhouse, brother Alfred, their parents having died, and the Bonds moved to Kansas. They always staid together and sometime previously had moved out to Kansas, Solomon River Valley and taken up some good land. The Stackhouses had taken their land up on the Divide, west of Solomon River. These two families Father had been acquainted with since boyhood days in Indiana. They insisted he come hither and settle in a new country, free from malaria and afflicted with all ails that people in low, damp country were affected with. After writing back and forwards a year or two, father, anxious to travel, decided to go out and look the country over in the fall of '73, or "Grasshopper Year", to see it at its worst. He took Tom Wilshire and Garrott Hurtzels, Ma's nephew, with him. They drove thru with a wagon and team, took their bedding and food and camped out on the way, about 800 miles. On arriving there, they visited the Bonds and heard their stories, then went to Henry Stackhouse's, visited a few days. Henry taking them over the Divide and showed them the land that was then open for settlement. There was then a few homesteaders already there trying to make a living.

Father went over and visited Alfred Stackhouse and family, finding such a large family of girls and boys, almost destitute of clothes and food, owing to the grasshopper raid. They hurriedly made their way home in due time.

Tom and Garrott were especially touched that the older girl, Nan, had no clothes fit to go to church and the others hardly enough to stay at home. As soon as they got back home, Father got a big wooden box filled with flour, bacon, and corn meal. Mother added weaving apparel such as she could spare and comforters. The first time the boys, Tom and Garrott, got to town, they bot yards of goods for Nan and others in the family. Emma remembers vividly the color of the dress goods; a black calico with vines of green thru it. To this, the others of our family twitted these boys about buying women clothes, "Practicing for the future, eh ? ?" This box of goods, when filled, was about all three men could roll into a wagon. It was taken then ten miles to Mitchell, billed out and paid the freight to Solomon City, with the bill [*of lading*] sent in a letter to forewarn them of its arrival. The Stackhouses had to take their team and wagon and go 30 miles for the box. This they received in due time and was very thankful for. I often wondered why I gave things to the needy. Now I can see by this act it was in the blood.

Ma sent Mary to Aunt Sarah's to go to school for a year or two. By this time she and sister then went to the Gulf school. Mary wanted to teach, so Ma spared her, sent her to school, a seminary in those days and fitted to teach a couple of terms of country school. When she finished there, she went again to Orleans, stayed with an aunt to get a higher education. This finished her with a certificate to teach. She then taught two summer subscription schools at the Gulf. For years a neighbor boy, which she had always known, had admired Mary and gone with her occasionally; Uncle Nat's youngest boy, John A. Wilson.

Sarah and Hattie took Mary's place at the house work and weaving. Hither to, Hattie had been the nurse of the family. Seth worked with his father and learned teaming when young and always followed it.

Father and Tom went back to Kansas with the idea of locating. Mother and all the children were left at home to do the chores and go to school. Mother and Mary ran the house and did weaving preparatory to going west.

In the spring Mary and John were married at home in the parlor, which Mother had previously carpeted with a home made rag carpet, which was beautifully striped in many colors. John and Mary had gone to school and church together. They were of the same age. He had been brot up on a farm clost by. Both were quiet, industrious young people, so it was quite right they should marry and go west. John wanted to go to California. The next day they took the train from Orleans to Stockton, California, where they lived there a few months. There they got work in Stockton. Mary longed to be with her folks.

In the meantime, father had written them of the possibilities of getting 320 acres of land in Kansas and they amediately came that fall and took up the land, tho lived on the place father had bot the relinquishments on. Then Father went back to Kansas again and staid there with them. He was there when Old Lady Peterson, an old swede woman, delivered Mary's first child, Enos. Later father came home and preparations were made for the final trip. He had now travelled this long road till he knew most everyone on the road. Travel lust had got him.

Herbert Briggs and the Knife

The second trip father made to Kansas, one day while looking around, he went over to Pierson's place where they were thrashing rye. Just then, when nearly done, Herbert, one of the Briggs men, cutting bundles, by accident let his knife go in to the machine. Father handed him his pocket knife to finish with. It had a peculiar short curve on the blade. That was the first time Herbert met his future father-in-law. [M*arried Emma Susan Halbert, Enos's 5th child - mc*]

Chapter VIII

The Move to Kansas

****

The "Go west young man, go west" would ring in Father's ear. With unwise adventure into farming and logging, father became involved in debt, then there seemed no other move but go west. For some years Tom Wilshire had been working for Father. He made his home with Father and Mother after his mother's death and some time a brother Henry came for a few days. Father and Tom went west for land. They found free land to be taken up in Mitchell County, Logan Township, Kansas. Father bot a relinquishment of a Mr. Veach. Mr. Veach had taken up a homestead that lay in the southeast corner of section (in Ureka Township's east corner) that gradually, in the center, raised to an elevation of five or six hundred feet. Each quarter section had about the same amount of the raise, making a hilly building place. The land, all the way up, was a deep black loam with not a stick or stone for miles till one struck a creek. Then there, one was sure to find a nice yellow lime stone. It generally was four to six inches in thickness with a white streak in the middle. It was often split with a wedge thru the white streak. Mr. Veach had another farm in the valley and wanted to sell his relinquishment, so Father bot. It was fairly built up for a new place in those days and there was 30 acres of land broken and some fruit and shade trees planted. Father had six months leave before he had to move on to it. Father took up a timber claim. It cornered with John [*Wilson*] and also lay along side of Tom Wilshire's land. This section our homestead was in. They came home, preparatory to move in the spring. That winter someone tried to jump our claim so father had to make a trip back to Kansas to straighten out the tangle.

One Friday night, Sarah, Hattie and Seth went over to Dr. Ritter's farm house to a party. On coming home, a storm came up of sleet and rain and turned bitter cold. In those days they had no over shoes and only shawls instead of coats. In the morning all took down with a heavy cold and was unable to be up. Mother administered her home remedies to no avail and Dr. Ritter was called. They were bad off and another doctor, Dr. Carter, was called of Orangeville. They took turns staying day and night. The colds developed into pneumonia and Sarah died. The others gradually got better. Sarah had taken Mary's place and was a lovely daughter. People those days did not know how to doctor that well. While medicine of herbs and bark were good, not so efficient all times. [*Sarah is buried at Wesley Chapel, United Methodist Church, Orange County, Indiana. - mc*]

This shock was almost more than they could stand. Father was in Kansas and we held little hope of catching him in time for the funeral. With the help of the neighbor that always helped in this hour of need, she was buried. Father got the word that was sent and carried along by word of mouth and came on the train a few days later. Then Tom came home with the team and wagon.

Reason Ma Concented to Leave Indiana

Southern Indiana had been a forest country for thousands of years. Rivers, lost rivers, creeks, rills and swamps had been formed there perhaps almost as long. Summers were long, breeding all kinds of bacteria in them. The first settler of those parts would contract malaria. When once in their flesh, was hard to get rid of. They thot it was caused from the water. Most every family had it, not all, tho several would take the malaria causing the victim to have chills, every third day. Then between time he would drag around, not able to do much. Some of our family had it and when gotten was hard to get rid of. Doctors could give medicine but none was good as quinine. Every household had to keep it and it was given to us all if we complained. I remember having to take it in the white of an egg so it would slip down quickly and not get the bitter taste, tho invariable that awful bitter taste. In many cases the victim of malaria crept around like a ghost. There seemed to be no cure for those. Some found out that change of climate cured them. Then consumption (T.B.) was quite common. So mother thot in able to escape these dread malady, she would go, as she had already lost one daughter.

The baby had grown into a child. That, on such a heart breaking scene and the loss of her sister, riveted on to her memory. A scene she never forgot. Then suddenly Uncle Silas and Aunt Rhoda's small daughter died. Tom Wilshire was no akin to us but he staid with the family. He carried me over to see Micha, Uncle Silas's child, about my age - took sick, died. Tom always admired me with my curls. It was a cold winter and much sickness and death that winter.

In the spring Tom [*Wilshire*] and John [*Wilson*] plowed and put in crops in Kansas, Tom having taken up a 160 acres, in the meantime, after father bot his relinquishment. When Father came home that early spring, he sold all of our stock but two good teams and wagons, a little claybank and a stallion for John Wilson.

In the spring, March or April, father and mother began to prepare for the long journey to our new home in Kansas. Mother wove up several lengths of chain to have to move goods. It would be needed. I remember well when piece by piece of our house furniture was sold. Annie's little chair, how she wanted to take it with us. She cried when the man took it away over thru the woods to his home. He said if a bear came along he'd set the chair down and ask him to have a seat. The framework of these chairs was made of poles with woven hickory withes for the bottom. They were sold and we were told they had no room to take them.

Some of the household goods were sold and the loom. Father had told Mother she would not need it as they would be well off soon and they then could buy everything. Mother was loath to believe all and kept many things he wanted to sell. Her chickens, turkeys and geese were sold and the money used on the road for expenses. The loom, the big wheels all went, the stoves and other things with the house. For a long time then a camp fire was to be our stove. Father had painted a very glowing picture of our new home. She would not have to weave or spin. Our crops there would supply all our needs in Kansas. No more slaving, it was such a wonderful place and in time it would be a paradise. I think he lost the love for the beautiful home we were leaving. We were leaving a lovely wooded and watered country for a prairie, no woods, no water. Tho at that time [*in Kansas*], before broke up by mans plows, was a wonderful grassy plains, cut up by river and creeks, sparsely timbered. In the spring was God's big flower garden stretching for hundreds of miles.

Boxes were packed, one to hams and bacon and other for feather beds and bedding. Big flat boxes contained four bedsteads, packed in and around with useful household goods, dishes, and others with more woven goods and the little wheel taken apart and put in when Father was out of sight. Mother did not wholly believe father's picture of Kansas, land of plenty, but she was afraid of want. So she secretly took apart her flax wheel and packed it, her card and various other things he said she would not need. Then yarns for socks and all the old socks to be footed. The little Howe sewing machine, which was new and a new invention, she packed in another box with the old hand machine she first used. These boxes were all taken, shipped at Mitchell for Solomon City, Kansas.

After these were shipped, next day the wagons were loaded. Our little cook stove was put in the wagon and other necessary things needed for our trip - bedding, clothing, food and seed were packed into the wagons, and made ready. Along with the other things she hoarded was a big wide poplar board saved from when father ran the saw mill. She saved it for a table top. It was wide enuf and long enuf for a fair sized table. That she stood in long side the wagon box and would use, propped upon stumps or rock, for her Sunday dinners to be spread on in the wide open on the trail. The wagons were finally loaded with the provisions for the trip and dried fruit, chucked into corners that would last till we gathered wild fruit. We had to have a plenty of everything as we would be 4 miles to the nearest rail road.

Neighbors knew we were leaving that spring, all thot it was a very foolish move. Those that had never left their old homes, but father was a traveler or empire builder. He liked the open road. Schoolmates, teachers, church friends, neighbors, relatives, clost and distant were all bid fare well. Pa's father was then real old. [*d. 2-9-1878, age 83*] . Was hard to leave him. Up to this time his father was active, tho now he was not even able to hunt for possum and the coon. His old hound sat around the yard all day watching for him to go on the trails.

These old hounds were our worst enemy, for when Aunt Rhoda would give us children bread and butter, if we did not stay in, they would take our lunch from us, often following us in the house and we would have to get on to the table and hold our bread away up high to save our bread.

Two wagons were made ready, a good team each and three loose young horses were to take the trail, along with old Watch, our faithful white Newfoundland dog. Father, Mother, Seth, Hattie, Emma, Annie, Maggie (the baby) all were to make the long overland trip.

The wagon had bows so the wagon covers she had previously made from heavy muslin were put on over the bows and tied down to the sides of the wagon boxes. Then the hind piece was drawed down and tied, leaving a small hole in the end of the bows and a similar one in front, only not drawed down so for the driver was to set on the seat. Often Mother or one of the girls sat beside the driver. The last morning everything was tucked in. We bid farewell to our home, went past Uncle Silas and Aunt Rhoda's, bid all a sorrowful farewell, all promised to write, which they did, and moved on up the hill past Bolton's. They were out to say farewell, then we faced west.

It only took a few days till we reached Vincennes and the Wabash River, a small river that starts in a lake in Ohio, flows the upper part of Indiana and makes part of the western border of Indiana. It and the Ohio form the toe of Indiana state, flowing in to Ohio at the toe. Father rather expected to encounter high water at the Wabash and so we did. It was on the rampage. It had washed out a bridge and a long high grade, the approach to the bridge. There was no way left for us to cross. He was advised to wait till the high water went down. We could come in an Emigrant Corral. It had a high board wall, was large, could drive in the wagon and camp there, but must be very careful of fire. So father drove in. There was no other alternative. We were protected in there. So we passed two weary weeks there. Between meals when time hung weary on we woman folk we sewed, knit, pieced quilts and Hattie even painted pictures. She painted on the wrong side of glass, roses and for those days we thot them fine. It was not so hard on Seth and Father as they would spend lots of time outside the corral, see the town and talk to the man that was to be our guide when the flood water subsided. The girls, by climbing up on cross pieces, could look out and get a glimpse of the town and river. One day they helt me up and I could see the big bridge swing out to let a boat go by. That glimpse, I never can forget. Finally the man told Father he thot the water had gone down enuf. By putting up our things we wanted to keep dry on poles, laid acrost the wagon bed, we called go. He had piloted a wagon train across the day before. So we were all up the next morning pleased to leave that stockade, not giving much thot to what we were to encounter later. Roads were muddy and deep rutted. At last we reached the back water area, tho it was down somewhat and was only backwater. The man assured Father it was the old road and he knew it well, so after all of our load was lifted up and put on the poles they drove in to the waters. Water, water everywhere, with scrub oaks on either side. Our guide rode along in front of the head wagon.

Just below us a few rods was the old grade - large section was washed out of it. One of the horses on the head wagon floundered and fell. Father and Seth jumped out in to the water and helped the struggling animal on its feet. Watch jumped out, swam around in the water, was very much disturbed at the incident. On and on in the water, then we saw land and a farm house, a joyful sight, a nice two story farm house with a fancy railed portico. It was past noon, we asked permission to camp, got dinner and were all refreshed and joyful that we had got safely thru the water. The men rearranged the load and threw away the poles. This was an over flow from the main river. Later crost the main river on a bridge in to Illinois State. As we traveled on yon, Sunday was our day of rest as well as the horses. Mother would have the board for the table brot out and we would eat from that instead of our laps. The day past quickly as our washing had to be done on that day and all made ready for onward on Monday.

One nice day as we trudged onward Father spied a little fluffy ball, a young chicken. Perhaps the mother left quickly and lost this little fellow. Annie and I were over joyed. Mother tended it till it became husky then she turned it over to Annie and I. When the wagon stopped, we would get out, take it and hunt worms for it. It proved to be a sturdy little fellow and was always ready for its bug or worm. Mother's brother's family, the Garrett Shirley family, lived clost to Olney, Illinois on a farm. They were waiting for us. They had a large family, Mag, Jane, Kate, Francis, Dell and two boys, Cliff and Henry. We visited there, did washing and fixed up generally, incidentally, rested our faithful horses, and visited a married daughter of Garretts. It was there they gave us our two buff cochin baby chicks to go with our one and two more white chicks what he thot would grow into a pair. Now we possessed 5 chicks for our new home on the prairie. Ma's sister, Margaret Kingsberry, lived in Olney. She had two grown daughters so our girls had a good time with their cousins. Some of the girls (Kate and Jan) worked in the woolen mills of the town. One day Kate took the girls and myself to see the woolen mill. I was afraid of the many wheels. They had a nice farm, well built up, good big house and barns, big broad field. Just at that time the corn was coming up nicely. Tho they had to watch closely and keep the crows scared away by changing scare crows and shooting them.

In our Aunt and Uncle's home was the loom and spinning wheel, where the clothing, bedding and carpets were made. Each girl learned the art, most common in those days. Our stay was only too short and we must be away to the new home on the prairie. Each day our chicks grew sassy and demanded more worms and bugs. Kept Annie and I busy at every stop, morning, noon and night.

On our way one evening we chanced to camp clost to the camp of two men, a sick woman and little boy, three or four years old. They asked Father where we were going and then told their story. The wife was sick and doctor said travel might cure her, so they had started. Just was traveling, so they asked Father if he cared if they go along with him. "No, no," was the reply, "we would be glad to have you." Our next big town would be St. Louis tho perhaps would be a week or ten days yet. Then one day another party fell in and traveled with us. Just parties going west.

Each night when we camped, the men would take down a large split bottom rocker which hung on the end of the wagon, spreading a blanket and carefully lift the sick lady out from her bed and place her in the chair alongside the camp fire. Then they would cook the meal and take her some food. Then fix the boy's meal, prepare their plate and all set around the camp fire relating incidents of the days trek. Mother seen at once that the lady was very poorly and offered any assistance she could give. In just a few days they would be in the city and Mother could see that the sick lady was growing worse. Then they might get something to help her.

They reached the city in the early fore noon and decided to get a few essentials for the larder. All the caravan traded some and decided to cross the river and go on till they reached the outskirts of town and camp at the first chance. Our teams were ahead. Father looked back. Grubb's, our co-traveler, was stopped, the other man running toward our wagons. Father stopped. He said, "Mrs. Grubb is real sick, won't your wife come back and see her." When mother reached the wagon, Mrs. Grubb was dying. Father went back to a house that set back a quarter of mile in a nice shady timber lot. He explained they were all travellers going west and those people were travelling for the wife's health and that she had just then suddenly past away. Father said they would like to pull off the main road and camp till they could bury the woman. In this extreme case they gave permission to drive in and camp. The body was laid out, a coffin from the city brot. Next day she was buried in the potters field.

We children and the little boy played in the grove and fed the chicks. In the morning all of the travellers in the train turned out in a body for the funeral in a lovely grave yard nearby. Mother, the older girl, Annie, the boy and I walked down thru the lovely sanded walks and stately monuments to a lonely grave in the potter's field.

We were all lonely travelers in a foreign country to us and we must hurry along. So they ate lunch, and pulled out after offering to pay the good people for giving us shelter in their forest. Then we all drove on and on the long road to our new home on the prairie.

The countryside now was beautiful. Missouri was a grand state, nice houses and farms, well stocked, seeing sights all along the way. One place we saw peafowls in the barnyard. Grass every where, lovely blue grass, high. One Sunday we camped in a lovely grove, blue grass knee high. Mother brot out the table board and we enjoyed a real Sunday dinner. Here Annie and I gathered up some wood ticks. Grubbs were still with us. Washing, sewing and patching done and all clean, Monday morning we moved out on the road. Some times the water was not good and the girls had to carry drinking water quite a way from some farm house. Mother often bot eggs and milk from farm houses. Now, with feeding the horses oats, they could get plenty of grass when herded along the roadsides. Then generally horses on a long trek are so broke to the road that they cause little or no trouble and are always glad to come back to the wagon for their oats.

We rested in Topeka. Pa went to see one of his clost army friends. The country here was more arid, only trees along the streams. The Kaw or Kansas or Smoky Hell River is in the valley here and runs into the Missouri at Kansas City. I believe this is the country where Paul Bunyan and his blue ox turned over all this prairie. There is a high rolling bluff at the north of town. It was a small burg at that time. We camped out in the commons and everyone went in to town, quiet and peaceful now. Thinking back in the 50's, I believe this is the town the question of slavery kicked up so much trouble? In earlier day a lot of good homes were over looked when the rush was on to California, Denver and a lot of gold country people rushed to. Now the big rush was over. The slavery question was fought over. Indians mostly were quieted. People went west to find a home, free land on the prairie. Horses rested, clothes changed and washed, chickens doing well by Annie, little boy and Maggie's watchful care. We pull on up the valley of the Kaw or as one old fellow called it, up the valley of "Smokey Hell" River.

The long open roads. We went slowly and often the girls walked. The young horses were broke to ride and all took their turn but Annie and I. We were too small. We found other amusements. Our noon camp was always made clost to the road, horses fed their oats from a box in the back of the wagon built on for two horses to eat out of and allowed to graze for a spell. Father built a camp fire, wood being picked up clost and Mother prepared the meal with the older girls help. We each one had our cup, knife, fork and plate, so sat any convenient place and was served from the pot or frying pan. A wagon tongue made a good seat or a grub box, a stump or an up turned bucket. Father always believed in giving the horses a good rest. That gave the girls time to pick up everything and carefully pack them away for this had to be done each day and every thing would be needed. Roads were rough and deep mud in many places. Then corduroy roads, tho mostly dirt road with little or no improvements. In the spring one was sure to strike swollen streams, with occasionally rains to make travelling slow and tedious. Even so, we liked the change in our mode of living, every one enjoyed the wide open road. Each turn in the road spread out a new picture before our eager eyes. We were all receiving an unwritten education, much more welcome than if by books.

In a day or two we would come to Solomon. There we would get our boxes of bedding and bed steads we had shipped. Would have to pack the wagon to the bows and sixty miles on would be crowded. From Solomon the R.R. went on to Denver. At that time there was no branch line, tho a few years later a branch line was built to Beloit and another one from the northeast part of the state was built down thru Cloud County, Concordia into Beloit. That one beat the other branch line and went up the valley to Stockton and there they remained just so for over five years.

At Solomon, Father bot the girls big straw hats. Most of the time the wind blew so they had to tie them up in the wagon bows. At Abilene, Kansas we began to see wheat fields as far as the eyes could see and for a half of a day at a time the road lead thru wheat fields like a sea. It was almost ready to cut. That was the loveliest wheat we ever saw in Kansas. At Solomon we left the Kaw River, the road led up the Solomon River.

At [*word missing, piece tore out of page*], we crossed and left the Solomon river going in a south west direction over plains and red sand cliff hills. Entered the little valley of 4th Creek where Levi Jones had preceded us by several years.

The last night out we spent in Jones' yard on the 4th Creek of the Solomon. In this part of the country they had a way of naming the creek by numbers. They had settled on a fine piece of alluvial land on the creek bottom. Was raising wheat and corn, had a fine garden, horses, cows, pigs and chickens. They were counted prosperous people. They burnt lime from the near by lime ridge and he had plenty of help - Jake, Joe, Sam, White, Nelson and Wilber, six boys. Father had met Mr. Jones on previous trips so we were welcomed that eve, June 16. Mr. Jones had come early from Illinois. They were there in the Indian raids. Tho was not molested being on a creek, the Indians over looked him and family, which concisted of six big boys, a wife and aunt. They were living in their old log house, had a nice orchard coming on the creek. Was thickly wooded with nice hard wood. He could raise anything on that creek bottom land. Three boys had land. The creek furnished fruits for summer, raspberries, gooseberries, plums, black walnuts. With so many boys in one family and being strangers in a strange land, the girls stayed clost to the camp and were glad to be on our way and away from their sly gaze. Mother sent up two of the girls to the house to get cooking and drinking water out of their well, which was lifted hand over hand by a pulley out of an open well that had a high curb to keep one from falling in.

Father visited with Mr. Jones that night, tho we were all too tired and anxious, for the morrow we would be home. Father thanked Mr. Jones for his hospitality and invited them to come to see us. In the morning everything was astir early, breakfast over and everything in place, horses hitched up and then came the call and to hit the road. The brush was full of boys trying to get a glimpse of Captain Halbert's family, especially the girls.

We crossed the creek near the lime kiln, wound around thru the timber and gradually climbed out to the crossing at Wanzers. There we stopped to wind the team.

From Jones' it was just seven miles to our new home. So early June 17 we pulled out up from the creek valley, up and over, up and over buttes of lime ridges covered well with all the conceivable flowers of today's flower gardens. Flowers growing every where, down in the sheltered places and in the ravines grew bigger, tender ones. Annie and I most lost our heads, gathered flowers for our new home. Up over the lime formation bluff, the wind began to blow and blew so hard it tore the wagon cover off the bows on the hind wagon. They finished taking it off and tucked it away, for we had not time to stop long. We must be at our new home by dinner.

Father forgot, in his haste, that his old Indiana friend, Henry Stackhouse, lived on the creek south of us. It was on the way and we would have to stop and see him. Their farm was on the same divide as ours. Being spring the country was at its best. As we drew near, Henry had spied us coming and was out to greet us, getting the latest news. Polly, his wife, came out. They both insisted that we stop for dinner. Father said, "No, when we get settled we will come to see you and you must come to see us."

Then we went on southeast over a nice level section of land. One quarter was owned by the Blotchers. We arrived at John and Mary's place before noon. We were all glad to see her and the new baby. John and Mary Wilson [*Maggie's older sister*] had arrived some time before us and were living on their claim two miles away from where our new home was to be.

After dinner we all got in our wagon and drove to our new home. Our crop was now doing fine. The trees made a homelike atmosphere and we soon settled down to home life again. It rather looked inviting, a house and a place we could call home. Tho we had really enjoyed the trip and if this had not been home, we would have been contented to go on and on and on.

Home, something we had planned on ever since we broke up in Indiana. So now we must settle and try our luck for at least a while. This home (160 acres) was in the south east corner of Mitchell County, Logan Township, 16 miles from Beloit, our county seat on the Solomon River, four miles from the post office at Coursen Grove, eight or ten miles from Asherville and Simpson on the Solomon River. These three places had water power grist mills, where one could get their wheat and corn ground. All this land was good black loam, every foot could be tilled and away a few miles on the bluffs of rivers and creek was fine building stone.

The creek south of us gathered its waters in adjoining sections clost to our place. At Briggs, one and a half miles south, it formed turning southwest in to Salt Creek, a larger creek, which run into the Solomon River. Then three miles west of us there were deep draws that gathered water for Salt Creek. North of us numerous draws and revines led off toward the Solomon, then east of us was 4th Creek of the Solomon. Solomon river drained a large area of north west part starting almost at the Colorado east line. At the nearest point, we were about ten miles south.

Chapter IX

Kansas
1875 – 1892

****

The second day at home word had been passed out among the settlers that Captain Enos Halbert and family had arrived the day before. Next day neighbors came in to see the family and have a visit. We were yet camping out as we had no time to clean the house and move in and when mother heard there were liable to be some company that day, she had the stove, which they had brot in the wagon all the way, taken out and set it up there in the yard. She began to get dinner, boiled ham and boiled some of her dried fruit she had brot with her, and made several pans of corn bread out of Indiana corn meal (that they had grown and had ground). By noon there was 15 or 20 settlers gathered. When dinner was ready she had that big piece of lumber brot out and placed on boxes for a table.

After the neighbors had visited, dined and drank black coffee, coffee which father bot as green beans and mother had roasted before the fire, as that was the way coffee was bot those days. All wishing the new family on the prairie the best of luck, they took theirs, departed, for all must go back early to their little meager start on the same prairie. Each one had horses, cows, pigs, and chickens. All must have feed and water. With no fences, horse and cows were tied up or put on a picket rope.

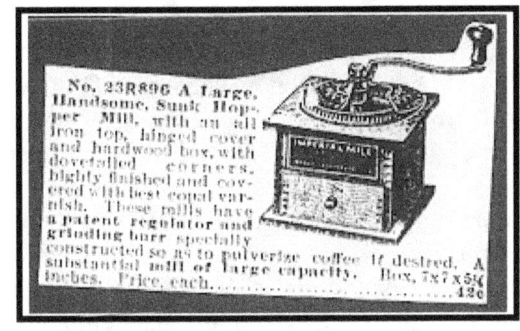

Coffee Grinder
Sears Roebuck & Company Catalog - 1902

The Grubbs had come along with us. After visiting for a few days and rested the team, thanking us, they took the little boy, bid us farewell and moved on. We never knew where as they never wrote back. Mr. Grubb gave mother the rocking chair. She was glad to get it as she had no rocker. The reed wore out in the seat so she put in a bottom of twisted slough grass, but that did not stand the wear. So she saved boot tops (boots were the universal footwear for men those days). When she had enuf, she cut the leather in strips, 3/4 inch wide and wove it in much like hickory splits. Other old chair bottoms were renewed later in that way. We all enjoyed the new country and led an easy time that summer. Men took fishing trips after the farm work was tended to. Mother and the girls often took a days trip to some nearby creek where wild gooseberries and grapes grew. Both fruit was used when green for pies and sauce, sweetened with sorghum molasses or brown sugar. Tho these articles were scarce and [we] never saw white sugar let alone have it in our larder. Then, when ripe, those fruits were gathered too, and wild plums.

Mr. Veach had planted cotton wood trees, plum trees, peach and they were a fair size. There was a house, one part cotton wood logs, with cotton wood shingles on the roof. They were worn then and curled up by the hot sun and let in the snow and rain. This part was about 10 x 12, with a door at each end. One window, two sashes, with six panes to the sash. This was built with the gables north and south. The logs were left just as nature made them with a little dobbing between, with no ceiling, so in time to make a ceiling, Mother took the two wagon covers and sewed them together and stretched it over for a ceiling. There was two hewn cross beams that held up the cloth from sagging in the center. Was comfortable in summer, tho the log part was so cold, like sleeping out doors in the winter with no heater.

The other room was made of stone laid up with mortar. Those days mortar consisted of lime and sand mixed with water. This was used in laying up the native rocks. The laying up of this room was rough. Tho strong, was not laid up by a good stone mason, as was the north end of the room was a fire place, ill constructed, most always smoked. Father thot the front was too high, so he managed to put on a board by putting the large nails thru the board and driving it into a crack between the stones. That did not help much so the girls took the chimney down a ways, then put it back with mortar in between the rocks. It never was a success, but some better. For a mantle, the man had used a big flat rock, longer than the width of the fireplace, using it as a wall rock log and letting it project over about 6 inches for a mantle. Then on either side he left a hole back in the wall to use for his pipe or tobacco or gloves, hearth of native flat rocks. The room was bout 12 x 16 feet, one long window on the east and a door in the west, with a doorway left in the south so as to enter the log part. This part had a dirt floor and a dirt roof. A ridge log was laid up on the south side on the square. Then a long ridge pole lay up on this one in the middle and extended to the wall at the fire place. This making a high place in the middle of the roof, then split poles were laid clost together on each side, reaching from the ridge pole to the outside of the wall. Then the split poles were nailed to the ridge pole to keep them in place. On top of this was laid willow, then slough grass hay and on top of that dirt. Did it leak? Yes, sometimes. Mother brot several books with her. They bear testimony to the question, did it leak? For a library she had a shelf built high up under the short ridge log. When it rained we often forgot about it. My book, she gave me and was hers given to her for spelling when she was young, bible, song book, [etc] bears testimony to the house leaking. Among the books was the large bible father had found when he was in the army. It was too large to be used and seldom ever looked into it.

When the men came back from freighting that winter they brot back windows and lumber to fix up the house comfortable. The stone part yet had no floor so mother took her good parlor carpet, put down a thick layer of hay on the dirt and stretched the carpet over the hay and took sharp small hard wood pegs, drove down thru the carpet into the dirt to hold it fast. This was the warmest room. To save fuel mother cooked on this fireplace all winter. Wood was scarce and had to be hauled from the river. In the south end was two beds, a door in the middle between the beds that opened to the cotton wood log part where in winter we girls slept, three in a bed to keep warm.

> For the Kansas Map and general locations see Appendix B, page 291.

One cold winter when John [Wilson] went back to Indiana, Mary and her children staid with us. Only one room was comfortable and besides the two beds, we had to make down two beds on the floor. But with Ma putting down straw on the floor thick and her good striped carpet over, sleeping on the floor was not too bad at that.

The third spring Mother wanted an el [L shaped addition] put on the house for a kitchen, a cellar built down in the ground and a door cut in the corner of the kitchen down in to the cellar. She planned and talked, [but] father said he was too busy. She went over to Charley Petersons. He was a stone mason. So she bargained with him to lay three stone walls and use the stone house there for one side, making a lean to which was dug down in the ground 6 to 8 inches. The west wall being lower and giving a slant enough for a dirt roof, about 16x16 on the west side of the stone part. Then Father bot a stove and a year after living on dirt he put in a floor in the new part and later put a floor in the old stone part.

This new last part was very low and one had to stoop to go under the ridge pole if tall. It was covered with dirt. Out of the northwest corner of the new part, going down a few steps, was the cellar where vegetables were kept from freezing. That made an L shaped house. There were to be two doors and two small narrow windows in the north, one in the south. The girls hauled most of the rocks from the state land quarry. The walls were built and the men folks put on the roof. So mother had another room. He had now flowered [white washed?] the stone room.

We still hauled water. Dry times in summer the well at Briggs's place often was baled dry each day for many settlers went there for their water. All the loose horses were taken and watered there each day and then as many barrels as would set in a wagon put in and filled. Often when home the wagon had to be used for something else. Then tubs and buckets were filled, then the barrel put down and filled from the one in the wagon. The process was repeated till all the barrels were on the ground. The next trip the barrels all had to be put in.

Mother liked the flat rock to build flower beds and walks. So when we could get a team and wagon, she and all the girls often went to 4th creek of Salt Creek. There were flat stones and all kind of plum sprout. The three corner place between the rooms, she and girls laid the stones together so as to make an outdoors floor. When one stepped out was not on the ground. Then they laid stones around the flower bed, brot in rich dirt and planted flowers.

All the homemade sheets, towels, flannel, linsey and jeans Mother brot with her came in handy. Every rag was saved for a carpet in the future, cut and sewed by the little girls. This became tiresome and often when down to small bits, which she said we must sew, we sometimes took a handful and buried them when we went out to play after we had sewed rags till our back ached. "Bad we whelps, so we were then too."

Annie and I often went to John and Mary's to see the baby (Enos), nicknamed Ena. Babies were quite an oddity for us - often we both staid with Mary. We seldom ever separated. Tho when we did, one or both were miserable with loneliness for the other. One time I staid at Marys and Annie went home. I was so unhappy I wanted to go home at once. Mary hated to see me go alone tho I told her I knew the way thru a section catacornered that lay between home and Marys. So I started out and made it in due time. When John came home that evening she sent him over to see if I got home. After this we never separated.

This wild new country fairly teamed with all kinds of wild fowls. Prairie chickens build their nests any place in the grass and such a glorious supply of birds everywhere. The spring then had advanced too far for eggs as the young had hatched and gone.

Father and Al [Seth] got hauling jobs the first summer and fall from Greenleaf, Cloud County to Beloit. (Some grasshoppers, tho did not destroy every thing like 1874.) Seth [sometimes] got work breaking sod from different farmers and was away a lot. Gradually he saved up money for a team of mules. He preferred them to horses. Then there was hauling over at Greenleaf and Concordia. Often came home between jobs. Henry Stackhouse had several boys Al chummed with.

In the fall '75 mother was determined to have a cow, pigs and some chickens. She went over acrossed the Solomon River to see some Indiana settler that had come to Kansas years before us. At Wash Teaslies she traded a feather bed, two blankets, and two comforters. She got a nice cow, a heifer coming two year old and a heifer calf, two shoats we fattened later for our meat, two dozen Plymouthrock hens. Hens were worth 3 cents per pound at this time in Kansas. With our crop of wheat and corn, we were able to keep our own four horses, the cow and calf, chickens and pigs that mother traded for. We were all so happy about this trade, as we had something to feed and care for that winter, even tho we had to haul water 1 1/2 miles. When it snowed we melted snow for our water for everything.

Our neighbors concisted of people from most every state in the union and several Swede families nearby and some quite English.

Mother wove linsey (linsey-Woolsey-linen woven with wool) for everyday dresses. Flax, kind grown for linen, was pulled, dried in shocks, seed taken off, then the plant soaked in river or slough till the outside came off. Then it is broke, scutched. Next step, fiber hackled, then bleached, combed short strand toe, from long fine kind and shirts, jeans, twill was spun, cotton chain for pants and suits. Then spun fine yarn for filling, then flannel, all wool in checks for dresses, and cotton goods for dresses and shirts.

Many men tanned hides and made the boots and shoes for the family. Then often in the settlement one man (shoe maker) made most of the boots and shoes in trade for other wares he needed.

Brooms were made from fine willows tied on a pole for handle. Then they were put in a clamp board and sewed back and forth to make a flat shape, then cut square off. If a few hills of broom corn was raised in the garden (as often was done) and saved at the right time, then a much nicer broom was made.

Men's caps were made from coon or other hides tanned with the hide on and then made at home. Summer hats were made at home, with some ingenious hands in the family, of rye straw braided into eight strand braid, more or less and then sewed together, blocked to fit and pressed ready to wear.

This part of the country was mostly taken up now. Our crop of corn was up and growing and a garden so there was not much to do till harvest. This summer Father and Seth got some freighting jobs. On account of cut rates on freighting from Solomon City to Beloit they hauled it to Greenleaf, Cloud County and then to Beloit. Part of the hauling had to be taken out in trade, balance in money. We had the two teams. Father and Seth could go together as there was no bridges and the Republican and the Blue River and creeks were often up. This was all the work that could be had. They worked at that most all summer and winter.

When wheat was ready to cut someone of the older settlers had an old wire binder. They would bind with wire. Wire was bot on spools. Later they discarded this, as wire was often swallowed by the stock and the stock died. Those days a homesteader would only have 15 to 20 acres, that would be bout all the land they having plowed. Then later they bot the March Harvester. It was so built that two men stood on the machine (third one drove) and made their ties by tieing two wisps of grain together and then tying the wisp around the bundle as they caught the grain coming over the elevator, throwing off the bundles at certain rows. Then men came a long and shocked the bundles.

Father had a lot of ground broke and the next year we put in wheat, corn, millet and potatoes. Of these we had enuf for ourselves, the stock and some to sell. Now it looked more like living.

In those days there was no ready made clothes. The cloth was bot and then hired made. Mother had made suits for Father and Seth so it soon got out she could make suits of clothes. George Stackhouse was a violinist and always tried to dress nice, so she made a suit for him and one for a brother Tom, then one of Myra Petersons men. They lived on a homestead 3/4 mile east. He was a stone mason. In the second summer she sewed for Mrs. Reins' family and took pay in setting hens and eggs. Many came to her for her to make nice quilted sunbonnets worn so much in those days.

Many people came to Kansas for their health. Our family had no more chills and fever and for twenty five years there was never a doctor called to our house. A Dr. Smith came in in earlier days, took up a claim north of Simpsons. Dr. Smith going where ever he was called horseback, conveying his pill bags in the saddle. Later years he moved to Simpson, a little town north of us on the R.R. and river. He was the first and only doctor for years above Solomon City.

I was very susceptible to bites and ivy poison when a child. Once I remember Father went to Simpson, told Dr. Smith he wanted something for ivy poison. He mixed baking soda and water, told father to have me keep the effected place wet with this solution. I was well in a few days. Formerly a plant called night shade, mashed up well, moistened in milk, often cured me.

The older women took care of the baby cases. I never knew how many times Mother was called as she never talked of such things to we children tho as I grew older one case caught my ear. Some foreign people lived north west of us. I heard her tell my older sister - "the bed bugs pested the poor sick woman so that they finally had to put her on the table for delivery."

Kansas climate had long been known as windy - there were hard winds, tho no dust storms and as long back as I can remember, cyclones on the divide. Tho there were some very bad in other parts on the river. These stories caused us to often go to the cyclone cellar.

Our winters were varied. The first winter was very cold and snowy [1875]. I believe '86 -'87 were about the hardest winters. The snow lay deep all over the prairie. The south roads were invariably impassable. Spring came early and the falls often long, summer long and hot. It was not till the ground was broke and fields plowed that the dust began to blow. The more they plow, the more dust. The rain was enuf to keep up a thick carpet of grass before the white man ripped open the sod with the two horse or mule breaking plow. Consequently upset natures equilibrium and made man to suffer. They took it from the Indians to give the white man a show to ruin it, other words, man is his own enemy.

> **No trees for fence posts!**
>
> *Trees were not available for fence posts but the settlers did, however, have a lot of limestone outcroppings in the area. They would quarry out 8 to 10 inch square by 6 or 8-foot long blocks of the limestone cut to length for fence posts. They would then drill holes in the stone, brace them or set the posts in the ground and string wire for their fences. - mc*

After the ground was turned under good, crops of corn, rye, wheat was raised. All kinds of vegetable, fruits and flower. The new settler set out shade trees, ash, elm, cotton wood, lombardy poplar, apple, peach and pear and small fruits of many kind. A peach tree would bear the third and fourth year and continue for years. Plums of many a good variety grew on the creeks that was brot up and cultivated. Wild grapes grew in abundance on the rivers and creeks of a good variety. Many planted Osage for hedge fence. The timber claims were mostly set to native trees, cottonwood, box elder. Some found a better set was got by planting black locust and others planted Osage. It made the finest hard posts. Also was a very excellent wood, tho hard to handle. Trees did well at first when there was plentiful spring rains. Many farm homes had groves, tho many only thot of getting money and moved on when it was hard to get. When we moved away in '87 the country was progressing nicely.

Churches in Kansas

Wanzer was the first to offer his home to the community for services and Sunday School. Wanzer was an old batchelor, lived on 2nd creek of the Solomon River. Also, before they built the church, a neighbor, Mr. Childs, offered his house for Sunday School and church. Prizes were given in Sunday School for the most verses of the Psalms committed to memory, in which my sister, Annie, excelled and received a nice new testament which she has kept and prized all her life.

After a year or two of holding meetings in private homes, the community decided to erect a central meeting place. Our first church was an old log building the community brot up from Mr. Jones. Mr. Jones, an early day settler, came to the community's assistance by offering his old walnut log house they had lived in for years and having erected a nice 1 1/2 story stone house, he needed it no longer. He had cut these walnut logs off of his homestead where he had first settled on Second Creek, Cloud County and had generously offered the old house if the men in the community would come down seven miles to his place, tear it down and haul it up and rebuild it. This was eagerly agreed to as most every settler had a team and wagon and would help with the work. In no time the building was up just acrossed on the section south of Henry Stackhouse's homestead. This being the most centerly located in the community. There being no money they would have to erect it on a very cheap plan. When finished it had dirt roof and dirt floor, minus a door and two windows, which was supplied later before winter coming on. Did not need them in the summer time. The seats was benches made of slabs. Sunday School and church was held here every Sunday tho not always a minister. We all went regularly. When winter came, they put in windows and doors. They used it that winter for all kinds of gatherings.

Minister of '75

When we first went to Kansas our part of the country was mostly Protestant (Methodists) and those of other faiths joined in. The minister, a Mr. Howe, from Ada, south several miles and having a large circuit to administer to, only came every two weeks to hold services. And, before there was a suitable building, held services in our house. My most forcible recollections of these meetings were the songs: "Rain O Rain Good Lord, send it down, send it down among the people in the army of the Lord", "When The Roll Is Called

> **THE SUNDAY HYMNS**
>
> We all sing hymns on Sunday eve;
> My daddy sings the bass,
> My mamma has the tune, and I --
> Oh, I sing any place!
>
> by Louise Gahnett
>
> From Maggie's Scrap Book

Up Yonder, I'll Be There", "Shall We Gather At The River", "Sweet Bye And Bye", and "There Is A Land That Is Forever Thou Day".

Mr. Howe was an elderly man with a wife and family of eleven, the youngest a baby. When coming up, he often brot his wife and all the children and staying all night with Captain Halbert and Aunt Susan. At that time it was a great hardship to our family, as beds had to made down all over the floor to accommodate this minister's large family. Normally our house was small for our family of four girls, one boy and mother and father.

The wife was a big fat woman and on those trips never had enuf diapers for the baby. And in order to save them and to impress on us she hadden enough, she often helt the baby out to the warm fire and with warmth on its hind parts, it would almost invariably urinate or evacuate before the fire. So, coming needy like that, the ladies of this sparsely settled community would all join in, make quilts and clothes for the preacher's family. And, for weeks and months they would knit, piece quilts and make Sunday things for the preacher's family. All the rag bags had to be hunted over and over for scrap for the quilt block and when the blocks were done with great saving, the lining and thread money was collected. Then the real work begun, quilting. There were two to quilt, so in order to have enuf quilters on each quilt, they decided to divide the community into two quilting places, ours over west and by then the log meeting house was up and one to be quilted there. Mother insisted that Emma go with her west. Altho Emma would much rather go to the log meeting house, quilting on account of the young folks being there. It turned out those in the west finished their quilt and bound it in one day, while the other had to take another day to finish theirs.

When the minister came again, the quilts, mitts, scarfs and many other needed articles were presented to them with O's and Ah's for thanks. The next time, here came the Howes all in the wagon box with dirty, muddy feet wrapped in those nice new white quilts. When Emma and Hattie saw this they were struck with horror. Right then and there they vowed never to help in those donations. When I drop off, [I] don't want to drop in with that preacher.

When church and Sunday school was held at Uncle Billie Childs' homestead our family all attended. It was there that Annie won her new testament by committing to memory 56 verses of the Psalms. Howe was minister with Hank Mallow, Secretary and placed his name in her book. John Wilson was the Sunday School Superintendent. When she left home she forgot her testament. When mother packed up the household goods to move to Beloit, she gave Mary everything she did not want. In some boxes of books and papers, when Mary came to look over the thing, she found Annie's New Testament with Hank Mallow's name in it and she at once mailed it to Annie in Arkansas where they had just recently moved. In two years she moved back to Kansas and she still has her testament, a precious treasure.

There also was another preacher that came some times with the Howes. Rev. Jim Lane - they often preached first one and then the other, making those afternoon sermons as forcible as possible. Mr. Lane would plead that the young folks be good, honest and true, pray the Lord for guidance. He seemed to be a little more anxious about the young folks than Rev. Howe. After long pleading and warning for them to keep the straight and narrow road, he'd say, "Boys, I tell you I was a sinner. Yes, I sinned and it was years ago when I was young, pealing tan bark away back in Maine. We had tan bark on our own farm but boys there were nicer trees over the line. I coveted them. That was wrong. Yes, I could not shake that desire off. I still wanted the trees over the line. I went over finally, cut the trees and pealed the bark. Boys, I pealed over the line. Will God forgive me for pealing over the line. Now will God protect and guide you and keep your minds a right and not covet your neighbors property and not commit the sin I have. And with Gods grace I beg and implore his gracious forgiveness. Amen. Brother Howe please sing 'Rain O Rain'." Consequentially our young folks called him "old Pealover". Howe, too, was much in earnest as to the boys' welfare. He often gave them fatherly advice.

In this new prairie country there were no other society and naturally every one, young and old. went to church and the young devilish fellow found thot and amusement to last to the next meeting.

Now that the church was done people came from far and near, filling it to its full capacity, morning services and Sunday School, afternoon meetings and then at night services.

Church Suppers

In order to pay the preacher a salary, suppers were put on. Mush and Milk supper, "Oyster Stews" and such but no chicken suppers as very few people had chickens in those days, having just recently came to the new country.

Our greatest blessing was good health and hopes - hopes in this new country of open range and as yet scenery of land of waving grasses. The breaks or draws were lined with choice flowers and shrubs. The black soil was deep with the turning over of the sod, abundance was assured. So these poor settlers all joined together in one solid body to keep up their church and society gleaning a few nickels here and there for its up keep by putting on suppers, selling ring cakes.

After church the older folks often called a business meeting and put the question before the congregation about funds for the church. If decided, younger folks were appointed to a committee to make arrangement for the supper. If my sister Emma was appointed, she often chose Winnie Wines as her help. If sister Hattie was appointed, she chose Mable Geering. The community was divided and each one took his appointed field to solicit. The radius of this community was about 10 or 12 miles and these girls knew the circumstances of about every family. Most every girl in early day were good horseback riders, so the soliciting was done that way. The first supper was a mush and milk supper. They only solicited for food we knew they could spare, so going to Lee Childs, they knew he was in very poor circumstances and only asked for milk. Other places and then again they asked for other articles that was needed to help out in the supper or added attraction. Most always they raffled off a cake with a gold ring in it. Some of the committee that would happen to go to Beloit, 18 miles away, would get a plain gold ring, perhaps cost $2.00 or there abouts and leave it with mother who always baked a plain cake with a hole in the center. This cake the night of the supper was cut in pieces. One was gently pulled out and the ring deftly pressed in so it could not be detected. Then the piece was put back and each piece was tagged by number tacked on. The ring piece was noted by one of the committee. Generally the boys and girls was eager to buy a piece of cake for 25 cents. Each number sold was recorded. When all was sold, the lucky number was called. This created a lot of merriment for the young folks and added extra money to their funds which was all used to defray the up keep of our church affairs.

> **Matrimonial Cake**
>
> 2 cups brown sugar
> 2 cups flour
> 2 cups oatmeal
> 1 cup butter
> 1 tsp. soda
> 1 egg
> 1 tsp. BP (baking powder)
> 1/4 tsp. salt
> 1 tsp. vanilla
>
> Mix above with hands. Place half in pans. Put in filling of 1 lb. dates, 1 cup water, 1 Tbsp. flour (cooked). Then cover with remainder of dough. Bake and cut into squares. - Maggie Hand
>
> **From the Susan Hand Collection**

Then they often varied the suppers, which added amusement for all, such as box suppers. Ladies filled the boxes with a dainty luncheon such as we had then, trimmed their box according to their fancy, thinking all the time hers would be the nicest.

Neck Tye suppers - Ladies baskets were sold [to the men] with a neck tye made from a piece of the dress she wore. When the box was bot and opened, he took out the tye and hunted his partner and they ate together. At one of these suppers, when my sisters were making their neck tyes, I was told to make one as every tye would count. I was quite small and bashful then - at first I said I would and then at once the thot struck me of having to eat with a man. And I said no, I won't.

They said nothing to me anymore about the supper. I had forgot about the eating with a man and went with the bunch that night. The auction began and 1,2,3 baskets were sold and what to my surprise, here a man came with a tye like the dress I had on. He says, " Won't you eat supper with me." "No, I won't", but finally went over and sat with him. But before we began to eat I saw how to slip away and went over to Mother. These sisters of mine had framed this all up and I knew it. I was about seven years old then and could not be teased and run on.

Oyster suppers - for these, oysters and crackers had to be bot and paid for out of the funds. Other needed articles were donated. Then just plain table, help yourself suppers were sometimes put on. Food was put on and every body helped themselves.

Coursens Grove was by this time a coming center of the community. It had the post office, a general store, a blacksmith shop and the school district had erected a nice large native stone school house furnished with good seats, desks and stove. They disposed of the solid black walnut log building to Henry Stackhouse and moved their place of meeting to the Coursen Grove Schoolhouse. There church and Sunday School was held every Sunday. Tho ere long it was not large enough to accommodate all the people.

Among the many ministers that preached here, I can only recall two, a Mr. Golden that lived down near Milo, Lincoln County. He often hitched up his light sorrel spotted mare to the buggy and drove up to the Grove to fill a vacancy in the pulpit. This preacher was quite different from others, as he could preach to the white folks in our community, then go down to Salina, black up, and preach to the negroes. In this way he pulled down double pay. This deception finally got out on him. Then there was a Mr. McDowall preached some and often conducted funerals.

Rev. Seaman came to our church, a very young man, inexperienced minister but seemed to be very sincere in his work. He married the oldest Wines girl and for a side line ran a blacksmith shop. Work was not so rushing there so between jobs he wrote his sermons and when alone delivered his sermon to the emptied church walls. He preached here for a few years and then went down the river to another congregation.

There were several leaders in our church, John Wilson, Henry Stackhouse and Mr. Mack and others. These men were Sunday Supterintendent at times and often lead in other meetings. Old Henry was so outstanding in his ways I can't help but speak of him. He most always was called on to give the closing prayer at the end of the sermon and often coiled his long legs up one, two or three seats and slept all thru services. Then at Christmas times he always gave the address and helped distribute the presents. He seemed to be a very devout member in the church as long as I knew him, tho he loved his liquor.

Once on a trip hauling lumber from Greenleaf to Beloit he accompanied Father and Al (Seth). Each had a team and running gears of the wagon and in order to haul long lumber they had to let out the reach as long as possible and when loaded, making the load still longer. As usual Henry got a bottle of liquor. After they had left town for some distance, Henry wrapped the lines to the standards of his wagon, took out his bottle, much to father's protest and began taking a drink. Then he raised his big frame up and began walking his load, all the time singing his favorite song, "When Roll is Called Up Yonder I'll Be There" and shouting "Come on boy" and lifting the bottle aloft shouting again, "Come on, lets take another snifter." Then father would say to "Put up the bottle Henry, you know that is not right to act that way." Then in heeding father's advice, Henry would walk the planks again, throw up the bottle and call out, "Come on boys and take another snifter." After this he'd sing another stanza of "When the Roll is Called Up Yonder". This all went on for some time, till the bottle was finished, while Al watched on with bursting sides of laughter.

On these trips he [*Henry*] took the cooking job. One morning he was going to have scrambled eggs. He got out a large frying pan, propped it up on the open fire and began to break the eggs one by one in to the grease. Father says to Henry, "Those eggs, you know, I got at the store so break them one by one in a cup at a time as you might find a rotten one." But Henry, unheeding, kept on breaking eggs into the pan. He now had almost two dozen and then, to his chagrin, pop, [*an egg*] went into the pan with such a smell. Then bacon and coffee was enough for that breakfast. They hitched up, pulled on by this time and all were sullen.

The one church dinner I remember most was a chicken dinner, as now by this time everyone had plenty of poultry in their yards. This was shortly after the church had moved from the log cabin one near Stackhouses to the Grove. It was decided that we have a dinner first. When the day came each lady brot her allotted amount of roast, fried or boiled chicken, as well as other food.

We children came too and played around. When noon came the older people all sat down and proceeded to do justice to the scrumptious dinner. When we found out they were eating, that made us all very hungry. We were told just as soon as the older folks were done we could eat so we waited patiently till the scraps were all cleared away. When we were seated, Mrs. Kinsey, a recent new comer to our community, proceeded to wait on us. The necks of the chicken with the skin on seemed to be our portion, much to our disgust. One filled up on what other food she gave us and hurriedly slipped away. The others perhaps had a good dinner, but we never to this day forgot ours.

In the new meeting place, with more active people, our church flourished under the leadership of active older ladies. Mrs. Caughey, Mrs. Wines, Mrs. Austine, Mrs. Rev. Seaman's wife, Aunt Susan (our mother), Mary Wilson, our sister and Mrs. Bayley, tho hampered physically, gave support by being in our midst. With all of these able workers the social side of this church flourished with entertainment of various social chicken dinners and suppers, & [*etc*].

This church flourished for a few years, then gradually times came on, people was tired of Kansas and its short coming. They, hearing of greener pastures, moved on, selling their place to other more prosperous people that would stay. Then the older young folks married and moved on, often out of this community. Then too, among some of the older men turned their heads to reading Mr. Coursen's paper the "Truth Seeker", which he generously shared with those that would read them. And by this time Denver, and in fact "West" lured away families and young men. So all in all our church dwindled, tho hung on going in 1893 fairly good, having regular meetings and its "Epworth League" Sunday School. Then to, in about 1886 new people from the states came of the Christian faith or Camelites and settled north of our place. They amediately set up a new meeting place, which detracted from the Grove and the community was split.

On one occasion we had come over to Stackhouse's on Saturday in a one horse buggy. The next day being Sunday there were several of us to go to church, so they thot we had better all go in the wagon. So we hitched our horse and one of theirs to the wagon, dressed up in our Sunday best and started. The horses were slow and we did not make any progress. Then the tire was so loose we had to stop every now and then and take a rock and drive it back on and by this process was repeated many times up and down over the hills to the creek school house. On the top of the last hill we saw, much to our disgust, that Sunday School was out. Anyway we got to see the folks and show our clothes. The progress was repeated going home but then we were content, we made the trip and seen the folks.

In early day, people were always welcome and they got the best they could afford and invariably beds had to be made down on the floor to accommodate all. No news papers, one was always glad to see someone. They could bring news from some place.

A Mr. Shirts and several other families came to Kansas from Iowa and settled over north of the Green Mound school house, buying a few sections of unused land and settled. They called themselves Christians and amediately Mr. Shirts, the older man, began holding church services each Sunday morning and evening. He, being the minister, at first only their folks attended. Gradually other church goers began to come and before long the school house was filled each Sunday.

In about 1905 the dwindling Methodist congregation at the Grove had now decided a new church more centrally located should be built on John Wilson's timber claim quarter of land 1/4 mile north of John's home. There they built a nice small church called Ureka Chapel. The country then being somewhat more prosperous these times and as long as John Wilson lived there it was kept up well as they hired more learned and able minister, which held the congregation together.

When we first came, camp meetings were held regularly each summer at Wanzer's Grove on Second Creek where family from far could come, pitch their tents and stay and enjoy all the social activities. Then some went from home and only staid a day at a time owing to their pressing home duties. Mother, rather tired of these meetings, discouraged the family's steady attendance, as they added a detraction to the home's quiet happiness. They were held for a few summers and then abandon there tho often at days dinner and picknick some minister other than ours would speak to the crowd in the afternoon. Then each family would go with heavily laden baskets for the dinner. After dinner, when all had done justice to the feast and the friends and neighbors had met and greeted each other, the crowd was all called. In order, each one took a seat. Mothers took their brood and sat beside them, both young and old, big and little, keeping quiet till the message was delivered and the benediction was pronounced. Then each family hitched up their horses to the old lumber wagon and mother and children took their place in the wagon. The better half would take up the lines, climb in to the right hand side of the board or spring seat, give to the horses the command to go and slowly and quietly drove away home, carrying each and all a new thot or message.

Pony Runabout
The American Peoples Encyclopedia
Chicago Spencer Press, Inc.
Copyright 1959

I remember vividly the last one of these meetings I attended in about 1886. There was to be a picknick held at Markley's Grove on the 4th Creek of Salt Creek. Mother and I hitched up the gray pony mare to the buggy and went. People by this time had phaetons, spring wagons or buggies, yet some wagons were still there. Sharkers, with long strings of phaetons, had gone thru the country selling their wares to each farmer that would bite, taking cash notes or whatever they could get, each time driving a good bargain in on their side. This picnic was goodly attended from far and near. Will Prewett, my old beau, was there. My older sisters never lost a chance to devil me about him. We had gone to school together and we rather liked each other. He had taken me to one or two night protracted meetings at Shilo at Walnut Grove. About three spring seats were put on a wagon box and two or three couples went. One night Annie went in the crowd and coming back Will put his arm around me. Annie saw that and she never let up on me. Once I was going to tell on her and her beau, Frank Briggs and then she said if you do I'll tell on you and Bill. That settled it, when Will asked me to go again, I said no. He never got over that for a long time. I evaded him on every turn. So at this picknick I spoke, tho gave him no show to talk. We moved away in '87. When in Beloit I always kept out of town for fear of meeting my old lover.

Some bunch of surveyors also attended this picnic from west of the creek where they were surveying for a new R.R. which never went thru. After dinner, everyone washed their utensils, as well as the surveyor cook. He polished his knives, forks and spoons by running them forth and back in the sand, then packed them away.

Obediah Bayley

Obediah Bayley took up a homestead four miles south east of Coursen's Grove on Second Creek of Salt Creek, coming to Kansas with a Mr. Rutherford from southern Missouri in 1871. There he built a half dugout facing to a small timbered creek a few feet back from the bank where the front door came out on level ground. There were two small windows on either side of the door. This was front room, dining room and kitchen combined and to a child's mind, all that was needed in a comfortable home. A partition cut off the bedrooms on either side of the front room. Then farther back was a store room with one small rectangle window put in sideways just above the ground. Then all was covered over with dirt. Made a very comfortable home for their family of two girls and three boys. Mrs. Bayley was a wonderful housekeeper and mother and a very good cook. One was delighted to be invited to the Bayleys for a Sunday dinner, after church, which was the custom among the early day's settlers. A special effort was made to have someone go home with you for dinner.

Bayley was not a farmer tho took this means to house and raise his family. He had taught school and was a fine scholar of his day and in the fall and winter resorted to teaching to help along. One fall he taught at Asherville, some 12 or

15 miles away on the river, walking home each weekend. He was a very deep thinker, always had his slate clost at hand to record big poems as they came to him. Then later copied them and later had a volume printed.

Once he taught singing at the Grove. Having lost a front tooth, he took a buffalo tooth, filed it down to fit the vacant place and slipped it in so he could teach the class and sing. Then when the whole world needed inventions, he invented the suction pump and while he was having some difficulty with the valve, a man stole the idea and had the patent recorded before Bayley had decided to patent it. Then a new Englishman in our community derided him by making a poem about Bayley's pump having the suction upside down.

He dropped out of going to gatherings to be alone on Sunday to write and think. Tho Mrs. Bayley continued to go each Sunday with her children till all were married, scattered and gone to their own homes.

Mr. Bayley had a timber claim up within a mile of Walnut Grove. Later he sold his home place on Second Creek on Salty and bot an improved place accross the road from the timber claim. Most of this 160 was broke up and farmed. There was a large apple and peach orchard on it and many shrubs and rare trees and vines and a small comfortable house, tho a very poor straw barn. By this time most of the children were gone and Mr. and Mrs. Bayley were not so young, tho both took hold to make a nice new home. Mrs. Bayley worked out a great deal till she found her eye sight failing. She began to doctor, tho to no avail and she lost her eyesight. Thru all she worked on doing all her work in the house, made her dresses, cooked, etc. Long after they gave up the place she still worked and washed dishes each day for her daughter. Made quilts, covered small fruit boxes with two colors, knit slipper tops, pieced up diamond pin cushions and made many other little commodities. At the fairs she won prizes over women that had eyes.

Once, when blind, she made a sheet. When Mr. Bayley came in she asked how it was made, he said fine but that did not answer her question. What color? Then he had to tell her it was made with black thread. Next day she ripped out the seam and made it over with white. All her sewing was done by hand. When she canned fruit, she put it away. Then anytime she wanted that particular kind she remembered just where she put it.

I think she was one of the most wonderful women I ever knew. They had 5 children, Hattie, Therne, Linlie, Della and Elgan. When Hattie married Frank Mack, they was married in his father's house east of the Grove. All the young couples that went to church were invited to the wedding and feast. Rev. Seaman (the blacksmith minister) officiated. After the ceremony was pronounced, Mr. Mack said to the minister, "Now give this young couple a lecture on the stern realities of married life." After a year or so farming clost to home, they decided to go to eastern Colorado with team and wagon and take up free government land, clost to Lamar. Times was none too good out there and Frank got work on a canal. Hattie staid on the claim. Frank took ill and before they could get a doctor, Frank died. Hattie sold out her holdings in Colorado, came back, staid a year at home, then got a housekeeping job near Glen Elder.

Grasshoppers

Grasshoppers came in 1874 in droves, eating the crops as they went. The Briggs' were living there in Kansas then. Seeing everything being ate up they thot by digging a big trench they could save their sweet corn patch by gathering the corn, putting it in the trench and covering it up. But the grasshoppers dug down in and ate the corn all up.

Stackhouses

In Indiana, neighbors of ours were three, grown up, married Stackhouses. Alfred, Henry, Stanford, called "Sant" for short. Henry and Alfred moved to Kansas several years before us, thru the years of hopper scourge. Both Henry and Alfred came to Kansas and settled in good Solomon River bottom land till the Indian raids. Several went back to the states. When the raids happened the settlers all went to high ground.

Alfred Stackhouse, Henry's brother, had taken up a good homestead in Solomon River Valley above Glasco. Indians raided the country, drove off settlers and killed several - one of the Bond boys. Alfred took his family and went to the Lime Hill on the north side of the river. When the raiders had gone all settlers moved back. Tho low and behold, some new settler had moved in on his claim. Alfred, being a good, easy going Methodist exhorter, would have no troubles so moved back on to the Lime Hills north of the river, dug out a good big dugout for an ever increasing family, raised whatever the Lord saw fit. I think he lived there till he died.

Here Alfred farmed, raised their food and raised a large industrious family of three boys, Milton, Drew, John and the girls were Nancy, Mary, and Lucy. Alfred was an early day Methodist Minister. Travelled to his outlying congregations horseback. They lived in a dugout built in a side hill, a window on either side of the door which came out on level ground. The dugout was larger than most of them, was divided in to two rooms by a curtain. The back room had one small window up at the gable which let in a few faint rays of light. Where the beds were they left in the solid dirt, thereby doing away with the expense of buying bed steads. This, with a corn husk mattress, made comfortable beds. Their good clothes were hung on nails on the side of the room and good hats were hung on the ridge logs, tied up in an old cloth. There was no bedroom furniture of any kind. The front room, kitchen, dining, sitting and parlor were all in one with a cook stove to cook on and heat the room. Above was a box cupboard, a rough table, chairs and benches constituted the furnishings. With a straw barn for his horses and cows, they managed to eak out an existence tho the farm implements only concisted of an old wagon, a plow, harrow and cultivator, and hoe. The children went to a country school and church over west on the creek. John and Milton went to Concordia, worked their way thru higher school. John taught school, Milton held a County office in Concordia.

John taught school for a while and then got acquainted with a school teacher. He decided he'd go to California and go in to the real estate business. So he wanted to marry her and borrowed money and went to California and as far as the school teacher, well, all she had to do was to make the move.

By this time Nancy had helped her mother raise the balance of the family and went over to keep books for John. Here she met a young man from southeast Kansas, Strong City, where he and his mother had a large cattle and land holdings. His mother, being an early day Kansas woman, foreseen the possibility of amassing an estate. They began humble, raised orphan calves given them by large cattle men. They had some land. Corn crops was good and then raised more cattle and corn. They bot more land till the mother Patten died and Nan [*Nancy*] became mistress of this large estate. Being raised so poor now knew how to save in her own household and amass more fortunes for their two children, a boy and girl. The boy chose to be a brakeman on the R.R. This most broke the mother's heart. After much educating and travel, the girl married an importer of fine horses.

Drew Stackhouse grew up with not much intentions in life. He said he wanted to see how long a good, healthy body would live good, taken care of. He often came over to see his uncle Henry, and incidentally, to see Captain Halbert's daughter. So after eating and feeding his horse at Uncle Henry's he came on over to our house. Not seeing the girls at the house, he asked mother where the girls were. "Well," she says, "I don't know but they were here not long ago." He staid a while longer tho the girls did not show up. Tho all the while they were in the grainary watching. When he got on his horse and rode away they came out. I have always been curious to know what became of Drew and if he really found out how long his good body lived and if he could give it good care rustling for himself in life. We moved away and never knew what became of the younger girls.

Henry took his claim up on the Divide west of Second Creek of Solomon. Water level on this divide ran all the way from 153 feet to over 200 feet deep. I only knew of two deep wells dug down with pick and shovel and the dirt lifted with a windless. Stackhouse's was dug before 1895 by two men that was willing to dig it for board and room and two oxen. Henry and Polly raised a large family of five boys and two girls, Jess, George, Tom, Hude, Azor, Jennie and Fanny. Jennie married Nash Teasly. Tom and Hude were Seth's running mates when we first came.

George had the only fiddle on the divide for years. Played by ear. He played for dances down on the river and any entertainment that was put on by Myra [*Peterson*] on the Divide.

Nice clothes and shoes to dress up in were scarce and hard to get in those early days. So on Sunday morning the first one up was the one that would dress up to go to see his girl. So one morning Hude was first to get up, so he went to see his girl, a Miss Londens, down on the creek. In the course of time Tom decided he wanted the shoes so he sent his younger brother, Azor, down to Londens for the shoes. He was too bashful to get off his horse and knock at the door so he drew up in hollowing distance of the house and hollowed, "Hude, O Hude, Hude, Tom wants his shoes."

The Stackhouses were easy going people and lived on this place long after the children had gone. Her husband often helped in the house and especially when visitors came, she being slow about getting the meals. He often, in summer, got the vegetables and prepared them.

Their log house was very plain - divide log house - built long with binding, 2 or 3 binding logs in the middle to hold it together. Mrs. Stackhouse always envied mother in her ability in making clothes for her family and often tailoring suits for men and one time made a suit for Tom. Then, too, mother made carpet and made carpet for others. In this she was very jealous of mother and when she wanted a carpet she says no, I'll not let Susan Halbert weave hers, she knit it. We were very interested in this new kind of carpet and went to see it when partly done. Only got a few strips done and she must have found out it was not a success as she never finished it.

Schools and Teachers

When we first came to Kansas, school districts in our part had not yet been formed in this settlement. In order to get state money, a three month subscription school had to be held, of $2.00 per child. This was state law.

Father took a great interest in getting this first school as he wanted his children to have an education. Mrs. Joe Thompson was hired to teach this subscription school. They had been living with her folks for a few years. The Speakmans [*Mrs. Joe Thompson's folks*] recently had taken a homestead, built a house and moved in and was struggling along trying to make a living. Mrs. Thompson needed the money.

Annie Speakman Thompson was a teacher in Pennsylvania years before. After her marriage to Joe Thompson, they and her father and mother's family came west to take up land and secure a home. They, her father and mother, owned 1/4 section of land west of us in the section we lived in. Then her brother had the east 1/4 acrost the corner from her folks in the other section and her land 1/4 lay south of her brother's. Not such a desirable 1/4, but they were willing to try to make a home. Mrs. Thompson was quite neat and clean and not having a large ward [*not having many clothes*] she often put on her wedding dress for school hours. Homer was a little fellow about 18 months or 2 years old and he was dressed regularly in a two motion frock, in a slip over, no diapers and he often ran around holding up his dress to the mortal imbarishment of the girls. In her kind, gentle way she would say, put your cuatty down Homer, put your cuatty down.

She was a fine scholar and a lovely penman. I remember later when we finally got a school established and our teacher put on a play one evening - the first of the kind in the new school house. The school house was jammed full that night, old and young. Older girls and their beaus all proclaimed it a big success. The Petersons with their children, Charley, Hanna and Lesslie, David and a lot of little fellows not of school age - the Pearsons, Laura and others, Prewett, Bill, Tom, Oilgal and Rose. The Francis, Etta and Adda. The Shirts's two children, Annie, myself and then all the parents and several visitors from other districts.

Later on when one of our teachers wanted to have a school paper and not knowing how to go about it, they sent for Annie Thompson to come over and set it up properly.

Both she and her folks had seen better days in Pennsylvania where she was educated and taught school. Mr. Thompson first built a dugout in a steep hillside. Having no place to hold this school, it was decided to hold it in Thompson's dugout, which was about 12 x 12 feet. The front was walled up with native lime stone, leaving the earth for the inner back wall, with dirt roof and dirt floor. The door went in on the east side. Then a small barren window lighted the dugout on either side, west and east.

The furniture consisted of a small wood cookstove. The table was made of native rough lumber (3 x 5 ft.) and poles for legs. The bed was the ox sled they had used in hauling the stones for the front of the dugout - now that the face of the dugout was completed, the sled could handily be used for a bed. In its making, a properly curved log was found on the creek and split for the two runners. Then proper stays were morticed in to make a stout frame, then with rough lumber, then presto, it could be used for a sled and then a bed and there by serve two purposes. With a corn husk mattress, blankets and quilts which was brot from Pennsylvania it was quite a comfortable bed and was a step better than the floor. There were no chairs, so wooden soap boxes made good substitutes, which were brot from Beloit 16 miles distant. As we had no desks or seats, each scholar were asked to bring a chair or box as their table for a desk. As Mother had brot several hickory bottom chairs from Indiana we were allowed to take a chair each and left them there the duration of the term and which Anna and Joe gloated over sitting in them whenever we were not occupying them. We did not begrudge them to her as she had a small boy of 18 months old to tend and hold. But he, the old fat lazy sided, would come in, make a dive for a chair if he caught us up reciting and sit and sit, rare back and smoke his corn cob pipe just as contented as if he was a millionaire. Then, when we were done reciting, we'd have to sit on a box or the side of the bed. When school was out, much to their pleading and begging to keep the chairs, Mother said no and we brot them home. We were glad when school was out. While we were there he never brot a bit of water from the well.

There were only five scholars. Win Chapin, two of Henry Speakman's children, and Emma and Annie. Mother thot it was too far for me to walk to school and I could learn more from her sewing and reading to her and playing at home.

The well at Thompsons was dug down about 10 feet in blue clay, walled at the head of a small pond so the water and frogs would seep in. Emma was about 13 years, tho quite an expert flipping the bucket on a rope so it would dip as soon as the bucket hit the water. Each morning, recess and noon, she and Annie would go down for the water. They abhorred the thot of the frogs swimming around in the well so she would flip the bucket and take out the frogs, one by one each time they went down, then draw a perfectly good frogless bucket of water and take it to the house.

The water was a milky color and when the weather warmed up we could hardly drink it, so Mrs. Thompson took black strap molasses and vinegar, mixed it all up and put it in our drinking water, making a vinegary, sweet taste, which we called frog julip. Why they did not all die with malaria or typhoid fever, no one ever knew in those early days.

Vin Cashman - After our first three months of school was finished we could get our state school money, so the next school was held in Rutheford's abandoned farm house 2 miles away. Vin Cashman, Mrs. Coursen's sister, was hired to teach a three month summer school at $21.00 per month. Mother boarded her for $1.50 per week.

The part of the house we used for the school room was built of boards straight up and down on a frame, then the cracks covered with batten strip. The teacher's desk concisted of a boot box stood on end. In those days men wore mostly boots and these boxes were packed full of boots at the factory and sent to the store for sale. In early days women liked to get these boot boxes for many purposes around the house. They were about four feet long, two feet wide and 18 inches thick, making "Kansas Tables". Sometimes a very handy table if legs were put on making table with nice wide and deep shelf underneath. This desk, she preferred to stand on end, drawing her chair up, putting her feet in and using the top for a desk.

Our seats were made of rough slabs with round poles for legs nailed to the wall. There were the following children that attended this school: Lillie and Alfred Abling, Fanny and Azor Stackhouse, two of Henry Speakman's children, Mamie Rutherford and Annie and Emma and myself. This was my first school. I learned very little and was often sent back to my seat to study my lesson over and kept in. The summer was very hot and I did not take very kindly to my books. Then Azor and Fannie would laugh at me.

No toilet here, had to dodge out in the sunflower patches in the field. Water had to be brot from home. Mother furnished bucket and dipper. In the course of the fore noon and after noon, some child was allowed to pass the water around, thereby keeping down the noise of each child going to the bucket for a drink.

Father took the most interest in the school as he had more children to go to school then. After the three month school was finished, he took his team and wagon and hauled eight cord of rock from the rock quarry where others had gotten out rock posts. He had given the district two acres of land in the southwest part of our homestead and placed the eight cord of rock on it. Then he got orders from the district to take his team and wagon to Greenleaf and buy the lumber needed for this stone schoolhouse, which concisted of lumber for the doors and roof, shingles, door and windows.

Men seldom went alone on those trips as there was simply no roads thru the prairies and river bluffs. Then no bridges over creeks and rivers. Neighbors had to help each other. So Father waited till another neighbor needed lumber and they went together for safety. This was a 180 mile trip. Men had to camp out at the Solomon and Republic Rivers, often having to wait two or three days till the water ran down before crossing. One of the men then would take a gentle work horse and ride back and forth acrosst the river till he was satisfied there were no deep holes or stumps or snags in the crossing and was shallow enuf for safety. The lumber was brot home and stored from the weather till needed. Father did this forgratis [*free gratis*].

The batchelor faction, north and west, came to a meeting, out voted everyone and decided they would sell the lumber. They advertised to sell all this building material at an auction sale to be held (much to father's disgust) in our yard. The time came, they sold it all at half price, on time, to some new settler.

These batchelors were afraid they'd have to pay more taxes if they let the school house be built. They, at each school meeting for several years (4 yrs.), held the balance of power. Tho each year a term of the longest possible duration was held, till they got married and there was prospects for their Johnnie or Mary going to school, did they relent. Some of the batchelor's wives were young enuf to go to school. And then when they saw money in sight in the form of teacher's keep and board they wanted them [*teachers to board with them*].

Mother had her hardships boarding the teacher. Food was so scarce those days and no sugar, tho molasses was used mostly. If we had lived any where else but our homestead and not had cows, pigs and chickens and garden, Mother never could have kept the teacher. One of our girls would rush back to the house for Vin's [*Vin Cashman*] hot lunch and grab a hasty bite and water, it all had to be carried from home. Annie would go back to the school house. Sometimes Mother would bake pies of vinegar, molasses and flour. Then I remember of going to the field and gathering sheep sorrel for tasty pie in the spring and rhubarb.

The next year was a repetition of the first. Mother was very tired when the schools were thru as Vin was queer and rather hard to have around. That fall the board hired Myra Peterson, our neighbor east 3/4 mile, to teach a four month school in her house providing that boards would be put in a rough floor on top of her floor, as there were now more big scholars to come and she did not want to wear her floor out.

The house was 14 x 18 feet, 1 1/4 story, a very narrow stair leading to the attic, built of native lime rock which was dug out of a quarry. Her husband worked as meed and was an expert workman in

---

Vinegar Pie

1 cup water
1 cup sugar
1/2 cup flour
3 tablespoons vinegar
Butter size of an egg
Pinch of salt
A little nutmeg

Stir all together and boil. When it becomes thick, pour into baked pie shell. Serve with whipped cream. - **Louise (Hand) Shafer**

[*This recipe was given to Louise by her landlady in Butte in the early 1940's, a Mrs. Valenaulf. I imagine in place of the sugar in the early days they probably used molasses, at least Maggie refers to molasses as a sweetener. - mc*]

that kind of stone and had built many nice stone houses up and down the river and in Beloit. The downstairs was all in one room. In the southwest corner was her bed, and over by the stair way a stove, [*and there were*] places under the stairway for sundry foods and utensils, except the place in the floor where her favorite female dog slept, then a table and two chairs. In the balance of the room was the pupil and slab benches - around the north and part of the west wall. We had no black board, but worked our arithmetic on slates and carefully guarded their care till we could present them to our teacher, at her one table that was used for a dining table, cook table and teacher's desk. It was made of rough cotton wood and pole legs. The board was sawed out rough by some early day mill run with water power.

Myra was born and raised in New Hampshire, came to a sister later at Mendota, a small town then in 1872, near Chicago. The sister owned and operated a store and Myra worked with her and learned the much needed art in dealing with people.

When in Mendota she met a very nice young man from Sweden and was married. He turned out to be a good citizen. An uncle had come to Kansas previously and settled on a nice river bottom homestead near Asherville. On coming to Asherville, Myra taught school there and John got plenty of work at his mason trade in the new country. When they took up land, all of the good river bottom lands had been taken, so they took up their homestead on what was called the divide near relatives between the headwaters of the Solomon River and the Salene River 3/4 mile from our homestead, tho they preceded us, coming in 1873.

Mrs. Myra Peterson was a shrewd business woman and made the mail route pay every time. She was the envy and talk of the country side, how she took a man's place, driving on the mail route or driving stage. She was a big, strong, raw boned woman. Went about business like a man and could talk to anyone on most any subject of the day.

She wore her hair cut like a man and was at that time real grey. To cut the hair at that time was questionable act. But Myra went along helping the needy. When Mary and John's twins came, Mary had only enuf clothes for one. Myra came to her assistance and gave her baby clothes. Then, too, Myra was childless and people talked, but she went along in her business like way, paying no attention to all the country gossip. When a school was too tough for other teacher to handle, Myra took the job.

In the fall when the school begun and most of the fall work done, wood from rivers or creeks hauled nine miles or more, enuf for the winter. Most of the boys entered school there being no other work to do.

The Swede boys came to learn the language which they could gather quickly by mingling with others. Mrs. Charley Peterson left her two children at home with her husband. He did carpenter work at home, kept the children while she attended school to hear mostly the English language spoke. Her husband had been here before and had learned the language while away on jobs. Mrs. Charley Peterson went to school till it was time for Mr. Peterson to begin to turn over the new sod. Then she staid home to take care of her children and run the house. Those attending school that fall were: Minnie Chapman - 15 yrs., Lillie & Alfred Abling - 6 & 8 yrs., Al (Seth Halbert) 19 yrs. old, Hattie, Emma, Annie & myself, 17, 15, 11, 7 yrs., Eddie Speelman 19 yrs. old, Peter Vance was 23 yrs. old - he was Mrs. Pearson's brother, Hattie & Frank Briggs 18 & 16 yrs. old.

This included the full school in the fall. Some dropped out, yet there was a good school the four months and everyone made good progress in their school. After the young children had recited their lessons, they turned out to play. We would gather up the chips from the building stones, pack them out in our aprons west of the house and would play at building houses and farms. Then when the geese would fly over going south in great droves, we would run and holler and try to change their course by youping and hollowing, which we never did. As the cold winter came on I did not attend very regularly as Mother was afraid I'd get too cold, so I played and she read to me. Then I'd sew, play with the cats and dogs, tho was very lonesome till the others would get home at night, for Annie and I were almost inseperateable.

I'M A STERN OLD BACHELOR

I am a stern old bachelor
My age is forty-four
I do declare I'll never look
At women any more.
I have a stove that cost ten cents
A table worth fifteen
I cook my grub in oyster cans
And keep all things so clean.

CHORUS

Little sod shanty
Sod shanty give to me
For I'm a stern old bachelor
From matrimony free.

I go to bed when e'er I please
And get up just the same
I change my socks once a year
With no one to complain
At night when I'm in peaceful sleep
My snores can do no harm
I do not have to walk the floor
With an infant in my arms.

On cold stormy winter's night
In my little cozy shack
I sing my song and think my thoughts
With no one to talk back
And when I die and go to heaven
Where all old bachelors do
I will not have to grieve or fear
That my wife will be there too.

by Clay Brown, W. Va

From Maggie's Scrap Book

This spring wild fowls were numerous, especially Prairie Chicken. There were very few animals on the farm that could as yet be spared for meat. One morning, while hitching up his horses to plow, Charley Peterson decided to take his shot gun along and get some chicken for meat. So he went to the house, got the gun, strapped it over his shoulders and went out to plow and in turning the corner of his land the gun slipped down, the hammer hit on the plow handle, which set the gun off. The charge shot thru the palm of his hand. He was rushed to the nearest doctor 17 miles away to Beloit. There being no hospital there, they took out the two middle fingers and drew the hand together, making a very small, unshapely hand, tho in after years he learned to work well with it.

All these people were new homesteaders so there was no money in the country and very few had a way to make any. So it became a quandary to his brother John, how that money could be raised to pay the doctor bill, when good old Myra thot of a scheme that would work. Yes, she thot, I'll take my goodly supply of older and young pupils and put on an entertainment that in one night will pay the bill and she did. She rallied her bunch of school children together, laid the plan before them and asked them if they wanted to do this for this man. Unanimously they all stood together, "yes". She gave each one a part or as many as she thot best. They then all began to learn and she had them to meet often on appointed day at her house, as her house was always quiet, there being no children. In two weeks we had the entertainment perfect, ready to give. Mr. J. Chapin had a large, low, stone house, the largest two roomed house in the community and he offered Myra his house for this entertainment, gratis. The entertainment concisted of dialogues, tabaloes, singing, violin music by George Stackhouse. He was a very good musician tho having no musical training what so ever. This was the only musical instrument in our community and he was the only musician and a very good one. He went far and near to play for dances. For the opening number Henry Stackhouse gave us a very appropriate, sincere, neighborly talk on the purpose of our entertainment. The entertainment went off without a hitch and everybody acted his part. The building was filled to its utmost capacity. This was all due to Myra's able ability in handling children and people. There were people there from a distance who asked Myra to take her troop and go to other community centers but some of the older heads thot we had accomplished the purpose we had set out for and they objected seriously in our going on any farther.

Myra kept this female dog. When the puppies came, she could sell them readily for $5.00 to $7.00 each to stockmen, thereby making more money from her pups than any other livestock and they were always sold before they came. One cold day the children noticed her old dog was quite nervous and uneasy. She would want out and would go out and roll in the snow, then want in and Myra would let her in. This kept up for some time and Myra let her in again. She went to her place under the stairs and settled down. Presently we all heard a small squeak. Every scholar ducked his head behind his book with chagrin, wishing he had a larger book to hide behind and then another squeak could be heard. The younger children would look from behind his book and giggle. Myra would scold them and say, "Now you study your lesson." The older ones were very studious thru the whole ordeal. School was out early that afternoon and we all cut for home. The next morning Myra happily announced the arrival of eight puppies.

We did not notice any increased good marks in our lesson of dogologic. These puppies, at $5.00 each, would make $40.00, the price of a good cow and if she got $7.00 each = $56.00, the price of two good cows. No wonder Myra was happy. This paid better than teaching, as she only got $22.00 for wage and house per month.

Eddie Speakman lived out west of us a mile. Bad, snowy times he often hitched up his father's sorrel mules to a sled with a wagon box on and drove to school and picked up all the children on the way. At noon, after we all had eaten our lunch, he tied Myra's water sled on behind his sled and would say to younger children, "Get on and let me take you for a ride." He drove up the well beaten road aways, would turn around and bring them back to the school house. The older boys would climb in his sled and he'd tell the girls to get on the water sled and a way he'd go, often to some cross road where the snow piled high in drifts. Then some of the boys would cut the rope, the'd drive on quickly leaving the sled and girls behind to walk home. The next time it was hard to get the girls to go but after much promising and persuading that they would not cut the rope again the girls went with them, if they would not cut the rope. No, they would not, if they would only go. So with their faithful promise the girls get on again and away they went. This time farther than before in the snow drifts. Then some villain cut the rope again and away they went. Much fun for the boys but not so much for the girls when they came in late for school that noon. But the boys were back studying diligently when the girls got in late.

School went on as usual till letting out time. Then Myra laid the law down to them. Ed must go at once for her water sled and this incident must never be repeated. She had to haul all her water a quarter of a mile from the Rain's place where the summer before they had dug a basement and they struck a spring that filled the cellar with nice, clear, good water. And several farmers hauled their water from there too.

We were still dragging along with a three or four month school. Several of the older ones lost heart and quit going to school. The state money was only $2.00 per school age. Many of the homesteads were not proven up on, many that had been there long enuf would not prove up, for if they did they then would have to pay taxes on their property and would defer it as long as they could. The lumber that they sold on time for half the value was not paid for yet. The batchelor bunch still held the power to keep the older children from getting an education and they did.

The Johnsons were thrifty swedes and had one child, lived on a homestead north of us. They first lived in a dugout, but recently had built a nice stone house with shingle roof. The district wanted Johnson's dugout to hold another four month school the next fall and hired Myra to teach it. The dugout was built on a sidehill with stone wall, plaster and white wash finished it and was quite respectable.

Mrs. Johnson was a very whinny woman. He built her a more palatable home of the native rock, he being a stone mason. This dugout was in the yard and of course we children vexed her in many ways. The first thing, we got on top of the dugout and peeped around at her husband in the straw barn to see how he did the chores. We were always a vexation. She was so clean in her household. She would scour every pan till it shown. Mother did most of her sewing for Mrs. Johnson, boy and man but for her, she was never satisfied. Mother made Johnson a suit about that time. She always complained of something being wrong. In Johnson's old age, he hung himself, drove to it by that woman.

The school room had a good pine board floor. The front of the dugout came out on the level ground. It was covered with dirt and prickly pears grew luxuriantly in the soil atop the dugout, which made it an unfriendly place to play. If we should have wanted to, I am afraid Myra would have objected. It was not far from their house and barn. Myra cautioned us all to stay clost to our school and not bother around the Johnson's premises.

School was held another three months in Johnson's dugout, 3/4 mile north of our house. Myra again taught that. Then by that time there were more children old enuf to go. A little Swede, not able to talk English, the Colling children, Tillie the oldest, a nice girl, and the Johnson's boy. I remember Hanna and Charley Peterson's children were young. Then, of course, Annie and I had to tease them. Hanna cried the first day and wanted to go home but her Aunt talked her out of that.

This school was quite different from the former one as all the older ones quit school. Hattie [*Halbert*] married Jake Jones and lived on Second Creek of Solomon. Al (Seth) went to Colorado, Pete Vance went home to Beloit and Andrew Peterson died. Hattie and Frank Briggs quit school and three of the Abling's children. Emma continued on and was the oldest in this school.

This school was taught thru. When done everybody was satisfied with the progress his children had made and everyone in the settlement was ready to holler Hale lagar, all power to Myra. After these many years holding schools from place to place and the [*batchelor's*] Jonnies and Marys began to arrive, they got interested and voted to build a lumber school house over on Johnson's northwest corner of his homestead. This suited father and he joined in with them, as he said he did not want to keep any children from getting a smattering of education, as his had been done. The school house was framed, about 14 x 20 feet and the outside weather board was put on and the shingle roof and new school was begin that spring. Myra was our teacher again, all the children that had gone formerly went there. Emma still went. Fanny Stackhouse came and walked four miles each way and Emm Mill walked three miles. This school went off quietly as before and everyone was pleased. Myra never whipped or slapped a child. She was respected and loved by all and her word was the law.

Our old benches were brot over to this new schoolhouse to sit on and an old table for a teacher's desk. Then in the northwest corner was built what they called a writing desk. A wide, rough, cottonwood board was roughly placed on a

---

The Old Slate

Say, what has become of the little old slate
That we used at school, back in, say '98?
The little old slate that was bound with red felt—
And don't you remember how musty it smelt?
Or, maybe, that smell that I'm thinking about,
Belonged to the sponge that we used to rub out
The Words and the numbers we'd awkwardly writ.
(But, some little rascals—my goodness!—used spit!)

And then, as they dried it—it's hard to believe—
They used nothing less than their hand, or their sleeve!
That seems like a terrible thing to be told—
But things are so different, before you are old.
And don't you remember that sharp little sound
The slates pencil made, as we scratched it around?
And oh, what a screech now and then we would make—
I'll bet teacher thought that her ear-drums would break!

What wouldn't you give to be back in that seat
With your little slate, when all life was so sweet?
And wouldn't you like to take back with you, too,
That same little happy-eyed gang that you knew?
But I don't believe we would be different men
If we could go back, and start over again.
But oh, if we could, it would surely be great
To start out once more with a new and clean slate!

(1930, Western Newspaper Union)

From Maggie's Scrap Book

slanting angle. Then a bench built underneath so we could sit, throw our legs under and write. There was no blackboards and we still used our slates. We got water from a nearby well and carried it over. This well was built in a draw so as to catch seepage. It was walled up with native rocks. A big, flat, rock covered up the well, all except a hole that was chizzeled out large enuf to let a bucket thru, and when done drawing the water with a rope and bucket it was covered with boards which was made to fit. To get water, one would let the bucket down that was tied to a rope long enuf to reach the water, give the bucket the proper flip at the end of the rope and it filled at once. Then one drew up the rope till the bucket was reached and lifted out. Then we'd pour the water in to our bucket and take it to the school house, leaving the bucket and rope there for the next fellow that needed water. In the spring these shallow wells were generally full, as were all creeks, sloughs, and buffalo wallows. There were generally plenty of rain. We children often went barefooted and enjoyed wadding.

The next year following, the school house at Green Mound was plastered, new seats were bot, a black board the full length of the west wall, made of wide plained boards and painted black, a teachers desk. Then they relegated the old seats and writing desk to the dark ages. School later was held six months, then as time went on, to nine months. We had several teachers in the meantime. The last I believe was a Mrs. Cotton from Beloit. Annie staid with Hattie on Second Creek and went to a Mr. Woodard. She liked him very much and learned well there.

Next fall Emma staid with Hattie and went to school there a few months till she took sick from wading deep snow, one mile and thru deep gullies and hills. After this, other teachers taught at Green Mound, as our school house was named.

About this time a nice big stone school house was being built at Coursen's Grove. This grove concisted of a few cottonwood trees. Coursen's kept the post office. It seemed to be a better center and served more people. It was four miles from our house. Then when the school house was finished, it was so much better than the old log building that the community center was changed to Coursen's Grove. People came for church and Sunday school. The ___person society concisted of young folks. They held their meetings there. The school put on plays there thru the school year. Then Christmas, always a tree. That was highly patronized. The tree was always a hardwood tree, as there were no spruce or fir in that country. It was draped in popcorn strings, bags and presents from mother to children, sweetheart to sweetheart, shy young lover, expressing their love to each other. Everyone went home happy, young and old lovers and sweethearts. Emma and Hattie got presents they prized from their beaus. Annie and I had candy and popcorn ball. Happy and tired, we would go to sleep in the back end of the wagon box on some hay, jogging along over rough, rutty road four miles. Hattie and Emma came back with their sweethearts. They, at that time, drove a wagon, as one was lucky to have a wagon.

**Maggie Ellen Halbert
Taken by W. H. Greenwood
Beloit, Kansas
From Maggie's Photo Album**

Thru all these times when Father was trying to get a better school and could only have but three or four months at the best, Mary and Hattie needed Emma or Annie to help and go to school in order to get more schooling. Myra [*Peterson*] taught at Coursen's Grove. Emma staid at Mary's and attended. This district had more deeded land and could have a longer term and more scholars. Among those attending when Emma went were Lizzie and John Coursen. The younger boy (Fettie) or Jeffie, was too young to go, but would run off each day and go over to the school house only a few rods away. One day he picked up his aunt's algebra book and came over. When school was called, he came in and presented his book to Myra. She had a good way with little youngsters and interested him that forenoon. The County Superintendent came to visit and in the discourse Myra told the Superintendent she had a class in Algebra. The County Superintendent wanted the class called. When Myra called, one small boy arose that did not know his letters. This was a stock joke on Fettie for some time.

[*These apparently attended Coursen Grove at this time - mc*]. The Caugheys, Sam, Mary, Violet and Kim Jennings, Bob, Bill, Cecil and another boy, Briggs; Hattie Bayley. Hattie, Theme, Linnlie, Della Elgan was not old enuf at that time. Blotcher, Ella, Lee Child's boys. Wines, Winnie and other. Each winter, as occasions permitted, Myra would put on a long entertainment with the school. Then Christmas, the Sunday Schools put in the tree and its merriments. As usual, this school activity was well and faithfully attended, with loud applause for Myra and her teachings and holding the school together.

Then the older young folks had a "Good Templers Lodge". Enos Wines ran the store. Enos Wines was head templer and often conducted the ceremonies at their lodge. Often at recess he would step out for a fresh breath of air. On coming back, his breath was noticed by the boys to have a very "rye" or vile smell. He was a good mixer with the boys and their nickles helped keep up the store. He also belonged to the lodge and was a right hand man when the boys put on a program, which was always good. Some times the girls helped on these programs. Tho once, I remember, the boys put on the whole show, which was a negro show. Each boy dressed and blacked up like a negro and Herbert Briggs gave a negro sermon. These entertainments always brot out an overflowing house.

Once, some of the boys and Enos (Sr.) went to town, getting things for these entertainments. On going to the wagon preparatory to going home, Enos would put a foot up on the wagon wheel, each time it would slip off. The boys, chuckling to their selves, says, "Enos, can't you make it?" "No," says Enos "there is ice on my feet." Whereupon the boys boosted him in on the seat. This was his besetting sin and one could always smell liquor on him even tho he was a "good templer".

With the church, suppers and dinners, the school and Good Templers entertainment, this was the hub for both education and social activities. People came to these gatherings from far and near. Emma staid on with Mary and went to school. When she quit, Myra gave her eligible grades for a teacher's certificate.

In those days psychology was not required. Annie staid with Hattie and went to log school house at the Second Creek. A Mrs. Woodward taught and she progressed. Mrs. Woodward wanted to take her to Jim's Creek, her to teach, but Ma and Pa protested, a sad mistake.

Time drug heavily on the trips over Green Mound and down to the little schoolhouse. Wearied me; cold sleety weather. Wearing boys overshoes, wearing two heavy underskirts, a flannel dress, a coat, a hood, and home spun and knit mittens. Was too much of a load to carry up and over the hill. So I grumbled. Emma and Annie had grown to womanhood and quit going to school. They could stay home and make quilts, knit, spin and weave, crochet, in fact, pass the time as they chose after the water was hauled. Then, too, if a wayfarer chanced to call, they were there to see him, answer his questions and pass on news. There was something lost for me when I came home in the evening and heard their stories. Going to school alone I did not like.

There was an old, gentle, foundered, crippled horse in the stable. I could ride her up over the hill then turn her loose, hook the bridle reigns over the horn of the saddle and head her for home. She could not eat in this way. All she could do was to go home. I asked father if he cared if I rode her to school. He said, no, he did not care, the exercise would do her good.

So, after bundling up good for the trip (as I believed I get colder riding than walking) I went to the barn, put the side saddle on, bridled her, lead her out, then tied up the halter rope, lead her over to the wagon and climbed on. Not far from the barn was a made pond, by damming up a small draw using the dirt in the draw for an embankment, therefore backing up the water accross the road that led to the field. I never thot of an icy place there as they had scattered litter over the road to make it safe. I was urging the mare on as I had spent some time getting ready. When all the sudden, Bess slipped and fell and I too. I got off hurriedly, took the bridle reins and tried to coax and pull her up. She struggled but each time could get no firm footing and would fall back again. O, my, such a dilemma. I hated to go to the house and tell Bess was down. What would father say and the girls. Well, I could do nothing else. Whenever she tried to get up my dog would bark hoping to be on our way.

At last I went to the house and told my trouble. I could not do anything but I waited around sheepishly and watched father and a man. They first took the saddle and bridle off. Brot straw with a pitch fork, and each time they coaxed her to get up and she struggled to her front feet they would shove straw under her so when she fell back she would have straw to fall on, not ice, for a horse soon gets cold and gives up. Finally by putting more straw and trash under her, she could rest and gather strength. At last, with one pulling on the halter, dog barking, she made a good struggle, got on her front feet. Father stood by her side and helped steady her and she got solid footing and got up. Wasn't I glad. Said nothing, turned up the road, over the hill sorrowfully, down to the school house. Late, of course. Not a child in sight on the playground. How I hated to go in and have the whole school turn around and grin and to face the teacher. Well, they never knew all the burning shame regrets I had gone thru with at home.

That ended my riding to school. Walked thru slush and snow, sleet and ice, hot and cold. When I got to school or home I was all drug out, made no difference. School, well, I went. Tho took but very little interest and learned but very little. All in all it was a diversion from steady home life.

Annie Rode Jones' Horse

Once, while on the homestead, Mr. Levi Jones rode a fine black horse up to our house. Then father took our team and they went to Beloit for the day. Annie was at home then and took a notion to go to Coursens Grove, four miles away, for the mail.

As Emma and Annie had ridden everything from an old plug horse, a blind horse, a cayuse, a mule, to a cow she thot that black horse was just her kind. But before she had made the round trip, found it was afraid of petticoats and perhaps had never seen one before, as Mrs. Jones never went to the barn and the Jones family concisted of seven boys. When Annie entered the barn, she could see at once it was afraid of her, for she had to pet and coax to get the saddle on and bridle in its mouth. She finally got them on, led him out into the yard and with more petting finally got into the side saddle and away he went. The first mile he thot he was going home and went good. When she turned him south he did not want to go and would try to shy at every weed that moved by the wind. When within 1/2 mile of the post office, the wind blew tumbling weed and cornhusks acrossed the road. Two men with team, picking corn, throwing the ears of corn against the bumping board, made a queer noise, [*along*] with the wind rolling weeds. All this, combined with my sister riding sideways, scared this black charger, so he decided to make one big leap. He squatted in his tracks and took a sideways leap and went from under the girl, leaving her sitting in the road so scared and shocked and hurt she could hardly get her wits together and seen the horse run off a ways, thinking he would go for home and all would be found out. But the men came over, wanted to know if she was hurt. They caught the horse for her and wanted to help her on, but she said she would walk to the post office. She tied the horse to the wagon and went in. She visited Mrs. Coursen, tho was hardly able to sit on a chair. She was so in fear the story would get out and go all over the country [*that*] she was hurt riding Mr. Jones's horse. After she rested, she got on the horse and rode him home, tied him in the stable and went to the house, never saying a word, tho hardly able to sit on a chair. She helped mother whatever there was to do that evening, tho she could hardly go. She felt that sudden jar for days afterward.

That night late Father and Mr. Jones came home. Jones was not feeling so well. He acted too full, but Father said to Ma, "make him some strong coffee," and later put him to bed. No one ever knew Annie had even ridden the horse or got hurt tho she told me. "We all knew before this to hold our own council."

Flowers

On some of Father's early trips to Kansas, he picked up a very large, round cacti and planted it in the yard. When he went again it had been kicked out. He replanted it. This was the starter for a large cacti bed, tended and gathered many more by girls. The prickly pare was a curiosity to them and they made a separate bed for them. The plains were really a big flowerbed as far as one could see, tho Mother longed for the Indiana flowers she had to leave behind.

The winter Mary's twin boys were born, John had to go back to Indiana to settle up the estate of his father and mother. While there, he packed two barrels of shrubs and plants for himself and Mother. They came in the spring. They were carefully unpacked and planted at both homesteads. Most all grew, tho only one cedar tree at our place. For the more cherished tiger lilies, roses, flowering almond, all grew in the new land. Mother and the girls took a team and wagon, went to the state land section for big flat rocks at an old quarry. Enuf to set on edge of a big round flowerbed 20 foot in diameter. Big, long willow to make a willow fence [*were gathered*]. The ground was dug up, richer dirt added. The precious flowers, bulbs and starts planted. The stones set on edge, which made a good outside support for the willows stuck in the ground then lapped over and put into the ground. This made a chicken, cat and dog tight enclosure. Tho once in a while a hen flew over, which was lifted out at once, or a new dog decided it a good place to escape from the stinging fly that settled on a poor dogs ears, stinging till blood stood out in drops. Dogs in that hot country suffered from the heat, flies and ticks and thru the hot weather would seek some dark, cool place. Well, he had to hunt other quarter. This was watered from the meager supply that Mother had to throw away after many usings. For water yet had to be hauled one and a fourth mile or if that well gave out, then three miles away to another well that had not had so many users. The rose moss bed, with its ever changing blossoms, each morning gave us a new language in flowers.

Birds

There were many birds on the plains. Of the larger kinds, the Prairie Chicken were numerous till civilization thinned them out. Tho at first they were everywhere and in the early morning in the spring one could hear their distant drumming in the grey morning, as if the cock were giving orders for the days work. Going thru the tall grasses, one often scared up a bunch and away they would take flight. In the early spring a settler often burned off a few acres of thick grass where he was going to break the sod for a new field. Many got eggs by hunting the ground over for Prairie Chicken nests. Eggs were scarce in those days, as few people had chickens and my, a fried egg or a custard was a delicacy not to be had often on the plains.

One evening in the spring, a prairie fire broke out in a piece of land lying between John Wilson's place and ours. The next morning Annie went to John's thru the burnt over ground. There she saw Prairie Chicken eggs, nests full by the thousands. The prospects of little chicks destroyed and old ones driven out.

Quails mostly inhabited brushy places and were hunted by many, tho Mother hated to have them brot in to cook. After we had our homestead planted they were protected there and never killed by home folks. Tho one day Jess Linnon was discovered hunting our tame quails in the garden back of the house. Mother told him to never hunt quails on our place again.

The Curlew family were represented in many species of their kind. How cunningly they would lead us on and on down the road, or in the fresh furrows behind the plow where we children trailed Father or Seth as the sharp shear of their plow laid open the new sod. Now we'd catch it as the poor thing must be lame. How it crippled and fluttered, hardly able to fly till we got nearly on to it. Then, out of reach again, cunningly leading us away from its nest.

The Meadow Lark came early so as to awake the farmer, remind him that spring was at hand. How we liked it's monotonous, cheerful sound-E, double gg, over and over again, sun and shine. The myriads of smaller ground birds twitted away, combing the grasses for their daily bread.

The Brown Thrush with its hoarse chitter, nesting in brush and hedges, all joined in to make the Kansas plains a wonderful country when new, untrampled, untrodden by man.

Coyotes

There were not many wild animals left in Kansas after the buffalo were killed off. Tho there still were a few small, skulking Prairie Wolves left to prey on the wild bird and an old woman's chicken coop after dark. The chicken that roosted in straw shelters were often picked up, but men often made drives, killing a lot of Prairie Wolves at a time, till they became rare sight to see one looping off in the early dawn of the morning. There were a few skunk, tho not hard to trap and get rid of.

The worst enemy to small chickens and pigs were the wharf rat that sometimes came in droves, caused all the trouble they could and passed on. One spring Mother gave me a few hens with chicks to raise for pin money. At nights I put them in boxes and put on a weighted down lid. In the morning early, she heard a commotion in the boxes, raised up the lids to let out the hens and chickens and found a few little chicks with their legs torn off. The rats had burrowed under the boxes, gnawed holes in the boxes on the cracks, caught the chicks by the legs and gnawed off the legs.

Once father thot an old stockyard on the Rutherford place would make a good rich piece of ground for Mother to raise squash, melons and cucumbers, being new ground away off there by itself, the squash bugs would not bother. Early one morning Mother went over before sun up to see how her garden was coming on. She saw something move in the big dark pumpkin vines. Must be a cat she thot, but getting up closter she found it to be a baby coyote. She tied it up with her apron string and brot it to the house. Being a very unruly and loveable pet, they soon decided one less coyote was best.

The summer proved to be very dry and very often we all, by hand, had to help carry water for the vines when in need of moisture from a made pond on the Rutheford place some 10 or 15 rods away. Squash bugs were very troublesome. Mother tried various home remedy to kill them besides going early, which was the best time to kill them by hand. Application of wood ashes or soot were tried when the dew was on and last she tried a solution of cow manure and water, which was effective to a small degree, anyway would not injure the vines. By fighting these pests and watering the plants well gave it a good start to outgrow the bugs and she generally had a good crop in the fall.

With the scarcity of fruits, these lowly vegetables filled a much wanted need, which I think lead to a winter pie filling called Pumpkin Leather. Pumpkins were cooked and ran thru a sieve. Then about the same quantity of sorghum molasses added, boiled and stirred till thick, spread on plates and put out to dry in the sun, up high away from cats, dogs or children. Taken in nights and replaced again in the sun till dry, put in a paper sack if possible (these commodities were scarce) and hung on the ridge log for pies. When soaked up in milk, an egg added, poured in a pie shell and baked, made a good pie. That year Mother tried to dry pumpkin leather but she had too many hungry, growing girls to ever get it into a pie.

Henry Shirleys wife was Mrs. Elrod's sister. They [*Elrods*] lived at Lincoln Center. The older folks were acquainted in Indiana, so when they found out we lived in Mitchell County they came up to see us. They had one small child, a girl, and twin boys that were exact image of each other. (Later when the boys grew up they came up and worked in broom cutting time, being likable chaps.)

Before they left for home they invited our folks down to see them. So that fall after the broom corn was sold and hauled to town, the corn in the bin and other smaller crops garnered for the winter, Emma and Annie asked father if they could have his team of buckskin mules to drive to Lincoln Center to see the Elrods. So, with his permission, we hitched the mules. They were perfectly matched, trim and sleek, ready to go and never tired. So next morning bright and early found us up, dressed in our best. After a hurried breakfast we put in plenty of comforters and wraps for the trip as no telling what kind of weather we could run in to on the three day trip. So when they drove out that morning headed south, they presented a very nifty appearance, mules hitched to a one seated buggy, with the mules groomed, main roached and tail cropped and sheared. Lincoln Center was just a little bit west of south from our place, 40 miles away. With a lunch for dinner, eaten on the way, they drove on and on only stopping to water the mules. When they reached the Salt Creek country, the valley lay stretched out before them, apparently level, tho just before entering Barnard they noticed a deep cut depression and on coming closter found it was at Salt Creek. To cross the creek, a narrow road lead down and down to the water and there a small narrow board bridge was crossed. Then on the opposite side of the creek a similar road wound up the bank to level ground. There was not a brush or tree in sight to warn them of this awful deep cut in the nice smooth valley. Grass grew up to the brink of the cut. When a prairie fire started in this valley, the creek was no barrier, jumping over as if the creek was not there.

The country abound in large flocks of Prairie Chickens and quails. A skunk was encountered on the way home, leaving its perfume on the buggy wheels. We arrived in Lincoln Center the middle of the after noon and drove down thru Main Street. A mule buyer was in town and saw the girls drive thru. He followed them out to Elrods, asked them if they wanted to sell them [*the mules*].

"These," they said, "are Fathers and we don't know."

"Well," he says "when are you going home?"

"Day after tomorrow," they said, so he went away.

They had most enjoyable time there visiting and seeing the new country. When we got home the mule buyer was there, had bot the mules and took them away as soon as we unhitched.

Broom Corn

Is of the sorghum group of plants, grown for its brush-like head used in the manufacture of brooms. (Brooms were also made of small willow twigs tied on to a small pole. The willows were cut square off at the bottom, made a very good broom.)

Pumpkin Leather

Cook your pumpkin, put through a sieve and then taking 1 3/4 cup of the pumpkin pulp, add 1/4 cup white sugar, boil together and then spread on cookie sheets and place in an oven, food dryer or in the hot sun to dry.

There will be a loss of approximately 1/2 of the bulk of the pulp due to evaporation of the liquid. It takes quite a while to dry, but when done makes excellent fruit leather. Store in a dry cool place. When ready to make a pie, follow the pie recipe. - **Myrna Carpita**

Pumpkin Leather makes excellent pies. I did not use the molasses as Maggie (Halbert) Hand stated her mother did. I do not like the flavor of molasses, but molasses may be substituted for the sugar. - *Myrna Carpita*

Pumpkin Pie (in a sack)

The night before you wish to bake your pie, tear pumpkin leather into small pieces, place in a bowl, add 1 1/4 cup water and one can evaporated milk, cover, place in fridge. Next day, stir until all pumpkin leather is dissolved. Add the following:

 3/4 C brown sugar
 2 eggs, beaten
 1 tsp. cinnamon
 1 tsp. nutmeg
 3/4 tsp. ginger
 1/4 tsp. ground cloves
 1/2 tsp salt

Mix thoroughly, pour into unbaked pie shell. Bake at 400 degrees for approximately 40 minutes or until a knife inserted in pie comes out clean. - **Myrna Carpita**

Homes

The homes of this community were very much like other early day settlements. A neighbor dug one on nice level land, down much as you'd dig a basement to a house. Then he run a way out with steps in it, put in four paned windows at the ground level and covered it with poles, willows, grass and dirt. Then storm doors over the stairway, so when it rained, it would run off. Grandma Speakman and her granddaughter lived there very comfortable for several years. Then some people built a big basement, covered it over and lived in it till times got better so they could build a good house on top of it.

There were three good shingle roofed buildings, Mr. Jones', Mr. Wanzer's, both on Second Creek and Mr. Child's, up on the Divide.

Some homes were built of sod taken from behind the breaking plow, cut 18 inches long and 10 to 12 inches wide, about three inches thick. They were nice handy slabs and laid up quickly. Places were left open the right width for the doors and windows and later door and window jams were cut to fit. The windows and door were placed in after the dirt roof was on.

Stone houses were often covered with dirt. John and Mary [*Wilson*] lived in one. A day after the rain it generally began to rain inside and made living in it miserable.

On the creeks and rivers where logs were plentiful, log houses were covered with dirt. Then again, dugouts were often built back in a bank and opening on the ground floor. Often eves were above the ground, giving an opening for a window. If not, the windows were put on the sides or often one on either side of the door.

Our farm buildings were built on the south east corner of the section. In those days all the land had been surveyed long before, tho the roads were only wheel tracks in a 60 foot space for the roads on each side of a section. Tho in many places where the land had not been broken up, one could take short cuts, when we first came to Kansas. The house set back a ways leaving a tillable space of four or five rods, which was planted to shade and fruit trees and gardened in between.

When we came there were several large cotton wood trees east of the house and some large plum trees which bore very few knotty gnarly plums. Mother admired the lombardy poplar tree over the river at their Indiana friends and got some cuttings. She planted them south out a ways on the line. They are a compact tree with their branches growing up which looked nice as specimen trees. Then west of the driveway she planted a box elder tree, it spread out nicely and gave a good shade. Then in the open space we raised Hollyhock and the sand plums Father brot up from Salina sand hills. Then there was other space between them and our flower beds, about 25 feet. We made a walk down thru it leaving 10 feet on either side for flowers - zennias, pinks, marigolds &, [*etc*]. Most of our seeds we gathered from year to year and then from neighbors that happened to raise flowers. Many did not care for flowers tho.

The flower garden was the first place visitors wanted to see. One day when Hattie Bayley came to see the girls, Annie was with her telling Hattie the names. "This one," says Annie, "is a Sweet William."

"O, yes," says Hattie, "I had a Sweet William once but he left me," and she fell sobbing to the ground. Annie knew about her love affair, it had been talked of far and wide the country over.

But Annie was made of different mettle. It had never occurred to her that the loss of a lover would still effect Hattie or anyone else. If it had been Annie in love, that loss of a lover would have never been concidered or worth

---

On September 15, 1879, Enos Halbert applied for a pension to be allowed him for his services to the Union during the Civil War. He completed the DECLARATION FOR AN ORIGINAL INVALID PENSION, in the District Court, Mitchell County, Kansas. In part, the form shows:

"Enos Halbert aged 54 years, who, being duly sworn according to law, declares that he is the identical Enos Halbert who was ENROLLED on the ___ day of August, 1861, in Company H of the 33 regiment of Indiana Infy commanded by James E. Burton, and was honorably DISCHARGED at Louisville, Ky. on the ___ day of _____ 1865, that his personal description is as follows: Age, 54 years, height 5 feet 11 1/2 inches; complexion, light, hair, light; eyes, blue. That while a member of the organization aforesaid, in the service and in line of his duty at Cumberland Gap, in the State of Ky on or about the ___ day of July, 1862 he contracted the disease of Fistula caused by constant riding while wagon master from Sept. 1861 to the fall of 1863. That said disease continued to grow worse from the time of its origin to the date of his discharge, and from that time to the present said disease has continued. That he was treated in hospitals as follows: Was operated on at a private house at Murfreesboro, Tennesee in 1863 by the Surgeon Robert Bents formerly of the 33rd Ind. This took place at Genl. Coburns Brigade."

It further shows him to have resided in Orange County, State of Indiana and his occupation being that of a farmer at the time of his enlistment and him being a farmer and his address at the time of this application as Coursons Grove, Mitchell County, Kansas.

It further states, "That he is now one half disabled from obtaining his subsistence by manual labor, by reason of his injuries, above described, received in the service of the United States; and he therefore makes this declaration for the purpose of being placed on the invalid pension roll of the United States."

The above is taken from Enos Halbert's Pension Records received from The National Archives – mc

while remembered. Annie stood there mad, shocked, disgusted and amazed at a girl giving away to love. No sir, not one minute would she have cried. Annie did not help her to arise or console her, just went on naming the flowers. She said "I can't see how Hattie could be so silly as to bemoan the loss of Sweet William = Bill Booker." To Annie he was just a great big silly nut. Tho Hattie never got over loosing him. All along thru life Annie would tell the story about Hattie and her beau with the most disgusting sneer on her face and laugh.

On the west side of the house we generally planted some kind of a vine, Cypress, morning glories or a Bermuda vine. Someone gave us a Bermuda Potato that had been carefully kept from freezing. In the spring I planted it, watered it, and kept a willow fence tightly woven to keep out the dogs. With any care the vine grew on heavy string up to the roof and lopped over heavy with lovely white tassels. The leaf was thick dark green and glossy. I don't believe one could find a nicer vine. I always felt sad in the fall when the frost nipped it for the first time. Then I cut off the vine, dug the potato in a few weeks when I thot it ripe, and stored it away in the cellar till an other spring, with the remembrance of its beauty.

When we came to Kansas in June [*1875*] it was then too late to do much transplanting, so we made the best of what we had at home and on the creek. Mary, John and Tom had our garden planted. Tho Mother had some seed that had been given her that she planted at once. A little melon called the vine peach, was one, squashes and pumpkins and mustard and turnip for greens. The little melon came up and with the nice rains grew abundant fruit. When ripe, they turned yellow, when pealed, sliced and cooked made a good sauce, which we all liked. From that day to this I have never seen it grown, tho it must be raised in warmer country. At that time, with the lack of all the common fruits of today, it filled a much felt need of the better fruits. There were some bearing peach trees that bore that summer. Then on the creeks were wild grapes which could be used early, when green, for pies and sauce, the wild gooseberry and later in the fall, wild plums of many kinds. This we gathered, marked well the best kinds to get starts from in the spring. The plums, mother dried all she could get for our winter supply. The grapes, when ripe, were dried and put in a large jar and sorghum molasses put over them. In this way they would keep thru the winter but some how I never relished them fixed that way but without cans this was the next best way to keep them. When fall came the peaches were dried. We all lent a helping hand at this. If the weather was not hot enuf out in the sun on top of the dirt roof they were dried in the oven or on top of the stove with a small low cob fire or chips.

Fuel was scarce even tho father got some wood from the creek. It was far away and scarce. People that owned wood on the creek did not want to sell any. So the early settler had to gather whatever they could for fuel. Later on when people had trees growing there was always some dying or needed to be thinned out. Then with the cobs from the corn they raised, they had more fuel. People that had come earlier, that had taken up timber claims and planted them, had plenty of wood such as it was. Every stick or twig burned and as an old lady once said, "her chip yard was scraped to the hard pan." When her old man was too lazy to provide wood, she got tired of scrapping for chips and came over to see if Father could do something, "perhaps a divorce". But as usual, Father talked her out of any such notions and she went home and under the yoke.

Many burned straw, even corn, which Mother declared a sin. Once a man came around selling a special devise to burn straw in, built of sheet iron like a wash boiler, tho deeper. The straw was pressed in by one foot, when full turned upside down over the first two stove holes. Father bot one thinking it a wonderful invention. Mother used it for a while, part of the time, tho it was not such a success. One filling tramped in tight would burn an hour. Such fuel was always littery, kept us cleaning all the time.

At first, before corn shelling machines, the corn was fed on the ear. Then it was Annie and my job to take baskets and gather cobs out of the horse troves and manger - then in the pig pens. Those there were generally filthy with mud tho we had to get them. They were fuel, even with mud on them. Father bot a corn sheller that was run by main strength putting in one ear after the other. That was laborious and was not used much. Then later years (1887 or about) there were larger corn shellers ran by a run around power. The corn was shoveled in, out came the cobs nice and clean. The corn was elevated in to a bin and some times the cobs were run in to a bin. Not everyone could own one of these so the man that could afford one went around from place to place and shelled their corn for a fee.

In later years I knew of one house, when it was built, had a cob room built in handy to the kitchen. A very sensible concideration for the women folks. Not many people could buy coal, tho some did for the winter and later when the run around power with its tumbling rod was supplanted by the steam engine for power to run the thrashing machine with. They had to have coal, so a few days before the thrasher was due at a farm to thrash their grain, the man of the house had to make a trip to town for a few pounds of coal, owing to the size of his crop. Sunflower stock made a good substitute for wood and were often used. They flourished every where they were allowed to grow. But Father's pride as to good farmer and a poor one, could not have one on the place. The crops were tended good to discourage their growth. Then twice or three times in the summer he'd hire the girls to pull all in sight on the farm. He often boasted of not having any sunflowers.

Governor Stubs

He [*Governor Stubs*] and wife ran the commissary on the U.P.R.R. [*Union Pacific Railroad*] that went thru Kansas in early day. Staid with the job as long as the job lasted. She was the baker and main cook. After this she baked for the home and always exhibited at the fair. They amassed a fortune, and built a mansion in Lawrence. When he was elected Governor he was expected to live in the state mansion, tho his children preferred to live in their own home. He was often called on to deliver speeches. He told he was uneducated, never went farther than the 8th grade. Then he urged the children to take hold of the privilege they now had at Lawrence.

Tom's Courtship

When Father and Tom [*Wilshire*] made the trip by team to Kansas, they always stopped at Uncle Garrett's [*Shirley*] and visited Mother's brother's family. Most of the girls were grown, so Tom at once became interested in one, Francis (nicknamed Frank). They were all a very industrious family of girls. Tom always managed to see Frank. After Tom settled on his ranch, Frank continued teaching school, tho they wrote often. Tom was often twitted about Frank by ones that knew Tom's intentions.

Once, before Tom had proved up on his land, while Annie, Emma and I were visiting the Caughey girls, they decided they would play a joke on Tom. About every six months, to comply with the law, one taking up a homestead had to stay on his claim three days. Tom had built a dug out, finished with a home made bed stead, slats for springs and a straw tick for a mattress, a stove, a box for a chair and another big boot box with four legs for a table, making a shelf of a cupboard below. The young folks thot it would be a big joke to make a notice saying a Mr. so and so, a name we made up, had jumped his claim, owing to his not complying with the law and tacked it on his cabin door. Tom was always so in earnest and never could take a joke. We were not satisfied at that. We pulled the staple, went in, put the stove lids on the bed slats, the coffee, up under the pillow, dishes hid in various places. Then we went out, putting the staple back as before.

In our devilishness we did not think about our tracks. From there we went home and the Caughey children went next morning on back their way. Staid all night with us. Somehow I felt very guilty. I had always been glad to see Tom before. He had been nearer to me than Seth. I did not sleep well that night.

In a few days Tom came back, went to the cabin and at once found the notice. He was taken back as if hit with a sludge hammer. At this time, so near the time of his proving up and he to be married. He went in, found everything disheveled. He was sick at heart. He knew he'd loose the place and spring coming on, he was planning for a crop. What would he do? Well, he got in his wagon and went back to Uncle Enos's and tell him. He had always been a good father to him. He drove in, Father went out and they talked a long time. Finally Father got in his wagon and they drove off. He surveyed the depredation that Tom was so upset over and said, "Tom, it looks to me like some kids joke being played on you." Tom's burden lightened. He could now breath a good breath. Do you suppose it is? Yes, yes, see those tracks.

They came back for dinner. After dinner Tom went out. Pa questioned Annie and Emma about where they had been the day before. No, they knew nothing about Tom's dugout. Later on he found me playing and asked where I was when with the girls. Why, at Mr. Caughey's. At last he questioned me more and said do you know anything about Tom's dugout and I said we did not hurt the old thing, implying we all were there. Nothing more was said. Tom went home happy, he plowed and continued as before. I always felt sheepish. Just to think I had been caught in the girls wilds, for I had always thought so much of Tom, as long back as I could remember. Tom rocked me, petted and carried me and was always my most humble servant.

One spring Father had had so much trouble with the well. A part of the rock wall had fallen in. He went to see if Tom would help him put the wall back. "No," said Tom, "I won't now that I have some one to love me." Frank liked teaching and the money. She was loath to come. He made trips to Illinois occasionally. Finally they were married in Illinois, then came out and lived on the farm. She took up her burden, milking cows, making butter, raising chickens and turkeys and each fall dressing the fowls for market. Ever ready to help in those trying days to make a living, always hoping some time in the near future to make enough to build a new house and be able to live easier, tho never reaching the goal.

Tom hated to take her to his little 12x14 dugout in the hillside, so he rented the stone Hull house, it being larger and more commodious. There being two large rooms and a full upstairs and a kitchen built on. Here they lived till shortly before the first child was born. Then she decided Tom had too much work to do to run back and forth when she was sick. She had come out to pioneer in the west, so she must be brave, bear her burden as many others had done before her. So Sister Mary and Mrs. Caughey were spoke to, to come when needed. So after the child was born, Annie went to stay with her to take care of the baby and do the housework. Frank and baby got on fine and all went well but they had one thing to contend with. The rats were so bad that in the nights the rats came out, ran over the bed and would try to bite the baby, so some of them had to be sleeping with one eye open to chase the rats away.

The next year after the baby was born, Tom made an extra exertion to get a better house. After the spring crops was in he excavated a part basement in a hillside a few rods away from the first dug out. Then built four stone walls with the front part having the windows and doors in. This opened out on level ground. The sleeper or stringer were placed overhead for an upper story floor later. Then he made a cheap board roof over all with gables at each end. This, when finished into three good rooms, made a very nice, cozy home. Tho even not so fine, it was warm in winter, being tucked in the hill and cool in summer.

After this they both worked hard. Tom never got a better barn, just the same old straw shed. I suspect he had to mortgage to get money to build that house, tho never knew. About '88 they then had two children, they left the farm and moved to Wamego, Kansas where her sister Kate [*Nancy Catherine (Shirley) Jackson*] lived. They bot ten acres. They then had two girls and a boy. Tom and the boy died, but Frank lived on and the girls went for themselves.

Mills - Grist & Saw

As the emigrants settled up the rivers and creeks, new dams were built. The grist mills were built to grind their grains and saw mills to turn the big cotton wood trees in to rough boards for the settlers to build with.

An old millwright by the name of Britt proceeded the settlers and built mills all the way up the river from Solomon City and had them in running shape hoping a homesteader might be interested in the mill business and would buy him out. Brittsville was on the south side of the river and was a little center where people came for their mail and other early day household commodities. Later when the R.R. came thru, a little town sprung up on the R.R. and was named Simpson. Later Mr. Simpson bot the mill, then the stores were closed, tho Simpson ran the mill for years. The town of Simpson was one mile north, also built on a gumbo flat. Wagons often were stopped by the gumbo, making solid wheels and sodding in between the wheels and the wagon bed, stopping the wagon. The team was unable to go on farther till the mud was dug out with a crowbar.

These mills were built at various places on the Solomon River and wherever they were there was a grist mill too, to grind the flour, corn meal and rye for the new settlers. When farmers took their grain to the mill a tole was taken out by the miller for his work of grinding the grain, corn, wheat and rye. Beloit, Lanquarried Mill, Asherville, Brittsville, afterward called Simpson, after the Simpsons of that place, Glasco & & [*etc*] all had mills.

Doctors & Dentists

Emma says she only knew of one dentist. At one time he had to do some work on Emma's teeth. He went horseback, carried his tools thru the country visiting around, in that way got his horse feed and his board and keep. If any one needed their teeth fixed he proceeded to do the work for them while there. Emma needed to have two or three filled. He hand drilled the holes, no pain killer, and filled them with his punches and hammers. Then he fixed mother's false teeth. He lived in Brittsville and made his regular interval visits. He was a good talker - entertained many a lonely family thru those early years.

Snakes

Once when Annie lived on the Jackway place, Lincoln County, Kansas, while hunting eggs in the barn, she put her hand under the feed box in the manger. Instead of eggs she felt something wet and slimy and on looking it was a big bull snake and it did not move but Annie did. She seized a pitch fork nearby, jabbed it clean thru its body, bringing it out in to the yard on the tines. It at once began to retch and threw up the whole nest of unbroken eggs.

Rattlesnake, bull snake, blue racer, water snake, and water moccasin were found in Kansas. The rattler was dreaded and hunted, everyone killed them. When they leisurely rode in a wagon or plowing they had plenty of time to dispatch a snake with a whip or rock. Therefore they were thinned out in the course of time. I was told they are seldom ever sighted, tho later they have again become plentiful on the plains, as everyone goes by them in fast moving cars.

Once while Emma was plowing a long with the mules on the sulky plow, the mules tried to shy. She looked down and saw a big rattler trying to wind his self around the plow beam and was nearly up. She was almost paralyzed with fright. She had nothing to kill it with so she set the plow a notch or two deeper, expecting the long farrow would knock it off. She drove off a few rods and stopped the team. She thot she got rid of the snake and that she'd stop and see if it was anywhere. If it was in sight she'd kill it. Just as she was getting ready to jump on to a small bunch of rag weeds, old Watch, our faithful dog, made a dive at the weeds where she had aimed to land, caught the snake in his mouth and shook it so vigorously that the snake came to pieces. The snake parts going everywhere. She was satisfied the dog saved her life, as she thot the snake was back a rod or two.

Many rattlesnakes were found in the prairie dog holes or out around them, as well as the owl. They inhabited those places in order to get their favorite food, small prairie dogs and onleggs. After the country became settled up several years, snakes, especially the rattler, became scarce. Clost to Concordia in Cloud County, just east of us, in a coal mining district, snakes of all kinds were found in an abundance by a man hunting horses. He saw several snakes around a hole and, killed them. Then so many more appeared [*that*] he called on the neighbors to help. They dug and killed and piled till they had a pile of snakes as large as a hay cock. On Second Creek a small boy was bitten on the heel by one and died almost instantly.

Once while Emma and Seth were planting the rows of cottonwood around the place, Seth saw a very large snake. He wanted to kill it so he could get the rattles and hide for a hat band. Watch all at once spied it and Seth could not keep him from grabbing it and shaking it all to bits, parts of the snake flew and hit Emma in the face. Watch got bit a few times, tho not always. To get bit only made him more vicious. When bit he'd crawl away in some dark place. Then we children would take him fresh milk and in a few days the swelling would go down and he would be ready for another snake. The only snake we ever found in the barn yard was a small one brot in with some hay. Annie and I had been playing there only a few minutes before. I only knew of but one woman that was snake bitten and she was living over about Delphis. Later she moved into our settlement and she told Emma that they put her foot into a bucket and poured hogs lard in to the bucket to above the bite. It did not hurt till they stirred the lard occasionally.

**Lucy Ann Halbert
(Aunt Annie)
Taken by W. H. Greenwood
Beloit, Kansas
From Maggie's Photo Album**

Annie

One cold, frosty, snappy morning, Annie decided a stallion that was in the barn and had not been out for days needed water. About noon she let him out, got on, and rode him to the pond in Ruthaford field. On the edge of the pond was shell ice for a ways and he would not go thru it for the water. He backed out, wheeled around, snorted and galloped away to the barn in spite of her coaxing and trying to stop him. That was the last time she took the stallion to water.

To Town

One time we decided we needed some ribbon for our Fourth of July dress so we hitched up a little buxskin pony to a one horse buggy, about three a.m. in the morning. After we got out a ways we saw a beautiful comet in the northern skies. At that time in the morning there was not many people out looking for comets. We never learned its name or never heard any one else mention it. We wanted an early start in order to get back and finish our dresses that afternoon. When we got in to town we found we were a little bit too early, as the stores were not open yet. When the store keeper finally came in and opened the door, he says, "girls you are a little bit early." "Do you live in town?"

Buffaloes

Just a few years before we came to Kansas the buffalo had roamed the plains country in large herds. The early days people secured all their meat from them. Coming in wagons from the valleys, men slaughtered and packed and dried all their winter meat.

> Relating to Enos's pension, there are four General Affidavits, all dated during November 1883 attesting to the knowledge of Enos Halbert's health during the Civil War. They are signed by a Fred D. Warner, resident of Hope, County of Bartholomew, Indiana, by a John A. Miller, county of Bartholomew, Indiana, a Joseph F. Wooley, county of Bartholomew, Indiana and the one signed by Lewis Crides, aged 53, of the Town of Martinsville, County of Morgan, State of Indiana which states:
>
> That he is personally acquainted with Enos Halbert, the claimant above named and knew him during the year 1862 and 1864 and during said time said Halbert was afflicted with Rheumatism and during said time said applicant used Linements and during said time this affiant has drawn this applicants boots and rubbed and bathed his limbs with liniments.
>
> That the above facts are given from personal knowledge of his own, he further declares that he has no interest in said case, and is not concerned in its prosecution and is not related to said applicant.
>
> [Apparently Enos was seeking an increase in his pension, as increase is marked on the outside of each of these documents. I do not find the amount of Enos's pension. – mc]

A mute reminder (piles of white bones) was scattered on the plains. Also plainly visible were their trails and wallows. The latter were made where a few buffaloes congregated, in self defense from flies and gnats that made life a curse, especially in day light, to all living beasts. By the continual pounding and milling, the dirt that was not blown away by the wind was mixed with their excrement and urine in to a thick impervious mixture like cement. So when the heavy rains fell, small little ponds were filled, lasting for days, a nice pool of water. It is quite evident they were used like the trails, year after year.

There were several wallows near our house. When it rained they were full to the brim. They were little oasis, fringed with small rushes where frogs, tad poles and mosquitoes lived till they had to migrate or sink deep in the mud till an other rain or next season. It was then that Mother did an extra amount of washing, filling all available barrels and tubs and other utensils full of nice softened rain water.

One [wallow], in the side of the road near our house, was large and deep with a hard bottom. The water staid in it for a long time. To reach out and get nice clean water, we threw in a bleached buffalo skull which had the dark outside shells on the horns. The wallows made nice wadding pools for Annie and me.

In earlier days, Jim Rieves was a scout and pilot for buffalo meat hunters for big outfits. He had come hither for a home on the river just a few years before the buffalo was killed and driven out. In the fall of '69, he and Herbert Briggs (then a boy) and others took five or six wagons, [and] went to western Kansas for their winter supply of meat, which they found plentiful. They soon loaded all the wagons and arrived before a hard winter set in. This was the last successful buffalo meat drive in these parts of Kansas. Next fall Rieves did not care to go but Herbert, being a young fellow, Mr. Coles, Billie Childs, and Padgett, insisted he go with them to the west for buffalo meat but they only saw three. Herbert got two of the bunch. On their return the weather turned bitter cold. The fall of '75 some one killed two cows and calf west of Salt Creek, the year we came to the country. That was the last buffalo seen in that part of the plains.

Later when the R.R. came in, ranchers that needed a few extra dollars picked the buffalo bones and sold them to a trader at Simpson and Beloit. From there they went to sugar refineries in the south. The only buffalo I ever saw was a lone one, out east of Beloit, in a big enclosure at a county fair with a bunch of cattle, when I was quite young. Tho we often saw buffalo coats and robes. They were a valuable asset to the Indians and early day explorers, trappers and trader, R.R. builders and settlers.

Herbert and Frank Briggs hauled the largest load of bones that ever went in to Salina, Kansas. In gathering, one staid in the wagons with a big sledge hammer and as the one on the ground picked up the bones and threw them in, he would pound the bones up fine. In that way they got in many more than if left whole.

Fences

The first wire fence we saw was up about Beloit, made of smooth wire strung thru holes in the posts. Horses and cattle did not pay attention to this, so later barbs were put on. As this was used, the barbs slipped into bunches so then they found by putting on barbs on one wire and twisting two together, that made a better fence. So all of those inventions finally evolved in to our present barbed wire fence.

With no fences, we could cut out distances by going catacornered over the country. When the fences came in to use we disliked them very much, as we had to go square cornered on the section line. To go square corners hurt the early day people's consciences, so when a man begun to turn the sod, travellers often would go over the humpty bumpty furrows, rather than go the square cornered road. Then, after the wheat was in, you could see the trail marks. Consequently fences had to be built. Then free pasture was cut off and everyone had to fence.

Christopher E. Coursen

Coursen and family preceded us by several years and kept the post office called Coursen Grove. On this homestead he planted a grove of cottonwood trees, built a small stone house and stables.

In those day, they generally built a stone wall on the north side as the beginning of their barn. Then with poles brot from a creek four or five miles away, they built a frame work using all the brush laying on top, then roughage of some kind was used for a cover. Generally the straw, when thrashing time came, was pitched on top and all around making a nice cozy comfortable shelter for stock. It was some years after that that the straw blowing attachment was used on the thrashing machines. The straw then was blowed on most any place they wanted it. Such barns often made a good hide out for skunks, which lived on mice, rats and chickens. It made no difference to Coursen what they lived on, they never were molested. When a better barn was built, the old wall, tumbled down, was left for the skunks. On my visits to play with the Coursen children we often seen them, tho kept our distance.

There were two boys, John and Jeff and a girl, Lizzie. Annie and I would go there and play with her and her dolls until mother was ready to go home. When Nora, the youngest, was born, Mother and Mary took care of Mrs. Coursen. Then if we would be quiet and play out of door, make no noise, we were allowed to go. The children were never asked to help. If they wanted to go to school or church they went on their own accord, often coming in late to school. They were led along quietly and gently till they wanted to help, then made good industrious men and women, helping their father and mother with their ever increasing acres. All worked together amassing a big estate.

Mrs. Coursen was a very competent and able woman to handle her part in household, no matter how many hired men they had. She managed the cooking, cleaning and clothing the family.

They soon added more rooms to their first small house. We were then all so glad they could build, as the children were growing up. Then too, as the acres increased, the more farm help to cook for, she hired an old lady to wash dishes. Mrs. Childs was then 96 years old but spry and active. Mrs. Coursen never had time to go any place, only to church. She took The Truth Seeker paper, as a few others did there in that community and for so doing was looked down on by the church going people and evilisized severely. When the post office was established here, the cross roads, Coursen's Grove, became a community center. A store on one corner, the stone school house and blacksmith shop on the other, where farmers could get a horse shod if needed, a plow sharpened or a piece of iron welded. Once a minister ran the blacksmith shop weekdays and preached Sundays.

When Lizzie grew up she married Frank Murry, brother of Mrs. Linn, they having come to the country later. Mr. Linn bot Father's timber claim.

Thru all the hard work taking care of her family, Mrs. Coursen still kept the post office and waited on the public. Enos Wines built a general store on one of the corners at the Grove. It was then Mrs. Coursen gave up the post office to the store keeper.

In the developing of this large estate, Mr. Coursen held mostly to one crop, wheat, as that seemed to him to be the most dependable and profitable year after year. He bot his machinery to run the farms with by the car loads, keeping enuf horses and mules for power. Then when not in use they were turned out to pasture. He also kept a large herd of fine cattle and sheep and handled the best grade of hogs. These found ready market in Kansas City. By his many trips there selling his farm produce, he became very well acquainted with one of the leading cattle men, being invited to his house often on his trips to Kansas City. John often went with him and in time John married the buyer's daughter. Country life after many years became unbearable. She preferred to live else where so an agreeable settlement was made. She went her way, John stayed on with his father and brothers.

Further documents from Enos's Pension File.

The following is taken from a document with the heading War Department, Adjutant General's Office, Washington, March 18, 1884. It reads:

Respectfully returned to the Commissioner of Pensions. Enos Halbert a private of Company H, 33 Regiment, Ind Volunteers is reported on Roll Nov. & Dec. 1861 (first on file) present - Jan & Feb 1862 Officially absent Mar & Apr 1862, present same to April 30, 1863, May & June 1863, absent, Wagon Master 1st Div. Reserve Army Corps since Oct. 21, 1862 - July & Aug 1863 present with remark: Detailed Wagon Master at Brig Hdqrs since Oct. 20, 1862, Sept & Oct. 1863 absent, detailed Wagon Master at Brig Hdqrs since Oct 20, 1862 - Nov & Dec. 1863 promoted to 2 M Sarg same Reg, Dec. 2, 1863 and is reported on Roll Field Staff Nov & Dec 1863, 2M.S. absent sick in Ind. Reenlisted as Vet Vol. Feb. 15, 1864 and is reported on Roll Jan & Feb 1864 present. The Regtal. Desc. Book shows him detailed Rgtal. Wagon Master Dec. 20, 61 promoted to Brigade wagon master Oct. 20, 62 advanced in Ky for forage Aug 63, was cut off from his command, had to abandon his wagon. Nature of sickness Dec. 63 not stated. The records of this office fail to show ordence of disability in spring 1863. The Rgtmt. Hospital records are not on file.

In about 1908 or 09 Coursen built a mansion on the home place. I say mansion for it has never had its equal. It is both big and strong, just the down stairs would make a big house alone. There was a large upstairs, with a wide spacious hall in the middle between the bedrooms. The dimension boards were all double in size to any other common house, the rafters being 2 x 6's.

Susan (Shirley) Halbert
About 1888
From the Susan Hand Collection

It had a furnace that heated it. Out of the kitchen thru a door was a cob room where the nice clean cobs were put for fuel. A wash room closet, something the poor pioneers never dreamt of to possess. A wind mill supplied the hot and cold water in this castle. Tho, as yet in 1910, the lighting system was somewhat deficient. As with all hard working people, Mr. and Mrs. Coursen did not live long to enjoy this all. Then Fettie or Jeff, the son, died. Nora and John ran the estate as ever. Nora had a good neighbor's daughter to do the house work for years. In the mean time a family (large) of boys moved in to the community [*Mr. & Mrs. Will Adams*]. They proved to be the good help John needed. John died Nov. 10, 1940. Nora was left with the estate, with only cousins and half cousins surviving.

In early days a trip to the county seat, 20 miles away, was carefully planned for the one going and the ones left behind. They had to have provisions, wood and water. The water had to be hauled from a distant shallow well in a revine or creek in barrels. If the wagon, in many cases, had to be taken on this trip, the barrels then had to be mostly emptied in other containers then taken out of the wagon and placed on the ground and filled again from the barrels on the wagon. In most cases there would be all the barrels that one could get in the wagon box waiting. Beside the household, there would be some stock that would have to be watered.

Enos Halbert
About 1888
From the Susan Hand Collection

When hauling barrels in a wagon, they had to be tightly covered. Hence a hoop and a piece of cloth was mostly used, tho often parts of bed quilts, blankets or coverlids or a grain sack split open. Anything to cover the barrels to save the precious water. Where thick pieces were used, a piece of rope was tied around the barrel to keep the cloth stretched tight. Care was taken in saving every drop of water, as over rough rutty road, if not tightly covered, they would lose a lot by jolting away a two or three miles. Being no shade or sheltered place in those early day, the water set out in the sun till used up. A bucket full was taken inside to keep cool for drinking water. In winter, the barrels often had to be brot in to keep from freezing.

As Mr. Coursen proved up on his land and his steady increase buying more, he always made a trip in the fall to pay his taxes and incidentally buy other needs for the farm and household. After every need was seen to at home, he'd hitch up the grey team of mares, colts following, to the wagon, fill the wagon bed with hay and oats for the horses. In the front he would tuck in his chest of food carefully packed by his good wife, rolled in the bedding. By sun up he would be well on his way. On arriving at the county seat 20 miles away (Beloit, Mitchell Co.), he'd camp on some vacant lot or alley, unhitch, water and feed his team, light a camp fire, take out his grub box, and proceed to get his breakfast. At night he slept in the wagon box. By the second day, having transacted all his business, the wagon loaded, he'd leisurely take his time home.

After Mother and Father moved to town, instead of camping he brot his horse feed and staid with them. He'd always tell Mother to go to no extra trouble for him and if she had others there, to make his bed on a day couch. He preferred to stay with old friends, tho he was worth more than anyone else on that wide divide.

The first time I saw Mr. Coursen, I was staying with Mary for a few days. It was a cold snowy day. He knocked at the door, yes, he'd come in. Took off his hat and a red, gray and white breakfast shawl from his head shaking off the snow. Said he was hunting a pig. He sat by the fire and chatted for a time and then went on. He was a small man, almost effeminate in his stature. Coursen was a good farmer, never was idle a minute. As times went on, he put all his strength and skill raising wheat. As he gradually accumulated more land, he raised more wheat and the fall and late summers he thrashed, hauled wheat to town to an elevator with a number of wagons, teams and men, while others kept the thrashing machines going. Not all was rosy in the wheat business. Once when wheat was low price he decided he'd hold for larger price. He built big granaries and kept his big crop. Price did not come up as he planned. Weevil got in the bins and to save it he ran it thru the thrashers again and then sold it at a loss. Also the cattle business, when a slicker once beat him on his own cattle deal, he never flinched or complained about his miss calculations or the other man beating him.

Mr. Coursen took up a homestead and timber claim. His sister-in-law, Vin Cashman, took up the same. Everybody had to build a house 12 x 14 to hold the claim according to law. She left and went back to New York and sold her land to her brother-in-law. This made Coursen his first section of land. Then he bot Warefield's 160 acres where the school house stood. This was the beginning of his many sections he accumulated in his lifetime. The last Annie remembered, there was 27, tho there perhaps was many more added.

Nade Robbison told his version of Coursen's trips to town. When Coursen got an extra early start to town, he would get in to town by 2 a.m. Then he'd unhitch, tie the horses to the wagon, roll out his blankets on the R.R. platform, not caring to disturb his friends at the early hour. He would unpack his sack of cucumbers and eat his frugal breakfast.

Coursen was very fond of cucumbers. Gardens, tho, thru the hot summer often dried up for the lack of water. He diligently hauled water to his cucumber patch. To each hill he rounded up a basin, like ridge of dirt, to hold the water he put on each hill of cuks, so he raised cucumbers when others failed.

Home of Enos and Susan (Shirley) Halbert, Beloit, Kansas

People in photo identified as, right to left, Enos Halbert, Lucy Ann (Halbert) Briggs, Frank, Ruby and Arta Briggs and Susan (Shirley) Halbert. The following was written on the back of the photo: I think this was taken about 1897 or 1898. Use magnifying glass to locate Frank Briggs in the chair in front, left of Aunt Annie, a small boy. Frank was born in 1895.

From the Susan Hand Collection

Songs

The song sheets had many old and new songs, just in verse without the music. They sung the songs they knew the tunes of. They would try different tunes till they got one to fit the verse. Most all the young folks sang and often exchanged songs with each other.

Paper of Early Days

There were very few papers and very few people had money for the subscriptions in the 1800's and very few books. We had quite a number of books brot from Indiana, tho most every one had a bible and if they went to Sunday School there would have been a quarterly and Sunday sheet each week. But there were a few papers in the community.

Father took a soldiers paper. I just can't remember the full title, perhaps it was a G.A.R. Tribune, tho can't remember where it was printed. But do remember that Annie and Emma sent for their song sheets out of it. Then, generally an old army song was printed weekly in it. Papers had but very few pictures in them. Father took the Toledo Blade, edited in Toledo, Ohio later and a Mitchell County paper from the County seat, Beloit, to keep up with the politic doings. He was a dyed in the wool Republican. The Republican candidates always depended on father to pull them a big vote from his section of the county.

I can remember very vividly, Father setting out in the yard as the suns rays were dropping on the horizon, reading out of the Ohio Blade about the awful earth quake that shook South Carolina in 1886. Then they took the Farm Journal - tho can't recall where it was printed.

Maggie Ellen Halbert
Beloit, Kansas High School
Graduation Picture - 1892
From Maggie's Photo Album

A Mrs. Kinsey came to the Grove, perhaps a year or two later and with husband, three children, Bill, Mary and Firatie, lived in Vin Cashman's house a while. It was there Mrs. Kinsey was the canvassing agent for the Home Hearth and Fireside Monthly. When you signed and paid for a year subscription, they gave you a large picture, highly colored and glazed. Then for her premium, selling a given number of yearly subscriptions, she could have her choice of several useful articles. The one she chose was a gadget to milk with - a hollar tube was slipped up the cows tits and the milk was suppose to flow, that is if the cow consented. As I remember, she had some trouble with the so called milker and I never heard anything more about the milker. The whole country near had lots to say about Mrs. Kinsey's gadget till it was a forgotten memory to many.

The fall of 1887 father sold out, moved to Beloit, where in October I entered the 8th grade at the age of 17 years. I continued my education there thru high school. Spring of 1892 graduated, went to Normal there a month, passed, and got a teaching certificate. I secured a school at Blue Hill for $28.00 per month, tho before school opened I resigned and went to Dewey's Flat, Montana.

Maggie Graduates

On July 16, 1892 Maggie received her Teachers County Certificate, Beloit, County of Mitchell, State of Kansas. It is Certificate Number 4. The original certificate is in Maggie's Bible.

From Enos Halbert's pension file from The National Archives, there are two General Affidavits, one dated February 6, 1893 from John D. Hiatt, aged 65, of Bethany, County of Harrison, State of Missouri; and the other one dated February 27, 1893 from Logan Tristler, age 50, resident of Des Moines, County of Polk, State of Iowa, both attesting to Enos Halbert's health during the Civil War. The Affidavit from Logan Tristler states:

I was intimately acquainted with the above named Enos Halbert while a member of Co. I, 33 Ind. Inf. war of rebellion. I know he was troubled with Fistula in ano and rheumatism while in the said Company and regiment. I also remember that Capt Halbert had several attacks of diarrhrea while on the Atlantic Campaign in 1864 and while on the march to Washington D. C. in the spring of 1865. I also remember that said Halbert had a severe attack of diarrhrea after we arrived at Washington D.C. in June 1865. I also now recall the fact that said Halbert was under treatment for diarrhrea while at Washington D.C. Then carefully read the foregoing statements and I know they are true. That I was personally present in the same and with said Command during the times the said Halbert was sick.

****

A document from the Bureau of Pensions, United States of America, Department of Interior dated May 27th, 1908, file No. 232369, (increase) reads as follows:

It is hereby certified That in conformity with the laws of the United States, Enos Halbert who was a Private Co. H, 33 Regiment Indiana Volunteer Infantry is entitled to a pension at the rate of Thirty dollars per month to commence on the sixth day of May, one thousand nine hundred and eight. This pension being for: Fistula-in-ano and rheumatism and resulting disease of heart.

Chapter X

Montana's Early Settlers

****

The Hand Family Background

The Hand forefathers were English men employed by the Kings as foresters. When the war of 1812 broke out, England offered their young men land in America if they would fight for England. The single men were to get 160 acres and the married men 320 acres in New Brunswick. At this time the New Brunswick interior was an unsettled wilderness only accessible up river and creeks by man power, dug out, boats or rafts which was a very laborious mode of travel.

Hand Family Tree Ancestor Chart may be found in the Appendix E, page 298.

There were four young Hand brothers that longed for adventure in America at that time, Richard, William, John and Howard. William was a bugler in the army. After the war was over, the first three came back to New Brunswick to settle on their land, preferring to live under the English flag. New Brunswick was an ideal country to carve out a home in and there in Queens County they would cast their lot. There was plenty of timber and water, land was rich when cleared, and yielded bountiful crop. The fourth longed for further adventure and settled in Ohio and but little was ever heard of him except it was that some of his offspring moved to South Dakota and later on one became Governor. Then two of his race appeared in Butte years later, a Carl and Ed Hand, noted assayers of Butte and mining men. They even had the racial resemblance of the Hand race.

William, Horace's father, took up his allotment of 160 acres near Plymouth, Queens County, New Brunswick. His two brothers nearby, each clearing ground, built a cabin. When money was needed they went to logging camps, often staying all winter and helping drive logs down the creeks and rivers, coming back in the spring to put in the crop and always clearing another patch of ground. In the meantime, William and Richard married two of the Wilson girls, Mary and Margaret. Mary was Horace's mother. The wedding day was set for in early spring. William had a call up the river to help drive logs. As the wedding day drew near, he found it would be impossible for him to get home in time for the wedding, tho the folks at home was preparing a big wedding day. The day came and no William. Mary never complained. He was not there and that was all. She did not break down and cry. Well, she said, he will come when he can. In a few days he made the perilous journey, afoot, thru deep forests, swollen rivers and creek, home. The wedding then took place quietly in the home church and Mary took her household goods, wheel and looms to his little new home in a clearing.

Many immigrants were coming from England, Scotland and Ireland, settling up that part of the province, then on the coast the French were early settlers. Prince Edward Isles had a mixture of all. In these settlements and other settlements near there were the Bells, the Wilsons, the McClellans, the Hays, the Lawrences, the Gentles.

Each little settlement had a name, many were designated as corners, Scotch Corner, McKinzie Corner, the Red Bridge, Plymouth, Richmond Corner.

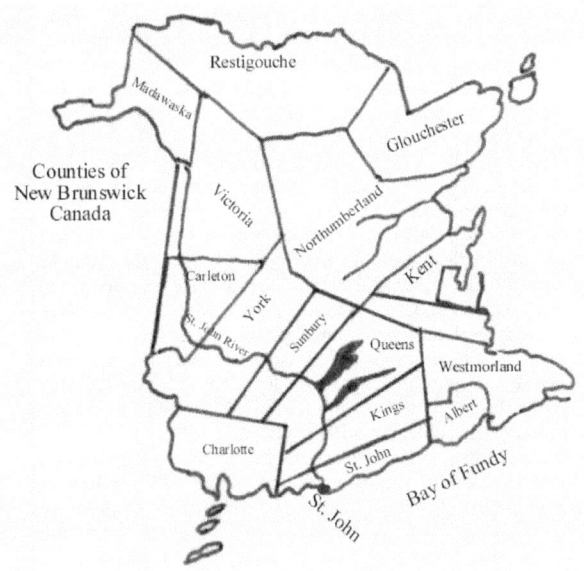

Counties of New Brunswick, Canada
For general location map of New Brunswick, see Appendix B, page 292.
Horace was born in Queens County
December 1, 1860

First Federal Census, Montana Territory - 1870
20,959 citizens

Second Federal Census, Montana Territory - 1880
39,159 citizens

Early Mining History of Beaverhead Reviewed

This article was taken from Maggie's Scrap Book. She clipped it from the Dillon Tribune - date unknown.

Interesting Article on Hecla and Glendale Compiled by George B. Conway

(Editor Tirbune: A few years ago when trying to gather information on the early history of Beaverhead County - especially seeking data on the origin and significance of place names, I asked Mr. George Conway who was identified with Hecla and Glendale during their boom period to tell me their history. Mr. Conway's reply, which follows, will, I think, be found of wide interest and value - Laura Tolman Scott.)

Montana and Idaho were part of the territory organized in 1853 and given the name of Washington. In 1863 Idaho (including much of Montana) were set apart from Washington, and in the following year Montana was carved from the year-old territory, by act of congress, and a territorial government was established at Bannack, with Sydney Edgerton as governor. Beaverhead came over as an organized county from Idaho, and has suffered no diminution in size, the only change having been the addition of several townships taken from Madison county, some years ago.

Although gold had been discovered a number of years earlier, at Gold Creek, by Granville Stuart, and placer mining had been carried on at the place and other localities in a limited way, the first discovery of sufficient importance to cause a "stampede" was at Bannack. Little attention was paid to silver and other metals until 1864, when rich silver and lead discoveries at "Frenchtown", later named Argenta, resulted in the opening of the Legal Tender and a number of other shallow mines, and the erection of several crude smelters. The ruins of three of these smelters may yet be seen on Rattlesnake Creek, west of Argenta.

In the year 1875 Billy Spur, while hunting horses, discovered the rich galena croppings of an ore deposit which he located and named the "Trapper" lode. The high grade ore, much of it worth a thousand dollars a ton, was hauled to Corrine, Utah, on the Union Pacific railroad, and shipped thence to Wales, for treatment. There was soon an inrush of prospectors and miners who pushed a little further into the wilderness and found rich ore in quantity on a high limestone mountain at the head of Trapper Gulch. While working on his prospect one of the miners who had strayed away from his partners was frightened by a mountain lion. Rushing after his partners he induced them to return with him with their rifles. Instead of a lion they found an old white mule munching the bunch grass. The mountain on which this occurred has ever since borne the name of Lion Mountain. Near Trapper mine a town grew up which was named Trapper City. There were numerous miners' cabins, several saloons, a "hurdy gurdy" and other accompaniments of a pioneer mining camp. As the importance of the ore deposits of Lion Mountain began to be recognized, the center of population shifted to Lion City, which soon became a camp of several hundred miners, merchants, gamblers, saloon proprietors, women of questionable reputation and a few families.

It was in 1875 that Charles L. Dahler and Noah Armstrong, realizing that the growth of silver-lead mining would make a smelter profitable, erected a small twenty-ton furnace at the crossing of the main stage over Trapper Creek. The name of the town which grew up around the smelter was decided by the flip of a coin, "Clinton" and "Glendale" being the names proposed. Glendale won. Two years later Mr. Armstrong, having acquired by location and purchase the Cleopatra, True Fissure, Atlantus, Hecla, Cleve Mine, Avon, Franklin and other valuable mines, organized the Hecla Consolidated Mining Company, investing Indianapolis and Philadelphia capital. Only a small amount of money, comparatively, was put in, the product of the mines paying for the development, opening of roads and conquering the wilderness. The ores produced were hauled to the smelter at Glendale, which was soon enlarged, by "bull teams" and mule teams. On the latter sometimes sixteen to twenty mules were used, driven by use of a single "jerk" line. The base bullion produced by the smelter was hauled to the terminus of the Utah & Northern railroad, a constantly diminishing distance, as the railroad pushed northward, furnishing back loading for the many teams which brought in freight from the terminus, until in 1882, the terminus was established at Melrose, which thereafter became the shipping station for Glendale. The bullion was refined in Omaha. At the furnaces in Glendale it was moulded into bars weighing about ninety pounds each, and there were sometimes thousands of such bars piled up on the smelter yards awaiting transportation. In 1879 E. C. Atkins, founder of the Atkins Saw Works, of Indianapolis, succeeded to the management. Two years later Henry Knippenberg, also of Indianapolis, where he was managing director of the Saw Works, also secretary of the Hecla Consolidated, became general manager. The real success of the company then commenced. Mr. Knippenberg arrived at Glendale April 5, 1881. By July 1st, a large indebtedness had been canceled, and a cash dividend of $15,000 paid. A like amount, being one per cent of the capitalization of the company, was paid each month thereafter over a period of twelve years, without a break, except to throw in an occasional "extra". The company during all this time never missed a pay day. The payroll often amounted to seventy-five thousand dollars a month. This was necessarily a large factor in the building up of Beaverhead county and southern Montana.

In 1881, when the writer came to Montana with the Knippenberg administration, Glendale was a flourishing town of 1,500 to 1,800 inhabitants. In addition to the smelting works there was a water works system and fire protection, furnished by the company. There was a church, built by union subscription, but dedicated by the Methodist; a good school house with accommodations for 200 or more pupils, presided over by John Gannon, who later became State Superintendent of Education. There were three hotels, two dry good stores, seven or eight grocery stores and thirteen saloons. There was a bank, that of N. Armstrong & Company, two drug stores, two shoe stores, a fine jewelry store, several confectioneries, a brewery, a photograph gallery and a weekly newspaper, the "Atlantis". A large business was done by a lumber yard conducted by William Thompson. One of his sons, now a multimillionaire, Colonel William Boice Thompson of New York, attended the school at Glendale, under Professor Gannon.

The Hecla company in those days employed at its mines at Lion Mountain, near Lion City, at its iron mines in Soap Gulch, its concentrator at Greenwood, and at its Glendale smelter five or six hundred men, and in addition a large number of Italian charcoal burners, who, scattered over the surrounding mountains, burned millions of bushels of charcoal, the fuel used in smelting furnaces until the coming of the railroad made it possible to secure coke from Pennsylvania.

The Hecla company's furnaces continued to produce bullion until 1900, when it became more profitable to ship the ore than to smelt it. Four years later the company's operations were brought to a close, through unfortunate litigation, and the corporation was dissolved. The smelter was dismantled, and the town of Glendale disappeared from the map. Its stores and dwellings were torn down and moved to other localities, until very little remains. Lion City suffered a similar fate.

........Continued - next page

> EARLY MINING HISTORY OF BEAVERHEAD REVIEWED - Cont'd.
>
> With the collapse of the Company the mines passed into private ownership, and for many years were leased to miners who produced hundreds of thousands of dollars worth of ore. They were finally sold to a syndicate of Philadelphia capitalists, who organized a new Hecla Consolidated Mining company. It is believed that the mines, far from being exhausted, are still the repositories of vast wealth. Glendale may not "come back", but a large population will again flourish and grow wealthy in this part of Beaverhead county.

> *Maggie wrote about many people who were friends and neighbors of hers and Horace's. These people touched their lives in many ways. Throughout these writings will be stories of these people, not necessarily in the order of their meeting as this was impossible for me to know. Some of these stories are placed before Horace and Maggie's arrival in Montana, as these people arrived prior to them. Throughout the following stories, Maggie covered various periods of time. They have been typed as she wrote them. - mc*

Alen Hay and Isaac Dodgson

Alen Hay, born in New Brunswick near Scotch Corner, was an uncle to the Lawrences of that place. I never met him but I have met many that knew this kindly old man. Leaving his native land, he went by boat to California by the [*around the*] horn, landed in the gold diggings. He worked and accumulated gold.

It was in this location that he met Isaac Dodgson. He was from Wisconsin. Isaac Dodgson left Wisconsin (Grant Co.) with his wife, son and baby in '70 [*1870*] overland to California. On their trip from Wisconsin they had missed Indian trouble by one day, the stage coach being shot up with bullet holes.

Isaac and Alen soon became clost friends and having money, horses and equipment, they decided to come to Montana, as they had heard of the gold finds there. So, well equipped for the trek, they set out for this far away gold fields thru Nevada and Idaho. When about 300 miles from their destination, Indians stole their horses, supplies and implements one night and left them afoot. With slow and careful travelling, they finally reached Bannack.

Always prospecting for gold, not satisfied, they went to Virginia City. The ground there being taken up, they went in to Butte and Highland. Stopped at the latter for a while and mined some gold. Dodgson, being a wheelwright, could find work at building arrasta and mills. Dodgson worked at his trade. Alen drifted in to the Flat [*Dewey*]. There he found ore at Quartz Hill and went to work. Took out a ditch above town and brot it around thru the Flat, then to the mouth of the canyon. There built his mill or arrasta and worked it quite successfully.

Dodgson, not being satisfied working at his trade, went to Radersburg gold mines. There he met with success, sold out after two years, went to Butte and finally to Dewey Flat. In the meantime his wife and children came. She was not satisfied with town life, so he moved them to a ranch and hired a man to help while he worked his trade. The winter of '72 they moved to Dewey's Flat. They were living there in '77 when the Battle of the Big Hole was fought, Mrs. Dodgson being the only white woman above Divide. News kept coming of the Indian trouble by traveler coming down the river. Being so frightened, she took sick and went to bed thinking any minute the Indians might be coming. Isaac was away that summer working. She and the two little boys, George and Tice, being left in this little settlement. They settled on Meadow Creek for their home, a lovely creek, coming from the near mountains. Not a long creek, but one that spread out into a wide grassy meadow affording homes for about six families, Robbins, Soper, Tice and George, Patton, and Sam Garrett.

After the boys became of age and married, the old folks gave up the ranch to the boys and they lived at the mill on Wise River or in Dewey Flat where they had a comfortable home. Tice and Maude ran the Bow place till 1922. They sold and moved to Butte where he passed away in '28 [*1928*].

In the meantime, Alen Hay's nephew and other relatives came out from New Brunswick. Clad Hay and family was a canivering young fellow and lent on his uncle. Alen being older now, became despondent and the story has it he took his life. Tho others even surmised it was not suicide. How be it. There was an estate to be settled. This happened before I came. I met his two brothers, Bob and Henry [*Hay*]. They came to settle the estate. John Lawrence had got his ranch and various things from Uncle Alen.

Clad took his family, after the settlement, and went to Aberdeen, South Dakota. Nothing was ever heard of them for a long while, till one fall one of Clad's sons came to see his relative, John Lawrence. He visited a few weeks. John came to see us, he seemed to be a likable young fellow. At last he decided to go. This day John was out riding for cattle. Thot nothing of the lad leaving. John continued to ride and round up cattle and horses. After this was all done, he had to go to Butte for provisions. Went into his room to dress up. Well, he looked for his good suit. It just was not there. It has always been a mystery. What became of his suit? Mrs. Gentle was doing the cooking and had been there all the time. If the suit had been taken out it must have been in the night. The boy was never heard of again.

Billy Vipond

Billy Vipond came to Bannack in the fall of 1864. He mined with varying success and later he and his brother John, in 1869, struck what ever since has been known as the Vipond District, south of Butte. [*From an article written by Susan Hand - mc*]

Sam Garrett

Sam Garrett was living on the ranch when Dodgsons came in 1872. He took up a ranch just east and adjoining Hugh Patton. He built a cabin and some sheds. Did not ranch very extensively. It served as a place to winter his horses and a home when he was not placer mining up French Creek.

One spring while washing gold, a neighbor miner ran short of water. He knew Sam had plenty of water, so he went down and asked Sam if he could loan him some water for a few days and finish up for the season. Sam says, "B-d, no. I'd not let me old father have a drop to drink if he came up from the bottomless pit of hell." So, I am quite sure he never let his neighbors have a drop either.

He was noted for being close and never caring to neighbor with anyone. Tho good and kindly to those he dealt with and peaceable with all. Tice Dodgson was about the only person who went to see him. One morning Tice went over to see him. Just had a hunch that Sam was sick and might need something. Sure enuf, Sam had been sick. Tice was going to Divide town and he asked Sam if he wanted anything. Yes, get me a can of peaches. In the evening Tice came back and brot the fruit to Sam. He gave Tice $10.00 that morning. After he died, the exact change Tice had given him back that morning was in a drawer. Some of the neighbor men came in and they found $10,000 certificates in his bed tick and other money, some two or three hundred around the house. When all was over, they found he never ate his peaches and that he had dug up something in the yard.

With the aid of the neighbor men, Sam was laid away. Dolman had the casket made in town. Isaac Dodgson generally made them. Dolman's son took it up in a wagon. Tice helped and the boy drove it down to the grave yard. No one was there to meet him, so he tied the team up to the grave yard fence and went down and got some men to help burry Sam. Jim Long was one of the men and he told how they let the casket down in the grave with the lines off of the team. They called for someone to say a few words. No response, so Jim took it upon himself to say the words:

> Here lies Old Sam Garrett
> He lived two weeks on a carrot
> And wither he goes, nobody knows,
> and no body cares.

Then, he says, we heaved in all the big boulders we could find and left. (true or not?)

Then, after all was over, a brother or uncle came from Pennsylvania and settled up the estate. Someone wanted him to put a stone to his brother's grave, so he went and looked at the grave and went away. No marker marks his lonely grave to this day and no one knows where he lies.

Al Cline bot the Garrett place and horses. Al improved the place and fenced it and he made a good living there for his family. Later sold the bottom land, then moved to a higher piece of ground and improved that piece of land and built a house clost to Wise River.

Al Brubaker

[*I believe portions of the following information on Mr. Brubaker was taken from a news article. I have been unable to identify with certainty where it came from. - mc*]

Al Brubaker came of sturdy old Pennsylvania Dutch stock. Being too young to join in the gold rush to California, he went to Colorado in 1859. Spent some time there, then went back to the middle west. There met Joseph H. Millard, a plainsman of Nebraska, later a senator in that state. Then later Al joined a party under the leadership of Millard headed for

Montana. He passed thru most of the stirring scenes of Alder Gulch, never tiring about the trip and the leader, for they escaped all the dangers that beset others who crossed the plains full of hostile Indians.

We started from Davenport, Iowa March 1864 with three wagons. At Grinnell, the terminus then of the Rock Island Railroad, we got our outfit in shape then took the mud road to Council Bluffs. We camped on the bank of the river, which was very high at that point. No wonder they called it the Big Muddy. A bucket full of water, when settled, would be 1/3 mud. At the rate the river banks caved off a farm would soon be taken away. We crossed over to Omaha and staid there till the second of April.

At the Cutoff

We made the acquaintance of a man "Jacobs". He told us about a new cut off road and advised us to go that way but after the first 9 miles (the first day) we decided to turn back and take the old road. As it afterward turned out, we got in to Virginia City before the man that took the cut off. The cut off must have been terrible. The wagons cut into the mud up to the hubs. Then at steep bluffs the wagons had to be let down by ropes, rivers to ford, and all kinds of obstacles to be over come by going the cutoff.

Our party camped at Independence Rock out in the open country. On its face are carved many names of those who had passed it going to California. Willard Barrows told us he camped there in 1849 on his way to California (4th of July).

The Sweet Water runs around one side of the rock at what they call Devil's Gate. It is said John Fremont went thru Devil's Gate in a canoe. From there we crossed the Green River and came to old Fort Bridger, 125 miles from Salt Lake. From there we journeyed on to Bear River where the Mormons had started to build. We crossed the Snake River at Ricker's Ferry. I think this ferry was at Eagle Rock or now Idaho Falls. Then on to Market Lake and Camas Prairie. Then on and on up the dividing line over in Montana and on past where Dillon was to be later on, arriving at Virginia City July 7, 1864.

No Trouble on the Trip

Unlike most outfits that crossed the plains, we got along without any trouble. In the outfit Joe Millard had a small safe which he slept on. When he got to Virginia City, he and B. F. Allen of Des Moines started a bank with the safe and what was in it.

It was at the last crossing of the Sweet Water that Barrows and myself came near losing our reputation as cooks. We camped there about a week to give ourselves and stock a rest. One day we thot we would like some plum duff or plum pudding as others call it. Barrows was cook and I the helper. We had some blackberries, very hard and dry. We mixed up the duff, put the berries in and then put the mess into a sack to boil. We only had green willows to fire with and they were wet. When we turned out the duff, when done, the berries were just as hard as when first put in. "A plum duff seemed to be Al's pet dish, as whenever you saw Al in his discourse he invariably would allude to his plum duff cookery. Having never tasted it, I could not vouch for his efficiency as a plum duff cook."-Maggie

John Bielenberg of Deer Lodge was in Al's party. We had started for the land of Gold - Virginia City. When we left Omaha, we kept on the north side of the Platte until we got to where the North empties into the South. When we got on the road the Mormons took at the time the women had to pull the hand carts, while the men looked out for Indians. Some of the poor creatures froze hands and feet. The party ran short of food. I hear had to live on rawhide soup.

We were right in the Indian country now. Sand from 6 to 8 inches deep. We had to pull thru and the weather hot. The teams were heavily loaded, which made hard pulling for the mules. When we got to Rushaw's Bridge (a Frenchman) we found a lot of Indians.

They were not on the war path, however, but were holding a council of about 600 Cheyennes, Sioux and Arapahoes, others coming in all the time. They told us they were going to drive the Snake Indians off their hunting grounds.

The Indians had a sham battle on horseback which scared some of our mules, which made them pull their picket pins up and run off. When the excitement was all over the mules came back. We had to watch our wagons pretty close as the Indians would steal things out of our wagons. The council was held right on the bank of the river and along the road. These were the first Indians we had seen so far on our trip.

We went on to Fort Laramie where Joe Millard got his last oats for the mules from the Creightons of Omaha, who was running a supply station there. Further on we had to go thru a canyon along the Platte very much like the one below Dewey's on the Big Hole. Here it was a habit of the Sioux to get up on the hills and shoot down on the emigrants passing thru. There must have been many a poor fellow killed there by the looks of the grave yard at Alder Springs at the mouth of the canyon. We were lucky to get thru unmolested.

Andy Jackson

Andy Jackson was an old timer, coming with Brubaker and Miller and was in the Big Hole a long time. Came from New York. Was an orphan. When small, a couple took him to raise (6 yr. old). The man was considerate of him and kindly but the wife was a tyrant, never considering the boy worth raising. The old clothes he wore, she begrudged them to him and the lunch he took to school was what ever he could grab and run. He was educated in the hard school of work.

When in Montana, he worked for Mr. Tong on both ranches for years. After Tong died, he quit and worked elsewhere. He got the logs for Tice Dodgson's house, now Husted's house. Once, when on Tong's upper ranch, he ran out of hay and the winter was not near over. (Tong was in Butte.) He got as far as chalk bluff and could not go any further. He came down to the lower ranch to send word to Tong to buy hay in the basin and keep the cattle there. John Hay was at the ranch and he had Hay write to Tong for him and tell him, "By God, there was no use, by God, to bring those cattle down, by God, as they could not be driven, by God, thru the deep snow." Hay wanted to leave out the swear words but, with Andy, it all had to be put in. So the letter was sent.

After Tice and Maude [*Dodgson*] moved to Melrose, he staid with them for a few years and then went to Medford, Oregon where he settled. He married and left all he had to a wife, but the wife died first and her sister got all he had left. He liked the climate there. In earlier days he had some money. Brubaker borrowed it, then Brubaker's venture failed and could never pay it.

[*Warren*] Churchill

Deweys Flat began to settle up about 1872 and Churchill came the year after, having come west to fight Indians from Maine - 1860.

The story goes he sent for a wife and in due time received one thru "Heart and Hand". She came from Pennsylvania and thru her coal land they lived well. He had taken up a small but nice little strip of land above town. There he built quite a nice log cabin for those days. He had cleared the ground and had water on it. Tho he had sold the water to the Butte Water Company twice, he yet used it as they failed to take it. I take that when he sold the water right is when he began to prospect for water at the big rock.

Churchill knew how to handle water. He had built a flume on two log piers to bring the Jerry Creek water over on his ranch. This he used as long as he ranched. When he wanted to go over to Jerry Creek he always used his flume for a crossing, a feat no other man would ever undertake.

Jimmie New

Jimmie New was born in England. When a lad, with his father, the father often pointed out to him the large mansions and say, "lad, these were built for you and I to look at."

He came to New York. When he grew up, he owned a livery stable, was married and had two sons and one daughter. When the gold rush in California was herald in New York, he left all and went, leaving when the children were all small.

After lots of hardships and privation there was not enuf gold for all and he followed other stampedes for Montana, arriving at Montana, Glendale '74 [*1874*] or about. No place was quite the utopia he sought. Rather than mine or work at the smelter, he took to fishing. The rivers were well stocked with white fish and grayling. That was before man came and fished them out. At that time trout was found mostly in the creeks. He caught fish and had a ready market for all. In his wanderings, he found land on the Big Hole River just below where Wise River emptied in to the Big Hole. Opposite the mouth of Wise River was an enormous big rock, sitting at the edge of the river. Then on his land was a large pond below a bluff and from it meandered a warm slough and emptied in to the Big Hole just north of his buildings. This seemed to be the ideal spot. Here he called home. In some way he bot an old buggy and a team - one horse was sorrel, the other white. I don't know the year he came to Wise River, but in 1877 he fenced Patton's place and among the barter he received for his work was a calf. The calf grew and increased and he traded with Gerry and Dixson and got a bull. From this meager start he soon grew a bunch of cattle and horses, and increased and grew. The cattle and horse knew him and they did not stray far away. He often walked out among them taking salt and talking to them like they were his children. The only besetting sin was drink. Often got on a spree, then went home. Tho never lasted long and was at long periods [*in between*]. As time went on, more people hearing of the good fishing on the Big Hole, came in to the country.

Griswolds and Jimmie New were among the first residences below Wise River. Then John Lawrence bot a piece of land below Jimmie and Horace traded with the Griswolds for the land above him.

Horace Hand
Houlton, Maine September 1876
15 years old

[*From Horace Hand's writings*]

I left Houlton, Maine with a lumber company and worked in timber the following winter at $13.50 per month - it looked [*like*] slow progress.

I left Houlton later and went to Denver, Colorado with a party of migrants by train. There was 28 in the party. The man that headed the party, name was James Carr. We got to Denver in 7 days. Then we all got work in a few days, most of us in a brick yard.

My next move was for Montana in 1879. Charles H. Webbe and myself left Denver by R.R. train to Ogden, Utah. Ogden was a small, rough looking place but the people was nice and very accommodating. We stayed at the Kinney Hotel and expected to outfit for Montana and went out where lots of covered wagons and emigrants was to see what we might buy. We got talking to 3 men. They had 6 mules and 2 nice covered wagons and was out of money and out of grub and broken hearted and was willing to go any place so they could get something to eat. We easily made a trade with them and gave them money and we all bought grub and the next day about noon, July 5, we started for Montana and found them to be very nice, kind Missourians. We traveled nicely and enjoyed our selves. The second day at noon we camped, lit fire and cooked and ate. Got up from dinner and not more than 10 feet from where I ate, there layed a big rattler on top of a sage brush. We shot it. That was my first rattler, but not the last. We got on the wrong road and was 2 days with only 10 gallons of water. About 3 miles before we got to water, the mules commenced to take on speed and the longer they went, the faster they went. When we came to a small creek they was on the high lope. In the creek, they ran up the creek. They went through the brush trying to drink. The check reigns were up on their necks, they had to go to their knees to drink. We had some time getting the wagon out of the creek. Got things together again. No damage, only to the wagon cover. It was tore some.

Same evening, while we was looking for a place to camp, cattle commenced to come in from all directions. It was a man from Oregon with 10,000 head of cattle going overland to Omaha. A sight like I never saw before - 300 saddle horses. The man had his wife and little boy, about 8 or 10 years and 28 cowboys. All steers from 6 to 10 years old he said. Lots of them would weigh 1800 lbs, with great horns. The next morning the boss sent 3 riders to escort us thru the cattle. They treated us very nice.

The thing of any concequence was at Roses Fort [*Ross's Fort, Idaho*]. We got too close to the reservation and the Indians gathered around us and got in our wagons and took all our grub. They left us nothing except a few potato and salt. 5000 Indians and us 5 whitemen. "Suppose if I said I was scared you would not believe me?"

Well, then we started with our potatoes and salt. We didn't know anything about the fort. No, I didn't know what a fort meant. We drove up a creek a mile or two and with chains we locked the mules to the wheels of our wagons. The next morning I got up at brake of day to cook potatos, all we had. I saw a nice pile of wood just over the little stream and went to get it and saw, I think a full acre of Indians rolled in their buffalo robes. I need not tell you how long I staid there. I woke the others up. We left without bidding our neighbors goodby. We didn't eat our potatoes that morning.

The next day, about 3 o'clock, we came in sight of a house. I was the youngest. They

Horace Hand at Glendale, Montana
Taken about 1880
He is braiding a whip. Stories are told that he was very good with a whip. He could use a whip to take a fly off of his horse's back and never touch the horse.
From Maggie's Photo Album.

camped at water and they sent me over to see about grub. I went to the cabin and found a man, told him our trouble. He laughed at me. He was cooking. The more I told, the more he laughed. I told him I wasn't broke, I could pay him but he only would talk about something else. Finely he had the meal ready. All at once he said to get a plate there and have a bite with him. I commenced to feel better then. I got the plate and ate. He would stop me from eating and then he would start me eating again. He kept this up for more than an hour till I quit of my own accord. He said you ain't hurt a bit. He took me out to his meat house. Their hung a nice fresh slattered [*slaughtered*] calf. He says how much can you carry? He cut me about 50#. He gave me about 10# flour. I asked him how much I owed him. Nothing. He showed me his horses, about 20 head. Nice ones. He said to me, I want you to take this chuck to them fellows and come back here and stay with me. I got a home for you that will amount to more than you can do working for wages. I never saw him since that I know of. We mixed flour and water, cooked flapjack and ate until daybreak.

The next place we came to was Eaglerock, now Idaho Falls, then the termise of the Utah and Northern. We got 2 pair of mules shawed and sold a dog for $10.00 to Con Orem - 2 mules for $250.

Nothing of any note until we got to Ryons Canyon. The stage ahead of us was held up and robbed. We heard about it before we got to the place. We saw the mask they used and some papers scattered about on the ground. We met bull teams. 10 yoke of oxen and 3 wagons to the team and 10 teams to the train and extra cattle - 25 head made 225 to each outfit. We also met mules - 10 mules, 2 wagons to the team. 10 teams made a train.

At Red Rock, Webber hired to David Metlen to do ranch work. I saw him next in Houlton, Maine in 1910. He was married and with 1 adopted daughter. He made his money in Montana.

We got to Glendale July 18, 1879. When we got to Glendale things was flurishing, a new smelter under construction. I got work making brick. Short job. Then I got work halling lumber from a sawmill for Wm. Thompson, one time mayor of Butte. I worked for 2 years for him.

I bought an outfit of my own and made lots of money on ore halling. Took another lumber contract and lost all I had.

I worked for the J. T. Murphy Transportation Company and worked for 5 years and 8 months without loosing one days pay. They sold the outfit. I went to work for them in Helena wholesale and retail store of general store. Didn't like the work. Left and worked for John Duffy, a wagon boss at Marysville, Montana. The R.R. came in. I left then and ran an ore outfit for A. L. Pickett at Dewey, Montana. The mill shut down. I bought a ranch at Wise River, Montana. Got some horses, hauled ore, logs and freight to Gibbonsville, Idaho.

When I write this and think and look over the trail which I have been all over, more than once since, and see the improvements that has been done. The whole country was wild. No settlers to amount to any thing. Now to see the farm buildings, rail roads, sugar factorys, smelters and city, roads and streets, schools, green fields and fence, ditches and so on. Some work has been done. What will it look like in 50 years hence? [*I found a note on some more typed information of Susan Hand's and she states, "This was written in 1927. Pa did this for me one winter week end because I had to bring a pioneer tale to some H.S. class." - mc*]

Glendale

Horace landed in Glendale 1879, a young man of 18. Got work at brickyard, the work he liked, having worked in Denver at a brick yard. The foreman in Denver begged him to stay, as he had a son of about the same age and wanted a companion for him and both grow in that trade. Hearing of greener pastures farther on he quit and started for Montana. Dan McMaster, needing miners, persuaded him to come up to Hecla and mine. One night was enuf in the dark hole with a candle and that ended his mining career. Gave up his candle to the next fellow. Having worked several years in the logging camp in Maine, it was an easier matter getting a job driving team hauling ore from Hecla to the smelter in Glendale. John L. Murphy of Helena hired him to run his stables in Glendale. He [*Murphy*] having the contract for hauling the bullion to Melrose and all freight back. At one time he ran the train way from Hecla to Greenwood. Ore was put in small cars on a track, which were drawn by horses down to the concentrator. That was dangerous - often killed horses. When the ore was hauled by team and wagon there were many dangerous places on the road, slick pitch where rough locks had to be put on the wheels before going down pitches then the rough locks had to be taken off. If a driver failed to do this, it was almost certain death to either driver, mule or horses. Then often a poor driver slid off of the road causing himself and neighbor drivers a lot of delay and extra work. These roads had to be kept up by the company. Men, hired with pick and shovels, to keep them as fit as possible. Then none too good as they, at that time, did not have machinery for road building as of today. In the later capacity of hauling freight Horace knew everyone in the town of 2000 or more. When in Glendale he was affiliated with organizations for the betterment of his country - was a vigilante.

When the smelter ran they used other minerals for fluxing - silica, iron ore and lime. The iron ore was mined in Soap Gulch above Melrose. They went by Pond's place, now Grant's, forded the river there. This was nearer and in those days they thot nothing of fording. It was on those trips Horace became acquainted with Jim Garrison, he being a farm boy from Iowa and only used to driving one span of mules. Jim had a lot of trouble with and invariably got stuck coming down in the McCauley Lane. Then there, Horace did not have the heart to see him stuck - would take off a span or two from his wagon and when he spoke out, Jim would come, mules and all. Then, times again, he'd have to pull him out of the river. Jim soon quit this job, went to Virginia City. Horace staid in Glendale till it began going down. No more hauling to be done and [*he*] begin looking for a ranch or a place to call home.

Narrow Gauge Railway

This photo is of the narrow gauge railway from the mines at Hecla to the concentrator at Greenwood, Montana. Length was about three miles. Horses were used to pull the ore cars back to the mines to be filled and gravity supplied the force for the trip back to the concentrator. Usually nine cars made one train, ridden by three brakemen.

From the Thelma (Hand) Kalsta Collection.

Big Al [*Seth Halbert*] had been teaming in Glendale since in the 80's and they became fast friends and both had the same notion. Work was slack one summer and they decided to take a trip to the Big Hole Basin and look for a ranch. At that time, [*it was*] mostly an open country. They took a camping outfit and went to look the country over good and take plenty of time. Passed the Wise River country, French Creek, Chalk Bluffs, Squaw Creek, Dolittle Creek. Camped all night at Steel Creek July 3. Was quite cold that eve. In getting supper and preparing for the night, a bucket full of water was left standing where they cooked supper. In the morning it was frozen so firm a man could stand on it without breaking. Where upon they both said no this is not a country to farm in. They continued their trip on thru Wisdom and Jackson country, Bloody Dick Creek, Rattlesnake and on down to Dillon and back to Glendale without finding a place any near to their liking. Horace had freighted thru Twin Bridges, Sheridan, Ruby River country before and there found nothing. He had been on freighting trips to Helena, Great Falls, Deer Lodge several times. Nothing looked good to him.

On one of his trips to Great Falls, they were crossing on a ferry, when nearly at shore the cable gave way. The instant they sensed the danger and by their hair raising yell at the horses in the time of need, the team jumped and gained the shore, saving all their worldly possessions, teams, harness and rigging of all kind for heavy freighting. This trip proved to be a failure. They went down to the Crazy Mountain country for a job which proved a fake. It was on this trip Horace

Dewey's Flat, Quartz Hill and Vipond Park Mining Districts

Dewey's Flat was located about 1876 or 1877 by Dave Dewey. This was before a wagon road was built up the canyon. He located it for a town and mill site. Later he left and took up the ranch known as the Farmer ranch near Feely, Montana.

Dewey's is on the Big Hole river in Beaverhead county, six miles west of Divide. The history of Dewey's is closely linked with that of Quartz Hill, which is located six miles south of Dewey's and is close to Vipond park on the south and west. The elevations is 2200 feet higher than at Dewey's which is about 5000 feet. There are four steep grades on the road from Dewey's to Quartz hill.

The Monroe company started work at Quartz Hill about 1877. They took out ore and built a 60 stamp mill at Dewey's but owing to some financial troubles the mill never operated.

In 1879 the Partridge brothers, Nick, Harry, and John owned the Lone Pine mill at Quartz Hill. Allen Hay, Jack Brodridge, George Pettingill, and Billie Spurr worked claims on Quartz Hill. The Partridge brothers had an arrasta where the pump station is now located on the Big Hole river. There they worked the ore from Quartz Hill and did very well. Allen Hay also had an arrasta at Dewey's at the mouth of the canyon. Here he worked his ore and the ore taken from other prospects at Quartz Hill. These operations were quite profitable.

I hauled ore from the mines at Quartz Hill to the mill at Dewey's. The surface of Quartz Hill and surrounding vicinity was literally covered with boulders that carried free milling silver ore. From one boulder I remember of hauling 40 tons good free milling ore.

In 1888, some developing company, I think it was called the American Developing company, bought the Monroe property, also the prospects since owned by the Partridge brothers, Allen Hay, Jack Brodridge, George Pettingill Billie Spurr and the One Pine and other property. They then built a new 120 stamp mill on the sight of the Monroe mill at Deweys. This they ran with some success for about five months. Then it was sold to an English syndicate for a large sum of money. They named it the Lone Pine company, after the Lone Pine mine, which was considered the best one of the group of mines on the hill. This mill paid well for about two years. But all these years the ore had to be hauled six miles over those steep grades to the mill at Dewey's. In order to eliminate this long haul they tore the mill down at Dewey's and moved it up to Quartz Hill on the Lone Pine mine. They operated it there about 18 months. They spend a large amount of money moving it to the hill, where they piped water from the Queen of the Hill in Vipond park, about six miles away to run the mill. Nothing was said about the returns from this mining adventure, but it was supposed to have paid very well. However, all of the sudden, and without any explanation, the mill was torn down and shipped to New Zealand. The manager of the Lone Pine mining company were Captain Harry and Captain Jim Prideaux. During the time that this company operated Dewey's and Quartz Hill were thriving little frontier towns, with their main street lined with thorough-brace stage coaches, ore wagons, passenger and express of all kinds and descriptions. There were stores, saloons, blacksmith shops, hotels, butcher shops and wagon repair shops in both towns. This was in the good old days when everyone owned and drove good horses. Then Dewey's had a population of between 500 or 600. Today it is not so flourishing, but there are still to be seen signs of what has taken place there. The old mill foundations are still visible and also the grade where once the heavily loaded wagons brought the ore to the mill. The mill tailings have been scattered to the four winds, though upon close inspection there are still to be found traces of these tailings.

John, Rod and Alec Leggatt, brothers of the Tobacco Leggatt company of St. Louis, Mo., worked property one or two miles west of the Lone Pine mine about 1879 or 1880. It has been worked off and on ever since with fair returns. Now all these men are dead. Last summer, however, it was worked by the son of the Tobacco Leggats of St. Louis, Missouri.

Another mine close to the Leggatt mine was discovered about 1888 and owned and operated by Professor Kinobby, a German assayer, for the Hecla Consolidated Mining company. This mine always looked very promising, but I do not know what ever became of it. Professor Kinobby went back to Germany and died there.

Continued . . . . . .

always said he could see the steam from the gysers at Yellowstone. He never rambled around after he settled down. Altho when the gold rush to Alaska was on, it was quite a temptation. Many men he knew were going.

There was a good demand for horses in the states so he and Al [*Seth Halbert*] bot up two car loads, shipped them to St. Joe, Missouri. They were all unbroke. When he sold a team, he went with the farmer and helped break the team gentle. This venture was not as paying as they anticipated. The expenses ate up the profits and in order to get rid of them all he traded for a nice stud horse. This he shipped back to Montana. All went well till one night out of Laramie, Wyoming. A train accident found him and his horse and car cross ways on the track. He got out, went to the engineer and demanded him to place the car in the train back of the engine, where it should have been in the first place. He then took the horse up to Wise River and traded it to Lew Griswold for the relinquishment of the homestead.

Griswolds

The Griswolds were early day people. They lived above the bridge at Wise River, going up the road. The family concisted of a father and children. They must have come from Missouri or Kentucky. Was slow, droll people. The father was born with a stub wrist. Must have been an awful handicap to a man with one hand before the day of inventions. They lived on the left hand side of the road at the crossing of Wise River. The corrals and barns then being down on the bottom and [*they*] being early day horse people before the open land was taken up and fenced. The sons were Al and Lew and a daughter, Tillie and son-in-law.

Lew was the most energetic of the bunch, was a teamster and went to the eastern part of the state when it was new and did well with sheep. Al worked around from ranch to ranch and drank up all his money he earned and then expected people to keep him. I don't know where he went to. The daughter and husband left and the old man was left alone. There was talk of sending him to the poor house. Mrs. Deno, being an old-timer and friend of the poor and sick, took him home with her up French Gulch and kept him till he died a few years later.

John and Walter Lawrence

......Continued
Dewey's Flat, Quartz Hill and Vipond park Mining Districts

Next to Professor Kinobby's mine is a mine owned by John Evans in 1890-95. This mine ran good in free milling silver. He shipped ore to Butte, but the returns were not very encouraging for some reason.

In 1885 Al Brubaker and Isaac Dodgson Sr., discovered the Keystone mine, in Keystone gulch near Wise River. They built an arrasta mill at the mouth of Wise River, where they ran the ore, but could not save it, though the ore was good.

Scot and George Galbraith in 1883 to 1892 built an arrasta three miles above the Flat on the Big Hole river. They picked float and mined it to run the arrasta mill. It paid for a short time.

Three miles south of the Lone Pine is the Grey Jockey, discovered in 1867 by John and Billy Vipond. Rich ore was taken out and hauled to Butte. This paid big dividends. It was patented by the Vipond brothers. In 1892 it was sold for $60,000 to the Grey Jockey company. They ran it 18 months and claimed they lost the lead. Then they closed it down. This was free milling ore, also.

The Queen of the Hill was discovered by a man named Cox, who died in about 1887. It is about one and one-half miles southwest of the Grey Jockey mine. It fell into the hands of Virgil Jennings and has been worked off and on ever since. Now there is a party from Butte operating it. It runs in milling gold.

R. Z. Thomas discovered a mine about two miles west of the Queen of the Hill in or about 1885. It yielded lead and silver. It paid well enough to ship the ore to Omaha. One car netted over all expenses, $1400. Thomas died. I still think there is plenty of ore in that vicinity. It is located on Little Sheep creek, which runs into Wise River from near the Vipond Park.

Signed, Horace Hand

Written by Horace Hand for the historical files of the Beaverhead Mining Association

---

Opposite of Honaker Creek where Vipond Creek came down, Walter Lawrence had a small place. The soil was gravel and flint and was not a good producing place. Never the less, John Lawrence's brother Walter and wife and family lived there for a few years. One year he raised oats and Horace took his binder and bound it. When he had to go a long distance, he put the binder on a wagon. Road was bad. They were not made, just traveled.

Men up and down the valley made no bones of telling how Walter killed Dodgson's cattle and took the beef out in the night and sold them in Butte. That kind of business was carried on a lot in those days.

Walter had married an older sister of Mrs. John Lawrence quite early and brot her out. Everyone liked Jennette and hated Walter. He moved. He took his family to Winnipeg, Manitoba and there got work at a R.R. yards. While there, he invented something on a Pullman sleeper and got good pay for his invention. He then went back to New Brunswick and bot his father's old home. He went so high there (women and wine), his children were big enuf to see his folly and ran him away. He went to Vancouver B.C. He soon found John Lawrence. When Walter landed in Vancouver B.C. and he needed work. John hired him to help on a house John was building. John could not get along with him. Later he [*Walter*] came to Mrs. Lawrence and wanted a saw - she lent it to him. Then later someone picked up a paper and saw where he was in a morgue, not a dollar or a friend, the last of crazy Walter. He was walleyed, very ugly. I can't see how Jeanette ever married him. His wife is dead. The children live in New Brunswick. Scotch Corner was where the Lawrences lived.

John Lawrence was born in New Brunswick at Scotch Corner. The Lawrences and Hays and a great many other families there, were intermarried in many families. It would be a large job to ferret them all out, as there were many of each family. John's mother was a Hay. John's older brother came out earlier, then John, and was never seen or heard tell of.

About this time in the east, New Brunswick, Nova Scotia, times were hard and the grown ups, as in all ages, wanted to go. Those days the west beckoned them on. So, with John, Walter and B.B. (B.B. was a cousin of Johns) Lawrence came to Montana. The same year Horace came, but a few months apart (1879).

They, too, came to Ogden, paid their way (paid 4 cents per lb. for extra luggage) with some teamsters coming this way. They were going to Dewey's Flat where their uncle, Alen Hay, lived. Uncle by that time was growing old. He had a quartz mill and mines (was thot to be wealthy). Some say it was thru Alen that John got a start and the ranch from Griswolds. But so be it, John stuck when he once got a foothold.

John was a tall, angular fellow, slightly bent with a bald head (early). When I first came to the country, he was the laughing stock of the country for he had often tried to court the girls - he failed. His team and rigging was always a misfit. A small horse and a large one or an old mare and a stallion that was never taught to behave and quit squalling when a mare was in sight. His clothes had seen many summers, so much so the coat was faded a shade lighter on the back. His face was hatchet shaped and when he got real interested in telling a story, he sniffed and twisted his nose. There was an old cabin on the ranch. I hardly think he built it as he never built much. An old horse barn and a few corrals, concisted about all in the farm buildings. They were built back a way from the road clost to the river. There was a spring a few steps away, up in the edge of a river slough, where they got their water to drink and house use. One could see at a glance he was not healthy (I believe it was the alkali water ailed them always). For all up and round there was deep alkalies to the edge of the hill and in the road. Sometimes one could hardly get thru the road for alkali boils.

He had a horse corral up on a knoll, clost to the road and out of sight of the house. The hay meadow was large but concisted of wild hay and sloughs. He had a ditch out of Wise River, came out just below our ditch a ways. He most always hired some old fellow to irrigate. When the horses and cattle had been turned out in the hills, then John rode the range continually looking after the horses, bringing in the mares to breed ever so often, whether his or the other fellows, they were seen to and herded well. So the colts increased. Mares from other ranges were kept herded in. He never talked about his business to anyone, but among the men this was known. Others said nothing either. After a time he accumulated a nice lot of cattle but he was so stingy with his hay he lost many each fall. Cattle and horses, alike, all looked fat to him. In the winter he often followed Horace to the hills for poles and sometimes stulls, but he either did not know how to get into the timber or was too weak. He invariably waited till Pa broke the road or made it in to the hills.

Friends and neighbors of Maggie and Horace's
Wise River-Dewey area
Identified as
Walter Hay, John Hay, Mr. & Mrs. Robbins,
John, Walter & Janette Lawrence
Photo taken 1892
From the Rock Hand Collection

Sometime after the freighting was no more for the winter, Horace went into the hills there above the John Lawrence house, looked out the timber he wanted for stulls and made the log road. They are generally made by falling old logs and brush in clearing the road and often up a ravine, throwing in brush and logs to catch the snow. When John found out Horace was preparing the road, John sniffed and twisted his nose and said, "I think I'll get out some stulls too. Times are hard and I could make a little money." He never would have tackled it alone. So Horace would not be mean to John and would say "Yes, come along, that will be fine." So John took his good team and old fussy mare and stallion. It was awful hard to make the grade and when he got up there he could only bring a few stulls. His team would not hold on the hill and was hard to get down, but John hauled stulls and so did Horace. He thot he was doing fine, and so he was as he had never growed up to logging as Horace had, from 13 years on. Horace always had new stories to tell about John and his team every evening.

John was always saying, ho, ho, to his horses, right or wrong it was always the ho, ho, ho. Horace did less commanding and the horses understood just what to do when spoken to. Even Horace's swear word they understood and stopped or started as commanded. A yell and oath, his team would pull to the very last, always things moved when he gave the word.

Time went on, John batched, sometimes kept a "who so ever", for he never turned anyone away. After a long days ride, would come back, often to a cold cabin, rolled out some sour dough bread that had been rolled up in a dirty dish towel, dug (blue) some boiled meat out of a pot and ate alone. No, with his faithful dog at his side. It was not his fault, he just seemed to be unlucky, yes, he had tried. E. G. Bryant said John had crossed the continent three times to get a wife and no luck.

When he became more prosperous, more hay, cattle and horses, John often hired a cook, once Mr. & Mrs. Percy Gentle and children. They were there several times, but Percy was one of the liquor loving and horse lovers. When he got a horse and buggy and a few drinks, there was no holding him. Then Annie and Dave Kennedy came out from New Brunswick and they staid two or three years. We thot he should have married her and drove Dave away, as Dave was rattled. Then he had a good, steady cook, clean, thrifty. The cabin was not too large either for their crowds, two bedroom hardly large enuf to get around in and one big room, cook stove, table and chairs and that was full. Then after they left, he had different cook till the fall of 1907. That summer the hay was good and good price so he got Pa to bale some hay for him. He always had more in the stack than it baled out. But even so, he sold his hay. Fred

School Meetings

For years John Lawrence and Horace were school trustees. The third one generally did not care and left all the business to Horace and John. The store keeper at the Flat was the clerk. So there were no call for a school meeting. Their school meetings were held wherever they chanced to meet on the road, thereby giving their horses a chance to rest. It was generally agreed that John hire the teacher with the hope that John might get a wife, often changing or as John seen fit. It was all right with everyone. This went on for years till about 1900 when we were in the Wise River District. Then I dare say John continued in the capacity of trustee till he left in 1918. School got along just as good as now.

From Maggie's writings.

Wilson was with John that fall and pretty good man to take care of things. John was going once more to New Brunswick for a wife. Fred took care of things and fed the cattle well. They faired better when John was away. After several weeks Fred got word John was married and was coming home and to meet him and wife at Divide a certain day. There had been a batchlor there for some time and as long as Fred was a lone he did not care. But a woman coming, with the cabin so dirty, that would never do. Johnnie Hand happened to be there and Fred said to John, you scrub and clean this house out while I go to Divide for the bride. When they arrived the cabin was as presentable as a boy 12 could make it.

That night or the next we were all going down to shivaree and meet the new bride but on going all the children were sick. They had planned so to go, was too bad. Mr. and Mrs. Davis and child and myself, I believe was all. We set, talked a while and went home (no lunch). We should have taken it, but did not.

December 24, 1909, Jessie was born. Before Jessie was born Mrs. Lawrence was poorly. Mrs. VanWart was with Mrs. Lawrence but she finally came to my house and left Mrs. Lawrence. Then when Mrs. Lawrence was sick, I often went down a day or two at a time and help nurse. She finally had to go to Butte and be cared for till the child came. Then it was comical to see those two old people take care of it. They still went a lot.

After a year or so, the house being so small, John got out house logs and built quite a respectable log house with more rooms, a basement and a well (in that alkali swamp) on the porch. Then one summer while driving a buckrake or derrick, an accident happened to John. His horses never were broke gentle or dependable. John was kicked in the chest near the heart. He suffered constantly and walked more stooped than ever. Good times came shortly after he was hurt and he sold to a Mr. Schmidt (a German). Mr. Schmidt worked and exposed his self while ailing from the flu and died. The wife, an ignorant German, and two children were left to run the ranch. A failure could not be averted. She could not speak English well or even understand it so she was an "easy mark".

John had sold the ranch to them on terms and when she was left she could not meet the terms. John had sold most of his horses and cattle at the high prices of the times, only selling a few cows and horses with the ranch. Then he had a sale and sold off all the household goods and machinery. We think this is where John coined his money. How much, might have been 30 thousand.

Anyway, now with John and Schmidt both gone and Mrs. Schmidt had to, after a year, give up the ranch. Mrs. Lawrence coming back each time a transaction was made. When Mrs. Schmidt moved away, at the time of the flood, Mrs. Lawrence got damages from the Power Company. Dana Miller, being a kin thru his wife Georgia to John, he weazled in Mrs. Lawrence to let him have the old place and he would make it boom. So Mr. and Mrs. B.B. Lawrence thot too, Dana was the man. He made all kinds of promises how he and sons would run the place if she, Mrs. Lawrence, would give him $2000.00 to fix it up. So she did as Dana ordered and he also got his clutches on the old Trueman and Jack Davis place, which John had bot on the verge of a boom. Well, with Dana's management and the two thousand, he built a milking barn, bot a power milker and separator and started up business in a business way. At times, when he chanced to milk a cow, he thot he could hear the stream say, Harry Gilbert, Harry Gilbert over and over again. Then he came to be thinking he could never pay Mrs. Lawrence for that with Harry Gilbert in the bank waiting for the payments, so when payments failed to roll in as due, Mrs. Lawrence too began to tumble. Then she came back (Pa told her to look out) with her dander up and took the place back and sold it to Joe Potts for $7000, which she got.

Dana's oldest son wanted to ranch the river place. She trusted him several years, got nothing and finally foreclosed.

After selling out and settling up his business, John thot his wife never would have any trouble. But this old changing world, John could not trust. He settled in Vancouver and less than a year he came back, nurse, doctor and wife and child so as to fix things safer for her. Got home in June 1921 and lived just a week.

Lucy Lawrence & John Robbins

Lucy was John Lawrence's sister. She came out a little later than John. Worked at the Flat and there met John Robbins. They took up a small ranch above Tice and George Dodgson, clost to the timber on Meadow Creek. Their only child died.

They had horses and cattle, and sheep, just a few, cut their hay. She sold butter and they lived there quite comfortable in a nice roomy cabin he had built. She was a good neighbor and everyone liked Lucy. They lived there several years, he sold horses. Often Dal More would stay with them and help break horses.

Lucy took sick and in about two years died. Lucy could never be equaled. But John must have a wife, so he courted a cook that was working for John Lawrence and he got her and a lot of hangers on, as she had several children. They came and visited, till they ate all the sheep up and she demanded more. So he had to let her go. He finally moved to

Anaconda. Then he began to ail. Came to Melrose about the time we sold the Donovan place. The spring we moved here to Lavon, he died. John Lawrence got word and buried him at Divide along side Lucy. What he had left, John got - much or little?

Mrs. Bertha VanWart

Mrs. VanWart came as far as Dillon on the train in the spring of 1881. The stage left Dillon for Glendale, nine passengers inside and nine on top. Roads were fearful, water high and in crossing a slough, the stage tipped over. Mrs. VanWart sprang out like a frightened wolf and was the first one on the ground. She came as a Miss Jackson to be the bride of Gilbert VanWart. The day she arrived, Gilbert was not expecting her, he was dirty and shaggy - she knew her bargain. Friends took Gil to the side and advised him to slick up and wait a few days till she got acquainted with him, which he did, and they were married in due time. He was a faithful worker all thru life. She did not like Glendale and they moved to Butte, never owned a home, moved 40 times in 60 years (or about). Made a good living and that was all. Raised one boy. Mrs. Van was about Horace's age or one year older.

Gingerbread

1 cup molasses
1/2 cup sugar
1 tsp. cinnamon, cloves, ginger
1 tsp. soda in 1 cup boiling water
2 1/2 cups flour
2 eggs beaten well and put in last thing
1 scant cup butter and lard mixed

- Mrs. VanWart - from Susan Hand Collection

Note by Susan Hand written to Janice Hand in 1989 states, *"Bertha and Gilbert VanWart were friends of Pa's from New Brunswick and Maine. She had the accent of East Canada. As a young woman she worked as a seamstress in 1880's or 90's for 50 cents a day and board. She was an excellent seamstress, slow, and particular. She lived to be in her 90's, died in 1950's in Butte. Sometimes she stayed with us after Gil died in 1925.*

When I brought in the cows on a summer eve I could smell the gingerbread almost from the barnyard! So good with a glass of milk! Maggie Hand baked this in a big cast iron muffin pan in a wood stove. No temperature given, probably 350. degrees."

Rebecca J. "Jane" Bryant

In 1882, Elbridge G. "E. G." Bryant, wife, Rebecca J. "Jane" (Howard) Woodson Bryant, and family moved to Dewey's Flat from Soap Gulch, where they had staid a year after coming from California to Montana. They had come to the new country by the advice of her brother, Mr. Howard, of Glendale. Times were good and she cooked for boarders wherever she was to help support the large family, Annie, Tillie, Sherman, Maude and Minnie. Mrs. Bryant had come overland in her younger day from New York state [*being married to a Mr. Morterman Woodson - mc*] with a child. After landing in California, Mr. Woodson died. Then she married E. G. Bryant, a young man from Old Town, Maine.

When a young man in the logging woods of Maine, E. G. got in trouble with another logger and felt like he would have to leave quick. He made his way down the river to Bangor on the Kennebic to the ocean, boarded a ship that was leaving port for San Francisco around the horn, as flunky in the kitchen. Naturally he entered the logging country on Feather River, California. There he met Mrs. Woodson and married her. Being an energetic woman, she still continued cooking for camps while he worked in the woods. They moved from Feather River to Placerville in the gold region. There she cooked and reared her family. At one time she traded her gold watch for a cow so her children could have milk. He often took long vacations. They then moved to Virginia City and Carson City, Nevada and other towns nearby, always cooking for boarders, school teacher or anyone wanting board and room, if she had it to spare, at the same time keeping her little brood clean and those of school age in school.

At Dewey there were 8 or 9 families, McKinzies, two Trueman families, John and Ed, Alen Hay and Clad Hay, the Denos, Lebos, McKays, Dodgsons. There were lots of men working in the timber, getting out poles and logs for W. A. Clark. They came and went. All had to eat and most of them slept in tents. Mrs. Lebo, a Flathead Indian, cooked, always had more than she could feed, so the Bryant's heard of this place and moved hither. McKays moved away and Bryants moved in the house the McKays lived in, which was Alen Hay's old two story log house used for a hotel. Before Mrs. Bryant and daughter, Annie, could get the house in shape for the first meal, there were hungry men wanting dinner, supper and [a] nights lodging. Annie and mother were taxed to their utmost to feed all that came. While they were yet unloading, the McKinzie children, Earnest and Mollie, came over from fishing and wanted to borrow potatoes for their dinner. Potatoes were high and scarce, as at this time a very few potatoes were raised in the territory.

Kept Corpse Packed in Ice While Bandplayers Learned Funeral Dirge

Dick Dawson, Veteran Montanan, Recalls Time When Famous Glendale Silver Cornet Band Came Into Being in What Is Now One of State's Ghost Towns

Free Press Bureau

ANACONDA, DEC. 15 - Back in the days before Montana folks condescended to regard the American penny as a medium of exchange and the man with a parched larynx was assured of a gargle of real tonsil varnish for a "bit", the bustling little town of Glendale came into being on Trapper Creek, about five miles above the present site of Melrose. The town' existence was due to the fact it furnished an ideal location for the smelter that handled the silver and lead ores mined at Mine Town, some ten miles further up the gulch.

About that time-- it was in the late seventies-- Glendale was regarded as one of the coming towns in Montana territory, and it was only natural that its residents were always ready and willing to boost any project that had a tendency to give the community a place in the sun. All of which accounted for the organization of the Glendale Silver Cornet band, one of the first musical combinations in this part of the state. During the course of its brief, but colorful career, the Glendale band was the pride and glory of the town it represented, and its fame soon spread from hamlet to hamlet.

According to Dick Dawson, veteran Anacondan and one of the former residents of Glendale, the band's repertoire was decidedly limited, but what it lacked in the way of diversity was more than offset by changing the time and tempo of such airs as the players knew. For instance, if the band was playing at some picnic dance, it would place a piece in two-four and four-four time for a march or quadrille, and then turn about and play it in three-four for a waltz.

But there came a time when none of the "tunes" known to the players would fit the occasion. One of the prominent residents of the community had died, and his last request was that the band play a dirge at his funeral. Provision for that ceremony had been made by the man, and the band was to receive a specified sum of money for its trouble. The trouble was, that before the dirge could be played, the band had to learn how to play it.

There was no licensed undertaker in the community at the time, and embalming was an unknown profession in these parts. The leader of the band, however, was a typical New England Yankee, whose ancestry ran back into the hinterland of Bonnie Scotland, and he had no intention of allowing the promised fee to find its way into other channels. He immediately assembled his musicians and they began practising on a funeral dirge.

Made Tin Coffin

The weather was warm, however, and while that had no effect on the musician, it did on the body. In order to keep the latter from decomposing, the bandmaster had Mr. Dawson, who followed the vocation of tinsmith, construct a tin coffin. The body was placed in this and covered with ice. There it remained for five days, at the end of which the band had progressed to a point where it was capable of playing the dirge.

Word of what was being done spread to all the outlying camps and on the day of the funeral, the entire country side was in attendance. It was the largest and most spectacular funeral ever held in the famous old camp.

On another occasion the band leader was seized with a brilliant idea. He decided that instead of assembling at the town hall for weekly practise, that the band visit the homes of different residents and double shoot the turn by turning the practising into a serenade. One day in particular the organization happened to halt outside the office of the justice of the peace, just as the latter was endeavoring to compose a legal document, resplendent with the proper number of "wherebys," "whereases", etc. The justice was a very irritable man who hated the band, its leader and everything else that was connected with it. Consequently, he was far from pleased when the sound of what was intended for martial music fell upon his ears.

"Look here!" he cried, pushing up to the bandmaster. "If you don't stop this infernal racket, I'll go and fetch my constable."

But the bandmaster was equal to the occasion.

"You can't do that," he replied, "That's him, over there, pounding the bass drum."

Continued . . . .

Business was good and Mrs. Bryant bot a lot nearby and built a big two story log hotel. For years Mrs. Bryant ran the hotel. When they moved to the new hotel, there was plenty to do - E. G. Bryant looked after the wood, kept fires and was general roust about in the winter. Early in the spring he would begin to plan on his trip up to his cabin, but was mostly plans, for as he grew older he staid clost to home.

A mill, being built by an English syndicate, bid fair to be a thriving little burg. In the meantime, the country above in the Big Hole Basin was being settled, and a saw mill below town on the river. Most everyone stopped at Bryant's to get a good meal and visit with E. G., as they often called Mr. Bryant. He always had a new stock of good stories that entertained all classes.

Transients coming thru, having heard of Bryant, was sure to find some excuse to stop and have dinner, wile away an hour or two and listen to Bryant's Bar [*bear*] stories or when he was in Maine on the Kennebec - always something, conversation never lagged.

When they run the old hotel, he ran a bar in it. An old wood chopper came in and got full. Bryant ordered him out, where upon the wood chopper shot Bryant in the arm. For some time he was laid up with a wound. A doctor was called, the wound dressed and cool water from the well was used on a cold pack to keep down the swelling, his younger daughter, Maude, being the attendant. Maude was a small girl at the time, running around in her bare feet with not much to do till then. She became both nurse and nursing maid to her father. She would bring cold water from the well, take a bleached flour sack, wet it and wrap the arm. No one thot of blood poisoning then. The articles were never sterilized, as such a thing then was never heard of in these out of way places. Soon the arm knitt.

Many good prospects began to pay. Alen Hay's arraster or mill had been worked steady also. Partridge, below the canyon, was getting good

> **Corpse in Ice - Continued . . .**
>
> **Into Oblivion**
>
> Like the town it represented, the Glendale Silver Cornet band is now only a memory. With the closing of the mines at Mine Town, Glendale went out of existence about 20 years ago, and according to tourists and others who visited the section during the summer months, nothing remains to cause one to believe the place was once the site of a town that was once predicted to be the metropolis of Montana.
>
> Anaconda Standard
> Date unknown
> From Maggie's Scrap Book

paying silver, and lead and a little gold ore from Quartz hill. [For] working men, woodchoppers and prospectors, silver was a good price and on the raise. Then there were men seeking ranches farther up the river where there was acres yet unclaimed. Onward they came seeking new environments and a living. The lone one or two arrrasterman worked, got out ore and run their mill or rustic. Soon the word got out and men with capital came, assayed the ore, found it good, bot out the little men and built mills. Men came with families and all their belongings, then log cabins went up as by magic. Store men came, blacksmiths to ply their trade, as the place swarmed with teams, horses and mules-all needed horses shod, wagons repaired, rough locks & [etc], various fixtures for wagons or sleighs. Butchers - cattle could be gotten almost anytime of year from ranchers clost by. With all this moving humanity, Mrs. Bryant kept steadily at work and sometimes as the work increased she had to hire cooks and even waiters, for in time her daughter married and left her to hire the help needed to run the hotel.

My Brother, Seth "Big Al" Halbert

Al [*Seth Henry Halbert*] was born at Orangeville, Orange County, Indiana in 1857. With his parents, he moved to Coursen's Grove, Kansas in 1875, when nearly grown - 18 years. In a few years he went to Colorado, worked in many occupations of the times. One time he freighted out nickel ore on a burro pack train in a very rough mountain country, then going from one camp to another, freighting most of the time. Later he went to Oregon, Washington and other states till he heard of Glendale and came hither in early 1880's. Here he drove 10 mule ore teams from Hecla to the ore camp and Glendale.

When Al drove the eight mule teams for Eliel and hauled the most of their supplies into Gibbonsville, Idaho for a branch store of the Eliels of Dillon, George Jewel, a Dillon blacksmith, did all the blacksmithing for the company. Anything the mules and wagons needed was made or mended by Jewel. They soon grew to be fast friends. The rough lock links were made and assembled by George. Sometimes one chain would weigh (?) 300 *lbs* [*300 lbs crossed out, so do not know how much it weighed - mc*]. Often two of these monstrous cables were fastened under the hind wheels to help hold the wagon from pushing the wheels down a steep hill.

The mules were shod here, also the extra saddle horse. All was made ready while the wagons were being loaded for the long trek over mountains and valleys that lie in the road to Gibbonsville. It took about two weeks for a round trip. Al was a good careful driver, always looking to the welfare of his team, which he was very proud of. When he took up the reigns, climbed to the seat, spoke to the leader, all fell into their collars. Bells pealed out the note of their starting on the long trip. Nothing daunted the team of mules, dusty road or wet roads, rain or snow, they would come in the little mining town over the continental divide on time, with the bells pealing out their glad herald of their arrival, after covering 120 miles.

Once Al's load concisted of barrels of whiskey. That night, to have something fixed he drove the wagons (2) into George Jewell's blacksmith shop for repairs. They both decided they would like to taste the stuff. George was wize, he drove a hoop back about 1/2 inch and then drove a nail in and thru the barrel, drew out a quart, then drove back the hoop in place. Neither one were drunkards, but could take a drink and go on about their own business and let it alone. Al, on these treks, always took a jug for a drink in the morning or to treat a friend on the road. He never got drunk, one drink was enuf.

> **DEWEY'S FLAT BOOMED**
>
> In April of 1886, according to the rural press correspondent, "business is ever booming at Dewey's flat, the Paris of the Big Hole valley. Kilkenny and Galbraith's mill is turning out some fine bullion as is A.M. Madison's mill. Brubaker and Dodson are erecting an arastra on Wise Creek. Immigration into the Big Hole basin is steadily increasing. Butte men are locating all the water rights for the purpose of starting an extensive lumber project. They will, it is understood, supply the Utah and Northern with ties for the purpose of widening the road" from a narrow to a standard gauge.
>
> ---
>
> The "biggest transfer of mercantile property that Montana has ever seen" is reported from Glendale. Knippenburg, Gaffney and Gates had bought out the Armstrong store at Glendale "with its stock of $50,000 worth of merchandise, a bank which will have a capital stock of $75,999, a store at Lyon City with a stock of $20,000 and a store at Melrose with a stock of $30,000". Knippenburg was the manager of the Hecla Mining company, Gaffney was a Glendale merchant and Gates was a Helena drummer.
>
> ---
>
> The third annual meeting of the Montana Stockmen's association was held at Billings in 1886 with an enrollment of 320 cattle barons. In the parade, which was headed by the military band from Fort Keogh, there were 100 mounted cowboys in line. Speakers, who were railroad men, favored the idea of making St. Paul a packing center in preference to Chicago.
>
> ---
>
> In 1886 the Moulton was making a good showing as a silver mine. On April 20 of that year it made one of its regular bi-weekly shipments; it consisted of 12 bars of silver valued at $18,507.76.
>
> Article found in Maggie's scrapbook
> Source Unknown

Another trip the load concisted of canned goods and some buckets of candy. Horace was with him this time. They both loaded at Divide this time. They had some trouble and if they stopped they could not make Hollinsworth's on Swamp Creek for the night. They must make it for the night, so they watered at the river crossing their teams and pulled on. Being used to a square at noon, they each one decided candy would be pretty good just then. So they opened a bucket and ate their fill. This called for water, so they opened a can of tomatoes which quenched their thirst. Eliel always told them that anything they wanted to help themselves.

A man by the name of Loren Jones was manager of this branch store, he had been a trusted employee for years of the management. After managing this branch store for a few years, Al noticed the orders seemed queer. Once his load was a full sized merry go round and baby buggies, a queer order for this mining camp where one never expected to see such luxuries. Shortly after their delivery, Mr. Jones took a trip and later found he was suffering from a serious ailment and he never was able to come back. Then gradually the mine failed to produce and Gibbonsville went the way of all other mining towns. Some few prospectors held on and made a living, others went to other camps. Some settled on little ranches where the opportunity afforded - along down the North Fork of the Salmon. Others went to Salmon City, a prosperous land mining center.

**Seth 'Big Al' Halbert
1881
Big Al and Team
'Ore Camp to Glendale
From the Rock Hand Collection**

The Sleeping Darky
George Jewell's Joke

While Dr. Bond was on the train at Monida coming in to Dillon, there was a darky on snoring away with his mouth open. A lady says to Doc, "I wish you would put a sock in his mouth, I can't get a bit of rest with his sawing wood that way." Doc says, "Yes, I can do better than that." Going to his pill bags, he got a dose of powdered quinine, stepped back to where the darky was snoring on in regular rhythm. He quickly and silently sifted the quinine into the darky's open mouth and sat down not far away. All at once the darky began to wake up, coughing and making an awful face, saying he had an awful taste in his mouth, that he was sick and that he wondered if there was a doctor on the train. Saying that he had an awful bitter taste in his mouth just like his gall bladder had busted. - True story told by George Jewell.

Clerk and Recorders Office, Beaverhead County, Dillon, Montana, Book 7, page 597.

This Indenture made the 15 day of May in the year of our Lord one thousand eight hundred and ninety. Between Alvin Griswold and Lewis Griswold of Dewey's Flat, Beaverhead County, State of Montana, party of the first part and Horace Hand and Seth Halbert of the same place, the party of the second part. Witnesseth, That the said party of the first part for and in consideration of the sum of ($700.00) Seven hundred Dollars lawful money of the United States of America to them in hand paid by the said party of the second part, the receipt whereof is hereby acknowledged, have granted, bargained, quit claimed and conveyed and by these presents doth grant, bargain, quit claim and convey unto the said party of the second part and to their heirs and assigns forever, all that certain lot, piece or parcel of land situated, lying and being near the Big Hole River and Wise River in the County of Beaverhead, State of Montana, bounded and described as follows: On the West by Dodgson and Brubakers Mill site, on the North by James New's Ranch and on the East by John Lawrences Ranch containing 160 acres more or less.

Together with all and singular, the tenenents, hereditaments and appurteuances thereunto belonging or in anywise appertaining.

In Witness Whereof, The said party of the first part, have hereunto set their hands and seals the day and year first above written

    Signed Sealed and Delivered }   Alvin W. Griswold
    in the presence of   }   Lewis Griswold
State of Montana
County of Beaverhead

On this 15 day of May A.D. One thousand eight hundred and ninety, personally appeared before me, a Justice of the Peace in and for said County, Alvin Griswold and Lewis Griswold whose names are subscribed to the foregoing instrument as the party thereto, personally known to me to be the same persons described in and who executed the said foregoing instrument as the party thereto and who acknowledged to me that they executed the same freely and voluntarily and for the uses and purposed therein mentioned. In Witness Whereof I hereunto set my hand the day and year in this certificate first above written.

                                    Allan Neay
                                    Justice of the Peace

Filed for record May 19th A.D. 1890 at 8:50 Oclock A.M.

                                    W. A. Jones, County Recorder

---

The Ranch at Wise River

[*In 1888 or 1889 Seth 'Big Al' and Horace struck a deal with Lew Griswold for the relinquishment of his homestead on the Big Hole River. Maggie writes that they traded a stallion for the property. The records at the Clerk and Recorders Office, Beaverhead County, Dillon, Montana, Book 7, page 597 provides the document of the completed sale in 1890. - mc*]

Now with a ranch there was plenty to do. A ditch two miles to be made and fencing and cabin so they both [*Al and Horace*] set to work with teams and soon had water. They took the irrigating water for the ranch out of Wise River 2 1/2 mile above. They built a log cabin 14 x 19 ft. and a barn for eight horses. Then, spare times when no logging or freighting jobs could be had, they stayed on the ranch, pulled sage brush, picked rock, and worked on ditches.

Up till this time they could come and go - lock up and go, but now with a cow and chickens someone had to stay or hire some trusty man to stay. It was a lonely place for one man but often a way farer came by - he was always fed. Except in two cases. Horace was irrigating, saw a poor fellow, asked him to go back to the cabin for lunch. [*The man said*], "No by G . This poor d-- fool got drunk and lost his money and now I'll teach him something." He was fixing a line so he could fish and get a meal that way.

Then one day Horace asked Pattengale [*Pettingill*] in and cooked some meat and fryed sour dough pan cakes for him. "No," he says, "I am not hungry you eat them." And no persuading could change him. There were not many people in the country, no fences to litter up the landscape - people only went when needcessity called them and people did with out rather than make extra trips.

People that lived on ranches went out twice a year to Butte to get food and clothing. That would take nearly a weeks time. The Big Hole basin people took longer - no roads to speak of. They most always had wagon sheets and bows to protect the load from rain or snow and also protection for the people from the elements. They quite often took their food and bedding and horse feed and camped out. Grass was plentiful if they cared to hobble their horses to feed.

The basin being a wild hay country, there was no hurry, just to get supplies in for haying, which began in July or August. In the fall the trip must be made before snow got too deep. Some did not camp out, made it to stopping house along the way for their night lodging. This was a rather pleasant trip. They came to know their distant neighbors on those trips.

'ECHOES Of the Long Distant Past'
From files of the Anaconda Standard, by Edward J. Hanmer and in the Montana Standard, May 20, 1956

"The above picture, taken near Divide in the 1880s, shows how they hauled freight in Montana Territory long before the modern 'gas wagons' were even dreamed of. The outfit of mules and horses belongs to 'Big Al' Halbert, known in this section of Montana and nearby mining camps in Idaho as 'one of the best in the business'. 'Big Al' and his helpers for several years were the principal freighters between Dillon and Divide, points on the old Utah Northern railroad, and Gibbonsville, a thriving gold mining camp in Lemhi County, Idaho, which at one time, was said to have a population approximating 3,000. Halbert is seen in the picture standing beside his team in front of the log building."

Photo from the Rock Hand Collection

The ranch so far was a constant drain to Horace and Al. One winter ('92) they cut stulls and hauled them to the bank of Wise River. Butte was in constant demand for logs or stulls for the mines. So they logged that winter clost to home and staid home. They hired a boy to snake the logs out to a pile or skid way. Bill [McClellan] and Al cut the trees, Horace hauled them to the river bank. Al said to Henry, "How many logs have you Henry [Overly]." "Well," he said, "when I get this one and two more I'll have three."

Their teams were true and willing and they could get more work out of them than any man ever lived. A big load hit a stump. The big grey mare pulled so hard she broke a blood vessel and died in the team standing up while they unloaded the logs. They did not realize it till they were ready to go. Others were putting in logs so they rolled them in the river after the scaling in spring and away they went down to Divide where they were caught in a big boom and ran thru the saw mill. When spring came, Horace staid on the ranch and Al, about this time, got a job from the Eliel Brothers driving a six mule team hauling goods in to Gibbonsville, Idaho to a branch store.

Gibbonsville was an old mining camp over the continental divide, a 100 miles from Divide. He kept steady at this till the camp began to go down. Next winter Horace logged with hired help on Jerry Creek. It had been logged before and dams were used to back the water at distances not large enuf to drive any other way. That was very hard dangerous work. One time he came nearly losing his life in trying to break a jam. There was good water this year and they made some money but the company, W. A. Clark, lost the logs. The boom at Divide broke, scattered logs along the river to the Canyon below Beehers. I believe they took a saw mill down there and picked up all they could find and sawed them. The high water took out the road at the Big Rock the spring of 1894. The County Commissioners gave Horace the contract putting it in that September after the water had gone down.

Billie Concella

The Moe place or Buyan place now [*late 1930's*], was once owned by Billie Concella, batchlor. He farmed some of the land. The summer when he was killed in his corral breaking a cayuse, he was alone and was not found for a day when some horse buyer chanced to stop and dicker for a team of horses.

New horses were always in demand in Glendale, hauling ore from Hecla mines to the smelter. And many tons of bullion was hauled to Melrose and shipped. Then the supplies that was hauled back to run the town, was no small item. The hills was open and Billie ran his band of horses on the range most of the year around. Tho he raised oats for his saddle horses and any of the weaker ones that did not fare so well. Before the estate could be settled, a sale was posted sometime in June. At the date set, people came that were interested.

Billie Woodward came down from Divide. Horace and Al were taking up their place on Wise River and needing many ranch supplies, thot they might pick up things there they needed. The sale began. Billie saw that the boys were not buying much. He stepped up, called the boys to one side and said, "Don't you need anything?" "Yes," was their reply, "but we haven't the money." "Well", says Billie, "buy whatever you need and I'll let you have the money." So they did. Bot a cow, a team of horses and the household goods, which was all put up as one, then the field of oats standing ready to be cut, the mower, rake and harness. They went home feeling happy in having a friend like Billie. Now they were in shape to farm. The oats was cut for hay, which they would need for winter feed.

Al mowed the oats down and they brot a boy from Glendale to rake it with a one horse rake. Horace did the cooking and made a hay rack in preparation to stacking the hay. Everything went well till one hot afternoon. The boy went to sleep and fell off the rake into the cup of the teeth. This woke him up and as he was bumped along he hollowed woe, woe, you old grey mare, woe, woe, but the mare kept on making hay and he could not get free till the mare had to cross an irrigating ditch and he escaped in the ditch. By that time Al had seen all the fun and tying up his team, headed the mare off. The boy wanted to go home that evening at Glendale. After this they got a man to rake and help stack till the haying was done. This is an old story I heard the boys tell often.

Dixon & Powell

John W. Powell was a white man married to a half or whole breed. They first lived in Deer Lodge. She was a very capable house wife and mother. They had several children and when Jinks [*a son*] was about 10 years old they moved to the Flat.

I believe Powell was a butcher. He had a steer in the slaughter house up the gulch and was going to butcher it, when a man name of John Rhoeder objected to Powell killing it. They had some words and the situation became tense, whereupon Rhoeder pulled a gun and shot Powell, killing him instantly. Rhoeder fled when he realized what he had done and never to this day was ever heard tell of.

Jinks then went to live with Jimmie New and his mother moved to Idaho, remarried and raised more of a family and their offspring still live there. In 1916 Horace went down with Jinks to look for land, a place to settle and there he met Jink's relatives. He spoke very highly of them.

Jinks grew up with Jimmie New around Wise River and the Flat. After rambling, [*he*] always came back to that country to live. He worked at almost anything, tho mostly gambling, punching cows, fishing and hunting was his long suit. He married a woman that located up Wise River, an all around cow girl, Eva Bennet. The marriage did not last long. She, after buying up ponies of various colors, string them out and started to Los Angeles. In about 1920 Jinks went with a party to hunt big game in Africa. After seeing Africa, the game and diamond mines he came back, had some money, but got in with two slickers in Butte and they got all his money. So he came back to Wise River country a wiser and poorer man. For some time he staid at the old Jimmie New place with Bill Dodgson, till Bill moved. Jinks moved to Dan Edison and Gus Staufferson's place. He liked the wilds of old mother nature and was none to anxious to work.

Dixon & Powell both lived acrost the river from Jimmie New and down a mile, more or less. The place was designated Dog Town. They hunted and sold game, dressed, to town and settlements or where ever there was a demand for wild meat. Later, as I have stated, Powell moved to the Flat and Dixon moved up in the basin [*Big Hole Basin*]. Located a ranch on Steel Creek and there went into the cattle business with Jim Garry as partner. Garry had a good hay ranch clost by.

Jim or James Long

Visiting with Andy Ray, he tells me Jim was born on Long Creek, clost to Bears Island, New Brunswick. Also that he came west about 1888 with some cousins, the Miles. When Andy first heard of him, he was cutting stulls up Seamore Creek for Frank Miles, a cousin. W. A. Clark hired Miles or gave him a contract to put in the stulls and thereby being clost to election, he would incidentally get more votes for Senator, if the foreman told the gang how to vote. A lot of that skulduggery was done in that way at that early date and no doubt bigger schemes are on foot today.

In 1892 Jim was one of several saloon keepers. His place of business was the first house going up thru Dewey to the left. The saloon faced the street, stable in back and then a long log house toward the hill. Jim barbered as a sideline. I often heard men remark how Jim could run up the bill on them by the adding of perfume and powder, plus the shave and haircut, $1.00, $1.50, or $2.50, according to the trimmings. Perhaps he could hardly help gathering money, as he was raised on a farm on Queens Island, one of the many islands in the St. Johns River. Coming to the west where men were free with their money and for him it was hard to pass up.

Up to about this time he was single. The attraction of a winsome divorcee over came him, with a good business, driving team and buggy, a home and being a very pleasant man. After divorcing her husband she soon found Jim. The long evenings they often drove afar. Once or twice called on Horace in his batchelor house. When he had just returned from a grouse hunt, they helped him prepare the feast and partook.

In those days birds were plentiful. Horace had an old grey horse called Sam. Perfectly gentle. Never bothered about getting off his horse when shooting. When fishing, rode the horse in and fished off of him. Saved wearing gum boots and in a little while could get all the fish he wanted at a time.

I staid with the Longs winter of 1893 and 1894. But the mills had moved to Quartz Hill, then renamed (Ronsomby). They moved to Glendale thinking it was a better place. However, it was going down too. She [*Mrs. Long*] died there and Jim came back. Then his mother came from New Brunswick, but being real old and the change too great, she went back. (He brot her up to see us once when John was a baby.)

For those days, Mrs. Long had nice furniture (a piano). In 1931, or about, I went to see Long and the piano was still there. I think this one was the only one in residence at the Flat at the time [*1893-94*].

About the time his mother left, the rush to Alaska was on and he left the house and belongings to his wife's sister, a Mrs. Scott Galbraith. She sold a few things, but other ways it remained the same till he came back from Alaska in 1922. Pa was in the hospital. Jim had heard of his sickness from Andy Rae, Wood, other old cronies and country men and came up to see Pa. I was there and he was the same Jim. He always was a good story teller, could exaggerate good and put in a spooky atmosphere in his stories and they went over good. He came from Alaska with some money, enuf to have seen him thru good, but thinking himself still young he planned on going back ranching for a livelihood the balance of his years. Meeting his old friends was too much for him and he gambled and drank. Soon called a halt, with some money yet to the good. He went back to the Flat, saying he was yet young and could do as much as a young man. When the Wise River dam broke, he worked for the water company and was here at Lavon with a gang putting back our flumes. That was good pay and he still had a little money left.

Shortly after, some crooks ferreted him out and others up there and in some fake exchange of his Montana Power stock for their stock, he lost all he had. This was too much for him and he gradually lost his mind. First going to Dillon poor farm and later to Warm Springs and there died. Pa and I felt very sorry about this but it was all over before we found it out. Last few years he was very saving and seemed to be needy, but it was his way.

Maggie Hater Williams and a girl wanted to find her sister's [*Jennett Hater*] grave at the Dewey Cemetary. She knew I was at the funeral (1893 fall of). I rode with Jim and his wife to the grave. But years effaces many things. We went to Jim's and told him we wanted him to come up, so he did. He took a short cut over the hill and we went the road. Our hunt was of no avail and no one seems to know where Jennett lies. That day he was real jovial and told about Sam Garrett's funeral.

After our search, he insisted that we go to his house for lunch. Maggie had prepared big lunch, but nothing would do but we go to his place. So we did. He set out old mushy bacon and bread that had been old and he had steamed the whole loaf to renew it. The table and dishes were so dirty and dusty we cleaned the best we could when he was out and put on our lunch. We all did justice to the lunch and he ate the food with relish. I had tasted the bacon and left it. I was going to throw it out but he said, "No don't, you know that is good" and put the slices back in the bowl with the balance. We gave him what was left of our lunch and was well pleased.

He showed us his scrap book and album and a corner in the house he had fixed up with a homemade barber chair and all the tools for barbering. His wife's piano was still there and the girl, being an expert pianist, played many fine pieces from memory. His eye sight was failing fast then, but the house was tidied up far better than the average of people that can see. At one time he had a notion he could find ore back of the cave at Dewey on the hill and he did quite a bit of work there, but nothing came of his hard labor.

Peter Dolman

When the Flat began to prosper, businessmen moved in. Peter Dolman came from Butte and set up a dry good and grocery store, with a Eugene Carver as clerk and Frank Ritschel as delivery man. Dolman often could come and go, having a home in Butte and other business.

His wife was a sister to Carral, the water man in Butte. Previously, before moving to Butte, Dolman came from some middle states, where in the Civil War he had enlisted and served as a colonel. The boys or men around the flat said that was the cause of his walking sideways and always looking back. Anyways, he was quite a shrewd man.

His wife often came and staid a few days in the Flat and especially over Sundays to help run the Sunday School. She was the life of the church interests in town, helping in many ways. Then Christmas times, with her help and Al Brubakers, they had a tree, gifts for all. She was an active social worker in Butte and often got gifts from Butte for Dewey's Sunday School in pamphlets and song books. Being a mining and mill town, it needed just such a Christian worker.

The summer of '93, Eugene Carver, Dolman's clerk, went to Gibbonsville to look for another location. He took sick, coming back from Gibbonsville, and by the time he reached the Flat, 3 or 4 days over, he was very ill. They took him to Divide, put him on the train, but he died before he could get medical attention.

They [Dolmans] had three children. The oldest boy was a very smart boy, having gone to Harvard. A girl and a small boy, Tommy, she often brot with her for a few days at the Flat. The winter of [1893] and 94, while getting a Christmas tree, also soliciting for the one at the Flat, she contracted pneumonia and never lived to see her efforts put thru.

Dolman had the town site platted, surveyed and took it up as placer claims. Then he dozed around the office of the Water Company - pretending to be asleep most of the time till he found out their intentions of building a dam on the Big Hole above the bridge down the canyon. So, he perked up, unbeknowance to the Company, got several old fellows to take up placer claims along down the river and kept them there working. When all of the sudden the Water Company found out they could not back the water up on free land. The Company built the dam in '97, fall and winter, but before they could back the water, Dolman sued them for intent of backing the water over his placer ground. In court he had the old prospector swear as to the amount of gold they panned per pan. Dolman had the dead wood on the Company and he got a goodly amount of damages.

The town being almost deserted, the store business was not paying but Ritschel stayed on a short while with Jimmie Wells. They did a small business and finally Ritschel moved away. Jimmie, with Dolman, occasionally still kept the doors open.

The store by now was not doing any business, so he had been carrying an insurance on it. One lovely, quiet, still, stormy, snowy night, when the snow drifted down like feathers, it suddenly took on fire. Jimmie left in such a hurry he left his hat behind and ran down town reporting Dolman's store was on fire. So it was, no fire fighter, engine or fighting equipment in town and the store went up in smoke, full stock. Word was sent to the insurance man. He came and looked over the ground. In the ashes he could not find any remains of goods or hardware stock. That was queer, as there are always articles such as buckles or buttons on clothes that can be found in the ashes and in the hardware department are many things that do not burn. Had Dolman hauled away all the stock in the store and hired Jimmie to set it on fire that favorable night? Or was the insurance man mistaken? We heard he was not mistaken. Dolman did not get away with this ruse like the placer ground. The outside store cellar and a big hay and grain warehouse remained standing in the Flat, mute remembrance of by gone days. There are still some that know this story, but to the majority it was only a cellar and warehouse.

> **Dewey, Montana**
>
> The Carroll Placer was taken up by Peter Doleman. The original survey of the Carroll Placer later became the basis for the town site of Dewey, Montana.

Bryant and the Chinaman

In about '89, when the boys were starting their new place, they came to the Flat expecting to get word about some contract. So they decided to stay a day or two, perhaps they would get the word. They had worked hard and decided to take a day or two off. As usual, they stayed at Bryant's Hotel. Bryant was a good talker. They enjoyed his type of telling his troubles, also the news of the town. Then too, he always kept in touch with the outlying country by people coming thru and stopping at the Hotel.

This day Bryant was up in arms at a Chinaman cook he had hired. He was a very good cook, but the thots of him eating food cooked by a chink. He was going to fire him, thot he would, so Horace agreed with him, saying "Bryant, lets go over to Bobbie's and have a drink."

When once there, that was all the boys asked for. They would certainly see that he did fire the chink in an under handed way. It would perhaps take all day, but what of that. They talked and drank with him. First one bot the drink, then the other one, then the house and the bar keeper. They never let the quest of firing the cook lag. Finally Bryant started back to the Hotel. The boys came back a few minutes later. Bryant says, "Boy, I am going to fire that son of a bitch of a Mongolian right now." He started down the hall, thru the dining room, to the kitchen where the Chinaman was getting dinner. "Yes sir, I will fire him right now. I'll fire that Mongolian. I'll kill him and tear out his entrails and put them upstairs for the cats to shit on." The Chinaman was so scared that he dropped the cooking job and took down the road as fast as he could.

The Wood [*Would*] Be Highway Man

Sherman Bryant had no particular occupation. He was a good worker when he worked. He drove cattle for the cattle buyers or worked any place he could get a job, as now the crash of '93 had put others going. He went too. One spring he irrigated for Horace, while Horace made a trip to Gibbonsville. After a month or two he moved on and again he worked on the Patton Lane, the first time it was heaved up in to a grade. He went to the basin thinking he could do better there. He was intimately acquainted with the freighting game and could see the men with good outfits were being cut in to by the little poor fellows that could not afford to get a good outfit. They would load more than their outfit could haul, get out on the road and invariably have to be helped out of every mud hole. Their wagons were old, horses poor and poorly fed, harnesses held together by baling wire. One such was nicknamed Bailing Wire Mitchell.

Dillon Examiner, Dillon, Montana
August 2, 1895

All of this Sherman knew and was then he thot of easy money and also help the better freighters. One evening Horace and Al had pulled into Pioneer to camp for the night. The teams were unhitched, watered, nosesacked, preparatory to being turned out on the luscious grass, knee deep nearby. The fire was built, grub boxes taken out preparatory to cook the evening meal. Spuds were washed to cook with jackets on, bacon cut, a can of corn and fruit were nearby for supper, when Old Ben took notice someone was coming. Ben boo woed, then was called down. A man horse back was coming that way. "Hello." Well it was Sherman. "Well, hardly expected you in these whereabouts."

"Get down and off," says Al, "and have some supper with us."

So Sherman says, "Yes, I am real hungry and believe I will." From this on they talked and cooked supper ready and they ate quite heartily, as when a skinner pulls the ribbons over a 6 mule or horse team for 15 to 20 miles per day, they are always hungry. Supper over, the dishes washed, they replenished the fire and all stretched out on the grass for an hour chat of news in various parts of the country. Sherman had been in the basin for some time and had taken note of the freighting situation. "There," he says, "is Baling Wire Mitchell not making much and is a nuisance to others. He'll be coming this way in a few days. If you fellows will pay me a good sum I'll see he is put out of business - right here in this timber, creeks, swamps and mountains. I could run them all off in one night and he would never get them again, then you would be rid of him and get more freight. That

THE LONE PINE

Hon. L. C. Fyhrie visited the Lone Pine at Dewey's Flat recently. To a reporter of the Tribune (1891-92) he gave the following facts:

"The Lone Pine mine is now down close on to 900 feet and makes a very fine showing clear to the bottom. Captain Prideaux, since he took charge, after the consolidation with the Jay Hawk company, had developed the mine from the 800 to the 900 foot level. He has in sight fully 2,000 tons of ore, more than was apparent at the time of the consolidation, notwithstanding the fact that both mills have been running since he took charge, and the character of the ore is much better at the bottom than at any place above. In my estimation the future of the Lone Pine is greater than that of any other mine in Southern Montana. The company is now running two ten stamp mills, which crush about 38 tons of ore every 24 hours. Five stamps are now being added to the Lone Pine mill and will be crushing ore in less than 30 days.

"The product of this mine is about 20,000 ounces of silver bullion and 8,000 ounces of concentrates per month, totaling about $28,000 and the total expenses are only $8,500 per month, leaving a handsome profit for the owners.

"I was in large measure responsible for the transaction by which the English capitalists became interested in this property and I certainly congratulate them upon having obtained one of the best mines in Southern Montana. But in this connection it must not be forgotten that to the economical management of Captain Preideaux the prosperous condition of the mine is due, and the company is to be congratulated upon having secured the services of such an excellent mining man. He thoroughly understands his business and is ever vigilant in looking after the interests of the company which he represents."

Southern Vipond Country

Few men have done more to develop the southern Vipond country than General J. A. Brown. He and William Vipond recently sold the Grey Jockey group of mines to a Michigan syndicate for $90,000. The General has more viable prospects in this location that he is fast developing.

Dillon Tribune
Holiday Edition
1891-92

---

would be the last of Baling Wire Mitchell." There the three talked to late in the night, when Sherman got his horse and rode away to his rendezvous, keeping back in the thick woods. He evidently did not persuade them in to his nefarious schemes, as Mitchell hauled on that summer as Gibtown was good. Tho when everyone was leaving the Flat, he too had heard of greener pastures, for he loaded up his wife and children and some household goods and went to Stykes, Washington where he got land and raised wheat on a big scale. Here he did well, accumulated a goodly fortune. Toward the last of his life he travelled, always going back to Stykes.

Sherman Bryant

While on the first day of a freighting trip to "Gibtown", Al pulled into Bryants to eat dinner. While watering the mules by a bucket and slipping on the nose bags so they could eat and be ready to go as soon as Al ate, Bryant came up, says, "Hello, Al, you big bastard. Did you see Sherman coming up the road?"

"No," says Al, "I haven't seen him."

"Well, if you should see a quid of tobacco on your way, just kick it over and see if Sherman is there."

Sherman always had a big chew of tobacco in his mouth.

E. G. Bryant and Isaac

Bryant owned a small wild hay ranch on the right hand side of the Big Hole River above Dickie's bridge. He built a comfortable cabin and a small stable for a team. He often spent some time up there away from the hotel. He would take his two dogs, a saddle horse and pack horse. Would spend a quiet time fishing, hunting and trapping, cooking delicacies of the camp such as sour dough bread, bean hole beans, delicious stews. He put up enuf hay in the summer to have for his horses in chance he wished to go there thru the winter.

Once in the spring he took Isaac, his grandchild, a lad of three or four years old. Isaac played around for a while then decided he would climb on top of the barn, being made of logs, easily scaled at the corners. A piece of liver attracted him and he thot the pup might like it, so he threw it down. The pup eagerly grabbed it and ate it. He got down then and went to the house. Presently the pup began to act queer. Bryant knew at once it had gotten some of his poison meat he had put out for the magpies. Where upon he said, "Isaac, where was you?"

"Up on the barn," was the reply.

"Did you throw my magpie bate down?"

"Yes, and the Son of a Bitch ate it," was the reply!!!

George Tong

George Tong owned the Goldsmith mine on the hill at Butte. He, like a lot of prospectors, had faith in this prospect, worked it thru thick and thin and it made good. He married Miss Lawrence of early pioneer stock. In 1892 they were quite prosperous with the mine, then they owned and operated two ranches on the Big Hole.

The one just above the old Patton place, Ben Mallon later owned. It concisted of 1200 acres wild hay adjoining a fine range on Johnson Creek. The other one was at Squaw Creek above Chalk Bluff and concisted of fine wild hay meadow, stocked with cattle and horses. In the winter he generally kept a foreman with helpers on each ranch. Andy Jackson being one foreman and a man by the name of Twig on the lower place. After the haying was done, the family, Mr. and Mrs. Tong, Georgia, Effie, Bud, Gladys,

Babe, Grandma Lawrence, the cook, old Lizzie and the parrot, moved back to Butte and the children went to school. In the spring they moved back again. The children were care free, never as much as cooked, washed, or any of the real work of life. Mother, Grandma and Lizzie could do it. As times went on, silver went down, money from the Goldsmith slackened. Tong grew older, drank a lot to help ward off trouble that stared him in his face, he failed fizicly [*physically*], nearly lost his mind. Mrs. Tong took him to the east. When money got scarce he could not pay his liquor bill. Things went from worse to worse and he died. Children were older and demanded more. Andy [*Jackson*] quit, would not be bossed by a woman. She hung on for a few years, sometimes they moved to the upper ranch.

On one of those trips, they loaded in their goods in three wagons. The last one was a spring wagon. Grandma was to go in that one but the parrot was there. Grandma would not ride with a parrot so the loads had to be rearranged. Grandma had ridden many, many, long weary miles in her day. Coming from the states over land to Montana. They had driven for days in the lonely prairies of Nebraska when one eve they were fortunate to come to a creek. Plenty of water and wood, something one could not always find on those long treks. That night twin boys was born to Grandma. There was the question of names for the twins. Grandma settled that. They should be called Atwater and Atwood. They both grew into manhood in and around Butte. Atwood was living in my day. Mr. Hand said he knew him. Effie married Ed Roe and lived at Red Rock on a ranch. Mrs. Tong sold the places and the family moved to Washington. In time she married. The other children scattered and married, all but Georgia. She travelled quite a lot and finally went to China. Shortly after coming back, she died very sudden and was buried in Butte about 1914. It was while Mrs. Wilkin was visiting me at the Donovan place, as she and I went to the funeral. Several of the neighbors from up the river was there (Ralstons, going home, met their death). Tice Dodgson bot the place from Mrs. Tong - lived there a few years. Sold it to George Dodgson, then George sold it to Christenson. He lived there several years. After his death the widow sold it to George Dodgson and Ben Mallon.

At both places, Tongs had prepared ample rooms for man and beast. They kept the stage horses and made the regular changes there. Then often the snow gave out there and the freighters were compelled to change loads there, wagon to sleighs or visa versa. In the winter a man cook ran the house. Their ranch barn set up clost to the hill. Just room enuf between it and the hill for a road. When Ben tore down one of the old cabins he found two ten dollar bills. Someone had put them away carefully in a crack between the logs in about 1900. Millie and Ben [*Mallon*] was married there in 1907.

Davis and Jones first took up the Tong ranch. They were cattle men. They wanted a bigger and better range, which they found on the Yellowstone River. So they sold this place and with local drivers, Tice, Sherman Bryant and others, drove their bunch of cattle to the new ranch.

Federal Census - State of Montana
1890
142,924 citizens

Chapter XI

Dewey Flat's New School Teacher

****

Divide
September 1892

This was my first time I was ever on a train. Three days and the third night, being worn out, I slept curled up in the day coach fairly well, tho the ever anxious thot of if it would only be day light at my journeys end? All of sudden the conductor yelled Melrose, Melrose, Melrose. I rubbed my eyes, yes, it was still dark. One or two passengers got off and one got on. The train pulled up and took on coal. The next stop was mine, Divide. The train started on. After some time the engineer gave the signal of stop at the next station. That was for me. The train wound in and out thru a deep canyon like a big snake for a long time. Then another long whistle and it began to slow down.

I had gathered my little possessions together at Melrose, put on my shawl and black sailor hat that Hattie, my sister, had worn when she came from California a year ago. I waited for the stop. The brakeman took my grip and the train stopped. He helped me off. "The Dewey's Flats new school teacher." It was still dark. Being put off at the depot door, I stumbled in the dark room and found a bench. Here at my destination, dark, not a living soul to be heard, only the train whizzing away in the distance. The sound growing fainter all the time. I sat and pondered. It was impossible to know which way to go to find the hotel so I decided to stay right there till day light came. After some time pondering on the situation I heard someone whistling. It came nearer, then I thot of the poem, "There Was No Harm In A Whistling Boy." As he stepped in the door he says, "Hello, well you got here at last." "Arn't you Big Al's sister?"

For the Montana Map and general locations see Appendix B, page 292.

I answered, "Yes, yes sir, I am."

In the meantime he lit a lamp. "Big Al said you was coming. If you like, you can follow the track to the crossing and then go up the road to the hotel or wait till it gets a little lighter." In a few minutes a man came over from the hotel for the mail sack.

The agent said now you can walk over with this man, which I did, in silence. He went in at the P.O. [*Post Office*] door and I followed. He gave me a chair. I heard the cook in the kitchen building a fire for breakfast. Presently Mrs. Pickett came in, we greeted, good morning and she said, "You are Big Al's sister arn't you?" I say, " Yes, mam."

"Well come on in the front room and take off your things. We will have breakfast after while. You are going on the stage aren't you. It won't be here for a while."

The sun was now up and what a wonderful sight spread out before me, mountains everywhere. I decided to walk out and see the yard. The main highway ran up to the front of the hotel, but on the upper side of the house was quite a little flower garden and the red, white, pink and mauve color poppies that greeted me in this high mountainous country - too lovely for description. Poppies was a flower I had never seen before. Ma said it was too windy for them in Kansas. Here they were in a riot of colors. That alone should take ones fear away of being in a strange country and not a face I had ever seen before. Breakfast was ready and there I met a young woman, Mrs. Bub Reynolds, of whom I was to know better in after years to come. Yes, she knew Big Al too. Breakfast concisted of oatmeal mush, bacon and eggs, warmed over fried potatoes, pancake and syrup, biscuits, prunes and coffee. After breakfast, time dragged slowly - I was anxious to go.

This was Saturday morning. I wanted to look over my school house and get some idea as to the number of children to go and most of all I wanted to see my brother. I had seen him 12 years ago. Finally, about 9 a.m., Mrs. Pickett said there was a stage coming, not a stage but a man with a spring wagon. He stopped at the Hotel for passengers. I was the only one. "How do you do, Miss. You are Big Al's sister, arn't you?"

"Yes sir."

After going over for my trunk, he got the mail then he was ready to go to Dewey's Flat. I bid Mrs. Pickett goodby. I put on my shawl and hat. He helped me in to the wagon and away we went up the road. For a few miles I could see where the road was going but at the river bridge all vizability closed in. We were going to cross the river and above was a saw mill. The stage driver kept up a continued conversation with questions. I answered mostly with yes and no. I learned from Mrs. Pickett that his name was Ed Vance. He told me his brother was clerk of the school and that the clerk had told him I was coming - Big Al's sister, the new school teacher.

As he talked I was taking in the hills, mountains, river, the canyon, ravines and rills. Sometimes the road ran along side of the river and again up on a very narrow grade cut in the mountain side. Then the river dashed in to a cataract with mountains towering high. Trees grew wherever there was a foot hold. Such lovely evergreens, wonderful to one from Kansas where all the trees are deciduous.

On we came to the end of the grade where the flat country greeted the eye. Tho framed as it were with trees and mountains and half mile distance the town of log houses. Nestled there that September in the warm sun shine, the cabins now up on row with the road that went on thru as main street. Bryant's Hotel was a big two story log house on the right hand side - a saloon and Bedard's Hotel opposite with Storie's Barber Shop above.

Crossing over Alen Hay's ditch on a bridge made such a clatter that warned the town of the arrival. As Ed Vance drew up to the hotel porch, Mr. and Mrs. Bryant were there to greet me. We three shook hands as friends. "And this is Big Al's sister, come right in. We have been looking for you." The stage driver drove on to Pond and Vances general store and P.O. News flew now, as men and children gathered around Ed Vance to hear him tell he had brot up the new schoolmarm and she was in at Bryant's now. Some children came right over. Others were shy and lingered around to see if I might come out. In the mean time Mrs. Bryant took me to my little room just opposite hers on the main floor down the hall that led to the dining room. She brot fresh drinking water, wash water, towels and soap so I could clean up in my own room.

Minnie Bryant came in, then a girl of 12, she was to be my pupil. Maude Dodgson, Mr. & Mrs. Bryant's daughter and her two children, Isaac and Hazel, was down from a ranch to visit home folks for the day. Bryant told me Al was working Vipond Park for Kelley and did not think he would be down for a few days, as it was several miles up in the mountain and that he had secured board and room for me there at the hotel.

To live in a hotel, well I hardly could bring myself to it, thot I, but I'll see when he comes. I shan't say a word to any one here about finding private boarding house. I would abide the time till he came. Mrs. Bryant tried to please me, gave me a table mostly to myself away from the crowd of men that ate in the dining room.

Over time I made acquaintance with the men and women of the town that ate there when ever occasions offered. Mostly, as soon as I finished my meals, I'd go to my room or school to escape the glare and remarks of strangers.

After dinner Minnie got the keys of Mr. Vance and we went to the school house. The school house was built of logs and it was about 16 x 20 feet. Was first built for a dwelling house. It had three 2 sash windows and a door in the end. It was cheese cloth lined and papered walls with no ceiling. The stove pipe was about in the middle of the room with a big large wood stove. I think it took two feet [*foot length*] wood. There was a teacher's desk and a straight chair. The black board extended the full length of the back wall. There was two rows of double desks and benches up two sides for six feet and a long bench under the blackboard. This was two years after the territory became a state and Mr. Knippenberg had not yet put thru his bill in Legislator asking to have the flag floated every day and used for an emblem. By this time most every child had heard about the teacher coming and there was to be school Monday.

Swept and put things in order. Then Mr. Fergusen and Brubaker on the board called to see me and we talked. They knew the school house was too small and tho hoped I could get along as there would be about 20 scholars. They would see I had plenty of wood and kindlings and if I needed anything or had any trouble to let them know. I was determined in my own mind I'd have no trouble. Tho I fairly trembled when I thot of facing twenty. I was thru high school (Beloit), had a 3rd grade certificate for Mitchell County, Kansas, but no training to teach. I had to raise up and teach, yes teach and face in tirely different temperament of children in Montana. Then, last of November, I had to take examination to teach in Montana. I had no permit to teach, nor no contract. I had the board's word and that was enuf?

The third board member, John Lawrence, I did not meet for some time. We went back to the hotel. I went to my room and rested a while, for the new scenes, I did not realize I was tired. Had supper. The boarders came, ate and went. This I disliked very much to be in the public eyes. I almost wished I was home again in our little quiet home with Mother and Father.

Horace rode down that evening, went to the post office and store. Vance said, "Miss Halbert, the new school teacher came this morning on the stage."

"You don't say."

"Yes, she is over at Bryant's Hotel."

After getting the mail and some supplies, he went down to the Hotel as he always did to talk and josh with Bryant.

"Hello, Bryant, how are you today?" says Horace.

" I am fine. Say, did you know Horace, Big Al's sister came today?"

"No, you don't say."

"Yes, I'll go call her."

So Bryant stepped to my door and gently knocked. I opened the door. "Say, Miss won't you come out?" So I did, he was always so confidential and kind, I most had to obey.

"This is Horace Hand, big Al's partner Miss Halbert." I stepped forward.

"Glad to meet you Mr. Hand." He extended his hand and we shook hands.

Bryant says, "Have a chair" and I sat down.

Horace asked me several questions about my trip. All the time I could not help wondering in my mind at the man. He was big, nicely proportioned (240 lbs), 6 foot tall. The color of his face was most as delicate pink, shaded in to a reddish color on his cheeks. He wore a light colored, heavy mustache - was slightly bald, tho he looked young. The sun of the summer had not burnt or tanned him. His manner was good natured, frank and friendly.

"I was in Divide yesterday and Al told me to look out for you. I was sorry I missed you."

"It took me three days and three nights. It is a long way. I was very much disappointed to not have met Seth."

"I dare say you must have been when they dropped you in the night. He is tending a whim for Mr. Kelley at the Grey Jockey Mine. Jobs are scarce now. When he got the chance to work a team, he took the job. He'll surprise you the first chance he has to get down. I have to be going Miss Halbert so goodbye, hope you get on fine with that school."

I thanked him and bid him good night. What that big strapping young rancher thot after his interview he never told any one. I yet felt distrustful of every one in this new, strange, tho wonderful country of my adoption. I was alone, three days had taken me from my little quiet home with Mother and Father. At home I could sew, weave or stroll, go horse back riding, out to view the garden, trees, flowers and shrubs. Here was no quiet little homes like the one in Kansas.

Everyone was curious at the new school teacher, Big Al's sister. I pondered about my brother's name. I had known him all my life and in the bible he had been christened Seth Henry Halbert. When they spoke of him as Big Al I had to think twice to know of whom they spoke. It was days, weeks and months before I gave myself over to address him as Al.

"I can't see why they call him Big Al?," I said to Bryant.

"O, I don't know, every body in this country knows him by that and very few knows his real name."

So many things had happened this day, was most exhausted, so went back to my room thinking of puzzling things to me as I prepared to lie down the first night in Montana. Then all at once I remembered that lovely garden of poppies and dozed off to sleep.

In the morning I heard the first stir. Bryant came down stairs with his dogs and went on out to feed Buck and Nig, his two horses and milk the twin heifers. Presently the cook and helper out in the kitchen were rattling pans and skillets preparing breakfast with Mrs. Bryant to over see the preparation and also to greet any new boarder that might come. I arose at the first sound, washed, combed my hair and dressed, polished my shoes. When I stepped out Mrs. Bryant greeted me good morning and asked how did I sleep. Just fine says I, thank you. As I strolled out the back way thru the men's wash room it was too early for the roomers to be up. What met my eye but poppies growing in a low bed 30 feet long, side of the hotel. I could hardly believe my eyes of all the big double and single purples shading down in to all the lighter shades, such a riot of color to gladden my eyes. I stood there spell bound for some time and Mrs. Bryant finally came out. I asked her how she raised them. "Last spring Mr. Bryant made me that bed and I had a package of seed here. Did not know how old the seeds were but sowed them there. Each morning and night I watered them. After they came up so nice, that gave me courage. I continued watering you see. It gave me a diversion from the routine Hotel life. Then with the watering chore morning and night I could get out in the sunlight," says Mrs. Bryant.

At breakfast I was given a table off to one side away from the men. Mrs. Bryant brot my breakfast, then her cup of coffee and ate with me. This was Sunday. In the afternoon Minnie and I took a walk, going up on the hillside so I could get a bird's eye view of the town. The little log cabin town lay there craddled in between the mountains. The sun shone down just a little brighter and warmer than I had ever seen before. The road going thru town wound out of town and up the marble grade and disappeared, as the mountain roads seems to have a freakish way of disappearing all of a sudden. As the sun dipped low in the western sky, we then went back to the Hotel.

Deweys Flat

Coming into town, on the right hand side, was a barn and corrals, then a street, then on the corner was Alen Hays old hotel. Bryant's new hotel was next to Alen Hays hotel, then the town well and Kinney's dance hall and saloon. Next was a very old dwelling; log house, tho always occupied. Then a butcher shop and a restaurant, tho not running in '92. And above that several old two stories and a blacksmith shop and scales. Jim Mitchell run a livery stable, lived in another one, and his wife kept roomer. Jim was a happy go lucky baling wire freighter, named that as his harness and all rigging were repaired with baling wire. He was a good hearted fellow and everbody was made welcome at his house by his congenial wife and children. In '94 Mitchell moved to eastern Washington, a new wheat country. This was when there was no more hauling to be gotten in and around the Flat and every body that was foot loose moved some place to find a more permanent home. Above these was a general store, Eliel, Tyrie and Burfiend Company, and a dwelling we bot and moved later on. There was a log building down on the river, Pete Woods built. Incidentally, it was told this was the house that the flood took whole down the river by the flood in "27". The piano played "Home On The Rolling Deep".

Then, back toward the river, directly behind the first barn, Leggate had a nice summer home and nicely furnished for those days. The fall of '92 it mysteriously burned. On the left hand side of the street was a Chinaman laundry and garden, two dwellings and a building used for a butcher shop and dwelling. Then another building, sometimes used for a shop and sometimes a dwelling and Joe Bedard's (a Frenchman) Hotel. It was nearly opposite to Bryant's Hotel, which caused a great deal of envy and strife, as one could see the other's customers coming or going. Above that was Bobby Shultz's Saloon and Tom Thomas' barber shop. Then the Vance and Pond General Store where most everything was sold or ordered for its customers, even to whisky. After the crash, George Vance moved back to Glendale and a man, Mr. Guy Ames, ran it till Lossel bot it out in about 1903. Then above that was a large skeleton structure made by hewed logs, with a two story center and on either side a one story leanto. Then came Dolman's store and large root house and warehouse in back. Then Jim Long's saloon/barber shop. They were on the corner and back was his stable where he kept a driving team and buggy and back of that still was his little low 4 room log cabin. Then in back of this front building, there were a number of dwelling houses and the school house. The school house set back a block from the street on a slightly rocky raise. Then a hill seemed to almost [en]compass this part of town on the west. Above the town a block or two, the mill set in the hills. The tailings from the mill, water and finely ground rock in a fine sand form, ran down nearly to the road and cord wood was ricked in clost available place to be used at the mill. Captain Prideaux lived above the mill in a log cabin. This was the little town of Dewey's Flat in '92.

It had progressed amazingly since '82, but then in '92 it was on the verge of toppling as many other mining towns of early day. There had been more saloons, butcher shops and restaurants but about the first of the year '93 there were several quietly moving away. There still were plenty of comers and goers stopping at Bryant's. The dances went on, tho only those that were on holidays were grand affairs. Music had to come from Butte and they generally played till 4 a.m. in the morning. Bryant's was home to the freighter. They nose sacked their horses, was met by a friendly greeting, ate a good meal, cajoled with Bryant, smoked and went away with a laugh.

**Dewey, Montana on the Big Hole River six miles west of Divide.
Photo courtesy of the
Beaverhead County Museum Archives
Dillon. Montana**

Bryant Hotel

With the growing little burg, with its many paying mines, the logging that was going on each winter, the ranching and cattle industry growing, it bid fair for Mrs. Bryant to build a bigger and better hotel, one that could handle the crowds.

The hotel was a big log building facing the street, the main thoroughfare. The main part of the building was two story about 60 x 20, of logs. The stair way entrance was built on the east side and was about 12 foot wide and 30 long. There was washing place for the men, a wooden sink. They washed in pans, towels were furnished. Places to hang harness, a place to store wood for the front room stove and under the stairway Bryant kept his traps.

The first room was the sitting room, generally occupied with men. It was het by a long wood stove of those day. An organ, a table and chair concisted the furniture, coil oil lamp were used to light the room. In fact, the whole house, and it was no small chore to keep these lights cleaned and filled each day for the coming night. There was two large long windows, one each side of the front door. Then a door out into the lean to. Going back to the large dining room was a narrow hall and on either side was a bedroom. The right hand room was Mrs. Bryant's private room where she and Minnie occupied. On the left hand side was another bed room. This was mine, by request of Al, that I should have a room down stairs. The dining room was long and full width of the structure, with two large windows on either side. Another large wood stove het this room. Homemade tables large enuf to sit four or possibly six chairs, coil oil lamps, Rochester hanging lamps and occasional reflector side lamp. When warm enuf Mrs. Bryant often kept a machine in a corner and between meals the sewing and mending for the house was done or whoever cared to sew. Then amediately back was a large kitchen, with a shed on the left hand side over the back door. Then on the right hand side was two rooms, one the cook's room, the other a pantry and an outside door for deliverymen to enter when bringing supplies. The kitchen was big and roomy, well lighted, shelves, home made tables, work benches and cupboards and a big range. The kitchen was large enuf with space to do the washing, when the weather was bad. Other times the washing was done in the shed by wash board and tubs and the boiling method when the stove was not in use. All this house was heated with wood stoves. Stoves, both up and down, were needed, so the wood that was used there was quite an item.

The upstairs concisted of several rooms. There were 3 or 4 fixed up with a botten bed, dressers and commodes, water pitchers and wash bowls of nice dish ware and I believe there was carpets on some of the bedrooms upstairs. These were kept for the better transient. Then there were several other rooms, plainer, she kept for men off the hall that ran south and north and in the back was one big room they called the corral. Men that traveled and carried their own bedding slept there.

There were no carpets or linoleums on the downstairs floors and the floors all had to be scrubbed spotlessly clean often. The sheets were changed and washed, ironed after each night lodging, the old laborious way and at times it took one woman on that job alone - keeping beds clean. Coil oil lamps and candles were used upstairs.

Water had to be brot from the outside well. The water drawn up by buckets and taken in to these rooms each morning and the slops carried down to the outside toilet. Then beds changed for the transients and all made up.

From my west window the visibility was shut off by an old log building about 15 feet away, but by looking slant ways to the street I could see a narrow strip of the pine covered hill and Tom Thomas's barber pole and shop and a side of a log saloon. This down stairs room was the only available room for a decent girl. Al had specifically stated to Mrs. Bryant that I must have a down stairs room if I boarded there. This she gladly arranged. Upstairs the riff raffs of the world often roomed there. My room window had no screen on, so I was afraid but said nothing to her, tho mentioned it to Al one day. He says, "You are all right, no one will bother you, just forget it."

Monday morning I arose with all the realization of the fact the day was here that I had looked forward to so long. I dressed in a plain gingham dress, polished my shoes, then took up a big bunch of books, paper and lead pencils and slate and went to the school house. Minnie was getting her books together said, "I'll be there later." Here I was with only the register, no list of pupils as to their grade. When they came, all I could do was to find out, as I taught, the grade they could work in or the older ones perhaps would know. In due time the children came, Linnie, Elsie, Charley, John Trueman, Lillie and Hugh Hay, Eva, Mable and May Lawrence, Lillie Overly, Ethel and Roy Vance. All came with whatever books they could find around home, left over from the older children; slates, pencil and paper, copy books. They chose their own seats.

I held some classes, tho most of the time was taken up in the forenoon finding how many pupils and books of a kind to make a class. Often pupils had to arrange their studies so other pupils could study the lesson.

Before hand, I had made a recitation and study program but found in many cases it had to be changed. Many times such lessons could be handled on the black board. I would put them on the day before, so they could be copied for the next day. I found too, papers, pencils and slates were sadly lacking.

There was no busy appliances for the little folk so I set my head to devising busy work for them. We always opened school each morning singing songs I had sung in Kansas schools. I put the song on the board and each one of the older ones copied it into a note book. There was drawing and speaking each 4th week.

I had by now quite a nice sized school - 20 and all was going good. Tho lacking books and many other things, I sent list after list to the parents of things needed. There was very little response. Most all the parents were idle. Tho some prided theirselves in supplying their children's needs and were able to do so. I was blind to the situation of town. Thot to myself a lot and just taught the best I could. So the first week of my school passed with its worries to the wind. Another Saturday and Sunday came, which was a welcome break. Each morning and evening I would go out and look at the poppies to see each days varied change.

Saturday I washed my clothes, ironed and got them ready for an other week. Saturday evening at dusk Bryant came in and said, "Where is Maggie?" Then he knocked on the door and said, "Maggie, Al's here and he is up at the store." My brother Seth had finally gotten a chance to come down and no sooner had Bryant told me, Seth came in to the hotel. Did I know him, yes, he had never changed, only in size. Now he was over 200 pounds. When I last saw him, 12 years ago, he was like a boy. Now he was 35, had gone thru a lot of hardships of the days gone by since I last saw him. He greeted me with a kiss, then we sat down and he enquired

> *School Outing*
>
> *There is a story told by Susan Hand and Louise (Hand) Shafer, that Maggie told. Maggie had taken her school children on an outing and while hiking in the hills near Dewey, found a Chinaman hanging in a tree. It is not known if he hanged himself, or if someone else hanged him. - mc*

about Father and Mother and all the relatives in Kansas and my self, the school, & [etc]. He had come down with Kelley and had to go back with them that night, tho said next Sunday he would come down and take me to the ranch. So I taught an other school week with the same struggle, tho the children were happy and that was some consolation. They wanted me to go the hills, so we did. I found out I could not climb as fast as they could. I had such a short breath but they waited and we examined prospect diggings and gathered flowers. Al came back the following Sunday, got a team and buggy in town. I dressed up in my cream colored albatross dress with a big hat to match. This was the first time over those scenic grades. Such a wonderful sight. It is all wonderful for one from the plains.

The oat crop on Al and Horace's ranch would soon have to be harvested, but, "I will work as long as I can up there at the Grey Jockey Mine," says Al. "There is not many jobs available just now and times don't look too good. We have been to a big expense getting this ranch ready to be set to grass. But we don't regret it, we just had to have a place to come to when out of work and a place to leave our tools and horses. There is nothing in these jobs, only to get some money when needed and then one must have a home when out of work." Al told me. I had always had a home so hardly realized the importance of his talk.

We drove in to the cabin, no one was there so he went on to Wise River. There was only a small cabin there then. So we came back and he drove down to Dodgson's and Brubakers quartz mill. There I met Brubaker and he explained the process and told me that they could not save the gold and there was plenty of it there. Isaac and Brubaker owned a silver, lead and gold mine up Spring Gulch country. When silver and gold was a good price they thot it would pay, so they built a water power stamp mill perhaps 1/4 mile below the Wise River Bridge. They ran the mill two summers. They once hauled ore to Butte when the mill failed to save all the mineral.

This mill was to be half and half. Brubaker borrowed his half and when it failed, he never paid the man anything. Dodgson lost all he put in it too and his work. Brubaker never quit doing assessment on his mine.

Brubaker's cabin was a little one roomed cabin with a very old, drab, rusty appearance on the out as well as the inside, with very little furnishings, a dirt floor, an ancient cook stove, home made table and stools. There was a bunk bed made of poles and very meager bedding, slough grass for a mattress and a few shelves to hold his meager larder. The one and only thing that was curious to me was an old iron chest on the floor, which was also a curiosity to his visitors. The lack in his cabin and furnishings was made up by Al's whole heartedness to the casual visitor, whether it be man, urchin, canine or beast. All were greeted with a jovial whole hearted smile. He was known to every man, woman, child for miles around, as they were all friends of his. He often visited neighbors in time of sickness of friends and neighbor. Al was a good nurse. His time did not count. He'd stay till his patient was well, ever looking to the comfort of his friends. Once when I was away, Horace had a boil on his hand. As soon as Al found it out, he came, made pollices, kept them hot and changed often till all the pus was gone and Horace was able to use his hand.

When a friend needs a man to stay in his home and look after things when he went by team to town for supplies, well, Al Brubaker would come and take care of the place. When the children was left in his care they were royally entertained and looked after with a watchful eye. Once his charges got real unruly with Al and would slip out while he was busy with the house work. Says Isaac, "We will go to the hen house, he won't find us there." But when in, they thot it would be real sport to chase the hens, for they could not be idle. So off went their coats. The hens took flight and what a glorious time they were having, as hens went round and round the house cackling, flying to get rid of those wild boys. Till all of a sudden the door opened and they heard Al call, "Quit that you rascals, come here." Where upon Al grabbed Isaac by the nap of the neck and gave him a sound kick for instigating such a rough house with the poor innocent hens. If this was an old trick of theirs, it stopped right there. In later years he often told the story and lay back and laugh: how he booted the Dodgson boys for hazing the poor hens.

Al was content to live in his little cabin home "enuf with sufficient". With a little home like this he could take his hat and go and come back when he tired of visiting his friend or going to town to gather the gossip of the berg. He seldom went farther than Dewey. There he knew everybody. When Christmas came, he always took up a collection so the children were provided with a well filled candy bag and an orange. This little obligation was his and he always encouraged and helped the teacher to have a tree, with a program suited to the occasion. Then after he saw the children had a good time, he'd buy some cheese and crackers, put it in a sack over his back, he'd trudge home to his little cabin home at the meeting of the rivers.

Al Brubaker
Long time friend of Horace & Maggie's at his home
From the Rock Hand Collection

A man on a nice black horse was there at Brubaker's. It was Copp [*or Kopp*] from the Copp and Jackson ranch below Divide. He had staid at Bryant's the night before. He was floating a pardon to get Mr. Clayton out of the pen at Deer Lodge. Clayton shot and killed Maddix for cutting a small strip of hay they both claimed on Camp Creek above Melrose some few years before. And that, the good people thot, he was punished enuf all signed it. Clayton was a good man from all accounts and had two small motherless children.

As we drove in off the road, we had to cross a strip of sage brush, "such a queer smell," I remarked. "Yes, it is sagebrush. People in this country use it for medicine," said Al. Ever since when I smell sage brush, the trip to Brubaker's mill comes to mind.

He took me back to the hotel and bid me good by. He took the team home and then went to Vipond and worked another week. In the meantime school progressed. Mrs. Dolman came to town, with her little boy, Tommy, to stay for a week to organize a Sunday School. The [*Billie*] Smails, a relative of Mrs. Bryant, lived at Divide. His niece from Montreal had come out that spring for her health. She was quite a lovely girl. She had been working in a garment shop in Montreal and contracted T.B. Thot this high altitude would be beneficial, which it was. She soon regained herself. When I first met her she was attending all the dances.

Up till now (23 years old), I had never gone to a dance and on no occasion set up all night or even till 12 o'clock. I never cared to congregate in crowds and as for dancing, I was taught it was a sin. It so happened, in our little prairie country in Kansas, there was no dancing minded people when we first went there. Late on there were some and in order to get a crowd, they would call their dance a party in order for our girls to go. All these ruses did not work for we had been cautioned that if we danced we could not stay at home. With love and respect for our Mother's teaching we never danced. When we were mislead by the dance party, we left and most generally came home.

Some years before in Kansas, the Bellow's were new German people, Isaac and his brother and wife. They lived on a poor farm, three miles west of us. Had walked over to our place. Father was sitting outdoors. Isaac says to him, "Where is Miss Maggie?"

"In the house," was his reply.

Isaac came to our front door. The log part of the house, we used in summer for a sitting room, even tho we had two beds in it.

He says, "Maggie come out here, I want to tell you some little thing."

I went to the door, he says, "We are going to have a party at Jim Speakman's, won't you go with me?"

I turned red and stammered, "Yes."

So next evening at the appointed time, he came with a two horse lumber wagon and he drove me to Speakman's, a mile away. I was so chargainned at the Dutchman I hardly said a word all the way over. The crowd had gathered. Annie, my sister and Frank were there. Since they were married she had gone to dances, for he was one of the dancing Briggs', as mother called the Briggs family. They were vivacious people, all ways happy and talking and laughing. Mother did not like that kind of people. Life was more real and sober to her mind of thinking.

Well, I sat in a corner for a while and then told Isaac to take me home that I did not know I was coming to a dance. He took me home and I did not talk. At home he helped me out of the wagon and I said good night. He turned the team around and I heard it rumbling away in the distance. Shortly after we moved to Beloit, he often came in to see the folks on his milk route to town, but I never saw him. I always managed to be out of sight when he called. He often asked father if I was home at the moment. I never could be found.

Each Saturday and Sunday in Dewey was much the same. Al came down one day, says, "Maggie can you sew up the lining in my best coat?"

"Yes," says I, "if it is not to bad."

"I'll want it in a few days when I go to town," he said. He brot it down. When I came to look it over, I decided to take the old lining out as it was badly worn and use it for a pattern. I went up to Pond and Vance's Store, got the goods I wanted for a new lining. I cut it out, then the first spare time I had, sewed it up on Mrs. Bryant's machine and basted the lining in place. Then took it to my room, away from inquisitive eyes, and did the balance by hand. Al took it home. The estimation of the new school teacher leaped in bounds when the men at the ranch saw the coat. But when he went to put it on, well, something was wrong. I had, in my haste, sewed the lining of one of the sleeves at the wrist in on a twist. Well, he brot it back and I soon fixed it and he went on his way, rejoicing. She could sew and really do things, what a sister.

The sun shined bright and warm each day, such wonderful weather, in such a queer mountainous country, where there were such lovely rocks in multitude of forms. I had never seen the likes before. Tho very few crops were grown, no gardens, no flowers, except those lovely poppies at the hotel and Divide and the wild ones on the hills. O, if only the folks in Kansas could have the waste wood in the timber. Yes, mum I must be - so my first September passed - would I stay? No, I was going back in June.

Hank Overly

Hank Overly was originally from Indiana. When the call for volunteers was made to go west and fight the Mormons, he enlisted and was sent to Salt Lake. (Morman War 1857).

There was never any fighting to be done, so when the time of his enlistment was done he turned to other occupations. While teaming at Salt Lake he got acquainted with the Mormon people and found them very congenial, hard working people. One man he knew quiet well had four wives and each wife had several children, some were nearly grown. He admired a beautiful, light haired girl with blue eyes and pink cheeks and finally married her. Then they started to Montana. She was always ashamed of the fact that she came from a family of four wives. He had a team of mules and a wagon working on the R.R. as it built farther north. He finally drifted in to Glendale. They then had three small children, Flora, Henry and Lillie.

When Glendale work became scarce, he went to Dewey's Flat where he could find work with his team. She was energetic, wanted a home that would shelter her children with a reasonable amount of comfort. They had always lived around, where ever they chanced to be, in little log houses. He was a fair worker, easy going and slow. His son, then a boy of 14 years old, was a chip off the same block. She was a good worker, washed, patched clothes and often cooked when she could get a job.

I first met them the fall of '92 when Al took me to the ranch. When Al and Horace was harvesting their first crop of oats, they had hired him and the boy to help in the field and Mrs. Overly to do the cooking. Al came down town one Saturday afternoon for supplies. He just had the running gears of the wagon and said, "If you can ride on this rig, I'll take you up, as Mrs. Overly is there, and you can stay till tomorrow evening." I much disliked the Saturday and Sunday at the Hotel and was so pleased to get a chance to go. So he drove over to the Hotel and I was ready. A gunna sack with some hay in side made a good cushion on the back hounds of the wagon. He sit on the front hounds on the horse blanket and a way we went slowly up the road. Al never believed in driving the big heavy work horses in a trot. They were for heavy work, not fast driving.

This was a wonderful fall afternoon and the sun shone down hot as we rolled along over the marble grade above town, past the Churchill place and in past an old cabin by the roadside in a turn of the road in a rock cove. We rounded another point and there was a man horseback coming. Al pulled out as the grade was too narrow to let a horse by.

"Hello," says the man horseback.

"Hello Horace." says Al. "Which way?"

"I broke a piece on the binder and was going down to have it welded. How are you Miss Halbert."

"Just fine, thank you."

"And how is the school? If you have any trouble just let me know and I'll come down and teach."

"Thank you, I hardly think I'll have any trouble."

I yet did not know what to make of that big man and was afraid and distrustful of him. In fact, that was an inborn attitude I held for all, both men and women I met. Being the youngest in the family, I had never met many people. And this Montana people thot and talked so much different than I. The best thing I could do, at least for a while, was keep away and talk but very little. Just now, the river, hill, mountains, rock and trees interested me.

**Cliffs above Watercress Spring,
along the Big Hole River near Dewey, Montana
Sketch by Louise (Hand) Shafer
From the Louise (Hand) Shafer Collection**

There clost by, where the sides of the river was low, was a ford plainly visible on either side, which perhaps Indians had first used. On our side, the red rocks in every shade towered their head, far above us, dotted with scrub. Scrub firs, litchens [*lichens*], mosses and ferns with wonderful formation, twisted and turned as if a big boiling pot had thrown up the rocks. Then a big warm spring gushed out from under a big lime formation along the roadside. It lay in a basin on the upper side of the road and filtered thru under the road and spread out fan like into the rivers edge. Then on the left edge of the road the river wound in and out of the low hills to John Lawrence's corrals. There the road took a straight course to the little cabin home on the ranch. We drew up to the cabin. Mrs. Overly came to the door. Al says, "This is my sister, Mrs. Overly."

She says, "Yes, she looks enuf like you. Come in and make yourself at home." The little cabin shone with her feminine touch. Supper was ready. Fresh bread from the oven, boiled beef, spuds, baked beans, tomatoes, white layer cake, coffee with cows cream, and the butter was brot from a bucket hung in the well. The men had washed at a bench where water, soap and towel had previously been placed by the cook, as the cabin was full.

After supper the men went back to the barn. Al came back for the milk bucket and asked me if I could milk. "Yes," says I.

"Well you milk for I haven't had any luck. I don't seem to get enuf." So I took the bucket. The cow was in the field above the cabin. Al tied her up and gave her a bunch of hay. After a due amount of rubbing and petting I finally got up enuf courage. I took the bucket in one hand and stood up and milked with the other. Being a western cow, I was afraid to sit down and milk. I finally got the bucket full - it was quite evident she would give no more. After all, that would be sufficient for then, as she would not always be milked on time. This was their first cow on the ranch.

That night Mrs. Overly and I slept on a straw tick in the corner of the cabin. She was about the largest woman I had ever saw. I should judge she would top the scale at 300 pounds or more. She was quick and spry on her feet. In the night sometime, Horace came home and slept in the barn and in the morning he came in with the other men for breakfast of mush, hot cakes and syrup, gravy, bacon and eggs, warmed

> . *In a conversation with Thelma (Hand) Kalsta, she tells me that Maggie planted the watercress in the spring that is today known as "Watercress Springs". She purchased the starts at Divide, placed them in a bucket of water, took them to the spring and planted them. Susan Hand wrote that "Watercress provided fresh "greens" early in the spring before there was any other fresh garden greens." - mc*

over spuds, coffee, and cream. After breakfast Horace stopped to talk to Mrs. Overly. Then he said to me, beaming with his deep blue eyes, "I heard you milked the cow."

"Yes, " I said, "I did, I have had to milk and can't remember when I learned."

Sunday they worked and after supper Al took me home. Tom Galahan from the Ruby Valley was a worker there and he went with us.

Next day was school day for me. I pondered on the word spuds, having never heard potatoes called that before. This was a queer country and most of all the people. I wondered, yes, I liked the country. What if I'd fail that examination I had to take in November? The thots fairly made me sick. I'd study every book thru and thru. O, I can't, I must not fail. These and many other bitter thots permeated my very soul and body, day and night. O, I must, now that I am here, I must pass. Then I must not say an idle word and keep my mind on the goal - the teaching certificate in November.

The mill still run. Old Captain Prideaux [*managers of the Lone Pine Mine were Captains Harry and Jim Prideaux*] needed drivers. The oats being cut and stacked, Horace was out of work, so he got a job driving the ore teams to Quartz Hill. There were other drivers that came from Butte, Frank Foley, Mark Hall and another man from Wisconsin, all strapping, big, strong fellows, good natured, ready and willing to do their work.

The mine was working steady at Quartz Hill, but the main body of the ore had pinched out. The foremen were working frantically to supply the needed ore to run the mill. Captain Prideaux was frantic. He had the teams and to bring the ore in, also the miners at work, coming and going. They seemed to be a discontented bunch. So he said to the haulers, "Bring me ore, I must have it." They did as they were bid. The next morning when they did not find enuf ore in the bin at the mine to fill the ore boxes on their wagons, they started down. The boulders on the side of the road looked good so all hand stopped and begun to heave boulders on. They loaded, heaved more than they ever brot down before. They were bursting with laughter when they drove into the grade above the mill and unloaded, never saying a word. They continued to haul. When the bin was not full, they stopped on the way and loaded more boulders. Next day Horace says to Captain, "How is the ore assaying?" "O fine," was the answer. The bunch hauled on a few days longer. Captain for some reason had been giving orders about the team ever since they took the job. So one evening when he had said too much to the teamsters they pulled in, put the teams in the stable and says, "Here's your outfit Captain. We are quitting." They knew more about the business than he as they had driven for several years over just such roads in all kinds of condition.

He had given them impossible orders. Besides, they were tired of the ruse they were playing on him. When they came down for supper they were jovial. They told Bryant their stories, as Bryant always enjoyed having them. "Well, the Bastards had quit," he told me on the sly. I had seen the four come and go to their meals, tho knew none then but Horace. I could not for my life see how they could be so hilarious over loosing the job, let alone quitting it.

To me it seemed they should be sorry. I know those big strong men feared nothing. What if times did look hard? They cared not? They would not work for Captain. Horace would go home on the ranch and the other three would go back to Butte where they could find something to do. They feared nothing. They were young and life was all before them. On occasions like this, I could hear all that was talked in the front room thru the thin partition. Each boarder that came in would have something to tell. Carver and Frank Ritschel from Dolman's Company Store, men from the Eliel, Tyhsie, Burfeind Store, saloon men, travelers, etc. would fill in the front room all talking and laughing. My, what would I give to be away. But Al says, "Maggie, you will have to stay here as bad as it seems. They won't hurt you, just keep in your own room."

There was a big cave on the lime hill just south of town and almost above. The children had pointed it out to me and wanted me to go with them some Saturday. I had never been in a cave and was a little afraid. They assured me they knew how and had been in before. So on Saturday they got candles and we started to tack the hill. They were like mountain goats, scaling the mountain face. It was real labor for me to climb, tho I rested often, yet I could hardly make it. Some of the girls staid with me and we finally made it to the mouth. I was tired out and sweating. The big boys went first with their candles. We had to almost bend double, then slip and slide down into the mouth of the cave. What a smell. What is it, mountain rats? When down, we could stand up, as the rooms were high vaulted overhead. I haven't any idea how far we went. One place was a narrow entrance where a small person could slip thru. All of the sudden the candles went out, a trick the boys liked to play. The darkness was intense. Every one froze in their tracks. When relit everyone wrote his name on the walls as other explorers had done before. It seems as if bear hunters in the early days had built a big fire in the mouth of the cave hoping to smoke out bears and all the ceiling, which had been pretty before, was smoked. We got a few specimens for the school of stalagmites and stalagtites.

The children brot all kind of ore specimens so we put up some shelves for our samples. I wearily dragged myself home and was almost exhausted - did not plan on doing anything that weekend any more than prepare lessons on Monday. It was a good thing, for Monday morning I had such a heavy cold in my throat I could hardly speak a word. But I taught as usual. Along in the week Al came down. "You should not have went to that cave, that is far too much exertion for you in this high altitude. Why, you are not acclimated yet. It is a wonder you are able to teach at all. You should have went to bed," Al said. However, with a little self doctoring I pulled out of it. Rubbed my chest with turpentine and lard. That was a burning lesson and never climbed that mountain again.

When the first cold arrived in November I brot out my heavy coat. Mother had bot it from the Annen Store in Beloit in March 1890. I had hither to only worn it in the coldest spells in Kansas. I had a short green jacket I had made and it was easier to walk in to school, a mile and a half. I had long needed a coat. One day Mother said it was now past the fall season and perhaps she could get me a coat cheap now. We would look around and see. She could not get it that day as she did not have enuf money just then to pay for it.

Sure enuf, Mr. Annen had just one left, a nice brown double faced cloth, a double box pleat at the waist in the back and a nice big cord and tassels draped over the pleat in the back. I tried it on and it fit. "To bad," the store man said, "you could not have it." It cost $18.00. Mother had $3.00, that was all.

"Well," says mother, "if you could take a roll of carpet later this spring?" The bargain was made. He could take 50 yards of hit and miss carpet at 45 cents a yard. She bot the chain, 4 pounds that day for the carpet. We took the coat. I was so ashamed, suppose some one would know, I thot, I was wearing a coat not paid for. So I only wore it the coldest days.

We went home, Mother begun tearing and cutting rags. She sewed the rags on the machine and father cut them apart and wound them in balls. Then Saturday and evenings I helped her put the warp on and evening I wove and she wove while I was gone to school. We soon paid for the coat. I wore it 12 years. That was my first expensive coat and you may be sure I wore it a long time. When John and Byron [*Maggie's first two children*] needed coats when they went to school I looked at my brown coat, yet good, tho some what to small for me then, and decided I could make two coats out of the one for the boys. It lasted them for several years. One day Mrs. Cline noticed the two little boys in brown coats and said, "There is where Maggie's nice brown coat went." I had a nice brown crochet hood I made. I wore it when it was cold.

Mrs. Cline's sister and father had moved from Glendale to Butte. She wanted to go to see them and incidentally shop. So she sent me word by Al that they would go on Saturday and if I'd like to go she would take me with her. So, of course, I would like to see Butte and was ready when they came. Her sister and father lived not far from the depot. We just walked over the back way north west a block or two to their house, a two story drab color.

On our way up a crost a vacant lot was a bunch of Indians drying guts on some willow brush. The day was warm and bright. The flys were swarming around and some dusty, dirty little Indian kids were playing. That afternoon we took the cable street car and went to town. It was such a dirty, ugly place, with houses jammed in together, no grass or trees or flowers any where to be seen. I went to Tiltons book store for I needed so much. I bot supplies needed, then books for prizes and also nature books for the children to read and other historical novels. I had not much time to decide, but bot all I dared to. I went to Hennesys store. It was on the west side of Main Street then and bot some black broad cloth for a shoulder cape that I would wear around the house and would be handier than my big shawl.

Years ago in Indiana everyone wore shawls. I can remember when Father and Seth each had a shawl and when very cold, wore it over a coat. Took the place of overcoats. The women continued to wear them. Mother always saw that each girl had a good sized shawl. They wove them on their looms at home. They make, even to this day, a very useful accessory to any ones wraps in cold climate - tho seldom used.

Next day was Sunday. We visited at Hulsizers. Ed Cline was a little boy, not quite two years old. His grandfather thot he was about right and he was a cute little toe headed lad. That evening we took the train for Divide. Mr. Cline met us with a wagon at the station in Divide and we drove to Dewey. After supper they drove on home.

I had brot a pinking iron with me and shortly after this I cut out my cape, which was cut on the bias and concisted of three graduated layers of capes and a small turn over collar. Around this all I pinked all the edges, which made the finishing. To pink on, lay the cloth on a block of wood and then put the iron and with a wood maul beat hard till the lower fluted edge cuts thru the cloth. Then move the iron over joining the previously cut scollop. It is a tedious process, tho a very pretty edge is made and was used years ago to edge such as broad cloth as it could only be used on fine, closely woven cloth. When finished I liked my cape very much.

Mrs. Bryant quite often went over to visit Mrs. Dodgson, Sr. They lived that winter acrost the street in an old house. I believed it had been used for a butcher shop. They liked to talk of days gone by and they were two very agreeable mother-in-laws. So they often chatted till 10:00 or 11:00. This was a good diversion for Mrs. Bryant to get away from the routine, worry and troubles of hotel life. When she would come home Bryant would say, "Well, Jane, when are you and the old lady going to get married, by the Jesus?" Jane would smile and go on to her room. Once in a while I went over with Mrs. Bryant if I had time. All I regret now is that I did not go oftener and write down the real history stories these two old timers talked over.

While visiting with Mr. or Mrs. Bryant once in a while, I learned of men that dropped in for a meal occasionally, their occupation and life in the hills. There was Johnnie Evans, a short, red faced Irishman that prospected in Triangle Gulch and had quite good holes that afterwards produced ore. Billie Vipond and his partner Joe Storm lived in a nice little cabin in the edge of Vipond Park. Billie had a good mine and that winter was taking things easy, his brother John was away. They generally worked together tho now he was away. Brubaker came in and I often seen him. Then Pattengale [*Pettingill*], the Wild Man of Wise River.

When at Mrs. Overly's one afternoon she was quite despondent. Lillie, looking out of the window, says, "Ma, I believe you are going to have company."

"Who?" says Mrs. Overly.

"It looks like the Captain."

Sure enuf, Captain Prideaux. She introduced him to me, he talked a short while and then went on. "O my," says Mrs. Overly, "I was afraid he was going to want me to cook for him."

"Would you have gone Ma?"

"No, I would not cook for him. I am afraid of him, for he said one day a woman would have to be good to him if they cooked in his house. So I tell you I'd not enter his house."

His double cabin was above the mill acrost the road on the bank of the river. That was the first and last time I ever saw him. The mill was just above Overly's house a short ways. One could look out of the window and see the ore team come up over the grade and stop to unload the ore and come on up the grade and turn down past their house.

The last of the month found colder nights, most all the lovely hued leaves on the alder, rose bushes, goose berry bushes, cotton wood, birch had all filtered to the ground.

As much as I disliked hotel life, Al said he thot I'd have to stay here as that was the best place after all. Mrs. Bryant was all right and would treat me good, my room was small that was true. If I did not want to mingle I had better stay there, which I did most of the time.

Most of the houses in town was small, even large families were crowded in to them in many cases. Then there was the question of the right kind of people to stay with? And every time one thot or pondered on the situation, Al had been there long enuf time to know what was best for me to do. And that was, "Stay right where you are. While you see a lot and hear a lot you have not been use to, they won't hurt you and you can get away by staying in your room."

The partitions were made of inch boards. The front part of the house was lined with cheese cloth and wall paper over. It was sight proof tho not all together sound proof. Often I could hear "God Dam it Jane, those beans were like bullets to day noon. I am going to pack up and go up to my own cabin and cook my own beans if you don't make that God Damed cook cook better." Jane seldom ever talked back. She knew she was running the hotel and was doing the best she could, and she always set up good meals. The trouble was his dyspeptic stomach was causing this out break.

There were Cornish miners coming and going most every day. Most every day some staid over night, most of them went on thru. Dolph Peterson and Shannon ran the Eliel, Burfiend and Fyrie Store. They boarded at the hotel but a little later Shannon moved his wife and two boys to town and the boys came to school, bright little chaps. I soon seen I'd have to stock up pencils, pens and various first grade appliances so the children could work. Some still borrowed tho others were independent. In many cases I still put lessons on the board and in many cases copied their lessons for them. There were now a few more people coming to town and some going out, tho the number increased.

The mill ran on, no indications of a shut down. I had a long talk with Al about getting another place to board and says, "No, there is not a place for you. You will have to stay in your room when they are here. What they say, don't notice." I never knew people could use such words. The poppies still bloomed on - I only wished that frost would never come.

Minnie always was nice to me and often come in, chatted with me in my room and always brot a treat. I stopped thinking about any other home and began studying all my books over and over for I must have that Montana Certificate in November. Then I must keep the children busy between times.

October 1892

October's bright blue weather came to Montana much the same as in other states, the mornings were tinged with light frosts.

The school moved on as usual, with now and then a slight increase in pupils, which made the job just a little harder on the teacher. But never a complaint I uttered as to the job for I would not let a soul know a thing. I thot, for if I

> **Deweys**
> Special Correspondence.
> Deweys, Oct. 8. -- Work has been suspended on the ditch at Vipond, and the mill closed for the winter and all work suspended except development work on the mine which shows a good quantity of free milling ore of superior quality.
> The Lone Pine Consolidated Mining Company keep steadily at work. The mine looks better than ever.
> The miners of the Tocquoholia, owned and operated by Long and Riley, are on a strike. The miners ask for shorter hours and a better quality of whiskey, while the muckers ask for increased wages.
> It is to be hoped that a speedy settlement may be effected between owners and laborers.
> We hope the genial N.A.J. of Wisdom will not over look his literary duties, now that he has entered the political arena.
> Now that the citizens of Deweys have at least given up the hopes of getting the World's fair, they are beginning the fight to get the capital.
> Mr. Vipond made the city a short visit to Tuesday.
> A sudden quiet has fallen on our city. The front window panes do not break mysteriously. The Chinaman is not frightened out of a years growth by a tick tack on the window; the tin does not push the canine down the street at the rate of 1.6093 kilometers per minute.
> The reason of this quietude is that school has commenced and young America is confined eight hours per diem.
> Verily the school ma'am is worthy of the remuneration which she receives.
> The game season was opened by Dan Doolittle who killed three deer within two miles of the public square. Mark Lefler killed a bear in Charcoal basin while looking for grouse.
> "Major Parks" made the city a short visit a few days ago.
> Mr. Guy Ames has severed his connection with the Dolman Mercantile Company and is going to Idaho. Guy has grown to be looked on as a fixture of the town and all regret his leaving.
> Mr. E. G. Bryant has delivered his first consignment of bear hides and oil. Four fine hides are on exhibition at Pond and Vance's. At present E. G. is up the river after more bear and is supplying the Travelers Hotel with trout, the smallest of which are 12 inches in length.
> The political pot approacheth the boiling point.
> Dewey's is in favor of Bozeman for the capital.
> A man never knows how much he amounts to or how necessary a commodity he is until the woods is full of candidates, each one of them willing to pronounce him the prince of good fellows - for his vote.
> Mrs. George R. Vance is home from her visit among relatives at Glendale, Melrose and Rattlesnake.
> Hand and Halbert have finished harvesting the first crop of oats ever cut with a self-binder this far up in the mountains. They were delayed last week by a snow storm but the bright, warm weather has fully ripened the grain and they will have a good yield.
> - Amos Keeter
>
> From the Dillon Tribune
> Dillon, Montana
> October 7, 1892

did, it would have been the town talk. Someone would say how's the school, have you licked anyone yet? "O the school is all right," I'd say. And with the bunch getting bigger each day it was really discouraging, but I had come so far I could not fail. "I must and I will" was old man Nugent's theory and I worked with that ever present thot.

Now the Hopkins family came in, six in all, with Etta, a sister, as mother, house keeper and counselor. When the Hopkins started [school], they came every day - Alfred, Mark, Harry, Arthur and Annie. (Incidentally, my daughter Susan taught Annie's children.) All with books, pens, copy books, pencils and slates. The father cut wood for the coke kilns in Canyon Creek and he clothed and provided them well for that day and they came to school with a purpose. They were nice and polite and ever obliging. There were some that would stay out, which made it harder on me. As when they were out, made draggy scholars. Then often those that I copied for would loose their copies on the way home or something, so they came without any lesson and then had to sit with someone to study with. All these were common occurrences. But I struggled on, worked at nights for them and studied diligently each night so I would not fail the teacher exams in November.

I went to school, came back, and staid in my own room, often hearing most disgusting talk from the front room. Bryant had the foulest mouth of all. Seemed other men delighted in provoking him in to such talk. If I had to go thru, on my way to school, I went right along, never noticing anyone.

Mrs. Dolman came out usually so she could be with us Sundays for Sunday School. She brot singing books and tracts for the Sunday School work and we had quite a good attendance. This we kept going most of the year.

One Sunday afternoon Al took me to Cline's. They had moved into the valley a short time before, coming from Glendale where they had known Horace and Big Al for several years. They had bot the Sam Garrott place and horses. There was a small log cabin on the place, a log stable and corrals. They moved in just as it was, determined to have a home of their own. So it was in this humble surrounding that I met Mr. & Mrs. Albert Cline and in after years to be friends and neighbors.

The First Bear Story

The first bear story I heard a day after I arrived in Dewey's Flat.

"Did you hear about that bear killing Ben Hamby up on the Big Hole near Jackson?" says a boarder.

"Your dammed right I did." says Bryant. "That old bald faced grizzly meant business. By the Holy Jesus," says Bryant, "it did not take him long to object to Ben's objecting to killing his calves in the pen."

Old Baldy, after coming nights and slaughtering two nice calves, Ben decided to take his gun one day and try his luck at tracking the bear to his hide out. Telling his wife of his intentions and not to worry, he shouldered his gun and he soon found the track of the big brute leading hither and yon in and out of a brushy patch of willows then disappearing and again picking up the track. Then the track was lost. Ben did not come home that night so in the morning the hired man, with a neighbor, decided to go look for Ben.

They finally picked up the tracks of the man and bear and in and out around willow clumps till finally both tracks entered a big clump of willows. They cautiously worked their way in a short ways. There stood the big bald faced grizzly in front of them and a few steps away the man lay dead. These two men were frightened at such a sight they beheld. They cautiously beat a hasty retreat out and home to tell their story of their gruesome find. With guns and ammunition they returned, prepared to meet bruin, but they found he had left hastily. Ben had evidently crawled in and taken one shot at the bear and then the bear rushed on to the man and killed him, bending the gun barrel then had kept watch over the man and had dug a hole, shoving the dirt to one side. Evidently intended to roll the man in the hole if he had not been disturbed.

This story was told over and over again by Bryant and damming Hamby for being such a dammed fool to crawl into a willow brush after a bar.

Giant Cap

One Saturday the boys of the town found some Giant Caps in a nice little round metal round box. They knew what they were as their father often used them in prospecting and always kept them up in some safe place where children could not get them. But these boys thot they knew how to handle them. Tho thot they would be fine to have a little fun with, so they took them out on this little rocky knoll by the school house. They found a nice flat rock, put one on the rock and then all threw rocks at the cap on the big rock. They had a lot of fun. All went well till Fred Mitchell got too near and was hit in the heal by a piece of the cap, which made a bad bloody wound. He was given aid at home tho Dr. Jones was sent for post haste by a horse back currier over the Vipond way.

November 1892

November marched in more sober, somber hues with cold blue air and occasionally snow. The nice fall days grew fewer with more and more darker storm clouds hovering on the distant snow clad peaks. The boys had gone to Laurin, Ruby Valley to see if Mr. Dupee would come up the valley and thrash their oats. Mr. Dupee was going to thrash at Melrose and would come as soon as thru there. The first week in November the boys were busy making ready for the crew.

They got an old Frenchman, Joe Buyan, from Jerry Creek to cook for the crew. He had formally told of his ability as cook so they gave him the job. Lucky for the crew the job did not last long and they got away to better cooked foods. Pea soup was one of his favorite dishes. He'd say," A little white bean he makes de best pea soup by gee." He made the bread for the crew, which Horace said was awful. They provided as much as could be bot those days of canned goods tho he had an awful time cooking for the crew. It gave them all new storys to tell even tho they did not fair so well.

This was the first oat crop raised and thrashed on the upper Big Hole. They had a good yield and was a saleable crop, as oats then sold from 3 to 4 cents per pound.

Bryant, Kizer and Nig

Bryant's Nig dog was a mongral tho in all appearance a black shepherd, a wise looking, knowing dog with tail curled up. Wherever Bryant went, horseback or afoot, Nig was at his heals. When his master sit down to toast his shins at the fire, he lay down with ever a watchful eye, lest his master should make a move. In the morning, noon or night, Nig would stroll down thru the house at his master's heals. There were always a few fellows sitting around in the front room,

---

Teachers Institute

The Teachers Institute of Beaverhead county will be held in the high school building in this city, Monday, Tuesday and Wednesday of next week.

Patron and all interested in the cause of our common school should make it a point to attend the sessions. The following interesting programme has been prepared.

Monday, 9:30
Opening Exercises
Primary Reading . . . . . . Miss Reininger
Primary History . . . . Miss Coffin
Busy work . . . . Miss Innes

1:30 p.m.
Primary Numbers . . . . Miss Brown
Factoring L,C,M,G,C,D, ... Mr. Bell
Primary Language . . . . . . Miss K. Coffin
Primary Geography . . . . . . Miss McStay

Tuesday, 9:30
Interm'd'te Reading . . . . Mr. Steere
Fractions . . . . Miss Staves
History . . . . Miss Coffin
Physiology . . . . Mr. Gates

1:30 p.m.
Interm'd'te Geog. . . . . Miss McStay
Interm'd'te Language' . . .Miss K. Coffin
Query Box . . . . Institute

8:00 P.M.
Teacher's Reading Circle

Wednesday, 9:30
Advanced Reading . . . . Mr. Steere
Music in Schools . . . Mrs. F. M. Thomas
Analysis . . . . Mr. Smith
Current Events as a Part of School work, ... Miss Geerston

1:30 P.M.
Penmanship . . . . Mr. Stouffer
Use of Blackboard . . . . Miss Call
Orthography . . . . Mr. Romney

8:00 P.M.
Address: Our Compulsory School Law
State Supt. John Gannon

Notice of Teacher's Institute
Dillon Tribune, Dillon, Montana
November 18, 1892

ever ready to provoke Bryant in to a storm of abuses. Men from out of town, having heard of him, would stop for a meal on a purposes to hear Bryant talk.

The harangue was on if someone said, "Bryant, what is that dog fit for?"

"Why, God dam your soul that dog is a bear dog, a real bear dog, I tell you." Then at the rattle of the traps he is ready for the trail. There upon Bryant would proceed to show the stranger other tricks he could do. Wadding up a piece of paper, lighting it, Nig would jump on it, scratch it, till all the fire was out. When a door was open and left again, Bryant would say, "Nig close the door," which he did by going behind the door and pushing it with his fore feet. Kiser was a quiet dog, larger than Nig. When he went up town the two were always at his heals. Nig, tho was a bear dog.

Nig and Kizer knew spring was just around the corner as they often sniffed the hot air of the old wood stove, stretch and went to the door as if saying, let me out. Bryant would let them out and say to the visitor, "Them thar dogs knows it will soon be time to go to their summer home."

When Bryant's dyspeptic stomach rebelled, he always was ready to go up the river and cook his own beans. He'd say, "Jane why don't you fire that cook. Why, she can't cook beans," then go thru the dining room with Nig and Kizer at his heals ready to start. Tho I don't believe he ever left all winter for he come to think this was much the best place after all. He had to come to the conclusion his self for no one of the amediate family coaxed him to stay.

> **Money Orders**
>
> "On the 17th instant, the Deweys and Argenta post office began doing money order business under instructions from the department."
>
> **The Dillon Tribune
> November 21, 1892**

Times when Bryant felt blues nothing suited him but his dogs. He dammed everything and everybody. Minnie, the youngest child was wayward and did about as she pleased, then Bryant would say, "Minnie God dam it, Minnie, mind your mother." Minnie never minded anyone. She came and went as she liked, tho always on hand when there was a dance. Would dance all night then at 12 and 13 years old. Then at times Bryant would dam the country saying "Who would live in the God dammed country. Why if a crow undertook to fly acrost those dammed peaks he would get his guts dug out." However, Bryant was not a young man anymore and he made no efforts to leave the country, bad as it was.

As the winter wore away the cooks could not cook grub fit to eat. "Look at those beans, hard as bullets," he'd say. He'd get his saddle horse and go to the ranch, that he would, yes he would. Then he often went to the wash room, pull out his bar (bear) traps and look them all over, Nig and Kizer at his heals. Nig would frisk around as if he knew Bryant was going on the chase or trapline.

When a stranger came then he would give a full detail of his trapping and bear hunting career, keeping his guest in hair raising stories all the time. If the man chanced to ask if the dog treed a bear, Bryant would answer with, "Why yes, God dam your sweet life."

Two waiters from Butte was waiting on the table. They went to Quartz Hill to a dance, got home late and was not able to wait tables in the morning. Bryant thot they had been drinking. Bryant hollowed to them, "you two jinnies, get up and get out and take your self down the canyon as fast as you can, do you hear me?" They obeyed and quick too.

This was election fall which gave Dewey's Flat two red letter nights. On these occasions liquor flowed freely and cigars were plentiful. Republican and Democrats, each one told how badly the other parties had run the affairs of county and state and how they could and would set things going aright if they could be elected. The Dillon Candidates, Republicans and Democrats, came by teams to Argenta, Bannock, Jackson, Wisdom and on down to Dewey's Flat, speaking at night in each place. The last night before election would hold a big rally in Dillon.

In those days campaigns gave an extra gala day that did not come every year. Both Republicans and Democrats came to hear the speaker, for in this day men tried to keep informed on the issues of the times on all questions.

The hardy, rough prospector, the lone rancher, took papers and kept up with the news of the world in general. They took time to go once a week for the mail on foot, horseback, sled or wagon or snow shoes. So, on these nights, ranchers up valley, miners from Quartz Hill and Vipond Park, lone gulches, where single prospectors worked outlying districts, Divide, all came. Some to keep up with issues of the day, others for the social part of the entertainment. Children of the town liked the bon fire that preceded in the early evening. They would work like troopers each time to make a big bon fire larger than others. Some men would help get big logs from the nearby timbered hills and build up a small pen like frame, up a few feet, then put in smaller logs and sticks on end in the center. Times if they could get wooden oil barrels, place two, one on each other, and use rubbish or sticks made a good lasting fire. When built right would last a long time and the children had a time gathering material to keep them going till late. At last, all tired out, they went home giving up the balance of the entertainment over to the grown folks.

On these occasions the Bryant Hotel got most of the crowd as this hotel was known far and wide. Most of the candidates came there for supper and a room if they staid over night, which most all of them did, as their teams as well as their selves needed rest. Then they liked to meet Bryant and hear him tell his stories about the trap line and his dogs.

At one of these gatherings a speaker failed to come on time. Whereupon George Vance, Horace and Al persuaded McKinzie to take the stand out in the middle of the street. They all imbibed quite freely. At last McKinzie mounted the stand and proceeded to give quite an eloquent patriotic talk. When all at once he was met with an onslaught of eggs. These three rascals had gotten every egg in town. Next morning it was ham or bacon, minus the eggs on every bill of fare.

When W. A. Clark wanted favors from the outlying precincts he went at it in a business like manner, putting on real work campaigns for his prospective voter. The boss always got big money. Clark always needed various kinds of logs and the mountains were full of timber, the streams offered transportation, all this, if handled right, meant votes. In '88 he began to put out logging camps, up many creeks and rivers, as well as several creeks that emptied into the Big Hole River. There were even camps on Jerry Creek, Seamore Creek, Wise River, Meadow Creek and along the Big Hole where logs could be gotten. In the fall of '92 he attended the campaign meeting at Dewey. I was introduced to him and danced once with him. He lodged at the Bryant Hotel. He 'lectioniereed also in his many logging camps. Every election year the camps flourished. He paid well for the times and he got the votes.

At another campaign meeting, I think it was a Republican gathering, I always laid this incident to the same crowd that egged McKinzie. The hall was lit with coil oil lamps, one on the speaker's stand and one or two side lamps. A pitcher of water and glass was also there. To make the meeting more impressive, Joe Buyan (the cook) (Frenchman) took his pet eagle, put it on the back of a chair on the rostrum and set clost by to keep it in place. The crowd had gathered. The Republican speaker came up and began to address the people. Such cheering and cheers again. He had to call the crowd to order time and again. Then he would proceed to talk on his subject, when Joe, having too much liquor to tend the eagle, would occasionally poke at the bird. It would raise up, spread out its wings as if ready to fly, then the crowd would cheer. When all quieted down the speaker would go on with his talk.

This act of poking the bird so it would spread its wings ended by the bird dropping excrement all over the chair. Then the more bolder of the crowd cheered more lustrously. Tho the others were too abashed to look up. Then the speaker, not seeing the joke, waited quietly till the crowd ceased cheering. In the meantime, Joe found that he had become suddenly dry and slipped out the back door to a near saloon to replenish his thirst. After this the bird sat quietly blinking at the lights and the speaker finished his talk and others came on and told how the country could be set aright if his party was in power and therefore told the voter who to vote for on the first Tuesday after the first Monday in November, Election Day.

When all the candidates had spoken, chairs and benches were shoved back to the wall and the dance was on till two, three or four in the morning. In the saloons liquor and cigars were dealt out to all. Very few showed the effects of liquor. Those that did never came back to the dance hall. In the late morning candidates ate a late breakfast and after paying their hotel bills and dealt out cigars, they quietly drove away down the canyon as that was the last night on the circuit. "Like the Arabs of old, folded their tents and silently stole away."

Bears

One morning bright and early Horace jumped on his saddle horse bare backed. Thot he would find his team up the gulch from town, going up Quartz Hill Gulch past the grave yard, heading for Swamp Creek. In passing the slaughter pen his horse became unmanageable. Two little black bears scaled the wall of the pen and took to the brush. After that he took time to saddle his horse.

Candidates

When the Dillon candidates came in November of 1892, Al Stone was with them. He was County Superintendent and was running again. Shortly before I let out school a gentleman called. I had never seen him before. Al Stone, the County Superintendent! He staid while I was hearing a class. Then I asked him if he would like to talk to the children. He declined, complimented me on my work. By that time school was out and he went over town. My, I was so nervous I could hardly contain myself. My face colored up like fire knowing that I would soon be taking exams from him. Seemed to stun me. Could I pass? Yes, I must, being so far away. If I failed? Those thots always confronted me.

Election day was a holiday for the teacher as the school house was used as a voting place on Tuesday. Booths were made of calico for the voter, so when voting their votes could be done separately and secretly - the same system that is used today in small precincts.

I did not know all the judges and clerks that were there that day but most always, George Vance, Al Brubaker, John Lawrence, Horace or Big Al, with others. After the votes were all in at 6 p.m., they were counted and some one of the officers took the returns amediately to Divide by horse and buggy or wagon. There they were telegraphed in to Dillon (county seat). These trips were often made late at night. They had to go no matter how cold the weather. Some times the trip was a real hardship to the fellow that took them out. Tho there were some recompense, as while at the depot there were a good fire and the R. R. agent often told them the flashes that came over the wires. In presidential campaigns they often got a good inkling as to whom would be president. Election after election came and went. John Lawrence and Horace Hand taking turns serving their precinct finally decided they would ask Jack Davis if he would take the returns. So he did and in the night some time it turned dreadful cold. Jack had a poor team and wagon which made the trip long. When arriving home in the wee hours in the morning he was nearly frozen.

When school resumed Wednesday I went early to get things put back. I suppose they thot they had left the school room clean, but tobacco spit was all over the floor. That evening I scrubbed. There was now nearly thirty scholars. Seemed most every family moving in brot more children which made more complication. Some had a very bad habit of staying out a day or half day, but I dare say on some of the poor mothers parts it could not be helped. I often talked to Al about the conditions and he said it could not be helped as many were so poor. These talks gave me courage to just do the best I could for them. That demanded more copying lessons such as arithmetic, spelling, then out lines on other subjects.

I often wondered if I was doing any good at all. Was I really teaching them anything? The only barometer of this was thru Al. "You are all right, just go ahead." The last of the month I arranged to have reading and recitations after recess. On Fridays we had oral and written arithmetic, sometimes spelling matches, then gave out report cards and prizes of books for good grades and perfect attendance.

The early winter of 1892, snow had fallen to such a depth that one could go most any place far or near on sleighs. Mr. and Mrs. Cline and baby (Ed) were coming back from a trip to Glendale, their former home, with household goods to their new ranch home. As they came up the grade they over took Big Al driving the stage, making his regular trip from Divide to Dewey. Cline wanted to talk to Big Al so he tied the lines together and put them over the dashboard and crawled up on the boot with Al. Mrs. Cline and the boy were sitting in the back of the sleigh box on some hay. Cline's team was perfectly gentle and would follow the stage. All went well for a time, but on coming to a sharp bend in the road, Cline's team, with the sleigh, took a short cut after the stage and away, the sleigh, team, Mrs. Cline and Ed, went over the grade and landed on rocky shore of the river. Without the deep cushion of the snow it would have been a hard landing. The men, seeing the predicament, stopped the stage, Cline hollering ho, ho, ho. The team stood still and were still hitched to the sleigh. Al and Cline jumped off the stage, slid down the grade. Big Al had tied his reigns to the hub of the stage, so if his team should start, the reigns would wind tighter and draw them back. It happened to not be a very steep place. The wagon box cooped right over Mrs. Cline and child, about two years old and when the men lifted up the box to see how they faired, Ed was laughing. All covered with snow and hay and around her was scattered bits of broken dishes and other belongings she was taking home.

One Sunday afternoon when Al was driving the stage from Dewey to Divide, he took Mag Nobern, a waiter, and myself down the grade a ways to show us where Al Cline's team and sleigh went over the grade. He let us out at the place and he went on, on his regular scheduled trip to Divide to pick up passengers and mail. He drove a regular concord thorough brace coach, only two horses for that short a trip. After we looked over the place we decided it was a very nice, snowy place to land. Then we walked back home (to the Hotel).

Shortly after this I was at Cline's one Sunday afternoon. Mrs. Patton came down with Old Brigham and the top buggy with Mary, Rose and Ethel, the baby. Soon after she came the baby began to be fretful and cried. Mrs. Cline had no medicine in the house for the baby. Finally she said do you suppose a toddy would help it. Yes, Mrs. Patton said. I'll give it some if you will make it and in making it, the water was real hot, so Mrs. Patton took the cup and placed it near by under the sewing machine to cool. The baby ceased crying and the two women began to chat and forgot the toddy. Rose was a little tot and had her eye on the toddy cup. When the conversation flowed freely, Rose slipped behind her mothers chair, took the cup up and drank the toddy.

Roads and Accidents

There were very few accidents. People became conscious minded and were careful on grades where there were no turnouts. Everyone was extremely careful. The long freight team with their bells warned one of their coming. Some times, on a two horse team, they unhooked the horses and set the wagon over by hand in a very close place. Passing that way was easier than to back a half of a mile and then too, some teams won't back and it was no place to teach them.

Below Dewey two men were in a cart. The horse took fright and went over a very steep place on the grade. The men jumped. Horse was drowned. Then another time two horses and spring wagon went over, men got out.

Another time Mr. Cline chanced to have some chain in the sleigh. Mrs. Cline got in at the Wise River bridge. Was a steep raise before getting on the bridge. She was sitting clost to the end, no end gate. She slipped out, next instant the hook on the chain caught in her shoe top. He looked around and there she was dragging, tho not hurt. Snow is often a good cushion.

About the spring of 1893 or 94 most everyone wanted to freight. Decker, a relative of Bryant's, had an outfit. He loaded at Divide. At the chalk bluff he decided the hill was too tough or snow on it too deep so he decided it would be better to cross on the ice. At that particular place the bluff came down into the river and if they went that way they were compelled to cross twice to keep to the only road. The ice gave way. Decker was not an experienced man with horses in this predicament. The horses drowned at once. No one knew how to jump out and hold their heads out of water. A horse drowns very quickly if their head goes under. So there he was, three drowned all at once, a sick man. With help of other freighters they helped him out, got more horses and made the trip into Gibtown.

Later when a few autos came, there was a very bad accident below, a short ways from Ralston's on a sharp little grade. Always bent the wrong way. A party of four were coming from Wisdom down the river to Divide. Their car slipped off at this particular grade and capsized in a slough, killing and drowning three. The forth man made his escape and ran to Cullum's place. All the while the auto horn was blowing just as tho a spirit or ghost had taken up the watch.

Cattle being driven down to market weekly and sometimes daily, were a detriment to those narrow grades that were carved out of sheer cliffs. Rocks of all sizes were rolled down, besides dirt slid down, filling in the upper sides of the road. Sometimes cattle went off the sheer cliffs into the river and times ice gave away and drowned some. Silver Bow Bill, Kip Mudd, Ike Edgger and many others bot and drove cattle in early days. Drivers were runners and reckless that plied the road day and night often making forced rides in order to be ready early in the morning to start the cattle out. Most generally they knew where they would stop to feed or pasture each night. When on the trail to market, drivers were reckless. Often in the spring when cattle were turned out for the summer they often drove in an extra one or two, made extra gambling money while in Butte. Some cattlemen had so many, one or two were not noticed but the little fellow with a very few had often suffered sorely from these losses. No record at the slaughter house was recorded and one could search in vain for their lost cows. When asked if they ever saw your cattle on the road, it was always no.

Since the auto ages there has been several autos to jump the grade below Dewey, either from icy roads or drunken drivers.

About 1911 or 12 autos were scarce, very few could have them. Ralstons, others and myself went to Georgie Tong's funeral in Butte. When I was going to the train I met Mrs. Ralston and she told me they had bot a new auto and Clarence Strowbridge was driving them out home by way of Anaconda and French Creek. Next morning news reported Mr. & Mrs. Ralston, Mr. Strowbridge being drowned in an auto accident. Mr. & Mrs. Bruce came to our house on the Donovan place and brot us the news. Stowbridge either dropped to sleep or the reflection of the light [*affected his sight*] and they jumped the gully. They should have gone around at the fatal moment or the gears might have locked. No one ever could tell. The car cooped them in the creek and they drowned like rats. A small boy Stowbridge escaped, ran to the ranch house a mile away, rang the dinner bell to wake the folks, awoke the sleepers in the home and told his story. Before this Strowbridge drove a freight team for a few years for J. P. Lossel Store Co. and he was often found asleep on the drivers seat. So we often wondered if he had fallen to sleep while driving them home that fatal night. But the roads were very poor those days, with sharp curves, narrow grades and such, and is a wonder more accidents did not happen. Up to the auto age I can't recall of anyone being killed on the road.

One exception - Bert Powell worked up about Ralston's, tho often drove team. He came down to our house with Ralston's wood saw and sawed our wood, went back and a few days afterward was driving a freight team up the road near Seamore Creek. The wagon dropped suddenly in a chuck hole, he fell off the seat into the horses heals and they took freight, either the fall broke his neck or the wagon killed him when it passed over the body. No one ever knew just how he was killed.

A Bath Tub

Yes, I really believe Tom Thomas, a barber, was the owner of the only bath tub in the town of Dewey's Flat. Being a barber, it was quite necessary to have one, for some of the boys whom had used them before in a more civilized country.

But the poor women, what of them? Cabins in those days were not modern. Well, they washed in a tub or wash pan or what ever came handy. They never thot of a bath tub. Perhaps they did not even know Tom had one. There were no water system in this town. One was lucky to have a well or was clost to a neighbor who was kind enuf to let them use water.

For Tom to prepare a bath, a fire was made in a stove, a wash boiler placed there, water brot from well and heated in the boiler. Then the hot water was put into the tub and more cold water left in buckets to cool the tub water to proper temperature.

Captain Prideaux hired an English man by the name of Willoby as bookkeeper. When Captain Prideaux's bookkeeper came to town, he and his wife stayed at the hotel until they could find a suitable cabin to live in. Their dress, speech, actions, and looks indicated very decidedly that they had just come over from England. Acrost the street Tom Thomas ran a barber shop and advertised baths.

Mr. Willoby and wife were used to baths. As soon as she came she looked around for a bath. Tom's being the only one, she went to Tom and ordered a bath. This was awful, for Tom was a very gentle, timid man and the thots of a woman coming to his shop, he nearly fainted. He hardly knew what to say, but in his barasment he said yes. He told her to come at stated time and it would be ready. There were several loafers sitting around, looking up at Tom, grinned. But, he thot, if she was bound to have a bath, he'd fix it for her. That was all he could do.

Here she came on time. Tom had put the hot water in the bath tub and cold water buckets sat by and all was ready. Tom opened the door for her and she stepped in. He explained to her she'd find cold water, towels and soap, then closed the door and went out. She was a beautiful, refined woman in all appearance. There were other customers and the loungers taking in the scene. All at once she yelled, "Tom I want a bath. Come give me a bath. I want a bath." What had he got in to by fixing the bath? He dared not go in. The men began to laugh at Tom. Then she called, "Tom I want a bath." In all his life he never was in such a position as this and she yelled again, "I want a bath." Then the men said, "Tom, go in." No, not for his life. Finally she got tired of calling for a bath, then quietly slipped out the back door mad as a wet hen.

Sears Roebuck & Co. Catalog
1902

Several loungers in the barber shop, or near, heard it all and began to guy Tom. As long as Tom ran the shop he was guyed about giving that English woman a bath. But I don't believe he was guilty. She either took it or not, no one could tell, but they do know she made a hasty retreat, mad as a wet hen. She never came back for any more baths. Town went down. Tom married Jim Friend's niece and later moved to Butte.

Willobys put on a whist party one night. I heard of it, tho was not invited. It seemed they needed a bell so Mrs. Willoby sent over for the school bell. I believe that was the only card party I ever heard of in all my life up the Big Hole. In those days cards were played by the men mostly when in the saloons. In January the Willobys moved away.

The Teachers Institute was set for the latter part of November, also the teachers examination. Al says, when I begun school, "If I were you I'd not draw my money till the end of three months and if you need any I can lend you some." So when I got ready to go to Dillon he loaned me $20.00 and took me on the stage to Divide. I really needed the money and my board money I knew should have been paid, but Al says no.

This was my first time in Dillon. Mrs. Axe was keeping a few out of town teachers and had sent down one of the girls to meet the train. It was lucky for me, as I was a complete stranger.

I attended the Institute, liked it very much and got new ideas about teaching. Now I can only remember very few of the teachers I met there, Mrs. Innes and sister, a Miss Humphry, she was teaching a private school in Horse Prairie, tho later taught at Melrose in 1899 and has been a high school teacher in Butte for years and is now [1930's].

Thanksgiving day I spent at Mrs. Axe's. She had some town people for dinner, besides teachers. She cooked a very nice turkey dinner with all the trimmings and served family style on a long table. Of the town people I remember was Mr. and Mrs. Lambert Eliel and son, a very bright boy of three or four years.

At dinner I wore a black cashmere skirt and a red waist. I had a silk black basque for the skirt but had made it too tight and the silk cut under the arm, so was obligated to wear the one outfit all the time when there. But many others had but very few clothes and I thot nothing of my deficiency of clothing.

The examination was held two days after Thanksgiving in a ware house acrost from Eliel's clothing store. I believe there were only two or three teachers to take the examination that time and Mr. A. P. Stone had us to come to his office there and take the examination. It was there at this time I saw my first typewriter in his office. The afternoon of the second day I had finished the examination and went home on the afternoon train.

Thanksgiving Dance
1892

When I came back I was told the following about the dance and fight that took place while I was away.

Bills had been out for a dance Thanksgiving night. It bid fair to be a big dance. The mill was running then in Dewey. The town teamed with men then, the Cornish miners at Quartz Hill often came and stockmen all up along the river. Thanksgiving was only once a year, then there was no other gathering to bring people out. Al was still driving stage. Horace came down too. The Hotel was full as usual, strangers filled the Hotels. A Mr. Bulpin, the R.R. ticket agent at Divide, the man that came whistling thru the darkness the night I landed, came. He was a cripple, having a cork leg, tho got around quite spry and could dance. The dances those days began around 10 p.m. and went along fine. The men that drank staid away. Ed Kinney kept saloon just above the dance hall. He was a tall angular man with a heavy beard. Before coming to the Flat, he killed a man but that was small significance in his business. There were not enuf room in the Kinney Hall for all couples to dance. Tho they crowded up as many square dances as they could get in. In the round dance more could get on the floor. Horace and Al did not dance so much tho went to see the crowd and visit.

Bulpin, as he was going out, motioned to Horace and Al. They went over to a saloon which teemed with Cornish miners. They knew him as they most all came down from Butte by rail and went back that way. They soon crowded around him and began pouring out their grievances and soon a fight was on. Bulpin flashed out a knife in self protection, cutting one man quite badly. Then the Cornish man's friends (about 40) tried to jump on to the agent and kill him. In the altercation that followed, Horace and Al took part standing the crowd back, giving the agent time to get to the river. He plunged in to the icy water and made the other side. Then he groped his way down the river and recrost. Horace and Al met him on the grade and took him to his room at Divide. Helped him change his clothes and made him comfortable, then went on back to Dewey's Flat. When they got back there was yet several that wanted to know what became of Bulpin and the fellow that got cut. No one seemed to know. Al went to his room, as the next stage trip came early in the morning and Horace slipped away quietly to his cabin home.

When I came back from Dillon everyone was telling about the Cornish man and the agent's fight. When Bryant got a show, he quietly told me "That those two big Bastards" (Horace and Al) had saved the agent's life in that cutting affair in the saloon the night of the Thanksgiving Ball. Not a word was ever told me from them what they did that night and I never mentioned it to them what Bryant had told me. They kept busy, Horace at the ranch and Al still drove the stage. They never feared any consequence as to what might happen to them later. Their rights were undisputed and they went any and all places at any time.

If the underdogs was getting the worst of a fight they helped him out and always stood up for their rights as well as the other fellows. If some drunken braggart got too boisterous he was put in his place by persuasion or main strength as the occasion called for. They never carried a gun as they never believed in that kind of bravery.

I had often been asked if I danced, being a newcomer. Everyone was anxious to find out something. No, was the invariable answer. Al asked me if I danced and I said no. Well, he said, that is best. So I staid home and thot nothing about it as I never had gone to a dance. I staid in my room and rolled in at bed time. There was a big crowd in the Hotel as usual such nights and the town was full of strangers. The dance was on at 9 or 10.

This was Saturday. I'd have to wait a few days before I'd get my certificate, that is (if). Some times I'd imagine myself going sorrowfully home. Then the chagrin of it all?

December 1892

Monday morning I was up early, the weather was real cold, so such mornings I made an extra effort to have the school house warm and my black board work done. My register contained now forty scholars within such a small school house. In some cases I had to set three in a seat, tho with these drawbacks we had quite a good school. I generally opened school with songs. I supplied many with leaflets or copied verses on the board for them to copy to a song book. Then when I could spare the time, I read each morning from some good book. I tried to follow with songs and stories, those that were used in my school day.

Monday after school I did up the janitor work and went over to the Pond and Vance store for my three month check, for now my three months was up. George Vance gave me a check for $195.00. The most money I ever possessed. I paid Mrs. Bryant $84.00 for my three months board and room, which she was glad to get. That left me $111.00. I sent my mother $75.00 and

> **From Maggie's writings:**
> At Melrose I shall never forget the hub bub there was at the train. People getting on all excited, talking about the big snow slide at Hecla.

UNDER MANY TONS OF SNOW

Monstrous Snow Slides Come Tearing Down the Side of Lion Mountain

Six Persons Taken Out Dead - The People of Lion City Abandon the Town for Safety.

Hon. Henry Knippenberg, superintendent of the Hecla Consolidated Mining company, while in Butte the other day, related to an Anaconda Standard reporter the details of the fearful snow slides at Lion City. His account of the calamity is perhaps the most authentic, hence we take pleasure in publishing it in full. The Standard gives his version of the matter as follows:

On Wednesday night at 11:30 o'clock a heavy snow slide came tearing down the side of Lion mountain, burying four men beneath a bank of snow between ten and thirty feet deep. A rescuing party, which was quickly organized, succeeded in getting one of the men out alive, but two men named Sparks and Rusk and a Chinaman who was asleep in the same house when the slide came, were dead long before they could be reached. Sparks' body was shipped to his father at Las Vegas, New Mexico, and the remains of Rusk were sent to his parents at Thayer, Iowa. The Chinaman's body was sent to Dillon. Both Sparks and Rusk were employees of the Hecla company.

The bodies were shipped from Melrose and when the party of thirty men who had accompanied them to the depot returned to the mines late at night they found that another slide had taken place at Lion City, which is about a mile below Hecla, a few minutes before their arrival, in which seven people were buried. The men quickly set to work again and succeeded in digging out four people who where still alive. Nick Bergstrom and two of his children were dead. Mrs. Bergstrom, who was sleeping in the same bed with her husband, and one of her children were taken out more dead than alive, but they will recover.

The snow around Hecla and Lion City is now all the way from 40 to 60 feet deep, and the condition of things is such that it is unsafe for people residing anywhere in the immediate vicinity. As it is well known to a great many people, Glendale, Greenwood, Lion City and Hecla are all on the side of Lion mountain, which is at an angle of about 45 degrees and very smooth, with but little timber and offers a clean sweep to a snow slide. Glendale, where the smelter of the Hecla company is located, is about five miles above Melrose and the concentrators is at Greenwood, seven miles higher up. Lion City, where nearly all the miners live, and which has a population of 300 or 400 is three miles above Greenwood and a mile below Hecla, where the mines of the company are situated. The side of the mountain is so steep that steps had to be cut in the side in order to facilitate travel up and down. Hecla is very near the top of Lion mountain, which has an altitude of 11,000 feet, and the snow gets very deep up there in the winter. This is the first snow slide that has ever occurred there, however, and is due to some very heavy snow falls during the past week.

After the last snow slide Mr. Knippenberg ordered all the families in Lion City to move down to Glendale at once, and they are out of danger by this time. Mr. Knippenberg also gave orders to Sam A. Barbour, the assistant superintendent, to try to shoot the snow down the side of the mountain by means of giant powder, and this experiment will be tried. Several heavy explosions of giant powder will be set off where the snow is the deepest, and it is hoped that the concussion will be sufficient to start the immense body of snow and send it tumbling down the side of the mountain so far that it will be out of danger. This experiment has never been tried and it is a matter of doubt as to whether it will prove successful or not. If it fails the people will be compelled to stay away from Lion City and Hecla until the snow goes off and the mine will have to be closed down. If the experiment proves successful the immense body of snow will do great damage to the Hecla company's property in its sweep down the side of the mountain, but Mr. Knippenberg is willing to stand this loss if the danger can be removed from the lives of the company's employed.

When Mr. Knippenberg went through Glendale on his way to Butte he sent a relief party up to Lion City to assist the people there in removing to a place of safety. Mr. Knippenberg has already returned to the mine, and he will give the attempt to shoot the snow down the side of the mountain his personal supervision. The telephone line of Lion City and Hecla was swept away in the slide, and it will be impossible to get further information from there for some days. The attempt to dislodge the big banks of snow will be fraught with great danger, and it is feared that some more lives may be lost before the impending danger is removed.

The Dillon Examiner, Dillon, Montana
December 6, 1893

kept $36.00 in my trunk, which I kept locked now. Then I bot 3 1/2 yards of black satin which had a nice white vine thru the black background for a dress I made up later.

It was quite a relief and satisfaction to know I had earned some money and could begin to help pay off the small mortgage of $320.00 which hung over my aging parent's home.

The Butte Butchering Company had turned out some cattle up Wise River Meadow in the summer. The snow had gotten deep before they could get them all out. They had gotten some earlier. Horace took the job of rounding them up and bringing them down to the ranch, then wintering those the company could not butcher. They took a team to take supplies for man and beast for a few days. Before they got up in the country some hunters had killed two, called the meat elk. He got out about 100 head and wintered some 25 head on their straw and some hay.

An Episode - E. G. Bryant

One day when Horace came down to Dewey, he went over to the Hotel to hear what ever news Bryant had to tell him and read the paper, as he often did and then get a meal that he did not have to cook, as he was baching then and was lonesome. Bryant was a good forcible entertainer. He, being from Maine too, had a first hand knowledge of this dialect. Horace, drawing up his chair to the fire while waiting for dinner, Bryant punched the big log in the old long wood stove. He squared his self and says, "Horace, I am going to Maine."

"Yes." says Horace.

"Yes," says Bryant, "that God Damed brother of mine is starving that mother of mine and I am going to Maine!"

Horace made many trips to the hotel after wards and that was the last he ever heard of Bryant going to Maine. Living was easier in the hotel and there he staid. For the men folks that came to the hotel, Bryant was an ideal entertainer. In fact, everybody liked him and he liked to talk to the women too, but he was ot quite so forcible and profane in his talk to them.

The Certificate

By the last of the week I should have some word about my examination and sure enuf a letter came from the County Superintendent's office in Dillon. I hardly dared to open, least the answer? What would it be? I went to my room to open it and set down for I felt weak. O what joy when I pulled out the Certificate. Maggie Halbert to teach for one year. Really, was it I? Yes, now I could cease my worrying for a little while at least and let the next years worries take care of itself.

> **Teacher's Certificate**
>
> Maggie received from the State of Montana, County of Beaverhead Teachers' Graded Certificate No. 42, dated 26th day of November, 1892.
>
> In the fall of 1893 Maggie again attended the Teacher's Institute in Dillon and again took her test to qualify as a teacher. Her second certificate is found in her Bible. - mc

Our Sunday school was progressing nicely under Mrs. Dolman's care. She was a real Sunday School teacher and one that could hold the children.

Brubaker came down and talked tree and Christmas. I really was not very interested, as with the school I felt like I had all I could do. So Mrs. Dolman and Brubaker took the lead and I helped all I could. They took up a collection for the tree. She donated, also got help from the Sunday School in Butte. I gave $1.00 for their nuts and candy fund for I did not begrudge the pleasures for the children and I was giving every day to books, pencils, and paper to keep the school going.

One day we heard a little voice out side saying, "O, Isie, Isie. Teacher, Ma wants Isie to go to the store to get some taters." Her Mom had sent her over and instead of knocking, she stood on the door step and yelled out her story.

Then quite often we had the oldest Doolittle boy that was deaf and dumb come over and peek in the windows. Then the school would laugh and to get rid of him I'd have to let one of the boys go and take him home.

On nice bright, moon light nights the children and young folks of the town had great sport tobogganing on the hill back of Overly's house. They came with all kinds of hand sleds and wanted me to go but Al always objected, saying it was too dangerous and I'd better not go. The previous mountain climbing was hard on me and I thot his advise all right. I was ever ready to obey and was content to stay in my room in the hotel, even tho it often was so cold I'd have to put on my coat and over shoes to keep warm.

The dances came regularly. There were always enough people to dance in the town. But there was no musician living there, so the musician most always had to come from Butte. There was a bill out for a big Christmas dance. Mrs. Dolman had the Christmas entertainment on another night so we could have plenty of time. She had a dialogue and insisted I be the new comer in the play.

I wore my pink striped wool dress. She had made up the dialog. Another lady and I were seated, talking about people we knew in and around Dewey's Flat. The other lady wanted to know if I had met John Lawrence, the lady crusher in the valley. Just then another lady rushed in, hollowed fire, we all ran off the stage. Poor John, every one talked and made fun of John. I had heard plenty, men seemed to delight in talking about his queer ways. The town was pleased with our entertainment and tree.

Up until now I had gone to very few dances. The Christmas dance bid fair to being a good one, so I went. For my life, I could not see how people could go spend all night and be all drug out for days and get any real enjoyment out of it, but they all did. This was a very queer country to me. I had never been trained that way.

Mrs. Bryant generally gave the dance supper, along with a Christmas turkey dinner Christmas day. It took a lot of cooking extra along with the regular meals. She had a fine cook, but she liked booze, tho she had shown no signs till Christmas eve. While working, she had over indulged. All at once she fell, taking a header under the serving table and lay there paralyzed. She left on the first stage out. Such a predicament in that rushed time. Happenings like these, I seldom heard of till Monday. I said to Mrs. Bryant, "Where is the cook?" Then she told me. She soon got another one. Then, when the house was so full, she hired a wash woman. It was not long till she got tired of washing the sheets after every guest, so Mrs. Bryant caught her ironing the sheets and putting them on again. Well, she did not last long. In the winter Bryant kept pretty busy poking the stoves and running errands. Such a big house was hard to keep warm and then it

School Monies	
Superintendent Stone had apportioned the school fund as follows:	
Dist. No. 1, Bannack	$865.72
" " 2, Bishops	184.20
" " 3, Poindexters	478.92
" " 4, Argenta	267.00
" " 5, Glendale	1,344.66
" " 6, Deweys	895.37
" " 7, Horse Prairie	322.35
" " 8, Hecla	386.82
" " 9, Birch Creek	296.03
" " 10, Dillon	3,840.57
" " 12, Lima	1,399.71
" " 14, Red Rock	202.62
" " 15, Big Hole	92.10
" " 16, " "	331.56
" " 17, " "	255.51
" " 18, " "	303.93
" " 19, Red Rock (Scotts)	156.57
" " 20, Medicine Lodge	110.52
" " 21, Grasshopper	198.41
" " 22, Dell	460.50
" " 28, Polaris	181.20
	$12,691.58

The apportionment is made on the basis of the number of children in each district between the ages of 3 and 21, $9.21 being allowed for each child.

School Monies
From the Dillon Tribune
Dillon, Montana
December 30, 1892

took lots of wood. Sherman Bryant and team brot it from Quartz Hill Gulch. Then it had to be sawed by hand and split. Mrs. Bryant generally kept a boy to do the chores and bring in wood.

In these days liquor was sold in quart and gallons in the grocery stores. When a man bot a bill of grub he need not go to a saloon to get it as it was at the store for sale. When Mrs. Patton bot groceries, she always bot a jug to be filled for papa.

So, December wore a way with its Sunday school each Sunday and the regular Saturday night dances either at Deweys Flat or Divide.

January 1893

New Years was celebrated as usual with a dance. Mrs. Bryant gave the dance supper. Charley Ralston, Dickie, Bob Beattie and numerous others, including the boys from the ranch, Quartz Hill people, and folks from Divide came. It was a big dance. The floor was full. I had made up the black and white satin dress goods and I wore that. Mr. and Mrs. Ralston came and Charley. I went over with the crowd at the hotel. There was many signs now that indicated a decline in the mines and mill. Then the freighter and everyone in general, was uneasy as to what would be the outcome of the little mining town and also the larger districts all over the state. Never the less the dances occurred regularly.

January was cold and disagreeable. Bryant kept the old long wood stove in the front room full from early morning to late at night and entertained the boarders with his stories. Mrs. Bryant and the cook and waiters kept the kitchen stove going and there by kept the kitchen warm. I was always up early, going over and building a fire in the school house, then coming back to eat my breakfast. After that I put on my coat and overshoes and hood and went back to get my heavy school work done by 9 a.m.

The routine of living in this hotel was much the same. I arose each day at the same time, ate breakfast, went to my little room if the front room was full of men. If all had gone, I often went in and chatted with any of the house hold that happened to be there. Generally in the forenoon all were busy, tho some times I'd chat with Minnie and Mr. or Mrs. Bryant.

All this had grown tiresome. Al had told me that Mrs. Overly was a good woman and she never talked about the other fellow. Thot I could go any time and be welcome. Also she and the girls had invited me to come. I liked them very much as new acquaintances goes, tho did not want myself to become a nuisance in their house or to common a visitor. This Saturday I longed for other scenes as it were. Picked up my quilt blocks and yarns, went the same street like going to the school house. Tho went past and threw the teaching trouble and ways to the wind, turned, went up the street past Sam Rhodes house, past Mrs. Galbraith's and Frank Ritcshel's cabin. His was the smallest little cabin I had ever seen, about 10 x 10, made of large logs. The next cabin nestled up against the hill, I knocked and a cheery voice said come in. It was Lillie just getting up.

Her mother greeted me, such a cheery good morning, giving me a cheer and taking my shawl. All at once my despondency lifted. They were glad to see me, as they were very lonely. Mr. Overly had gone to stewart a little place on the R.R. where he had gotten work with his teams. Flora had got work at Mrs. Mitchell's. They kept a few boarders and he ran the stage barn along with teaming business he kept up. The Mitchells were happy go lucky people.

Lillie was going to school with me. A very nice girl about 12 or 14. Henry, or as the boys often called young Hankens, about 15 years, had been going to school, tho he was a very poor, backward scholar and staid out a lot. When the boys, Al and Horace, began to log in Triangle Gulch, they hired him to snake logs to the skid way. He could do the work, so this day he was up at Big Al's and Horace's place. She seldom seen them, only when they brot their clothes to be washed and get their clean ones.

THE STATE LEGISLATURE
THE LATEST DOINGS OF
MONTANA'S SOLONS

Bills Introduced - One Locating the Normal School at Dillon - Standing Committees Appointed - Balloting in Joint Session - Hauser Men Now for Clark

A Helena special, in this morning's Anaconda Standard contains the latest news from the legislature, from which we take the following:

The house, in its morning session, transacted considerable business. The following bills were introduced: By A.F. Bray, notice of a bill to provide for the location and purchase of Warm Springs as an insane assylum, and a bill providing for the relief of Emily Swan, et al.; by Scharnikow, an act regulating licenses, another providing that the per diem of members be limited to $8 per day and mileage fixed at 20 cents per mile, and a bill to repeal the estray law; by Monteath, a bill regulating primary elections; by Burns, an act creating Bear Paw county from a part of Choteau county; by Metzel, a bill locating the normal school at Dillon; by Babcock an act amending section 595 of the fifth division of the compiled statutes; a bill locating the state prison at Billings, and an act to amend the revenue law; by Tierney, an act legalizing the funding bonds issued by counties; by Lewis, an act locating the county of Valley from a part of Dawson county; by Lockey an act amending statues 533, 534, and 538, concerning articles of incorporation, concerning the use of water in ditches, and making females eligible for notaries public respectively.

The Tribune
Dillon, Montana
January 13, 1893

As we set there by the wood fire of pitch pine and fir, I enjoyed the quiet of the little cabin. Lillie was washing her face. When done, combed her golden hair and braided it in one long big braid which hung below her waist.

Mrs. Overly was patching some mens clothes that she had washed and was getting them ready to send out. I took out my quilt and began to work. She never gossiped about anyone and when needed, she made kind excuses for everyone's short comings, but what worried her most was the out look of the times. The mill was not putting thru as much ore as usual and she hinted that the town was going down. It was now January and general business was slacking. Lillie was fixing over a dress and not having any breakfast, she says, "Ma, I am hungry."

"Yes, Lillie, but your ma hasn't felt very well this morning. I seem to be so dizzy this morning, but I'll get dinner soon."

So she took the butcher knife and saw, saying, "We haven't any place to keep a quarter of meat, so Galberths let us put our meat in their meat house and I'll have to go down and get some for dinner." She was only gone a few minutes when Mrs. Galbraith came running up. "Lillie your mother is sick. She came near falling. I told her to hang on to the block while I got some one." We all ran down, which was not more than 2 or 3 hundred feet away, to the meat house.

I stayed with her and kept her from falling while Lillie ran down town for Mr. Galbraith. Mrs. Galbraith had to go back to the house to take care of her two babies. When Lillie and Mr. Galbraith got back we helped her back to the cabin by being careful, resting her every few feet. I on one side and Mr. Galberth on the other. We got her in and put her to bed with her clothes on and for about five hours I had all I could do to keep her from getting out and falling on the floor. We three decided to send for Dr. Jones. Galbraith went to send word to Divide. The message had to be telegraphed to Melrose and then by phone to Glendale. He hurried back to help Lillie and I. Lillie was so afraid and she would only hand me water and towels which we put on her [*mother's*] head. Being paralyzed on one side, she would want to get up, when up she would try to get out and then down again. I worked with her gently as I could and tried to do everything she seemed to want me to do. Nothing suited. This lasted till dark, then she became more quiet. We were a bout wore out.

About 8 or 9 p.m. Dr. Jones came. He ordered crushed ice. I made a sack for it, then he placed it on the back of her neck saying, this may remove the blood clot. He went down town for supper. When he came back she was steadily sinking. By this time, other friends came in and then Horace and Al and Henry. They had heard she was sick and came at once.

In my mind I was quite sure she could not last much longer. Tho I had never been at a death bed before. Yes, I could not leave as long as Lillie was there. The men had held council outside, finally about 12 p.m. she passed.

When all was over, Al, Horace and Galbraith, Dodgson and a few others decided there would be no watchers, as the weather was turning cold. They could keep no fire to keep warm with the corpse in the cabin. Lillie and I put on our wraps, preparing to go to the hotel, as Lillie would stay with me. Horace walked down with us. In the front room we bid him good night and went to my room, tired, hungry, two sorrowful girls. I had lost a true friend and Lillie her mother, which could never be replaced.

Some man in town took the message, horseback, that night to Hank Overly.

They placed the corpse on a strong board between two chairs and took measurement for the coffin. They screened the windows, put out the fire and all went home. Galbraith was close, so he watched the cabin.

Next morning early, Dodgson Sr. was at work on the casket. That evening, as soon as it was finished, we covered it with black calico on the outside, inside was lined with bleached muslin. For trimming, we bot several yards of ruchings from Pond and Vance store to go around the upper part of the coffin. A pillow of wood shavings was made and covered with the white muslin. That night the boys, Al and Horace, and others took the casket to the cabin and placed her in. Hank had arrived and arrangements were completed to enter her in Divide Cemetery and to hold a short service by Mrs. Dolman, in the morning at the cabin, before starting to Divide Monday morning. The school board gave me the day off. Al and I went to the hotel to dress me up for the trip, as the weather had turned bitter cold. Over my over shoes he tied on the three cornered gunna sack over shoes. Then a fur coat over my coat. I wore a hood and took my shawl for further protection and two pair of mitts. Men were dressed accordingly.

Horace drew up to the hotel steps and Al helped me in on the seat. I had so many clothes on I could hardly move. We took the lead, as Horace had the corpse. The sleigh was made with two bobsleds, with the wagon box on the bobs, with a generous amount of hay in the front end of the wagon box to help keep out the cold and draft. Then a heavy robe spread over the seat, coming well down behind our feet and then a big robe over our laps and tucked in well under us on either side. Al and Dickie followed with the family. Snow was deep, the air full of frost and the river boiled and hissed and ice cracked. The horses were cold and impatient to go and they struck a brisk trot. Horace said, "You will think this awful, but with the distance and the cold, we will have to go fast and get this over and back to shelter."

As the team dashed along over the grade in the canyon, the bell ringing out merrily, he began to talk about their work, places he had been and his lone wonderings. They, their settling on the ranch up the river and the hardships they had encountered. All was news to me and I listened. Then he says, "Maggie some time I'll tell you my story."

"Yes," I says, "O, you need not mind."

We were then about to cross the bridge and conversation seemed to lag. I did not realize how my answer affected him. We were nearing the road that turned off the main road and up, up to the cemetery and nothing more was said. He drew up along side the open grave. He got out, unbuckled the two reigns while the other men took the casket out. Then the reigns were placed under the casket. A man to the four ends of the reigns, carefully let the casket to its resting place. I did not get out. Horace replaced the reigns and got in, drove off down a different road to the Hotel (Divide). The steepest road I ever rode down and came near slipping off, down to the heals of the team, had it not been he held me fast.

At the hotel he blanketed his team and we went in and got warm and incidentally to see Lou Pickett and his wife Laura. Horace had worked for Pickett when Pickett had a contract hauling freight in and out at Glendale from L. C. Pourers, the head contractor, a few years before. They were fast friends. Pickett was where he could learn more of the general trend of affairs and Horace wanted to get his opinion of the times. This was just before the Panic of '93 and all seemed to sense the situation. Horace, too, had been to Butte a few days before and got the contract to put in the stulls and they were then logging in Triangle Gulch. Then we all started back to the Flat. Dinner was over, tho Mrs. Bryant fed us. She never let anyone go away hungry. Al, Horace and I visited for a while and then they went back to their little cabin home.

Fred Dickie

When I first came, Fred teamed some. He went with Horace and Al when they took the boiler over to Gibbonsville. He did not care if school kept and often staid for a day at Ralstons or at the Flat, boarded at Bryants. There I met him. He was friendly and often wanted to take me places.

Dickie was staying at the Hotel for a few days, waiting for a load of freight. He says to me, when you want to go to Clines, any time, I'll take you. So one Saturday I had some sewing to do and he took me up. Mrs. Bryant had Jennet Hater there then sewing for her and I did not want to bother. Mrs. Cline had invited me to sew on her machine any time I came. Sunday night Mr. and Mrs. Cline brot me back to the Hotel. By the last of the month, the town had decidedly began to go. A few families and children went down the canyon to various towns for work. Others staid, hoping by spring something would open up. Then, too, winter is a hard time to move. Those that had cabins staid on.

Fred Dickie lived acrost Dickies Bridge in a log cabin. There were nice barns and corrals and was quite a liveable place. The farm land widened out, extended down the river, but was narrow and steep up at the upper end, just room enuf for the buildings. And finally the land pinched in to a steep side hill. He and Fred Vaughn were partners. Vaughn living down the river where Babe Dodgson lived. The land extending along the left side of the river for two miles, lower and near Alder Creek.

Fred was from Nova Scotia. Came to Montana to work when so many in the far east came. While hunting horses and cattle once, his horse stepped in a badger hole, threw him and hurt him. He was alone at the time it happened. Then after that he took fits and had to have a man to stay with him. A Belgian, Joseph Vanvincent, staid with him a long time - 1908 or 1909. Then, after that, he was worse and he went to Ralstons where she cared for him till he died. I think the Vaughn place was the first place old man Dodgson took up. Afterward sold it to Dickie and Vaughn.

After Vaughn's wife died in 1895, he married again and finally left his wife and went to Alaska. The partnership between Vaughn and Dickie was dissolved, Dickie still lived on his place, had some cattle. The Vaughns had a son and when about three or four years old, when Vaughn left for Alaska, he gave him to Mr. and Mrs. Ames. They had two children and wanted to raise this boy with theirs. When Mr. & Mrs. Ames left the Flat and went to Chicago about 1896 or 7 to make their home, they took Norman and educated this boy along with theirs. I have never seen him since a baby. Some years later he came back, married one of the Anderson girls (a second cousin). They lived in the Big Hole or Anaconda - tho did ranch in the Basin at first.

Vaughn sold out to Ralstons and Charley Ralston and wife lived there for several years. You would hardly call it lived, as Charley would hitch up, go to Ma Ralstons and then stay all day at home and take back everything that was needed (even to the stove wood) to keep Mildred and kids alive. Then the next day was repeated, day in and out for years and Pa Ralston put up the hay and Charley and Mildred lived there. When Ed and Sis grew up to school age, they kept the teacher (summer time) and she drove to Meadow Creek and took the children to school.

February 1893

    The snow was still deep and the bitter cold held on with an icy grip and building and keeping the fires was a steady job. Tho I really believe Bryant enjoyed it. The chore boy [*kept*] the wood piled handily in the hall and Bryant fired. Then occasionally a new man would drop in for a meal and Bryant would entertain him with a hunting story or logging on the Feather River in California or whatever the conversation might turn to, as in those days he might have been called a versatile man. He often did the buying for the house, then on his way home he'd call in to see Mr. Marstin, the barkeeper. He had a pretty wife and Bryant would much rather talk to her. Tho if he went to the house to talk to her, those infernal dogs, Nig or Kizer, would follow and sit on the top step and then that was a dead give away and Jane would twit him for that. He'd much rather she came to the hotel. That looked better and folks would not talk. However, the Marstins jollied him along as they might need him in time. Mrs. Marstin had two nice little girls that went to school.

    Now one and one or two, quit school, the parents were leaving. This relieved the crowded pressure and gave more time to those left.

    Among the folks at Divide I made lasting friendship with was the Forrests and visited there. William Forrest and wife were married in Illinois 1865, just at the close of the Civil War and started overland for Montana. He mined in German Gulch for a few years, then moved to the stock ranch above Divide in 1869 on Divide Creek. The ranch concisted of a wild hay meadow, was quite easy to care for. They built a log cabin and, as was needed, built on more till it was quite a nice sized house. The increase in size was due to [*it being*] a stage stopping house. It was a change station for years. Horses were changed and a fresh team hooked on, passengers often ate there. This was before the R.R. came in 1881.

    Mrs. Forrest was a good cook and an agreeable hostess. Mr. Forrest was a fine man, tho not given to talking. One had to know him to appreciate him. They had two children, Johnnie and Mary. Johnnie married. The woman did not like ranching so they moved to Anaconda. There he worked for the Company and while in their employ he lost an arm, then they lived in Butte. He ran a grocery store and served as secretary in the court house and finally went to Wenatchee, Washington and then to Oakland, California.

    Mary married a man from Illinois and they have always lived on the home place.

    Mr. Forrest was a good irrigator but he often got thirsty when in the lower field clost to Divide. He would go over and drink too much sometimes and as he grew older he was quite a toper, much to Mrs. Forrest's disgust. Tho she kept clost tabs on him, he often evaded her and sometimes got as far away as Melrose on a spree.

    They had the oldest water right on Divide Creek. The Water Company finally got it away from them after she died and he was too old to fight for their rights. The old house burned down, burning most everything they had. The gatherings [*they had accumulated*] for years all went. They had many priceless relics, besides fine quilts Grandma Deno had made in her declining years, which represented hours of toil besides the money they cost. Some were made of scrap and many of botten material which came high in early days. In time a nice big modern house took its place.

    The old man was very cross to Fred [*Dickie*] at times but it was Fred in later years that took care of him to the last. George Forrest, a brother to William, came to Montana in early days, settled at Melrose. Their mother came and married Stone from Arkansas, the first man to raise potatoes at Melrose. Everybody thot it was a wonderful thing to raise potatoes at Melrose.

    Later in February, Kennie advertised for a masquerade ball, suits were for rent, many made theirs. On Friday night Al came down to see me. I told him I wanted to make my masquerade suit.

    "Well," he says, "I will take you to Clines. You can have it done by Saturday night, can't you? You know Mrs. Cline would be glad to have you come. Get ready and I will take you tonight."

    I sewed like a trooper. When he came for me Sunday eve, my suit was done and I laid it away in my trunk till the eve of February 14.

    Dickie says, "May I take you to the dance tonight?"

    "Thank you, but I am going with some ladies here in the house," I said. I did not want him to know me.

    Before I dressed, Mrs. Smock came in dressed in disguise. She and her husband had moved into the Overly cabin later. They were a jolly big couple from Missouri. Never tired of dancing. I remember one eve she sent for me, after this dance and wanted to buy my suit, which she gave me $2.50 for. At that time they were out of work and they had danced in various burgs for five nights straight. He was a good dance manager, caller and singer. In the years following they cooked, logged or worked at most anything. When W. A. Clark built the Utah Cut Off they went there and then we never heard of them anymore.

    We waited till the dance begun and then we went over. At the door we had to tell the door keeper, Oscar Vance, who we were. Then went on in and soon we were in the swing. With some dancer but who? Some times we could tell our partners, tho not often. The hall was crowded. Ere long I could tell several people I knew. Ettie and Frank Ritschel were hard to disguise as they both had quick, jerky movements. There were many nice costumes, tho some horrible. There was one in particular, dressed buffalo coat and pants, the tail of the coat was tucked in to the pants, making the man look much larger than ever. The pants had been gnawed into several holes. The wearer had a horrible face and carried an umbrella all the time. Once I was sitting down and the fellow came over and tried to set down with me but I amediately got up and moved on. I heard Shannon, store keeper for Eliel, say, I believe that is the school teacher and the wooly fellow laughed. I was disgusted. Never gave a thot to who it might be. Next day I heard some of the boarders talking about that Buffalo suit. One says, "That was Big Al." It was so hot he could only wear it but for a short while, so he went out, took it off and someone else wanted to wear it and I bet a half dozen fellows wore it before 11:30 that night. Then when "mask off" order called out, the buffalo suit wearer disappeared.

Wearing a mask and being corseted up was an awful punishment for two or three hours. When they called "masks off", gentlemen chose their partners for supper. Scot Galbraith chose me. Those days, after supper, they all went back to the dance hall and danced till 4 a.m.

Each time I'd go to a dance I'd be so all in the next day. I was disgusted for I'd hardly recuperate by Monday morn. I knew it was foolish and a curse on both body, mind and soul. Tho I was not like others, going to every Saturday night's shindig - I managed to make an excuse to Minnie and others when they would say why didn't you go? I still know my mother's teachings were right. Horace at this time, too, had long time passed his foolish age. He went as he felt he had an interest in me – then, too, he wondered what I meant by cutting him off short by saying "O never mind!" He wondered if I had someone back home that "Thot more of her than I," says he to himself. "I'll just bide my time and see. I won't bother her nor push myself on her. I'll see, I'll give her time." Each time he came to town he came down to the Hotel and would say to Bryant, "How is Maggie?" Then once in a while we would meet at meal hour. The logs being most all in he was looking out for other teaming jobs. Horace often staid a few days at the Hotel to meet men. In this new country could it be possible that I should meet a man that I really admired. I never was interested in one before and I was determined I should not let any one know my thots. I was here to teach school. Then I expected to go home, tho I should never forget him.

Undoubtedly now the town was going for the mill and mine had shut down. There was nothing to do now but hunt other jobs elsewhere but winter was getting on and most waited and in the meantime tried to find a place to go where they could find security for their selves and family. The destiny of Dewey seemed to be doomed tho Captain Prideaux was still in town. Had the mine failed? The Cornish miners had gone down the gulch. Every little enterprise felt the shock. The Hotel, too, cut the waiters, did their own work. About this time, in Dewey's darkest hours, came word that in Gibbonsville, Idaho they had struck gold and surly there would be lots of freighting to be done there.

Gradually the news spread that Horace and Big Al had a contract to put in a big boiler before the snow went off. Those that owned a wagon and team of horses and harness that had freighting blood in their veins, picked up their ears and took new hope that they too could haul and get something to do the coming summer. Dickie came down, staid for a few days, again looking for a job. He had several good teams he kept in good shape. The harness even showed care. In those days a housing were put on the horses, two large pieces of leather were put on the harness, hanging down and over the shoulder to keep off snow or rain from the horse's shoulders. They could be trimmed up fancy, as his were with brass buttons all around the housings, then his initial F.W.D on the housing in brass leather buttons. Then, with a set of bells and celluloid rings in the lines for trimming. His team was sure to attract ones attention as they stepped out.

Often when he spent a few days, he would sing or whistle or clog dance when only a few were in, then grab Minnie, who most always was in, whirl her around in a waltz. Then Minnie would fight to get free. Then hearing the noise, Mrs. B. would call out from the kitchen, "Minnie come here" and Minnie would dash away to her mother. School, had [*for a*] long time now, held no charm for Minnie. She went for a while, then all of sudden she would stay out part of a day or late or not come for day and then come again after some time. She then finally quit with the excuse to help her mother. This I did not believe. Tho could not say, my, that she was getting too worldly wise to go to school. There were young, worthless fellows hanging around. She would rather go with them and then the dances, etc. Pulled her down and she never went to school any more. If her parents could not make her go, then 12 years old, it was not my part and at that time had no truant officer or any one that would say a word but Brubaker. He always gave the children good advice.

Quite often when a boarder would be seen going to Bedards, the hotel acrost the way, you could hear Bryant call, "Jane come here, Jane come here - see that son of a B going in to that fisheaters place to eat. Well, I hope he gets his fill."

Lou and Laura Pickett was giving a dance at Divide in the hotel. Horace always enjoyed visiting his old Glendale friend. He was taking a sleigh load down and said to me, "Maggie, won't you go with us?" "Yes," says I, and was ready when the sleigh drew up to the steps of Bryant's Hotel.

A sleigh in those days was two bob sleds chained together and a wagon box put on, then as many could go as would fit in a wagon. With spring seats, hay in the bottom to keep out the draft, plenty of robes on the seats and over the lap and well dressed for the occasion, it was a very comfortable rig to go in.

I believe there was but one bottom cutter, built for two, in the town. Jim Long owned it and with his driving team it was a fancy rig for those days.

When riding in an open sleigh one had to dress warmly. Horace and Al wore heavy woolen cloth, then over the suit pants a heavy overall. The best that money could buy "Levi Staus". I had never saw man wear such a brand of overall. In fact, men in Kansas seldom wore overall, mostly pants made of jeans, some dark color. With Al and Horace's experience of being out in all kinds of weather they found that a light wool or cotton sock, with a medium thin shoes and then a high top overshoe over, was the warmest rig they could get for their feet. Quite often in severe weather they would rip open a gunna sack, fold it three corner ways and use each half as a wrapping over the overshoe. When put on right they helped keep out the cold. The buffalo coat was put on over a top coat. Then the scotch visor cap on the head seemed to be the ideal head covering. On the hands they wore various combinations. Silk under gloves, when they could get them, and a heavy buckskin over. They generally had various combination of gloves of several pair as the hands suffered most on long drives. After I came, I knitted them several pairs each, then the under glove out of black knitting silk.

The provision I had made for the winter was two piece suits of knit red flannel under suits, and a pair of over shoes. I had brot home knit mitts and stockings and crocheted a wool hood to go with my heavy brown coat and shawl. I was healed for most any trip nearby. There were always heavy robes in the sleigh to wrap in for further comfort.

When going on a long trip women often het a big rock, wrapped it good and put it in the bottom of the sleigh which helped a lot to ones comfort. Tho men never resorted to such comforts.

My dancing education had been neglected, I must confess. I would stumble around in the square dance, but in the round dance I was so self conscious of my shortcomings I would not try. Those that tried to dance with me gave me up and I was not bothered until after supper when Pickett was tread upon. He wanted me to dance a shodish. I declined, he insisted and fairly drug me out. We were the only couple on the floor. He was a good dancer and fairly drug me around and then gave me up as a poor dancer. By this time a lot of the men were getting too full [*of liquor*] and Horace could see that it was no place for me. He slipped out and told Laura she had better give me a room as he knew I was tired. She took me to the southwest corner room up stairs. It had no outside door and the one she took me thru had no occupants then and I never gave it a thot. The room was cold. I never was in a colder room. I took my shoes off and corset and dress and lay down. I knew I'd nearly freeze there from 2 p.m. till six. I put in a terrible night. I never got warm. As soon as I dared I got up, opened my door and what to my surprise, there were two fellows in that room dead asleep, Ches Keller and another fellow. I was there and slipped out of that room quietly and downstairs. Laura was up building fires. She was surprised to see me up so early. I made no excuse tho hung clost to the stove. Breakfast was late. In the meantime I passed the time away reading.

After breakfast, when our crowd had taken on a moving, Horace drove to the steps. All got in and we dashed away over the frozen ice and snow, bells ringing merrily - on the river ice at the saw mill to the bridge, over the river at the dam and from there we took the icy grade four miles to Dewey.

Little did Horace think I had put in such a miserable, cold night nor would I have had him know. It is a wonder I escaped pneumonia.

On the whole, Dewey was a very quiet little town. Men drank and gambled in the various saloons, Kinney's, Pat Lillis and Sutherland and Boby Schultz's. But of all the women, I only heard of one who drank and got on a tear but I never saw her on a drunk.

It is true, in a long winter there was one big scandal, much to the disgust of the berg. One woman would leave her three little kids at home when she went to the dances. Her husband often came over from the store. When she asked him to go over to the house and look if the children were all right, he would say "Go your self." The town was dark and she hated to go alone - she then asked a kindly man to go with her. Finally he was her steady escort and often hung over the fence to talk with her. Then at last they decided to stay home and look after the children. When the father found a man in his house, he blew up and there was a terrible scandal which spread all over the town. The father was more guilty than the mother. The mother and children left town for Glendale to her father's arms. In time, with the town going down, the husband followed. The wife's father, so stricken with the daughter coming home with this scandal hovering over her, that he at once took to drinking and no one could console him. They sent for Horace and he went over and staid with the father a few days and got him to straighten up and make the best of the situation.

Now that the Flat was going down, Vance went to Glendale. A Mr. Ames was put in charge of the store. The store drug on a year or so and George Lossel bot the remaining interest of Pond. But it was almost a total failure. Eliel, Fyrie and Burfiend had closed their doors the summer of '93.

The school now was diminishing slowly. Most all the transient families had gone.

On every occasion when Horace came to town for supplies and the mail, he invariably came to the Hotel to get some of Bryant's stories and eat a good square meal. It tasted much better when he did not have to cook it. After dinner he would read the paper.

This time Bryant seemed to be wrought up more than common. Horace dearly loved to draw him out on his stories. For Horace could then go home and reproduce them again and again in Bryant's Maine dialect. Horace was perfect at this, as coming from New Brunswick and Maine hisself, he could copy Bryant's stories perfectly.

Pat Lillis was a knowing Irishman. He and Sutherland ran a saloon acrost the street and boarded at Bryant's Hotel. He was quite a reader. Horace used to go to Pat's just to get Pat to talking and then he could go away and repeat Pat's stories and have lots of fun to Pat's back. McKinley was President then and there was a lot in the paper about the McKinley bill. They would argue about the administration for hours. When all at once Pat said, "Well, Horace, if they owe McKinley, why don't they pay him?" That was one of Horace's stock stories on Pat. Pat sold to Tom Brown and moved to Divide.

Tom Brown was a queer, knowing fellow. He borrowed money off of his half brother to start and run on for a while. He ran the saloon and gambled. All went well till the borrowed money gave out and he could not get any more. Then he told his friend he did not care. He had learned the saloon trade and when he started up again he would make money for now he had learned how.

Like most all pioneer women of every state and territories, those of Dewey Flat were much the same. Living in small log cabins, with one stove or fire place, a homemade table and chair or boxes and a very meager collection of cooking tools, a wash pan, washboard and tub, tho some times the wash board had to be borrowed from a neighbor on her off wash day. Also a pole bed or ancient wood bed that came with the bull team and a few other accessories that had been left her by those moving away. She stayed home with her meager supply of clothes and food to keep the home fires burning for the husband that was out looking for a job. Or he might be a more fortunate one, working a prospect, which he hoped to turn into a real mine, one that would give the family a better house, clothes and a good living. The cabins were often put up in haste with logs showing in the inside making a dust catcher. Too, if he had time, the logs were hewn inside and cheesecloth lined, then wall paper finished it in to a quite respectable house. If he had time, log partitions were put in tho if not, calico partitions were added on or they done without a partition. I had the pleasure to visit many that were finished in that way, but I can't recall of any with fireplaces. Those days wood was plenty, but seldom ever a big wood pile.

Women in this town were in general a happy, easy going kind - most, young and old, attended the dances there. I often visited with them. Mrs. J. B. Trueman had a large family and times were hard for them. She was a kindly soul. I went to see her one day. I could not see how 10 people could live in such a small two room cabin. It set up clost to the hill and in the winter time the sun could not reach it.

Most everyone lived in the "tomorrow" such are, most invariably, in a new mining/mill town. The clothing was meager. Men, to stand the rigors of the cold, had to have better and costlier clothes. If a woman or girl got a new dress, a cheap pair of shoes and cotton stockings in time for the next dance, that was most important. This was all the social life the new country could offer. Men, perhaps, spent more than was wise at the saloons, meeting with other men in view of a much needed job. They were the bread winner. Some were judicious, while like many frail, weak minded people, some indulged too freely and lost their hard earned money. Tho the married men were more stable knowing the responsibilities of housing, feeding and clothing a bunch of little hungry mouths. On the whole, Dewey was a remarkable camp of 200 to 300 souls, more or less. While I was there, there was no sickness to call a doctor for except in the case of Mrs. Overly and Jennett Hater, a T.B. victim. And as for maternity cases, some of the older women took care of them and [there were] no deaths from any maternity cause (Mrs. Dodgson, Mrs. Bryant, Mrs. Overly or Mrs. Trueman were midwives in the area). Jimmie New's grandson, a doctor, up Wise River officiated at two maternity cases in that vicinity tho not at Deweys Flat.

Mrs. Trueman told me about being called to Sam Rhodes's wife's bedside before a birth, March 17, 1893. As soon as the pains came on, Mrs. Rhodes sent to the saloon for whiskey and drank and drank till drunk, all the time haranguing in the most vile talk and drinking till the child came. Says Mrs. Trueman, "I never want to be called there again."

Mrs. Rhodes had been a prostitute in Glendale and ran a house till she married Rhodes. She was a well educated Russian. She gave birth to four and Mrs. Trueman had to go each time.

Jennett Hater came to Dewey a TB victim and died in the fall of 1894. She came to Divide to an Uncle, Billie Smail, in the summer of '92. She was a very sick girl from a sewing room in Montreal, thinking the change would cure her, which it did for a while. Then she began going to the dances and over done. She tried to sew for a while and then went to Anaconda for medical treatment but came back ailing. She staid at the Hotel and sewed for Mrs. Bryant, and to save a room when she had many boarders and transients, Mrs. Bryant put her to sleep with me. However, she did not stay long and went to her uncles. When Al found out Jennett had roomed with me he was furious and said never, never. She did not come back.

When I came back the second year she was very poorly. [*Maggie went back to Kansas the summer of 1893*] A sister, Maggie [*Hater Williams*], was sent for but got there the day after she died. I set up with her half of the last night she lived. After, I asked Mrs. Smail if I could do anything for her to help fix for the funeral. She said "Yes, Billie's suit needs cleaning." So she gave me a bottle of Benzine and the clothes. I took them to my boarding place and got an old table out doors and tackled the job. I had never seen a dirtier suit, let alone clean one before. I aired them well after cleaning, then pressed them and took them back clean and respectable.

Like all other boarding houses of those days in a mining camp, this one was no exception with keeping the help that was needed to keep it efficient enuf to take care of the regular boarders and transients. A likely cook would come, then stay a few days, week or months and away. The waiter was much the same. There were times when two waiters and a wash woman were needed. Many times Mrs. Bryant and others was overworked keeping the house running till they could get other help. They came to Divide, from there by stage and it was many an anxious look to see if help was going to get off of the stage each time it drove up. The year I boarded there, they had several cooks, waiters and wash women. One, a very nice woman and good cook, worked for some time.

Josie, The Cook - February 1893

Josie, the cook, was just one of many cooks and staid longer than the general run of cooks. She was generous, good hearted, a good worker, always happy and sang as she worked. When alone after the meal was over, you could hear her sing "Three Leaves of Shamrock," "Coming Thru The Rye," "Two Little Girls in Blue," "After the Ball" and many other popular songs of the day. She was a good dancer and often went over to the dances when all her work for the night was done.

She wanted a new dress. The Pond and Vance store did not sell ready made dresses. She knew I made dresses for myself so she asked me if I'd make her a new dress. I told her I had so little time that I could not get it ready quickly and she had better get someone else to make it. "No," she says "you make it."

"All right, I'll do my best." So she sent to Butte for the goods and pattern, thread, hooks and eyes, whalebone stays, crinoline and braid for the bottom of the skirt. It was a beautiful piece of cashmere cloth, a blue green color. With Saturday to cut and fit, I worked after and before school and within a week she had a lovely new dress. News filtered out I had made the dress for Josie and my, how the women talked. "Did she not have enough money?" "And did she not have enuf to do at school?" "That was why my little girl did not learn her A B C's," says one mother. Well, it was a good thing I heard no more. I fairly boiled. I was teased on the sly. One day Brubaker came into chat with Bryant as I came from school. I was rather down hearted looking. He says, "How is school coming on?"

"Fair, tho there is a lot of talk about me making Josie's dress."

"Well," he says, "don't you mind those people, you just teach and don't pay any attention to what they say."

"Thank you for that concideration Mr. Brubaker, I'll remember I have one person to stand up for me."

"Yes," says he, "you would have a lot on your side if it came to a show down." All this soon blew over and I was happy again at my work, in my room away from the gossip of the town.

Josie was so happy with her new dress, it was a pleasure to work for her. Now she could go to the dances and enjoy the short stay at the hall with her lover, Ed Cramer. He was driving stage from Gibbonsville to Dewey Flat. When he came to town she would cook him a good supper with some extra daintys. There was always some extra dish for him the evening he came in. And, well, he deserved it, coming from Gibbonsville over that high range of mountains thru all kinds of severe weather with snow deep, deep, deep. Often ranchers had to put a fence on top of the snow to keep the cattle out of the hay stacks, the first fence being covered.

Sitting on a sleigh drawn by a pair of horses, with no shelter but his overcoat and robes on this long hundred mile trip, he became so snow burned he resembled an Indian. Boarders began to josh him about getting married, till some of the boys had came from Wisdom and Gibbonsville. There they found out Cramer had a girl at each place that he liked equally as well.

The boys around town often wondered when he and Josie would be married or which one of his sweethearts he really would choose. They knew he had one at Wisdom and another at Gibbonsville that loved him dearly. At last the boys say, "Cramer, which one are you going to marry?"

"Well," says he, "I love them all and I can't decide which to marry."

Cramer quit stage driving and then Charley Ralston took the job, a boy then 17 years old. It really was a mans job to sit in the seat from morning till night in the cold weather (1893).

The stage drivers were supposed to board at Bedard's Hotel, much to Mr. and Mrs. Bryant's disgust. Charley ate there for a few trips and then one evening as I came from school, I see Charley come out of Bedard's with his arms full of clothes, go acrost the street and to the side door at Bryants and on upstairs. From that time on he ate and slept at Bryant's. There was several reasons for that.

There being three saloons in Dewey at that time, it was quite a temptation to a boy to mix with the older boys and drink. Charley's mother told him if he would quit drinking she would give him a nice gold watch for his birthday.

The stage drivers always ate dinner at his father's place going both ways. When Charley pulled in for dinner, his mother met him with a hug and a kiss, then presented him with his birthday present. "Thank you Mother and I'll try to go straight from now on." When dinner was over, with a change of new horses, Charley was ready, dressed in his buffalo coat, visor cap, over shoes and gloves. He took the whip and reins and mounted to the seat of his sleigh and away he went over French Creek bridge and away down the road, around a turn in the grade and was soon out of sight. His mother looked longingly after him, thinking, if he can only withstand the temptations of that little mining town with its rough and toughs.

There was a dance in town that next night. Mr. & Mrs. Ralston decided to go down town, take their extra supply of butter [*to sell*] and shop for groceries. Mrs. Ralston was the best butter maker on the river and her butter found ready sale. Everyone spoke very highly of her butter. After the chores were done for the night, Mr. Ralston hitched up a good driving team and they were not long on the way to town. The shopping done, the team taken care of at the livery stable, they came down to Bryant's as they always did and got supper.

Bryant greeted them with a hearty welcome and gave them chairs at the stove, then hung up their wraps. He went back to the kitchen, "Jane, Mr. and Mrs. Ralston will be here for supper, along with Charley." This was an indication for Jane to do her best as Mrs. Ralston was noted for her cooking all up and down the river, far and near.

Bryant punched up the coals in the long wood stove and stepped to the next room for more wood, all the time old Kizer slept peacefully behind the stove, while Nig followed every step at Bryant's heals. "Nig, God Darn you, why don't you lay down? You know, Mr. Ralston, that dog is half crazy to go on the trap line."

"When do you think you will go?" Mr. Ralston said.

"O just as quick as the snow goes off." Bryant sat down then. He and Ralston talked about the snow, ice, road, the times and cattle conditions, the beef cattle. Hardly time for the beef cattle to be trailed out yet.

I had been in my room preparing for supper. When the Ralstons went in I followed and greeted them and they invited me to sit at their table. As the supper progressed, we talked about everything in general of the town. Mrs. Ralston said, "This is Charley's birthday." Then Charley took the watch out of his pocket and showed it to me. A lovely Elgin and he was very proud of it. After supper we all visited for awhile. Then Minnie came in and said, "Maggie, arn't you going to the dance?"

I replied, "I hadden thot of going." She was dressed, ready to go and in a few minutes she and Charley left the room.

Mrs. Ralston said to me, "We are going over for a while, come and go with us." So I did.

The dance hall was about 75 feet away. The crowd was coming in and before long the dance begun. This being Saturday eve there was quite a crowd. Soon Horace and Al came in. They, too, had come for supplies and thot they would come over to the dance before going home. Next day was Sunday. They would rest. We danced in several square dances and then Ralstons thot they had better go home, as there was several stoppers that night at their house and she would have to get early breakfast for some cowpunchers going up the river. They wanted me to go home with them that night. No, I thot I'd better not go. Mr. Ralston says to Horace, "Can't you come up tomorrow and take her home tomorrow eve."

"Why sure," says Horace, "if she wants me to." So it was agreed that I get back that way.

Mr. & Mrs. Ralston and I made the trip in due time. The horses were lively and wanted to go home, over a good snow road with bells ringing merrily. We soon came to the Dickie Bridge, from there took the only road open on the river ice. This was the road in the winter as the grades were snowed full.

Early in the morning everybody was moving at the ranch. Mrs. Ralston had prepared a good breakfast. There was a stage horse tender, a hired man, two cowpunchers, a choreboy, Mr. and Mrs. Ralston and myself. Breakfast was wheat mush, pancakes, syrup, ham and eggs, butter, white home made bread, warmed potatoes, dried fruit - two kinds, and coffee and cream. Time passed all too quickly to me, visiting, and helping her with the morning work.

In this country, the home, the surroundings, the people, their ways were all so new and foreign to me. Yet, I liked this new country, with its mountains, rivers, bitter cold and deep snow. Tho I soon found out I was just an oddity to them, a green tender foot whose every word and action gave them something to think of, and talk of, which when I was wiser made me mum. I learned to be careful and talk very little, as perhaps I was really queer, just as they were queer to me.

After dinner Mrs. Ralston wanted me to go over the river to the Hugh place, then called Bryant place as E. G. Bryant's brother formally lived there. Old Mr. and Mrs. Lewis lived there, also Mr. and Mrs. Hugh and Brown and Frankie, the younger of their ten children. The cabins were small and old. They all were just wintering there, hoping to get work in the spring. The Lewis's ancestors formally was Virginians and they were directly related to the Merryweather [*Meriwether*] Lewis that played a part in the Lewis and Clark Expedition in 1803. These old folks were quaint Missourians, having owned a big estate in Missouri before the Civil War. With the emancipation act they lost their negroes, then no crops, they sold the land for nearly nothing. They then decided to take their teams of mules and wagons and go to Texas to make a home. But the hardships of making a new home at their age was too great. One of the older sons had gone to Montana and he wrote back that Montana was the place to get a start, so they came hither. Mrs. Lewis never could ride on a train so they drove their mule teams all the way from Texas to Montana.

On alighting from our sleigh, we were greeted in a friendly way and ushered in to their little home. In those days not many took a daily paper and all the reading material I saw was a stack of cheap dime novels.

Horace met us at Lewis's and as it was time to be going home, we bid farewell to the Ralstons and Lewis's and many thanks. He helped me into the sleigh and wrapped the robes around, took up the reigns and away he drove with the bells ringing merrily, as over the deep snow we fairly flew. We travelled the river ice to Bob Beattie's. He was out feeding his cattle for the night and waved us to stop and invited us in. His cabin was low and blackened by smoke, two small windows. It seemed quite large, when inside, for one lone man. A bed and cook stove, table and a few chairs was all the furnishings. The walls were hung with his traps and furs of his kill. At his bedside was a bears hide for a rug on the puncheon floor. The bedstead was made of poles. Web snow shoes hung on the wall, the first I ever saw. I asked if they were hard to travel with? "O no," says Bob," won't you try them?" I stood up and put them on. I was afraid to sit down for fear I could not get up. I carefully walked around the cabin snowdrifts and came back and took them off. I believe they were the first and the last ones I ever tried to walk on.

Apportionment of School Money
Miss Millie Coffin, county superintendent of schools, has completed the apportionment of the school money among the various districts of the county. The total amount of the school fund is $11,887.94, which, divided by the number of school children in the county makes the apportionment among the various districts as follows:

No. 1, Bannack	$760.90
" 2, Bishops	266.81
" 3, Poindexters	434.80
" 4, Argenta	227.28
" 5, Glendale	1,126.53
" 6, Deweys	602.79
" 7, Amesville	260.81
" 8, Hecla	316.22
" 9, Willis	434.80
" 10, Dillon	3,685.05
" 12, Lima	1,314.69
" 14, Red Rock	197.63
" 15, Wisdom	138.34
" 16, "	355.74
" 17, Bowen	227.28
" 18, Fox	177.87
" 19, Scotts	167.99
" 20, Medicine Lodge	118.58
" 21, Grasshopper	171.87
" 22, Dell	464.45
" 23, Polaris	247.14
" 24, Alamo	177.87

The Dillon Examiner
December 27, 1893
****

There is a drop of $292.58 in the amount of monies spent in Dewey from 1892 to 1893.

The evening was bitter cold and we bade Bob fare well and continued on down the river ice road to Dickies bridge. There we crossed on to a snow road on the other side. Darkness now over took us, while Horace told me about the happenings after we went home the night of the dance. Some of the boys thot it would be good time to get Charley drunk, so one treated him and then another for his birthday, just for sociability sake, till at last Charley slumped over. Then he took pity on the poor foolish boy, picked him up in his arms, like a baby, and walked upstairs at Bryant's Hotel and put him to bed. Charley had a headache the next morning, but his mother always told how Charley quit drinking when she gave him the gold watch.

On our way down we passed Vaughns, Tongs, Pattons, Clines, Wise River, then the little log cabin on the ranch, John Lawrence's place, the big rock and the spring, Churchill's and past the marble grade. Soon we could see the faint flicker of the candle and coil lights from the cabins that dotted the Flat. Thanking Horace as he helped me from the sleigh, I bid him good night. Turning his team, he drove back to the road we came on and I heard the faint tinkle of the bells as they faded in the distance.

Along in the week Al came down town and came over to see me at the hotel. He came in to my room to talk. In the course of his talk, he said he could not see why Horace had to take that heavy work team and go clear to Ralstons Sunday. He said Horace knew the team was working hard and needed that day of rest and that Horace did not care a thing how he abused a good team.

Bryant

Bryant was a very ardent user of the weed, in both chewing and smoking. Some of the boys often said when he was at Dolman's store, coming out and the wind blowing down river, they could scent Bryant's departure when he opened the door, so strong was the nicotine scent that penetrated his body and clothes.

When at Dolman's he often entertained the help by telling "Bar" stories. On entering he got the story started off just right. He would pull out his pipe, then a plug of horseshoe tobacco, put the pipe in his mouth, take out his pocket knife and going over to the stove, he'd begin to shave small thin slices of the plug, laying the pieces on the edge of the stove so as to dry out the tobacco. Then the Bar story started a way back in Maine on the Penotseat above Old Town.

He would scrape out the pipe, saying, "The Bar then was just coming out of his hole."

When the tobacco would start to burn, he turned it over, put it in his pipe, light the match, "Then the Bar was sniffing around for food and I would be watching him." Just then the match burned his finger. "Dang that match," says Bryant and throws it away.

"Just then says I, I get that Bar," and lights the match and tamps down the tobacco. "Yes, if I know anything about Bars, I get him. Darn that match went out. Conner, get me sum other match?"

"Thanks."

Now, says the boys, go on with your story. This time he got a light and puffed away. Says he, "I get him. So I got a quarter of beef - Ding that pipe, it won't draw - give me a broom straw." Then he puffed and the pipe wheased.

"Yes, I knew he just smell at first. Another match, please. Then later I get my trap."

Puff-puff-puff. "Something the matter with that tobacco, burned I guess, so I got a hundred pound trap with big heavy bradded jaws."

Then he scrapes out the tobacco into the stove, takes out his pocket knife and begins to shave off more. This time, again tending it closely, turns, twisting his knife blade, getting it just dried out to the proper concistancy - "And set that trap right under the quarter of meat." Another match was lit. "Then the Bar took another circle around, whiffing - Ding, that match, it burnt my finger - Bar don't eat when they first come out fellers, no sir, is they don't." Conner gave him another match. This time he had better success, "And the Bar was circling again---", when Minnie came in panting, says "Papa, Mama wants those potatoes for dinner!"

Boiler

In March of 1893, Horace and Al got a contract to take a big boiler into Gibbonsville. They had taken in other machinery but this was the largest piece. Snow was on then as in midwinter and they took it in on the snow crust. They had quite a bit of trouble. It took 40 head of horses and besides their selves, other helpers.

After loading at Divide, the first night they got as far as Dewey. I was staying at the Bryant Hotel that winter. Horace and Al always stopped there. By that time I had became quite well acquainted with both and they talked freely of their plans, hopes and aspirations in general. I had found out, too, to keep my own council. I spoke of getting acquainted with Al. Yes, it was a way back in Kansas in the early '80's or late '70's when he left home and went into the far west. I was only a child then. So it was as meeting a stranger when we met here in the fall of '92. Fred Dickie was to go with them with his teams (to help). Fred was very nice and sociable all the time and once in a while had taken me to Clines, five miles up river, or walked with me over town to Mrs. Deans. Once he wanted to take me to the dance there in town but I declined and later in the eve went with a lady there in the house. In a short time, someone told me Fred was drunk, well I could not help that. We were good friends just the same and he had hopes he could take me yet.

There was to be a dance soon in the Flat. Dickie thot Horace also would miss it, for they could not possibly get back in time from that awful trip to Gibtown with the boiler. Horace came to see me that night before he left. He saw some green chalk lying on my table. He said he wanted it, so I gave it to him. In the morning there was written on the table, "Be in Dewey for the dance April 1." None of the crew ever dreamt of any of the party being there, seemed impossible. Dickie knew it could not be done. Tho down deep in Horace's mind he knew he would be there and take me, so this he planned with decision before hand. Leave Dickie and the crew so wore out it was not possible for them to come.

They were up and gone long before I was up the next morning. Mrs. Bryant always made an effort to serve meals to her borders, early or late, so as to help them on their way. After feeding, watering and harnessing, they ate. By that time the faithful teams were hitched to the load and when the command was given, each horse bore their weight forward in the collar, bells rang out merrily in the snow and the load rolled on steadily with Horace's watchful eyes scanning every move to avert any delay. He knew the allotted time it would take for the trip, barring any misfortune or delay.

> **Trees for Brakes**
>
> *In going down steep slopes with heavy loads, they would cut trees, tie the tops of the trees to the wagons, thus dragging the butts of the trees behind them in order to slow the wagons. - mc*

Once, on crossing the ice at Tongs upper ranch, they came near letting the boiler go in the river. Two of the helpers became so cold they would have frozen if not found in time. Cheo Keller and Fred Dickie, they sat down in the snow, had lost all feeling and thot they were warm.

Gibbonsville is just over the continental divide and when on top of the range there is a drop of 8000 feet in three miles. With all the big loads that they took down, ruf locks alone would not hold the load. So they had to cut down big trees and tied top down to help keep back the load and keep it from not running the horses. With a horse down on a decent like that, was sure death to the animal.

Main Street, Dewey, Montana
Courtesy of Beaverhead County Museum
Dillon, Montana

Fertilizer at the Hotel

One day a man drifted to the Flat and joined the crowd in the lobby just before dinner. There were often strangers from a distance which were brot in by the four time daily, four horse stages that plied between Divide and Dewey as long as the mill, mines and prospects flourished. There were the steady boarders and those ranchers or prospectors that were going farther up the country, who made Bryant their regular stopping place. The food was excellent and they knew if Mr. Bryant was there they would come away with a good story and a big laugh. Something they could entertain others [*with*] for days, all winter, perhaps by the fireside of some poor snowbound trapper, prospector or rancher.

The regulars always knew how to start Bryant off as with a harangue about somebody or place. As he poked the fire in the old long wood stove, went to the wash room for more wood, he heard the stranger speak of crops, the possibility of better crops by the addition of a new kind of phosphate that was on the market, giving wonderful results in many places. The steadies knew by now that they had struck a new line of thot as Bryant was unconsciously listening. This new stuff, well, he had lived in Maine where the ground was poor and had to be manured each spring. This new kind was a needcesity, was kept under shelter to keep it from bleaching by the weather and gave results when properly scattered on the ground in the spring. As he listened to this man expounding the good qualities of his new kind of fertilizer sprinkled on in each row, Bryant knew he was a cheat and imposter, a scoundrel and everything but a good, honest man. Finishing building up the fire, he lay down the poker and squared himself before the new comer and said, "Mr. fertilizer, fertilizer, fertilizer. God Dam you, your fertilizer is worth about as much as a pigs fart in Hell." The uproar nearly raised the roof and the phosphate man had nothing to add after the "horse laugh" he got from the regulars.

Bryant Up the Woodpile

On another occasion, Horace stopped for dinner. There had been trouble this time with Jane. Mrs. Smail happened to be there for a few days and she thot they had better put a stop to it. So when Horace appeared on the scene, Bryant was up on a pile of wood. Evidently from all appearances, he had to run to safety, for the woman had him treed and Bryant was saying, "I can lick any son of a bitch on this bar."

Stages

In the boom days at Dewey Flat, miners and businessmen and rif raf came in by stage. It met all passenger trains at Divide. The stage was a thorough brace coach like was used in earlier day - generally drawn by four good, fast horses. Express was brot and the travellers luggage. The stage held from about six inside, one on the seat with the driver and in urgent cases, passengers on top, but not often, only when crowded. There were many good drivers, tho not everyone could drive a stage. The driver of the west has never been excelled. These trying days developed drivers of the very best that it has ever seen produced in any epoch of the world history. The horses received the impulses, the word of praise or curse and obeyed. The driver knew the exact time to start and when they would arrive at a certain place. They were exposed to all kind of weather, cold to the extreme or hot, rain or snow and they dressed for all kinds of emergencies. Dressed in his fur overcoat, with plenty of good woolen clothes on, chaps or buffalo pants, wool socks, shoes, overshoes and gunni sack wrapped and tied over the overshoe in the western fashion. A wide eight inch leather belt on over the overcoat, a good heavy wool visor cap with ear warmers [*completed the outfit*]. Then he was ready to take the lines and whip in one hand and mount the boot, release the break and give the word of command to go. Such was the dress to withstand 40, 50, 60 below zero. There were still some stage routes in the early 1890's. Tho the long routes were supplanted by R.R. Tho still there were numerous lesser routes being kept up by horses and stage coaches. Now the gas auto has taken the place of the horse.

The Wisdom line was in its infancy in the 1890's. Mail twice a week was hauled by the contractor that furnished his own transportation. In the winter the lone stage driver saw untold hardships for in those days few people went in and out of the Basin. Everyone laid in his winter supplies and there was little need of the outside world. The stage driver, in the winter, became so tanned by the action of the sun on the snow. In color he was a genuine American. Sometimes they became snow blind. The remedy for that was to blacken a wide ring around the eyes. There were times in the summer when the trip was delightful when the air was free from mosquitoes, as that country seemed to have no equal in certain times of the summer.

Stories have been told of lone footman carrying the mail in earlier days. Lebo carried it one winter on snow shoes. From Wisdom there were other Post Office mail routes to various parts of the basin, Trox, Bowden and others. Once the Wampler girls drove a tandem team hitched to a log over the Bowen, Wisdom route. Then Jackson got its mail in over the Jackson, Wisdom route which becomes almost impassable in the winter at times.

When Gibbonsville began to thrive there was a daily mail route from Divide to Wisdom and on to Gibbonsville, Idaho. The road was desperate over the hill, but they made it. The route manager tried to have the drive as equally divided as possible so as to keep his stock able to go the distance each day, about 15 miles. At each stage station a tender was in full charge of the horses. At each stage station was a good barn, horse blanket put on each horse when he was taken off the stage by the stable man. If the horse was warm, he was not fed or watered at once, but allowed to cool off. Then he was watered and fed, rubbed off and bedded down for the night. This kept them in trim for the next days trip. At Divide was a stage stable, one at Ralston's, sometimes at Tong's and at Tong's upper ranch and Wisdom. [*Also there was*] one at Swamp Creek, Harry Neal's and sometimes at Swamp Creek at Hollinsworth. Then one in Gibbonsville. There was a blacksmith that went from stable to stable along the line to keep the horses shod and stages in repair. There were four horses to a stage. Extra horses had to be kept, so at a notice a new one could be put in place of one disabled. Feed, hay and oats, and straw for bedding were kept in abundance and a new supply on the road. Contracts were let by the government, to reliable men, that could give bonds and the mail had to go thru regularly as ordered.

One bad winter about 1903 or 4 the snow drifted so deep at Chalk Bluffs that the contractor could not get the mail thru. The mail was piled up for two weeks till the storm abated and they could exchange the piled up mail on either side of the drifts. When the mail went daily the ranchers along the Divide-Wisdom route got their mail daily. Each farmer furnished a small sack with drawstring top. The stage driver distributed them from the Post Office, then on his return trip he picked up each sack, hanging from a crain [*crane*].

When the daily stage was put on, they used the old thorough brace coach, 4 horses, there being more travelers going to Gibbonsville and Wisdom. In the years that followed there were several contractors, most all (Anderson, Lossel and others) put the mail in on time. One, I can't remember his name, was a failure from the start and he did not last long for horses, harnesess and wagons were borrowed and scattered a long the line. Then the contract was turned over to Al Anderson, things were soon put aright and the mail was put in on time.

These storms did not come so hard every winter, tho from reports of those day the snow fell very heavy each winter. From the time the river froze over in the fall, till late spring or breaking up time, the river, in many stretches, was used for a road. It being level on a water grade and when the snow began to fall it packed in the tracks, making a good, visible grade all the way.

It was true there has been some accidents, such as slipping off the grade and upsetting a load. Tho not often as a good driver kept his team, six or eight horses, in the road, being constantly on guard as to the road and teams.

There were no serious accidents on this stage line that I recall. Once the regular stage making it's down trip, one afternoon, was not loaded and coming along briskly, hit the ditch culvert. Suddenly the stage parted, leaving the coach and hind wheels and driver. The four horses, with front wheels, naturally took fright and ran just as hard as they could down the road. I was out in the road and saw the team go past. A wicked sight. They finally were found down the road near the big rock. One horse was down and others tangled up in their harnesses, tho none hurt badly. The queen bolt either broke or slipped out of place.

The stage ran several years after 1910, with horses and coaches, till automobiles became more numerous. The roads of those days were not good, as the new and better road and jeme [*pavement*] had not been thot of then.

When the auto stage took the place of horses, they still had to resort to the horse stage when the snow was deep. Then later a man invented what they called a snow mobile, which worked with note worthy success.

About 1908 or there about, a woman from Gibbonsville rode out on the stage, seemed ill, tho talked to no one. Then too, she was the only passenger that day. The stage stopped at Ralston's for dinner and to change horses. This woman got out and went in. Mrs. Ralston was very busy preparing and serving the meal, as there always were several for dinner. The woman ate but very little and seemed very reserved. When the stage was ready she got in. She seemed in pain, tho said nothing.

The stage made good time and met the up going train at Divide. She still looked haggard and worn, but she got on the train. No one knew her and no one was interested in this unfortunate woman. When she boarded the train, the world closed behind her. When the driver drove the stage to the stable he noticed blood in the stage, tho said nothing to anyone. At this time Ben Mallon was driving Lossel's freight wagons and the next day came up the road. At a turn in the road, he saw something lying at the side of the road like. Well, he stopped the team and examined the queer object. A baby, yes, still born - dead - yes. Well, with the help of his freighting companion, they dug a shallow hole and placed it in and covered it up. This mystery had never been solved.

Freighting Dog

There are all kinds of dogs. I admire the intelligent one, one that understands and picks his occupation. I believe Old Ben typifies the kind I mean. I don't know his ancestor or how exactly he was brot up. A mongrel I think, light brown in color, rather heavy set, tho strong and wiry!

Sam Rhodes was a freighter when I first knew him. He, with a family, lived in Gibtown, then coming to Dewey. Like many jerkwater freighters, came there for freighting job, mostly hauling ore from Quartz Hill to the mill, but would work anywhere. Sometimes Al or Eliel would hire him to help Al in with a load to Gibtown, but his teams and rigging was poor and if they could get better freighter, Rhodes was left out. However, he got some hauling for other concerns.

Ben seemed to sense all danger. When they camped out, made the fire, took out the grub, made ready for a meal - he was clost about. They often left the food left from the evening meal at the camp fire for the morning meal. Ben was fed well. Whatever was left, no one could touch. If a stray horse or mule came too near, Ben was heard in the dark of the night driving them away. Al bot two stag hound pups, and kept them in Gibtown till they were grown up. Then he had a man train them to catch coyote. In a few months he brot them home, as coyotes were thick in our country. At their first camp in the timber near the Abe Dean place, on this side of the big hill, they camped as usual for the night. The hounds were let out. Ben kept a jealous eye on them, as he had all ready made up his mind he did not like them. Things were taken out for the evening meal as they always did. The boys cooked supper, ate, fed Ben and the hounds. They had boiled enuf extra potatoes for breakfast and laid them out, when hot, on the grub box lid as they often did. Just then a mule needed their attention a little way off and then they thot they would step over and see Abe Dean. All of the sudden they heard an unearthly yell from one of the hounds. Just as a hound had decided he would take one of the potatoes, old Ben thot differently and nailed the hound. Gave him an awful trouncing. The hound never bothered again. Al would laugh and tell this. Old Ben was next to human. Just leave it to Ben. He followed these teams as long as they freighted, always the same. I often wish I knew, but I think he finally made his home with Al, going always to see if he could be of help. Often rode on the seat looking ahead.

Ben not only knew human kind, but he harked to the call of the wild of his own kind. Once coming out of Gibtown before the usual picking up of the things at the camp fire, Ben jumped up in the wagon seat and sniffed the air. All of the sudden he got down, made a line down the road and was not with them any more that trip. But normally, he was regular as a clock on the beat, trip after trip. That time his lady love called, they said. When Al got into the Flat three days later, Ben had been there two days. When bad roads were encountered and the wagon dropped in a mud hole, he was busy and anxious till [they] was a going again.

The Oat Thief

Quartz Hill was producing some good ore with no adequate facility in transporting the ore to the small mill or arrasters. Word came into Glendale of their wants. Horace amediately prepared to go and haul the ore. Horses were shod, break blocks repaired, rough lock, worn out links replaced, last but not least, feed for the horses while there. He could get hay delivered from a rancher, but the oats he had to take in, as in those days no one had bothered about raising any grain. On arriving, he rented a barn for his horses. It had a feed room to store the oats in.

Bryant ran the hotel where Horce secured board and lodging. Everything went well till one morning the part of the sack of oats he had left for the morning feed was gone. He casually mentioned the fact to Bryant. He thot a while and then says, "Horace, I'll tell you how to catch the son of a bitch. Take charcoal and scatter it all around the sack."

In the morning, sure enuf, some one had been there and got oats. In the snow, the foot prints showed up plain. They led to the stable in the back of the hotel. Bryant kept transient's horses and Sherman often kept one or two of his own.

GLENDALE ODD FELLOWS

Their Public Installation and Ball is a Great Success
Special Correspondence
Glendale, Mont., Jan. 1, 1894.

The public installation and ball of Bannack Lodge No. 3, I.O.O.F., drew one of the largest and happiest gatherings that Glendale has seen for years. Miss Clark Sharkey presided at the organ and a quartet consisting of the Misses Grace and Luella Terry, Tulip Jennings and Mr. Ed Harvey, singing the opening and closing odes of the order. The installation of the officers by Frank P. Tate, D.D.G.M., assisted by John Bergman, G.M., John Rhino, G.W., Peter Laybold, G.T., N.I. Hungate, G.G. followed the opening exercises. The following officers were installed for the ensuing term:
  H. K. Bateman, N.G.;
  G. R. Vance, V. G.;
  Peter Laybold, Sec.;
  K.N. Hilbinger, Treas.;
  D. Gist, R.S.N.G.;
  Theo. Leybold, Con.;
  Jno. Rhino, War;
  Jno. McCarl, I.G.;
  George Howard, R.S.S.;
  G. R. Hardisty, L.S.S.;
  Wm. Jennings, R.S.V.G.;
  Horace Hand, L.S.V.G.
The music for the ball was furnished by the Dewey's String band and the supper by the Hecla Mercantile company's restaurant. The ball was held at the rink, and was crowded. Sixty couples were in the grand march and they danced until 5 o'clock this morning.

Dillon Examiner
Dillon, Montana
Janary 1, 1894

Fish in the Milk Can

While driving team on the Glendale road, Horace often watered his horses at the creek that runs in the edge of the road, up a turn, and around a jut of rocks. Coming back the long, steep, up hill grade fagged a team out. Most teamsters that took good care of their horses always carried a water bucket and stopped at a creek or water hole. While watering, the team was refreshed and given time to take a rest. Other teamsters watered there too.

Pickett's wife, Laura, had become an inveterate kicker. She growled at this and that. She said Mr. Howard, the milkman, watered the milk he sold her. While Horace worked on the transfer for Pickett, he became fast friends of Picketts and he came quite well acquainted with his wife. He told her he thot Howard watered the milk too and in order to make his thots come true, one morning while watering his team, Howard drove up and stopped to water his team. Thot he, here's my chance. Seeing a school of little fish, Horace scooped them up with his bucket and when Howard's back was turned, poured them in the milk can. Sure enuf, Laura by chance got a fish. Then Howard did catch it. She'd tell him, yes she would, and she did, but the poor man could not account for the fish, and he never did. She always blamed Howard. Horace told Pickett and they kept it a secret, just to hear her rave.

Ames and Wife

Guy Ames and his wife came to Dewey Flat about 1890. He came first from near Chicago. He worked mostly as a clerk in stores and when the town went down he ran the Pond-Vance store. She came out shortly after he got a steady job. He was a good store man. They had a boy, Claud, and one girl.

They used to tell how the people on the lake lived, always paying for their back winter debt. Tho always got work on the lake in the summer.

He was a spiritedly man, tall, bald headed and red headed. She was a very nice woman. Everything was kept sewed up, in order, and the log house well kept.

I boarded there about six months. Their house was just a crossed the street from the school house. Vance built it and lived there till the store changed hands and they moved back to Glendale. After Ames went back, we did not hear of them any more.

Chapter XII

Maggie and Horace

****

A New Life Together

We decided to go to Dillon July 6 [*1894*] to be married. When the time came, the R.R. strike shut up travel, so Horace borrowed a two horse buggy and having a good driving team, we went to Dillon and was married by Shannon, then Judge of the court there. The third day, got back as far as Dewey's Flat. That night a bunch of the rounders shivareed us. Cost Horace $3.00 in drinks to get rid of the bunch. Next day we went on home to the ranch. That year there was not much raised on the ranch and after putting in the piece of the road at the Big Rock, Horace got contracts to haul in supplies to Gibbonsville. This he worked at till the next spring. Then for a while he worked on the ranch, seeding to hay and oats, but occasionally took a load in as needed. This helped run and improve the new ranch. We had lived in their first cabin the winter of 1894. In early 1895 Horace thot we needed a better house, so he went to work and got out the house logs from Triangle Gulch (that was our nearest supply of timber) for our new house. The logs were 32 x 1 foot. Nice big logs and when hewed they laid up fast and looked nice. Some time that winter, after hauling the logs to the yard, he hired Jimmie New to help hew and lay them up. The house soon started to take on the looks of a dwelling (was 15 feet south of our original cabin, toward the road). The upper sides were in line with the cabin. The house was 15 x 30. Made two big rooms, one for a kitchen and one for a bed room and combined sitting room. That left the cabin for a constantly growing need of a bunk house. The old well had fallen in, so a new 60 foot well had to be dug in the summer. There was plenty of water, but no drinking water. The first summer the cow died, so the next fall Horace bot two of Park's cows. I had a good saddle horse so put in a good time going places, but soon tired of that, staid home when he was gone - always busy sewing, making clothes and quilts.

Horace and Maggie (Halbert) Hand
July 6, 1894
Dillon, Montana
From the Susan Hand Collection

Wise River Meadows
1894 - Summer

After we were married 1894, July 6, we came back from Dillon, and cleaned up the cabin.

Horace had went into Butte the first of the month to settle up with W. A. Clark for the logs he and Al had cut that winter and drove to Divide that spring. When in Butte, he bot a bed, dresser and commode. We used a home made table they were using and a nice set of dishes (not china) we bot in Dillon (like my old brown and white begonia leaf platter). There was an old rocker the boys bot at Billie Concella's sale a few years before and an old cupboard bot at that sale - was no paint on it. I used it all the time. [*We built*] a few shelves on the wall and in the corner behind the stove, a three cornered shelf or two for the groceries. The walls were left natural, and another shelf over the table. Of course they had some dishes, knives and forks, pots and pans, which I used too. Then we bot two good sitting chairs, while in Dillon, and a platform rocker. People thot nothing of going long distances and the radius of places and country and towns has no bounds. But for me, at that time, my radius was small. Melrose, and Dillon, Glendale, Divide, Butte, back to Divide, home and upriver to Ralston's, Gibtown and Virginia City. That was as far as I knew or had been up to 1910 when we moved away. Some of those places I only seen once, and not to Butte for 8 years. Horace had been many places before settling down. We never went for pleasure, all business.

The cabin being small, there was lots of time on my hands. The crop was small and Horace and Al, being away all spring, did not expect much. Then, too, it was this spring that Al got the job from Eliel's to freight mostly from Dillon to Gibtown by way of Jackson. Sometimes he was sent to Divide to load and then quite often Horace got an order to load too. Horace began to look around for something to do. One day, bright and early, we saddled up to take a look at the Wise River Meadows. He had seen them before, but he wanted to see if the ground all over (160 Acres) was level and could be mowed.

Horace always had a big saddle horse. He had just traded a horse Cline had given me to Hide Ordeway for a broke strawberry roan. Baldy had a nice white strip down the forehead. Was gentle, tho tough as leather. I liked him and he must have liked me, as I could go to the field, take my apron off (talking all the time) and put it around his neck and lead him home. The boys soon hated him, for he was a signal and always lead the bunch in the field. They often had to come to me to go and catch him.

We went up the ditch for a mile or more, then went down thru Trueman's field to our old ford, the roughest I ever saw, boulders large as a bucket, which a horse had to feel his way slowly acrost. Up at the end of Walter Lawrence's place we crossed over to see his stand of oats. It was about the poorest, thinnest I ever saw. The ground is mostly flint rock, does not show so much till it is plowed. Walter and family must have been away this day. I thot it a lovely place, as clost to the house Vipond Creek came tumbling down from the near high hills - the finest, purist water ever.

From there we went on thru a nice strip of land and I remarked how nice a field it would make if the rocks that had rolled down from the hill were cleared away. Some few years after a Mr. Richardson took it up, built a big house and afterward had to abandon it.

We came to Hugh Thompson's place next. He was not there, perhaps away haying for someone. Just a lone cabin with a beautiful little rill coming from the high mountain, rushing to the river. On farther he had a hay corral and a nice little patch of ground he had raised some hay on for his mules. This is the place Butler took from Hugh in about 1906 and staid and raised their family till they tumbled out of the nest and scattered, an ignorant bunch.

The next place is the Pattengale [*Pettingill*] Meadow and Creek. His hillside shelter and a foundation of a barn which he had begun - we hurried on, trying not to look at things too much, for Horace said he might be there hiding and see us. We did not terry, crossed the river there below the forks and continued on up the right hand side of the fork.

Soon we came to the meadow, a lovely strip of hay - mostly sloughgrass. Here we ate our lunch and after resting and giving the horses time to eat, we went up over the field. [*It was*] lovely soil that had rotted there for years. The snow protected it in winter and it [*the grass*] fell down and a new crop came up thru the old year after year. On going over it, there were deep gullies cut thru it by the high water in the spring and we would have had trouble taking the machine over the meadow, so Horace abandoned the idea. Tho the hay was nice. A few years later a man by the name of Kingsberry went up and put up some hay, just shortly before the Wise River dam was built there. It would make a fine dam - the water company soon found that out and in 1901 began to build a dam (that is another story).

We turned our horses down the river on the west side and for home, past a lone grave. In about 1880 Clark hired men to put in stulls on upper Wise River, Seamore Creek. Smallpox broke out in this camp and claimed this victim, a Mr. Palmer from New Brunswick. He was buried just where he died, as was the custom of the times.

➤DOWN THEY GO!⬅

WE make prices within the reach of every purse. To see is to believe.

NOTIONS.		DOMESTICS.	
White Tape, 3 for	5c.	Bleached Cotton Flannel,	10c. per yd.
Dress Shields,	10c. pair.	Unbleached " "	8c. "
Curling Irons,	5c. each.	Best Shirting Cheviot,	15c. "
Curling Irons,	10c. "	LL Sheeting,	6 c. "
Waving Irons,	25c. "	Small Linen Towels,	5c. each.
Mourning Pins,	5c. box.	Large Linen Towels,	15c. "
Corset Clasps,	5c. each.	Skirt Cambric,	5c. per yd.
Corset Clasps,	10c. "	Grass Cloth,	10c. "
Finishing Braid,	10c. piece.	Linen Canvass,	15c. "
Dress Stays,	15c. per set.	Hair Cloth,	12½c. "

MOST COMPLETE LINE OF

Men's Underwear, Shirts, Gloves and Socks.

To Be Found in Dillon and Prices Lower than the Lowest.

Trade where you can get the Best Value for your money. We Know that we give it to you.

Mail Orders Promptly Filled.

THE C. O. D. STORE,
MASONIC BLOCK, DILLON, MONT.

Dillon Examiner
Dillon, Montana
August 21, 1895

On the way down, Horace spotted a nice patch of poles. He afterwards got the poles and hauled them home for fences.

We rode down over that rocky road to Stines. Seemed to be a day when all were gone - and so with Stine. We let our horses drink out of his creek. It twilled down past his cabin and into the river. Below his cabin is quite a nice little meadow [*where*] he generally went thru the motions of cutting a little [*hay*]. Then we and horses wearily plodded home, past Honacre Creek and a nice strip of ground where Vinyard later farmed - there was no one then living there before Stines. We all were tired and glad to get home.

Warren Churchill had a team and saddle horse and a few cattle. He ranched in his queer way, she [*Mrs. Churchill*] getting money occasionally from the east. In 1894, he raised quite a patch of oats. He got Horace to come and bind it for him. The grades being so narrow and roads so poor, that Horace always loaded the binder on a hay rack when he went any place to bind grain. It wasn't till then that Horace got so good acquainted with Churchill and his wife. He ate dinner there and each time he came home had a lot of new stories to tell about Churchill and the family. One morning he went down early and they invited him in. The two little boys, Warren and Russel, were up to the table in their night clothes, hollering "Papa, give me the hot cake first."

"How can I," says Churchill, "how can I?"

They kept up their plea to have it first and finally he divided the cake. Then they howled.

Churchill would putter around, nothing was quite right. He tried to shock grain as Horace bound it. That noon the children both set up a howl for pie first and kept it up till they gave them pie, tho not till after Warren had measured the pie with his fingers.

Old Rona was a gentle roan saddle pony, perfectly gentle for the Churchill boys to ride. The boys often came out to the field where we were at work. Once they found some mice under a shock and in catching the mice, one bit Warren. He cried and boo hooed. Churchill quit his work and tried to console the boy, saying "God Dam Christ" for putting a mouse in my field to bite my poor little boy. Then the wind blew. The boys could not keep on their big straw hats. Then Churchill would dam Christ again. Churchill was an old man and he took all adversities to heart.

He never was a teamster and seldom drove out on the roads. One fall when Horace went to Melrose for winter potatoes, Churchill wanted potatoes. Horace says come with me, you have a team, go get your winter spuds. He finally decided to go and one morning when Horace went, Churchill followed. He was so nervous going down the canyon he would sit on the edge of his seat, peering around down the road, fearful lest they meet a team coming up. O, my, what would they do. Horace came home from that trip with many more stories.

People in those days visited but very little. Once Mr. Churchill took his family to see the Dodgsons at Meadow Creek. This time at dinner the two boys set up a howl for cake first. Mrs. Churchill was ashamed of them and left the house saying she was leaving, tho came back presently and gave them the cake.

When Mrs. Churchill's money ran out and the ranch would not pay, there was nothing else for her to do but leave, taking the only girl, Maggie. She went from place to place. It was hard at her age to make a living. Finally she came back to Dewey, rented a shack and took in washing. He stayed on the ranch and kept the two boys, washed and cooked for them and mothered them well. It was said, when he had to go to Dewey for supplies, if he saw her on the street, he would wheel in his track and go the other way. He so resented her leaving him in his old age. It was about this time Horace and Al got the County Commissioners to give Churchill the road job, which he held faithfully till the day he died.

Mr. Churchill finally, in his old age, passed -1907. Churchill had called at our house one morning. That evening he took sick and we were very much surprised to learn, by Brubaker the next day, that he had died. Everyone was grieved. There was a large funeral. The VanWarts were with us that summer, so we all put on our best clothes. Horace hitched up the horses to a wagon so we all could go. Nettie [*our daughter*] was a little girl and took in everything. Mrs. Churchill and Maggie were standing at the turn of the road where the road turned off the main road to the cemetery. After the procession moved on, she and daughter followed on foot to the grave. The mother was heavily vailed and Nettie heard someone in the procession say, "I bet she has an onion in her hands to make her cry." The boys grew up and were able to shift for their selves.

Citizenship

That fall Horace finished getting his citizen paper. He was always rebellious at the fact he had to get them. He had been here some time before he and others found out [*they needed papers*] (even voted) and was concidered as a citizen. When all at once a lot of them had to get their papers. He never kept them and when needed I had to produce them.

Horace's Citizenship

Horace Hasting Hand became a citizen of the United States on September 17, 1894, Dillon, Montana.

Fall 1894

> *The Citizenship Story*
>
> *The story behind the citizenship papers was that Horace wanted to homestead some property adjacent to the ranch at Wise River. Upon applying for the homestead, it was discovered that he was not a citizen of the United States and therefore could not homestead the land. Horace had migrated from Canada some years before. The filing for the homestead was done in about 1894, but was done under Maggie's name, as she was a citizen. The papers showing the completion of this homestead transaction were "filed for record May 10th, A.D. 1910 at 10 o'clock a.m." Patent Number 118266 was recorded this date showing Maggie Hand as sole owner of the property. This is recorded in the Clerk and Recorders Office, Beaverhead County, Dillon, Montana, Book 57, page 517. - mc*

Once, that fall of 1894, I wanted to tack a comforter. Horace, being home for a few days, and this day he was going early to hunt a good patch of poles to get out that winter for a new fence. With him being gone all day I would be alone, so thot I could not tack a comforter alone. He said get your horse (Baldy) and come as far as the turn of the road (Jones place, tho no place there then), then you can carry the quilting frames from there to Clines (or Sam Garrott place). They lived there then down in the wild hay meadows. I knew Baldy was skittish and hardly thot the plan would work, but newly weds dare not say much. So went along as meekly as I could. At the turn of the road I took the four quilting frames under my arms and started on, when all at once Baldy kicked, bucked a little and did everything but keep straight in the road, as Horace said he would. He said I cried, but I don't believe I did. Anyway, I hollowed for him to come and help. He did, [*and*] laughed at me for not disciplining the horse and going on. Well, it ended, and he finally consented to go on with me to Clines and carry the frames, which I thot he should have done in the first place. He never got done telling this story, laughing at me. Now if this incident had happened before we were married, how eager he would have been to go all the way with me, and besides carry the frames without saying a word? Makes some difference of when and how's?

Trueman

One time when we first moved up on the farm I went up to Trueman's horseback. This was in the winter when they were cutting logs (stulls) for Trask. Mrs. Trueman was a kindly soul. I always liked her. She asked me to stay for dinner. Being hungry, I was glad to stay. All she had was beans and salt pork, soaked together, black coffee and bread. I never tasted better beans. They were equal to the bean hole beans or at least, just then, when I was hungry.

Mrs. Trueman washed for the boys [*Al and Horace*]. After I was married I went up for Horace's clothes. She was so little, she could not wash those dirty clothes clean, so I washed them over and patched them. Then was the beginning of my patching days, made over and patched. I mended shoes till we came to Melrose. It was there my right arm bothered me and I gave up the cobbling to the cobbler in Dillon.

Another horseback trip to Trueman's, Linnie was going to dress a chicken, tho never had. I took hold and showed her how it was done. Then that summer I often went up and bot peas and vegetables. We did not plant any that year.

There were not many women living in Wise River country at that time and were not very sociable, owing to the distances from one an other and the poor road. Became a habit to only go when needed. Mrs. Cline was the nearest neighbor and I went there quite often when left alone for a week. I would often go and stay over night. Finally I thot it foolish and staid home. Then Clines came down and told me to not stay alone, as there had been a queer fellow in the country and it was not safe to be alone.

Powder

Shortly after the quilting episode, Horace got wind to load a six horse team of various articles needed at the Gibbonsville Store and mines.

In those days one did not get mail so often, so the parties needing the freight depended on the word of mouth chain to get their orders filled. Horace generally got word in time to fix up and repair rigging and shoe the horses. This team was seldom turned out on the range, only in the spring when the roads were bad, but always were fed their three meals per day and watered regularly. So within a very few days, they were ready to go to Divide and load and [*were*] back home by night. It was a long day, but by getting up at 4 a.m. the load could be back by night. Then it generally took 5 to 6 days to pull into "Gibtown".

One day when he was gone, Cline came down and stopped on the way. He says, "Maggie, what is his (Horace's) load this time?" "Oh, I said, "groceries and the like." I noticed a queer twinkle in his eye, nothing more was said. I knew they used powder in the mine, but Horace had always told me he'd let the other fellows handle that. I lived happy all these years, never thinking that he and Al were about all the freighters on the road in and around that time. Years after, I heard him tell how one box of powder had broken open going down that awful hill into Gibtown. One stick [*of powder*] rolled out in a crack of the box and was ground to pieces. When he got to the foot of the hill to knock off the trees he drug behind and also knock off the rough lock, he was with horror what had happened and drove on in the three miles, while aghast, thinking, tho, with all that, he was safe.

Chick

We [*Horace and I*] seldom went places together, being cheaper for one to go than two and [*in later years with*] the children. [*It was*] only when there were papers to sign that I went. This trip was in the late spring and we did not have to load ourselves down with clothes. In Dillon it was really hot that day.

We got a room at the rooming house where most ranchers got rooms. I was going to trade in the afternoon and Horace said he would get me a chick. Mr. and Mrs. Hirschy had rooms there too. Neither one of us knew her, but Pa knew him and had seen her on the stairway.

Those days women wore shirt waists and skirts and we both were dressed similar. We were both upstairs in the washroom, when she turned to go into the sitting room. Just then Horace came up behind her and in a rather loving way held the chick before her eyes, all the time thinking it was I. Just then I accidently appeared on the scene. Mrs. Hirschy resented a stranger giving her a chick in a loving way. We all three had a good laugh and then got acquainted.

Horace's Cousins

Bill McClellan, Fred Wilson, Wilnot, Fred and Ed, (can't think just now their names, tho cousins). All three families were born and raised clost to the Red Bridge, New Brunswick, Canada.

Bill's mother and Horace's mother were sisters, Eliza and Mary Wilson. Most of the early settlers of this part of New Brunswick were English, Irish and Scotch. The Wilsons were Irish, Hands English. Putting it as Willie Hand quoted it, "Take away the Irish in our race and you would not have much left."

Bill was not a large man, tho strong and wiry, a good worker on most any job he set his hands to. When a young lad at home, was an alert youngster, picking up bits of news in his community and all other news that might be brot in from the outside. Evenings he often spent at a little settlement center. There fell in to mingling with older men, and soon learned to like his rum - a very bad habit which followed him to his grave. Men those days drank on the sly. Acquiring the habit of carrying a bottle, taking his friend away out back in some secluded place and taking a drink, then hiding their bottle in a manger. This was a sure sign they were from the Red Bridge. Their main pride and delight was to dress up, get a horse and buggy and go some place to town or to a relatives and always a bottle stored away for a friend, mostly tho for himself.

He first went to Pennsylvania to work in the lumber wood, coming back to sport around. He, being the oldest of a large family, was the apple of his mother's eye. After a trip or two to Pennsylvania, he and Horace went to Colorado (Denver). The Westward Ho fever struck Bill, after working for a while so he could go on farther, leaving Horace in Denver.

Glendale, Montana was his next stop. There were many New Brunswick friends he had known in and around the Red Bridge. He got work as everybody did, saved up enuf money to go back home, get a wife and come back again. He could get work, [*and had*] no worry about the future. They lived there happy, tho soon Bill's drinking fastened on him. She learned to drink too. By and by there was not so much work and they went to Anaconda. There they saved and bot a home, tho both drank. She finally left him, taking the two children and later married a black man she had known in her younger day in New Brunswick, not as good a man as Bill. Then they went to the coast and Bill lost track of her and the children. With the home broke up, he turned to Horace for a home, tho still continued his drinking. I first heard of him was in the fall of '92. Having been on a big spree, he came in to the Flat and got a horse from Jim Mitchell, rode it up the road toward the ranch. But in some way, the horse and drunken driver went into John Lawrence's field. Bill and horse parted there and Bill came up thru the sage brush to the cabin. Men guyed him, but he kept mum, and later found out about him getting a horse from Mitchell. They told him Mitchell wanted him to pay for the horse. Bill said he could go to the devil, he would not pay for the horse.

After he drank, he was a very penitent, disgusted man. As soon as he was able, he would go to work again and be so saving, you would think he would never drink again. Later on in the summer he took another big spree, going to Dewey, Butte and Anaconda. The saloon men and hotel men were always glad to see him on a drunk as then they were sure of their money. He was always sure to pay up later and they knew he would work for Horace and then they would get their pay. It really became a game for them to get money later on.

This time he did not terry long in the Flat. Not fairing very good in Butte, he went on to Anaconda. As long as he was able to handle his money, he was very stingy and careful with his money, only buying a bottle and going into a barn or chicken house and drink till the bottle runs empty, and then getting another. If some pilfering kid or unprincipled man never found his money, it would last quite a while. When in Anaconda the first night, he had all of his money taken, [and his] clothes and shoes. Being on the outskirts of town, he went to the city dump for clothing and shoes. He dug around, got an old dirty pair of overalls and a ripped shirt, which he tied up the rips to put on. The best he could do was to find odd matched shoes. There he was, 20 or 30 miles away from that cabin and Horace. All he could do was walk, weak from not eating for days - a garbage can looked good to him just then, weak and sick. He grabbed a few pieces of bread and started. There would be water on the way. If only he could get home to Horace. Horace would laugh, but then, he too would take care of him, give him a bed to lay on, peace and protection, clean clothes, food and he would get well. Then never again.

Next day Al Cline was fixing fence and saw a man coming down the road. Sure enuf, it was Bill. He had known Bill in Glendale - just another spree Bill was on. He was too dejected for Cline to josh, but Cline offered to feed him if he would come down to the house. No, Bill could not do that and then too, to have to face Al's wife in such a plight. "No thank you Al. I'll make it on to the cabin."

Horace was out irrigating, looking up the road to see if he could spy someone he might talk to for a while. Who did he see - why it must be Bill, but I'd never look for him coming that way. Sure enuf. Tho he looked like the worst beggar he ever saw.

There was no use scolding or saying a word. They both went in silently to the cabin - by and by when Bill was getting better, he would tell it all and be so sorry and such a sorrowful character when better. All he needed then was food and drink and kindly concideration, by not saying a word. With rest, feed, and a caring companion, Bill gained strength and soon was quite his self again, ready to take up life anew, taking interest in the new fields. When Horace had work for him, Bill worked for him. If not, he generally worked for Pat McKinney in Idaho but often he took those trips when he became more ambitious, having saved his wages. He always intrusted me with his money. Till the day he saddled up his horse he was to ride and packed the pack horse, then he would have me put the money he wanted to keep in a muslin poke and pin it securely on the inside of his undershirt. Then he would take the amount he would need for his journey in his pockets. With hopes high, Bill would ride away, assuring us he would make the trip safe and not spend this savings this time in a saloon. If starting early, he might reach Wisdom that

---

From the charge account ledger of the Hecla Mercantile and Banking, Inc., Melrose, Montana the following charges are shown:

September 19, 1895:
   To A. L. Pickett, Account # 502:
      3 1/2 doz. eggs - $0.65

September 26, 1895:
   To A. L. Pickett, Account # 502

100 flour	- $2.75
3 brooms	- 1.00
10 butter	- 3.00
10 cans lye	- 1.00
500 oats	- 6.50
TOTAL	-$14.25

To J. Hartwig, Account # 345

1 pr. Olls	-$ .75
1 C.P. Tea	- .60
Candy & Nuts	- .50
1/2 Nut Meg	- .50
200 Flour	- 4.50
TOTAL	-$ 6.50

A few other items and costs found in this book, dated August 30, 1895 - 3000 ft. of fuse cost $18.00, bale of hay cost 90 cents, 16# ham cost $2.08 and 5 cans of evaporated milk cost $1.00.

This just shows the cost of things in 1895. This ledger book is at the Silver Bow/Butte Archives in Butte, Montana.

night, tho perhaps he would only get as far as Tong's upper ranch at Squaw Creek, or as far as the Callen Ranch on Doolittle Creek. A man could get feed and shelter at most any place, but Bill liked the hospitality of little towns. He might gather news.

Arriving in Wisdom, tired from the new exercise, as he was no rider, he would resort to a bracing drink of rum. One was never enuf, so he ate his supper dazed, got a bottle for the night. Perhaps the horses were unsaddled and fed, tho if he met old cronies, they stood all night at the hitching rack without feed or water. Then some kindly horseman would take pity on the poor dumb animals and feed and water them, till Bill spent all his money or someone rolled him.

Then in an other day of hard riding he might get to Dean's place clost to the continental divide. The third or forth day arrived at Pat's, tired and sick with all his well laid plans all crushed and a guilty conscience. He straightened up with these friends as they were always glad to get news from Dewey and vicinity.

McKinneys, in their younger day, both worked at Quartz Hill, he as cook at the miners boarding house and she as a waiter. They were a bright, courageous pair, willing to tackle most any job in order to get a chance to build a home with enuf worldly goods to raise their small family and keep theirselves. Bill always found work there and could stay till he had recuperated. He loved their children and was at home again, often staid a year or so, would amass a few dollars, "a nest egg", and start back to see us. He generally fell prey to thieves and robbers on the way home and came in an object of pity. Loosing his money and clothes, sometimes even a horse, and then make the last leg of his journey with a freighter. That was the cheaper mode of travel if one did not have a price of a stage ticket. Then the stages stopped at the regular change station and one would have to have money to eat on. When coming with a freighter they often camped out, and cooked their own food. Then he would help round up the horses, harness, hitch and be a congenial companion to the freighter. Once again regained his health, being very penitent and when once told of his fault, he would say, never again.

Dillon Examiner
Dillon, Montana
January 10, 1894

When I came to the ranch, not being used to a drunk, I was very bitter about him acting that way. Then when he sobered up someone had to give the whiskey, on a schedule and just so much. He often was so sick, he had snakes, dogs and fishes. They appeared all over the floor and on the ceiling. He was afraid to stay alone and Horace would have to sleep in the cabin with him. In the day time they gave me the liquor to deal out, tho he would pester me for a drink often and often [*I would*] have to drive him out of the house. When he could not get the liquor as often as he wanted it, he would drink boiling hot water. Often found the medicine chest and drank 4 H liniment, or pickled red hot pepper of ketchup. I was disgusted with him and told him what I thot of a man that would let his appetite get the best of him. When he finally recovered and was not yet able to work, he would take care of the children while I worked or carry water, hang out clothes or anything to lighten my load. Then I would feel ashamed of abusing him. After all was over and he was himself again, I have heard him say, "A good big drunk was as good as a course of medicine." Then I'd say, "Bill you ought to be ashamed of yourself."

He often said I needed a harness and one horse cart so I could take a child and go visiting. There was a nice little cart and harness at Ames for sale. "No," says I, "I don't care, for a cart is too small." So he bot the cart. The little sorrel mare would make a good single pony for his cart, so the sorrel was broken. All went well with the cart and the sorrel. He could go to Butte, Anaconda, see friends. As he had some money, he dressed up as he liked to do in starting on these visits. Bid us farewell and that he would be back safe in a few days. A week went by and a few days. A neighbor going home stopped and told us Bill was at Dewey and he wanted to come home. With all gone, we were disgusted. Horace was busy and did not go down for a few days. When he did, Bill said, "I want to go home." Horace was not in a hurry. Bill followed him like a whipped pup all round town. A very dejected, disgusted, sick man, old sores on his head, forehead, arm and hand. Everything had slipped away from him, money first, good clothes, all soiled and torn. Finally, in Dillon the horse was sold, then the cart, harness, not getting scarcely anything for them. Then saloon men and other thieves got his money and a friend of Horaces put him on the train, paid his way to Divide. From there he either got a ride or walked to Dewey. For over two weeks he had slept in stables and chicken houses or any place he could crawl in. Sleeping a drunkard's sleep, with clothes and shoes on all the time. Horace always had to buy whiskey to sober him up, then he would follow like a lamb.

[*Bill was*] a very sick man. Horace bathed him like a child and put him to bed, administered the right amount of liquor for two days and fed him regularly. Beside the other sores, bruises and cuts, they found on him was a very bad swollen, sore arm that did not yield to salve treatments. One morning he got up, dressed, came to the house and says, "Maggie, I wish you would take that razor and lance my arm. There is puss - should come out."

"Yes, I see, but what if I cut a nerve, might disable you for life," and I begged off. That day Dr. Townsend from Melrose was called on a case farther up the river. Horace happened to be on the road and told the doctor to stop, as we had a sick man with a bad arm and to be sure and stop on his return. So he did and found Bill suffering from much pain. Yes, local blood poisoning, good thing it has not scattered. Dr. Townsend called for a pan to sterilize an instrument in. In time it was sterilized. Then he cut open the swollen place and a cup of pus flowed out. He gave me instruction how to keep that place open so it would drain for several days. I went by his instructions and it finally healed up.

I told him if he ever got on another spree like that, it would kill him. For a year he went straight, staying home with us. [*By this time,*] Roscoe [*Maggie's fourth child*] was the baby now. Bill thot a lot of all the children, especially Roscoe. Finally in early spring, he decided he could go with Al, Fred Wilson and others that were loading cars for Cody, Wyoming, to work on a big ditch there. I always told him to spend his money for a good bed and bedding. We rather objected, but he went, taking his only possessions (two double blankets), bidding us all good-by. When out in the yard, Roscoe still followed Bill. When they got in to Butte, for some reason the fireman did not load as planned, but got a contract to put in a viaduct there, finishing it before they left. All the men were given work there. Bill was driving a scraper team, sleeping in a lean to next to the stable where they kept the teams. This was in a bad place and bad company, with the other boys drinking, he soon drank too. He wanted the boys to bring him home but they were too busy having a good time theirselves. So poor Bill was neglected, and having a scratch on his leg, blood poisoning set in again and Bill passed away. After Horace, Al and other boys buried him a daughter wrote to Horace from some place in Washington enquiring about his estate. Horace answered the letter, telling her a few pennies and two double blankets constituted the estate. [*Bill died 1908 or 09.*]

We hoped his poor old mother in New Brunswick, Canada never found out the full truth about her dear boy, the apple of her eye.

PROPHESY

Oh, the Twentieth century girl!
What a wonderful thing she will be!
She'll evolve from a mystical whirl
A woman unfettered and free;
Not a corset to crumpen her waist.
No crimps to encumber her brain.
Unafraid, bifurcated, unlaced,
Like a goddess of old she will reign.

She'll wear bloomers a matter of course,
She will vote, not a question of doubt;
She will ride, like a man, on a horse.
At the club, late at night, she'll stay out.
If she chances to love she'll propose,
To blush will be quite out of date.
She'll discuss politics with her beaux and out-talk her masculine mate.

She'll be up in the science of things,
She will smoke cigarettes; she will swear,
If the servant a dunning note brings,
Or the steak isn't served up with care.
No longer she'll powder her nose
Nor cultivate even a curl
Nor bother with fashions or clothes,
This Twentieth century girl.

Her voice will be heard in the land
She'll dabble in matter of state.
In council her word will command
And her whisper the laws regulate.
She will stand 'neath her banner unfurled
Inscribed with her principles new
But the question is: What in the World
Will the New Century Baby Do?

(Chambers Journal, Sept., 1895)

From Maggie's Scrap Book

Jimmie Wells

Jimmie Wells was an old timer of the Flat (Dewey). He told me once he went with a horse buyer in the Civil War times. They bot horses in the north and took them to the south, New Orleans, and sold to the rebble [*rebel*] officers. He seemed to know all about the Mississippi river trades. After the war he drifted north. In his old age he had accumulated quite a bunch of keyuses (horses). They ran on the ranges and he lived in the Flat. When the winters were hard and snow deep, horses could not paw the snow. He would buy a few loads of hay and feed them in some convenient place till the weather cleared or warmed up and took the snow off. Then they could rustle their feed. Horses, uncared for, often become small and not marketable stock. (Jimmie was often in debt to Horace for hay.)

Maggie and Horace's first child, John William Hand, born August 30, 1895.

The summer of 1895 we had our new house done. My mother came out and staid a while. Our first child, Johnnie, was born August 30, 1895. Our home was established. Then Horace did not do so much freighting, as the ranch was made to be a paying investment. Later he did make several trips, the first and second summer. Cattle and horses increased and soon had a bunch, as our hay fields grew in size.

Al Griswold

Maude tells about Al [*Griswold*]. When he was working for Patton, Mrs. Patton would give Al some good advise and try to straighten Al up and make him quit drinking.

She would say, "Al, don't you see drinking is no good."

"That's right," Al would say.

"Don't you see these people never amounts to much?"

"That's right" Al would say.

"They never can have a home and drink."

"That's right." Al always agreed, no matter what she told him.

One time Horace hired Al to split wood and do the chores. That was the fall John was a baby and Ma was here. Horace was away on some hauling job. Perhaps a trip to Gibbonsville. Al took the job all right. By that time we were living in the new house and the cabin was used for a bunk house for the men. He had his bed there and a stove where he could toast his shins and snuff, as he chewed tobacco and spat in the fire. That aught to be enuf of one good thing and it was for Al. After the horses and cow was tended late in the morning (had to call him for breakfast). He would split two small arms full of wood, bringing one to us and lay on the floor, and one to the cabin and lay on the floor. Then, there he would sit. Ma and I were flabbergasted. We had been used to having the wood box filled. Well, when we wanted more wood, we'd have to go and knock on the cabin door and tell him we were out of wood. We would have gladly gone and got the wood if it had been split at the pile. He would drolly say yes and, after a time, would get the arm full of wood. Well, when Horace came back, his term of office expired. Then he went to John Lawrences. There he could get shelter, for John would never put him out. Ma and I were glad to get rid of him, for everyday was the same, never had wood, only from one armful to the next.

**Wild Man of Wise River
George Pettingill - Right
Photo taken from a post card
From the Thelma (Hand) Kalsta Collection**

George Pettingill
Wild Man of Wise River Country

[*George Pattengale [Pettingill] was a neighbor of Horace and Maggie's. Note that Maggie spells his name Pattengale in all of her writings. Pettingill Meadow and Creek are named after George Pattengale [Pettingill]. He was known as the 'Wild Man' of Wise River.*

According to an interview with Maggie Hand by the "Standard", Maggie's husband, Horace, met Pettingill along with his young son – mc]. "The man and the boy "holed up" in a cattle dugout near Twin Bridges where the boy contracted diphtheria and died. Pettingill then drifted over to the Big Hole country where he made his home, although he always declared that he had "considerable" mining property in the Twin Bridges District. No one, Mrs. Hand said, knew anything about Pettingill's alleged mine but he did own a few horses that ran wild over the prairies and valleys. He sold an occasional one but even this source of revenue dwindled to such an extent that, when he died, he owed bills to practically every dealer in the entire district over which he roamed. His wants were few, however, and his bills were not large."

[*Pettingill apparently came to the Montana Territory shortly after the Civil War. - mc*]

Maggie states in the newspaper interview, "The story, as I remember it, stated that Pettingill, a Wisconsin farmer, married a girl with one small son, became a soldier in the Civil War. He may have been drafted or he may have enlisted as a result of a family quarrel. At any rate he entered the army and saw much service. When peace was declared he returned home to find another man in his place.

The inevitable clash followed. One of the two proposed that they fight the matter out with pistols, the story stated. This proposal was accepted and the two men, armed with pistols, went down in the adjacent forest to shoot it out. Only one of them returned.

When Mrs. Pettingill saw that it was not her lover but her husband who had survived the duel she seized a pistol and blew her brains out. Pettingill was apparently not disturbed by her action. He gathered his boy in his arms and struck out for the West to keep a couple of jumps ahead of civilization."

Maggie further states, "People passing along the road near Dewey have undoubtedly noted a high marble cliff with a cave-like opening in its upper structure. That cave was one of Pettingill's homes, his chief home, it might be said. He also had a cabin which he probably used in winter--when the snow was too deep to permit him to reach his cave. The cabin, my husband and I saw, was shaped somewhat like an Indian teepee except that the structure was entirely of medium sized logs. Pettingill had cut a sort of circular trench, stood the logs in it and then brought them together at the top like a pyramid. The teepee was large enough to allow him to lay at length with his feet to the fire which had burned in the center of the tent-like structure which was built against a hill.

Pettingill always ate his meat raw. He would shoot a deer or elk, sit down and make a meal of it and then go about his business.

Pettingill's hair hung in ringlets about his shoulders. It had not been cut or combed in ages. He was very timid and not very communicative. It is possible that his days of solitude in the hills had made it difficult for him to carry on a conversation.

He was on his way to his pretended mine when he suffered his last illness," Mrs. Hand said. "He passed a ranch where the owner was slaughtering a beef. Knowing Pettingill's fondness for raw meat he gave him the liver. He gorged himself on it, was taken ill and died.

In another news article the person (unidentified) being interviewed states, "When Pettingill visited Dewey's he always collected every paper, every periodical that he could find. These he read avidly and was consequently well posted on current events."

The dilapidated hat he wore, together with his pose on horseback, made him strikingly resemble an Indian. Graying curls more than a foot long hung in front of either shoulder. Possibly the most unusual thing about him was his low and wonderfully modulated voice."

[*At the time of Pettingill's death he was believed to be about 75 years old. - mc*]

Lost Years

About 1892 or before, a Drummer, being tired of city life, came for a few days up the river to fish and rest. While up the river he chanced to meet Jimmie New and chatted for a while. A paper those days were rare. The Drummer gave him a New York paper. He was glad to get it. On looking thru it, something took his eye - coal and wood ad, proprietors, his very own sons, Edd and Tom. That was like a letter from home and he broke down and cried. Had he been away so long? Sons growed up and in business? At once he wrote a letter and in due time came the reply from a Grandson Edd, also grown up and thru medical college. He wanted to come to his grandfather in the Wild West. Yes, he came in due time. Staid all winter and practiced his medicine in the neighborhood. But it was too healthy a place for a doctor. I think he had a few confinement cases was all. So he went back and a younger brother (a veterinary) came out and staid a while and then a friend came, but the place was too quiet for an active youth and they all left. Jimmie was then alone on the place for a few years, but before (1888) Horace had started his home. Horace then being his closest neighbor and being on a piece of land that was higher than Jimmie's, Horace could look across the field and always kept a look out for him and could see if there was smoke in his cabin. Horace often went down, took his mail and often traded for him in town, for by this time Jimmie was getting feeble and one leg bothered him so he used a cane - even when irrigating he drug his leg and used a cane. - From Maggie's writings

---

Jim Redfern

In the spring of 1896 or '97, one bent of the Dickie bridge went out on the Beaverhead side. For a few days all teams going over were obliged to ford. The river was high and it was a dangerous feat to take the stage over. Isaac Dodgson was hired to put the bent in and was at work at once. He managed to put in a plank walk for the passengers to go over on and Jim Redfern was hired to drive the stage over each trip. Times were good then and many crossed this way till the pier was built and proper connections [*were made*]. In the long, narrow canyon above, ice often broke up in the late spring and ice jams often covered Bob Beatties ranch and often it joined on to the bridge causing danger to travel. After this, for several years, Horace was hired to blow the ice at the bridge so it could move out without piling up on the bridge. Jim Redfern was a very reckless bronco man.

The winter of 1897, Pa [*Horace*] had put in logs from Jerry Creek and had driven them down to the dam - a small dam then with a saw mill attached. In the summer he had taken me to Mrs. Forrest's till the baby came. Horace, with help, had to saw up the lumber and float it down the big flume to the lower saw mill, and there put [*the lumber*] in R. R. cars for Dillon. Trask was interested at that time, the father of Henry. Horace had to have a man to irrigate the hay and keep the home going. There were a few things in the barn yard to feed and see to. He knew Al [*Griswold*] would irrigate, so he got him. I gave orders to tend things in and around the house, especially water the flowers. I had nice flowers and thot lots of them. Ma brot many starts from Kansas. When Horace went home, he saw to it but along to the last it was neglected (the orders never given Al). When I came home they were flat. I was mad and said so aloud, never thinking Al cared, but he did and at once pulled out for John Lawrence's where there were no women or flowers. Horace said, "There, see what you did?" But I was too busy with two babies then to care.

In the summer and fall of 1897 Jimmie [*New*] was not very well. Horace watched and often went there to see him. Could tell he was failing. He had always lived hard. The cabin was one room, a cook stove in one corner, might say this was his kitchen, a rough table of hewed pole and three cornered shelves for cupboard with home made chair, made of slabs with poles for the legs, with slough grass for the mattress and a few dirty blankets. The dog, he kept in the house most of the time and always fed him on the floor. The sour dough keg had never been cleaned or restarted as there was not much space left for the dough (it grew up).

In earlier years he must have worked quite a bit as he had lots of corrals, sheds and a stable all made of logs, and pinned together. The hinges to the gates were made of wood. He must have had help. Someone said a man by the name of Sanburn helped him to build the buildings.

That was no place for a sick man, Horace said one morning to me. So he brot him [*Jimmie*] up and we gave him a good spring bed. Next morning he said he slept so good and that was the first time he ever slept on spring. He had Horace write to his son in Long Island, New York. In due time the son wrote him [*that*] he would come for him at once. In the mean time Jimmie was thinking of his cattle and horses he loved so well. He thot Horace and Al would be the ones to sell to - so when his son came, the sale was made and in a few days they were on their way back. His wife was still living but she would never see him. The boys kept him. We never heard any more.

> **Jimmie New Place Purchased**
> *In 1897 Al and Horace bought the Jimmie New place, which was adjacent to the original ranch at Wise River. - mc*

Dams

The Big Hole Dam was begun July 1897. It was built on the sight of the old saw mill dam. That spring Horace and crew sawed lumber there and ran the lumber down in the old flume to the track on what is now Cullum's place and from there shipped it to Dillon to Henry Frank, then dealing in lumber there at Dillon. Those days news travelled slowly. Horace was about thru sawing when he took me to Forrest's. He finished up in about two weeks and all of the sudden teams, men and every thing was on the ground, breaking sod for buildings to house the men to come later. The bunk houses were about half way from the dam to the pump station. Horace sold the stove and wood pile to them and all the lumber he had left. Horace got his money for his run of lumber, paid his men and store bills, came home and finished irrigating his crop of hay and put it up.

Horace sold hay and meat to the company till we left in 1910. As the fall and winter wore away with a big crew of men, Winters, Parsons and Boomer sunk the foundation to bedrock, built and dug the tunnel on the opposite of the river to let the river thru and filled in the dam - supposed to be filled with dirt and concrete, but when the bosses backs were turned they hoved in ice, manure and any thing to fill in and make the job progress. The ice was handy at the face of the dam and the boss was too full of whisky to see or care. Some folks, Mr. & Mrs. Rodgerson, and Mr. & Mrs. Wilkie had house tents in the first turn above the dam, where a little rill trickled down the gulch on the left hand side of the road. There they staid, after the men were gone, as watchmen. Their son is the boy that gave me my toothpick holder.

When spring came there was the critical test. Those that knew kept mum. Finally the dam gave way, one foot, but held, tho it was unsafe and the over flow tunnel took out the water till it was all out but the natural flow. Every time our men went to Divide I was in fear of some accident. When it first began to give way Horace was loading cars of baled hay at Divide for Butte. The foreman of the dam wanted his

> Maggie and Horace's second child, Byron Hand, born July 2, 1897.

load, which they put in the break, whether it helped I do not know. Tho they took several loads. The next summer and winter they worked, after reorganizing the company and getting more money, to straighten it. They straightened it some and filled in dirt at the face - had two dirt boats pulled by a tug boat. It was that time Horace sold Joe horse to work on the scraper. He knew his freighting days were nearly over so let him go - he remained a faithful horse for the company for years. Joe had made many a hard trip, always up and coming. He knew more than the average horse.

The third spring the dam held and was concidered a wonder, as this was Montana's first dam. Roy Wells worked there for years. Roy owned and operated the first small car to ply the roads and it was a scare crow to most every horse and cows on the road. The roads were so rocky. Roy carried a garden rake and often raked out the rocks on the worst places. It was handy for him to go to Divide and see his girls at Woodward's but a nuisance to the teamsters. When John and I went up in the fall (September 1910) for our last load of household goods, it scared our team on the grade. I got out for fear our nervous mare would jump the grade. He saw our fright and helped us pass his machine.

P. Demmins came, I think, about the time the dam broke. He was a good waterman and had grown up with dams from the Maramashe River in New Brunswick. He had worked on that line so they sent for him. I think he, with the help of other men, have built most every dam in Montana up to 1920 or about. It was he that gave Pa the idea of a dam for our ditch. Dams, small or big, Demmins was the man. In a few years other dams were built in the state. But in 1900 or 1901 a dam was built in Wise River (20 miles) to help regulate this one. The Wise River meadows was an ideal place for the backwater. At the lower end, a mountain closed in clost to the channel on the east side. The west side was sloping back to another big mountain - there a big grade was all that was needed - so one early fall, men, teams, provisions, all kinds of tools, foreman and beasts were sent up and work began. Mr. and Mrs. Wilkie went up after a cookhouse and other buildings were up. She cooked there. Al and our teams worked there. When spring came everything was done, the dam completed, the headgates let down. Gradually the big pond filled, all the willows and lovely meadow grass was to be killed by the ever deepening water. Finally it was full. Full to the over flowing. This was the test, if it was well built and would it hold? Gradually little trickles of water burst thru the slide rock of the embankment and the mountain, as the formation up there was largely composed of slide rock, a very hard ground to hold water.

**Hand Ranch at Wise River
About 1897
Home in foreground, small original cabin, center and barn in background
From the Rock Hand Collection**

Finally it poured thru in torrents - the watchman became alarmed and thot the dam would break, so he mounted Old Bess, a white mare and away he flew down the river spreading the alarm. The dam had broke and for everyone to go to higher grounds. He came in to our place and yelled the dam is broke. Horace said we were safe there and he took his shovel, went out to turn the water and then on over to the river to see how it looked. Then down to the Dodgson/Brubaker mill and tell Brubaker and warn him. He found Al at work at the mill. Then went down to Al's place to warn Wolf. All the time I could imagine him drowned. I took the two boys and climbed up the steep hill clost to our house to keep from being drowned and see if I could see him. After a long, dreary wait here he come - laughing at me. Told me he was at the Wise River Bridge when the quick raise came. Just like him. He had to be in the most dangerous place if it had come. Then he never got thru guying me about going up the hill. Al came home soon from freighting and he and the teams were sent up to the dam to mend the break and make stronger embankments.

From our place the man that spread the alarm rode Bess on to the lower dam, never giving a thot to Bess. She was fed and watered too soon after that awful fast ride and she was stiff ever afterwards. Later Pa bought her for our children to ride and drive, as she was perfectly gentle. One spring, lambs would play on her when she was laying down.

First School at Wise River

We were not concidered in that district and not having children of school age did not help. But the Pattons, Roth, George and Tice Dodgson and Clines with children old enuf to go, something must be done and done at once, in order to have a spring term. [*A school was held for a four-month term in 1897 - info taken from "**The History of Beaverhead County**." - mc*] So each family looked over their woodpile logs and took out such that was fit and the contribution from all built the first log school house that stood at the foot of the Patton Lane. Brubaker was greatly interested and helped, with the other men, build it. He always was foremost when it came to children, school, Christmas, all holidays. That served the purpose a few years and later built a better and larger log cabin not far from the other one.

When John was old enuf, we found out we were in that district. The summer before John was six he went a few days on the stage. That was not good. He and Byron went on an old horse a while the next term and he walked alone. We were too busy to take them and a lot they did not go. From here Nettie can tell better than I how the three went. I hate to think it all over. What fools we were for ever sending them at all in that awful old times.

When we found out we were in Meadow Creek District, it was some time afterward that Horace had any thing to say about the school. In time he was trustee, tho did not want to have a say, as the others had older children and left it to them. One spring they hired a teacher from the southern part of the county - a Mrs. Marcasau, an older lady and they thot this time we have the woman. As time went on, there were complaints she and Mrs. Patton were drinking Papa's [*Mr. Patton*] whiskey after school on her way to her boarding house. Then occasionally the stage driver (Winnie Todd) was bringing her a bottle now and then and finally she drank in school. The trustees became alarmed and called a meeting. They had evidence enuf so what should they do? The trustees all wanted her fired and that they had a right to, but who would?

Winter of 1898

When Horace went to the hills, he batched and cut the stulls. He had to leave some fellow to take care of the stock and saw and split wood. An old man, Mr. Orsburn was hired. He did not do much, nor was expected to. Well, this time I was told to have Orsburn hitch up the team, which consisted of a big rangy saddle horse, and another smaller horse, my saddle horse, Baldy. (By this time, with two small children, I could not ride anymore.) We hitched up the two horses to the sled, with a wagon box on for a bed and went to the Flat for some supplies and tools.

I wrapped up the children and tucked them in the hay, took the ribbons and away we went (lots of snow). Everything went fine. At the big rock, the clip on the end of the singletree came off. I could not get out to drive it back on and leave the children in, nor take them out. The grade was none to wide, river below a sheer wall and the clift of rocks on the other side. If I went on, the clip on the end of the lug might hit either horse and I knew they would run, and I could not hold them. I happened to be in the cove of the rock, a little wider place and drew the team in and in the distance, coming around the grade, I heard the bells of a big team.

**Byron and John Hand
At Wise River Ranch
About 1898
From the Rock Hand Collection**

When they came up, a late rancher, returning from Butte with his load of supplies for the winter, Elliott. He saw me and stopped, so I told him my troubles. He tore off a piece of gunnysack, put it over the end of the singletree, took a rock and drove the clip on - many thanks and I will always remember that man. I made the trip down and back safely enuf with the ponies chewing the bit and wanting to go.

Horace took a man or two, horses and feed oats and hay - cut stulls on Meadow Creek above the ranches. There was an old cabin or two there and they batched there and cut the stulls. When sufficient snow came they hauled them by sled to the river in Patton's field, having got permission from Tice and George to go directly down thru their meadow on the river. They only did a very little of the cooking. I cooked bread, meat, fruit, spuds and rutabagas and when they came in they warmed up their meals and with the addition of coffee, a meal was soon gotten. One day Horace said I could bring up the food and see where they were at work. It was a nice day so hitched two small wiry horses, one was a saddle horse, to a sleigh with a wagon box on it. Put in the food, plenty of old comforters and wrapped John and Byron (Byron was a baby) in, and dressed warm myself and away we went. Went up over the Robbin's bench as we called the country then. The road left the Wise River bottom just behind Jones' house and climbed up on a long bench. That led to the timber and found the cabin. There being no other road in snow open, had to find it. Got there as the men just came in. The cabin was cold and had a dirt floor with pole bunks for beds. I thot "My, such a place" and pitied anyone having to live in such a place (no windows). Well, it was no place for a baby (cold, fire just started in the old stove) so I decided I'd better go back. Horace said "You had better go down and see Maude, the road is open." So I did, glad to get away from that cold, dismal place and being in the thick timber made it more cold and lonely.

I got there all right and went to tie my broncs to a fence. Just then they saw a blanket on the line flying in the wind. I was on the ground, had tied the lines to the dash board and had hold of the halter of the left hand horse. I talked and coaxed them and finally the blanket eased flapping and I calmed them down and tied them. The two boys lay in the wagon bed not knowing how they had escaped being in an awful run away.

All the time I was hoping Tice or someone would see my predicament and help me. They had just moved in their new house and she was working inside. Maude never busied herself any with the big out doors, so no one saw me in that trouble.

When they hauled the stulls to the river, the snow was poor - getting late and they had an awful time, but they always finished that they begun.

George Dodgson, the oldest son and Tice lived on the old home place, cut the hay and ran cattle on the nearby hills. Tice sold his place to Obe Lewis and moved to the mill for a while. It was there Tice and Maude's children used to come over to see ours. I often sewed for Maude. One day Maude sent Sherman over with some goods for Sherman a shirt. I was gone to Lawrences. Horace said, "Give me the cloth and I'll cut it for you. I make all the clothes anyway."

"No," said Sherman. "I won't, you will spoil it," and away he went, saying "you darn fool, I won't let you cut it."

Tice and Maude Dodgson bot the Tong ranch from Mrs. Tong and moved there. This was a stopping house for the freighters and a large hay and cattle ranch.

Maggie and Horace's third child, Nettie Mae Hand, born November 19, 1899.

Cattle

One fall after the hay was bailed and shipped Al, Fred Wilson and Horace, not having anything to do that winter, decided to get saw logs out of Triangle Gulch and saw the lumber for home use and sale. Horace wanted to build on to our house, for a growing family needed more room. Al wanted lumber for a big irrigating flume and also for an addition to his house. Then there was always ready sale for lumber to other ranchers. The three worked away. Cut, sawed and hauled logs for a month or two. In the meantime also feeding the stock cattle that we had. Finally there was a sea of logs across the road in a little flat. Shortly before they got thru, Fred, in binding the logs on the sleigh, threw a binding chain which had a hook on the end over to Al to catch and bind the logs. But instead of catching it, the hook hit Al an awful whack on the thumb. He did everything to relieve the pain, but as day by day went on it got worse. Could not get a wink of sleep and finally Horace took him to the doctor at Melrose, 30 miles away, to have it lanced. He poulticed it and went to the doctor again. Finally, after nursing the thumb two weeks, it began to get better.

Pat McKinney and wife came to see us. They had been out to Butte and were on their way back to their home at Salmon, Idaho. When the Quartz Hill went down, they heard of the Salmon country, so went and found a place they could call home and develop a good cattle country. They had been there then several years. Had two hundred head of cattle and they wanted to sell them. Thot Horace and Al might buy them. We thot cattle was going to drop in a few years. McKinney was shrewd, he thot they would raise. Finally Horace and Al decided they would take the cattle as there was plenty of range and they were cutting more hay each year and we had just bot the Jimmie New place and had it paid for. Al's thumb was getting better. He thot he would go along with Horace and could do something to help bring the cattle home. So I wrapped and rewrapped his thumb and whole hand and finally tied a small breakfast shawl over the whole hand. They went over with the McKinneys. Tho took their own team, sled and saddle horses, leaving Fred Wilson to do the chores. To the Salmon River ranch must have been 150 or more miles. Thru deep snow, road was good to Wisdom. After that the road to the top of the range was not so good. They, being lightly loaded, made the trip in about four days. After a few days of visiting at McKinney's, the deal was closed and they started back. Al drove the team, Horace and a man they got at the ranch drove the cattle. They were just stock cattle. To bring them thru a heavy snow country was a desperate undertaking at that time of year. But they made it up the awful hill to the top of the range, as yet the snow was not so deep. Then, after they came off the hill, the snow was deep and the travelling became more laborious. First night over they stopped at Hollinsworth on Swamp Creek. Next night they reached McKeys. There the cattle showed signs of fatigue and in the morning they were obliged to leave two or three. They would give them good care and later put them in a bunch coming down. Yes, that was fine. Then, each day and night as they came on down, they had to leave a few at various ranches they passed. Finally they got home with 185 head. The balance they would get later. A few of those left died, but they never got many from those left at places. Whether they sent them, as agreed or not, they never knew. We were the losers. Those that we got home were jaded by the long drive thru the snow. They had to feed them well so they would be strong when they turned them out in the spring.

Byron, Nettie and John Hand
Taken 1900
From the Thelma (Hand) Kalsta Collection

When turning out time came the cattle were in good shape. That spring was very rainy and when turned out they had to be herded as several bloated and died. But all they could find in time and bleed would get well. The loco weed, when pulled up and eaten, is very poisonous to cattle in the spring. So we lost several that way.

Jimmie Dodd wanted the fat cows. Told the boys to bring them in and put them in the meadow. They waited and waited, he never came. Just an old gag of his but they were not wise to cattle buyers then as they had always teamed. In the fall, when they rounded up, they still had the McKinney bunch of cattle and our own. Price of cattle did not look good so Horace decided they had better sell. He found a man over the Cascade that wanted 200 stock cattle so he wrote many letters and finally made the deal at $31.50 per head, with calves throwed in. Al was away on contract getting out poles in the Basin. Horace, with help, drove the cattle to Feely stock yard to load on a certain day.

> **Partnership Dissolved**
>
> *In 1903 Seth "Big Al" and Horace dissolved their partnership. Al took the Jimmie New place and Horace stayed on the original ranch. This was recorded April 17, 1903, Clerk and Recorders Office, Beaverhead County Court House, Book 52, pages 354 and 364 - mc*

About two weeks before he sold and drove these cattle away, our cattle dog (big black shepherd) bit Johnnie in the back as John ran to catch a cat. The cat got under the barn and John reached under after the cat and at the same time the dog wanted in the hole for the cat. The dog, in his fury, bit John in the back. Johnnie now came crying to the house and the dog followed. Horace scolded the dog and reached down to cuff the dog's ears. When all at once the dog lunged at Horace and it was with all his might that he kept the dog off. Then Horace grabbed a chair and drove the dog off. All the while I was frozen with fright, having started to push the three children in the cabin. Horace ran for a gun nearby but now the dog was going away rapidly. He shot, only crippled him. Horace wanted to follow the dog to John Lawrence's and kill him but we all begged to let him go. He had always been so faithful and everyone wanted him. So the dog got better and when Horace sold the cattle the man wanted the dog. Said I'll keep him if he eats a man for breakfast every day. So Horace took him and drove the 200 head to Feely and loaded the cattle mostly with the dogs help. One cow broke the fence and he brot her back and put her in the car. Horace liked the dog but he did not want him around the children. So at Cascade, when Horace delivered the cattle, he gave the dog to the man. With the cattle delivered he could breath a sigh of relief and he went to Dillon, paid off his note for the cattle he bot from McKinney even tho it took a few of our very own cattle to pay the debt. He and Al were wiser, nothing gained but experience. It was yet open weather and we had not begun to feed the cattle hay as the after grass was good and no snow yet to cover it up.

We had had a good crop of timothy and alsyke [*alsike-a type of clover*] that summer on the home place and there was good demand for that kind of hay in Butte (1903). Every vehicle was horse drawn then. The Jimmie New place cut 50 to 70 tons wild hay, which was about enuf to winter the stock, providing we sold off 150 head more of cattle. If we kept the cattle they would eat most of the good hay and only have the cattle in the spring. Then too, cattle had fallen in price decidedly since he shipped the 200 to Cascade. They thot they had better sell. So, Johnnie Peterson was buying and selling cattle in Butte. He drove a bunch past most every week to Butte so Horace told me to write to Johnnie and tell him we had cattle to sell and if he was interested to stop in some time. So he did. Horace was away hauling poles so I told Johnnie where the cattle were. He looked the bunch over, said cattle was down and all he could give was $14.00 per head [*for a*] cow and calf, and a few two year old steers in the bunch. If Mr. Hand wanted to sell at that he would take a few each time he came down and pay for them after he sold them. Horace and Al decided to let them go and then bail the hay and find a ready market for it in Butte. Then later in the winter the hay price was good. They had their own bailer, horses, teams and rigging and they could put it on the market cheaper than other farmers could. In the spring they had a bank account instead of having a cheap bunch of cattle. Thereafter hay prices declined.

Horace gradually raised more cattle and often bot a bunch to feed thru the winter and sell in the spring, as fat cattle was a ready sale. Did not have to drive them off of the place, as there were buyers on the road often looking for such a buy. One winter after Horace and Al divided the ranch, he went to Butte horseback, thinking he might pick up a bunch of calves to fatten. When he got there, a man told him he could buy calves, all he wanted, at Whitehall from a Mr. Tube. So he sent word, by a man that was coming out our way, that he had gone to Whitehall and to not look for him. So in a week here he came driving a bunch of white face calves. These he vaccinated for blackleg and put on feed at once and found a ready market for them in the spring. He had a feed lot and sheds over at the warm spring and they did fine. By this time John was a big help to his father, helping feed and do chores.

A Trip to Meadow Creek Timberline
Late Winter, Early Spring 1904

Up on Meadow Creek was a good pole country and easily gotten to with a sleigh. So, early in the fall before snow came Horace hired two men, Bill McClellan and another man to go up there and stay till they got out the amount of poles he needed for a fence, posts, jack legs and poles. They had been up there for quite a while, but needed supplies and came down over the weekend. Monday they were to go back. Horace was hunting cattle and wanted to get them all in before snow came and snowed them in as it often did. So he said to me, you take the team and sleigh and take them [*the men*] up over the bench and on up to the edge of the timber. Then they can walk the balance of the way. We then had three children. I did not want to leave them all alone in the cabin, so wrapped them up warm, put hay in the wagon box, filled with hay and plenty of quilts and took them along. The men drove going up, but coming back I sat in the seat and drove. About the time we got at the place the men were to get out I could see blue haze in the air and as we started home it turned colder and colder. By the time we got home, I was chilled thru and thru and felt the effect of that cold trip for days after. That was the beginning of a very cold spell and was thankful I had no farther to go. I had a new neighbor at Wise River crossing but was too timid to ask her to keep the children for me. Tho, they did not suffer the cold down in the wagon as I did up on the seat driving.

Coyotes

In early days, coyotes were a menace to ranchers. They often came quite near at nights, their howls made the nights seem lonely. Dogs stood no show with them as their savagery always drove the dog into the shelter of the barn.

One fall they were so thick, [*they*] came to the butcher pen each night. I said to Horace, "Why don't you set some traps there and catch them." I did not realize it took a real trapper to catch them.

"O," he says, "I could not get them."

"Well," says I, "I will."

After supper the children and I took the traps out and set them where they had butchered. There were some chains clost, [*that*] they had left at a derrick, so we picked up a nail and a file to toggle the trap to the chain. Coyotes are very wily creatures. They can scent a person and often does not come the first night to eat, tho the neighbor's dogs are not so careful. Tho they did come and fought with the dogs and howled, made the night hideous. We forgot to tend our traps the next day.

Tice and Maude lived at the mill on Wise River that summer and fall. Tice came down that afternoon, stopped in to see us. Got out of the buggy and said, "come here Maggie, I have something for you." He pulled out the trap and said, "Here it is Maggie."

"Well, how did you know I was trapping."

"Well, Boon came home in the night dragging this trap. We knew you had butchered too."

That was the first and the last of my trapping.

E. G. Bryant Funeral - Dewey, Montana - 1904
Written on back of original photo,
"The man who is in the middle of the street is Johnnie Evans from Quarts Hill."
From Hazel Maddon Collection, courtesy of Thelma (Hand) Kalsta

E. G. Bryant

Mr. Bryant being poorly, Maude helped care for her father at the Flat. In the meantime, Tice helped Horace a few days to put the fence on our desert land we had taken up at the mouth of Triangle Gulch. Tice had bot a ranch, the old Bow place at Melrose, and occasionally took care of Bryant. Horace, too, took his turns, as Tice had most of his household things moved down to his new home at Melrose. Bryant passed [*d. 5-28-*04] and was buried June 1st.

Maggie and Horace's fourth child, Roscoe "Rock" Konklin Hand, born June 8, 1904.

Jimmie New Creek

After the hay crop was bailed, hauled and shipped to Butte and sold, the cattle were gotten all in from the range those years. Those that did not come in were often left until hunting them was no pleasant chore. Often snow fell so deep that when found was a task to break the snow trails in order to drive the cattle single file out. Then, with the river frozen over with glare ice, to cross them was equally as hard.

Wise River Ranch
The following is taken from a note that was attached to the original photo: Al's place is down on the river. The goats are grazing in the pasture. Horace is mowing down in the field with a pair of white horses. You can see where it is mowed for it does not show all. The day was very smokey. The post at the road is mail post. Lumber lays around in the foreground.
From the Rock Hand Collection.

This winter the river and creek was froze over good by the time the other ranch jobs were done, then the snow and ice was just right to get out poles for fencing. The road running thru the ranch made two extra fences this time, the road fence from John Lawrence's west fence to our house, on thru right hand side coming up was to be fenced. When hunting cattle, Horace had often seen a nice lot of poles on the west fork of Jimmie New Creek. Horace decided that was the place to get them. After repairing the sleigh or front bob, fitting the horse shoes with heavy calks and shoeing the horse - sharpening a good ax - he prepared for a good early start next morning. We always arose early - he would build the fire in the cook stove, then got water, fed and harness his horses. By that time I would have his breakfast of mush and milk, beef steak, pancakes and coffee ready. He would eat while I put up him a lunch, for as usual when he cut his load of poles (80 to 100) it would be noon, so he ate his lunch feeling better not having to hurry. This winter the creek froze over and bulged in ice terraces, making the coming down dangerous.

He fastened the tops of the poles on the bobsled and drug the hind ends, making a good brake. Tho often in steep places, the load ran the horses and it was only a skillful driver could keep the load, team and all from upsetting. Each day I waited with anxious glances thru the field for his return at last. Then when I heard the sleigh bells I'd return to my work. The poles and posts were all down, the poles strung and the posts in the yard. The posts were there, as they had to be bored and jacklegs shaped to fit in the holes. After that was done they were taken and placed about 16 feet apart preparatory to setting up the fence. For this he had to have help so we wrote to John Sinnbaugh, Melrose. He had just returned from Alaska, yes, he would come. Johnnie was a good worker and understood building fence, so when he came the fence was "just so" on its feet. The rider poles were double lengths and took two good men to put them on as for the size in proportion of the fence. I invite my reader to look it over and see if the workmanship is not a monument to a pioneer of the Big Hole.

When it Rained -1905

As a rule, each spring and summer, the Big Hole Country has a general amount of rain and the hills are well clad in grass thru the spring months at least. Tho often in August, when we were putting up hay, rain would fall so it would stop their operations for a few days. Once I remember snow falling so deep and lodged the oats, so in order to cut it for hay they had to cut it one way.

In earlier day, a man (restaurant man Darcie)

Soft Cookies

1 cup sugar
1 egg beaten light
1/2 cup butter or lard
1/2 cup sour milk
1 tsp. soda, nutmeg & vanilla
Flour to make dough soft

I found this in the Comfort Magazine in 1896 or about. All who have used it since have liked it - Grandma Hand [*Maggie*]

In a letter to Janice Hand in 1987, Susan states, "Flour to make soft dough (2 1/2 cups, about right.) No temperature or time was given but we find 350 degrees for about 15 min. O.K. These were the standard on-hand cookies in our household. Mother was a great cook but a free hand cook. She left us only 3 recipes. She could make a delicious pie out of most any fruit, fresh or dried. Her mince meat most special." Further she writes, "Maggie Hand made acres of these, cut out with the top of a big baking powder can."
From the Susan Hand Collection

---

used to bet money that it would rain every day in June. Often he won till after a time his bet failed owing to dryer Junes. But this June of 1905 was different. It begin first of June, rained continuously every day and every day roads became almost impassable. June was the month the ranchers from the Basin went in to Butte and Dillon for supplies and they must get them in before haying time in later July and August. That included everything needed for mowers, rakes, and harnesses. That would give them time to make the necessary repairs and be all ready when the time for haying came.

As usual they made the venture to either Butte or Dillon. Horace was road supervisor then. There were other freighters on the road – Lossel's trains, and others. The rocks and slides falling from the steep grades often filled the road. The longer the rain poured, the softer the cuts became, till some one had to accompany the trains down each morning and coming back the same - everybody got off their wagons and worked. This was a common chore each day - to help the teams over the grade.

Work on the ranches was at a stand still. If one did the regular chores that was enuf.

While all this was happening on the outside, the dirt roofs on all the old log cabins began to leak like sieves. One neighbor with a small creeping child was at her wits end to know how to keep dry in their cabin. She put the child in the bed and put an umbrella over it. They put a heavy tent tarp over the roof, put the bed and all under it and here they kept the child for days. But what of the other part of the house? Just about like outdoors! Then another neighbor with young ladies had bot a new piano. The rain poured on it. And still another neighbor could not let his neighbor out do them, and they got a piano - it was soaked too.

We were not fortunate, could not own a piano, but we did have a good shingle roof and thru it all we were dry, never giving a thot of our neighbors. But when Horace learned of their pianos being wet, didn't he laugh, for he had no sympathy for anyone what bot a piano in those hard times.

The effect of those June rains were marvelous. Flowers jumped up as by magic. Hills and valleys were purple, white, pink, blue, yellow, red and magenta. In fact all the mavelus hues that nature could concoct sprang up and showed their colors. And grass covered the hills and dales, one foot to 18 inches high. At a distance in the valley, it looked very much like a wheat field.

When Bill Did Not Take The Saddle Mare

The effect of drinking followed Bill [*McClellan*] all thru life and he became a periodical drunkard. Being a cousin of Horace's, after his wife left him, he made his home with Horace or as soon as Horace had established his home at Wise River. In time, after several of his drunken episodes, I got tired of him taking a saddle horse. When ever he wanted to go to town, he went to the stable and took a horse with good intensions on coming back each time, tho invariably leaving the horse tied to the hitching post in front of a saloon. Then it stood till some kindly soul turned the poor horse loose to let it come tearing home to be freed of the bridle and saddle and to get its feed.

After a year or so of these episodes, I finally told Horace that Bill should not take that horse again and if he could not stop it I would. He always said Bill was such a good hearted fellow and could not help it. I said if I can, I am not going to let him have the horse. Then Horace laughed at me. This made me mad. He did this just to see what I'd do?

In a month or two the time rolled around. Bill went on another drunk and in a few days came back. We thot he had come home to sober up but not so. He wanted more liquor and after storming around, got none. He made for the barn. "There," I said to Horace, "he is going to take your saddle mare. Why don't you stop him?"

He answered, "You said you would stop him, now why don't you?"

Bill was just going in [*to the barn*]. I grabbed an old broom handle nearby and went to the barn, just then he was saddling the mare. I said, "Now Bill, you are not going to take that mare."

"Yes, I am" was his reply.

"No, you are not," says I, and he kept on preparing to take her.

"I never got in to such a bunch of thieves as you are, you stole my money and I am going to leave" says Bill.

"I never," says I, "and you are not going to take that mare."

He kept right on in his drunken way. I see he was going by [*his*] declarations. He was cinching the girth. He soon would be thru and to my chagrin he was surely going to take her. Horace and children were standing outside the house waiting to see how this jangle was to come out. To be called a thief was an awful disgrace by one we had taken into our home as one of the family. Generally he was very concidterate and kind. No other time would he [*have*] ever called us names like that before. It was quite evident to me he would take the mare. Horace, outside, was wondering which would win out in this jangle. Just as Bill started to mount the mare I jabbed him in the ribs, several times in a quick succession. This was such a blow to his pride he dropped the rope, made down to the road fast as he could go, calling me all the names he could think of. By this time, with one man licked, I turned on Horace and told him what I thot of him for not helping me. He says, "Woman, what more do you want, you have licked one man?" Horace never got thru telling this story when he wanted to dampen my courage.

Wolf and Hank Sperrier

Hank Sperrier camped up the river some time in the first of the 1890's. We heard he left his wife and children in Dillon and worked at various jobs on the ranches and the roads in the summers and holed up like many an old fellow in the winter in some cabin. He was a big, husky fellow capable of any kind of hard work and a very good worker. Tho as time went on was found out he was very temperamental and often indulged in fits of temper, mostly when by himself.

John Lawrence, Al and Horace employed him when an extra man was needed. Then one spring the neighbors hired him in putting in the community telephone line. With men on the job he generally was brave and liked to do daring jobs. When they got to the river, he gave up the pole climbing job to ride our Maude mare with a coil of wire acrosted the river. The river being high, this a rather dangerous attempt.

Then he [*Hank*] had a cabin at the lower Joe Young cabin, clost to where the old bridge crossed the river. Hank wanted a telephone box put in his cabin, thot it would be so handy when alone. Then, when there was a prospect of a job, he could locate it without tramping all over the country. This phone worked fine for a while. We all had separate rings and there was no way to shut off the other fellow's rings. He objected to that extra amount of ringings. After a time it became unbearable for Hank and in a mad fit he tore it off the wall. Later a neighbor bot the box off Hank as he wanted on the line.

Horace hired Hank the spring he and Al sawed the lumber. The job was nearly finished when Fred Woods and the other kid stole some horses in the valley and was leaving the country. Fred and his gang had previously terrorized the country. Once [*they*] killed a calf of John Lawrence's on the hills, took off a few steaks on the spot and had fresh steaks cooked over a camp fire before leaving the country. The citizens thot these escapades of Fred and his gang should be stopped, so Sperrier was deputized as sheriff in the valley. He was big and husky. They all thot [*Hank was*] just the man to stop the marauding young chaps, just starting out in lawless career, using the old sturdy rancher to practice on. When a new case of stealing happened, Sperrier said, "I'd go and get them but haven't a horse." Horace spoke up, "Take my Maude mare, she will outrun anything they have." Horace saddled the mare and made ready. Hank went to the cabin, got his gun and mounted. He followed thru at top speed for a few miles, sure he would catch them, but the yellow streak began to get the best of him and he held Maude in. Then when in sight of them he turned around and came home, making some flimsy excuse. Horace was furious at him for not catching them, as well he could. Horace paid him off and let him go.

Al always liked such old Bull shitters, so Hank made his home at Al's that spring with a prospect for a good job later on.

Hank bot some lumber, packing it down to his cabin on his back. He was going to make a nice large cupboard to put his lovely set of dishes in which he had got in some drawing, buying goods. The lucky man got the set. That spring Al built a long flume thru a swamp on to a dry patch of land. He and another old fellow Al had picked up worked on a flume. While sharpening tools in the shop, Hank took a mad fit, took up a sledge hammer, hit hisself in the forehead such a blow he fell over unconscious. Al and Wolf picked him up and put him to bed. Took care of him till he recovered and went to work. Then later, he took another mad spell, took the dishes and cupboard out on the bank of the river and broke them all and threw them in the river. At another time, while mowing hay at John Lawrence's, he took a mad spell, said people were fools to use new inventions like mowing machines and the like, and would be better to use a scythe, etc.

Wolf was not so temperamental, tho he could not always get along with Hank. If Wolf and Al would pet Hank in his mad fits, they could get along with him. But Wolf would not always give him his way so there came a day when they quarrelled. Hank would not fight, was much like a cur dog. So they growled around for a time, then Al got them to agree to be friends - "Bury the Hatchet". Nettie was a little kid those days, spooking around listening to men talk. She heard Al say, "Wolf and Hank had buried the hatchet." She got it in her little head they had buried the hatchet at a gate on the line fence between our place and Al's clost to the Jimmie New warm slough. So she was hunting one day for it. When asked what she was hunting, she said I am looking for the hatchet Wolf and Hank buried here.

After a few years no one could get along with Hank. His temper spree worsened on him. He went up Wise River where he could be alone and there, in some of his mad fits, was seriously hurt and died.

Wolf staid on with Al and took care of the place and stock when Al was away on other jobs. He had drifted into the Big Hole about the same time Hank did, was temperamental, tho not so desperate. Tho was hard to get along with people. So long as he was left alone, he got on very good alone.

John's Trapping Coyotes

When John was quite a lad, he often trapped. Horace sometimes would help him and sometimes caught one. Tho often they got away. Once one staid in the trap a few days, finally chewed his leg off and got away. Then they caught a three legged one once after that.

They finally got a good one, a very cold time, and John was so proud of the hide, so they tacked it up on the inside of a barn door. He would get a bounty, $5.00, and then sell the hide for at least $2.50. Then he would have some money for something he had wanted.

When a real bitter cold spell came on, coyotes are generally easier to catch. Seems as everyone had caught a few that winter. No peddler had come thru yet, buying them. All at once, everyone all up and down the country had lost all their pelts. A mystery. No one dared say, tho all understood who was the guilty thief. Sleigh bells, robes, whips, harness, chains and the like all went. Finally Horace saw some of his things, went to the guilty party and took his things, tho they never found the coyote hides.

Millie & Ben Mallon

After the wedding in 1908, Millie and Ben took up housekeeping at Divide. He working in the Mercantile store there, freighting then to the Basin was yet quite heavy. Ben had served his time stage driving and driving a six horse freight team for the company. He was tried and true. They often drove back to see her father's folk, so one Sunday there was time to make this trip. Ben hitched up a supposedly gentle horse, with another, to a spring wagon he had got from a man a few days before. Millie went with him. They had gone several miles up the canyon when all of the sudden the horse began to take fright and became unmanageable, pushing the other horse over the grade. Ben could see they all would go over and took the situation in hand in time. He pushed Millie out on solid ground and jumped just in time to see the two horses and spring wagon go over and in a few minutes both horses were drowned.

Saving the Tadpoles

Maggie and Horace's fifth child, Thelma Victoria Hand, born January 12, 1909

Horace told John, then a mere lad, to hitch the Robin's grey horse to Bill's cart and take some piece of machinery back to Cline. He started out in the early forenoon, taking Nettie with him, and could have been back in an hour, anyway. Horace did not state definitely just when he should be back. When he did not get back we thot it queer, tho we felt no alarm. As the afternoon advanced I began to worry, but could not go for him and the men were all out in the field.

It was August. Cline had turned the irrigating water off - preparatory to begin haying. This left little pools here and there in the lane to the house. Sis [*Nettie*] proposed to John that they take the tadpoles out of these pools and across the meadow to the river, a distance of nearly a mile. They got old pans and buckets to collect them in and worked steadily all day - except for a few minutes off for dinner.

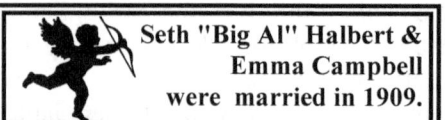

When he came home late in the afternoon, he was all tired out from the heavy days work under Sis's supervision. She was afraid the pools would dry up and the tadpoles would die.

The Swimming Hole

From an interview with Rock Hand in 1992 at his home in Helena, Montana. "He [*Uncle Al*] married a widow woman with two kids. This was great for me 'cause they were right there. I can remember we wanted to go swimming but couldn't find water. We had a bunch of pigs running loose there and the pigs had a wallow that the darn pigs laid in on hot days. We ran the pigs out and went swimming. My mother whipped the devil out of me. We had taken our clothes off. We'd got them dirty then and we were going to wash them in the pig wallow and hung them on the sage brush to dry. Then Al's wife come up. Mom whipped the devil out of me and sent me home, but the other kids, they got off free."

The Chicken Thief

Late one evening, after the chickens had gone to bed, Roscoe went out to shut up the chicken house door. He heard something thumping around inside. Previously we had lost chickens and of course at the first thot was it must be someone inside.

He ran back to the house, told his father someone was in the chicken house. Where upon Horace grabbed the gun and ran out to the chicken house. "Ha, you damed scoundrel, come out of there. Ha there, I finally caught you, come out." All the time a scuffling kept on behind the half open door. By this time he wondered what it might be, pushed the door farther open and the old sow ran out with a dead hen in her mouth. That was a joke Pa and Roscoe often told on their selves.

Dirty Jack

Going up Camp Creek early one morning, Roscoe, with his father, thot they would stop and see Dirty Jack. Perhaps he could tell them about the bunch of cattle they were looking for. Then, if he could not, they could always get a good laugh out of their casual visits. Jack had a small place up the creek he called home. A cabin, a few head of cattle and horses, a few acres of hay land and a prospect in the hills clost by where he could spend his lonely hours mining, mostly boulders. In his mind it was very rich. Once he took a load to a smelter and had to borrow money to have it smelted. That did not daunt his faith, he mined away just the same. Jack built up a good log face with a strong door on it and kept it locked for fear someone prowling about might get in and steal his gold.

Reigning up they hollowed, "Hello?" Finally he came out. "How's things going Jack, these days?"

"Bad, bad, enuf," says Jack. "One of my best cows bloated, bloated and died. Then I cut off the tip of her tail to bleed her and it didn't help."

Horace looked real sympathetic. "Too bad, Jack, too bad." But Roscoe could not contain his self and ha ha'd right out. This seemed to be Roscoe's stock story.

In the spring, when the earth was soaked deep with rain, cattle grazing often pulled up the loco plant, eating the top and root which contained a poison causing death, tho if found and bled the critter often recovered. Jack just had not understood when to bleed them.

Divide to Wisdom Stage Line, Early 1900s

by Roscoe K. Hand

*The following are excepts from this article. Taken from **The History of Beaverhead County, Montana, Volume I**, Copyright 1990 by the Beaverhead County History Book Association, and also given to me by Rock Hand.*

By the time I was five years old I can remember that my job was to meet the stage as it went up or down the road that passed our ranch and pick up the mail sack for the ranch. The drivers were all friendly, liked kids, and passed along any late-breaking news.

As a rule the stage drivers were young men. I have heard it said that drivers as young as 16 would take the stage out. No doubt this was true because the one driver that I particularly liked was very young. I have forgotten his name, but when I talked to Dave Hirschy about him, Dave verified what I have to say about this man. He may have been 20 years old but I doubt it. Anyhow, one evening after he made his run he was murdered at a bar in Wisdom by a young Mexican. Dave said the stage driver was quite a fellow to kid around with people and something he said to the young Mexican fellow was taken in the wrong way and the Mexican pulled his gun and shot him.

Although I was only five years old, this fellow was my friend and my parents allowed me to go to his funeral. I can remember that experience as plain as if it was yesterday. The funeral, held at what is now known as the Vern Stanchfield place just out of Wise River, was rather late in the afternoon because they had to bring the body from Wisdom that day. There was no mortician. The body had been prepared by his friends and it was long after noon when the spring wagon showed up from Wisdom with his body. They drove beside an outside porch and proceeded to remove the body from the big box filled with ice and place it in a homemade coffin that had been built, lined and prepared by some carpenters in the neighborhood.

It was a bad time for me and I insisted on seeing the body. Some men tried to keep me from seeing him but my father said to let me have a look, which satisfied me. It was the first dead man I had ever seen. After the funeral, when the body was taken to the graveyard, I remember a grown lady crying and I couldn't understand it because I thought that old people didn't cry. My mother explained to me that this lady was the boy's mother and it was all right for her to cry.

In later years I talked to Otis Mudd and my friend, Dave Hirschy, about what happened to the fellow who killed my friend. They both told the same story about the posse that followed the murderer and how they corralled him in a patch of buck brush as he fled, and before they could capture him he committed suicide. That may have been true, but many people doubted it.

Doctors of Early Day

There were no doctors in the Big Hole or Basin. The country was too thinly settled to keep one. Then there was no one that needed a doctor. Each one took it on his self to doctor each other when needed. They did not think of running to a doctor for aches and ails.

In the care of broken bones, most anyone could set a bone, and a childbirth, any older woman could, and did, take care of those cases. There was no death in that case, no infection or blood poisoning. Glendale afforded two or three doctors when it was at its height.

Sagebush tea was a panacea for all fevers, rocky mountain (typhoid), rheumatism, stomach troubles of all kinds, in fact all aches and ails to which human beings fell heir too, even falling hair.

In those days, all sicknesses were doctored in a very crude way. The method was crude indeed, as they thot that pneumonia had to be doctored by moist heat applied to the chest, [and a] mustard plaster to their wrists and soles of the feet. To apply moist heat, they boiled corn on the cob, then wrapped the corn in a cloth and applied this to the chest, letting it stay there, tho often changing to keep up the heat. Quinine was the panacea for all aches and ails and diseases. Each household kept large bottles full of it on hand. We all can remember how bitter it was and how we hated to take it. Mother would put a little white of an egg in a spoon, then the quinine, and more white to cover it up. Then if taken and let slip down the throat, one would not get the taste. Tho often one would make a miss swallow, then it would take apple sauce and bread and a lot of things to cover up that awful bitter taste.

Roads or Trails Up The Big Hole

This subject I hardly feel I know.

In 1892 the road from Divide to the dam at the mouth of the canyon was dirt road - some places bad. From the pump station to the dam, the road had been graded out above the Wanderlie and Woodward ditch, which the boys, Al and Horace, had made before I came. The river bridge then crossed above where it does now and there was a small saw mill dam just a ways on above the bridge. Then the road was down clost to the river and only a grade where the bluff hugged too closely to the river to permit a wheel track. The early day residents built these grades - Alan Hay, Dodgson, Brubaker and others who had gone in there and found mines, ranches & [etc].

In Early Days

In early days when the country was new, prospectors had no time to build roads so in order to get to Dewey's Flat they came to Glendale, then into Canyon Creek, up a very steep trail to Vipond Park and down Quartz Hill Gulch. Then when at Dewey, one could make their way by fording the Big Hole many times to the upper country of the Big Hole Basin. When the prospectors found good ore, people came hither, each one seeking in his own way a part of the world's goods.

Early day road near Dewey, Beaverhead County, Montana
Courtesy Beaverhead County Museum
Dillon, Montana

Then such as Isaac Dodgson, Partridge, Hay, and Brubaker dug out a narrow road long the rivers edge of the mighty canyon towering hundreds of feet above them. Others then were eager to come.

John Hay tells how those men had improved the road. Others flocked in and they naturally felt peeved about it. Once Legatte had a mine at Quartz Hill and he came loaded with his winter provisions. They had previously put in a post on each side of the road and put a gate and locked it. It being early fall, the man could not get thru and being too far away from legal help, the wagon stood and the perishable goods froze. Legatte went to Bannack or the nearest legal help. He had Alan Hay, Dodgson and Brubaker and others called for trial. I am not quite sure, but think this was the time Brubaker took his sack of cheese and crackers on his back, with the others and started to walk to Bannack and arrived the day after the trial was set. He was coming just the same. Trial was dismissed and nothing came of it, only they had to take down the gate - posts stood for years afterward as a reminder.

When they took up the monument [*Big Hole Battle Field Monument, established in 1883*], I have heard told they had to cross (ford) the river 17 times in taking it up with the bull teams. I believe a Hungate, the one that worked for Thornson at Dell, went with Bales when they took it in. Evidently there must have been no road nor bridges then. Before the marble grade along the river was made, they had a road up graveyard gulch, then to the right over the marble hill or ford twice. That must have been bad when high water was on, then over the hill. Then on past Churchill's place, one had to go up Triangle gulch, cross the ridge and zig zag around and come out a way above the present road above a spring and then on in a half moon coming out at John Lawrence's corrals. Then the road was fair, except some alkyd holes along John's fence to Wise River. There was a bridge over the main river and the slough on the other side of the valley. From there it was fair. Sometimes rocky, sometimes good till one struck Patton's and Dodgson's lane-nothing had ever been done to it, it being a mile, or nearly, long. With good native sod on it, it was passable with light wagons. But it was soft alluvial soil, sub irrigated from the creek as it spread out under the ground. When the freight wagon, heavily loaded, went up in the spring and summer, they invariably had trouble and it was there the hoarse yells and crack from the whip asounded again and again. Many times the team could not pull the load out and they had to double. They often resorted to the lane fence for pries. That was a place freighters dreaded. If once thru that, could count on no more troubles. At Dickie's there was a long pole bridge on the river.

When across the river there were grades in many places up to Ralston's. There was not much work done on the roads in early days, if one could get over, that was all. Then from Ralston's on one encountered creeks, bridges with poles, and also long stretches of bad soft roads to Chalk Bluffs. There the river hugged the white bluff, so there was a heavy grade over the bluff and good roads to the river ford at or near Squaw Creek. Now there is a bridge over the river there. From Tong's upper ranch to Wisdom, there was only a couple of grades sharing Rock and Steel Creek. The roads up there being on the level, did not require much work. At Wisdom, the river, being small, was forded and one could go for a half day over the plains country road till one struck the timber and the road wound in and out crost Swamp Creek. Up, up, thru tall white pine, zig zag up and around, till one was on top of the continental divide, with scarcely no road work. Perhaps trappers and prospectors made the trail, if not made by Indians or game. Most all of the white man's roads were Indian trails.

Patton's and Dodgson's lane, being an eye sore for a long time, each spring it being almost impassable. The County Commissioners hired Horace, first time it was ever graded, to grade it. He, with two or three men, graded it up. They camped there, took feed, hay and grain and staid there till the job was done. I did most of their cooking, sending up a new supply every few days. Well, they made a nice road, one to serve the people for a long time. But this was nice for Hugh Patton. A big ditch to catch his irrigation water and all he had to do was to dam off where he needed. All he did was to haul out a big load of manure and dam the water off, throwing it out to his thirsty ground. They had provided him his culvert he needed. Mr. Hand had predicted this and told the commissioners just what would happen. So sure enuf, next spring Hugh set up his irrigating system. The commissioners told Horace if this happened to notify them. This he did and they sent word by Horace for Hugh to discontinue using the side of the road for his ditch. Hugh agreed and said he would obey orders, which of course he never intended to do. And that was that. Hugh continued as long as he lived to use the side of the road for his ditch. The road soon sunk, being of gumbo clay, and the commissioners still, as far as I know, build up the grade. But poor Hugh passed on about the summer of 1909 - to make ditches in a far dryer clime?

When Churchill sold his water right on Jerry Creek, he thot he could tap the water above the big rock on the road and take it down in a flume on the edge of the road grade, on down to his ranch road in that way. I mentioned before about he and John Hay working on this project. Who built the grade from the upper end of Churchill's ranch to the big rock I don't know, but it was there in '92. Perhaps Churchill, for his flume he never built. That was a good addition to the road, as it was a water grade most of the way. Shortly after that, the citizens built a short grade, just a short ways above the big rock, called the Citizen Grade. It was a bad little grade. Then on farther, Galbraiths had a rock crusher - the road went above that on to another poor piece of road - Galbraith Grade it was called. The road was made in a shear butt of a hill that always seemed to lean the wrong way. They built up a log cribbing on the lower side and worked the dirt out over it. That took the

---

Bryant's Hotel

I'm a Canadian; my name I shan't say.
I arrived in Montana quite early in May.
I went to Butte City, and stopped there
a spell; then I came up the Big Hole to
Bryant's Hotel.

This place, it is famous, you may bet
your life. Old Bryant has left and
it's run by his wife. Burnt biscuits
and beef steak, which grew by the bell,
is a dish that's quite common in
Bryant's Hotel.

The eggs that we get; they are rotten,
I swear. They look more like chickens;
the feathers are there. It's a pity to
break them and make such a smell, and
disturb the boarders in Bryant's Hotel.

Old Mrs. Bryant, she sniffs and she
sighs. She brags very high on her
beans and her pies. But her aim is
starvation; the plain truth to tell.
She's the devil's own cook in the
Bryant Hotel.

Old Bryant is sick; Dyspepsia quite
bad. He swears like a pirate; this
old gray haired Dad. No wonder his
stomach has taken a spell; since he
boarded so long at the Bryant Hotel.

For fear of old Bryant, I'll finish
my song. If he'd happen to hear me
I could not live long. When his
tongue once gets started, it runs
for a spell, and makes them all
laugh at the Bryant Hotel.

This house has changed hands since I
started my song. It's run by McKinzie;
he's seven feet long. He keeps all the
books, and he cuts a great swell; since
he got to be foreman at Bryant's Hotel.

McKinzie knows all things. He's wiser
than Saul. His learning is great, though
his brains, they are small. If I ever
come back; I will fill his glass well,
and drink him a toast to the Bryant Hotel.

-John Carmont

Toast

"Here's to the Mammoth, the pride of the Flat; where nothing could live but a dog or a cat. If this house has an equal, it must be in Hell; for there's nothing on earth like the Bryant Hotel."

"Here's to old Jane, as I finish my song. The person who boards here must be mighty strong. A toast to the house as I bid it farewell. May the Devil set fire to the Bryant Hotel." -John Carmont

[*The poem, Bryant's Hotel and Toast are taken, with permission, from Rock Hand, from* **"A LIFETIME OF NONSENSE" With Me & Ed & Ray by Rock Hand,** *pages 173, 174, Published by Thurber Printing Company, Helena, Montana, Copyright, July 10, 1980, Registration No. TX 580-735. - mc*]

road back away from the river into the half moon curve and came out at John Lawrence's. Road building in those days was hard, not many knew how to go at it and very few had the teams, plows, scrapers and rigging. A lot of it was done by hand and they did just as little as they could to get by. The other fellow could do the same. Now this strip of road is put down along the river edge. Later, and after we moved away in 1910, and is much shorter. They had better and bigger machinery when it was put in.

Horace was road supervisor for years. After the ranch began to produce, he turned the job over to Churchill. In the fall of '94 Horace put in the strip of road under the big rock. The high water took it out that spring. Then when the dam was built in '97, that fall and winter, he, with a crew of men, built the present road above the backwater line of the dam to within 1/2 mile of Dewey. The crew was so large he boarded them at Bryant's and Joe Bedards Hotels. That was why and how John Carmont wrote the famous poem "The Bryant Hotel". He happened to be a boarder there.

Just later than this, the roads being in fairly good shape, Horace and Al thot Churchill needed a job. He had a team of old horses, Darbs and Rosemary by name and in his way could make a living for himself and the two kids, since the ranch would not afford a living and his wife had left him. The road needed someone to roll out boulders on the grades and fill in a few chuck holes, so Churchill took it. They told him to take his team each day and [even] if he did not work it, charge for it. But Churchill was too honest to do that. He took a shovel, pick and wheel barrow and worked away. In time they told him they would not go on his bonds if he did not take his team. He says, "Jesus Christ, that ain't right. I can't do that." "Well, if you want the job, you can't have the job unless you do as we say." So he finally concented, tho it hurt him to be so dishonest.

Then as time rolled on more people came out that way, [there was] more traffic and so people wanted better roads. And there was more money to pay for roads. Al took the job. Al had put the ditches on several big ranches in the Big Hole before this time, which took several summers, besides road building and grading the awful hill on Bloody Dick Creek on the Jackson to Dillon present road. Gibbtown freighting jobs was over and the town gone down, no big store. There people simply lived on what they had, or went down to Salmon or over to the Bitterroot for needcessities of life. Then the heavy freighting days were over in these parts. Al never was much of a rancher. Tho he had the Jimmie New ranch, horses and some cattle. So the road job was quite the thing. He could hire men to do the work and he could be out among people that were doing something or that is, making the world go around. He could not be happy if he did not have several around to cajole and tell his stories to.

In this capacity he worked the road for several years, fixing many poor places, so those places troubled teamsters no more. About all the big teams were a few from Wisdom and Jackson, run for the stores there, for by this time they sold a lot of haying tools. Tho there still were ranchers that did all their own hauling, going out twice a year for provisions, etc. About 1915 or 16, Beaverhead hired the convicts from Deer Lodge [prison] to work the grade over and make wider, which improved it. Cost a pretty penny making it wider, with more turn outs on the grade so one could see in time to let a team from the opposite direction pass, without one or the other having to back to the nearest wide place as formerly was often done.

In the winter of 1934 or 35, now that the gasoline supply and money was available to help build roads, the road building administration graded off this grade with the road building machinery, nice and wide, and also the marble grade above town (Dewey). Then later they oiled from the turn off of 91 to the bridge, over the Big Hole below the old dam. There it seemed to be at a stand still tho there are hopes of having a good oiled road up thru Wisdom to connect with 93 [at the] top of the continental divide and last to the battle ground and in to the Bitterroot.

Roads and grades like these seldom come when most needed. The old freight roads were very bad as a rule. The Big Hill going down over the Divide to Gibbonsville is a fitting example. It was like taking a man's life and all his possessions in hand to go down it. A man had to brace his self with feet and both hands to set on the wagon seat, which was almost up and down. With his hands he drove the team and braced, while putting on the break with one foot. Then two big trees were lashed behind the trail wagon for further brakes. After the turn, [the road] went down, then there was a 3 [%] grade (road) put down the hill and one that is easy travel.

In the years that Horace and Al freighted thru that country, they often had call to bring in a load any time in the winter. Generally there was no snow at Divide to speak of or for sleighs. So the load had to go on to wagons, taken to Tong's if the snow was deep from there up. If not, then they would have to transfer at Ralston's. This extra loading and unloading took a day longer. Grades were often filled with snow. Then the best road was in the river. The ice being deep, deep, could go as far as Tong's upper ranch on the river, then generally took the road from there on. A snow road gets hard by travel and this now blowing in [with snow] often forms a grade. When they loose that grade they often set up and have more trouble, tho on the whole, winter is a fine time to haul freight.

General Joe A. Brown

It was said he attended West Point and got the title General.

George Bryan built the first toll bridge on the Big Hole River, just above where the bridge is now. Then he sold it to Joe Brown. There being need for a stopping house/stable, Brown built to accommodate the traveling public. Then there was need of hay and oats, so the farmland was developed. Cattle in those days were expected to live winter and summer on the range.

Brown had an ever flourishing trade. The toll for a team of two horses was 50 cents. Many two and three wagons were drawn by 4, 6, or 8, sometimes 10 horse teams. With the toll, meals, beds, if over night, teams to feed and over night, the money literally rolled in for about ten years or till the train came in 1880. Even after that time they did a flourishing business till about 1890. The state charter for toll bridges ran out about that time. They continued collecting toll for some time afterward.

The toll gate was between the barn and the house, built so it was handy. Every team had to come thru it or go thru the hills by a far road to Glendale. Tho, if the traveler was headed for the upper river country, it was nearest thru the bridge.

The house was built of four log cabins joined together to make room. The south cabin logs were brot from Argenta in 1860. The barn was large, mostly of logs, with a loft for hay. At one time Brown owned and operated what is now the Woods Livestock ranch, this a ranch on lower Rock Creek and a resort at Browns and Agness Lake. Built cabins that are still in use today [*1930's*]. He built the first road to the lower lake and the trail to the upper lake, with lookouts in various places on the road and trail. He was concidered to be a wealthy man. The boys rode the range and took care of the cattle. The girls helped in the house work.

Joe liked company and often drove his fast driving team to Glendale. When his boys or hired man (Floyd Langley) happened to be riding, they were permitted to go to the Hotel for meals and put the horse in the livery stable for food. It was said he was very exacting with his family. It was also said when Vipond left for health on a sailing vessel to Australia, Vipond gave him charge of the mine at Vipond Park to look after. Brown gave Hugh Patton the right to sell the rich ore, amounting to several thousand [*dollars*]. For this Brown took the money and he gave Hugh cattle to stock his ranch up the Big Hole. That was Hugh's nest egg or start.

When Vipond left, he said to Brown, "What can I bring you from Australia?" Brown said, "Bring me an oruo Thorniness (bird & animal) combined." So Billie did. He bot one and had it mounted, but Billie said if he had known Brown had stole his ore, he would have never bot it.

In years after, Hugh often remarked that Brown would give you everything you wanted, provided you did not want anything.

In his later years he was on the go a lot. Most every paper you would see where he was in Dillon or Butte. The R.R. gave him special privilege to run a one man hand car on the R.R. so he could go to Melrose often. They also built a small station house for him and his guests that he took to the lakes.

After his death, Joe A. Brown, Jr. operated the ranch for years. May married Hagenbarth in 1894. Frank was accidentally electrocuted visiting a plant in Butte. Fanny worked around Dillon and then married and went to California. When he died, his fortune, land, and cattle, was most depleted, till the old home ranch was all that was left. The wife died shortly after Joe's death.

The spring May Brown was married, Mrs. Patton had her up there for a week, and in the meantime, Ralstons gave a dance and she was there at the dance. A very nice looking girl, rather pretty. Then, the day we went to Dillon to be married, she came out to the toll gate for the toll. Mr. Brown was a good friend of Horace's and he told Horace to not pay the kid's toll, but he did.

The day Horace came to the country, he was with a team and other men. The stage team became frightened, became unruly and the stage went into the river, just in the narrow place in the road before coming to the bridge. The driver was drown - was buried on the hill clost by. General Brown was helping build the barn. Afterward they became friends and later he wanted to stake Horace to a bunch of mares and go in to the horse business [*with him*]. But Horace preferred to make it alone. Then it would have been a bad venture as that was a few years before the auto began to buzz in everybody's head. On this barn Brown built a lookout. People said [*it was*] so he could watch the hired men at work in the field.

– mc

Picnic

Thelma (Hand) Kalsta told that just a ways and across the Big Hole from the ranch at Lavon, on Rock Creek, Maggie and Horace stopped for a picnic on their way back from Dillon when they were married. Unknown to them that some years down the road they would live right across the river and build a large new home there. – mc

Joe H. Browne

Joe H. Browne of Glendale, Montana was born August 1, 1831 near West Alexander, Washington County, Pennsylvania. He left home March 14, 1859 for the Rocky Mountains, prospecting and mining in Colorado and New Mexico until May 1862 when he started for Salmon River mines. Arrived in what is now known as Beaverhead County, Montana in July 1862, and continued to prospect and mine until 1870 when he engaged in stock raising and ranching in the Big Hole Valley, but retained a large interest in several valuable silver mines. He was a member of the Territorial Legislature for five terms, serving in both the lower and upper houses. Mr. Browne was also a member of the Constitutional Convention that convened in the Capital of the Territory, January 14, 1884, to frame a constitution for the future state of Montana. Mr. Browne has held other responsible positions and has been prominently dutiful with all acts of benevolence in his district.

He married April 9, 1872, to Miss Agnes M. Murray of Dubuque, Iowa, by whom he has four children. It is to be regretted that he will not permit anyone to publish his adventures during the past twenty five years in the Rocky Mountains. A man of his known love of adventures and unquestioned courage must have witnessed some thrilling scenes.
- From Montana History (Beaverhead Co.) 1885.

Ben and Stage

When Ben Mallon first came to Divide, he took the first job he could get driving stage from Divide to Wisdom. The Post Office, first P.O. above Dewey, then was at the old Ethridge place.

While he was taking out the mail bags, a man rode up on a horse and says to Ben, "You are going in and I have a bronco, so if you will get me my mail I won't go in."

"Yes," says Ben, "I'll get it if you will tell me your name."

"Mudd," says the man.

Ben went in and keeping an eye on his team all the while, exchanged the mail and came out without the man's mail.

"Did you get my mail?" says the man to Ben.

"No," says Ben "you didn't tell me your name," and climbed on to the stage and drove on.

Then Mudd had to get off his horse and go in and get his own mail. That was what he got for having such a dirty name.

Ben Mallon and the Bear

Once while on his regular trips hauling freight from Divide to Wisdom for J. B. Lossel, coming thru the Dewey's Flat, near the mouth of Quartz Hill Gulch, Ben's saddle horse, that was leading behind his six horse team and two wagons, broke loose and made a dash up the canyon.

Knowing it would be useless to go on foot, he stopped and took out one of the horses in his team that he knew he could ride and in his haste and not thinking he'd have to go far, left the harness on and hurriedly took after the saddle horse as fast as his work horse could go. Tho he never could get ahead of him and if he could, the canyon was so narrow he never could head off the horse. At Quartz Hill the horse still gained ground on Ben and on going around an old, rotten, deserted cabin, a big mother bear with cubs jumped out of an open door, almost into him and made for Ben. This frightened the horse and it almost got away from him. By this time the saddle horse had disappeared into the timber and he knew it was not wise to follow, so he came on back, put the horse in the team and made his trip to Wisdom. Time went on, no word of the horse. Was a long time, till one day, almost a year later, Fred Dickie and George Dodgson found him in the hills, up the country. The new saddle he had on when he broke loose was now battered and worn, for in his travels on the range it had slipped in under his belly.

Bob Beattie and Brother Ed

When I came to the country (1892), Bob was living on a small farm just above Dickie's Bridge. There the hill and river bowed back, and left quite a little piece of land. With careful managing he could keep 50 or 60 head of cattle and a team of horses. He was an honest, reliable, sober man in every way. He stayed with the ranch. His brother worked but always needed help from Bob. When Ed worked, he drank and gambled all of his earnings up, which kept Bob worried. In

1903, when the pump station was built, Bob had to get a man to take care of his things while he worked and paid off some worthless debt of Ed's.

Horace and Bob hayed together. In the summer when our hay was ready to be put up Bob would come down with his two white ponies and help. Then Horace would send up a team and rigging and help put up Bob's hay. Then when he went to the Flat, he always stopped to pass the time of day. Children liked Bob.

When we rewalled our well, Ed was the only fellow that Horace could get to wall it up. When once he had a job, he knew how to hold it, for he was weeks walling 60 feet. That time I was away with Byron in the hospital, Thelma was a baby. I had my hands full too.

Rean Flannegan did the cooking (cooked the hard beans). After that some time, Ed died and then Bob was free, but not for long. Before this some time Bob expected to get married to a Miss Galholly. He had been living in a very large, comfortable cabin, low and warm. So, he thot he must do better and built a nice small frame house. The wedding failed to materialize. He lived there a few years after we left. Some infection on a thumb caused his death. They came from London, Canada.

Bob often got game - deer were thick and closet. He told Pa a story about going out on the steep sidehill once, seeing one deer, he took aim and fired. When it fell he ran up to cut its throat and bled it. While doing that he saw another deer down, so he went and bled the second one and just then he saw a third deer struggling. By this time he thot he was beside his self or was he seeing things. But sure enuf, his shot had killed three [deer] instead of one.

In the spring he turned his cattle out on the rough hill adjoining his home where they grazed all summer and until late fall. Bears were plentiful too. They often killed three or four of Bob's cattle, besides neighbors cattle.

In the early stage of the game, Bob built a big log pen with a trap door that tripped the trap and the bear was [caught] in the pen. Then it was an easy mark for Bob to shoot. Some times the bear would die of starvation before a rider would find him. These were only two of the many hunting stories he often told us.

Years ago, J. B. Nose [Gnose] (late) of Anaconda gave a full, large set of dishes for the person trading so much at his store - prizes were given. These people often traded groceries with Nose [Gnose] in Anaconda. It happened Fred Dickie drew the prize. Bob told Dickie he had seen in the paper where he had the prize. "So, Dickie, you write to J. B." and explain he was the man [who won] and to send the dishes over. In due time the dishes came. Dickie gave Bob half of the set. They were so nice. Bob did not care to own them in his cabin so he gave them to me. Delighted, yes, to get these nice dishes. I am sorry to say I only have two pieces left of the set, one plate (dinner) and a large platter. I have guarded them with care. They are blue and white, a grape vine leaf pattern. Bob and Dickie lived closet for ranchers in those places.

Bob and Ed owned a mine in the hills near. Later years Tom Pelton took good ore out.

Madison

Madison was an old man, wore glasses, and previously had served four years in the pen [prison] for killing a man. When he got out he came to Divide. A dance was on and Mrs. Forrest got her name up by dancing the first dance with him. Was a odious thing to do for a respected matron.

Hugh Patton

Hugh took up the piece of land at the mouth of Meadow Creek along the Big Hole River. It was a nice alluvial meadow. Below the road it widened out. Sam Garrot had a nice piece of meadow adjoining Patton's on the east, also at the mouth of Meadow Creek.

John Hay was staying at Robbin's one winter. Patton often came to spend the evening. Brubaker lived closet at his mine on Meadow Creek and would come down to Robins in the evening. Brubaker would wash the supper dishes while John Hay would read to them from Patton's favorite book. "Chiniquies 50 Years A Priest" was the book. Brubaker would go out to throw the dish water out and if he did not see anyone, he would say to Patton Ba, Ba, Ba. The others was afraid Patton would hear Al, but he never

$1.69 PERCALE HOUSE DRESS WITH DUTCH NECK.

This neat and serviceable one-piece House Dress is a very good value for the money. Made with four tucks in front. Dutch neck is finished with band of self material. Three-quarter sleeve with plain cuff. Nice full skirt is gathered on to attached belt. Sizes 32 to 44 inches bust measure. When ordering, state bust measure.

No. 38K7228 Color, black with polka dots. Price..$1.69
No. 38K7229 Color, blue with polka dots. Price..$1.69
No. 38K7230 Color, red with polka dots. Price...$1.69
If by mail, postage extra, 21 cents.

Sears Roebuck & Co. 1908

happened to. When Patton came, they hid the book under the dish rag and read other books or talked.

After a time of living alone, Patton began to look around for a wife. A Molly O'Harra was cooking at Bryants Hotel. After courting for some time he proposed to Molly, but Molly did not seem so inclined. So he says "Molly, all right, if you won't have me then I have another in view." Which he did, for Maggie Murphy was then cooking for her uncle at Feely Ranch on the old dirt road to Butte. Feely station on the R.R was named after this man that owned the ranch and stopping house near by.

Patton's first residence was a small log house. The new one was a larger log house set nearer the road. It was more commodious - at the time the nicest house on the road - having five rooms and a porch. The family came late in the lives of both, three girls and a boy, Mary, Rose, Ethel and George, the youngest. Mary grew to be ten or twelve years old, was sick for some time and passed away. She became ill after returning from a trip back to Buffalo, New York. She had T.B. Rose was a very nice girl. From grade school she went to Salt Lake to school, later kept books for the Murray Hospital. There she met a doctor and married.

Ethel was smart, but too smart to make a success anywhere. After the father died in 1909, George and the others persuaded the mother to sell the ranch. They took the money and put it in a garage in Whitehall. Well, under their management, the ranch floated out in thin air. Mrs. Patton then ran a small store at Wise River for a few years, sponsored by Ethel. Failing health forced her to abandon the store. Then she lived with the children till she passed away in 1935.

When Patton was a bachelor he often hitched up and drove to Glendale, then a flourishing berg. There he would meet the boys and have a good time for a few days. One time he had such a good time, he got too full. So the boys, Al and Horace, thought they would pull a good one on him. One of them went down to a negro who did washing, secured a bed and took Patton down and put him to bed. When he got up the next morning and found he had slept in a negro wash woman's extra bed, Patton was furious, but the boys were no where to be found. So rather than stay and have the men make fun of him, he left town at once. After that he was very careful when he went to Glendale. The boys never quit telling about Patton sleeping at the negro's shack.

He often told about playing marbles, when a child, with Queen Victoria's children when she visited Ireland.

On coming to America he worked and traveled in many states. While down in lower Georgia, he got mixed up in a fight with a negro. Seeing it was sure death for him if he did not kill the negro, he did, and saved his own life. He made for the swamps as fast as he could and stayed there for days before he could escape. Then he came to Montana in order to escape the vengeance of the southern negros.

Patton, like so many other men, wanted his first born to be a boy. Mary came - he was disappointed. Then came Rose, and he felt no better and finally Ethel. My God, three girls! The morning Ethel came, he hitched up old Brigham (the old grey horse) to the buggy and went down town for some supplies and to replenish his jug. With this last blow he needed more toddy. Horace was up on the field cleaning off sage brush. He heard Old Brigham's feet coming down the road and over the Wise River bridge, clump, clump, and a "Get up, Brigham, get up". Horace thought something was up so ambled over to the road to learn the news.

"Hi, Hugh. What is it?"

To which Hugh replied, "O, the dammed thing is a girl." And quite enough, that expression went down through the years, "The dammed thing's a girl."

Finally he was rewarded when George came. George was the apple of his eye.

In those days, with a good hay meadow, one could make a good living with hay and cattle. The summer range was clost, just put them across the river and they would come home in the fall, fat. Patton was a very poor feeder. As Callen often said when the cattle were poor, "They ate too long off the top of the stack" or if they died it was "willow poisoning". So, with Patton, his cattle died like flies in the spring. When asked how they wintered, he invariably said, "Why they are thick fat," and he never admitted that he lost any. When one chanced to go through his field, dead cattle lay everywhere and the willows were eaten off to stubs.

He ranched year in and out with very little effort. He hired a man to help clean ditches for a month and a few men to help put up the hay in the summer. He milked a cow or two for the home milk and butter, had their own meat all winter and corned a barrel full for summer use. Then the balance of their needs were bought. No one seemed to work hard. They enjoyed reading books and when the daily mail came they had a Butte paper which gave them the news of the world.

Early in the spring (before the fair at Buffalo, New York), Mrs. Patton went to Butte [and] stocked up with enough dress goods for each girl and herself, several dresses apiece. Then, after she had dragged them out and showed them to the neighbors several times and got the royal brand on them (cow manure), she brought them down for me to make (1902). This was quite a chore for me, with three children and some men to cook for, but I did it by the time she was to start for the fair. She visited the fair and some of her relatives in New York and Jimmie New in Brooklyn. She left George with "Papa".

The girls often came down to see us. Horace would ask them, "Where did Hugh board when you were all gone?" "Why for himself," they would say, "But he only used one dish rag all the time we were gone."

Al Griswold often worked for Patton. He was very fond of buttermilk. One day he came in from the field very dry and asked Mrs. Patton for a drink of buttermilk. She went out to the old cabin. In the summer she used one half for a bunk house and the other side for a milk house. That year she was raising turkeys and in some way the door had been left open to the milk house. The young turkeys had gone in and one flew up on the edge of the buttermilk jar and slipped in. The sides were perpendicular, so it could not get out. When she went in, there it was, nearly drowned. She picked it out, squeezed the milk off of it, saying, "You dirty thing." With this she handed Al a dipper of buttermilk.

One time the ladies of the valley put on a supper and dance in the school house. They put up a tent for a cook shack. Patton seldom went to a gathering. Maggie Patton insisted that he should go, so he did.

I could not get my man to go either, so I hitched up an old gentle horse to the buggy and took my children. They were small, but this being the first entertainment of the kind they wanted to go. There were several young people up there then, May and Millie Dodgson, Ben Mallon and the McVey boys and others. So it bid fair to be a big occasion of the season, nothing quite like it at Meadow Creek School House, at least.

Along toward midnight the men seemed to be quite jovial and they often made trips out between dances. Hugh Patton did not act quite right either. Wonder what could be the matter? On one of Hugh's trips out he got tangled up in the tent ropes, falling and picking himself up on every rope as he made a circle of the tent. Yes, he was drunk, but no one dared to say it!

Mrs. Patton was always so nice to me. I went to see her and she came to see me. Invariably she would hurry up and make me stay for a meal, when I just wanted to call.

As our children grew and went to school, there were many differences between the families. But all in all we were good friends and enjoyed having the privilege of living along side of them in the quiet little valley.

Asbury Stine

Years ago June was a wet month. Teamsters on Wise River, if possible, laid off hauling and gave their team a needed rest, taking them to pasture and keeping watch so that none strayed away and were ready at a few days notice.

So it was Horace was herding a bunch [*of horses*] one spring on the Vipond Meadows, a high plateau, surrounded with lofty wooded mountains with many a mountain rill or creek dashing to the rivers below. For a helper and company, he took the Longley boy. Domiciled in an old cabin, they could enjoy a long earned rest for a while. One day a few head of horses were missing. So Horace decided he'd get up early and hunt them. Possibly they had gone to Wise River Meadows and, as he had never been there, he would go down and look the country over. Having heard a great deal about the country, he had an urge to go. Would be killing two birds at one throw. He choose Vipond Creek trail as the best way down. It proved to be only a game trail. Down timber and rock made it most impassible to ride down, so he had to walk and lead, and in places make the trail. Going was slow and dangerous. Finally in the afternoon he came to open ground and went to Pattengale [*Pettingill*] Creek. Thinking there he would find the horses, but no, not a sign of one. Then he crossed the river and it was there he ran on to Pattengale [*Pettingill*], sunning himself on a log. He had not seen any stray horses. Said he had bunch farther up the river. By this time it was getting late, [*and Horace*] must be going as the sun was low and nothing to eat since breakfast. That trail was too bad to even think of going over it again. So he turned down the river road which wound in and out along the river and a big mountain that hemmed it in. Could hardly call it a road as it was over broken boulders, which in ages had crumbled off and fallen into what was called a road. Finally he came to an opening, and to his surprise, a cabin with smoke coming out. And as he came nearer, a man came to the door.

"How do you do?," says Stine. "Come right in, you must be tired, come and have some supper with me," says Stine.

This was certainly hospitality, and in such a lonely new country, Horace could hardly believe his eyes. After hobbling the horse in a nice grassy place, he went in and sat down to supper. Stine said he was most out of grub and that he had made some pine needle tea and that it was good for rheumatism, which bothered him. This Horace partook. It had a very fine aroma, if one liked that kind. With sour dough bread, the supper was complete. Stine talked all the while for he was a kindly man and a very interesting conversational. Time past quickly by, but being so tired, Horace again looked after his horse. Brot in the saddle and blanket, climbed up in his sleeping apartment, pulled his blanket over him and used the saddle for a pillow. Soon was off in sweet sleep. Stine crawled to his perch and slept soundly.

In the middle of the small cabin was an opening or cellar, a few feet below the floor, where he had his stove. Did all his cooking there. Then up on the upper floor he used for his bed and to store things. The cabin was built of small logs that had been uprooted years ago. These roots all were used, the roots making corner decorations. Perhaps saws were scarce or he did not care to go to more labor than necessary, how be it? It was a shelter from the elements and a home sweet home to Stine. He had chosen a lovely little mountain creek that came tumbling over itself to empty in to Wise River. He was long side the road so to be a friend to man, for he liked company, to meet all wayfarers that had come from down country.

Horace was always an early riser, so this morning he thot he would quietly slip away for by this time there was pangs of hunger. Stine awoke and insisted he stay for breakfast. He made some urgent excuses, thanking Stine for his supper and nights lodging and then he quietly saddled his horse and rode away down the river. Never over that trail again, fearful if he staid he would have to drink more pine needle tea. He always said that was the first and the last pine needle tea he ever drank.

A few years later when Horace and Seth Halbert (Al) took up their ranch on Wise River, Horace renewed his acquaintance with Stine. He often stopped to chat with Horace and after Horace was married he would drop in to see his wife and family. He would often get a lunch and when I had buttermilk he heartily enjoyed buttermilk and the lunch.

Once, I recall, Horace complained about his hair needing cutting. Then Stine said he had barbered when in the army and he would cut his hair. Whereupon Stine got the scissors, took Horace out in the shade of the house and proceeded to cut his hair. He told at length of the Battle of New Orleans, (Civil War), all the time entertaining Horace by telling an army story about the capture of New Orleans. Horace was bald on top of the head, not much hair to cut, but by and by Stine had nearly run out of hair, leaving only a narrow vine left. After that Horace never wanted a hair cut when Stine came. Pa said, "My God Stine, you have ruined me!"

Then at another call, Horace was building a blacksmith shop. They spent some time visiting and in the discourse Stine said he too had been building, had put up a house. He generally averaged three rounds of logs a day and had been working 30 days. I don't believe he ever finished that house as at one time they said to get out of his house, this was his new dwelling house, he had to climb over on a ladder and crawl thru a wide place between two logs.

One time a young man and wife called at our house enquiring the way to Stines. Said they were going to stay there and help him ranch. Uncle had sent for them, but the next day they came on back. The lady said, "O, my we could not stay there." Others had tried to stay before but all went away. This building idea with Stine grew when he saw others building in the country.

Then he later decided to build what he called a hay "barrack". This he built with poles, roof and all, but it never was chinked. The roof poles were laid about six inches apart. It also served as a chicken house and milk house.

Campers used to come up the river and often camped clost to Stine to hear his stories. When once camped, they always came back for more. They often left him food and one party gave him a buggy, old but intact. He took great pleasure in hitching in his old gray mare and coming down and going to Dewey. After many, many trips the seat came off, but he was equal to the situation. He sawed off a block of wood and placed it on the floor of the buggy and nailed the seat to it. This worked for some time and finally the box of the buggy refused to stay on and he discarded the whole thing. So, he tied a board on the full length of the hounds or running gear of the buggy and road astride the board. This worked well till all at once it all gave out at the forks of the road. Just like the "One Horse Shays". Then he walked and rode his horse home and thereafter depended on catching a ride or walking.

Stine was a large man. He had served in the Civil War and while there was severely wounded on the cheek and drew a pension. After the war had farmed in Kansas before coming west. He had a few horses, a wagon and mowing machine. In order to keep his stock from straying and others out, he had a gate in a narrow place on river bluff on the road. Neighbors told the story about Stine using his mowing machine for 15 summers without sharpening a sickle. He cut a little hay each year and generally stacked it on top of a pile of brush. The first year he ever sold any was the winter when the Water Company built the dam on Wise River.

The Water Company that winter kept quite a crew of men and horses to work, so they bot Stine's hay. The snow was deep and they needed hay. They measured up and paid him but when they began to haul, they found only a few loads on top. So they sent post haste for Horace for hay. It then was the dead of winter and in one of our worst cold snaps, but hay had to go to the work animals at the dam - at once. It was late afternoon and Horace only had time to load and be ready to go early next morning. Tied [*the load*] down securely. In the morning bright and early, Al dressed extra heavy for the trip and Horace hooked to the wagon four of their best horses and all made ready.

I shudder as I recall that morning. All the thermometers had failed to register any farther than 60 below, how much more we never knew. Snow was deep and the air was thick with the cold. They put a comforter on the load to wrap up in and all was ready. An awful undertaking, as it was 15 miles or more up there and up hill every step of the way. The water in Wise River descends at the rate of 60 feet per mile. When the order "git up" rang out, the horses bent theirselves to the load, and the sleigh bells rang out merrily - sorta cheered us all up.

Then another winter Horace needed more poles for fencing and had found what he wanted above Stines on the river. He hired a man (Ben Butler), this time to cut his load each day as he hauled. Getting up at 4 a.m., getting his team ready and ate breakfast, he then was on the road miles away at sun up. At Stines he would leave his lunch so it would not freeze and when he came back with the load he would water his horses at the creek, and slip on their nose bags. While they ate, he would go in and Stine would have coffee made and both eat the lunch. I always sent a pie. Horace generally ate a slice and Stine would finish it. One day he said, "Maggie, I want you to make me a big mince pie in a milk pan." So I did, but Stine could not eat it all that day. Said he'd have to wait til another day to eat such a large pie. Big eater. Horace thot he would stall him that way.

This was the last winter Horace ever hauled poles from up there, tho Stine never failed to call on us once in a while. He was still there in 1910, but we learned shortly after that he went to the soldiers' home at Columbia Falls, Montana and there after a few years passed away. Pa often told the pie story and would laugh how he stalled Stine on the milk pan pie (mince pie).

Judge Wilber

Judge Wilber lived in and around Divide. (Pa knew him)

He was noted for his marriage ceremonies. When the bride and groom asked to have the nuptial knot tied, he would ask the groom if he liked her and where upon the groom would answer yes. Then he would ask the bride if she loved him and of course she would say yes. Then he would say, "By God you are married!" and throw his hat on the ground.

Maude tells about him going to see Hugh Patton when Patton was a batchlor. He would stay and stay and finally say, well I must go and after repeating that declaration time and again, Patton would say, "By God, if you don't go Judge, you won't have a chance to come back."

Jones Ranch

Farther down below Vineyards, Charley Moore took up a 320 acre ranch. Most of the land on the bench. Built his ranch building under the brow of the bench hill and clost to the Big Hole road. He built the ditch mostly and built a house, but the undertaking proved too great in time and Charley sold out to Walter Jones. Jones has improved it and has made a good ranch for [*in spite of*] the sage brush and rocks.

Ditches

Before 1892, the Dodgsons and Robbins on Meadow Creek saw the need of more water. They were then taking a ditch out of Wise River over to Meadow Creek. Then later Vineyard took his out and then later Moore. All three came out clost together and ran to the various places.

I believe our ditch was the oldest taken out on the opposite of the creek above the Clad Hay ranch. Then came John Lawrence's clost below and Trueman's ditch. Horace foretold trouble and could see it coming afar - scarcity of water in Wise River, but we were away when the trouble came. Every little farmer that had taken up a rock pile wanted water and so they took it to court in '34 or '35.

Frank [*Reitchel*] Ritschel

[*Maggie spells the name as Reitchel but marriage and land records show it to be Ritschel. Also she indicates that his wife's name is Etta but research shows it is Esther. I would suspect "Etta" was a nickname – mc*] Frank Ritschel was a young lad when he came from Hungary to Minnesota, to an aunts. Her husband being a contractor, he found work with the uncle and saw to learn the language and the way of the new people in his adopted country. He was a very young, earnest boy and wanted to please the uncle. The uncle was a hard master, put Frank to too heavy of tasks for his age, packing candy baskets of mortar up ladders to the second floor. Soon he gave out and was compelled to leave in order to live with the meager wage his uncle had allowed him. He came to Butte 1885. In '88 Dewey was a berg by that time and he went there. He worked at anything he could get to do and built a little cabin which he could call home. When out of work, he could eat and sleep at a small expense till he could secure another job. But Dewey was good. Dolman set up a store there and Frank got steady work with him. Frank was dependable and he needed him as Dolman had other things to attend to and Frank staid on till in '93. Most all industries in Dewey closed or knew they could not hang on much longer. A great many of the people were moving out to other frontier, some going to the wheat country in eastern Washington, others to logging camps in Idaho and Washington and some to other mines, then some to ranches. In the meantime, Frank married Etta Hopkins, the oldest daughter of a large family of 8 or 9, a motherly girl having to help raise her brothers and sisters. They were English, having come from England in early days. Etta brot her pony and often rode horseback. One time she loaned it to me to go to Clines on one Saturday.

Mr. Hopkins cut cord wood on Canyon Creek and Vipond Park for the smelter in Glendale. Work at the smelter was not so good for a few years, so people began to scatter from there. Now that Dewey was on the decline, they all must move. Gibbonsville looked prosperous and that was not so far away, so both families decided to go there. Etta wanted to be near her people. In the Big Hole country land was yet vacant. They could get here in only two or three days travel, so they went there. All took up land that they could and had their rights. They chose land clost together on the upper north fork. Frank and wife then got work in "Gibtown". A man just below town needed a good man. He was working a gold mine there by hydraulics. Frank was promised good wages at the clean up. The house and garden were nearby the workings. They could have a cow, all went well. Frank worked diligently for his employer. This man had been in Gibbonsville for a few years and had quite a good standing in the town. In lodges he was quite influential. Frank liked him.

In the fall when they had to close down for the winter, Frank went up the creek to shut off the water to let it go back in the creek. The boss said to Etta, "Why don't you go, you could get some fish when Frank shuts off the water?" Well, she had the baby to pack and did not think she had better go.

Frank says, "I'll carry it if you will go," so she went. "How much," says Frank, "will we make, a thousand dollars?"

When they cleaned up, Frank's share only figured out to $2.50 per day. He thot surly he had ought to have had more, but it just was not there. The dirt might not have been as rich as he figured it was, for Etta did digging on the side with a small pick and often got nuggets. She saved them and gave them to the boss, whereupon he put them in the sluice.

That fall they moved back to the ranch below the battlefield, built a house, got out fencing. The little money he saved from the summers work helped to tide them over, but in the spring they must hunt a job again. The old mining man promised more money if Frank would help him another summer, so he agreed to try another time. Yes, he would work harder, surely he could make more. So he moved his little family back to the bar - cow, chicken and garden. Ettie tended to that, for Frank worked early and late, sluicing down the gravel bar into the troughs. Fall came, ice and snow forced them to quit and once more to go to the head of the ditch to turn out the water. She went and on the return picked up fish while he carried the baby. This time he thot he could go home with plenty of money to carry on a winters work on his ranch. When they cleaned up the sluice troughs, alas no better than the year before. The old man was so sorry but there it all was. Frank could see for himself. Yes, yes, yes, they faced what seemed then the stern facts. Frank picked up his meager belongings, wife and child, and made it back over the continental divide to his little home in the valley. He resolved never to leave again to work for wages and, if possible, to stay with the land the U. S. had made possible to acquire. A home where he could live and raise their little brood. Next summer Major Smith, thru his management, took up a large tract of land on the bench. He hired Big Al to put on a big canal to water this bench and also hired him to cut off the many knolls that dotted this prairie. Here Frank and many other struggling new ranchers got work and eventually made the money to help them improve and stock their places.

But what became of the mining man that Frank worked for on the bar? Not long after Frank and wife moved home, he disappeared. Not a soul in and round Gibbonsville ever heard a word from him. No one heard him say he was leaving or seen him leave. This remained a deep, dark mystery even to this day. In his room was found an iron rod loaded with a magnet. It was what he drew the gold from the sluice with this rod? But the gold, no one seemed to know how he got away with it. This same bar today is yielding good money. It did then and has since.

Some time before Frank came to Gibbonsville, this same man and Mr. Mulcy, an old placer miner, were sluicing one summer for gold. Mulcy's sluice was in line with his cabin above the works. One morning quite early Mulcy arose and went to the door. In looking down at the sluice, he saw a man bent over with a rod load stone working the riffles in the flume. Stepping back fully in his cabin, he reached for his shotgun and leveled it on the bend in the man. Bang, filling his hinder parts full of buck shot which caused him to quickly disappear down the hill. Knowing the culprit, he craved no other law for his revenge, knowing he'd have to see to it immediately.

Frank did not know this till after he had quit working for him. The story came out when he disappeared so mysteriously. He was treasurer for the Rebecca's and Odd Fellows Lodge and seemed to be a very respected citizen.

Joe Zeigler

Having more cattle one year than he thot he could handle, Joe offered 300 head for sale at a little misgiving as to whether he should sell. It had taken a period of years to accumulate the bunch. He knew each cow, calf and steer at sight. Then [*he considered*] the many weary days, early and late feeding. Then looking after them thru the long summer days on the range. Another rancher and cattleman near Dillon soon heard of this bunch that was for sale and came hither, eager to buy. Tho being willing did not push his bargain too hastily. Before night fall Joe sold the 300 head. The man was to come for them the next day or two, or just as soon as the buyer could get help to drive them away. Enuf money was paid to hold the bargain. The buyer had no sooner left than Joe's regrets began to gored him. He had sold them too cheap? He could not afford to let them go at this price. When the man came back to pay the balance and drive them out, Joe offered him $2.00 more per head for him to take his money back.

The Lewis Sr. Family

The Lewis family were natives of Missouri and before the war 1861-65 they owned slaves and were quite wealthy. After the war was over they were broke and from there they went by mules and wagons to Texas. After staying there a few years, they came to Montana by mules and wagons. They were at Quartz Hill one fall. Horace and Al were hauling up there. They had often brot hay and oats up for Mr. Lewis. This day they had an extra heavy load and they thot of course we can get Mr. Lewis's team of mules to hitch on and get the load up. So they asked him for the loan of them a short time. They got the load up and thanked Mr. Lewis for their use.

In a few days they got a bill of $8.00 for the use of the mules. They paid it. The Lewis's finally settled on a piece of land above Bob Beattie's and over the river. A nice, big wild hay meadow. They had 10 children, all eventually came out and settled around. The old man and woman and Frankie, the youngest girl, moved to Dillon the fall of 1895.

Kate had gone to Dillon a year or two before and settled there, taught music. Then after the old folks moved down, they kept boarders and did a good business for years. Mr. Lewis died in 1904. Mrs. Lewis lived till nearly 100 years. They gave up boarders and kept some roomers. The summer of 1936 Frankie was very poorly and she and Kate died that winter. No one thot Kate poorly, but she did not last long after Frankie died.

Kate was a remarkable woman. Nettie and Roscoe, Thelma and Susan all staid with Kate. They had their ups and downs, but all liked Kate.

Mr. and Mrs. Hughes staid on on the old place. Mrs. Hughs was one of the Lewis girls (Cary). Then Mr. Drake came out and another daughter. Mrs. Brown was another daughter, raised her boys and lived in Gibtown. She died at Ralstons in 1935. (Mildred) Charley Ralston's wife was Mrs. Brown's daughter. Then there were five boys. Addison, married Lillie Bryant and afterward left her and went to Butte, worked in the mines. He killed his mistress and then his self. Joe Lewis was at the flat, died later of pneumonia. The other boys I did not know. Once Ernest lived in Gibbonsville and Obediah Lewis, the oldest, moved out here from Missouri about 1902 and bot George and Tice Dodgson out. He was well to do. They lived on that place till 1915, moved to Portland and later died there.

Mildred Brown was left with an aunt and did not come till later, about 1905 or there about, and she was such an odd girl. Never was taught to work. Charley Ralston soon picked her - she was as good as gold, but (doolers). After the children began to come, she learned by hard knocks. They were a good hearted bunch. Tho craved the nickles, almost too much.

Obe [*Obediah*] was clost, too, was a pain to see him connive. Obe had two sons, Max, up the Basin and Glen in Portland. Then their girls, Maxine and Louise. Maxine married a sailor, then annulled the marriage. She went to Hollywood, died before she went on the stage. Louise married an (Ice Cream) man and they are wealthy on the coast somewhere. Obe sold to Hustead. All the children were natural musicians.

The Lewis' were direct relatives of Merryweather Lewis, explorer in 1805.

Mama's Vaccination

Jr. says, "Mama, an't you going to be vaccinated this time?"

"No," says Mammy, "makes me have sore arm and hi can't wash."

"Well, how about your leg."

"Then I can't stand and wash the clothes."

Well, Mammy, can't you think of some other place on you, you don't have to use so much."

"Yes," says mama, "and I don't set down much."

From Maggie's Scrap Book

Sopher

Sopher was from Kennebeck in Maine, where he spent his early days, then came west and spent some time in the RubyValley, before coming to Dewey's Flat vicinity. He and John Robins took up places above the Dodgson ranches on Meadow Creek. He never was married, tho according to his stories he left several girls in Maine.

Living alone, he was quite a burden on his neighbors. When he came to visit, often staid up most of the night telling Robins or Maude and Tice his experiences. Being closter to Tice, he made them more calls. Often Brubaker would be there visiting and the trio would sit. Sopher would hold them there, telling his younger days experiences, till finally Tice would say, "Sopher, there is a bed, go to bed and I'll have too." But, still he rambled on. Brubaker would listen and ag him on. Then Tice would say, "Sopher, go to bed." Finally, about 2 a.m., Sopher would go home. Tucked under his arm, a loaf of Maude's good bread, as he always had a kindly way of inveigling her out of a loaf each visit.

He had a comfortable log cabin, stable and corrals. Gradually accumulated a few head of cattle and lived quite comfortable there all alone.

Finally, a relative came out, tho did not stay, and later one came from Massachusetts. He had been raised in town and knew nothing about ranch life, had never harnessed a horse. He was rather indignant, tho gradually learned the ways of the west. When the old man passed, he inherited the place. He sent for a wife. Without the old man's guidance he soon decided he could make more money in town, so he sold and they moved to Dillon. Here he lost all he had gained by inheritance. They raised two boys.

George Grown

George Grown was quite a rustler, worker, promoter, but mostly drinker. He built a monstrous large house at the mouth of Fish Trap on the road. At the time, they passed a law that to obtain a liquor license you had to have a hotel with a given number of rooms. It stands today as his monument, gaunt and stark, with only liveable residence in one corner.

One time Grown tired of his own kind of liquor, saddled his horse and went down the road to the first bar. There he imbibed quite freely and started home feeling just right. On the road, not far from his home, an old, simple minded fellow lived in a small cabin. Everyone, in order to keep out of trouble, gave in to his whims. On the road, out a ways from his cabin, he had a mail box, tho seldom had any mail come. Here came Grown, uncoiled his lariat rope, made a swing at the mail box and away he went, dragging it up the road. The old fellow was standing in the door, saw this, grabbed his long range rifle from the wall, making the dust fly all around Grown, tho never hit him.

Westside - Wise River

Below Honacker Creek was some good land closter to the hills and bench land. Mr. George Vineyard took that up in the early 90s and made a good hay ranch from the rocky soil. Being a scavenger in Butte, he hired all of this ranch work done. This is a hard way to make a ranch. Tho he built lots of buildings up closter to the hill. A well had to be dug. The first one was abandoned and a second deep well dug before they could get enuf water for use. He often had questionable characters there. Cattlemen soon begun to miss cattle. On request from the people, the place was searched and the first well yielded the hides they were looking for. The brands were cut out and being so decayed, they had to let the matter there rest. They knew the culprits, but could not ferret any one and the matter dropped for the time. The place was far away, which made a good rendezvous for cattle rustlers.

Finally the place passed one from another till I believe the bank has it now [*1937-38*]. This land, like a lot of bottom land, raised good crops for a few years, then if not fertilized every year it becomes poorer.

John B. Trueman, Sr. (Tax Joke)

Being an old, stooped, grey haired man in the first of the '90's, enjoying the comforts of a saloon in Dewey and taking in the situation, as an assessor had come to town enquiring of those there about their taxable property. John, thinking of his past career, he had not gathered much of the world's goods, to be sure, and it seemed awful to be setting there. Possibly his turn would be next. Just what had he; to be sure he had eight children and wife. What else? Yes, a log cabin he called home.

Thot John, "I must be a man among men, but how I never thot of this before and wish to be a man with property, especially at this time. " He could not possibly say no, I haven't a thing to be taxed after these long years of hardship in those 'Thair Hills'." Finally, after seeming hours, the assessor said, "Well, John you haven't anything to be assessed, have you?"

"The Hell I haven't," John replied.

"O excuse me," the assessor replied. "Well, I take it now, what have you?"

"A home here in town, a house and a [*unknown word*] block, wagons, horses and saddle horse, cattle, horses on the range, 2 milk cows."

Yes, John really had them in his mind. Now his mind was relieved. He had made a clear breast of the whole thing and the assessor thot he really was a man of influence and means.

He never thot of the consequence of such a declaration. In time he found out when his assessment came. There it was in white and black. $30.00 taxes for things he did not possess, tho he had gained in rank as taxpayer. But how could he manage to pay it? As it then was a hard scrabble to clothe, feed and house those eight children, he and wife. Even then they hardly could find the needcisity of life. The two older boys was then bringing in all they could working. Then work was not steady, but what of the taxes. $30.00 must be paid; if left over due, 10% added there too.

John Lawrence then often needed help. Dick [*Trueman*] was able to work, tho young and inexperienced. John Lawrence would over look his short comings if he needed a man. So Dick was told the tax secret. He got work at John Lawrence's and in the course of time paid the taxes, even tho he hardly had clothes to cover him. This was a burning lesson to John (Sr.) and never again did he want to pay taxes.

**Nettie and Roscoe "Rock" Hand
From the Susan Hand Collection**

John B. Trueman (Jr.) Fish Story

John B., Jr. was the baby of the large family. He spent his boyhood days on the ranch at Wise River. There being older ones to do the work, left him free to chase the hills for flowers, birds nests and like enjoyment. Fishing often, as that was a very much needed food in his mother's larder. Then, too, hunting was usually a needcisity, tho there was often leisure times. He enjoyed relations to such an extent, till all of those pleasures finally became a burden. Later, other brothers went to Butte and he soon followed, finding work in the mines. With so much money, he wooed a wife to help spend his money.

He longed for the freedom of the hills, with the wide open country, and they moved back to Wise River. The freedom of the hills there failed to provide food for the body. At the last resort he rigged up his fishpole and fished. Soon his hunger was stilled, catching a large mountain trout, he hurried to his cabin, built a fire and cooked and ate it at once. Maude, on awakening after he had finished his last bite of fish said, "Where is mine?"

He replied, " Maude, if you want a fish, there is the pole, go get it."

Shortly, I heard she left his board and bed.

Brubaker to Butte

In 1910 Al Brubaker decided he'd like to see the Buffalo Bill show, which was showing in Butte that July. Al never had any thot of dressing up in his house. But to go to Butte, he'd just have to have better clothes to go to Butte in. For this he'd be apt to run in to some friend.

He paused from mining labors in time to go to Meadow Creek and see Tice Dodgson. Tice always had a good suit and he believed he could get it and then it was his fit too. All dressed up next morning, he went to Divide early to catch the train to Butte. When a young man with his pack of cheese and crackers on his back,

---

Buffalo Bill Show

In visiting with Rock Hand, he told of going to the Buffalo Bill Show in Butte as a child. It seems that his uncle, Seth "Big Al" Halbert, had known Buffalo Bill from somewhere in his travels and took Rock to meet him. – mc

he'd not have taken the train and by walking all night he might reach Butte in time for the show. Now he was older. Then to impress his friends, he would go by train, not as he had 44 years ago. Well, what a change there would be?

Federal Census - State of Montana
1900
243,329 citizens

McKinzie

McKinzie was a Scotchman coming west quite early. He worked in Glendale at odd jobs. Married. Mrs. McKinzie came by stage in early day to Alder Gulch.

McKinzie worked for the Montana Mercantile Company in Melrose. Later moved his wife and family to Melrose. In '92 he had gone over to Gibbonsville and worked there; the wife and children were still in Dewey. There Jim, the oldest, a very good boy, could always find work. Laura was a waiter. Maude was a school girl of about 12 years. Earnest was a lad of eight or nine. Years passed on, the two oldest moved to Anaconda, Maude married and went to Canada to live. Earnest staid with his mother till she finally divorced her first man and married a Mr. Cross and they moved to Butte. After his death she lived on in Butte.

McKinzie never met me till that trip I went over to Gibbonsville on the freight team. When he found I was in town he made special effort to see me. He talked all the time, telling me what a good teacher I had been, coming up so clost to me he fairly spit on my face when he talked. Yes, it was quite a surprise, for I knew others that did not think so much of me.

Byron Hand
About 1910
From the Rock Hand Collection

Chapter XIII

Off to New Brunswick

****

Looking for a New Home

In 1910 Horace and Maggie sold their ranch at Wise River with the idea of moving back to Horace's native land in New Brunswick, Canada. - mc

Excerpt from a letter written by Susan Hand to Horace Hand April 9, 1991 - "They left there [*Wise River*] in 1910 and Pa traveled back to New Brunswick where he took an option to buy a farm. Mother followed, spending some time visiting her folks in Beloit, Kansas. John was 15 going on 16, Byron 13, Nettie 10, Rock 6 and Thelma 1 1/2 years of age. Mother carried, pinned in her bodice, the actual money they'd received for the ranch."

The following information is taken from "Our Hands", a brief story of the family based on Faye's memories and written by Faye Thompson Fleming and Vera June Thompson, March 1973, page 8. *These are relatives of Horace's living in Maine - mc* "On coming home from school one afternoon in September, we found there a big, blond, blue eyed man who looked as if he had just come off the range. When Uncle John Wilson asked mother if she recognized this man, she said, "If he isn't Horace, I would not know him." She had seen him only once in thirty years when he had made a short visit home. Mary and I were just overwhelmed with the "goodies" he brot, candy, nuts and bananas, more than I have ever seen except in bunches hanging in stores. He had sold his ranch in Montana and had selected a place above Woodstock, planning to bring his family shortly -- Aunt Maggie, John, Byron, Nettie, Roscoe and Thelma.

In those days the B & A Railroad always had a special round trip to Millinocket for $1.00 on Labor Day. (That is the truth.) Uncle Horace took Faye and Aunt Annie. Mother would not allow me to go and I surely felt abused.

At last the family arrived and plans for a home in Canada evaporated. Never underestimate the power of a woman! Aunt Maggie was homesick and refused to live in the east, but agreed to stay until after Thanksgiving. We were thrilled with these western cousins and listened eagerly to their stories. They rode horseback to school, since home was four miles distant. I can still picture John sitting on a chair tilted back on two legs and leaning against the kitchen woodbox. At fifteen he seemed very grown up to us. Nettie had her 11th birthday during the visit and we had a little birthday party for her. However, the gala event was Thanksgiving dinner, which was held at Aunt Edith's. We experienced quite a let down when the family returned to Melrose, Montana. Susan was the latest addition to their family, born not long after their return home."

> **Chinch Bugs**
>
> When the family visited in Kansas in 1910 there was a large infestation of insects, mainly chinch bugs. My grandfather, John Hand, always had the story told of going to church with the family during their visit. Upon the congregation singing "What Will The Harvest Be," John jumped up, yelled "Chinch Bugs" and jumped out of the church window. - *mc*

> The Horace and Maggie Hand Family Descendent Chart may be found in the Appendix E, page 299.

Excerpt from letter written by Susan Hand to Horace Hand April 9, 1991 - "John told me in 1968 that Mother wouldn't stay in that country where they had to tie the cows in the barn all winter and had to put "dope" (fertilizer) on the land in the spring."

So they got home to Melrose before Christmas of 1910 and continued looking for a location. They bought the Donovan place about 1/2 mile north east of town and moved there by the spring of 1911."

[*Upon the family's return to Melrose from New Brunswick, John was of the age to go to the various dances in the area. He sometimes would go by train, but most often would ride horseback. John, my Grandfather, related to me one such dance that he went to in Glen. He and Pat Smith decided to go, saddled their horses and took off. The only problem was they did not have the money to get into the dance. They went anyway and as they were riding along, a coyote chanced to run in front of them. Their immediate thought was "money for the dance". They proceeded to chase the coyote and roped him just as he went down a hole. When the horse came to the end of the rope, Grandpa said the coyote went "pop" right out of that hole and they had him. With the money received for the hide, they got into the dance. - mc*]

Chapter XIV

The Donovan Place

****

Mary E. (Raker) Speelman Donovan

The following is an interview conducted by Nettie M. Hand, Melrose, Montana, Assignment III - a school assignment (undated) - mc In an interview with Mrs. James Donovan in regard to her experiences crossing the plains and early life in this part of Montana she said, --

"I came to Montana by ox-team with my father from Topeka, Kansas in 1863. My father's name was George Raker. There were 100 wagons in the party, of which he was wagon boss. At Fort Laramie our party split up; many went over the Oregon Trail to Oregon and Washington. Only seven wagons remained, bound for Montana. The authorities at the Fort would not allow my father to leave with the seven wagons because of dangers from Indians, so we were forced to lay over in the Fort six weeks waiting for more emigrants going to Montana. Finally a party of 60 wagons was organized and we started. The party traveled too slowly to suit my father and he and six others started out alone. It was a dangerous undertaking. On our way we met Mort Lott, an old time resident of Montana, and party on their way east to spread the news of the discovery of Alder Gulch.

We arrived in Bannack August 1863. It had taken us six months to come. We just stayed one night in Bannack. Everyone was on the move to Virginia City and we followed the crowd. Virginia City was just one month old when we arrived. There were no houses. People were living in tents and shelters made of brush.

Father did very little mining. He cut timber, snaked it down the mountain and built cabins for the growing town. The buildings were all one-roomed log-cabins with dirt floor, a fireplace, a sliding board for a window and a slab door. Only one or two families in Virginia City had stoves."

Mrs. Donovan lived in Virginia City several years and says she well remembers when a hundred pounds of flour cost $75 and potatoes sold for 50 cents a pound. She says that for the first few years before people got to raising vegetables they bought sacks of dried peas and beans. They lived principally on wild game, coffee, and flour. The sorghum and bacon that they brought from Kansas became exhausted soon after they arrived. A few families were lucky enough to get through with a milk cow or two. Her father brought one and they had plenty of milk. Fruit, even dried, was unheard of in those parts at that time.

> **CARROT PIE**
> Two medium carrots grated and cooked in a little milk, then 2 eggs well beaten, 1 small teaspoon ginger and cinnamon each, 1/2 cup sugar, 1 cup milk. Bake in 1 crust.
> **From TESTED RECIPES by the Ladies' Aid Society 1st Baptist Church, Dillon, Montana, Tribune Publishing Company, Dillon, Montana 1913.**

When questioned in regard to entertainment Mrs. Donovan said, "I can remember of many times going ten miles by ox-team to a dance. Our evening lunch would consist of deer, antelope or elk meat, coffee and carrot pie. We danced old fashioned dances on the hard sod floor. When the sun came up we started home."

Mrs. Donovan remembers about the activities of the Vigilantes and was present at the hanging of the seven desperadoes in January 1864. She was well acquainted with Boone Helm, the outlaw who was hanged.

After the gold rush in Virginia City Mrs. Donovan moved with her father to Twin Bridges and tells of plowing a truck garden there for her father with ox team. Later she married James Speelman and they came to the Big Hole valley, where they took up the old Speelman ranch a half-mile north of the present sight of Melrose.

Regarding early days in and about Melrose, Mrs. Donovan said, "We came to the valley by ox-team from Twin Bridges in 1875. The only ranches in the valley then were those owned by Stone and Bow. Stone kept a stage station on what is now the Jack Smith place. The old stable is still standing. The Bows kept a hotel on what is now the Connor's place. Hecla and Glendale were at their best then. A little placer mining was being done around Butte but no copper had been discovered. All the provisions came up the Big Hole river from the South by freight teams. They crossed the river at the old Brown place eight miles south of town. Joseph A. Brown kept the toll road and bridge there. Food was about the same as we had had in Virginia City only wild game was not as plentiful. A good deal of bacon and cured meats were sent in from Utah. We gathered wild gooseberries and as soon as possible began raising gardens.

Occasionally the Nez Perces crossed the valley; they never camped for any length of time and they never caused any trouble. At one time they gathered and had a war-dance. The people organized a party to go and ask them what they meant. The chief replied that they meant no harm. The next morning they were gone.

Each day the stage met the freight teams that came in from the south and carried provisions and men to Hecla and Glendale. Hold-ups and robberies were daily occurrences. The Vigilantes did their last work in and about Glendale and Melrose and restored order in the valley.

The Oregon Short Line built to Melrose in 1881. Melrose was the terminus for about a year when the road was built on to Silver Bow. Melrose was a lively town then. There were fourteen saloons, two hotels, two stores, a bank, a school house, post office and dance hall. The population was about 400." [*Nettie received a B for her effort. - mc*]

Melrose, Montana
From the Thelma (Hand) Kalsta Collection

Mrs. Donovan & [*William*] Lacy

In the early days people "bear and forebear". So it was with her. She and Speelman were settled and had sufficient means. Cattle, horses and hay and only two of them, both hearty and strong. Lacys were new neighbors with a family. Mrs. Donovan helped them in many ways, loaning machinery, horses and even money. When the sheep bands came in, she furnished money while Lacy fought to drive them off of the range. Later the forest [*service*] helped to settle the range dispute. Then by that time she had sold the place and cattle to us. Lacy then would not stop fighting so he turned his attention to us. As usual, Mrs. Donovan would not see her friend run over and abused. The place had been hers and now she would not stand any of Lacy's abuses on us. Lacy claimed the line between us and him was not right. He had land in our field. He got a surveyor, then she got one. She came each day to talk things over and find the old corner stones. It took days to find them, as they were covered over by time. Finally, once found, she put up white flags. Mrs. Lacy had noised about that old lady (Mrs. Donovan) had packed those corner stones till she was bent over calling her the old woman, old hag and so on.

> *Mrs. Donovan must have helped more than just a few by loaning money when they had financial troubles* -**From the writings of Mary (Zunino) Carpita,** "Dr. said if he [*Cesare Carpita, Mary's husband*] din't leave the mine he won't live long so he gave all his tools to Lena and he went back to work on the section with Mr. Pach. He gave his share of the mine to Pit Lena and the 2 houses we had [*at*] Hecla we had borrowed money from Mrs. Donovan when Cesare was sick so we turned [*houses*] in to [*over to*] Mrs. Donovan for the money we had borrowed and that was in August 1918." - mc

Mrs. Donovan stalked over the fields and one day met Lacy. I saw her stand for an hour talking to him. She had known him and said, "No God Dam you, you want to ruin those new folks on my place. I've even gone down in my jeans and given you money to help you over your troubles and now God dam you, you quit." So he did. Lacy quit fighting.

Rebecca Jane Bryant

Rebecca Jane Bryant, widow of E. G. Bryant, passed away at the age of 73. [*January 22, 1911 - taken from Hazel Madden's records, Hazel being Mrs. Bryant's granddaughter - mc*].

From a letter written by Susan Hand to Horace Hand, April 9, 1991 - "I was born there [*at the Melrose Ranch*] that fall - the only baby Mother had a doctor for, Dr. Mueller of Melrose who had graduated from medical school in Montreal and spoke with a French accent. He had one of the first cars in Melrose but also kept three fine driving horses for some time.

Mother said Dr. Mueller was out with Pa looking over our horses when I was born. Mrs. Thompson, mother of Bertha Streb, was the midwife. Mother was 42 when I was born - it must have been a hard spring and summer for her. She suffered from anemia after I was born and Dr. Mueller prescribed red wine. Nettie, near twelve when I was born, cooked the breakfast that morning and she is in my earliest memory as my caretaker.

Maggie & Horace's sixth child, Susan Edith Hand, born October 1, 1911 at the ranch at Melrose.

On the Donovan place we had a grove of big black willows, imported from Oregon to early Montana. In the willow grove we had a spring, a hammock, a teeter-totter, and an old tread mill to play on - really a fine playground.

There was a big red barn, cattle sheds, wagon sheds, granary, and bunk houses which probably had been the first home buildings. The house was too small for us so the boys lived in the bunkhouse. Mother kept out there the two harness rug loom Mrs. Donovan had given her.

The house had a small lean-to kitchen but it had the convenience of a sink and a pump. There was the old kitchen range, the noisy coffee hand grinder that was my alarm clock. The dining room was large - was the center of all activity besides the meals - I played dolls or with pups, which I preferred. Then the table was for homework where Nettie earned her pins for Palmer Method penmanship. Always there was reading aloud in the evening - often from the Youth's Companion where good authors were published. And there was story telling, too. I can remember Magic Lantern pictures - stills, of course, as a special treat. We always ate, all 3 meals, in the dining room as the kitchen was too small. I can't remember but I think there were 2 or 3 bedrooms. (Later, 2 Rock says). This house burned maybe 1940's.

We also had a gas lighting system which Rock can describe. Gasoline I mean. And there were lightning rods on the house."

CAPT. HALBERT DIES

Soldier Passes to His Last Resting Place This Morning

FUNERAL THIS AFTERNOON

It was a shock but not a surprise this morning to learn that captain Enos Halbert had breathed his last in yielding to the call of the great commander whose final order cannot be disobeyed.

Captain Halbert was one of the best known of the Mitchell county pioneers and one of the most highly respected. Most of his life was spent in Kansas on a farm in Eureka township; there the captain lived as a highly prized and influential part of his community winning the esteem of his neighbors in the civil life as he won it from his comrades in the military life. The title of Captain, won in the army never left the soldier.

Captain Halbert at the time of his death was 87 years of age and had been in poor health for several months.

He leaves to mourn his death, his wife and six children. One of the children live in Mitchell county. Their names are Mrs. Mary Wilson and Mrs. Hattie Jones of California, Mrs. Emma Briggs of Rooks county, Kansas, Mrs. Maggie Hand of Montana and Mrs. Annie Briggs of Lawrence, Kansas, and Seth Halbert of Montana. Some of Captain Halbert's grandchildren, children of Mrs. Wilson, live in Eureka township in this county. At the time of his death his daughter Annie--Mrs. Briggs of Lawrence--was at his bedside. None of the others will be here. Enos Halbert was Captain of Company I of the 33rd regiment of Indiana Volunteer Infantry.

At the close of the war he was mustered out with the honor and lived in Indiana in private life until 1875 when he came to Kansas and settled on his farm in Eureka township.

The funeral was held this afternoon at 3:30 by the I.O.O.F. Lodge of Beloit from his residence at southeast corner of town where the deceased had lived the last few years. Burial was in Elmwood cemetery.

The pall bearers were A. Daugherty, J. W. Bartleson, Wm. Widger, Wm. Houghton, E. B. Williamson and W. C. Hoffmeister.

Enos Halbert
Died October 6, 1911 - Beloit News, Beloit, Kansas
From Maggie's Scrap Book

Mrs. Donovan and the Ghost

We bot the Donovan and Speelman place, in 1911 in January and took possession at once. They [*Donovans*] lived there with us for two months and then bot the Ladue Saloon. Sometime in the late summer she said to Horace, "I sold you this place and forgot to tell you about it being haunted."

Horace says, "Well, I am not afraid of a ghost, he and I will get on together all right, now don't you worry."

"Yes, but I want to tell you so when it comes in about September you will know what to expect. It will thump, thump on the roof and I know it is Jim Speelman's ghost. Now if you are afraid I'll do most anything to make it right with you as I meant to tell you and am so sorry."

Horace says, "Don't mind that, as I am sure you, Jim and I were always the best of friends."

She went home and in due time the ghost came just as she predicted one night shortly after I was in bed. I never yet let a ghost get the best of me so I'll see what this one is.

I slipped on my clothes and went cautiously out doors, all the time looking closely as possible in the dark night. Finally I located the thump, thump, thump. Must be on the roof. I first thot it was in the thick clump of trees nearby. Watching and waiting, that thump, thump, thump came again. Sure enuf, there was something small like an owl, yes an owl. Marching back and forth on the eve of the house, he would dance back and forth, then thump, thump, thump. Jim Speelman's ghost, sure enuf. Quietly going back in the house, getting the gun and tip toeing out, I shot the ghost. It tumbled down. I hung it up to show it to Mrs. Donovan the first time she came up. When I showed it to her and told her that was the ghost she said, "Of course it was, any damed fool aught have known that!"

From the Christmas Letter written in 1993 by Thelma (Hand) Kalsta she states, "When I was three, we lived in a long old house. During Christmas there was a tree in the corner, and believe it or not, Santa Claus came with a big gunny sack full of gifts - oranges and coconuts. Santa was wearing a big buffalo coat just like my Dad wore. His shoes looked just like my older brothers! That sack full of gifts was a wonder, a big bag of hard candy, a little cellophane bear that if you held it in your hand it would turn over, and a big teddy bear and a buggy for him to ride in. We had no candles, only old kerosene lamps lit the room. Santa didn't have any sleigh bells, but cow bells were used and seemed to do the trick. We found out many years later that Mrs. Donovan from Melrose had sent all the gifts to us children."

When Automobiles Came to Melrose, Montana

by Rock Hand

The first car that came to Melrose area was a Sears Auto Buggy. Frank Tate showed up with it. These cars was sold on a 10-day money-back guarantee. Tate didn't have much luck with it. He had a hard time getting it over the Big Hole River bridge and out to his ranch. In fact he had to have a team of horses pull it to the ranch after the salesman demonstrated it, and in a couple of days it was setting out on the road abandoned. Someone came out from Dillon and started it up and took it back. Then Tate showed up with a new Apperson touring car. This was a big car with a 4-cylinder engine and it ran for many years, winding up at our ranch with the engine made into a motor to run a wood saw.

Shortly after Tate bought the Apperson, a salesman brought in a new Hupmobile touring car and sold it to Streb brothers who ran the Iowas House in Melrose. In a short time afterward he sold a Hup roadster to the saloon keeper, Jim Donovan, and another Hup roadster to Dr. Mueller.

I think it was sometime in 1913 or 1914 that the next cars to show up was the Model T, brass radiator, Ford. My sister, Nettie, and I went to Dillon by horseback to bring back some horses, and as we went into town the Montana Garage in Dillon was unloading a carload of Model T's and they were shipped in crates stacked one on top of the other.

Mr. Evans, who lived at the mouth of Cherry Creek, bought the first Model T, as I remember it. Mrs. Reynolds, the grandmother of Benny Reynolds, bought one, and was probably one of the first women in that area that learned to drive an automobile.

In any event the Model T's weren't too popular because the only way they ever got over a lot of the hills was either by a team of horses or by some horseback rider that gave them some help with a rope on the saddle horn. Sometimes they could make a hill by backing up because the reverse gear had more power than the low gear.

Horses didn't have much use for automobiles. One day I was riding up the road with a friend I was visiting with and had my roan saddle horse tied behind his wagon. Mr. Evans came along with his Model T and as he pulled out to go around the wagon my horse swung and kicked out one of his brass headlamps. I didn't have to pay for the headlamp but I took a good cussin' bout it because I was leading the horse instead of riding him.

By the time 1917 rolled around many makes of cars showed. The Model T became quite popular because a touring car sold for around $295.

In 1915 the Dodge touring car showed up and it proved to be a sturdy car that could pull most any hill that had a road on it. It was popular with sheepmen because they could pull their sheepwagons when they moved camp. They weren't so good in the high gear but the low gear was very popular.

The livery stable man in town bought the first Dodge touring car that came to town and paid for it in a short time by taking people from place to place. One of the Slater boys bought a new Dodge and was telling people about how it pulled the hills in high gear as he drove it home from Butte, but when he showed the livery stable man how well it ran he found out that he had driven it all the way from Butte and never had shifted higher than second gear.

Later on someone came out with what they called the Rukstell rear axle and that could be installed on the Model T and that made it easier to pull the hills in our area. A sheepman by the name of Fisher was the first one that I remember with one of these Ford Model T's that had this type of axle, but later on he bought a 4-cylinder Buick that was very satisfactory for his work. When he sold his sheep ranch he bought a big 8-cylinder automobile that I remember was a National. Then, because he had money he bought two big trucks, one a Republic make and the other a Kissel. He hauled ore for the mines, but even with hard rubber tires they didn't last too well and soon all the ore hauling in our area was left to the horses.

In 1917 when I was working for Vince McCauley, he traded in some horses on an automobile. It was an Overland, and that was probably where the idea of trading in your transportation for some that was new and modern started.

The Chicken Gulch Sheep and Cattle Fight
Spring of 1912
by Rock Hand

Recently my friend Eugene Dunlop, who is just two months older than I asked if I could remember the sinking of the Titanac. I certainly did remember because it was about the time of the sheep and cattle fight over the Chicken Gulch grazing area in Silver Bow County. The Camp Creek Stock Association of cattlemen were all gathered at a miner's cabin in Old Soap Town. They were afraid to move and were out of grub because there had been a killing of sheep and the cattlemen were getting the blame for it.

Our ranch was just 1/2 mile north of the town of Melrose and one evening a man came to our house and asked my mother if I would take a pack horse with provisions to the men that were at Karl Christian's cabin in Old Soap Town. My mother said absolutely no, that I was not to get mixed up with their fight because of my age. But I was sure ready and between the visitor and I we convinced her that there was no danger. I was ready far before daylight when they brought the pack horse for me and I took off with a feeling that I was the most important man in the world. Just leading a pack horse for about six miles wasn't much of a chore and in less than 3 hours I was at the camp. However at the mouth of the canyon I met up with two men who asked me where I was going. I didn't know them so figured they were just inquisitive.

I was met with a lot of praise for a job well done, but they were more interested in a big baked ham and many loaves of bread but most of all with the evening before newspaper which had an article about the sinking of the Titanac. That is how I remember the approximate date of this sheep and cattle fight.

The people at this miner's cabin were my father, Horace Hand, who was president of the Camp Creek Stock Association, Jim Brown the forest ranger for that district, a Mr. Stockdale the forest supervisor (Stockdale drove an Overland roadster that was quite an automobile in those days and the only automobile there). Then there were the following cattlemen, Pat and Jack Smith, Pat Connor, a Mr. Allen and John Collins, a Montana Stock Inspector. The forest service men were there in the interest of the cattlemen that had grazing privileges in the Chicken Gulch district. The Montana Stock inspector was there as an officer to keep the peace between the two factions. During this meeting there was another Soap Town Miner by the name of Louis DeRivers that kept walking up and down the road. Some people thought that he was on the side of the sheep people because he had mining claims in the area of where the sheep were. The people thought that he might cause trouble, but nothing came of it. What transpired at this meeting I never learned other than the fact that there was a sheep killing and it was blamed on the cattlemen.

Prior to this argument between the cattlemen and the sheepmen an outfit from someplace in Idaho had shipped a train load of sheep over the Oregon Short Line Railroad to Divide, Montana where they unloaded them along with a camp tender, herder and a sheep wagon. They proceeded to move this band to the Chicken Gulch area a matter of 6 or 8 miles. As I remember the name of the sheep outfit was Dansie.

I never found out how this sheep killing came about until 40 to 45 years later. Patsy Streb, who was retired and living in Dillon and who was the cook at the Iowa House Hotel in Melrose clued me in on all the details. It appeared that sometime during the day someone set the sheep wagon on fire and it burned pretty much to the ground leaving just the wheels and running gear of the wagon. The herder had bedded his sheep down for the night and the remains of the wagon was setting on a hill above the sheep. Then sometime during the night someone removed the wheels and rolled them down the hill thru the sheep. This killed some of the sheep but from up on the hill many shots were fired into the band that resulted to more dead sheep. Evidently this made the herder or camp tender or whoever was looking after the sheep mad and they shot back in the direction of the firing. My brother John, who was 9 years older than me disappeared and wasn't located for a time, along with another young man, but they were found at one of the ranches asleep later on. At the time of the meeting at the Old Soap Town they didn't know what had happened to them.

Late in the day of the meeting the crowd dispersed and I went home with my father. It was then we learned that brother John was ok at another ranch. What was decided at this meeting I never knew but two or three days later a sheep train came thru Melrose and the Idaho sheep loaded up and headed for home. I was in town, in fact it seemed as if everyone was in town to see the sheep train pull out and as it left the depot the owner stepped on the caboose and waved good bye to Montana.

The one person that wouldn't discuss this incident with me was my brother John who never seemed to have a good word for Dansie or any of his relation. If he knew any of the details he never would talk about this Chicken Gulch Sheep and Cattle fuss and he has taken it to his grave.

The sheep and cattle range that existed in 1912 was where you could ride from the Big Hole River to the Highlands out of Butte, from there to the towns of Old Rochester and Twin Bridges along the Big Hole River. You could do this without opening a gate and besides the cattlemen I have mentioned the Sidenstickers, Seylers and other cattlemen used this area. Also there were many sheep outfits sharing this range like the Schultz brothers, the Hamples, Fisher, Vanoy and others I can't remember. There was a struggle for range but it seemed that they all managed to respect each others rights. They would help each other in need and seemed to visit with each other when they came to town.

One way the cattlemen stayed alive and I presume that the sheepmen did the same was to control the water holes. The cattlemen grubstaked people that had mining claims with water on them. For instance Bill Fleming had the Barrel Springs, Bill Moore had water on Corral Gulch, Jimmy Lamb, a placer miner had a reservoir that impounded practically all the Soap Gulch Water plus other miners in the area. Then there was the Forest Service that allotted land on the forest for grazing. Now it is a different story, the entire area is fenced.

From writings of Rock Hand, dated 1989, titled "The Horace Hand Family", Rock states, "John, the oldest, was born in 1895 and was a great older brother for the entire family. He was put to work real early. Early in life he fed cattle, opened water holes in winter by chopping ice and in all really did a man's work by the time he started to public school and even before he was in school. He grew up fast. I can still remember one day when Dad led the colt out to a patch of plowed ground and John got onto the colt while Dad held the colt. The colt bucked John off but John got back on and this time he stayed on. I was about 5 years old at the time. John broke and trained our saddle horses as he grew up. Two of the finest horses we ever owned were horses that John had broke, Nig and Baldy. We had them for years."

Hand Home on the Ranch at Melrose, Montana - 1911
From the Rock Hand Collection

From an interview with Rock Hand by Myrna Carpita in 1992, Rock tells about his brother John leaving the ranch. "John went to a dance one time and never come home. There was a masquerade dance and he had his suit case with his masquerade stuff in it. He never went to the masquerade, it was his traveling suit case. He grabbed a freight train. I guess Pa wasn't going to let him leave the ranch, and the next morning when we woke up John wasn't around. What had happened is he had grabbed a freight train and what was suppose to be his masquerade suit in there but it was his every day clothes. So he made it into Butte and this old guy had a ranch, he was running the Pittsburgh mine, and he was over by Whitehall somewhere and John had known him and he got him to let him work on this ranch over by Whitehall and John disappeared. Dad went to Butte and he guessed it right, this fellow Ray was the foreman of the Pittsburgh. So he went to see Ray first as he figured John was there. But Ray wouldn't tell him that John was over on his ranch. It was quite a deal. Susan was just a little youngster. She was just all for John. John had her spoiled rotten I think. And by gosh, it just made her sick cause she lost John. Couldn't figure out why he wasn't there."

Later in the interview Rock stated that John was not yet 21 when he ran off and his Dad figured he could get him back but that was the last time John lived with his folks. Rock further states that "It was shortly after that he was going with Ida [*Hartwig*]. They were pretty thick, and he brought Ida up to the ranch. My Dad thought a lot of Ida. She was a likable person."

It was in the Melrose area that John became interested in mining. Hecla and Glendale had been good producers and he liked what they had done. He went to work in the mines at Butte and attended night school to become a hoistman. John helped off and on at the ranch and also worked in the mines to make extra money."

Nettie, Thelma and Susan Hand
About 1913-1914
From the Rock Hand Collection

From a letter written by Susan Hand to Bernard and Annette, (undated) she stated, "When I was very small, on the Donovan Place at Melrose, where I was born, we had an old cylinder type phonograph with the cylindrical records. It wasn't much of a recording device. I was more interested in the trade mark, showing a terrier listening, "His Master's Voice"! When we were in high school we fell heir to an old hand wind job with flat disks and used to play it when we cleaned house mostly."

From a letter to Bernard and Annette dated 1975 from Susan Hand states, "The money for the piano was Mother's, about $300, which was a large sum in 1915; it may have been from Grandma Halbert's sale of the old home after her death. We never knew about the arguments and differences of our parents but the argument over the purchase of the piano, I do remember, and remember when it arrived."

"The Piano Box"
by Thelma (Hand) Kalsta

> **Susan (Shirley) Halbert Passes**
>
> Susan (Shirley) Halbert passed May 2, 1915 in Beloit, Kansas. Susan was born the daughter of Henry and Catherine (Wyman) Shirley on February 17, 1828 in Orange County, Indiana. She married Enos Halbert on January 16, 1848 in Orange County, Indiana. She came to Kansas in 1875 with her husband and family.
>
> She was proceeded in death by her husband, Enos Halbert, and her daughter, Sarah Elizabeth Halbert. She is survived by daughters Mrs. Mary Wilson and Mrs. Hattie Jones of California, Mrs. Emma Briggs of Rooks County, Kansas, Mrs. Maggie Hand of Montana and Mrs. Annie Briggs of Lawrence, Kansas and a son Seth Halbert of Montana and numerous grandchildren.
>
> Burial was in Elmwood cemetery in Beloit.
>
> **Beloit News, Beloit, Kansas**

The piano mother bought, from Ortans in Butte, when we lived on the Donovan Ranch north of Melrose. She got the money from her mother's estate. As I remember it cost $100.00. Mrs. VanWart worked for the Ortens and got a good deal, but mostly a high grade instrument (Reed & Sons). It came by train (freight) to Melrose freight station in a box and was hauled the mile or so on a lumber wagon. That was a Big Day. It filled up a space that was empty. Sometimes the couch was there, but when winter came it was moved to the other end by the stove. Nettie was suppose to learn to play. We were too little. She did, Mrs. Heinz taught her - got even up to Humerske and any church music. Then we sold and moved to Melrose. They put the piano back in the box and moved it again on the lumber wagon. I can well remember the party they had in the bunk house for the boys who were going off to war - World War I. They sang and laughed and played the piano. One boy played a mouth organ. I liked the sound of that. Otto Harvey and Henry Eighorn never came back. Otto Harvey's remains was finally sent to Arlington Cemetery (Nettie may have gone back there as she was engaged to be married to Otto prior to his leaving for the war). In about 1 1/2 years in Melrose we moved here (Lavon), Earls Ranch. They put the piano back in the box and loaded on the same lumber wagon and brought it here. April 1, 1918 this was a new house. McLaughlin from Dillon came with 12 men and they stayed until they finished, there was a few shavings and smell of fresh paint when we moved in. The grandest thing of all there was a (new fangled) piano window so the piano had a place to go. I can't remember anyone playing it but it sure looked nice, along with the brand new davenport, wood arms but real leather. And a brand new oak dining room set, a shinny new wood stove with a see-the-fire window and a lot of chrome. You feed the cottonwood thru the top door. It was on the other side of the room from the piano. And the piano box, well dad put a door on the side and we put the chicken feed (wheat) in it.

Nettie, Byron, Thelma and Susan Hand
At the Donovan Place, Melrose, Montana, 1916
From the Rock Hand Collection

Well, that was only for two summers because in the fall of 1919 he sold the ranch and in November 1919 struck out for Oregon to find a place where he could live with his rheumatism. He found a feed store in Junction City, Oregon and bought it. Well, they returned the piano box and put the piano back in it and loaded it in a box car on the Lavon siding along with most of our furniture (don't know what it cost) - all carried to the siding in the lumber wagon. We found an old mansion the banker owned to live in, plenty of room for the piano and it looked nice in the big parlor. There was a big barn on the square so Mother had the piano box put away and there it remained until we moved back to Montana in 1921. At that time the box was brought back to the big house in Oregon, and put the piano back in it, carried it to the railroad and shipped it back to the Lavon siding. Again it was loaded onto the wagon and taken to the big white house where it was uncrated and the piano put back in the house under the special "piano window" that had been especially built in the house for it. The piano box was retired and was used for a grain bin.

Trip to Moose Creek

From a letter by Rock Hand to a "Briggs Relative", written September 11, 1984 states, "In 1916 Harry and Bert [*Briggs*] drove into our ranch in Melrose in an old Model T Ford roadster with a box, but no top. I was 12 years old at the time and any kind of an automobile was interesting to me. They wanted to see my Mother and the family, especially John who was 21 and had left home. He happened to be firing a sawmill engine up in the Moose Creek Country some 20 miles over 1916 mountain roads. Knowing the country, I drew the job as guide. (40 mile round trip in an automobile!) We started early in the morning and got to the Gold Hill some 13 miles in about 5 hours. But here the joy ride ended. I don't think any Model T with conventional axle had ever made it. We pumped air into the gas tank to get it to feed, we backed up, zigzagged thru the sage brush, chucked the wheels six inches at a time and in about 5 more hours we made the top. As we headed down the other side it was as steep as a waterfall. Harry was driving and by the time we got to the bottom of the hill the brake band was gone in the transmission and he was using the reverse for a brake. Harry's one remark was "WOW". We spent the rest of the afternoon with John, had supper at the mill and headed back with a team of horses hooked to the Model T to get us back to the top of Gold Hill. By the time we made the bottom it was dark and there was just enough adjustment left in the low gear to keep going. In order to have lights on those machines you had to speed the engine, so when Harry ran out of road he would speed the engine and go another piece ahead. The following day the boys put new bands in the transmission, with several hour delay of fishing for a nut that dropped into the oil pan."

Pushin' it Home
From the Thelma (Hand) Kalsta Collection

[*In 1917 Horace and Maggie sold their ranch at Melrose to Patrick and Ora Connor along with 275 head of cattle. They then moved into Melrose and began their search for another ranch to buy. – mc*]

From the Dillon Tribune-Examiner, February 3, 1966, "John Hand Recalls Lifetime of Mining"

I grew up fast and my needs were for more money quicker, so I decided to try mining in Butte. I was to rest long hours and to only work eight hours, and I hardly knew what to do rest of time. I enrolled in Butte Business College two hours a day. It was a class for workers when the day shift went in the evening and our night shift went in the afternoon.

Then things went better. The least wages I got in the mine were $3.75. This was for only one month then wages went to $4.00 and again to $4.25. I worked all Sundays, I got in quite a lot of overtime, in nine months time I had taken in $1100. This was much better than I could of done as a cowboy at $40 per month.

I liked the mines. I also liked outside but money was the key. The next six years I would sometimes get out of mines and help fire sawmill boiler, but when it got cold I would go back in mines. Then I took a steam engineer's course in Butte Business College. I got to be a hoist man, and thought I would stick with it, but after I learned how things worked and had run different ones, something told me that I wanted to operate my own business of some kind. I tried stock raising but the price kept going down and I would have to go to the mines again.

United States Enters World War I
April 6, 1917

From a letter by Susan Hand to Bernard and Annette, (undated) - "Reader's Digest says people who were under 10 at the time don't recall the war. Well, I do and I was under six when it started for the U.S. I also remember the outlaw horse, Riley, that John couldn't break -- Pa sold him to go overseas before we got into the war - must have been 1916 or earlier. John told me when I was in Sheridan that horses were gathered up and shipped out of Dillon and he helped in the horse drives. I can remember feeling bad about Riley going to war, maybe to be killed with a cannon. I understood he'd have to cross the ocean by boat. I wish I'd written down about who bought him -- John knew the country that purchased the horses -- I think France.

From writings of Rock Hand, titled "The Horace Hand Family" dated 1989, Rock states, "John married Ida Hartwig at Reichle, Montana, on April 11, 1917. People came from miles away by train on the Oregon Short Line. The party lasted all night and the next morning everyone went home."

GLEN NEWS

(Special Correspondence)

Reichle, Po. O., April 12 [*1917*] -- a very pretty wedding took place Wednesday evening at nine o'clock when Miss Ida Hartwig and John Hand were married at the bride's home. The ceremony was performed by Pastor M. Hudtloff, of the German Lutheran church of Butte. The bride is the daughter of Mr. and Mrs. Julius Hartwig, and was born and raised in our midst and is esteemed by all. The groom formerly lived in the Big Hole basin, where his father owned a ranch, but sold out there and bought another near Melrose, where his folks Mr. and Mrs. Horace Hand, are living now. He is a young man of sterling qualities, and both young people have hosts of friends and are highly esteemed.

The bride wore a white crepe de chine dress with a flowing veil attached to a wreath of white flowers and looked very charming. She was attended by her sister, who wore a beautiful gown of pale blue radium silk, trimmed with lace of gold and pink silk. She carried a large bouquet of pink roses. Miss Juanita Fitschen, a cousin of the bride, was ring bearer, the double ring ceremony being used.

The groom was attended by Carl Hartwig, cousin of the bride. The ceremony was performed under a big evergreen arch, put up for the occasion. White carnations, also were used for the decorations. Over two hundred friends and relatives attended the wedding, people from Butte, Big Hole, Melrose, Dillon and all in the neighborhood being present.

A very sumptuous wedding supper was served to all present. The large dining room was then cleared for dancing and everyone present had a glorious time.

How well liked the young people are is shown by the long list of handsome and useful presents they received. From Mr. and Mrs. Julius Hartwig, two cows and a horse; calf from Julius Hartwig, Jr.; cow and calf from Mr. and Mrs. Al Halbert, also a casserole; twenty dollars cash from Mr. and Mrs. Jacobs of Kuna, Idaho; aluminum set, Peter Spritzer; chest of silverware, Thaddous Mauz; sterling butter knife, Mr. and Mrs. Ed Nikel; water set and butter dish, Erneat and Jack Waters; cut glass jam jar, Mrs. J. W. Grant; cut glass salt and pepper shakers, Miss Sybil Grant; Aluminum percolator, George Beehrer and daughters; pie server, Mr. and Mrs. Frank Beehrer; silver cut glass castor, Mr. and Mrs. J. W. McLean; china creamer and sugar bowl, Mr. and Mrs. L. R. Foote; silver cream ladle, Miss Maude Jones of Walkerville, silver butter dish, Mr. and Mrs. John Waters; silver fruit dish, Vincent McLean; cut glass fruit bowl, F. R. Gaines; cut glass bowl, creamer and sugar bowl, Mrs. Sheehan and family; bed spread, Mr. and Mrs. H. Cannon; Mr. and Mrs. F. Gransberry; hand embroidered pillow cases, Mr. and Mrs. C. Sassman; patch comforter, Mrs. Jacob Hartwig; sack of potatoes, Mr. and Mrs. K. Hauser; dresser scarf, Mrs. Gladys Oliver; cut glass spoon tray, Mr. and Mrs. Fred Oliver; sterling sugar shell, Mrs. and Mrs. Alois Fassler; sterling silver cream ladle, Huber Bros.; linen table cloth, Mr. and Mrs. John Lenkersdorfer; cash, $5, Mr. and Mrs. Geo. Gross; two picture frames, Mrs. McGowan; embroidered pillow cases, from Mrs. Meade; cut glass creamer and sugar bowl, Miss Hazel and Babe Hand; table linen, Fred Hartman; cash, $20, Mr. and Mrs. Laurenz; gasoline iron; Mr. and Mrs. Allen and Ralph Dutch; percolator, Mr. and Mrs. Wm. Lacy; berry spoon, Mr. and Mrs. Arthur Jones; pickle fork, Mr. and Mrs. Delbert Jones; berry spoon, Mr. and Mrs. Marlow; embroidered pillow cases, Mr. and Mrs. F. Dodge; percolator, Mr. and Mrs. N. Ahers; one set silver salad forks, Ladies Social club; carving knife and fork, Mr. and Mrs. Frank Bryan, berry spoon, Miss Cora Bryan; small cut glass bowl, Eliza Bryan and Pat Schmid; embroidered pillow slips, Mr. and Mrs. A. C. Hood; piece-quilt Miss Zerr and school children; glass table set, Mr. and Mrs. Robert Joy; cut glass salt and pepper shakers, Misses Mary, Anna and Angela Buyan; china plate, Mr. and Mrs. Jake Mittelmier; china plate, Mr. and Mrs. F. C. Green; aluminum tea kettle, Mrs. Eliza Garrison; carving set, John Halls and daughters; table cloth, Wilfred Lewis; cash, $5, Ernest Zabel; three comforters, Mr. and Mrs. H. Hand; table cloth and napkins, Miss Nettie Hand; carving set, Roscoe Hand; pair pillow cases, Mrs. G. VanWart; table cloths, Mr. and Mrs. A. Maier and son; percolator, Joe Wample; set of dishes, Bluebird pattern, Mr. and Mrs. Gus Fitschen; three sacks of potatoes, Hartwig Bros.; two guest towels and flower sifter, Mrs. C. L. Jellison.

THE DILLON TRIBUNE
Friday, April 13, 1917

John and Ida Barbara (Hartwig) Hand
Wedding Picture
Aprill 11, 1917
Courtesy of Louise (Hand) Shafer

Our Wedding

From the Dillon Tribune-Examiner, April 20, 1967 - By John Hand (as related at the Golden Wedding Reception – 1967 at Argenta, Montana)

On our wedding day – April 11, 1917 – at the home of Mr. and Mrs. Julius Hartwig in Glen, 50 years ago, I will recount different little things that happened.

The main travel was on the railroad; there were two passenger trains past Glen each way, 9 a.m. and 7 p.m. southbound; 3 p.m. and 2 a.m. northbound. The 50th anniversary was to be on the same line so our family has gone to work and has brought things in shape for this day.

The Hartwig family worked hard to prepare for the wedding and there was a big gathering. They had a large house with a spacious dining room and the stairway to the gable room above entered from the outside. The dining room was used for dancing.

Rev. Hudtliff came from Butte on the 7 p.m. train and he told us what to do. My wife's sister, Louise Hartwig Hirst, was bridesmaid and their cousin, Carl Hartwig, was best man, so we gathered up that trail of wedding gown and started down those stairs.

Entering the front room from the rear we faced the crowd. Everyone was looking at us and, as the minister began I had a curious time at trying to see how everyone was acting.

My bride didn't seem to be very nervous and Carl was pretty calm, but my wife's sister held a big bunch of flowers on her arm and those flowers were dancing around like magic.

- - - - continued

Our Wedding – continued

It was soon over and we started off the dancing. My pals were all set for me. They had a pole with a mountain sheep hide on it and were going to carry me down to the bar about 1/4 mile. I put up the best ride I could and then they said Eliza Bryan could haul all in his auto. There were 14 in it and after they had a couple of rounds they brought me back, but Eliza's car took him to Dillon and never ran again.

Eating and drinking and dancing went on till the 2 a.m. passenger train took most of the crowd. The hotel at Glen was full and some stayed at the Hartwig house. During the evening two switch engines came along and stopped. The four men came in for refreshments. The engineer's names were Charlie McGee and John Cosgrove; I did not know the firemen.

Carl Hartwig took us to the place that was to be our home for a while. I had rented this place, bought livestock and feed, had the horses in and was plowing so we had to be there next morning to take care of the stock.

My wife did not think much of my bachelor set-up – it had to be changed right now. We had new furniture at her home so I went out and caught two black horses that were pretty snappy. We only had a hay rack to hitch them to and about a mile and a half to go. We both got on and went to Hartwig's house and when we got there, there was help to load. We went up to the top place for some things and laying on a bed there was Matt Summers, his head in a dishpan and his feet in an ice cream freezer, sound asleep.

Some neighbors came by and helped to get the stuff straightened in the house and this, I suppose would be called a "Honeymoon."

From an interview by Myrna Carpita with Rock Hand in 1992, "I remember Mother and Net chasing me all over Butte for clothing for John and Ida's wedding and I wanted a pair of long pants, something different from the pants that they bought me. Oh hell, they looked like little Lord Falteroy pants and they made me so darn mad and when I went to the wedding everybody was bragging about how cute I was and that made me mad you know. I thought I was a man grown up. I didn't appreciate any part of it."

From an article titled "John William Hand" - by Louise (Hand) Shafer and used in the History of Beaverhead County, Montana, Vol. 1 1800-1920, copyright 1990, John and Ida "made their first home at the Foote Ranch, then the Hand Ranch and then to a ranch of their own across the Big Hole River. This was only a few of the many moves for John and his family. In Hecla he worked in the mines and Ida ran a boarding house, then back to the ranch where hail and water problems forced him back to Butte and the mines, then to Rocker, Montana just out of Butte where he worked in what he called the "slave station". This was where timbers were framed for the mines in Butte. He worked 16 hours a day, seven days a week, for $4.75 a day. From the "slave station" he moved back to Reichle to work on the bridge gang that was repairing the railroad bridge that was damaged in the Wise River flood. Then to Brown's Lake to mine for himself, then to Argenta to do some work for a mining company.

Ida was a very good cook, cooking for family, friends and boarders. She was noted for her pies of which she made many. No one came at mealtime and went away hungry. She always said there would be plenty, she would "just put another bean in the pot."

TIME MARCHS ON
by Rock Hand
Helena, Montana

Some people like to talk about the "Good Ole Days". But there is a vast difference between then and now. In those days when you wanted to go to a Saturday night dance, you got ready by takin' a bath in a washtub with water you had heated on the cook stove, dressed up in a suit you had owned for the last ten years, put on a pair of shoes that hurt your feet and took off with a horse and buggy to pick up your best girl after you'd have curried, harnessed and hooked up your best driving horse. At this time of year you had to have your earflaps, sheepskin coat, mittens and overshoes. Then you picked up your girlfriend who bundled up so much you couldn't tell if it was her or her grandma. The main thrill you got was from bundling her up with the lap robe.

Now days you call on the lady in an up to date automobile enjoying the music from the radio, with power steering you can drive with one hand, enjoying the comforts and romance of the modern age.

After you return home instead of unhookin' and feedin' the horse all you have to do is to drive up to the house, turn off the ignition, and call it an enjoyable evening.

Ed says the best part of these modern machines is you don't have to pitch fuel to them and then next mornin' shovel the exhaust out of the barn.

****

The Madisonian, Virginia City, Mt. December 15, 1983
[Note at bottom of the original to Shirley (Hand) Groff from Susan Hand - "Shirley, I copied this for you because John was the one who went courting in the buggy. I can remember it being washed and shined up for a date - Susan" - mc]

Reprinted by permission from The Madisonian, Virginia City, Montana

Chapter XV

Lavon

****

The Earl Ranch

The following information about the Earl Ranch, 1885 through 1887, was provided by Thelma (Hand) Kalsta to me. She received the information from the **Massachusetts Audubon Society**, August 24, 1973. The cover letter states that the information comes: "from the Journal of Henry S. Reynolds who was born in Providence, R.I., educated at the University of Illinois and worked as an assayer at Glendale, Montana Territory----"

"Mrs. Adelia Reynolds, wife of Henry, was a writer and included in the Journal as entries are occasional articles written by her for various newspapers and magazines in Montana Territory and outside of it."

Mr. and Mrs. Henry Reynolds had two small sons, Vinton and Ernest. On February 12, 1885 "Henry walked down there [*from Glendale to Earl Ranch*] again and Vinton, baby Ernest and I went by stage and train. We had a pleasant visit and came back on Sunday. We intended to come back Saturday night but no train came on account of a snow-blockade in Beaver Canyon south of Dillon. On Sunday before we came away, Mr. Earl had made a distinct proposition which Mrs. Earl acceded to, to sell an undivided half interest in the ranch, house, barn and other buildings, cattle, horses, pigs and poultry for $3500. Five hundred dollars down and the rest in ten percent interest bearing notes, with five years margin for the completion of purchase. To be more explicit: 3 horses, and 48 head of cattle. Later Henry went down and he and Mr. Earl worked on a plain board cabin to make it suitable for us to move into. It stands in the yard near the log house occupied by the Earl family. The fine large garden patch under the ditch is in the same enclosure with the dwellings. Mr. Earl arranged with his wife to buy her half interest in the heifers that she claimed, so all seemed well arranged. I anticipate much pleasure in our new home, God willing, although our house will be very small, and we must live very economically until the ranch is paid for. It is a beautiful spot for a farm home with the river in the foreground and the picturesque McCarty Mt. in the background, and includes every variety of scenery, and all changing with the suns rays in the morning, noon, and night. The R. R. swings around the curve as it crosses the river on the bridge just in front of our dwelling. There is a switch and flag station in the meadow field above our house. The station and post-office is at Willis station down the R.R. south from here three miles. Item. A cow was killed on the place by a train Friday morning." *Mr. Reynolds' Journal further states:*

"Geographical Location of the Ranch, Madison Co., Montana.

This country of varied scenery and of varied interest occupies a novel place in the physical features of this territory of Montana. It is bounded on the south by Idaho, on the west by the Beaverhead County and Silver Bow County, on the north by Jefferson and Gallatin counties and on the east by the National Yellowstone Park reservation and Yellowstone county. Its principle town Virginia City, county seat, was formerly the territorial capital. Twin Bridges, Sheridan, Ruby, Silver Star, Iron Rod, Pony, Tidlewave, Summit and other mining camps. The physical features are very diversified: mountains, broad bench lands, and valleys all giving grassy pastureage for herds of cattle. The marked feature of the county near our ranch is McCarty Mountain encircled on three sides by the Bighole river forming with Beaverhead river where they unite to form the Jefferson river north of Twin Bridges. The Central ridge of the county is the Virginia City uplift mountain range extending across the entire county from north-west to south-east. Next comes the Madison valley and beyond that the Madison range extending from north to south through the county. The Ruby Mt. being a spur from the Virginia range. Besides three main rivers and valleys there are numerous minor streams. If we start a section line from west to east we have first to leave Bighole River and our farm, next the McCarty Mt., then the Bighole River again, then the valley east of the Bighole, and then to Beaverhead River, then the Virginia range, then the Madison valley and river and then Madison Mt. and then the National Park. The Bighole river enters the county from Beaverhead County to the west of us. The Beaverhead river rises south in Idaho and runs northward across Beaverhead County, and then to Madison County at Point of Rock. The Ruby River is the main branch of the Beaverhead in Madison County and the Ruby River has a few branches of interest, the Alder Gulch noted for the rich placer mines below Virginia City and Georgia Gulch noted for its rich gold-bearing veins. Also Mill Creek on which is situated Sheridan. These streams all help the industries of mining and irrigation. Our ranch as we have said is located on the western plain lying at the foot of McCarty Mt. and is irrigated with the water from the Bighole River. A beautiful situation for a ranch and good for us for the next five years. I had the satisfaction of being able to eat the vegetables from the soil of the fertile Madison county. The chart accompanying this description [*we did not receive chart*] shows the location and tributaries of the Madison River as one sees them passing from Virginia City to Ennis on the trail to the Park. After leaving Virginia City the first is Bear Creek, Indian Creek, Wolf Creek, Squaw Creek, Pappose Creek. All these rise in the Madison Mts. and falling westward to the valley empty into the Madison River. One rises on Bald Mt., called the White Meadow Creek, flows eastward and empties into the Madison River. There are various hot springs which are found before we reach the National Park reservation. All curative and resorted to by patients. Various lakelets nestle in the basin areas through this county, well stocked with fish. One in particular is surrounded twice, a sort of natural refrigerator supplied by nature.

From what is known as the High Ridge mine, a person gets a most interesting view of valley, meadow and of the eastern plateau of the county. This mine is situated on the mountain side, a spur which breaks off from Virginia range near the head of Georgia Gulch where last year I had charge of an assaying plant of Armstrong & Hardesty: while at its base the billowy foothills of gigantic structure are streaked with mineral veins, the miner's dumps showing up in profusion. This Georgia Gulch is fringed with willows and aspens as well as the other creeks of this region. Just beyond we note the woodsy winding Wisconsin Creek, meandering in its course westward to meet Ruby River, while beyond we see the irrigated fields and ranch buildings showing well inhabited valley lands. Away southward the great snowy barriers shut out from view the National Park domain. At this time that I write Montana and Idaho are both territories. Bald Mt. is a land mark in this section of the country, a kind of nucleus for the mining prospector and mineral surveyor. On its southern flank lie two branches of Nugget Creek, and further south Wisconsin, Indian and Mill Creeks. Westward thirty miles away may be seen the Bannack range of Beaverhead county and this in plain view from our ranch. I can almost pick out the location of Lion Mt. with its wealth of mines on the western verge of our horizon lying at the head waters of Trapper Gulch. Just on our border McCarty Mt. with its wooded sides supply us with fencing and fire wood. Besides these scenic features and agricultural beauty spots for ranches, the geological structure is of equal interest. The lowest horizon of geologic times we find of gneiss granitic structure, then the slates overlying these, the coarse, gritty, sedimentary sandstones, then above these the lime-stone of dolomitic structure, but of carboniferous origin. In these we find the more marked fossils quite interesting for study. Then in the terraces bordering the river the later quaternary accumulations. At High Ridge, Bald Mt. station the sedimentary rocks show a dip southward 70 degrees west. The dip is light near the bench terraces and increases as we reach the central of upheaval in the mountains.

Can I reproduce the thrill of gratitude as we, a united family, open up this interesting home ranch life. I came down Wednesday with the furniture in our ranch wagon, and on Thursday Adelia and the two boys landed from the train at the Earl's Siding. I had carpets and rugs laid down and the cook stove set up and supper ready for their arrival. The next day Adelia's 32nd birthday, March 13th and a Friday. We are busy these early spring days getting settled in our rude cabin on the ranch. Our books, etc. The R.R. section men coming up the track on their hand car from Willis brought us our mail each day from our many friends east and west and also from publishing houses who from time to time are taking Adelia's stories and poems. We may say a word of interest concerning the Earl family. Mrs. Earl was our son Vinton's former Sunday school teacher in Glendale. There were two daughters Edith and Mabel. At first they were very friendly perhaps gushingly so and then there seemed to develop in Mrs. Earl's mind a settled purpose of antagonism akin to insanity that made kindliness and Christianity a back number in our experiences. Nature however has done its best to spread before us its rich stores of hope and gladness and in this store house of nature we revel for the space of five years in spite of evil corrupting influences springing from this unneighborly source.

Our early spring work began with the dairy, milking cows, butter making and the like. We had three horses, Billy the Indian pony for rounding up cattle, while Maid and Nellie were the two mares constituting our team. I never appeared on Billy in the towns or camps of the country, with his glossy, black, flowing mane and tail, with an impish cunning in his eye of doing surprising stunts and creating interesting situations for his rider, without eliciting interesting inquiries as to what I would take for him, and if they had seen him with me on his back tailing the wild cattle through the brush they certainly would have wanted to possess him at any cost. For he was indeed a treasure in cutting out cattle from the brush or from the pack. As a cow pony he knew his business even better than his master. Under many trying circumstances I can witness to the truth of this. He would quite frequently buck his unsuspecting rider from his back evidently to break up the monotony of the trail or for sheer fun. Sometimes he got clear away from me and galloped home, at other times I held on to his bridle as I went over his head. Only once was I ever hurt by these antics. Often his lariat rope would get loose from the saddle and dropping to the ground with me I would remount all right. His arriving home without me would not create a very great disturbance, for my wife and boys knew his tricks and expected that I would turn up in a little later all right.

The hens were provided for with nests so that we had a good flock of young chickens. Our poultry had to be guarded well from the prowling coyotes. We shut them up very securely in the henhouse every night. We had young pigs also to feed regularly, thus we had good meat supplies along with the fish of the river. The best feature of farm life was that the father could have the companionship and watch and care of his son Vinton in teaching him farm wisdom and noting his active interest in all farm matters.-----

The wagon trips to town with farm produce were also welcome past times. God made the country for parents to rear their own children and man made the town an artificial substitute for child culture. We had fences to build, irrigating ditches to dig and keep in repair, we had storage cellars to build and we had to supply ourselves with wood which we cut from dry timber on the public domain, McCarty Mountain. These logs had to be worked down the hill side and the butt end laid on sleds and the whole tree dragged down to the ranch a mile and a half or two miles away. New fields had to be cleared from greasewood and sagebrush, and they had to be ploughed and laid out for irrigation purposes, and then carefully seeded to wheat or oats or rye. We select favorable potato patches and from them we are able to glean

Train at Lavon pulled by a Steam Engine
From the Thelma (Hand) Kalsta Collection

shipments of potatoes for the Butte market by the car load. We aim to preserve our Sundays unbroken from the new routine of work, there being enough necessary work to keep the animals on the farm comfortable: but we had many pleasant family rambles on the hills. The ducks and geese on the river and the Jack Rabbit ever ready to spring forth from his form under a shrub. These wild creatures and many others we saw on our walks. "The Island" at the lower end of the farm and "The Canyon" and Brown's bridge at the upper end serve as trips for Sundays, while McCarty Mt. and Rock Creek one to the east and the other to the west of us supply us with one or several full days outings, camping for Fourth of July at Rock Creek Lake in the very heart of the mountain ridge. Each season of the year has its special call of the wild for nature revels in variety. Our work on the farm varies with the seasons. The plow and the seeder for the spring time, irrigation stunts for the growing time, and the harvest home, each has its special beauties. The reaping and mowing machines gives characteristic music in mid-summer time and the noisy music of the threshing and bailing machines of autumn, while marketing of produce, the sale of fat beefs and fishing break up the monotony at all times. We often take our lunches with us and make an all day job when the work is in a distant part of the ranch or we are chopping down timber in the mountains. Happy days and peaceful nights reward the diligent rancher. The river is engaging in its annual spring freshet and the big gate at the head of the irrigation ditch is opened to let in early irrigation waters. When Earl's ranch was located and the water right on the Bighole River, the mouth of the canyon was wisely chosen where an island divides the river into two portions. The part on our side of the island being the one we dam to throw the water into our ditch. There is hardly a road left for the railroad to come between McCarty Mt and the Bighole river at the place where our head ditch is located. Mr. Brown on the west side of the river gets his head ditch from Rock Creek instead of from the Bighole River. Our ranch broadens out into a broad grassy meadow after the canyon has been left behind. Our ditch supplying water for this meadow land and for the narrow bench land toward the southern part of our ranch, so our market crops are grown favorably in both sections of our ranch. Corn is not a product for market in this mountain valley of Montana but grass, wheat, rye, oats, barley and flax are abundant crops for the market. The ranch is capable of giving industrial support to our two families and one or two farm laborers as well the year around, but as Mr. Earl can make good money at his business of superintending the mines and reduction works he has been engaged at in Colorado and soon after we moved upon the ranch he went to Curay mining district and left a man to work on the farm in his place, a Mr. Carley. He was to work with me in ranching. Mr. Carley and the Earl girls came over to sing in the evenings. My wife playing her organ for the improvised chorus.

Adelia kept up her writing for the Montana papers: her stories, poems and reviews appear in the Butte Miner, The Helena Herald and the Dillon Tribune. Quite a number of newspapers outside of this territory are also publishing her writings both on the Atlantic and Pacific borders, also in Chicago papers and The Sunny South. She enjoys this literary work and shows literary skill in reviewing current literature and in the Christian tone that she always uses in her original stories."

[*Excerpts from Mr. Reynolds' journals go on to show that there are many tramps that come along the railroad track. They feed them and often the tramps will work for a few days and then travel on. Their livestock herds continue to grow, with the major problem being their cattle are often killed by the train. The garden continues to produce, supplying them with "a fine crop of potatoes, peas, radishes, lettuce, beets, tomatoes, onions, cabbages, turnips; all showing very* beautifully under irrigation." Both Mr. and Mrs. Reynolds continue writing, collecting plant and insect specimens and they "organized a home chapter of the Agassiz Ass'n. for our own interest and our neighbors become interested in nature study too. The neighbors often bring in or send to me specimens." The specimens collected were not only for their own interest but for various Universities in the midwest and east, including specimens from Yellowstone Park. –mc]

The Journal shows that "about the middle of August the twelve tons or so of meadow hay was cut and stacked from the railroad meadow north of our houses and then the timothy meadow lands south of the building was harvested also. Thus the chief crop of the ranch was quite a success and later was bailed and loaded into cars at Earl's Siding and sent to the Butte Market. The same was also done with vegetables, potatoes being the chief item. Several tons of turnips were not marketed but were used for the cattle in winter.

In the spring freshet much drift wood comes down the stream and we can catch it on the side bushes on the piles of the railroad bridge, thus adding to our firewood materially. We use the river water for all household purposes although we have a well on the place. In winter we keep a hole cut in the ice near our shore of the river. November days see us in the potato patch harvesting our crop and also taking them to market at Glendale and Melrose as the prices there are good this season. Mr. Earl has returned from Colorado and is here again at his house on the ranch. We are looking up the prospect of keeping the water in the river from receding from our gate in the canyon as the water has been doing - the other side of the island promising a scant supply in the future. The high floods of the summer just passed swept out some of the dam rick work that had been placed in the river on the ice the previous winter and there dropped in place. It is a problem to take water successfully from the river bed that has a pitch like the Bighole River and has floods of high water in the spring. Our first year at the ranch has been a series of variety phases. The worse phase being the Earl family. The mother and her two daughters. We close these notes of the first year with hope for the future. If we succeed on this ranch it will satisfy our physical desires for a pleasant rural home life, and if other plans come in we await the Divine Leading, for we seem unable ourselves to trim our sails to catch friendly breezes and to escape cyclone visitations."

The situation with the Earl family only worsened as time went on. Mrs. Earl apparently became more and more erratic in her actions and talk. Upon Mr. Earl's return from Colorado he found the situation, "uncomfortable at his house and attempted to get possession of the girls legally, taking the ground that the mother was mentally unbalanced. First on the farm and then in Virginia City the doctors and court agreed with our nearby neighbors' judgment that she was not insane."

As matters progressed, Mrs. Earl was given a court hearing. Mr. Reynolds writes, "The following week Vinton and I as well as Joe A. Brown, our nearest neighbor, was present on the day appointed for the trial. It lasted from Thursday to Saturday evening. The doctors agreed that she was a lunatic and not fit to have charge of her children but not altogether insane and not to be placed in an insane asylum. We arrived home on Monday morning by train. Mr. Earl kept himself in a room upstairs in his own house, getting his own meals, etc. Mrs. Earl immediately instituted a suit for divorce and guardianship of the girls and support of the girls and herself from Mr. Earl. Ten days after she entered the pleas, Mr. Earl was served with papers of arrest for cruelty. Mr. Brown went to Glendale and got 45 men to sign a bond for Mr. Earl and then went home and brought Mr. Earl home with him. This because Mr. Earl would not give bail and so was a prisoner of the county. Trial postponed for some future time, and Mrs. Earl was completely non-pulsed at the proceedings. Mr. Earl takes his meals with us but sleeps in the garret in his own house through February. --------- The neighbor that had helped Mrs. Earl in her lawsuit against Mr. Earl was forbidden by Mr. Earl of coming on to the place. He comes however twice a week as far as the boundary of the ranch and Mrs. Earl or one of the girls meet him on the range. He brings her mail, packages and fresh meat."

Railroad siding at Lavon
From the Thelma (Hand) Kalsta Collection

Work on the ranch appears to go on as normal, with spring planting, new calves, etc. taking place. One note that was made by Mr. Reynolds is "A stage robbery was attempted upon the Glendale and Melrose line of coaches a few nights ago and George Ferguson, a stage driver was murdered, shot in his driver's seat. A passenger on the seat with him caught the lines and brought the team and coach through into Glendale without being robbed."

The Reynolds' have visitors at various times, which they enjoy. He further writes, "I have not spoken of another set of callers that we entertain on the ranch from time to time, a bunch of Bannack Indians under the leadership of Major Jim. They come about every summer to camp here. The Indians are polygamous and Major Jim wants Adelia to meet his wives and children. Major Jim waxes quite indignant if any one shows fear of him or of his people. Mrs. Earl tries to make out that she and the girls are afraid of them, shutting the door in their faces when they ask for biscuit or salt and various other things. "They are great beggars." Major Jim tells Adelia in a scornful tone -- "The Earl woman afraid, afraid of Major Jim." The tone of voice that he uses shows that he is very indignant over the matter."

From Mr. Reynolds' Journal dated September 24, 1886, "Mr. Carruthers, sheriff of Madison County came down from Virginia City and served an arrest notice on me for assault and battery on Mrs. Earl. The idea; like her trumped up charge on Mr. Earl. She charged him with cruelty, binding her with a heavy binding chain, etc. I had never touched her, had always walked off when she dared me to a tussel or opened an altercation with me. No specifications or details or time or place was in the summons at all. The sheriff took dinner with us, and then kindly offered to go up to Glendale with me to get bonds or decide what to do. Mr. Earl being at this time re-employed by the company at his old job. We took Billy behind us and at sundown I rode home alone. Everything being fixed up for the present. Mr. Earl and Joe A. Brown signed the bond for my appearance when I was needed at Virginia City."

A note made further on in Mr. Reynolds' Journal states, "Our Glendale house is now rented at $7 a month and some little repairs are to be put upon it by the new tenant, Frank Tate. His wife is Mr. Carley's sister. Her name was Nina Tate. I bought a piece of meat at 18 cents per pound, also a pitch fork at Glendale. Frank the new man, was greatly amused at some of Mrs. Earl's antics which he witnessed her going through with some days ago."

November 7, 1886, notation in Adelia's Journal notes, "Henry has been at Virginia City some days at court. His assault and battery case was dismissed and he got home last night. Mrs. Earl was not on hand to appear against him. It had been set three distinct times. The divorce case comes off tomorrow, so she probably had too many irons in the fire at one time to attend to them all."

November 13, 1886, "Mrs. Earl has secured her divorce and secured permission to stay on the ranch until next term of court when the alimony question will be settled."

November 23, 1886, "a copy of the Earl Divorce Decree and an order for us to leave the ranch. Word from Virginia City however comes to us that the Court Decree does not interfere with us. We are busy getting our wood down from McCarty Mountain for our winter use."

[Thus ended the information from the Journals. Thelma (Hand) Kalsta states that Mrs. Earl did eventually end up with the ranch and letters to Horace Hand from Mrs. Earl show her as sole owner of the ranch. As to what other settlements were reached with Reynolds and as to the total outcome is not shown in the Reynolds' Journals. - mc]

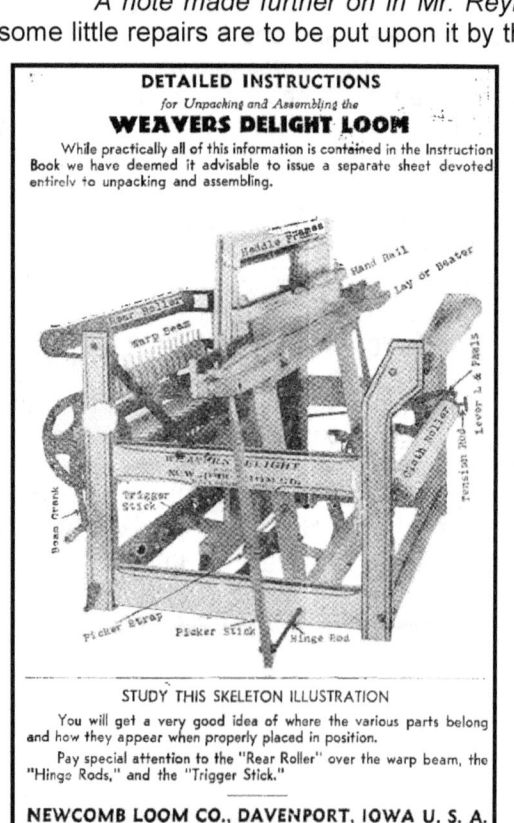

Newcomb LoomCo., Davenport, Iowa U.S.A.
This was pictured on the front of the envelope that contained the instructions for the
WEAVERS DELIGHT LOOM.
From the Susan Hand Collection

From a letter written by Susan Hand to Janice Hand, dated March 14, 1983, Susan states, "In 1917, Mom came over to the state fair at Helena and saw a display of four-harness pattern weaving, put on by Mrs. Mary Atwater, who was just then reviving the old art -- this was before her book which is basic to a weaver." *[This was apparently the beginning of a long friendship between Maggie and Mrs. Atwater, as I find a lot of correspondence between the two ladies. - mc]*

[Horace and Maggie eventually purchased the Earl Ranch at Lavon, a flag stop on the Oregon Short Line. There they built new fences, ditches, cleared land and built a large new home. - mc]

From writings of Susan Hand, dated August 15, 1983, she writes, "When we moved to the Earl Place at Lavon, on the Big Hole River, north of Glen I was only six. The place had a reputation as a snake infested area. Pa had spent 18 years on the road, freighting, camping out, and he knew how to be on the lookout for snakes. They put us in overalls, Thelma and me, so we had protection from the mosquitoes and also to provide us with pockets for jackknives that the old man gave us "to cut and bleed a snakebite" if we were ever so careless as to get bitten. When we were older we wore heavy, knee high hiking boots or gum boots. The tool shed off the cellar stairs at home was called the Snake House so we would think how they sought out a cool spot to rest, and not reach in for a board or a hoe without a cautious poke with a stick first.

Chickens were good to set off a snake alarm and also guinea hens, which set up a big racket like a rusty pump. We kept guinea hens a few years. What we liked about them was the little, brown, hard eggs --you could play ball with them and they would never break! Of course we used those from some abandoned nest and there was always the awful possibility that one old, rotten egg might break when batted with a board. You had to use a board for "balls" so small. The folks kept the guineas as an alarm system--snake alarm. Gee, they were mean little birds. Just loved to ride on the peacock's tail. Tatter, tatter. The poor male, so proud--the geese ate off his top knot. The geese and guineas went and Old George the peacock stayed.

Horace and Maggie Hand's new home
at Lavon, under construction, 1917
From the Rock Hand Collection

The snake I killed when I was ten was quite near the house, up over the ditch on dry land where the gophers lived. That was the year I became wise about which cat was expecting kittens and managed to find them first. Then nobody had the heart to drown a batch to keep the population down. This went on until I went away to high school and in four years the cat population boomed. Before I left for high school there were wild cats in the woods along the river, north and south of the house. But during those years we had no close encounters with snakes in the yard or garden, that I recall. When we had that army of cats the gophers were kept cleaned out in the immediate area and the snakes were not attracted to the vicinity of house and garden."

From a letter written by Susan Hand to Bernard and Annette, (undated) she states, In 1917 "we were living in town, [*Melrose*] between sale of Donovan place and the purchase of the Earl place at Lavon. Then in February, [*1918*] when Thelma had what they thought was scarlet fever, the house was quarantined. Rock went to the ranch at Lavon where the house was being built, the big white house. I was farmed all over town, then Net came and took me to Lavon when only the front, kitchen and workroom section was complete. That was probably when Rock missed out a year of school, or half year. Nettie cooked for the carpenters, who by spring could sleep in the barn or maybe a tent. The barn was left over from the Earls but the original house had

Susan & Thelma Hand
From the Rock Hand Collection

John Hand, first child of John and Ida (Hartwig) Hand, was born on February 11, 1918 at Reichle and died on February 19, 1918. He was buried February 21, 1918 in the small cemetery located on the Gus Hartwig ranch at Reichle, Montana.

been burned; the ranch was unfenced, not cleared, no ditch. Pa was 56 going on 57 when he cleared, fenced and built the ditch. Well, anyway, Nettie was home; I remember her substituting once in the first four grades in the 2 room school in Melrose. So since the flu started around Armistice 1918, that must have been the year she started teaching; first

> **Horace Hand's Will**
>
> *On November 6, 1919 Horace H. Hand wrote his Will. The document is just a straight forward, simple Will. It states he was 58 years of age when the will was written. The will further states,* "I declare that at the time of the execution of this instrument my wife, Maggie E. Hand, is living and that I have the following children and none other, Viz: John Hand, a son, Byron Hand, a son, Roscoe K. Hand, a son, Nettie M. Hand, a daughter, Thelma V. Hand, a daughter and Susie E. Hand a daughter.
>
> I give, devise and bequeath to my wife, Maggie E. Hand, all of the estate, real, personal and of whatsoever character and wheresoever situate, of which I may die seized, to her and her heirs, forever."
>
> Signed
> Horace H. Hand

at the Hoffman school with the bedbugs. Then she was home with the flu; everybody was down sick, Rock and Thelma and I didn't get it. It was awful, everybody so sick and only a young teenager to take care of stock and see to it all. Then an old prospector came down on the train from Melrose and took over the household until things got better.

Then it was that the Reichle teacher did not return so Net took that school, I don't know what the deal was on the Hoffman school, and anyhow she got out of the bedbugs into the awful Dutch cooking that almost killed her. She attempted to go to Normal that summer of 1919 but got what they called yellow jaundice but was hepatitis and came home. The Normal was closed."

> **John & Ida (Hartwig) Hand's second child,**
> **Alvaretta Pauline Maggie Hand,**
> **born December 25, 1919.**

> **Fruit and Nut Christmas Confection**
>
> 1 lb. raisins   1 lb. brazil nuts
> 1 lb. dates   1 lb. shredded coconuts
> 1 lb. figs   1 pkg. All Bran
> 1 lb. walnuts   1 cup honey (clover)
> 1 lb. almonds
>
> Grind, mix, pack in cake pan about 1 inch thick. Let stand in cool place, covered about 2 weeks. Cut in bars. If sticky roll in finely chopped nuts or coconut. Can add or omit any dried fruit or nuts. - Maggie Hand
>
> **Susan writes in a letter to Janice Hand in 1987,** "Mother made this before Christmas. Total of 7 lbs.+. We loved it. Honey we bought in 2 [*two*] 5 gallon cans. Raisins and figs by the lug. This fruit-nut confection and taffy are about the only sweets I remember at Christmas. There were always lots of nuts in the shell. And mince pie of course - just the best. No way could I ever make pies such as she made so easily. Perhaps the greatest memory is the open door hospitality. One week I counted over 24 extra meals - drop ins - from a tramp to neighbors, to a Dillon minister and his family (not of our church). Then there was one day after Christmas when Mom put 2 turkeys in the oven, saying, "Somebody may come." Over 20 people did that one day! No highway then - they drove over the frozen river!"
> **From the Susan Hand Collection**

[*In the late winter of 1919 Horace and Maggie sold the ranch at Lavon to Bill Harvey and brother Herb Harvey. Bill had just returned from France, WW I. This was one of coldest winters on record. - mc*]

Chapter XVI

New Home In Oregon

****

In January of 1920 Horace, Maggie and their family, Byron, Rock, Thelma and Susan, moved to Junction City, Oregon (about 14 miles north of Eugene) where Horace had a feed store in a dairy area, in partnership with Tommy Williams of Melrose. Pa would be 60 on Dec. 1, 1920. Both he and mother felt better in lower climate. Susan finished 3rd, Thelma finished 5th, and Rock finished his first year in high school in the spring in Junction City. - **from undated writings by Susan Hand.**

From a letter by Susan Hand to Bernard and Annette, (undated), she states, "Nettie came to Oregon and taught a 7th grade at Junction City, where we lived, and stayed at home. Some difference from the awful winter

**Nettie, Thelma and Susan in front of home in Junction City, Oregon
From the Thelma (Hand) Kalsta Collection**

**Delivery Truck for Oregon Feed Store
Junction City, Oregon
From the Thelma (Hand) Kalsta Collection**

of 1919-1920 when she rode old Nig the five miles to school - one of the worst winters on record. If she hadn't come to Oregon she probably would have married Bill Harvey, the oldest of the Harvey boys; she stayed on with the Harvey's at Lavon after we left for Oregon, and finished out the term at Reichle. But in the year she was away in Oregon another woman, a widow, took up the chase and married Bill."

"In those days, getting remarried was a business for a widow and the main aim for most women. They were failures if not married. Only a few went on to make a living alone. It was changing a little as I grew up - 12 years behind Net's venture into independence."

"After Oregon, maybe because she could save money teaching and staying home, that year at Junction City, Net went the summer to Normal in Bellingham, Washington; then the winter of 1921-22 to Dillon, and graduated from the 2 year course, which was all required then for grade school, in August 1922 and took a job at Billings. In 1925 when I started to high school, she went to Ogden to teach and kept working summers, at Missoula, by extension in Utah, and by correspondence to get her degree in 1929 as I graduated from High School. That made it possible for her to get a job in Dillon as a teaching instructor affiliated with the college - training the college students to teach. She had a 3rd and later a 4th grade there from 1929 until she married in 1935. I took my training under her and one other - but the only help on instruction I got was from the work under her. After that they passed a rule that no one could train under a relative -- I'm glad that I beat them to it for I know I had the best of the instructors. She made $1800 a year when she built the house; that was top wages - ordinary teachers did well to make $1300 or $1400 in town schools. One of us poor beginners made as little as $85 a month!"

From writings of Susan Hand, undated, she states regarding automobiles, "Nettie learned to drive in Oregon. Rock taught her on the Maxwell. You know, then, you couldn't use a car but a few months - no paved roads in Oregon - mud too deep in winter. Junction City was so small you could walk everywhere. We used to go on Sunday excursions into the country after church. Pa was 60 when he bought the Max and figured he was too old to learn to drive but mother learned to drive our Model A Ford when she was 62. Only trouble was she always thought a car could go anywhere a buggy or a wagon could."

Byron Hand
Junction City, Oregon
From the Rock Hand Collection

The Maxwell in Oregon
From the Thelma (Hand) Kalsta Collection

Nettie Hand
Daughters of the American Revolution Colonial Party
February 22, 1925
From the Rock Hand Collection

Byron, Susan, Rock, Maggie and Thelma Hand
Arriving back at the ranch at Lavon after traveling 1050 miles in 10 days
when moving back from Oregon to the ranch at Lavon, Montana in 1921
From the Rock Hand Collection

Chapter XVII

Back at Lavon

****

The buyers of the ranch at Lavon were unable to make the payments and Horace and Maggie took the ranch back. Horace returned to the ranch at Lavon in January or February 1921. - mc] "I remember he wrote how they plowed in February 1921." - **Susan Hand**

From Susan Hand's writings, undated, "--- in June 1921 we, Mother, Rock, Byron, Thelma and I, backtracked on the Oregon Trail in that Maxwell from Junction City, Oregon to Glen, Montana with Rock, then 17, the driver. Pa had returned in January or February to repossess the ranch. It took us 5 days with overnight stops at Hood River and Baker, Oregon, Gooding, Idaho and Dubois, Idaho and home to the ranch at Lavon the 5th day. We got stuck in the mud at Spencer, Idaho. On the Monida Pass into Montana and the car turned around on the muddy grade above the Beaverhead River near Beaverhead Rock south of Dillon. That scared me - probably all of us - those old cars had only a cloth top like a covered wagon, and snap on side curtains against cold, rain and snow.

Ranch Home at Lavon
From the Thelma (Hand) Kalsta Collection

When we got to John's place across the river from home we were a rough looking crew! We'd camped out enroute at the towns mentioned where tourist parks were maintained by the town with water and toilets. Dillon even had one in a vacant lot across from the courthouse.

We had no road into the ranch, no bridge across the Big Hole except the R.R. bridge so we must have driven as near the bridge as possible and walked the R.R. bridge to get home. Later Rock brought the car home via the Glen bridge."

Letter to Shirley (Hand) Groff from Susan Hand, June 23, 1982, Susan states, "Pa lost his second cutting of alfalfa and his grain to hail in August 1921. Nettie graduated from the 2 year course at Dillon Normal that August and Mom took me to the graduation, by train, just a few days after the hail -- that I remember - I was not yet 10. The only other time he lost a crop was when the rail road put in a new culvert for his ditch under the tracks and had the downstream end higher than the upstream end. There was no lawsuit -- the rail road company paid for the lost crop. But the crop was a total loss -- no insurance. The ditch, the original, was there before the rail road -- so there was a clear case about the culvert. In the '21 hail we lost our talking magpie."

In a letter from Susan Hand to Shirley Hand on January 22, 1949, Susan writes that "of course we may have an April like the one in 1922 when it was 18 below on the 18th of April and the old sow had 18 pigs and lost 17!"

[*In the spring of 1922, Rock was a junior in high school, Susan in 5th grade and Thelma in the 6th. The teacher was Gen O'Leary at Rock Creek School. - mc*]

John and Ida (Hartwig) Hand's third child, Louise Mae Hand, born June 23, 1922.

"Some Afterthoughts About Rural School Education"

From writings of Susan Hand, she states, "Transportation, you transported yourself. Usually on foot. Sometimes on horseback, or larger families in carts or buggies. At Rock Creek there was no shed or shelter for horses as there were in older more established schools. Riebers had the farthest to come - from the mouth of canyon leading to Browns Lake, 2 1/2 or three miles. Chris used to bring kids, especially when they were younger, team and spring wagon

Rock Creek School
by Thelma (Hand) Kalsta

"I went to the Rock Creek School in the 20ties (the learn'in was thin). We struck out at 8 a.m., over the river and west for a couple of miles. We either crossed the river on the railroad bridge, or rowed across in a boat, or slid across on the ice, even sometimes forded the river and rode a horse, up to the 15 x 18 log schoolhouse. Inside there was two long windows on the South and East, and a blackboard across the north side. The floor was plain wood, no covering. Our desks were double ones, the teacher's stood up on legs, with a hinged top. The stove was suppose to keep the room warm - here there were difficulties. The teacher was a poor fireman, the wood poor, or the nights and days just too cold. It did happen that we sit with our coats on. At one time the bigger boys led a protest about the cooling system. They made paper windmills and stuck them in the crack in the walls; they ran like mad and caused a lot of noise and confusion. The teacher laughed, and promised to report it to the Trustees. The next week the schoolhouse had a new daubing job inside and out. Compliments of the trustees. There was two little houses out back that said Boys and Girls. Later they built a coal shed and added a lean-to for lunches, coats and overshoes. They also added a big crock to drink from, you just turn the handle and the water ran into your cup; that is after someone had gone to the creek for the water. We had to remember to empty the crock or our water system would freeze. We managed our own school lunch program, the best ones were cooked outdoors over a bond fire. When the season was right the boys did some trapping at recess time, they were always anxious to show the rest of us their catch. Here the whole school was viewing the dead skunk, the teacher was inside, to our great surprise the skunk came to life and ran into the schoolhouse; out came the teacher screaming and accusing all of us of chasing it into the house. Our education stopped short for several days, until the odor vanished. Try as we could we never did convince the teacher that it was not done on purpose; and it wasn't. I now often wonder about the life the poor teacher had. She walked to school with the rest of us. She boarded and roomed with any neighbor who would keep her. I have no idea how much she got. We most always had a Christmas Program, exchanged gifts, decorated a tree with our own hand made ornaments, and had candles that we lit for only a short time. We did have a flag pole so the flag went up each day and usual allegiance was said."

From Thelma (Hand) Kalsta's Christmas letter of 1982

maybe -- later a Model T Ford. Sassman's had a long hilly trail over the foothills, around 3 miles. We walked -- mile and a half up creek, same back; took most of an hour, because of crossing river and travelling a rocky trail and road. Cattle in the fields sometimes caused us to take north side of the creek -- for fear of range bulls -- but mostly Wood's Livestock company had sheep in the fields when I was small. We gathered wool from the barbed wire fences, pocketsfull a trip, and Mom either carded them at home or sent it off to a woolen mill for bats to put in quilts for the many beds -- 6 bedrooms and bunkhouse bedding. So the school district had no transportation costs. Parents supplied the sole leather, and shoes were resoled. My mom had a shoe last and sole leather and could do it if we couldn't get shoes to shoemaker. Sometimes the tacks worked through the soles and that was hard on a hiker! Weather reports, there were none -- papers came days late. So you were your own weather prophet. I remember one April blizzard that came in afternoon (maybe it was May) and the neighbor from Wood's Livestock, near the school brought an assortment of coats and wraps. We left school early, but our folks had sent someone with a horse rig, which we met half way, having left early. I suppose the ice was out of the river and the river still low or they could not have come. Usually you had to have almost winter clothes in the cool of morning, even in spring, so you just carried them home if it warmed up in the afternoon."

[*In early November of 1922 Horace had a ruptured appendix and was taken by Gransberry over 40 miles of dirt road in an open car to the St. James Hospital in Butte. There he developed pneumonia. He spent a good number of weeks in the hospital in Butte. Also during this time, the economy of the area and, for that matter, of the nation was in a general down turn. Times were hard economically and with Horace in the hospital for a good number of weeks, Rock had to leave school his senior year of high school and run the ranch. Nettie was teaching in Billings at the time. - mc*]

From Nettie (Hand) Garrison's 1922 diary:
Dec. 3 - Went to church and SS [*Sunday School*]. At 2:30 p.m. had phone from Mother calling me to Butte. An afternoon of suspense! My train left at 9:45 - A cold hard night.
Dec. 4 - Arrived in Butte at 5 a.m. - Rock met me - a cold blizzard was blowing. Went to hospital as soon as possible, felt too badly, could not stay in room, finally braced up enuf to stay with him [*her father, Horace*] in the P.M. Surely is a sick person.
Dec. 5 to 10 - Stayed constantly at his bedside - going home late every evening, worn out and discouraged.
Dec. 10 - Dr. says I might just as well go - leave Butte at 10:30 - train late. Cold ride.
Dec. 11 - Arrive in Billings too late for school, luckily my room had been dismissed on account of cold weather.
Dec. 12 - Have a severe cold and am not very enthusiastic about anything - 23 below. - No word from Mother yet.
Dec. 14 - Word came that he is still holding his own.

From Susan Hand writings, undated, she states, "I can't remember much about the Maxwell after we got [*home*] to Montana. One very vivid and painful memory was of the trip home from Butte at Thanksgiving, 1922. I think we went up on the train. Pa was not expected to live - pneumonia and complications of a ruptured appendix. Rock came up in the car, weather turned cold, snow and below zero. We had the side curtains on but there was no heater. I froze my right foot - heel and side.

When we got home the kitchen door had blown open and water was frozen in the water bucket (no other plumbing) but the old parrot was still alive and I'll bet she was glad of a fire. ---Those were grim days - Pa pulled thru - home after 3 months in the hospital. Rock was 18 and had the work of the ranch on his shoulders. Of course he lost a year of high school."

Taken, with permission, from an interview with Rock Hand for the Montana Historical Society Oral History Project, dated March 10, 1987, when they were talking about the depression and how he learned to survive in tough times he said, "Well, what was it, I was on the ranch. I've seen days on the ranch where we couldn't pay the taxes and my sister taught school and paid the taxes and my mother raised turkeys and we butchered those turkeys and take 'em into Butte and peddle 'em one at a time around Thanksgiving. And uh, we had my dad in the hospital one time there and I didn't [know] what the law was or whether you had to pay the bill when ya took 'em outa the hospital but I was pretty young and I never had any experience so I sold a bunch of hogs. Another fella and I butchered em, thirty somethin' hogs and I had 'em sold to the Metropolitan Market in Butte. That's the ACM [Anaconda Copper Mining] company's meat market, but they turned 'em down, and I had, I was just butcherin' the last hog when they did, so I put 'um on the train and I billed 'em to myself in Butte. All but about six or seven I put them in an old Maxwell car I had, got in there early in the morning, I went to Butte and I peddled them. I'd sold a half a one for six and a whole one for twelve [dollars]. And the miners were glad to buy 'em because they had families to feed and they could buy all the meat they'd want there for a month or so see, and I caught it from the railroad company because they was afraid that I was gonna walk off and leave 'em with a bunch [of] dead hogs on their hands. I'd go down there and I'd catch it every time I'd go down to get a dozen a those hogs, 'when ya gonna get 'em outa there, we're not gonna put up with this very long.' I just stalled um off and I got it done and between the turkey money and the hog money that mother and I could get together, we got my dad outa the hospital and the bill was four hundred dollars. He'd been in there about six weeks and the people in the hospital, when we paid the bill, had said, "Oh my God, it's been months since this has ever happened to us, that anybody paid their bill." But we didn't know, I didn't know, I was ignorant, I guess I figured they'd keep my dad for storage or something. But, ignorance don't seem to bother you when you don't have any brains."

> **From Nettie (Hand) Garrison's 1923 diary:**
> **June 29** - A very unusual day. Pres. Harding's special train passes thru Lavon at 8:30 o'clock preceded by an advance guard train and followed by a rear guard train. The track was patrolled for 24 hours previous to his arrival - all bridges were guarded. The Pres. train stopped at Melrose for some time - many of the residents of the town and vicinity shook hands with him. The special train went to Butte, Helena, Livingston, Billings and Great Falls.
> **June 30** - A busy Saturday. Coyote took turkey hen in door yard.

> **From Nettie (Hand) Garrison's 1923 diary:**
> **Aug. 5** - Little Joe Kambich was drowned in river near Glen. Others narrowly escaped. George Ferguson rescued Carl Kambich. [Kambich's were neighbors who lived nearby. - mc]

> **From Nettie (Hand) Garrison's 1923 diary:**
> **Aug. 22** - At 11:30 a.m. Mama, Susan, Thelma, Dolly and I left for Lakes [Browns and Agnes Lakes - mc] - Up hill drive - made camp at 3:30. Went up to lake after supper. Rode in motor boat.
> **Aug. 23** - Went to upper lake in a.m. Ida and babies came up in p.m. Home by 8:00 p.m.

[In February 1923 Horace got home from hospital and continued to recuperate. Rock continued to work the ranch and in the fall went back to high school in Dillon and went on to graduate in May of 1924. Nettie was still teaching school in Billings and Thelma and Susan are going to school as usual. - mc]

From interview by Myrna Carpita with Rock Hand in 1992, he tells that he worked for Pearl I. Smith at his abstract office in Dillon while going to high school. After high school Pearl and Rock went into the sheep business and he said, "by gosh I made money on those sheep. I got the money made, I sold those sheep in Omaha, Nebraska, loaded them on the train and took them to Omaha. When I got back from Omaha I think $2000.00 of that was mine, which in those days was a lot of money. I wasn't even 20. But anyway, I put the money in the ranch account in the Dillon bank. Then that was fine until I started to write the checks on that money. Then my Dad got mad and kicked me off the ranch. I said I have too much invested here. He said 'you don't have a damn thing invested here.' And he just booted me off the ranch and I took off."

> **From Nettie (Hand) Garrison's 1923 diary the following account is found:**
>
> Owe me:
> Roscoe $70.00   Winter 1921-22
> " $55.00   Suit
> Mama $40.00   Fall 1923
> Roscoe $14.00   Coat
> Roscoe $33.00   Evans Note
> Taxes $73.90   Spring 1922
> Pa $200.00 Spring 1922

[*Upon Rock leaving the ranch, he went from the ranch to Butte and then on to Rocker where John was living and stayed all night with John, then went on to Missoula. - mc*] He states, "I had the old Maxwell car cause I figured that Maxwell was mine because I paid for it and I took off with it and I wound up in Missoula."

In writings of Rock's, undated, he states that because of raising the sheep south of Dillon on Axes Canyon, "I had to pay taxes to Beaverhead County. As a result I was called on the fall session of the jury in 1925. When I explained to the Judge Rogers that I had only turned 21 in June of that year and I had doubts as to whether I should be on the jury. The judge's only remark was that it would be good experience for me.

As a result one of the cases I was called on was a fellow by the name of Hoffman who was suing his brother-in-law for $14,000 for the loss of his thumb. It was the most entertaining experience I ever had.

It was developed that in order to settle some sort of a disagreement they had decided to shoot it out. They agreed to meet on a side hill in "Axes" Canyon. Hoffman rode up on his horse looking for his brother-in-law who had tied his horse in the brush and was laying beside a big rock. When Hoffman rode up on his horse the brother-in-law took a shot at him. When the attorney asked the brother-in-law if he had shot to kill, his reply was that he wanted to warn him that he was ready, not to kill him. The attorney then asked the brother-in-law what happened after that. His reply was that he took another shot at him because he drew down on him and he was still coming on his horse. The attorney then asked if it was with the intent to kill and his reply was, "Your Damed right, I was getten right down to business." When the attorney asked him what happened then, his reply was, "That turned him, because I shot his damed thumb off". That ended the testimony and after due deliberation the jury awarded Mr. Hoffman nothing and I always figured he was lucky."

> **Home Made Crackers**
>
> Sift 2 cups white flour with 3 teaspoons baking powder and 1/2 teaspoon salt. Add 1 cup milk and 4 tablespoons melted butter or lard. Mix in the white of 1 egg beaten stiff. Now add more flour to make a stiff dough.
>
> To knead, pound with a rolling pin and then roll thin and cut into squares and sprinkle with salt and prick with a fork and bake in a moderate oven.
>
> -By Alma Snall, Billings, Montana, - Note by Susan "In 1916 this recipe was given to me by a woman who always made her own crackers. Not because they could not be bought in a store, but because in those days of homesteading there was no bridge across the Yellowstone River near Pompey's Pillar. So every family used this recipe on the day soup was served. And these crackers were the best, even better than store bought ones."
>
> **From the Susan Hand Collection**

> John and Ida (Hartwig) Hand's fourth child, William Murray Hand, born August 21, 1924.

Thelma Hand
From the Rock Hand Collection

[*Thelma started high school in 1924 in Dillon. She stayed with Mrs. Harwood, worked, but was not well treated. She then moved to Billings with Net to attend school after Christmas. A Miss Larson is the teacher at Rock Creek School 1924-25- mc.*]

From Susan Hand writings, dated June 30, 1974, "The 4th of July in Melrose was some celebration; the unscheduled events were more memorable than the scheduled ones!

Pat Smith, on his Appaloosa, almost always won the horse race-down the main street - and almost always got into a fight--always got roaring drunk. One generation removed from the "old sod" Pat was still a true Irishman! I can still see the blood on the white shirts -- men wore their suits and white shirts, took off their coats as a signal of battle!

I'm remembering prohibition days but there was no shortage of good spirits!

With the locally borrowed rodeo stock in the R. R. shipping corrals, and the spectators behind the "fence" of parked cars (Model Ts abundant) -- a real western rodeo was free entertainment. Even 12 year old boys took a try at steer riding. I can still see Bud Gransberry flying off, unhurt. I don't think there was a doctor in town but nobody got hurt.

On the sidelines you could watch the romances in progress, look over the new babies, catch up on the latest gossip. And look over all the new dresses -- everybody in something new for the occasion -- but all skirts, for the ladies.

After the 4th of July you started haying, and until that was finished you worked right along, maybe even Sunday, because the rain might make a mid-week "Sunday". The clatter of the mowing machine was sure to be answered by thunder and lightning and rain.

Circus time usually was August and you might get to Dillon or Butte, or might not. Most likely a picnic or work on the irrigation dam with picnic lunches and water fights were the only diversions -- maybe berry picking. This was in the lull between hayings -- the two crops of alfalfa.

Although we didn't get away much, we always had lots of company, not callers, visitors who stayed a while. They came by R.R. to Lavon, the station given to the old Earl ranch in the '80's in exchange for the right-of-way, or as part of the agreement. We really ran a free dude and summer boarding place, but we looked forward to our visitors, all were welcome. No doubt they enjoyed the fresh vegetables, butter and cream, eggs, fried chicken, ham and home made ice cream. And Mother's pies, fresh bread, foods almost extinct!

The greatest was when some of Mother's sisters or cousins came. Only Annie and Emma visited, and then Enos, Mary's oldest son; but they were all such fun. Emma's boys came to the Melrose ranch; Arta and Ken were there at Lavon in the later times when we had a highway.

We used to have company by car before that but they had to park across the river and walk the R.R. bridge. Of course it was unlawful, but everybody used it as a foot bridge, even we kids, if we didn't use the row boat – which due to high water or ice had a limited season of transport.

**Getting ready for winter at the ranch.
Cutting cottonwood for the winter to stoke the stoves.
From the Thelma (Hand) Kalsta Collection**

Late August, when the blackbirds gathered, the grain was cut and shocked, chockcherries gathered from the lower pasture, was the foreshadowing of school. Before high school days summer pleasures extended into September and even October, with really more time to enjoy the outdoors on our 3 mile hike up to the log cabin school in Rock Creek. We had the added enjoyment of recess and noon games and rambles with the other pupils. Our teachers never bothered us, nor we them, we took off and lunched in the creek bottom, or at the watercress spring, nearby.

Taxpayers didn't have to buy us any playthings! We used broomsticks or sticks for bats. Some kid brought a ball, and when it lost its stitches my mother usually repaired it, probably it was our ball. We played steal sticks, hide and seek, run sheep run, anty, anty over did take a ball, which was thrown over the school house with a team on either side, if anyone caught the ball the team could run around and tag players on the other side. Sometimes we fished all noon hour, no poles, but in low water we could run brook trout into shallows and catch them by hand. Sometimes we could take home a treat for Pa that fall [*as*] he was ailing before the appendix attack and operation in Butte. Once Rock killed a willow grouse, out of season, with a sling shot, but we were afraid to take it home -- he never expected to hit it, was just shooting at it; we gave it to some other kids whose folks wouldn't quote the law.

**Roscoe "Rock" Hand
At Hand Ranch at Lavon
From the Thelma (Hand) Kalsta Collection**

In winter we had our own hot lunch program. We built a stone or brick fireplace, placed large stones as a circle of seats, built our fire, toasted our sandwiches on forked willow sticks. The teacher could join us if she wanted to on a sunny day. On a cold day we had to eat inside. Then we played button, button, who's got the button, hide the thimble (even if it were a piece of chalk). Other days the kids who had skates skated on the pond in the creek or on an overflow from the spring in the field back of the schoolhouse. (The teacher couldn't get her shoe skates off one noon, the big boys had put glue in them). Most kids had to slide on their shoes. One or two had clamp on skates.

Everyone had apples for lunch, you put the seeds on the top of the stove and named them to see which one would pop first.

Our water system was a big 5 gallon crock in the cloakroom, filled by bucket from the creek by the kids; or they went to the creek and drank. I don't know whether the state board of health ever tested the water. Above us were two ranches, with corrals near, or on the creek I suppose; and campers, a few up the gulch all summer, but none in school year.

The kindling and coal was brought in by the kids and often the fire was built by the kids. Usually the boys took care of the coal and kindling and often the girls took a hand at sweeping and tidying up the school room after school, cleaning boards and wiping desks.

We teased our teachers, but mainly took pretty good care of them. We loved to put up and take down the flag, and the pledge of allegiance recited just after putting up the flag had real meaning, every morning.

The county superintendent was supposed to call twice a year, and would be sure to make it in the Indian summer days of autumn; spring was not so sure, roads, dirt roads might be impassable with mud.

I'll never forget the time the county "soup" as we called her, came the fall of my 5th year. Miss O'Leary asked, in our history class, "Who was Sir Walter Drake?" Elizabeth Rieber answered, "He was the duck who sailed around the world for England." Now you have to understand that smart alecks were not tolerated in those school days, and you have to understand what a shy little girl Elizabeth was, having learned English at school as German was the home language. Yet she was smart, and full of fun.

The school year ended soon after mid-May. We always had 2 weeks off at Christmas. You started after Labor Day in early September and that meant May closing. After the School Picnic, at which the teacher was guest of the community with no duties, you could look forward to the Fourth of July.

When we were in 7th grade we had to go to the county seat, Dillon and take state tests in geography and hygiene as those would not be in 8th course. Then to finish 8th you had to go and take state tests, in the county superintendent office in all subjects.

Johnny, Elizabeth (Rieber) and I took the 8th grade exams in January 1925, and we all three passed, leaving Miss Larson with maybe 4 pupils for the remainder of the year. I had the highest grades in Beaverhead County, including the May tests. Nothing was made of it. I rode up to Brown's on old Nig and picked up the letter from the county "soup" with the grades and the 8th grade certificate and that was the extent of it.

I did have a half year off - the most wonderful half year in memory. I was alone at home. Thelma was with Net in Billings, and was very ill with scarlet fever that spring but finished her first year of high school. Rock was home, it seems to me. I rode the hills all that spring. Old Nig was still spry at 13, he and I were the same age; a little part cayuse, part race stock from a Daly stallion, the story was, wild on Red Mountain back of Melrose. It was a very wet year, and flowers bloomed that had never bloomed before on McCarty. I had an issue of National Geographic with wild flowers of the Rockies and rejoiced in being able to name them. --- I learned to cook, to bake bread. ---- I looked forward to summer when we'd all be home and haying. And Net would be there to play the piano evenings --- Story telling, reading, and some harmless practical jokes along with home made music and ice cream were all wholesome diversions."

Sweet Beet Pickles

5 lbs. beets. Cook in salted water until tender. Peel, set aside.

1 1/2 cups sugar
3 1/2 cups pure cider vinegar
1 1/2 cups water
Stick cinnamon
1 tsp. allspice, whole or ground

Boil sugar, cider vinegar, water, spices. Pour over peeled beets. Bring to boil. Can. – Maggie Hand

From note to Janice Hand by Susan Hand in 1987, Susan states, "Coming home from Rock Creek School in the fall you could smell Mother's pickling from the river. These beets are so much better than commercial. Mom made a great variety of pickles, (dill) sour and sweet, pick-a-lili, mustard and chow, chow from the fall garden. Aside from a huge mixed pickle recipe, this is the only recipe that survived."

"Also she made real mince meat (with meat) for the best pies. Then there was head cheese at pig killing time in the fall - so spicy and tasty. We weren't much for sausage but John learned that from the Hartwigs. I should also mention the wild berry jellies, gooseberry, current, choke cherry."

From the Susan Hand Collection

Billy Vipond

From the Susan Hand Collection - *The following is from a handwritten copy of a 1924 account of the death of Billy Vipond at the age of 77. No date given for the paper from which this was copied. The date of Vipond's birth is 1847.*

According to a long distance telephone message received by Alex Johnston, cashier of Clark and Brother's bank, William C. Vipond died in his sleep some time Sunday night or early Monday morning in the cabin he was occupying at Bear Gulch near Twin Bridges. With the passing of Mr. Vipond one of the most notable of pioneer prospectors passed across the great divide. He was the last of a rapidly vanishing bank of hardy gold seekers who were either present at the discovery or put in appearance immediately afterward at every well known Western mining camp.

It was such men as Vipond who first uncovered the wonderful mineral resources of Montana. Mostly after finding their pay dirt or veins to let others develop the mines. As a rule they asked little for themselves and restlessness kept them always prospecting and seeking for mineral in more or less unexplored fields.

Maggie wrote the following about Billie Vipond:

There are good articles on Billie and John Vipond. But by his many visits to our house I might add more. Billie and John first went to the Black Hills from their home in Galena, Illinois, preferring going West than to staying on his father's farm. At the Black Hills they did well tho after they had made money it was hard to stay alive and keep it. The country was infested with thugs and road agents. They thot up a ruse that threw that element off their guard and quietly slipped out, doing prospecting near by and made a clean get away without being molested.

From there they went to Salt Lake thinking to settle down but after buying a house they soon left for Montana. Billie was clost friend to J. A. Brown (tole bridge on Big Hole). Some reverse came over Billie and he nearly lost his mind. A doctor prescribed a long trip on a sailing vessel - freighter. He sailed from San Fransisco to Australia.

He would set till late at night telling stories about the long trip. Once the sailors caught a shark and brot it on deck. They wanted him to kill it. When he hit at it, it was not there so after many unsuccessful attempts the sailor showed him how to kill a shark – cut its tail off and it died at once. They stopped at Tasmania – saw the burning lake. In Australia he hired a man to catch him an ornithorhynchus, or platypus, and mounted it. This was Mr. Brown's request of Billie that he bring one for him. Had he known what Brown was doing to him he would have never gotten the bird and beaver.

Brown played traitor, took the ore out and sold it. Brown was to look after their interests while Billie was gone. Instead of looking after theirs, he looked after his. He got Hugh Patton to do the dirty work and divided the spoils. Hugh had a ranch up the Big Hole then, but no cattle. After this Hugh had plenty of cattle. After that Billie was Brown's bitter enemy.

The winter of 1892 Billie and Joe Storm wintered in Vipond Park. They often came down to Dewey - generally came to E. G. Bryant's to eat. I saw him quite often. Then we did not see him any more till he came back from Mexico. I think 1896, 97 or 98.

I remember he came to our house, staid a week or two. Horace and Al insisted he should stay. Two meals was all he would eat. In the evening I'd go in the bunk house with the men to hear him tell his stories about John's death. He said after he got no letter, as he should, he began to have misgivings. One day about noon he sat by a camp fire at Wise River and dozed for a second, woke with a start, heard John cry as in pain. Then at once he started and arranged for the trip to Mexico.

I think the conviction of John's murderer cost near $1000.00. I remember him telling about getting his last $20.00 gold piece changed on the last end of his journey home. In the fall of 1910 he came thru Melrose, while we were in Maine. We told Tice Dodgson to give him the gun if he saw Billie, which he did. I think it was on his return from Arizona. He went up to Big Al's place and camped there for some time in his meadow and complained often of not being able to sleep. He was glad to have men come and sit at his camp fire and talk. We told him to write a book and he laughed. We did not see him any more tho knew of him going to Bear Gulch.

Story Reveals Vipond Had to use Great Strategy to Obtain Justice in Mexico

Montana Standard, Butte, Montana, Date unknown

By MARY A. GALLOGLY, Sula, Mont.

The most interesting story, as told by Ruby McIntyre Dennis in the Sunday Montana Standard of August 1, recalls details as told by Mr. Vipond on his return from Mexico to the late Guy Ames, then manager of the Eliel-Burfiend general store in Dewey's Flat, who reported the incident to me.

The story told by the Mexican who saw the murder of Mr. Vipond was verified by the finding of the victim's watch in a pawn shop, thus pinning the crime on the man accused by the Mexican.

Then began for Mr. Vipond a long and almost baffling campaign to overcome the indifference of the sheriff, owing to the influential standing of the murderer's family. The sheriff was hostile to any plan involving justice. To win him, Mr. Vipond began by winning his family, especially gaining the love of a tiny girl, dear to her father. Mr. Vipond wrote to a member of his family in the East: "Send me the finest, best dressed doll you can buy". In answer came a marvel of dolldom, costing $50. This was given to the child, and that, with other acts of friendship, won the sheriff and the arrest was made.

Prisoner Had File

The man was found guilty and sent to prison to await execution. Mr. Vipond visited the prison daily, and on one visit found that a few more rasps of a file would liberate him. Mr. Vipond then had him changed to another cell and had himself appointed deputy marshal. From that time until the end he guarded the prisoner.

According to Mexican law the criminal must be executed in the district in which the crime was committed. This necessitated a long and dangerous journey through a rough and sparsely settled country. It was whispered to Mr. Vipond that in a very wild, unsettled portion of the road the prisoner's friends would attack the party and rescue the prisoner. He requisitioned a company of soldiers to see that the prisoner was taken safely to the appointed place, where the penalty for the crime was paid.

It has been said of the Vipond brothers that the profit or loss of any business venture undertaken by one was fully shared by the other.

Justice imposed the penalty of death upon the greedy assassin who struck down his unsuspecting victim -- but it could not restore the wreck of a beautiful brotherhood that did not know Self.

[*Nettie continued to teach in Billings and at the end of the school year in the spring of 1924 accepted a job to teach in Ogden, Utah beginning that fall. She taught in Ogden for four years. - mc*]

[*In 1925 Susan started high school in Dillon. Thelma also went back to school in Dillon. They stayed with Kate Lewis. - mc*]

Susan Hand has made notes in various places, on various things and some are as follows, "Pa was a bachelor of 34 when married. He never complained about anyone's cooking if it was clean and on time and with plenty for all, the dogs and passing tramp. His aversions were few - gravy, frosting on cake, which he called calf slobbers, too much hot seasoning. He wanted natural flavors. He loved cod fish or any fish. Thot western fish soft from warm pacific waters. Old hired man fished for him all during his last illness. We kids caught trout - against the law, for him when he was sick from chronic appendix. [*We*] fixed fish dams, wet our shoes, brought fingerlings proudly home for his supper."

In writings by Susan that appears to be a journal of sorts, not dated, she writes regarding the work horses they had on the ranch, "We had Clydsdales, a Percheron, Belgians that I remember. Grand, gentle animals. Percherons were more spirited. ----- In 1925 I had a scary trip from Melrose, in a hay rack with Old Newt, the Percheron and Judy, a big sorrel Clydsdale. They were gentle and steady around home but headed home from Melrose, they gave me a fast ride, I struggled, standing all the way, 8 miles, over rough dirt road - and a right angle turn off Brown's Bridge! There was a chair for me but I never dared sit down - they would have upset the hay rack! I was a sturdy 14 year old - almost adult height - but it was all I could do to control them. My arms were sore a week after. ---- I think old Newt and Judy were about my age but headed home they were 3 year olds."

John and Ida (Hartwig) Hand's
fifth child,
Earl Seth Hand,
born March 23, 1926

Byron Hand
From the Rock Hand Collection

Byron Hand

From "The Horace Hand Family", written by Rock Hand, 1989, he states, "The second child in the family was Byron [*nicknamed "Stub"*] who was the unfortunate one in the family. Early in life after an appendix operation and an accident or two he began to show epileptic indications which as time passed developed into serious convulsions."

Rock notes in other writings, undated, that in the "spring, 1926, he went back to the ranch because of Brother Byron." [*This was when Byron was committed to mental hospital at Warm Springs according to information received from the Department of Institutions, Montana Mental Health Division in Helena. Byron was committed to Warm Springs on April 11, 1926 and remained there until he was paroled on March 30, 1927. The research by the Department of Institutions found only the dates he was confined to Warm Springs. Records on patients were not kept in an orderly manner at that time; therefore the type of treatment he received while in Warm Springs is unknown.*

We know that after Byron's release from Warm Springs he returned to the home of his parents at Lavon. Very little has been said or written about Byron by family members and it appears to be very upsetting for the older members of the family to discuss. It must be remembered that in that day and age, before there was any treatment or understanding of epilepsy, to have a family member with this type of an illness was viewed as a disgrace. From what little I can glean from family members, apparently Byron's seizures became more and more severe as time went on.

Thelma (Hand) Kalsta, in a conversation, did say that her mother had a very hard childbirth when Bryon was born. He was a large baby. The actual cause of the epilepsy or information as to the onset of the symptoms seems to be unknown. There is one mention in Maggie's writings that she was in Butte with Byron as he was in the hospital. This was in 1909. Whether this was connected to his epilepsy cannot be confirmed.

In a conversation with Rock about Byron, he told me of staying with Byron one night in particular. In the morning when it got light, there were 13 matches near the candle, which counted how many times Rock had lit the candle during the night when he had to get up to help Byron due to convulsions.- mc]

Washing

[*The methods and equipment for washing clothes have varied over the years. In the very early years there was the scrubbing of the clothing, by hand, in a stream or in a tub. Then a little improvement came along with the advent of the wash board. An even bigger improvement was made when the hand operated agitation washer came on the market. There were several varieties of this new invention, but all required arm power – you grabbed ahold of the handle and moved it back and forth in order to operate the agitation device in the washer. The washday work was further lightened with the invention of the gas operated washing machine and then eventually the electric agitation washer. Of course, with all of this equipment the water had to be pumped from the well or hauled from the creek, poured into a wash boiler, heated, then hauled to the tubs and washing machine and then the washing done. The rinsing was generally done in tubs filled with cold water that had also been hauled.*

Wash Boiler
Sears Roebuck & Co.
1923

Early on, the water had to be wrung out of the clothing, by hand, after the wash, and again after each rinsing. As the mechanical age progressed there was a new invention that simplified the "wringing". This was a hand-operated wringer.

Of course, after all of the water hauling, heating, hauling again, washing, rinsing, and hauling the water out of the house when the washing was done, there was the chore of getting the clothing dry. Mother Nature was used as the dryer, even though she was unpredictable.

The clothes were generally hung outside on a line to dry. This worked well except in the rain or in the dead of winter when the clothing would freeze in whatever shape they happened to be hung in. Then there was the chore of getting the frozen, misshaped clothing off of the line and into the house. If the clothing had not gotten dry, the living room, or whatever other room might be available, had to be converted into a clothes drying "parlor".

The soap that was used for doing the washing was also made at home. That, too, was another ordinary chore in the early days.

All in all wash day was a major undertaking. And then the chore of ironing! - mc]

'Agitation' Washer
Sears Roebuck & Co.
1902

In a letter to cousin Arta, dated April 22, 1982 Susan Hand states, "How well I remember the big washings, the wash boiler, wash board and hand wringing. Mom wasn't very well and we got broke in early.

In late spring, summer and early fall we washed down by the river because the well water was hard and had to be packed further. And also it kept the mess out of the kitchen. We had an outdoor fire - great fun! When we kids were in high school we took turns going home weekends - or both went - to help with or do the washings.

In 1927, when I was a Junior, the gas powered Maytag was bought and the sales man packed it on his back over the R.R. bridge. (We didn't have the highway until 1929.) But washing by Maytag was still a lot of work so we continued going home to help. A pump in the house helped.

And the ironings with the old sad irons! I can remember two ironing boards and then someone doing the flat goods on the end of the table. And the men's overalls were also washed and ironed."

Sears Roebuck & Co.
1902
Sad Irons were placed on the surface of the wood stove to heat before ironing. Several irons were placed on the stove and then used as needed. The handle was removable.

Wise River Dam Breaks

The Dillon Tribune
A REPUBLICAN PAPER SINCE 1881

Dillon, Beaverhead County, Montana, Friday, June 17, 1927

TERRIFIC FLOOD TAKES TOLL OF FOUR LIVES IN WISE RIVER SECTION EARLY TUESDAY MORNING WHEN UPPER RESERVOIR DAM BREAKS

WATER SWEEPS DOWN CANYON, DESTROYING TOWN OF WISE RIVER AND WASHING OUT BRIDGES, ROADS AND MILE OF O.S.L. RAILROAD TRACKS

Railroad and Highway Crews Are Working Day
and Night Repairing the Extensive Damage

TRUEMAN FAMILY AND CHARLES FERGUSON ARE FLOOD VICTIMS

Wise River, Montana after Wise River Dam broke.
June 14, 1927
From the Thelma (Hand) Kalsta Collection

The Wise River Dam held water for years but it was not a success and finally they opened the gate and it was pronounced unsafe in about 1925 or before. Then the farmers struck upon a plan to fix it up to help out their water supply. So they shut down the gate and stored water. When the flow of the river slackened, there now being more water users, that it would afford the older and bigger water rights come first, and everybody wanted water and took all they could. This idea of catching the water looked quite feasible.

The last week in May, 1927, snow began to fall and morning of the 30th it was so deep, cars standing out in the streets of Butte were almost covered. The snow was general in these parts of the state. Was said new snow fell three feet on the level at Wise River. It was a wonderful thing for the range, tho no one dreamed of what might happen to that condemned dam full of water. In two weeks time they would know what an awful catastrophe was. On June 14, early morning, a man up the river started in an old car to spread the alarm. This time no fooling, no time to warn a man in a mill or stand on the bridge and watch an 8 inch rise. This time it came with an awful roar, bringing rocks, trees, cutting a path with a 20 foot breast of water ever gaining power and speed as it tumbled down the 60 feet per mile decent, on and on taking everything in its path. The little place of Hugh Thompson's, later Ben Butler's place was so torn up, it was most worthless. The Butlers had come out to Melrose a year or so before to work and the place was vacant at that time.

Tearing on to Young's place, being built in the river on a slough and hit there hard, tearing his log buildings down like kindling wood, committing an awful tragedy. Tracy Trueman, wife and three children lived there at the time and heard that awful roar. He tried to start the car. The two girls were in it but the boy was so frightened his mother could not get him in [*the car*], in the awful excitement. (Youngs had moved away several years before. The family married, scattered when Young died.) The avalanche [*of water*] caught them trying to get the car started. The water caught them. Some few hours later searching parties found the two girls on the west bank and the auto with all four wheels torn off it. They all were in their night clothes and the girls were found nearly naked. Tracy, wife and little boy all drowned. The boy never was found. Tracy was found somewhere below Wise River in a pile of brush.

[*Charles*] Ferguson was in a small cabin. Even with all the hurried calls for him to come, he slept on. [*Lovell*] Pool jumped into his truck and made it acrost the lowland and acrost the bridge, taking up the warning that the other man could not do. Just after he crossed the bridge the flood hit - taking it out. He never stopped but tore on spreading the news as he went. The flood hit the Hotel. Some logs lodged on the porch, tore the posts down, letting the porch roof act as a fender and the flood rolled on. When it was built the sills were laid in the mortar foundation and that is one reason it stood and the porch roof veering off the worst impact of the flood.

The shack Ferguson was in was taken down a few rods. Rode the waves well as a coil lamp on the table still set there in place but Ferguson was drown. The drunk man upstairs in the Hotel slept in his drunken stupor till all was over.

From the road the valley widens out, which gave the flood water a chance to widen out and somewhat slacken the onrush of the flood. Al's house and barns being located at the east side of the mouth of Wise River also on the bank of the Big Hole River. It did not get the main force of the flood. Tho got its share. A large, long log was thrust under the kitchen the full length of the house and everything flooded - filling the ditches and tearing out flumes.

At John Lawrence's place it cleaned the barnyards. There, too, the flood had a wider scope to spread out. Mrs. Schmidt was there at the time, Johnnie Hand had gone up to help a few days till Mrs. Lawrence could sell or rent. He went to Wise River as soon as he could get there and helped parties over thru the torn up fields. All the time Pool raced ahead of the flood, spreading the news: "the dam has broke - the flood is coming". Spread the alarm in the Flat [*Dewey*] as he dashed away, determined of wheels, cogs, gas, tires and body

**Railroad bridge at Lavon after the Wise River Flood
June 14, 1927
From the Thelma (Hand) Kalsta Collection**

held together to beat the flood at the dam and get across the river before the flood, as it was sure to take out the bridge he had to cross in order to get to Divide. Warn the people on the way, and stop the oncoming trains, because if they were allowed to go past Divide and into the canyon it would be death to all aboard the trains. After delivering his message to the section agent, he dashed acrost the bridge at Marrows farm house to warn them of the flood and then back, just in the nick of time. The bridge went out behind him. Then exhausted, he rested at Divide.

At Deweys Flat it did little damage. The old log house down clost to the river was lifted up and taken down. A family by the name of Dillons lived there and did not have time to take anything out. The story was told (I can't vouch for it) how it rode the crest of the flood thru the canyon and when it went over the [lower] dam, a piano in it was playing "A Home On The Rolling Deep, A Home On The Ocean Wave". The dam [lower] was not jarred.

The county bridge below the dam was taken out and the spans taken down the river 1/4 mile or more. The main lot of the debris was dropped in Marrow's hay meadow and along the R.R. track before it entered the canyon, tho it gathered more on its way at Maiden Rock. It tore out the R.R. track and dropped it on the opposite side of the river. The section crew only saved their lives by taking to the nearby bluffs (hills). Some of the farmers had sawed and split stove wood on the islands. That was all taken.

About eleven o'clock, we noticed the river being full and very rapidly raised carrying everything that could be picked up by a flood. The river seemed to be full of stove wood. By noon we were alarmed, tho knowing it was one of the dams broke loose. We thot the lower one. The section men had picked up the news and hurried to the R.R. bridge over the river at Lavon and we learned from them it was a dam brake. It came on, flooding the upper meadow and field, even then the river grew higher. Finally it came over the banks into our barnyard and left it clean, not a fence board on anything left. Then it was up to the R.R. bridge floor pounding away. Finally the bridge gave way, taking the end pier down the river and leaving the middle pier down stream. The lower abutment tore away. This was a trying day for all of us - trying to save things from the flood. In the upper field, ditches were filled, flumes taken away and post holes for a new fence were all filled, besides the meadow land was filled with silt, which made the mowing job a hard one for man and beast, as well as scythes. But, I'm happy to say our dam was made better.

From here it widened out, losing a lot of force. This side of Glen the water went down in the Wood Livestock field and tore out a strip of embankment below the section house. At the forks of the river in Myers' field, it filled in the east fork, so the Garrisons and Beehers had to later work that fork to get enuf irrigating water.

Dad Corder's place was vacant. The only damage, other than filling the cabin, an outhouse was floated away. At Mrs. Alder's it flooded the place in general. At Twin Bridges the flood water covered the grounds at the Orphan Home and farther on down the Jefferson it flooded LaHood's Campgrounds. Finally it lost it's force and entered the Missouri at Three Forks.

Three bridges withstood the flood - but in each case the water had to slow to spread out. Brown's bridge, the old bridges below Glen, and the Pennington bridge. The latter was leaning from a high water in 1916.

For 60 to 70 miles the flood lashed, filled and tore down property. Damage to a (million dollars worth)? It was done and all that could be done then was to compensate the owners for their losses and put ditches, flumes and such like back in working order as soon as possible so the farmers could reap as reasonable a harvest as could be under the circumstances.

REVIEW OF DAMAGE DONE BY FLOOD

- Dam breaks at Wise River about 6:30 Tuesday morning.
- Wall of water 20 feet high rushes down canyon carrying everything before it.
- Wise River bridge washed out.
- Flood strikes Wise River engulfing buildings but all occupants with the exception of Charles Ferguson saved.
- Waters enter the Big Hole river and race towards Dewey - town is partially flooded and several buildings damaged.
- Roads and telephone lines as well as small bridges washed out.
- Montana Southern railroad bridge carried out.
- County wagon bridge at Divide knocked to pieces by hurtling timbers.
- Substation and pumping plant at Divide flooded and badly damaged.
- Cottages at pumping plant suffer.
- Light wires and trees toppled over near Divide.
- About a mile of track of the Oregon Short Line washed out from Maiden Rock in both directions.
- Parts of Melrose flooded and several small bridges washed out.
- Part of railroad washed out near Browne's station as well as small county bridge but Browne's steel wagon bridge stands strain.
- Railroad bridge at Lavon swings out into stream at 1:30 but north end holds to abutments.
- Valuable farm lands along the Big Hole flooded.
- Buildings at Zeigler Springs under water and badly damaged.
- Several ranches in vicinity of Twin Bridges flooded as well as county road and grounds of the state orphan home.
- Bridge across Beaverhead at Twin Bridges reported unsafe.
- High Water general from Iron Rod east.

The Dillon Tribune
Dillon, Montana
June 17, 1927

Montana Power paid damages and in most cases both parties were satisfied. Then they hired men and set them to work on the ranches where they needed ditch and flume repairs, cleaned debris off of meadows, etc. They did all they could for the people along the flood path.

The dam was never rebuilt, was given up. Fact was that these two dams were past their useful days. The machinery was taken out of the lower dam several years before and a section of the upper part taken off. By this time the water company had bigger and better dams on other rivers in the state and they did not need these two.

In talking to Louise (Hand) Shafer, she recalled that she was staying with her other grandparents, Pauline (Pfeifer) and Fredrick Julius Hartwig the day of the flood. Their place was located further down river from the Hand Ranch, at what is now Glen, and on the opposite side of the R.R. tracks from the river. She recalls going with Julius (her uncle) in a car up to Navy, where R.R. section houses were located. They went up there to help Piccones (Mr. Dan Piccone was Section Foreman) put their piano up on blocks so it would not be damaged by water. She said she stayed in the car while the piano work was being done and remembers seeing the water coming. The piano being placed on blocks, her uncle then got back in the car and drove them to high ground. The Hartwig house was protected by the R.R. embankment and thus did not receive any damage. She said they went up to stay with Aunt Eddie [*Louise (Hartwig) Kambich Hirst*], as her home was on yet higher ground.

[*In a conversation with Rock Hand, he told me that the truck Lovell Pool drove to warn people of the coming flood was the truck that Lovell and Rock owned jointly on a delivery service they had going from Butte to the Big Hole Basin. The truck was ruined from the wild ride ahead of the flood and thus the "delivery" venture was also gone.*

The railroad crews moved in immediately to repair the railroad track and bridges that had been damaged in the flood. One of the fellows working on the Lavon Bridge was destined to become a part of the family. His name was Lars Kalsta.

In the fall of 1927 Susan began her junior year in high school and Thelma began her senior year in Dillon. They rented a small house that year from the Hildreths. Nettie was still teaching school in Ogden. - mc]

Byron's Homestead

In Book 112 of Patents, page 227, in the Court House in Virginia City, Madison County, Montana it is shown that it was recorded on August 27, 1927 that, Byron Hand has been established and duly consummated ------- for the S 1/2 of SW 1/4 Section 26, the E 1/2 of E 1/2 of S 34 and NW 1/4, N 1/2 of SW 1/4, the N 1/2 of the NE 1/4, the SW 1/4 of NE 1/4 and NW 1/4 of the SE 1/4 of S 35 in T 3 S of R 9 W of principal Meridian, Montana - 640 acres ----. [*This is a record of a homestead that Byron had taken up and the patent that was granted to him on this property. – mc*]

Byron Lost

[*In the late part of February in 1928, early one morning, Byron went down to the Big Hole River to cut ice so the cattle could get water. When he did not return, his father, Horace, went looking for him. He was not to be found. Horace found that a hole had been cut in the ice and a lantern was setting beside the hole. As to what happened is anyone's guess. At first they speculated that he had ran away. A search was conducted, but no trace of Byron was found. The following June, Byron's body was found several miles below the Hand Ranch in the Big Hole River. He had drowned.*

There was speculation afterwards as to whether Byron had had a seizure and had fallen through the ice, or if he had committed suicide. Apparently there had been some discussion of sending him back to Warm Springs. The actual happenings of that morning will never be known.

In the spring of 1928 Thelma graduated from high school. Nettie was attending summer school in Missoula. In the fall of 1928 Susan began her senior year of high school. She lived first with the Fairbanks and then moved in with Kate Lewis.

Horace and Maggie continued to improve the ranch, continued raising their family and watched their children grow, mature and go their own ways. Some of these partings were not always of an easy nature but as time went on some of the differences were settled and there appeared to be normal comings and goings of the children, their spouses and grandchildren. - mc]

NO TRACE IS FOUND OF YOUNG RANCHMAN

More Than a Week Has Gone By Since His Sudden Disappearance.

Byron Hand, son of Mr. and Mrs. Horace Hand, prominent ranch people at Reichle, who disappeared from his home early on the morning of February 28, is still missing although an extensive search has been in constant progress and circulars have been sent out to police officials in several northwestern states.

Friends have thoroughly combed the country for miles and have discovered nothing to aid them in the clearing up of the mystery and the theory has been advanced that the young man secured a ride from a passing motorist on the morning of his disappearance and made his way unobserved to some distant city where he would be recognized with difficulty.

**Dillon Tribune
Dillon, Montana
March 9, 1928**

From an interview by Myrna Carpita with Rock Hand in 1992, Rock told me that he worked the winter of 1928 in the mines in Butte. He mentions working in the Mountain Con Mine. He rented a room to stay in and had his lunches prepared at a restaurant on the corner of Park and Main each day. He tells that there was a gambling game called the "Butte Pool". He did not say what it was based on. He said the winnings could run from $50.00 to several hundred dollars.

One morning on his way to work he recalled, "I had just got in front of 123 North Main, walking up the hill and I saw a lunch pail come out the doggone door. I had to back up from getting hit. It hit the street car track and broke open, the sandwich run one way and something else and something else. The guy come to the door at 123 North Main and I said what's going on, a fight in there? "No", he says. This fellow was going to work this morning and he stopped to check his ticket and he found out he won $500.00 in the Butte Pool. He said he was through with the mine as he had won the $500.00 and I guess that was good enough for him."

[Later in 1928, Rock started working in Helena for the Bensen Carpenter Company selling Willy's and Wippit cars, Reo trucks and International Harvester farm machinery. He started working for them for a wage of one hundred and seventy-five dollars a month, with a car furnished for a demonstrator and expenses for his out of town trips, which he made to call on customers.

On April 14, 1929 Thelma Victoria Hand and Lars Kalsta were married in Ogden, Utah.

Nettie made all of the arrangements for Lars and Thelma's wedding and wedding breakfast. Lars and Thelma took a very extensive honeymoon trip to Los Angeles and up the California coast, seeing all the sights and visiting with various relatives that lived in California.

Susan graduated from high school in the spring of 1929. Nettie also had a graduation. She graduated from the University at Missoula and accepted a position as training instructor for teachers at the Normal in Dillon. Susan started college at the Normal in the fall of 1929. - mc]

**Lars and Thelma (Hand) Kalsta
1929
From the Susan Hand Collection**

BYRON HAND'S BODY IS FOUND IN RIVER

Mystery Surrounding Young Man's Disappearance Cleared by Two Fishermen.

The body of Byron Hand, 25-year-old son of Mr. and Mrs. Horace Hand of Browne's Station, prominent ranching family of that community, who has been missing from his home since early on the morning of February 28, of this year, was found in a clump of driftwood in the Big Hole river last Sunday about noon by two fishermen about seven miles south of the Hand ranch.

Frank and Carl Kambich, two young men of Reichle, made the discovery while fishing in the river and phoned to Sheriff Orr here who with Undersheriff Carl Hartwig and Coroner James Phillips drove to the scene and extricated the body from the water where it had probably lodged for several months. Identification was made possible through parts of the clothing and dental work by the young man's father.

It is believed that he fell into the river the same morning he was missed from the ranch and was unable to save himself, probably becoming cramped by the cold water.

Byron Hand was a native of the community where his parents have resided for a number of years and is survived by his mother and father; two brothers, John of Reichle and Roscoe of Butte and three sisters, Nettie of Missoula and Susan and Thelma of Reichle.

The funeral was held Monday afternoon from the family home and interment was made in the cemetery at Melrose, the Rev. Edward Smith of Butte officiating.

**Dillon Tribune
Dillon, Montana
June, 1928**

On April 3, 1930 in the District Court of the Fifth Judicial District of the State of Montana, in and for the County of Madison, in the Matter of the Estate of Byron Hand, deceased, the final account and decree of distribution was acted upon. "It was adjudged and decreed:

1. That the said final account be, and the same is hereby approved.
2. That the residue of said estate be, and the same is hereby distributed to the heirs of said decedent equally, share and share alike, to-wit:
   To Horace Hand, father of decedent, an undivided one-half interest thereof, and
   To Maggie Hand, mother of decedent, and undivided one-half interest hereof.
3. The real estate affected by this decree is situated"---

[Listed as the same as Byron's Homestead Patent - mc]

John states in "John Hand Recalls Lifetime of Mining", Dillon Tribune, February 3, 1966, that he had visited with various mining men and "I asked them where would be a good camp to try leasing. They mentioned several but I can remember a place called Argenta, and they said no use to go there as this had no chance to ever make ore.

I kept clear of Argenta for a long time, until I agreed to come and take a look with Mr. Decker and Mr. Herndon. I came to look at Ferdinand Mine and it looked promising. Things seemed like metal would be good. Mr. Herndon made me acquainted with the people. There was a school here which looked good as we did not want to be away from the family.

This was late in the fall of 1929 when I moved here [*to Argenta*]. Things went down in metal prices and we did not do any work on Ferdinand Mine. I did some shaft work for Bill Cushing and worked a little that winter."

[*On October 10, 1929 John and Ida's little Earl died at age 3 years of spinal meningitis. They were living at Argenta. - mc*]

Louise (Hand) Shafer, talked to me of Earl's death. She related to me that the day before his death he seemed okay. That evening when he went to bed he was fine but during the night he started running a fever and by the next day was dead. It was very quick and unexpected.

She also went on to tell, and I remember Grandma [*Ida*] talking about this, that the night before Earl's death Grandma woke up in the middle of the night to see a woman standing at the foot of the bed. This woman told Grandma that Earl was going to die. This was very vivid to my Grandmother.

> **EARL HAND VICTIM OF SUDDEN ILLNESS**
>
> Earl, the three-year-old son of Mr. and Mrs. John Hand, prominent ranch people of Reichle, succumbed at the Barrett hospital Friday evening following an illness of less than two days. The child was brought to the hospital Friday morning in a critical condition. The funeral was held Saturday afternoon from the Brundage chapel, the Rev. L.M. Wilenius of the Lutheran church officiating.
>
> **The Dillon Tribune**
> **Dillon, Montana**
> **October 1929**

Louise said Earl was a cute, fun loving child. Earl and Bill were nearly inseparable. Louise said she was staying with her grandparents, the Hartwigs, when this happened. When she found out about Earl's death, she cried and cried and there was no way to console her. She also describes the funeral. He was buried the day after his death and she remembers viewing him in his casket. The casket was covered with a domed glass. This was because he died of spinal meningitis and it was a highly communicable disease.

[*The spring of 1930 found John and his family moving back to Reichle. - mc*]

In "John Hand Recalls Lifetime of Mining", Dillon Tribune, February 3, 1966, John states, "We were in the beginning of the depression in the spring."

"I got a job with Mrs. Carrie Keith of Butte on her Vermont Mine at McCarty Mountain at $5.00 per day and $1.00 per day for my compressor. I went over and got started. When school was out here [*Argenta*] our family moved to Glen. I had made arrangements for an empty farm house to live in, about five miles from the mine.

When I took the job silver was 50 cents per ounce; lead was about four cents per pound; gold was $20 per ounce. The ore was very high grade, 200 to 600 ounces per ton, 40 to 50% lead.

Mr. & Mrs. Jim Donovan
"She may look rough" but she had a Heart of Gold in her "own rough way". At 16 she saw the 5 hanged by the Vigilantes". - Thelma Kalsta
Thelma (Hand) Kalsta Collection

> **Mrs. Donovan's Parrot**
>
> **Louise (Hand) Shafer tells a story about Mrs. Donovan's parrot**. When Mrs. Donovan went some place she would leave her parrot with Horace and Maggie. Louise said she remembered the parrot well. She said the parrot could talk and would! He would say, "Polly wants a cracker, Polly wants a cracker" over and over and over and then pretty soon would say, "Polly wants a cracker you bald headed son of a bitch." Then "Polly" would get a cracker! The favored cracker was a saltine.

Lead was small. We would ship about 15 ton at a time. I would bring down a ton at a time on my old Dodge truck, stack it at the ranch house till Mrs. Keith wanted to ship it. She would get a railroad car at Glen, and we would load sacks in for East Helena Smelter.

The price of silver kept dropping, and at 40 cents per ounce she leased the mine to three Butte men. They got me to stay with my compressor and we worked about six weeks. Winter was near. We shipped about 10 tons of ore, 250 ounces silver, 45 of gold.

Well, I got some groceries, and about $30 money for that venture. We piled 15 tons of 100 ounce ore on dump. Silver continued to go down to 23 cents per ounce. Lead was 3 1/2 cents. Then we were in for hard scratching."

OLD-TIME FREIGHTER CROSSES THE DIVIDE

Seth Halbert, better known to old residents of Beaverhead county as "Big Al", passed away at his home in Hot Springs, Montana, Saturday morning, April 11.

Mr. Halbert was born in Orangeville, Indiana, in 1857. In 1875 the Halbert family moved to Kansas where they settled. Later, when a young man, Mr. Halbert went to Colorado. There he packed ore out of the mountains on burros. From Colorado he followed the western migration to the coast states.

He came to Glendale, Montana when the "ghost city" was in its prime. Here he engaged in hauling ore from Hecla to the smelter in Glendale.

With the decline of mining activities in Hecla, Mr. Halbert with other freighters saw possibilities in farming in the new state. He took up land near Wise River, Montana. For several years after establishing his home there he freighted from Divide to Gibbonsville, Idaho. He hauled freight for Eliel Brothers' store in Gibbonsville.

He was a lover of horses and always kept a fine driving team and good draft horses.

In 1909 he married Mrs. Emma Campbell.

About five years ago he sold his ranch at Wise River and moved to Hot Springs, where he has resided since.

His death followed a lingering illness and although he suffered much he retained his genial disposition to the end.

Besides a host of friends both in the Big Hole valley and at Hot Springs he is survived by his widow, Mrs. Emma Halbert, two step-sons, Wallace and Chester Campbell and five sisters, Mrs. Horace Hand of Reichle, Mrs. Lucy A. Briggs, San Jose, Calif.; Mrs. Emma Briggs, Colorado Springs, Colo.; Mr. J. A. Wilson, Folsom City, Calif.; Mrs. Hattie Jones, Dinuba, Calif., and a number of nieces and nephews.

The following poem is dedicated to his memory by a niece, Nettie M. Hand of Dillon

> Here's to you, old-timer!
> The battle is over now,
> You've driven the mules on the freight team
> And followed the harrow and plow.
>
> Your maker has called,
> And you've answered.
> The hands that once toiled
> Are now still.
> The journey was long,
> You were weary, now rest --
> "Tis God's will.

     Dillion Tribune
     Dillon, Montana
     April 1931

**Seth 'Big Al' Halbert
From the Rock Hand Collection**

[In the spring of 1930, Susan was still attending Normal (Western Montana College) in Dillon and Nettie was teaching there. The fall of 1930 Susan started a teaching job at Duncan School, in the Ruby Valley. At Christmas she resigned and had her tonsils out and a sinus operation. Spring of 1930 finds Thelma and Lars on the Brown place. Rock is in Helena working various sales jobs.

In April of 1931, 'Big Al', Maggie's brother and Horace's early day partner passes on.

The year 1931 finds Maggie and Horace with no children living at home. They have a hired hand, a fellow by the name of Bud Masters. Times are tough economically but they continue with their everyday lives. Maggie learns to drive in 1931. She is 62 years old. Horace has his first stroke, though a light one. The children and grandchildren come and go.

Susan returned to school at the Normal and in the spring graduates from a two year course. She signed a contract to teach at the Gibbons School in the Big Hole Valley in the fall of 1931.

Nettie is in Dillon working at the Normal.

Lars and Thelma are on the Lavelle place at Divide. Thelma is pregnant but loses her baby in the summer.

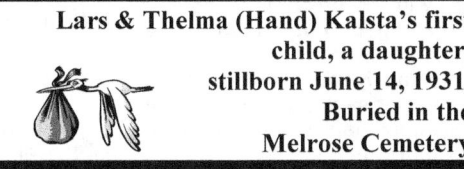

Lars & Thelma (Hand) Kalsta's first child, a daughter, stillborn June 14, 1931. Buried in the Melrose Cemetery

John is struggling to find enough work to support his family. He is working every chance he gets.

In the fall of 1931 Rock took a trip to Cuba. Upon his return from Cuba he returned to work at Bensens. He worked for them until they closed in 1932. - mc]

Federal Census - State of Montana

1920 - 548,889 citizens
1930 - 537,606 citizens

Chapter XVIII

Tough Times

****

In 1932 Nettie built her house in Dillon. It was made of squared logs, except on the outside which were rounded and varnished. This home is located at 120 South Dakota St., Dillon, Montana. She was teaching at the Normal College in Dillon.

In the early 1930's Horace had begun to start to suffer from strokes. The strokes were mild but they affected his health and his overall abilities to do the necessary work to keep the ranch going. As a result, he began to consider the fact that he was going to have to do something with the ranch. Apparently he began to approach his sons about taking over the ranch. Very little is known about all of the circumstances of this. From the information available, it might be surmised that John had a deep interest in mining and was not interested in the ranch or there may have been other circumstances. At any rate, he did not take over the ranch. Nettie, of course, was teaching and was not married, so her circumstances and interests were not such that she could take the ranch. Susan also was single and just beginning her teaching career. She was not in the position to manage the ranch and probably for most unmarried woman at this time, it would not have been a consideration. Rock states in some of his writings that his father approached him, but he felt he could not get along with his father, so he said no. He suggested that Lars and Thelma be approached. This Horace did and on March 28, 1933 an agreement between Horace and Maggie Hand and Lars and Thelma Kalsta was signed. It is as follows. - mc]

> From "John Hand Recalls Lifetime of Mining", Dillon Tribune, February 3, 1966
>
> I had to work at anything I could get the second year at Glen. We had to pay advance rent on house, and place was old run down ranch. Rent cost me $125 in advance. We got it, and after the year rolled around we had only handled $325. We had lots of garden stuff. I still got half-time on government fence jobs and got one-half compensation on a road job which lasted four months.
>
> Next spring I was recommended to three New York men who wanted to drive a tunnel and raises at Moose Lake. I got the contract. I moved in that May. Lots of snow and mud. Got going in about three days and completed the job first of August. I never thought I made any money there. I had two shifts going and watched both during that time.
>
> When we cleaned up last round I told them not to wake me up till I got my sleeping done. I slept 36 hours, then left my compressor and went home. Harvested what crop family had raised and no more work in sight. I went back with an old car I had bought for $35. It ran good but had some tire trouble.
>
> I took the family with me. Kids would blow up a paper sack and bust it. I got so jumpy about flats thought I would never get there. In one place road ran through cattails and seemed to be crawling with small ducks, and kids needed a run, so I stopped and away they went. It took about one hour to run them down, wet and muddy, but no ducks.
>
> All the money I could spare off that job was sent home and when I got home they had new clothes, shoes, flour and sugar to the good. I never knew what I had realized out of that job.
>
> I rented my compressor to a gold mine at Pony. They were supposed to pay me for pipe, but never did. I got the compressor back, but no engine, and compressor wasn't worth hauling home. I had lost my tools and was everything but happy about that.
>
> The next year [1933] was a bear cat. I had to raise something to eat. There was a Government loan for fuel for tractor and seed. I qualified for $275. This time rent went to $150 which I managed to get.
>
> The old tractor I had gave out. I bought a tractor that had not run much, but was a pile of dust. I got it from State Bank of Dillon for $5 and give a trucker $20 to haul it to Glen. Next day I was plowing with it. We had accumulated chickens, turkeys, pigs, and we were not bad off only for money. Family was getting bigger and it meant move again, and some money must be made.
>
> The only source was ore. I knew by now where lots of ore was in different places. Had records of all my assays, also description of each place, and what it would take to get it.

ESCROW AGREEMENT

HORACE HAND and MAGGIE E. HAND, his wife, as first parties, and LARS KALSTA and THELMA KALSTA, his wife, as second parties, AGREE:

1. That the first parties have sold to the second parties all of their lands, now occupied by the first parties, in Madison County, Montana, for the sum of $20,000.; and have included in said sale all farm machinery, livestock and other personal property except two horses and all household furniture. The same are reserved by the first parties. Ford truck also reserved.

2. The first parties reserve for their own use, during the term herof or for such less time as they may require, four rooms in the northwest side in the dwelling house now occupied by them, comprising two rooms upstairs and two rooms downstairs.

3. The ordinary supplies required in the livelihood of the first parties during the term of this contract shall be supplied to them, or the survivor thereof, by the second parties. This shall not include medical services or medical supplies, nor hospital bills, nor hire for trained nurse.

4. Upon the purchase price the second parties will pay to the first parties, or the survivor thereof, on the first day of January of each year, beginning January 1, 1934, the sum of $500.; and such payments shall continue for twenty years, and until the sum of $10,000. is paid. The supplies above mentioned shall be provided and accepted in lieu of interest for said period of twenty years.

5. After the first $10,000. of said purchase price is paid the second parties will pay interest at 4% per annum upon deferred payments. They shall, on January 1st of each year, beginning January 1, 1954, pay at least $1,000. per year on the last $10,000. of said

purchase price. However, the second parties, may upon any payment date, pay any additional part of the purchase price, in excess of the amount herein required. No interest shall be chargeable upon any such sum after the same is paid.

6. The second parties shall, during said term, pay all taxes that shall be collectible upon any of said property after May, 1933. They shall maintain insurance upon said property in a sum equal to present insurance and have the same payable, in case of loss, to the first parties.

7. The second parties shall, at all times during said term keep up the livestock and other personal property, in amount and value, equal to that which is now delivered to them by the first parties. They shall keep the premises, including ditches, fences, corrals and buildings in as good state of repair as when received by them, reasonable wear, deterioration and loss from unavoidable causes excepted.

8. The first parties have signed, acknowledged and caused to be certified, a deed by which said lands shall be conveyed to the second parties. Said deed, together with this agreement, shall be deposited in escrow at the First National Bank of Dillon, Montana; which bank is hereby constituted the depository. Said bank is authorized to receive all payments required hereunder. The second parties shall deposit with the depository receipts for taxes and insurance as paid. When all of the terms of this agreement shall have been performed by the second parties, said depository is authorized to deliver said deed to them.

9. Time is of the essence of this agreement; and in case the second parties default in any payment required hereunder, or fail to perform any of the terms hereof, then and thereupon the first parties, or the survivor thereof, or their representative, may terminate this agreement and may withdraw said deed from escrow, and resume possession of said premises and of the said personal property, or other personal property substituted therefore, and may retain as rental for the use and occupation of said premises, and the use of said personal property, all payments made hereunder prior to default.

10. The lands affected by this agreement are described as follows:

S1/2 SW1/4 Sec. 26;
SE1/4 SE1/4 Sec. 27;
E 1/2 and all that part of E1/2 NW1/4 and E1/2 SW 1/4 which lies
east of the Big Hole River, Sec. 34;
NW 1/4, N1/2 SW 1/4, N1/2 NE1/4, SW1/4 NE1/4 and NW 1/4 SE1/4 Sec. 35; all
in T. 3 S. R. 9 W. M. M.
All that part of E 1/2 Sec. 3, T. 4 S. R. 9 W. which
lies east of the Big Hole River. All of said lands
are located in Madison County, Montana.

11. This contract shall not be sold, assigned or sublet without the written consent of the first parties, or the survivor thereof, or the representative.

Dated March 28, 1933.
Horace H. Hand   Lars Kalsta
Maggie E. Hand   Thelma Kalsta
First Parties   Second Parties

[*Lars and Thelma soon moved into the ranch house at Lavon with Horace and Maggie. Horace's health continued to deteriorate, as a result of more strokes, but he still was up and around and active. Monetarily times were tough. This was the depths of the depression. Things appear to be inexpensive, but there was not any money to be had. They struggled and got by as best they could. By this time each of Maggie and Horace's children seemed to be set on their own course in life and everyone's world was ever changing.*]

[*On August 7, 1933 Roscoe "Rock" K. Hand and Verna Marie Ogilvie were married in Helena. - mc*]

From Susan's writings, undated, she states, regarding the trip to Helena to Rock and Verna's wedding, "Net arranged for Jim Garrison to take us in the Garrison car - Mother, Net, Ella and me. Jim Garrison and I needed to go job hunting and their's was the only big car in the "family". Net was going with J.B. then."

[*In 1933 Rock worked a short time for Bergenden Walker Company, a Buick and Pontiac dealer in Helena. He felt he was not getting paid enough so he quit. Shortly after that he acquired the Pontiac dealership, with the help of two partners, a few hundred dollars from Verna (who was working for the Montana Power "and had a good job") and a loan for $3500 from Bob Barrett of the State Bank in Dillon. - mc*]

Rock stated in his interview with the Montana Historical Society, "I lasted just a year and I lost all the money that my wife had and I lost all the money I borrowed from the banker in Dillon and I was years gettin' it paid back but I paid him the interest every year and I was stripped."

Roscoe and Verna (Ogilvie) Hand
August 7, 1933
From the Rock Hand Collection

[*After Rock lost the Pontiac dealership in Helena, a friend approached him about constructing a building on some lots on Main Street in Helena. The friend gave Rock title to the four lots and Rock, along with a building contractor, borrowed the money and built the building. At that time Rock acquired the International Harvester Agency dealership. - mc*].

John & Ida (Hartwig) Hand's sixth child, Shirley Ann Hand, born August 27, 1933

From the Montana Historical Society Oral History interview, Rock states: "I didn't know where I was gonna get the money to pay for the Harvester machines. I was in lots of trouble from time to time, but we got it up between Ustead [*his partner*] and me. I was out peddlin' somethin' night and day and some way or other I got it."

Winter of 1933

Susan [*Hand*] taught school at Gibbons. That included the families of Willies, Topes, Ritschels, Else and others. This is a very snowy part of the Basin over on the North Fork of the Big Hole. She often relates how she suffered and nearly died teaching the school that winter. The school house was cold and the boarding quarter were no better. She paid a high board and room to endure these physical and mental agonies to freeze both day and night, in school and out and to make it more agonizing, Mrs. Tope would not allow her to wash even a handkerchief in the house. A fire had to be built in an outhouse, heat the water and wash there.

This was called a very bitter winter and many speak of the hardships in that winter. Mr. Byers [*Bayers*] lived on the North Fork. He went into the basin in 1928, bot a place and kept thorough bred white faces. He did well with his cattle while there. Says there is no other place where cattle do better. At the high quality of the hay, pasture can't be excelled anywhere else, tho the winters are hard on people - those that really get out and tries to do something.

He related an experience that decided the question of staying longer in the Basin or moving out. It was the winter of '33. They had had several days of real cold weather (36 below). A man was coming to look for some good cattle and told Byers he would come anytime he sent for him. While this cold weather was on, Byers decided to wait for better weather so the first nice day he telephoned the man to come. He should be on the 4 p.m. bus, but the bus was late, so finally he hitched up and drove two miles to the Walker place to the road. Was 9:30 p.m. No bus yet. The weather was none too good; finally about 11:30 p.m. the bus came. The man got off, got into Mr. Byers sleigh and away they went and all of the sudden a terrible blizzard came out of no where from the north. The worst he ever saw. He knew where to head the team to some bars in a cross fence, but when they got there the bars were not there. So he tied the team to the fence to make sure and felt his way along some distance and finally found the bars. Then thru, the storm still raged on, but he was quite sure this time he could head them straight to the barn a mile away. In this field there were 14 hay stacks, so away they went and the first thing they knew they were back at the bars again. Each time he thot he surely knew how to reach the barn. Finally, the third round and no where yet, the blizzard still raged, he was cold, exhausted and wanted to sleep. So he told his companion it was no use, he had almost given up. He pulled the robes up over him and gave the horses the reigns and did not try to drive. Strange, they had never, in all this travel, seen a hay stack or come near one, tho there were 14 in the field. Finally the team felt or sensed an old sleigh road. The ruts being froze with ice, the horses felt their way to the barn but they missed it by a few panels of fence. Then Byers got out and felt his way, panel by panel, till he found the gate. It was 2 a.m. The horses' eyes were frozen over with frost. His face and nose, hands and feet were frozen. The other man did not fare quite so badly. In the morning the thermometer stood at 62 below, clear and cold. (The blizzard ceased.) He sold some cattle to this man and later moved to Twin Bridges and bot a place there.

In another writing of Susan Hand's, she states, "J.B. [*Garrison*] was a speaker and organizer for the Farmers Union --- I often went with them [*Net and J.B.*]. J.B. was so haphazard in taking care of a car. Once we ran out of gas

**Susan Hand
1933
From the Susan Hand Collection**

Mild Weather in Winter '33-'34 at Lavon

From Maggie's Diary - April 1, 1934 - No moisture has fallen here all fall and winter. No ice to stay on the river all winter - never saw such a nice winter.

Further notes in her diary indicate that the rhubarb is up enough for a pie on the 12th of April and the gardens were being planted. By the 24th of April it was dry, dusty and hot and the, "River is high - measured 4.10 at 9:15 o'clock - too high for April." In June the rains finally came and there was a fair amount of moisture, but lots of forest fires in the area - "Smoke got thicker and thicker all day - looked like the whole world was afire."

The summer months were hot and dry, although there was sufficient water for irrigation. The weather continued to be nice until into October. On the 13th of October Maggie's Diary reports snow on the ground and continued to snow and be cold for some time to come. She noted concern about the potatoes - if they suffered damage or not - later she writes that the potato crop was in good shape.

The weather turned nice in the latter part of October, but became quite cold in November and December.

when near Dillon - late at night. Another time, probably fall of 1933, when J. B. was driving, the steering gear broke and we drifted into a cut bank on the road out of Sheridan. A neighbor and John Hand came along. John tied the steering gear together with strips of strong linen cloth Net had brought to cover the seats to keep our clothes clean. I abandoned them and rode with a neighbor in a new car."

Excerpts from Maggie's Diary - April 15, 1934 – "Branded cattle (crop calves 25 to 30). **April 25, 1934** - Stung by a bee. Thelma irrigated garden, I had to play lady, owing to bee sting, but got better by evening. Thelma got ready to wash. **April 26, 1934** - Water higher - 4.45. Thelma washed. My bee sting still swollen badly. Discovered my iris along fence ready to bloom - a month early - columbine most ready to bloom - 2 goslins hatched. **May 1, 1934** - Lars sold steers 4 3/4 cents [*per pound*] 1 bull - $35.00, 1 cow - $35.00. **May 2, 1934** - Sold steers, drove to Beehers to weigh - averaged (1271 at 4 3/4 cents) 14 head (12 head ours, 2 Lar's). Steers averaged $60.37 each. Car quit on road - John hauled me in." [*A later entry shows the cost of car repairs being $22.00 (parts) plus cost of labor.*

Throughout the diary there are entries where Maggie sold eggs at .15 to .25 cents per dozen, cream at .50 cents per quart, plants at various prices, and later the produce and flowers from the garden.

Entries in the diary show 42 rows of spuds planted in the upper garden patch, north end, 25 rows of Golden Bantum corn, 25 rows Sunshine Corn, and another 30 rows of other corn to be ready in June with pumpkins planted in between. Also, acres of potatoes being planted, along with sugar beets and soy beans. There were also tomatoes, squash, string beans, spinach, radishes, lettuce, carrots, kolaraba, peas, cabbages, cucumbers, parsnips, peppers, egg plant, pie plant (rhubarb), asparagus, garlic, onions, and flowers planted in other gardens, along with strawberry and raspberry patches to be cared for. There were also apple and plum trees. The planting of the gardens went on in various stages so they would have produce available throughout the summer and late into the fall. - mc]

From Maggie's Diary - May 28, 1934 - "Delivered flowers, came home, went to bed. Shortly Clifford Reid and family called on way home from Dillon - discovered a reck on the bluff, came back here, left family with Thelma and Lars went with Clifford to the scene -2 drunks driving wild, tore out 8 posts and leaped in air, lit 80 or so feet away on R.R. tracks down a steap imbankment. The machine was an awful reck. One man unconsious - other cralled back up grade. Men were taken to Dillon by passers by."

From Maggie's Diary - May 31, 1934 - "Dr. Hall came to see Pa and I. Gave him treatments." [*There are many notations through the diary of helping Horace bathe and take care of himself. - mc*]

From Maggie's Diary - June 18, 1934 - "Went to Dillon with Pottson - law suit of Wise River waters. Every rancher taking out water on that river was there to defend their rights - and get all the water they could - supper at Nets and came home. Bot the linnen for Julius's [*Hartwig*] bride [*Isabell Mast*] - we gave (Net, Thelma, Susan and Ma) a table cloth (linen) and napkins."

From Maggie's Diary - June 26, 1934 - "Prepared more spinach - canned 15 cans [*canned 40 more cans the next day - canning and food preparation was constantly being done. - mc*] Susan and I started for Shultzes on McCarthy to see Jess Swafford and apply for school. Such a day - the wind blew at the rate of 60 per or more - cold and fits of rain. Such a day long to be remembered - almost recked the top of car. We went to the flat rock field and got all [*rocks for the rock garden Maggie is building*] dare bring. Got home - the

From "John Hand Recalls Lifetime of Mining", Dillon Tribune, February 3, 1966:

GOLD GOES TO $35

Then came the raise in gold to $35 per ounce. Next came a job at Argenta, working for ACM at the new gold mine on French Creek. The pay was $3.50 per day. The place we were renting at Glen was sold, so came one more move. Family got situated in old farm house in February so they could finish school. When school was out they came to Argenta.

I did not stay working for ACM long. Canadian outfit was in a process of starting Ground Hog Mine to mine gold and they offered me $5 per day working for them. I closed down all hand drilling. Had them take me to Butte. There I picked out the stuff they would need. I got some men and we were finding pay ore in less than a week. I ran two shifts and had 1100 tons of ore in less than two months time. They then got to running too high. I was in process of leaving them when attachments were placed on them, and I was put in charge to take out enough ore to pay up the debts. I only had a small tonnage -- two cars, if I remember right -- that paid all gas and hardware bill, 86% of dead payroll and I left then.

When I was employed by them they furnished me with a pickup truck, which I used while in their employment. My old truck I gave to a member of a family which had bad luck, so, when I left them I was on foot. The court paid me, and so did one of directors that came here from Canada to take it.

drain plugged up. They had a time fixing it - a dress peddler called - crow killed large chicken - my little ducks are all scattered."

From Maggie's Diary - June 28, 1934 - "Haying started - picked currents and put up - 8 quarts and juice. Susan tried to ride the horse Robinson is breaking and she never got in saddle - was luck to not get killed; all bruised up, will be sore."

From Maggie's Diary - July 7, 1934 - "I believe this is the 40th anniversary of our wedding day. - If so tomorrow we took our dinner on Rock Creek where the old road crosses Rock Creek. Turned the horses out to eat while we ate and one did not want to be caught in the open but finally Horace did catch it. Went on to Dewey Flat and next day home on ranch.

Nettie and I picked currents for her. Nettie made my (our) garden cards. She went home loaded [*with garden produce*] on bus. Susan cooked. Turned hay till noon, stacked afternoon and made a killing (7 men) at work."

From Maggie's Diary - July 9, 1934 - "Hoed all morning. My knee has gone lame again. Hoed in afternoon, not nearly done."

[*Other entries show that Geneveve Squires came to visit and stayed. - mc*] **Diary states**, "Susan and Gen went wading in sloughs. Girls sick for their folly."

From Maggie's Diary - July 14, 1934 - "Spent all day in bed with my leg. Thelma hoed most of day, Susan cooked. Nettie came on 2 p.m. stage." [*Further entries show that Maggie finally went to a Dr. McGill for her knee. She had arthritis. Other entries also show she had problems with her knee all summer, but still worked daily in the garden and did all her other chores.*

It was a rare occasion that there were not visitors of some kind - friends, family, grandchildren, and business people, many of them staying for meals and staying over night. Also, there was a daily flow of people coming to the house to buy plants, produce, eggs, hens, and geese. Entries show Susan punching cows and keeping them in the proper grazing areas, helping with the cooking, gardening, cleaning, and canning. Nettie visited regularly from Dillon, going back and forth on the bus or train and Maggie and Thelma were always hard at work in the gardens, washing, cooking, canning, cleaning and sewing. Rock and Verna visited occasionally as did John, Ida and their family. As the garden matured, the produce was loaded into Maggie's little car and taken to Butte, Dillon, Glen or Melrose and sold to their various customers, sometimes house to house, sometimes to stores they contracted with.

Lars was busy with the haying, fencing, irrigation and cattle. One entry shows, "Susan and Lars went to hills for horses - came in late with them." *They used these horses for haying.*

Diary entries also show Susan, Nettie, Thelma and Lars all very active in the Farmers Union organization, attending meetings, pie socials, plays, fund raisers and other get togethers. They attended meetings state wide and did a lot of promotion. Maggie attended occasionally. Horace occasionally took a ride with family members to see neighbors, but was pretty much homebound.

Susan was attending summer school at the Normal college in Dillon during the summer of 1934. In the fall she began teaching at the Drummy School and stayed with the Staudemeyers. She apparently only taught there for a short time and then accepted a position with the Farmers Union Group to prepare and distribute a newsletter. Various diary entries show her living part time at the ranch and doing some traveling for her job. - mc]

From a letter by Susan Hand to Bernard and Annette - "In 1934 Pa wanted to protest our ranch taxes, which meant a trip by Model A over dirt roads to Virginia City; a hard day's travel. He thought we needed a man along and J.B. wanted to protest their taxes, was glib and knew men at the court house in Virginia City so Pa sent him with Net; and I went as chaperone!"

Just Off The Sunshine Trail

Just off the famous Sunshine Trail
You'll find some vegetables FOR SALE
In limousine or dyspeptic fliver
Drive down, good friends, to the Big Hole River.

We guarantee them fresh, you know,
Because they stay in the garden row,
Until you call for them and say,
"I'll take some vegetables today."

Some perfect peas in firm, green pods,
And crispy spuds beneath the sods,
A head of rotund cabbage green,
And those oft called for stringless beans,

Then later on when Old Friend Sol
Works on that corn so green and tall,
We'll have that luscious ear for sale,
All wrapped in its green coat of mail.

Tomatoes, cucumbers, carrots, and such,
Will all be ready with Nature's touch;
To complete this menu you'll want a fry,
And a bouquet of flowers to please the eye.

Thelma Kalsta '34

"Garden Card"
This is a copy of a card Net, Maggie and Thelma made and used to advertise the garden produce from the ranch.

From the Thelma (Hand) Kalsta Collection

From Maggie's Diary - October 5, 1934 - "Loaded cabbage, squash, rutabaga, parsnips and carrots for Melrose. Susan and I went to Melrose in afternoon - did very good - saw Hubers new fireplace - certainly a fine structure. Saw John, Ida and Shirley at Melrose. Saw Mrs. Boettaker Sr. (96 yrs. old I believe)." [*Further notes show the breakdown of money made for the year from the garden. They made about $402.50 cash* "plus food for house use from the garden."

Maggie was interested in a variety of things; gathering rocks and building a rock garden, fossils, arrow heads, sewing, weaving, knitting, reading, to exchanging starts of plants with neighbors. - mc]

From Maggie's Diary - October 12, 1934 - "Columbus Day. Susan did house work - looks like storm but is warm. Billy Malory came and rented the house (Corder). Paid $2.50 per month in advance. Pa feels quite good these days."

From Maggie's Diary - November 4, 1934 - "Pat Smith came with a cattle buyer. Lars sold 7 cows for 2 1/2 cents and 2 for 2 cents [*per pound*]. Nettie did not come. Pa did not have a very good day. Susan exercised her new typewriter." [*Susan is preparing the newsletter for the Farmers Union group. - mc*]

From Maggie's Diary - November 5, 1934 - "Cleaned and fixed front room of cabin for election - Thelma and I. Weaned calves (28) (should have had more?)."

From Maggie's Diary - November 6, 1934 - "Election Day from 8 a.m. to 6 p.m. in Cabin. Frankie, Mrs. Garrison, Mrs. Hoffman Jr., Ralph Streb and Susan [*must have been election judges*]. Bernard [*Garrison*] got 29 votes." [*Bernard or "J.B." Garrison was running for state legislature - he won the election. - mc*]

From Maggie's Diary - November 8, 1934 - "Cooked dinner while the girls cleaned and painted kitchen. Lars took up 7 fat cows, averaged about 2.9 cents = $203.00. Also got $100.00 for the dry pasture."

From Maggie's Diary - November 16, 1934 - "Cattle buyers came - bot 10 steers - good ones. Weighed 1050 - 9 and one smaller. (4 cents for nine - 3 1/2 cents the one). $411+ for steers."

John & Ida (Hartwig) Hand's Seventh child, Horace Delos Hand, born December 18, 1934.

From Maggie's Diary - December 18, 1934 – "Thelma worked on bath room and pantry. I helped a little and cooked. Mrs. Phil Nye came for Thelma to go to Dillon and take care of Ida but before they got there Isabel took Ida to hospital and the baby boy (9 lbs) was born at once. John was in town and Susan arrived on the stage. Julius Jr. brot John and Thelma home about 9:30 or later. All were glad the job was over so nicely and quickly. Susan staid in town."

From Maggie's Diary - December 31, 1934 - "The last day in 1934. A nice winter day. Bernard and Net stayed, figured gas all day until late in the night. I made 3 aprons - now the dresses next. Lars has a cold. Pa is not so good - Susan still in Dillon. Good By '34."

From Maggie's Diary - January 1, 1935 - "My window garden is fine. Several jars of paper white narcissis in bloom along with my other flowers. Net, JB, Jen and Mary came a minute on their way to Butte. Tomorrow they will go to Helena to get ready for Legislature to begin 7th."

From Maggie's Diary - January 5, 1935 - "I am still piecing quilts at odd moments as Pa won't let me get away to do anything and doesn't want me to work at that. Lars put in cattle scales."

[*Further diary entries show Maggie still cooking, washing, ironing and housecleaning. It shows she is sewing for the family, making dresses for herself, Susan, Thelma and Net, as well as aprons, quilts and scarves. She is also making baby clothing, doll clothing and sewing rags for rugs. She also makes notes about working on her scrap books. - mc*]

From Maggie's Diary - January 7, 1935 - "Lars paid $500.00 on place. Put in bank."

From Maggie's Diary - January 17, 1935 - "Men finished putting up ice. They put up Julius Hartwig's ice. He is getting too feeble to do much hard work. Old age is an awful thing when left alone to carry on the work to live and no money. Everyone should guard against it in that form."

From Maggie's Diary - February 5, 1935 - "Sorted and arranged my flower seeds in envelopes - ready to give away. John, Ida and little ones came."

> *There are numerous notations where they had butchered beef and hogs, both at the ranch at Lavon and at John and Ida's. Then, after the butchering, a large portion of the meat was canned as a method of preservation. Some of the meat was used fresh and a small portion was put on ice in the ice houses and used fairly soon.*
>
> *While butchering hogs at the ranch at Lavon, Louise (Hand) Shafer, a young girl at the time, was riding a large black horse. It ran off with her, down across the meadow and across the frozen Big Hole River into a plowed field. Everyone went running to see if she was okay, but her dad, John, kept right on with the task at hand, saying, "Oh, don't worry about her, she will be back." He was right. She rode the horse out and then brought him back, with neither being any worse for wear. Louise loved horses and would ride any horse she could get on. - mc*

From Maggie's Diary - February 23, 1935 - "We all cleaned house. I got dinner and then Susan and I went to Grandma Beotticher's funeral - a large crowd. Met Miss Umphery, a teacher of long ago - she taught school in 1892, so did I. We met at Mrs. Axe's boarding house in Dillon for the Teachers Institute. She was teaching in Horse Prairie in a private family and I at Dewey."

From Maggie's Diary - March 1, 1935 - "I quilted. Susan helped deliver sheep to Lucy and Frank's [*Kambich*] at Glendale. Thelma fed the bunch and cleaned. John and Frank Kambich loaded 2 slag pots - just the slag 250 pounds each in the truck and Susan brot them for my rock collection. They are odd and rare – the only two up there. She also brot pudding rocks. All went to county Farmers Union meeting at Melrose."

From Maggie's Diary - March 14, 1935 - "Monkeyed around, crocheted and embroidered some - started a doll dress and finished none. Pa and I went to Butte with Net to get Bernard home from Legislature. Pa got real tired."

From Maggie's Diary - March 15, 1935 - "After dinner went with Lars to Dewey - saw the road men working - 1 power shovel and 2 trucks, 1 air compresser - 8 men."

From Maggie's Diary - March 17, 1935 - "My birthday also St. Patrick's Day. Roscoe and Verna came, Net and Bernard, the Katoes from Butte. I got a new dress from Net."

[April and May diary entries show the usual spring chores of the garden plowing and preparation, planting and getting ready for the summer. There was also the chore of raising more chickens and geese. All of the family was busy with their day to day lives. In late May, Thelma had the measles. Lars attended a cattle meeting in Great Falls. Entries show that Horace is getting around better. He is doing some walking, to the fields, mail box and around the yard. There are numerous visitors to the house, both young and old. Preparations for Net's upcoming wedding are in full swing in May. - mc]

From Maggie's Diary - June 5, 1935 - "Worked at everything to get ready for the wedding. Susan came home with the newspapers to mail - Prickly Pear Post - a dandy big issue. Better than last month. Rained last night, dampened things up."

From Maggie's Diary - June 6, 1935 - "Worked all Hands for the wedding. Tired tonight - finished the waist for Net. Nettie & Esther Snodgrass came up in evening, brot lilacs, a big tub full - goslins hatched 8."

From Maggie's Diary - June 7, 1935 - "Worked all Hands to put on the finishing touches for the wedding. Freda came early to help me get supper for our gang. Supper over - thus the gang [*was fed*] - 25 in all - 3 did not come. Thelma and Susan rested while Freda and I got supper and the men ate, then all dressed. Dressed Pa early. Bernard was in hot water all the time for fear the boys would pull some jokes on him. Roscoe and Verna came early too. Rev. Tradgett said the words - a nice ceremony - music by Mrs. Redburn and 3 Normal [*Normal College-Dillon*] boys. Then congratulations and getting the guests names in a book. Supper - 2 long tables (chicken creamed - salad, ice cream, strawberries, bride and groom cake - Thelma baked and decorated) reading the place cards and contents - jokes. Boys were fixing their suprises in the meantime. Well wishes and most all went away. Bride and groom were started out with much difficulty with his new cupe [*coupe, which*] failed to pull the hill - the drag, [*it*] was decided [*was too*] heavy, [*and*] at the gate they stopped [*to*] take it off. At this juncture some high jackers or kidnappers grabbed him, rushed him into another car, took him to Browns for games and drinks - left bride in car with one lone watch (Mr. Squires). After a long time he came in and reported the situation then some of the girls went to Browns to see. Finally persuaded them to bring Bernard back and put him in the car and [*the groom was*] warned not to stop till he reached Dillon. The boys followed. They soon turned back, came home to report. Some got lit up [*drunk*], all left were tired and rolled to bed. One poor soul spent a very miserable night from the effects of too much eats and drink on the groom."

J. Bernard and Nettie (Hand) Garrison
June 7, 1935
J. Bernard photo
Courtesy of Floydena and Bill Garrison
Nettie (Hand) Garrison photo
From the Susan Hand Collection

From letter by Susan Hand to Bernard and Annette, (undated) - "They had a home wedding, mostly because my Dad could attend as he was in poor health due to strokes. The lilacs were blooming, purple and white. I was the bridesmaid, Bill [*Garrison*] the best man. They had a new, blue, I believe, Plymouth coupe and went to Utah, where she had taught, to the Tetons and back up north, maybe Glacier and I know Holland Lake. There were no good roads in Tetons or Holland Lake area. Just June mud.

She had the house paid for soon after they were married and sold it to buy their first home in Butte on Gaylard St. She sold that and moved to Garrison Ave. soon after 1942 and did a lot of work and repair and finishing on that. The upstairs was unfinished when she bought it. They made an office in the back porch and later enclosed but did not heat the front porch."

From Maggie's Diary - June 9, 1935 - "Roscoe, Pa and I went over to see John and Ida and kids at Argenta - a lovely trip. Hills so green and flowers in bloom. All fine in Argenta - little kids growing."

From Maggie's Diary - July 20, 1935 - "I forgot to record (a few days back) Mrs. Patton's death. I first knew her in 1892, afterward my neighbor for years and years. Very sorry to read of her passing. She was with me when Roscoe was born on the ranch and walked down several mornings to see me and help."

From Maggie's Diary - July 21, 1935 - "Last evening Lars, Thelma and Susan went to Garrisons & Frankie's. On their way home [*they*] got run into by 3 Butte youths. All got shaken up. Susan got baddly bruised on hip and car was disabled so had to be hauled home. What next. 2 of the boys came here tonight to bluff them by lies & bullying."

A note in Maggie's Diary reads, "To be in a garden where the reward of work is the joy of the work itself ", a thot - seems very fitting for a gardener." [*The garden work continues as usual, with planting, watering, hoeing, harvesting and the selling of the crops .- mc*]

From Maggie's Diary - July 28, 1935 - "We learned yesterday Mrs. Hartwig was sick. Today John and children came for a short while. Baby [*Horace*] is so fat."

From Maggie's Diary - August 4, 1935 - "Mr. Hartwig took Polly to the hospital in Dillon. Not so well."

From Maggie's Diary - August 8, 1935 - "Grandma Hartwig died yesterday at 10 a.m. Poor soul - had been down sick 2 weeks. Emma Halbert sent me $20.00 to pay on debt." [*Records indicate Emma, Big Al's widow had borrowed $120.00, I believe for Big Al's funeral expenses. -mc*]

From Maggie's Diary - August 9, 1935 - "I went down to Grandpa Hartwigs with Buyans. Polly was at home all day today. Julius brot me back and took Lars and Pa to Melrose. I picked a few currents - was a very hot day. Billie and Shirley came with us and staid all day. Billie mowed lawn and she had a big time. Susan made her a sun dress. Julius came for the girls. Lars to call on the Hartwig home a while. Certainly a sorrowful house and will be lonely after this."

Susan Hand at Lavon Ranch
Notice chaps. They are made of hide with the wool left on and were her father, Horace's, chaps.
From the
Thelma (Hand) Kalsta Collection

From Maggie's Diary - August 10, 1935 - "We burried Mrs. Hartwig today. Susan and I went down with Julius to the house at 12 o'clock. People had begun to come by 2 p.m. The main room and parlor was full, all friends and neighbors far and near were there. The Lutheran minister from Dillon gave the sermon. They took her to Dillon graveyard. I rode with Earl Fitchen and family. Isabell's [*(Mast) Hartwig*] baby [*Carl Julius Hartwig*] born."

From Maggie's Diary - August 17, 1935 - "Picked strawberries and raspberries - Susan and I. Thelma took a load of vegs to town. Cooler today. Reported a good trade. Vance's house burned - everything. Mary Vance had lovely old time furniture. Paper reported Will Rodgers and Wiley Posts deaths this morning. Too bad they had to be killed in a plane."

An **August 18, 1935** note in her diary states, "Went to see Dr. McGill in Dillon. Dr. very busy - found me fine, weighed 136 lbs. - advised to stay at about that."

From Maggie's Diary - August 24, 1935 - "Eugene Mulleur bot a plot of land just entering Melrose to right for a tourist camp. Will tear down the Boettiker house and Harvey house and build camp. The river measured 1.22 on bridge, the lowest of the season so far."

The Chicken Business

When people came to the ranch to buy fryers, the chickens were caught, butchered, plucked, and cleaned while the customer waited. There was no refrigeration in those times so nothing could be prepared in advance.

From Maggie's Diary - August 28, 1935 - "Thelma and Lars went to Dillon. I did the work. A lady from Butte came for chicken, corn and berries. Another called for corn. 2 men came for work - haying begins. Haven't seen the cat for 2 days. Think him dead. He came to us a small starved kitten about a year ago. Because he was so needy of a home we befriended him and gave him food. For our kindness he soon grew fast friends of the women folks of the house and answered us with his tricks. Toward spring he developed stomach trouble from which we think he died.

From "John Hand Recalls Lifetime of Mining", Dillon Tribune, February 3, 1966:

MINING ON MY OWN [around *1935-36*]

It was now that I stood in the road at Argenta asking for someone to give me a ride to Dillon. I was going mining on my own alone, and stay alone. I had $190. All went well. I looked for some kind of a pickup. Good ones I could not have. They were too much for what I had. I finally found a very new model. International, which had been treated pretty rough. I finally got it of $25 and balance of $150 in three months.

I got powder, groceries, 30 gallons gas. I had worked about a week on Midnight Mine. Had two cars sorted from dumps and started shipping. I had found ore in a little hole and was in process of sinking. I had got down to where if I threw a shovelful out, part would come back. I got together some gears and made a hoist, using old auto engine at a cost of $15.

Returns were coming in from first shipment when one evening I was sinking alone, had about 10 tons out. Here came two men from Ground Hog Mine. They had worked for me there. They said "We come over to see if we could go to work. We are quitting that guy. We don't know mining." I told them I wanted to finish this shipment and be sure I had money to work on. They said, "We will be here in the morning; we are not afraid of you. We know with help you will make it." The men worked till spring and went ranching. They were good men.

I finally sunk that shaft 200 feet. Managed to keep going till I got a better ore producer at Argenta Springs, belonging to Ed White and ACM. At this time we got 90 cents for silver, $5 per hundred on lead, $35 per ounce for gold.

LEASES SHAFER MINE

I then leased Shafer mine, in meantime ACM had given it up. Some outfit had leased it, built a mill at Argenta and went broke. I do not remember how many had it long before I had it. How I come to want to try it, when there the boss had me digging, trying to uncover lead.

It was in February, frozen ground. He laid out a trench, told me he would be back in a few days and if I did not uncover it in that place to try my luck somewhere else. I moved about 30 feet further up and when I finished my cut to depth there, I found the ore after a hard day's work was just about done. He came and said there was no ore, that it couldn't be. I had four feet showing and one rock 4x4x7 feet which I could see gold in. He never looked at it, just had a fit, walked off, and at quitting time I walked down and quit.

When I got the lease I took a carload of ore off that went 2.12 ounces gold, 3 ounces silver. This was a real boost. I took out $2200 that summer and had to quit on account of bad weather to grade ore. I mined at various times around Argenta for a while, and one spring Jack Shafer said, "I have a compressor, and you have hammer and hose. Let's try and get some ore at 'the Shafer mine'."

We went at it. After a couple of shipments of awful low grade ore, we felt like we were beat. While waiting for smoke to clear, we climbed up to a rock sticking out of the mountain. With us we had a 10 pound sledge. Jack hit it. I picked up the piece and it had lots of gold in it.

HIT PAY DIRT

We went to digging and before night we had a seven foot face of ore you could see gold in. We got about $8000 each out of it. We had one assay and 25 pound carbide can full that went 563 ounces of gold and 20 ounces of silver.

Winter came on so we got out. I went to work for an eastern outfit, which was looking for lead and copper, and worked till December. I was looking for mines with ore. One I found they wanted but they were too slow. It was taken away by another company. Then I came home.

Jack Shafer and I had some high grade of 1200 pounds. We split it up even to try and see what could be gotten out of it. As we had lots of it go in our shipments and we felt we never got any good so I said I am going to have a sample assayed and see what is in it.

At this point I got the assay, handed it to Jack. His wife was looking over his shoulder and her mouth started to open and shut four or five times, before she could speak. The assay was 249 ounces gold. I took my share, pounded it up, screen pounded it out. I don't recall how many ounces I shipped to mint but I took 640 pounds to East Helena Smelter, and they paid me for 14 ounces of gold, in what I could mint, got out with pan. Winter was here again, I and Bill Gardner took out two cars in Gold Finch Mine. I helped Flemings take out a car on Silvia Claim, which netted them $6000.

The house is lonely without him. Coyotes have begun their killing - chickens and goose have been laid to their door." [*The cat apparently never came back, but just a couple of weeks later there is a note in the diary – mc*], "A yellow kitten was thrown off and Susan got it - nearly starved to death."

From Maggie's Diary - September 14, 1935 - "Thelma still swollen bad - in bed most of the day. We pronouce it Mumps."

From Maggie's Diary - September 19, 1935 - "Girls washed a big 4 week wash. Mrs. Williams, Mrs. Gleed and Mrs. Pierce from Lima came for chickens, veg and strawberries. Staid for dinner."

From Maggie's Diary - September 25, 1935 - "Heard that Frank Kambich died last night. Had been operated on for appendicitis on Sat. Poor Frank, Lucy (Hartwig) [*Kambich*] and Pauline."

From Maggie's Diary - September 26, 1935 - "Thelma fixed boquets and they will go to Glendale tonight where Frank Kambich's body is at house."

From Maggie's Diary - September 27, 1935 - "Woke up, everything white with frost. Certainly made a good job of it, everything gone - a sickly mess - was so cold when they came home from Cambich's. Was a big crowd there. Lucy was so tired and so broken up. Poor Frank. They got back 2 p.m. Thelma was so tired - All the Cambich brothers were there (6), 1 sister. Mrs. Garrison and Katy took me to the funeral in Dillon. A big crowd - Old Lady Cambich left church, broke down and Lucy was bad at the grave. Carl broke down and Lucy went in to histerics, had to take her to hospital to rest her." [*Lucy remained in the hospital for over a week - mc*]

Wakes

It was the custom at this time to have the body of the deceased prepared and laid out in the home where it was watched over by someone 24 hours a day until the funeral. The wakes could go on for several days. Friends, neighbors, and family visited during this time at the home, bringing food and often staying with the bereaved family. - mc

---

From Maggie's Diary - October 12, 1935 - "Andy, Susan and I heard the earthquake last night shortly after midnight." [*Referring to the Helena Earthquake. Roscoe and Verna were living in Helena at the time. A note on 10-21-35 indicates that they received the first word from Rock and Verna. They were okay but,* "The house was wrecked. They saved most everything." *There were numerous aftershocks that continued for several weeks. Verna and the two love birds, in their cage,*

From the Helena Independent, Helena Almanac, October 28, 1989 - Oct. 28, 1935: Helena's temperature dropped steadily all day on Oct. 28, 1935 -- from the high of 71 degrees on the 27th to a low of one degree below zero on the 29th -- a drop of 72 degrees.

finally moved to the ranch at Lavon until things settled down and Rock could get the house back together. - mc]

From Maggie's Diary - October 29, 1935 - "Awoke and a cold blizzard was on in full force - cold. Snowed and blew all day - cold - had to move my chicks all in the hen house and keep up all day. My, we were all glad to stay in and sew. I patched and knitt. Susan wove - has 3 pieces done now."

[After the fall work was done and all the garden prepared for the winter, Maggie again took up spinning, knitting, sewing, weaving, and other handcrafts in her spare time. There are notes telling of people visiting and learning how to weave. In various letters found in the Susan Hand Collection there are many references to Horace's failing health. Apparently he was becoming more frail, he tired out easily and his health was an ever present concern. Notes indicate that he occasionally still rode to Glen for the mail and went to visit friends in the area. - mc]

From Maggie's Diary - October 30, 1935 - "Cold - 13 below this morning - cold all day. Lars hunted cattle all day - was bad on the cattlemen. Susan wove - I started the tomato can stool and did various odd jobs."

From Maggie's Diary - December 1, 1935 - "Had turkey dinner. Pa's birthday - 75 years old."

From Maggie's Diary - December 25, 1935 - "Christmas, Nettie and Bernard came up from the Garrison ranch for dinner. Esther and Mrs. Snodgrass came with Rock. Verna already here. We had a Merry party and the short day passed too quickly. Net and Bernard went home. John and Ida and children came for a few minutes. The little ones are cute - Grandpa Hartwig came with them. They had been up to Lucy Cambichs for dinner. Thelma and I received more cups to our new blue set."

From Maggie's Diary - December 31, 1935 - "Today puttered around - cleaned 3 bureau drawers."

From Susan Hand's writings she noted: Sometimes milked as much as 6 cows. We had a Galloway separator that cost $40.00. You were lucky if you could get $5.00 for a can [*5 gallons*] of cream - that was about all and often not that much. Sometimes was the test* that told how much you received. I did lots of milking. Used karosene lantern for light. [*The test determined the butter fat content in the cream and the price was based on that. - mc]*

Nakuka and Son

Louise (Hand) Shafer related that this gentleman and his family lived at the section house at Lavon. When he and his wife were married the neighbors decided to give them a shivaree. It scared Nakuka and his wife as they thought they were being attacked as they were Chinese and sometimes not well treated. After it was explained to them that it was a party, everything was fine and the congratulations and party proceeded and all had a good time.

From the Rock Hand Collection

Chapter XIX

****

Home and Garden
1936

The following is Maggie's 1936 diary, Home and Garden. This is the entire 1936 diary, as it shows how they lived, worked and what was going on for them at the time. All entries are as Maggie had written them. The recipes were not in the diary but are Maggie's and relevant to the time. - mc]

"**January 1, 1936** - Goose for dinner. Susan got ready to go back with Nettie & Bernard in the eve. Nettie had a sore neck caused from tooth.

2 - Cleaned my room. Went to Todoviche's. They were not home and came back and Fergusons came - had a good visit with Mary. Finished the foot stool. Was all in, lay down before supper, cut carpet rags.

4 - I went to Dillon. Thelma and I have a cold!

5 - John, Ida and little folks came and he butchered his steer. Lucy and Pauline and Billie came for dinner. The little folks had a good time.

6 - School began everywhere today. I am on my second scarf - a little colder today. Susan came home on night train from Butte.

7 - Finished the scarves and Susan is putting in 20 yds. Egyptian cotton chain for Whig Rose. Lars and Thelma made lard and sausage.

8 - Helped clean kitchen and got supper - mixed sausage. Susan threading loom. She went to Garrison's for meat.

Horace Hand in the potato patch
Taken in late 1920's
From the Thelma (Hand) Kalsta Collection

9, 10, 11 - Susan put in "Lover Knot" [*on loom*]. We all cleaned and got ready for Sunday visitors. Thelma made lard and sausage. I got 10 eggs today and McPherson's came for dinner. I would like to weave on this pattern - lovely.

12 - Sunday, Thelma's birthday. Mrs. Mezel and Elwin, Net and B. came. Net brot Birthday cake - after dinner all went to Melrose to the Farm U. County meeting. Mrs. Van staid with me - glad we staid home for they staid and staid till 8 or 9 p.m. Then Susan and balance (4) squeezed in the car and went to Butte. Haven't heard how they made it.

13,14 - I made a sugar sack sheet. The pillow for Mrs. Squires and split yarn and twisted. Susan hasn't showed up yet.

15 - Lars and I went to see Mrs. Tadovich - down on the world and its workings. Afternoon went to Dillon, traded and saw Mrs. Boetticher. When on arriving Susan had just blown in from Butte and Alder.

16 - Twisted more yarn. Jimmie McMeekin came. Susan worked cleaning clothes. Men are putting up ice. Snowed quite a snow.

17, 18, 19 20 - Susan cleaned and fixed to be ready for a call but alas none came. We did the usual loom work, housework, &, & . Thelma, Lars and Susan went with Mr. and Mrs. Smith to a F.U. meet in Dillon. We all got more colds - such a mess of colds.

22 - Washed a 4 week wash.

24 - F.U. meet in Melrose. Was able to go but a lot of others failed to come on account of colds.

25, 26, 27 - All had colds. I went to Butte on stage and snow storm began in morning. Bot my dress, black silk.

28 - Bot single bed. Came home on stage. John Cummins is hired man. Kato and Maude [*Keith*] are in the cabin.

29 - Snow plow went over the road.

30 - Warmer today. Calves are coming.

31 - Gale Dickenson came from Butte, Susan weaving.

> In a letter from Rock Hand to Myrna (Shafer) Carpita, dated November 14, 1960 he states, "after 1927 I never got to see much of Louise but can remember how much fun it was to have any of the kids visit us on the ranch. John used to get mad because we wanted them to stay with us so much. We always had a good time with them. The thing I can remember best about your mother [*Louise*] was that she liked to go with me at milking time so she could play with the cats. We always had a lot of them around the barns. I used to get after her for kissin' the cats and she said it was all right because her Grandma Hand used to kiss cats when she was little."

Feb 1, 2, 3, 4, 5, 6 - Turned colder. The old river heaved and boiled. We are all glad to stay in doors and work and sewing, weaving. Gale cut and made my new dress. I work at one thing and then another.

7 - Cold 40 below in evening. Susan sick. Keiths tried to start the car and leave but a good thing they could not start it.

8 - 24 below in morning. Lars took Susan to Browns. Took train there to Butte. Keiths finally got away at 3:30 p.m. God help them - not quite so cold this evening. Todavich came to get men to doctor a cow. No paper for two days. Would like to know how the balance of the world have faired in this storm. Girls kept fires for two nights to keep the pipes from freezing and plants alive.

9 - Still cold 40 below - cold everywhere all over the state. Gale wove.

10, 11, 12 - Gale made me house dresses. All worked to keep fires going and house warm. Nettie came thru an awful storm. Will stay all night. Still cold.

Some of the many baskets that Maggie made.
She used various materials - cattail reeds and leaves, willows, pine roots or other materials that may have been available to her.
From the Thelma (Hand) Kalsta Collection

13 - Car cold - men worked a lot to get car going by 1 p.m. Susan and Gale left - still cold and cold and snow everywhere.

14 - Cold 15 below and cold all day and tonight. Men went to Glen got a letter from Susan. Cold there - Well pleased with her venture. I finished putting on all the silk scraps, a quilt, afghan and several pillow tops. Men learned that Keiths were still in the valley and MacIlvath beat Smith in water case.

15 - 30 below this morning and o boy so cold only got my chores done by noon. Mr. and Mrs. McPherson stopped in - car froze up. She staid while he went to Dillon. Cold again tonight.

16 - 20 below - got letter from Susan. Likes her job.

17 - 36 below - and a cold day all day.

18 - 12 below this morning and warmed some all day and evening. The cold grip seemed to loosen - no ice on the windows. John Cummins went to Dillon and got two letters from Susan. Harriet Schuler came last eve - Will and Rosenta went up to his ranch. They came at 12 p.m.

19, 20, 21 - Warmed up a bit. John Cummins moved to Glen to go to work on road - took cat.

22 - A lovely day - snow melted. Thelma got ready for the card party (23 came including ourselves) kids all had a good time. Went home 1 p.m.

23 - We cleaned up room and discussed the news gathered. Ida, John and little kids came. Kittos, Thelma and Lars went to Verbances tonight.

Feb. 24 - Made my underclothes 4 pieces 30 cents each. Can you beat it. Mr. & Mrs. Miller called and Mac Pool. We got letter, picture & clipping from Susan. Still glad she is there.

Feb. 25 - Thelma cleaned bunk house.

26 - Ash Wednesday beginning of Lent. Lars went to Dillon to Mrs. Gordon funeral, a large one - I sewed. The Miller boy came to work.

27 - Thelma went to Butte on train, back in eve on bus. Met Maud & had a good visit with her. Thelma got 30 yds. sheeting, dress goods, towels. Saw Net & B. Mrs. Francis Brown died, Mildred Ralston's mother.

28 - Frankie & Jen called to tell me Mrs. B died. Was going on train & then went with them & they brot me home - visited Mrs. Squires. Got letter from Susan & Annie & Emma.

29 - A big wash day. Lars & Jessie Miller helped. Got done by night. Mr. & Mrs. McPherson called. She brot me some red pieces.

March 1 - A nice day. My, lots of ice in the river. Billie called McPherson. Well is still frozen up. Lucy Kambich, Pauline - got a card from Susan and Annie.

2 - Ironed with new iron - did not get done. L went to Dillon. Albert Streb called - a lovely day - my well still frozen up. Measuring on ice at river.

3 - A lovely day. We got up late. Thelma went to Glen. After dinner rested, helped iron & finished hemming sheets (10). Mrs. Garrison called & D. Doblier.

4 - Another lovely day. Ice still holds in well. We ironed some more & I patched & made bunk house sheet & the day was gone.

5 - Went to Dillon with Lars in afternoon. Forenoon gave Pa a bath & helped in house while Thelma finished the 4 part of day ironing (12 steady hours in all). I went to see Kate Lewis & Frankie. A pitiful pair of old folks. Kate don't know what to do? Traded for the house & L was busy and we got home late. Saw Mrs. Miller & Mrs. Fiddler, Mrs. Sheelar. A lovely day. Florence Frassler, 2 girls & two old maid Aunts came while I was gone - Mande and Mrs. Lester was here (peddler). Man from Helena came & set clock in well going so now measuring on water.

6 - A lovely day. Dr. Morrow called early. We cut & sewed Thelma's new dress, hope to finish tomorrow. Got letter yesterday from Della - a lot of news in it. Susan is on her way home, will be on the road tomorrow & till 12+ p.m. Sunday morning.

7 - A nice day finished the dress for Thelma. Some fellows came to fish, sold five doz. eggs to them. L & Thelma went with Jen and Frankie together to Shulers card party.

8 - Sunday a nice day, turned cloudy & windy in evening. We looked for visitors, only men came. Bill Ferguson & a horse buyer & some 3 cars, one woman wanted a goose to be delivered, C. V. Dixon 1905 Monroe St. = Telephone 6273. One woman wanted eggs, lard & parsnips, another eggs, just then we ran out of eggs. Planted tomato seeds & celery (7th).

9 - Finished patching & made Thelma's dress. Horse buyer came & went & came for several days. Susan failed to arrive. Thelma & L went to Glen. Colder & windy. Would prefer to stay in doors. Ice cut thru in a channel.

10 - Cut 7 made 2 dresses for Thelma today. Horse buyers & every Tom, Dick, & Harry came. Lars & Jess butchered 6 pigs. Jen & Frankie came to operate on a bull. We looked for Susan, but never came.

11 - Cloudy day, not cold. Men cut up pork. I made Thelma's white skirt & sewed on other things. Susan did not come home today. Minie came for the horse. The river holes went dry - often happens when channel breaks thru ice. Men have to dig ice & haul it back to the water holes. Caswell, coffee man called, found out how Mrs. VanWart is by him. She is 75 years old or there about & sewing, making $48.00 every two weeks.

12 - Cold windy, some clouds - men & Thelma worked with the men. L went to Glen for mail, got card from Susan, said would be here today but failed to come yet (late night). I did not get any sewing done. Mrs. Stanley sent me buttons & buckle for my dress. Very pretty, no one called today. Melrose people fishing, ice gone out of river.

13 - Susan came with Bill Garrison from Butte. She & Jess worked in lard & sausage most all day. I finished my dress & worked on Louise's quilt.

14 - Susan all in but helped some. Thelma went over for Mrs. Todovich to help & teach how to fill casings, so filled a lot of sausage & finished lard. I helped all I could clean house. Lars & Jess went to Dillon in afternoon. Roscoe & Verna came after supper. Roscoe, Lars, Jess & Susan went to Farm Union Dance. Thelma & Verna & I staid home.

15 - 2 hens (7 1/2) lb - Katto - 1 goose, Mrs. Dixon - sent by Nettie. As my birthday neared (17th) a combined force of children & relatives came in to give me a surprise dinner today. Roscoe & Verna came last night, Net & Bernard this morning & Mrs. Garrison & Bill about noon so with our own folks there was quite a dinner party. Lars & Bill felt badly - to much booze last eve - Roscoe, Jess, Lars & Susan all went from there to F. U. dance, reported a good time & made good for F. U. Treasury. Pa went with the men to Garrisons to see their steers. Verna brot oranges & candy, Net apron & things for dinner. Mrs. Garrison brot lovely stationary. Been digging & eating parsnips for some time now. Set 3 hens (Friday 13) have tomato plants up. Men brot Lar's Holstein cow yesterday.

16 - Monday - a windy day, burned chips - just puttered around - cut 3 aprons - Jess & Susan dug parsnips. Thelma canned meats.

Gamers Mocha Cake

Cream 1 cup butter (part lard) with 2 cups sugar
Add 1 cup mashed potatoes
4 eggs, beaten
1 cup sour milk
1 tsp. soda
2 or 3 tsp. baking powder
2 squares melted chocolate
1 cup nuts
1 cup raisins
2 tsp. cinnamon
1 tsp. ea. cloves, nutmeg and allspice
2 1/2 cups flour

This makes 3 layers. Bake in moderate oven. Chocolate can be melted in hot potatoes as you mash them. Cake has good keeping qualities - except it is too delicious to last long. **In a letter to Janice Hand in 1987 by Susan, she states**, "This recipe came into our valley with a cook hired by Garrisons, who's been let go by Gamers [*Gamers Bakery, Butte, Montana*] in the depression. It's an expensive cake now but we surely made a lot of them on the ranch." "No baking temperature given - who knew with a wood stove? You felt the oven with your hand and knew how many sticks of wood to burn to keep the temperature. I suppose 350 degrees is about right. With frosting add cream to melted caramels 'til they spread."

From the Susan Hand Collection

17 - St. Patrick day & my birthday. Mrs. Stanley sent me a card. Susan & I took the parsnips to Dillon. Traded for Thelma. Visited Mrs. Snodgrass & helped her quilt. Saw Kate Lewis - went to Squires for Susan, had tea, started for home called on Mrs. Miller. Wind blew so hard was hard to keep the car on the road, bad both ways.

18 - Sewed on apron & quilt & cut night gowns, a busy day - girls canned meat.

19 - Wash day. I worked dinner while girls washed & sewed - finished the block of Louise's quilt. Made Susan apron & did other odd jobs sewing. Mac Pool called in eve. I made out order for yarn, Bartlett, Harmony, Me. 1 lb 1.00 for me, balance of $6.00 for Thelma.

20 - First day of spring, they say anyway. Was a nice warm day - wanted to work out but busy indoor. Tho did not do much. Girls ironed. After dinner Susan went to Butte on bus. I rested, did the evening chores - only made one apron.

21 - Cold windy day, nice to stay indoors. We finished ironing & patching & other odd jobs. Sent quilt scraps to Mrs. Snodgrass (Dillon) made one night gown. Susan came on evening train. Lars & Thelma went to Beehers to a card party. Old Lady lost her colt. I now have 5 hens set, geese laying somewhere.

22 - Cold stormy windy day. Cleaned all fore noon. Kitto's came & visited a while. Susan & Jess went to Miller's Junior F.U. meet. Frankie & Verbance called - a quiet day.

23 - Monday, cold, cloudy & windy. Sewed on Thelma's night gowns. Susan typed & went to Glen. Found 11 goose eggs. Jess helped me get those under the granary. Bill Malory came to work.

24 - Still cold cloudy & windy, finished Thelma's night gowns, all but the embroidery on them.

25 - Weather cold, cloudy, windy day. Made over an old woolen blanket. Susan wove some.

26 - Cold, cloudy. Clouds hung low, snowing on mts. Very cold all day. Susan wove & poisoned gophers. Lars & Verbance went to Apex for a sale, got there late, came home late, no mail to speak of. I embroidered on Thelma's night gowns. Pa put in an awful day with the cold. River is very low, all ice gone except a skim each morning & thaws each day.

27 - Still cold cloudy & windy. Storm in mts. Finished Thelma's night gowns (embroidery) & worked some on silk bath robe. Susan poisoned gophers, wove & helped with house work. - (a new colt)

28 - Puttered around. Wind blew cold & storm in the hills all day. Worked on robe. In eve Lars, Jess, Susan & I went to see the Townsend Play at Glen - was good (11 players) dance after. John, Ida, two little kids & sister were there & everyone else far & near.

29 - Sunday – looked out, ground all covered with snow & snowed all day. I thot it would finally come to a big storm before it quit. The old goose that Patsy hurt came in tonight. This evening a big flock of blue birds. Susan said they were blue buntings. Lit in the yard & garden - just hundreds of them & some ate the blue berries on the vines. Storm must have brot them in. Have 14 goose eggs to date.

30 - Monday - Just puttered around - worked on the robe - was 6 below this morning - cold, even ice in the well. Too cold to work so the men took down the old log cabin (glory Haleluga) - seems so much more room in the barn yard. Saw some of the little blue birds today.

31 - Made out my gauge book. [*Maggie measured the level of the Big Hole River for years and the guage book she refers to here is her daily recordings - mc*] Too cold to mail it. Woke up in the morning, another cold blizzard had been raging most all night. Seemed worse as it came from the north, a driving blizzard - fired all day hard as we could and every room was cold except the kitchen. Girls canned meat all day. I finished the ecru cotton I had on the robe. Now have the back to do, glad for a rest. Hard for Pa to keep warm in the house. Men had to lay off - too cold to work. Little blue birds are still here they ate all the berries off of the vine.

1 - April - Cold, ice frozen well. Zero this morn. Puttered all day. Lars & Susan went to Glen, Garrisons. Got mail and the yarn from Maine (12 day) quick service. Lovely yarn. Man & wife were selling onion plants from Wn. [*Washington*] Thelma got 1000 to come May 15. I am still looking at catalogs, not satisfied to give us, want some more flowers. Net sent Enub thread by Mr. Garnet - I got letters from Annie & Emma in the mail.

2 - Cold, cloudy day. Girls canned meat. McPherson's came in afternoon and ate supper with us. I began Thelma's bed jacket. Pa don't feel quite so well. Men sorted spuds.

3 - A cloudy snowy day, in evening the snow came thick and fast. May Dodgson McKinzie died, was hard to believe - stroke. Mr. & Mrs. Rife called - going to Butte & brot me a note from Net on their way home about May's funeral. Did not accomplish much today. Knit a little. Miss Stone the extension agent called & staid till Susan and I could not go to Melrose today as planned.

4 - Snowed quite a bit this morning & snowed all day - was cold too - Susan & I went to Melrose in afternoon for oil & grub - took wrong barrel (so got none). Visited with Mrs. Peterson. She is poorly, called on Violet McCauley & thot we had better go home - so cold. Got 8 chicks hatched & more setting. Took eggs (15 doz) to town. Violet loaned me large wood needles so I started an other bed jacket - have two on the way - Susan, Jess & Lars went to a card party at Schulars.

5 - Sunday - Cold & frosty, turned warmer and sun came out bright. Set 4 hens on goose eggs (12 eggs). More to set, have 14 chicks, a few more to hatch. I got home 2 p.m., Jes & Susan went with a bunch to Delmont park dance after party. Jess came home & Susan staid, hasn't showed up yet at 8 p.m., no one came, a quiet day - Susan got home.

6 - Monday - Susan has a cold for her galavanting to card party & dance & Union meet at River Side. Knit on Thelma's [*bed jacket*] went to Butte on bus - arrived on train, made a flying trip, saw Dr. McGill, Net & the gang at the F.U. A quiet day otherwise, rather nice day but minus the sunshine.

7 - A nice day. (George) Elder came to survey. Thelma & Susan washed. Susan poisoned gophers.

8 - Lars & Elder & Bill Malory surveyed the new Marlow ditch and went to Dillon in the afternoon, Susan poisoned gophers. Got my blue yarn, worked a little on Thelma's bed jacket.

9 - Thelma & I finished ironing, Susan helped cook. I did not do much. Jess filled the hot bed (late). Elder & L. & Bill surveyed in the jungle between Woods Livestock & Marlow place. A nice day - buds have not started yet - a few perennials are showing up.

10 - Good Friday - Mr. Elder & men finished surveying. A nice day. Thelma & I planted hot bed. Susan went to Dillon to speak at Riverside. Steer buyers, Mr. & Mrs. & children, McPhersons came.

11 - A lovely day - Mr. Elder went home. Cleaned my room & swept large room. When all at once Maude & Kato Keith came. Mrs. Geo. Huber came for a chicken & people at Browns came for eggs. Then Susan came home on train.

12 - Sunday - a lovely day. Net & B. came. Linnie Moor & Elsa & son came then Florence & Bertha & little girls. Then Mr. & Mrs. Miller & 2 boys - made a full day. Did not get to rest. Susan went with B. & Net to Garrisons to a turkey dinner. Susan missed Mrs. Miller. B. & Net stopped on road home. They brot me & Thelma a box of apples & oranges, all dead tired.

> **The Song of the Robin**
>
> The April rain in torrents fell
>   Against my window pane,
> The sighing wind rose high still
>   And shrieked and shrieked again;
> But in the lulling of the storm
>   That held me 'neath its wing,
> Just like a messenger of joy,
>   I heard a robin sing.
>
> Oh, help me, Lord, when terror falls
>   Across my rugged way,
> When sorrow chills and burdens press.
>   And skies are cold and gray,
> Tho every friend should prove untrue
>   And mean no more to me,
> To sing above the storm and strife
>   A lilting melody.
>
> ---Zula Lloyd Leach
>
> **From Maggie's Scrap Book**

13 - Another lovely day, the river has been on the rise for several days & today the river bed is full - geese laying again. Planted Leucretia dewberries at the two willow stumps. I hope they grow, cleaned some iris, burned a little, put the chicks on the ground. Tony & Josie called on way to Butte - are rooming in the same house that B. & Net are in. They wintered in Washington on coast (Bremerton).

14 - Thelma's & Lar's anniversary wedding day. Warm, nice, sunshine today. Lots of water going down in the river for this time of year. Lars & Susan went to Dillon & Millers for spuds.

15 - A lovely day - water very high. 4.80 on bridge at 7 p.m. I made soap - 1 large bbl & 1 small one - just started - burned some & cleaned yard. Esther & mother & Mrs. Forester called late in evening (all tired). If water keeps raising over night it will go in the goose nest on bank of the river.

15 & 16 - And so it did go in the goose nest and in the fireplace where I boiled my soap. Also in the lower door of the measuring house and at 8:58 a.m. bridge measured 5.00. I don't remember of it being so high in April, boiled soap. Esther & mother came. I mixed this up a little owing to my neglect to write each night.

16 - Bridge 5.00 at 8:58 & the river is on a terrible rampage. Another lovely day - helped Thelma clean garden some - tested soap. Susan cooked I finished Thelma's bed jacket. Planted a plumb bush "Red Wing" & some shrubs. (86 degrees) - hot.

17 - Friday - Lars went with Todovich to Butte. Another lovely day. Thelma & I cleaned yard a little & went to view the stakes of the new ditch at the Marlow place & poison gophers. Susan cooked, after I rested I boiled the soap again. Hope this finishes it. Pa don't feel so good.

18 - Another lovely day, in evening & night wind from south & cloudy skys. Took out soap, 1 bbl, to dry. Puttered around (10 cars in) sold steers to Hansen Packing house for 6 1/2 cents per lb. Gedona & girl & a man, Frank Lishner. A truck from F.U. Butte delivered spuds. I started Susan's bed jacket (10 for dinner) Lars went to Dillon with a man. Susan cooked & cleaned & washed her clothes & we ironed them. Pa is about the same. Jack Smith called. Ruth Morris Nester died, left a baby 6 day old - to bad.

> **Hard Soap**
> (without boiling)
>
> Melt 5 1/2 pounds of clean grease - tallow or lard - in a pan over the fire until dissolved. Set aside to cool. Empty the contents of 1 can of lye into 2 1/2 pints of cold water. When the grease has become cold or about 120 degrees now slowly pour dissolved lye into the grease, stir until it mixes thoroughly and also mix with this 1/3 box of 20 Mule Team Borax. Let stand until it begins to get thick and then pour into mold -- a wooden box will do. Cover with an old blanket, carpet, gunny sack, etc. and cut into squares. - **Aunt Net** [*Nettie (Hand) Garrison*]
>
> **From the Susan Hand Collection**

19 - Sunday. Puttered around all fore noon helped what I could. Thelma cooked while Susan got her papers ready for the Junior (F.U.) program (after dinner). We, Susan & I went to Miller & on to Nelson School where they met (15) in all young & old folks. I went to Schulers for a visit while they held their meeting & went back to school. We got home 6 p.m. Mrs. Stanley & boy & Katto came while we were gone. Several cars went thru - Frankie called late at night had been up all last night & days work yet to do tonight.

20 - Monday. Cleaned yard a little & went with Susan to Melrose to Ruth (Nester) Morris funeral. A large crowd, saw Maud & Mrs. Shepherd. Then later we called on them, got groceries & came home. The trucks came for the steers, at Todoviches they had an awful time loading, beside stuck in the mud & had to be hauled out with the teams, finally got started & went to Butte. Mr. Miller & Lowel called, brot the fertilizer.

21 - Another lovely day. I cleaned & burnt more trash in the yard. Susan went to Glen & brot me a package from Gale (small iris roots) she sent seeds & wrote a letter. Frankie Beeher came in eve & Lars took him home. Men manured this garden here. Kinkades called. Thelma & I moved the new babys breath. We never had any luck so we will hold our breath till they start growing.

22 - Cleaned & burned in forenoon. Another nice day. Clouded up, looked like rain. Mrs. Williams and Mrs. Gleed came for plants, sold $3.00. Thelma went to Verbances & staid 3 hrs. Mrs. V. was sick. Frank Lichner was here for supper.

23 - Rained all last night & today - let up a little & men plowed a small piece of the garden but rained again so they cut spuds forenoon & part of afternoon. Old goose had so many eggs & other laying in all the time & river nearly up to her so we took all out & set under hens (4). I wound the blue yarn & Susan began a piece but felt so badly she quit. Soaked clothes. Lars went over to Verbances. My this rain is doing a lot of good. Pa is not feeling so well. A good time to transplant things. Knit some on No. 2 bed jacket.

24 - Friday. Rained last night & all day showers. Thelma & I washed & Susan cooked. River high, men plowed a little in the garden. Jack Smith came for eggs. Susan, Lars & I went to F.U. meet at Glen, a good meeting, entertainment. People are having a time getting a crost sloughs below Glen.

25 - Sat. Skys are clearing, a heavy frost last night. Girls are baking. Thelma & I dug a little, started to clean strawberries but Bill finished the job. Finished plowing & leveling the garden. I fixed flower beds, planted Oriental poppy seed, Salpiglossis, Snap dragon, started to clean iris, my but the rot is working on them. This spring a lot of transplanting to do if I ever get it done - River real high 5.55 on bridge. I went to Dillon.

26 - Sunday - cloudy, cool, rainy all day. Nettie came after dinner. Then Schulers just a minute to see the river. A quiet day, men worked in a hurry to plant spuds.

27 - Cold & cloudy, I puttered & cooked. Thelma ironed, Susan wrote and went to Glen. I went to Dillon.

28 - Cold but turned off warm in afternoon. I put in 2 double rows, radish, onions, & beets in garden and off day. L. went to Dillon, trouble with spud planter, finally got one, patched.

29 - Wednesday - went to Farm Union meeting at Country Inn, rode down with Mr. Rolk & Mr. Garnett, staid all day. Roscoe & Pa drove down, saw every body & his dog. Rode home with Frank Buyan. Nettie brot down 50 little Rodeisland chicks, put 3 old hens with them in the evening.

30 - Planted glads & Dahlias, sweet peas. Went (Thelma & I) over to see Mrs. Todovich about our chicks (lost one today). They all look nice. L. got new horse today, started (finally) to plant spuds. Jack Smith was getting cows home by truck.

May 1 - Thelma & I finished spading & planting sweet peas, zinnias & other flowers. Susan & I went to Dillon. Got groceries & came home - shower everywhere but we got the nicest shower here, chicks are coming fine.

2 - Sat. Planted peas, spinach & beets. Chickens coming fine. Esther Snodgrass stopped on her way to Butte to see Nettie. A Big party at Mrs. Garrison's tonight. Lars, Jess & Susan went.

Rich Shortcake

2 cups flour
1/2 tsp. salt
4 tsp. baking powder
1 tbsp. sugar
1/3 cup shortening
1 well beaten egg
2/3 cup milk

Sift dry ingredients, cut in shortening until like coarse crumbs. Add combined milk and egg, stirring until just blended. Turn on lightly floured surface and knead lightly 1/2 min. Pat out dough 1/2 in. thick and cut with biscuit cutter - a big one. Can stack two together with a brush of butter between. Bake at 425 for 20 minutes. Serve hot. **Susan writes in note to Janice Hand in 1987,** "The only real shortcake is rich biscuit dough like our mother made. Now she didn't leave a rich biscuit dough recipe, so I had to go to my 1938 Better Homes and Gardens Cookbook for what would have been hers had she written one."

"As you may know we had a big strawberry patch and lots of strawberry shortcake. There was also a patch of raspberries. Used to the old fashioned shortcake I never could enjoy it with angel food or other sweet cake."

From the Susan Hand Collection.

3 - Sunday. Thelma & I planted carrots & I gave Pa a bath. Susan was all tired out after the big party at Garrisons last night. After dinner Jess & Susan went to Millers & Riverside to a Junior meet. All was quiet and we rested then Violet & Marion McCauley came. Lois & Mary Reid & boy came to show fancy work & Marion wanted to know about strawberries. Egg woman called. Frankie Beehers & Louise called. Had a lovely rain & hail some. Everything is coming fine.

4 - Monday. A hectic day - dug some, mowed a little & Susan finished the job. Men branded. Rosetta & Bill took up Rosetties cattle. Frankie brot his cattle up this far to stay over night. 2 goslin hatched, more to hatch. Mr. Lively came to visit Pa. I loaded him up with shrubs for his and her mountain home. Then Maud & Kato came. They ate & staid. I was so tired, half past two they left & I tumbled in to bed. Then Lester called with his wares, got up bot stockings & went back to bed, got up 5 p.m. & did the chores and Katie & Jen & kids came. Then the Rutledge boy from the Big Hole. Lost some chicks, not bad tho - knit some.

**Maggie at ranch at Lavon with chickens
From the Thelma (Hand) Kalsta Collection**

5 - Rainy, cold & stormy, windy. Puttered around all fore noon - rested & planted nasturiums, red beans & holly hocks, spaded the ground along the fence more to do - Frankie Beerer came early & got the cattle started for the Big Hole. Bill Malory uncovered the raspberries & sure enuf it turned cold just like it always does when they are uncovered. Bernard sent a man with another cow. Came at 9:30 p.m., will stay over night. So windy I could not sow the parsnip seeds. Have a few goslins, not a howling success.

6 - Cold, cloudy & windy, so did not work out. Men worked in the cold. I puttered with the chicks & knit. Susan & Thelma did house work. If all goes well, will finish the cape tomorrow. Drove the chicks to the old cow barn tonight.

7 - Did the regular chores & after dinner cleaned yard. I went to Garrisons.

8 - Did regular chores & helped get ready to wash. Then after dinner Thelma & I washed a big wash in 3 hrs & was all in. Susan did housework & cleaned house got ready for the Junior class after supper - Mary Smith & two girls & boy. McCauley girl, Billie Buyan. Mr. & Mrs. Piccone & Geo Fergasons wife came. I planted one row of beans. Brot little chicks down to the yard.

9 - Planted parsnips (3 rows) ground so dry can't come up till get moisture, rested after dinner. Susan & I went to Livelys to visit. Mrs. Lively gave us plants & we brot home flat rocks & picture rocks. So I have more terrace gardens to build now, have 4 goslins - goose business early a failure. Went for mail & got the plants I sent for. Mr. Lively gave me crystal specimen, rose quartz, other rock, green granite from Nigger Mt. [*mountain*].

10 - Sunday - planted the plants Mrs. Lively gave me & the ones I got from state nursery (phlox) (perennial) busy all morning. Kitto came after dinner visited with her. They left & John & Ida & kids came, staid for supper. Lars & Susan went to Ramsey with the Garrisons after dinner. Louise got flowers to plant. Little kids had a good time. Mr. Miller's car broke down & Buyans had to haul them home. Verbance called.

11 - Planted soy beans & other beans. After dinner Lucy, Pauline and Billie came, bot current plants, raspberry plants. Florence & kiddies & Bertha & kids. Florence brot me bluebells, climbing rosebush and another shrub - planted them out after supper. Susan did'nt arrive yet. Water man called. Planting spuds. A nice day - we need rain.

12 - Helped a little, finished Susan's shoulderett. Susan came home with F.U. accountant & wife, they staid for dinner. After dinner I rested most all afternoon. Then did the chores & helped water the plants. Joe Buyan, mother & father called. Then Ralph Streb came, a lovely day - ground is dry. Men finished most of the field planting.

13 - Cleaned porches. Todovich came for planter, onion plants came and my phlox from Kundred, must plant tomorrow. Men irrigated garden above.

14 - Planted phlox (Thelma & I), Susan was sick. Irrigated a little. Jess did the heavy irrigating, he set onions (2 rows) & leveled garden. I see the beets coming up - rested a lot. Lars went to see Churchill about lumber. Three school teachers from Butte came to see Susan's weaving, ordered a bag - a lovely day.

15 - Real windy & cold in morning. We (Lars & I) went to Dillon. Rained hard while there, rained everywhere, got home at noon. Thelma & Jess planted carrots & beans in afternoon, set cabbage & cauliflower. I planted 1 1/2 row cucumbers -

men made head gates at blacksmith shop, cold and cloudy. Bernard & Net came. Susan went with them to the May fair at Dillon. Apple trees in bloom & my bleeding heart. Plumbs did not bloom so vigorously this spring.

16 - Cool & showers, some hail - Nettie, B. & Susan came home in the night from Dillon. Susan brot me a amaryllis from Mrs. Squires. Net & B. went back to Dillon. Thelma & I planted cuks [*cucumbers*]. Jess leveled spaded & hoed, now the south garden is planted. Susan helped with housework. Mac Pool called and an auto dealer & man for spuds.

17 - Sunday, nice. Frosted last night hard, several tender things showed it. A quiet fore noon. After dinner Susan & Jess went to a Junior Meet at River Side. Nettie & B. stopped on way in to Butte. Bida [*Alvaretta*] and a Mr. Konklin [*Conklin*] called a few minutes. Bill went to Glen. Mr. Hartwig Sr. & Carl Mast came in fore noon, otherwise quiet.

18 - Monday - dug in flower beds. A lovely day. Mary Reid & Louis came for straw berry plants and perennials. Men plowed upper garden & began to plow in the berries but had to quit. They marked the upper garden. I finished a new bed & planted to Oriental Poppies & rose moss & some other flowers. Susan spaded some & helped in the house.

19 - Men finished plowing in shrubbery & Thelma & I planted the corn - 63 rows. Susan did the house work & went to Glen. Men worked on the Marlow place. Killed a rattler, turned windy & cold.

20 - Rained last night & was snow clost on the hills. Cold & cloudy most of the day with shower in the hills. Susan did the house work. Thelma & I planted squash & beans in upper garden. Some potatoes are up and my row of early beans, expect they will frost tonight. Set 4 hens, one goose & I gave it to the old goose under the grainary. Men worked on ditch below, turned horses out to rest on the hills. Tommy Zimmerman & another man called from the pump station.

21 - Cloudy & cold all day. I planted the shasta daisies, beets, carrots, & spinach, hollyhocks. Rested, cleaned hens nests, got straw for nests, moved the hen off the porty & scrubbed it. Mrs. Todovich & Katy came in the afternoon & Susan went to Glen for mail. I got a letter from Gale Dickenson. Susan rode the new saddle mare. She feels her oats & is hard to catch. The cannies and dahlias came. I planted them.

22 - A nice day, reset some cabbage, kohlrabi, planted peas (2 rows) and 2 rows cuks & flowers. Rested. Mrs. Piccone and Geo Ferguson's wife came. Lars, Bill & Susan went to F.U. meeting tonight in Melrose. Norman Grant came for plants, late $2.00.

23 - A nice day - finished planting cuks & cleaned my rooms - washed my head. Susan & I went to Glen - got Thelma new coil oil stove. Planted out my Geraniums, irrigated the garden.

24 - A lovely growing day - helped clean house & get in order (Susan got breakfast). Thelma rested & helped with dinner. I rested after dinner. Meyers & wife & girl, her sister & their father came from near Galen. Norwegian people to see Lars. The sister lives in Oregon, east of Eugene on the McKinzie river, farmers, she came over to see the father, no one else came - a quiet day - but a lot of cars on the road & fishermen on the river & canoes. They were interested in the weaving.

25 - Monday a nice growing day. Irrigated the garden & Jess set cabbage. He helped wash in the morning got a good start & finished before noon. A big wash. I had to stay home with Pa & made cushion top, pealed spuds & Carl Kambich came late in eve & Lars went to Melrose. Susan went to Glen for mail, got a picture from cousin Artie of her boy Kenneth. My the iris jumped today, have some early ones in flower & soon will be more. Snowball winter killed a long with a lot of other things last winter. Have Lilacs, tulips everything I bot & set are coming good, have beans up for over a week.

26 - An other lovely day - I finished mowing the yard & paths to road & toilet - Mrs. Verbance came & ran over one of my pullets - had 2 doz lovely ones. Ralph Streb and after dinner Eva & Mrs. Jones came. Susan went to Glen - no mail & Thelma & I ironed & I patched.

27 - Helped finish ironing, patching, after dinner planted out the tomatoes. A picture man called a quiet day (Susan cooked). A nice day, looks like rain tonight. Cut the flower for Mrs. Ahders, one early kind of iris, lilacs,

---

Homemade Wall Cleaner

The following formula makes a cleaner which is effective for removing dust and smoke from papered or kalsomined walls:

One and one-third cups flour, 1/2 cup warm water, 2 tablespoons salt, 2 tablespoons vinegar, 2 tablespoons ammonia, 1 tablespoon kerosene.

Combine these ingredients and cook in a double boiler. Stir as long as possible. Then cut and fold until all raw flour appears to be cooked. Be sure the product is stiff, not sticky. Remove the mass from the kettle and knead in the hands for few moments until it appears elastic. Place in covered can until cooled. This to be used as any cleaning dough. Clean a strip of surface at a time, working from the top downward without pressure on the dough and finish the strip with the arm in action instead of stopping abruptly. Slightly overlap each strip.

Fold the dough over as it becomes soiled. If the dough becomes too dry during the process of cleaning, work a few drops of water in by folding and kneading, but make sure this is uniformly blended, as a moist spot will mar the wall surface. The dough still cleans well after it has become black with wall soil. To absorb a small grease spot coat it with talcum powder or powdered chalk. Allow the powder to remain for a few hours. Then brush off.

From Maggie's Scrap Book

tulips & yellow buttons. Susan & Jess went for ceder boughs.

28 - Susan delivered the flowers to Mrs. Ahders 7 a.m., Pa went with her - flowers 1.50. I set asters. Mr. & Mrs. Rife called on way to Butte. They stopped on way home for aster plants. I rested & Jess & I planted out the late cabbage also planted 5 rows rutabagas. Susan washed windows. A road man left the road machine here this evening. Regina Rieber & Miss Larson & her man called - din't know her name since she married, but she taught two terms of school on Rock Creek 10 years ago.

29 - A lovely day - irrigated some, hoed cab [*cabbage*] - Susan & Lars went Dillon & brot me a letter from Net. Pa not so well. Went to Verbances (Thelma & I). Dan Smith sent for cab & planter. Iris coming (new ones every day). Lars brot me a new hoe.

30 - Arbor day - windy & warm 92 in shade. Warm for this time of the year. After supper very windy & stormy but no rain here. Nettie came down. She & I went to the cemetery. Saw several friends, Boettichers, Jack Smith & Donald. Saw Si Flemming, he enlightened us. Mrs. Hoffman moved in the Harvey house & Bill Harvey moved in to the old Wold house. Got home for dinner. Deda Gilbert, Mr. Gilbert & girl were [*here*] came to see the weaving. After dinner Nettie, Pa & Susan went to Glen and on to Garrisons. Net is always disgusted at her (Mrs. G) when she goes down. Thelma went in to Butte with Nettie. I hoed peas & cab, planted pumpkin & squash above here.

31 - Wind blew a gale all day & rain clouds but no rain. Looks like rain to night. Beat the iris so & everything else. I turned water on the iris was so dry, hoed a little, Kitto's came - staid all day, fished & we women visited. John & Ida, Pauline & two kids came in after noon late - staid for supper. Susan & Jess went to River Side FU Junior meet. Lars irrigated all day. The terrier learned to chase the chicks and catch one.

Building an irrigation diversion dam in the Big Hole River

This photo was taken at the diversion dam in the Big Hole River just above the ranch at Lavon where water was diverted from the river to the ranch. Note that this work is being done during high water with horses hitched to a wagon to haul the necessary materials for construction. The people in the photo are unknown.

From the Thelma (Hand) Kalsta Collection

June 1 - Rained last night & on & off all day. My this is the greatest thing for the country & raining tonight. Wound yarn for Netties shoulderett & knit some on it. Susan cooked I slept a lot & felt better. Set out the marigolds. Mrs. Todovich came for plants & Ferguson - must get busy & plant the balance - rained too much to set out plants. Bernard called late on way from Dillon. Pa not so well, gave away two pups to people at Brown's.

2 - Rained most all day & snowed in hills. I set balance of cab plants, looks too cold to plant out tomatoes. Doll came on bus - was glad to see her as Susan was all in, I knit on Nets Cape - Frankie came and Churchills man. Carl Kambach came & L gave away two more pups.

3 - Cold & cloudy - did not frost but was cold & cloudy all day expect a big frost tonight. Snow every where but here. Knit. Doll cooked, Susan finished the bag & I made it then knit some. Lars went to Don Smith & got 2 pigs. Jess cleaned chicken house.

June 4 - Did not frost as I expected last night. Clouds still hang low must be raining or snowing in hills. River on the rampage. Bridge 5.90 this morning. Got cellar cleaned & aspargrass [*asparagus*] patch cleaned, planted celery plants & shut that head gate water. Susan, Lars & Jess went to the FU meet at Dilmont park. The new tractor was demonstrated. Susan got her shoes. Mr. & Mrs. Dan Roskie (The Nomads) came in. I bot stockings.

5 - A nice day - hoed a lot in the garden & from now on will be plenty of hoeing. Set out the last plants (peppers & tomatoes) Susan & Doll went to Mr. Foots funeral at Dillon. Men worked below.

6 - Rain, hail & an electric storm last eve just after went to bed (very hard) rained all night, cloudy today & started to rain 5 p.m. & looks like a rainy night again. Susan finally got ready & on the bus 2 p.m. for Butte. Elder & a boy came for dinner. Esther & mother called on way to Neb. [*Nebraska*]. We were sorry to see them go - Jess worked for me today. Want to finish planting peas, beans. Everything looks bad after the hail. Iris was nice. Will be again in a few days. Columbines blooming, everything was fine. The cuk took an awful beating, look bad, too much rain for them, whitish green.

7 - Sunday rained all night & off and on all day - ground all soaked up. Knit in fore noon & L & I went to Butte just after dinner went to McRaes. Nettie came & I went home with her - L & Thelma & B came. Linnen Weaber (Mr. & Mrs.) all ate dinner (one yr anniversary) at Netties. Came home, stopped at Linliefs to see Fred - he is bad off - came on home. Kenneth Davis wife & child & Bill & Mrs. Garrison were here, so ended the day. Pa was put out I went today. At a theater saw a wreck of a car fly off in space & roll on face of cut like - was a few rods away, car was unhurt.

8 - Bright sunshine early - too bright to last - clouded up by noon & rained off and on all afternoon & evening - river raised up. I knit at odd times & finished Netties shoulder cape - the water man came.

9 - A lovely day, went out raked over beets & carrots & see was no use. The cuks had to be replanted so did that then planted beans & hoed corn, cab in upper field & planted some squash seed - a full day & am weary now. L. went to Dillon, took Toby to Millers. Went for wire - men are fencing on the Marlow place, ground in good kilter to hoe.

10 - A lovely day - I planted 5 rows peas, hoed cab above here & hoed peas. Men cultivated spuds & peas in our garden. They are cultivating their spuds below, did not do anything after I rested but work on the silk robe - took off one hen with chicks.

11 - A nice day - the hen has 19 chicks. I hoed 2 long rows parsnips & carrots, cleaned cedars & planted hollihocks, dug in flower beds - a little work on robe - Mr. & Mrs. McPherson called, Jen & Frankie.

12 - A nice forenoon, Bill hoed garden, did such a nice fast job - he is the man to work the garden. Jess finished spuds - below & began on the garden worked he & L. till in afternoon, rain drove them in - Bill kept on hoeing. Almost finished it Jossie & Tony Linnewealz came and staid all night. Picked some flower - staid up late talking to the folks. Worked some on the robe - Bill came in eve.

13 - Miner Union Day - a nice day. Looked like rain but did not. River is going down. Gave Pa his bath. Tony and Josie went on to Garrison's. Nettie & Thelma came in afternoon, staid till after supper - went to Glen, Nettie took Pa & I for the mail. A porcupine got up an ash tree last night, when men found it they finally shot it. Got a card from Susan.

14 - A cloudy but nice - planted more pansys. Kittoes came - all anxious to Thelmas welfare and L came in with a dish pan of mushrooms. Doll & I were cleaning them when Johnnie Verbance came with a call from Butte. So Lars & I got ready at once and went to Butte. Thelma was in Hospital. I went on home with Net & rested. Mrs. McRae called on way to hospital. We went back to hospital at 4:30 p.m. then went to Columbia Gardens. Thelma was progressing but I could not stay, could not leave Pa over night & my little chicks. I came home on train - arrived on train at 9 p.m. - to bed.

15 - Lars came in the night 2 p.m. to tell of the new arrival (a boy 7 1/2 lb) just a little after 12 p.m. after midnight. We went back in the morn & staid all day at hospital & Netties & up town, traded a little, got lining & setting for sisters quilt. Went to hospital again to see Thelma & Lars came after 5 p.m. I saw Mr. Late & then the baby, started home, went to see Nettie & she was almost with cold, it had been coming on for

Lars and Thelma (Hand) Kalsta's second child, Gunnar Kalsta, born June 15, 1936

several days, was worried all day about Pa but he got on fine, got home about 7:30 p.m. & L went on down to Bills, mostly to tell the news and see Bill about cultivator & take those blooming chairs back. L in his excitement only got 4 & should have gotten 6 so guess she will have to get them her self.

16 - Lars birthday - a son yesterday will be old now soon - puttered around tending new chicks, Pa & rested, I planted turnips, hoed a little & Frankie Beeher was here. L went to Dillon. Doll & I were hunting up things to wash. Got card from Susan. Wonder how Net and Thelma are to night & the new baby.

17 - A lovely day - cloudy toward night. Jess & Doll washed in fore noon. Doll gathered clothes & I rested. Florence Fasslet came to see my flowers. I finished etching the robe - Doll brot in folded & dampened the clothes. [*Dampening clothes was sprinkling the clothes, that were going to be ironed, with water to "dampen" them. They were then rolled and placed in a sack until ready to iron. When a hot iron was applied to the cloth steam was created to ease out the wrinkles when ironed. They were using the old metal irons that were heated on the stove as there was no electricity for an electric iron, nor was there such a thing as a "steam" iron. - mc*] L, Jess & Doll all went to Brown's to phone to Thelma. She is fine. Roscoe had been over to see her.

18 - A nice day finished cleaning the walk at north end of the house & started east side. Lars went to Big Hole with Lee Joy to see about the cattle. I rested. Mrs. Todovich & Katy called. I started my shoulderett. Doll ironed part of ironing, one more hen off - 18 chicks. Bill went to Glen to see about the prize fight - was called off. He got the mail & I got 2 letters from Susan & other letters.

19 - Worked with my chicks & cleaned my rooms. Doll & L went at noon to Butte. I rested, we are all alone save for Jess. He took sick last night and is all in, in bed. "To much night work?" I got supper, Doll & Lars came late, stopped at Linliefs, he is better, heard the fight over the radio, Whiteman, German beat the Negro - 16 rounds. Nettie came just after Doll & L got here. Must go to bed early - find some things to wear & to bed for in the morning we pull for the Yellowstone Park after over 44 years in the state.

20 - Got up early & a way, stopped in Butte, saw Thelma. We left Butte over the Harding way, a lovely man made drive over the divide, went thru Whitehall, stopped at LaHood. Saw the LaHood girl, crossed the Jefferson, went to Harrison, Norris, Ennis, Jeffers & on & on miles & miles past Hebgen Dam & on & on to West Yellowstone. Ate our lunch at Paisleys grove. That is a nice town, paid $3.00 entrance fees & went on to Madison Junction up Fire Hole river. Saw the steam as we neared the lower Geyser Basin. Saw them working in many forms on to Old Faithful, got cabin, rested & after supper took in the sights there. To bed early & slept the sleep of the just.

21 - Up early & on our way, saw a deer on the grounds out. No use my readers perhaps won't care for my description but will go & see it & describe it better than I can - saw deer again on the way. The road to the turn is under construction a lot of places & is a one way road. Stopped & saw mud pots there, bot gas & oil. Then to the Dragoons Mouth & on to Fishing bridge & the Canyon. Saw the sights, raven pass & buffaloes & a bear. There & on to Tower falls, saw buffalo in the distance. Passed mountains that form the opposite bank of the Yellowstone River, has rocks that put you in mind of pipe organs for miles, saw Petrified tree. Ate lunch at Lava Creek & on to Mammoth, a wonderful sight, more geysers, mud pits & terraces, devils kitchen, went thru museum there, wonderful sights there - saw the house of deer horns & on thru silvergate, deep canyons, walled rock, work for roads, meadows, forests, saw moose, elk, deer & bear. At the Polanaris Springs a begger bear & 2 cubs, cut up for the traveler. She finally came up to the car, put her two feet & nose in our car window, wanting feed, did not know she was scaring us stiff & instead of shutting the window, Nettie rolled it down. Such a time we wanted a drink of that water & she came for us again. We went to the car & others called her attentions & we went on wonderful beaver dam country. Heard the roaring Mt., The Glass Mt & the Norris basins, a wonderful sight, & on to Berryl Springs (very hot). Then to Glibbon Falls, lovely falls (I lost my glasses there) & to Madison Junction then down the Madison & out of the entrance gate. Got ice cream, cars & started for home, sun was still high. We ate our lunch before we left the canyon of the Madison, heated water, made coffee & ate a good lunch all by our lonesome. At Jeffers we went to see Mr. & Mrs. Mitchell, a very nice visit for an hour & on for Butte. 11 p.m. arrived in Butte, saw the lights of Butte coming down Harding way. O so tired. Susan was there, dead to the world, so crawled in and she found out in the morning we were there.

22 - Rested all fore noon & afternoon went to see Thelma, then Susan, Net & I came home, all went well. Roscoe & Verna came & took care of Pa. They had car trouble & got there Sat 1 p.m. They did not know we were in Butte Monday & went on thru. Maud & Kato came, brot me a lovely specimen.

By the Road

I live in a house by the side of
   the road
   Where scores pass by every day
Some in their cars, some on the
   train
And some are thumbing their way.

I see 'tis the man with the battered
   old car
   That stops for the one that's afoot
With a smile and a nod, as he opens
   the door
And gives him a lift on the road.

Such is life, we will find, 'tis the man
   who is rich
   In love, compassion and cheer
Who passes it on to the one down
   and out
Not he who has plenty to spare.

We will find when we come to the
   end of the road
   When life's sands have run out the
   day
That all we will get, when They open
   the gate
Is what we have given away.

Fannie Chenoweth

From Maggie's Scrap Book

Haying Time

Mowing alfalfa with a team of horses. Person unknown.

From the Thelma (Hand) Kalsta Collection

Stacking Hay
Unloading hay net from the hay wagon to the stack.

The hay was cut, raked and then hand loaded with a pitch fork on to a "Hay Boat" or wagon. A net was spread in the "boat" and the hay was loaded into it. The net ends were then pulled up, attached to a rope which ran through the pully on the top of the pole. The hay was lifted into the air and swung over the stack. A rope was pulled, tripping the release on the net and allowing the hay to drop on to the stack. Note the man on the left holding the release rope.

From the Thelma (Hand) Kalsta Collection

23 - I puttered around all day in garden & yard. Took care of chicks (a nice bunch) gathered strawberries (second time) started water, came slow. - Things are too dry. Mr. & Mrs. Richell came on way from Dillon home.
24 - Rained in night. Ken & wife & Mrs. McRae brot the new baby & Thelma home last eve. I tried to irrigate a little, did not feel equal to the job - hoed a little.
25 - Rained in night. Lucy & Billie called. I did not feel good - puttered around. Thelma poorly, but likes our grub, baby cried. We think he is hungry. Doll, still sweet on Jess - good thing this love. Gets ice, wood, water & & & ---- Mrs. Garrison & Katy called (picked strawberries). Mrs. Todovich & Kate called.
26 - I puttered around in fore noon. Went with Lars to Dillon - bot groceries, sheets & &. Visited Mrs. Jones & Mrs. Squires. Mrs. Jones showed me thru the house (Foot) furniture, rugs & & & - she gave me the piece of petrified wood, a lovely specimen. Arrived home a little after five p.m. The water man was here, picked more strawberries. Jess & Doll are star gazing this eve.
27 - A nice day, Bill worked in the garden which needed it, more & more - I puttered around. Thelma is getting better, baby fine. After supper Jess drove Doll & I to Melrose for Susan's bed roll. I took Mrs. Peterson some flowers. She is very poorly - in bed. Drove over to see Mrs. Farsher & her flowers. Nice garden. Mrs. Garrison & Josie & Katy called.
28 - Sunday, a lovely day - Roscoe & Verna & two friends came early to fish. I puttered all day. John & Ida came -

Nettie & Susan, Mr. & Mrs. Linenweaber all came in afternoon. Picked strawberries again. - A lovely day tho I thot a few bean leaves were frosted last night, a cool morning. Frosted just what we could notice.

29 - Doll & Jess washed & I cooked. Thelma took care of the boy, good this fore noon but cried & was hungry in afternoon. Mrs. Piconne called - Frosted a little.

30 - A lovely day for haying, plowed upper garden & begin to cut hay after dinner. Irrigated garden. Susan came home with Mr. Rife, Thelma & L. went to Brown's to phone Dr., men brot home a turtle, everything is growing.

July 1 - An other lovely day. Jack Horup irrigated garden good. I puttered. Mr. & Mrs. McRae came. Nettie came on way from Twin Bridges. Thelma went in with the McRaes. Mrs. Todovich & Katy called. Doll & Jess still sweet.

2 - A lovely day. I slept most all day, helped a little & hoed a little. Jen & Frankie called. Susan & Jack took cattle to Keiths, took all day & was tired as the dogs on the return late p.m.

3 - Irrigated & hoed a little. Nettie brot Thelma & baby home in p.m. Pa & I went on down to Garrisons with Nettie. Took Mable O'Lera down to Jens - came home - Bill & Mrs. G called, had supper. Nettie went on to Butte & baby was cross. Doll & Jess still star gazing. Mr. & Mrs. Ferguson came late. New spuds & peas dug & & &.

4 - Fourth of July - a big time in Butte. Men stacked hay with their new machine. Georgie Slate called for hen & vegetables. I irrigated & hoed, went to Glen late for mail. Mrs. Langdof called for eggs. Doll & Jess star gazing. Had new peas & potatoes for dinner.

5 - Sunday, nice day, windy in afternoon. I am still irrigating & hoeing a little. Nettie & Bernard came in afternoon, went down to see the spuds. Some folks came for veg.

Molasses Pie

3 eggs
1 teacupful of brown sugar
1/2 of a nutmeg
2 Tbsp. of butter

Beat well together, stir in one teacupful of molasses and then add the whites of the eggs; bake on pastry. The juice of one lemon will improve it very much. Syrup is better than molasses for this pie. It is a great favorite with children.

From the Susan Hand Collection

---

6 - Irrigated above, see corn tassels this morning. Looked like rain - men got up all the hay they had down & started to cut again. Rained & a heavy thunder storm tonight. Susan went to Dillon with J.B. this morning & came back, weighed baby, 7 1/2 lbs. - has not gained any but had had a tough 3 weeks. Circumcision was hard on him. Smokie horse died in hills.

7 - Irrigated, two heavy rains. I shut the water off in gardens. Stopped the haying. Mrs. Lindlirff called for eggs. Mrs. Jones for veg & to see the baby. Looks like rain tonight. Sewed some on Louise's quilt. Doll & Jess mooning or spooning. Jen & Frank called for a few moments.

8 - Rained twice, put a stop to haying. Earl gulch & other gulches ran heavy streams of water, fill ditch all went to look & see the rush of water. Susan & I went to Country Inn to a Farm meeting. The readjusting man from Lewistown was there & several other, lasted till 12 o'clock, we left before it was out. We went to see the Whale at Dillon before the meeting was over - a good crowd was there. We got home at 20 min to 1 o clock p.m. I hoed some - sewed up several things.

9 - Rained - men could not work. Finished the bed roll cover for Susan & hoed some in the garden. Doll staid in, what can the matter be?

10 - Hoed in forenoon & started to rain about noon. Well such a rain. Water came down in a river at kitchen door & everywhere else. Did all kinds of damage to the ditch in places, filled in the ditch & run under the R.R. track and road from that cut in the bluff. Dugan Luban came from Dillon on his bike - his mother took him in car on to Butte & back to here then he rode bike on to Dillon. People from Lima called for veg. Doll & Jess took a walk to night - Susan not well.

11 - Rained, cloudy most all day and rained in the night. Everything suppy. Men worked repairing ditches. Susan packed, cleaned & & & - getting ready to go to Lewistown. I puttered around. Mr. & Mrs. McRae came - he is very poorly. Mr. Rife called late in eve with note from Nettie. Lars went to hills. Doll and Jess spooned till after 11 p.m. New cabbage for supper.

12 - Sunday - did not rain, men worked on ditch. John & Ida & Horace called on way to Lucy's then stopped on way back. Billie went home with them. They had Shirley to, she had been at Lucy's. John brot me two rocks, one from Gibbonsville Idaho & one white lead from Argenta mine. Schullars young folks called on way to Butte & Susan went with them to Butte. Tomorrow she and Mildred goes on to Lewistown camp - Farm Union camp. The first of the kind ever held in U.S. Doll & Jess still loving.

13 - Monday - rained a little toward eve. Cloudy, nice in forenoon. Thelma & I washed. Jack helped a little - men moved & turned hay. We picked a mess of string beans & hoed a little.

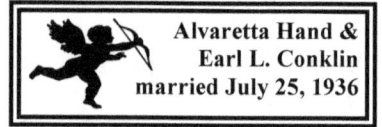
Alvaretta Hand & Earl L. Conklin married July 25, 1936

14 - Tuesday - Rain in afternoon (just a small) shower with a little hail & thunder. New green beans for dinner. I staid in bed most all day. Jack & Thelma weeded carrots. Should have been done two weeks ago, some job. She & I weeded a little after supper, men raked, mowed, turned hay. Doll ironed some.

15 - Wednesday - Rain, sprinkled in forenoon - afternoon hail & heavy rain, stopped the men haying. Certainly disgusting can't get ahead haying that way. Mrs. Jones came for peas & too wet to get them. Rey McPherson went home & forgot his veg. We finished cleaning the carrots & parsnips. Mr. & Mrs. McPherson called late at night. Doll staid in?

16 - Thursday - Rain to day haying stopped all day - Banker from Helena called for veg. Mrs. Piccone, Mr. & Mrs. Kato & Mrs. Stanly. Jess mowed the lower lawn & raked it. Mr. & Mrs. Kato, Keith called & she brot me a nice sample of Hematite & jasper. Started Sylvia's bag.

17 - No rain today, nice day, men put up hay with the (Gas buggy) put up a big bit. Eva Jones called for veg, man & wife from Bob Beatties place, Kattie & girl. I planted Iris roots.

18 - Sat. A nice day, men stacked hay most all day, heavy dew in morning. I made the bag for Sylvia & packed it. Roscoe & Verna came about 4 p.m., staid for supper & went on to Rock Creek with some others from Helena. Ray McPherson went to Dillon, took Red down, he gave out with the heat on stack. Jess & Doll swimming.

19 - Sunday, a lovely day men stacked hay all day. I made a bag with imitation bottom. Art Peter's & wife came. Roscoe & V came from the lakes and another car was with Roscoe called. Jess & Doll went swimming tonight. Mr. & Mrs. McLane & 2 babies came, wanted to buy a place.

20 - A lovely haying day, men worked furiously but did not get all up, take tomorrow - picked beans. Thelma & I went to Glen. The loveliss are still mooning, no one came today, mowed lawn & washed toilet, cut out limbs on road to toilet - we'en getting ready for election tomorrow.

21 - A lovely day, Election day, a small pole [*poll*] tho good. Thelma & I cleaned cabin after men had packed bed & bedding out. Thelma & Susan were clerks. Doll went to Butte with the man from Helena. Susan & Net & B. came late. Mr. Rolf's daughter & husband came that eve late.

22 - Another nice day but indications of rain. Rolfs folks drove me to Dillon in afternoon to trade for Thelma. Rained a little while there & blowed a gale on way home. Susan cooked. Doll came late with Kenneth.

23 - Nice in fore noon - Rained good & heavy - garden needed it. Lightning struck a post. Mrs. Jones came in forenoon for veg, men dug spuds for FU. They came for them & only got part of a load - rain stopped them. Rae & boy went home this eve. Susan & Mr. Kenfield came home with some finds at the "Buffalo Trap". Must be a lot of things there to be found. Rained in the night. A man from Butte. "Safeway Mgr." had taken Frank Lichner & groceries home & on way down ran in a deep ditch, could not get it out alone. The night was so dark, he made his way thru fields & ditches to the R.R. switch light thinking it was a house so he, after finding his mistake, found our house. Dogs barked & he rapped, finally I got up & found out his troubles, got the house up. Susan and Mr. Kenfield went in the rain to find his car & finally found it. With all three, 2 pushing & one steering, they got it out & sent him on his way rejoicing to his wife & 4 children. He was very grateful for their help.

24 - A nice day. Thelma & Jack & Mr. Kenfield plowed the garden & we all hoed some so the garden is looking better. Men mowed & Susan & Kenfields went to Browne's lakes - got home early & they all cleaned house. Mr. Squires & girls & Rinkie Miller came for a few minutes. All of our folks went to FU at Melrose this eve.

25 - Sat. cleaned & baked. I did not do much - explained the weaving to Mr. Kenfield & about 4 or 5 p.m. the New York car pulled in - 5 in all 4 ladies & 1 man. Lar's sister & her friend & cousins & cousins, all the way from New York.

26 - Sunday (visited) (hayed above here) Several called, Mrs. Kambich & Molly baby & 2 boys. The first time she ever called. Mr. & Mrs. Kile

---

Green Grape Preserve

Either the fox or Concord grape may be used. The fruit should be cut when it has attained its full size, but before it begins to ripen or turn color. Each grape must be cut in half (hold the grape with the end of the stem up and cut around it). Take out the seeds and throw the cut grape into cold water at once, or they will discolor. When seeded weigh them and allow one pound of granulated sugar for each pound of fruit. Cook as directed for other preserves. The grapes do not need to be taken out of the syrup like strawberries or peaches, for, being firm, they do not break.

This is an excellent preserve, but very hard to make because of the time and patience required to seed the fruit. It's flavor is like fine gooseberry.

Grand Union Cook Book
Compiled by Margaret Compton
From the Susan Hand Collection

NICKNAMES

In an interview for the **Montana Historical Society's Oral History Project, March 1987**, Rock states that everybody seemed to have a nick name. "My brother next to me was called 'Stub' and his name was Bryon. I didn't like to spell, so it was just natural that my nickname was "Rock" as my initials were RK, so it was natural. It was a name that was easy for people to remember. My brother John, well John was just 'John'."

[*The grandchildren of Maggie and Horace also had nicknames. Alvaretta was 'Bid'a, her husband Earl was 'Miggs'. Bill was 'Plug', Louise was 'Little Guy', Shirley was 'Sister', and Horace was 'Booky', Virginia was 'Ginny', and Annette was 'Bobbie'. - mc*]

& two children in evening. Mr. & Mrs. Kenfield came back from Garrisons & went back next day.

27 - Company & Lars & Susan went up Birch Creek to salt cattle, staid for dinner (camp). We got a chance to clean up, visit, then picked berries. Mrs. Molleur & Ailene came for spuds - Frankie Beeher called. Company still here, preparing to go to home marrow. Washed & ironed for return trip. Susan went to Georgetown FU camp. Kenfields called on way to camp. Pa as usual.

28 - The company left for Butte on way home. I went along to get new glasses, had been a month since I lost them & needed them badly. Pa got up as usual. I helped him dress & wash. Then ate breakfast & about 9:30 a.m. we left, asked me to come back as usual & hoped I'd not stay long, all bid him goodby as well as I. I showed the company where to find souvenirs while the Ford shop serviced their car bout 12, drove to Farm U Trading Co. & saw Nettie, only stopped a few minutes & then they were on their way. After dinner Bernard took me to town & I shopped, got my glasses and about 5 p.m. I got on street car, stopped at Kittoes. While there Nettie called & said must go with her as Pa had passed about 5:20 p.m. An awful shock. We went to the ranch at once. Sick only 20 min., heart. Thelma said he ate a good dinner & had held the baby as she ironed. Then lay down a few minutes, called her & went to his chair. He turned sick, she called Lars from other room. She bathed his head & he said "it is coming, "Let it come" - talked up till the last two breaths & was gone. Thelma & Lars sent Ray McPherson to Glen to telephone Nettie & Roscoe & sent him to tell John at Argenta. After dinner Bernard had taken me up town & I was to shop & come back after getting my glasses & shopping for other things. I went down on the street car, being put off at Kittoes. I thot I'd go in. Nettie called for me at once & told me of the sad happening at home. So we went down home. Found it all too true. Poor Pa was gone, free at last from all this worldly trouble. He had requested me to lay him away on the hill by Byron & Willie & Mark, the spot which we will. We went back to Butte to get the Richard undertakers to help lay him away. They took him to Butte till Friday afternoon when they brot him back. Then that night & afternoon friends & neighbors came in - the girls got midnight supper & then some of the friends set up. Mr. Hartwig Sr., Lee Joy, Mr. Todovich.

31 - Nettie & Bernard staid & Maud Dodgson, Mrs. Julius Hartwig Jr. staid over night. John [*Hand*] & Isaac Dodgson dug the grave (Friday) in the morning, I was with them and we went down to Isaac's for dinner. Then they went back to the grave. I traded some & John & I came home before the undertaker came with Pa. The girls had been real busy cleaning house, getting every thing in shape. Susan came from Georgetown night of 29th.

Sat. Sept. 1. A hard day as that was [*Horace's*] the last day here. Many friends

---

PIONEER RANCHER CROSSES DIVIDE

Horace H. Hand Summoned at Home on Big Hole River After Long Illness.

Wednesday, July 28, Horace Hand, aged 75, passed away at his ranch home at Lavon on the Big Hole river. In failing health for the past five years, he was stricken with a heart attack about 5:20 in the evening and death came almost immediately.

Born December 1, 1860, in Woodstock, New Brunswick, of English and Irish descent, Horace Hand's life spanned the era that saw the change from hand labor to the domination of the machine. One of his most vivid childhood memories recalled the time his father brought home the news of Lincoln's death.

Soon he was to take part in the stirring events of the times, when as a lad of 15, after working in the lumber woods of Maine for two years, he joined the Westward movement, going first to Denver.

His next move, a couple of years later, was to Ogden, Utah, where he and Charles Webbe made a deal with four other men who owned a six-mule team and two light wagons, and together these six men outfitted and headed for Hecla mines and Glendale smelter in the Montana territory. Starting July 5, 1879, the party reached Glendale July 18, taking 13 days for the journey. The railroad had not yet reached Montana. The tale of this trip reads like a romance, and is the only written account which Mr. Hand left, of all his adventures in early-day Montana, tales he loved to tell, and told with skill, but which are now lost, save for scraps remembered by his family.

Though only a lad of 18, he was noted even then for his great physical strength, and in the years that followed was occupied as a freighter for the J. T. Murphy Co., the Helena Wholesale and Retail Co., the John Duffey Co., and at times worked independently, or with his partner and life-long friend, "Big Al" Halbert.

In 1889 Al Halbert and Horace Hand took up the ranch now owned by Joe Potts at Wise River. Over a period of five or six years they worked at improving the ranch, and at freighting and logging, until the ranch was on a paying basis.

On July 7, 1894, Horace Hand and Maggie Halbert were married in Dillon, and made their home on the ranch near Wise River until they sold out in 1910 and went back to Houlton, Maine, to Mr. Hand's childhood home. Soon discontented with the East, they returned to Montana to purchase the Donavan place near Melrose and there made their home until 1917, when they sold that ranch, and bought the old Earl place at Lavon, an abandoned ranch, which in the last years of his life, Horace Hand reclaimed from a desert, and made into a productive ranch.

Saturday, Aug. 1, scores of old time friends and neighbors gathered at the Hand ranch at Lavon and paid their tribute to one of the last pioneers of the valley. Rev. H.M. Tragitt of Dillon conducted the services.

The pall bearers were Arthur Jones, Jack Smith, Isaac Dodgson, Ralph Streb, George Eighorn and J. C. Ferguson.

Honorary pall bearers were George Vance, Frank Tate, Billy Lyons, Berl Lively and Otto Boetticher of Melrose, Julius Hartwig of Reichle; Ben Mallon, George Dodgson of Wise River, Quitman Owen, Clark Anderson, John Gelhaus, Joe Gelhaus and Carl Mast of Dillon; John Kambich of Glendale; Charles Ralston of Fishtrap; Louis Wanderlick and Charles Woods of Divide; J.P. Lossl of Wisdom,; Charles Woods and Andy Ray of Butte; Tommy Bird of Twin Bridges, and George B. Conway of Helena.

Horace Hand is survived by his widow, Maggie E. Hand; two sons, Roscoe Hand of Helena and John Hand of Argenta; three daughters, Susan Hand, Reichle, Mrs. Nettie Hand-Garrison, Butte and Mrs. Thelma Kalsta of Reichle and six grandchildren.

Dillon Tribune
Dillon, Montana
September 3, 1936

called in fore noon. Services conducted by Reverend Tradgett from Dillon. Two male singers sang & played. The house was full & the yard. After services we took him to the cemetery at Melrose & laid him away in a steel vault. I tried to fulfill his request as best as I could. Poor Soul, he was a good man and tried to live a just life, but the best at times, such is life, will ere. All the friends & children scattered & the house was lonesome and still.

Sept. 9 - Staid two days in Butte with Maud & Nettie. Then home - could not stay longer, have helped here all I could but that is not much as my side bothers.

Sept. 15. A vacancy seems to still fill the house. I am trying to pick up the broken strands and weave them together, but it can't be done, try the best I can. I have neglected to keep up this diary as I should, seemed as if I could not write this all in till now. There will be slips which I can't remember & fill in. Maud Dodgson stayed with us a few days & Mrs. VanWart a few days & later I went Helena Sept. 4 & came back.

Sept. 17 - Cleaned my rooms, put stove up, patched & looked over my rags. Girls cooked for haying hands, have been haying two weeks (rain, bad weather)."

[*September 17, 1936 was the last entry Maggie made in her 1936 diary. – mc*]

Horace Hastings Hand
December 1, 1860 – July 28, 1936
From the Thelma (Hand) Kalsta Collection

Chapter XX

And Life Goes On

****

Maggie and Horace had been married 42 years. They had a good life together. There was the good and the bad of life but they had made the best of it. Maggie now had to go on without Horace. She relied on friends and family to inspire her life and she kept busy. It was at this time in her life that she started her writings at the urging of various family members. She wrote of her memories of the stories of her parents and her own life stories. She corresponded with her sisters, Annie and Emma. It appears that if one of them could not remember something specific, the other one did. Maggie also used various books and news articles she had gathered as a part of her research. Now she relied on all of this to do her writing.

In October, 1936, Susan and Maggie made a trip to California. They traveled from Lavon to Bonneville where they visited with Lar's brother, Aystein. - mc]

In a letter from Susan to Thelma dated October 22, 1936, "We enjoyed the visit with Aystein [*Kalsta*] at Bonneville, Washington. It took me about a half an hour to find him, and when I did knock at the bunkhouse door they were asleep and were't going to bother waking, and when they did wake thought it was kids and weren't very cordial but I just stayed with it until they got up and let me explain myself. Then he took us up to a lookout on the Oregon side, we saw the works and he explained much of it to us, then we visited their recreation hall, a beautiful building, saw models of the dam, looked over the fish hatchery, took a picture of Aystein and Mother and used up about two hours. We wanted to make Junction City that day, Aystein said we couldn't and wanted us to stay for more sightseeing from the Washington side and go in to Portland the next day but we had just come from the two day visit in the Dalles and were anxious to be on the road so we left at noon, and we did make Junction City about seven that evening."

[They stayed with friends at Junction City, Oregon and visited with many other friends they had made while living there. From the letters it is obvious that they enjoyed themselves, picked berries and visited various sites in the area. - mc]

In a letter from Susan to Thelma from Sacramento, California dated October 26, 1936, Susan states, "We came down by the coast road part way, stayed one night at Gold Beach in cabins near the ocean, so near that we could hear the roar all night. We did not get in any rains, and the ocean was quiet calm all the time, but we could not see far out in to it, either smoke or slight mist or both. I just loved the ocean, could have watched the breakers for hours, but I do not think it held the same fascination for mother.

Then for two days we drove in the redwoods, and words can scarcely describe them. They are much like the picture, but their size and height and the miles and miles of trees, hours and hours of driving in them is something a picture can't tell. The country is much in need of rain. We drove thru heavy smoke and near some fires and thru some burned over country and thru one town that was almost wiped out by fire.

Besides the redwood, we saw myrtle trees, a rare tree that grows only in Coos and Curry counties in Oregon and in Palestine. It is a beautiful wood and we picked up a few polished pieces, as well as a bit of redwood the next day."

In a letter from Maggie to Thelma dated November 3, 1936. [*Maggie and Susan are staying with Annie, Maggie's sister. Maggie describes the various aspects of their trip and some of the sight seeing they are doing. She further states, regarding Annie, - mc*] "tomorrow we will take Annie to the hospital to get her knees treated. She simply has run them weak. I gave her flannel to wrap them and she says they feel better. She has had to give up work and take the old age pension. Her house is awful poor and the yard is set with everything that will grow."

[*She further states in this letter*], "We haven't decided yet just where we will go from here but would like to stay but you know why. Perhaps will another winter. Marcia and Tom want me to stay with them but no one is ever satisfied. I am not either. If I staid here I'd want more fire and better house. I have a fire and home up there and looks like I'll have to

---

COURAGE

She strung a warp of
   courage
   Upon her loom of days,
And wove her love in cross
   threads
   Of gratitude and praise.

In faith, she tended weaving,
   And spliced the woof
     with song,
Aware that on her day loom
   The warp thread
     must be strong.

The color of her living,
   When woven, was as fine
As if a Master Weaver
   Had patterned the design.

The fabric was so lovely,
   That no one ever guessed
How underneath the pattern
   The warp thread
     held the rest.
     ---Jane Sayre.

**From Thelma (Hand)
Kalsta's Diary
May 28, 1940
Publication Unknown**

go there to get it, besides my money won't get me the things of life I like here. Wish I had an island somewhere. Well, I am a little tired tonight must close. Love, Ma."

In a letter dated November 7, 1936, Maggie states, "went to garden stands for vegetables. Bot bunch of large carrots (4 & 5) to a bunch for five cents, green beans 3 lbs for twenty cents, l doz. oranges for fifteen cents. Went to next stand and looked around. Each had a garden in back with veg growing there. I also saw men plowing and the ground turned over nicely. We went to a farm union store - been in operation for years. Annie and I went to trade a little then visited three different strange people. We pick our company --?

Annie has the gaul of the devil. She knew of a coverlid a woman had, a friend told her about so she went there. We viewed the coverlid, a very lovely blue and white only. Different pattern. Then we saw a white counterpin with heavy french knots used in the design. This woman told us of a woman three doors down who had coverlids. Annie went there and the lady was pleased to show her her coverlids. She and her family had been reared in Canada. She had blankets and quilts and 3 coverlids of new designs to us. Very pretty and simple with a border all around. We talked and talked then she showed ancient china and glass ware and a table made of birds eye maple. She invited us to come back Tuesday afternoon. That would not do Annie so she said she knew or had heard of a woman on 334 3rd St. So we drove there and found the place correct and the lady was glad to show her work and looms. Quite different. A nice girl, perhapse 25 or more and her mother to help as I did and a father that made the nice looms - 3 in all and he made looms for sale. Were nice pieces of furniture, far different from mother's old looms. They wove scarves and drapes. Had nice scarves and handbags. Her father made the handles. We learned something there, they were pleased to show us. They lived in a big ancient house. They wanted to sell it for a little place in the country and get out away from the noise of town and still follow weaving. Well, by this time I wanted to go home, was feeling lank so we went back to Annie's and had supper. I am teaching Annie the popcorn knitting and she is having a time. Susan still working on her pine needle baskets. Must go to bed."

[*Maggie describes the area, the lovely flowers and the interests she and Annie share - rock collecting, knitting, sewing, pottery, pine needle baskets, gardens, friends, family memorabilia and sight seeing. She tells of many trips and people - it would take another full book to include it all. - mc*]

In a letter dated November 12, 1936 from Susan to Thelma, Susan states, "you see we are now leaving for Los Angles, to be gone two weeks and mail that comes here will lay here until our return, tho you might drop a post haste to us in care of Frank Briggs, 6133 Monterey Rd. Los Angeles. Will be glad to hear from you.

But then there is this, I have a chance to work here with a weaver, near San Jose, a teacher of weaving and in weaving and working for her can earn a three months course in weaving, a course that costs $50.00 in tuition alone, and besides that she will give us private living quarters in her studio and workrooms in the remodeled garage. Mama wants to stay and the climate has done her so much good so far, that I believe I will take the chance and work there for the next three months. The whole thing seems ideal, the woman is genuine, and anyhow she is taking as much chance as I in the bargain. She will teach me everything from the details of warping and dressing a loom to rules of color combinations. She has had extensive art courses, canes, weaves baskets, models figures, turns pottery, does lovely needle work and of course weaving of all kinds. Her house is furnished with all objects of her woven goods and it is neat. All furniture is upholstered in her own woven goods. She used to have a large business in selling woven goods before she began teaching, and I think it is to keep up this business that she wants me as a weaver. She said she used to sell materials for womens suits at $50 for material for one suit, unmade. I am going to chance it for the good it may do mama, if I were to come back to the lecturing job it would automatically take her too, she just doesn't want to stay down here alone, everytime I suggested it she had some excuse to go with me. She will stay if I take this, and we can be together. And I will stay even if the other job turns up, if I miss out on that for her sake, I am sure I can make a way into it later if I need a job, and will have my weaving besides. I am just doing what seems best for her now, and I am willing to stay and with the opportunity feel it is no sacrafice whatsoever, would not anyhow if it would give her what she needed, for she has done much for me. And so have you, but maybe that will have to be repaid at some later date.

Will write more fully later. Know you won't understand all this about the job. Have to do up an interview I had today with a cooperative for dried fruit marketing. They are all so nice to me. Will investigate in Los Angeles. Expect to keep up the cooperative study if I stay. Intend to visit a Farmers Union official tomorrow morning before we start if I can. Love, Susan"

Letter, in part, dated November 14, 1936, Madera, California from Susan to Thelma states, "Yesterday before we started out from San Jose we drove out to Mrs. Badger's (the weaver) and agreed to stay the three months with her. I am to help about the house, but she says I am not a servant and I won't be treated as such. I can earn my course in weaving and color work, a fine tapestry embroidery, and can take a course in pottery with her at night school, and that will only cost $1 for as long as I take it no matter how long we stay. She is interested in me it seems, and I feel that all will be fine. We will be comfortably fixed in a two room home, with fireplace and wood cook stove below and little heating stove above, and a 45 inch loom to work on. The weaving will be my own, tho I could weave for her, yet she says she wants to see me possess for myself and my home, the work of my hands these three months.

So we will have to ask you to send all our yarns, and weaving materials of all sorts. Also want all rags, except I suppose those of Mrs. Hall's, tho I could do that here, but will write her first and see about prices and so on. The rugs Mrs. Badger weaves of rags she gets $18 for, but of course I can't ask that much yet I must earn a little for more materials. Will make a list and attach it to this with approximate locations of all things we want and will send you postage.

Want to do something for you or the baby during these three months, and want you to tell me what you most desire. I could make a nice large crib coverlet, could make it large enough to do him for years, could make coat material, well almost anything you ask. And if you dig up enough rags of one sort or another will do you a rug or so in pattern weaves. I plan to do a coverlet, possibly two. Wish I could stay here and weave a year, would like to make you one, but they are a lengthy job, and Mrs. Badger wants me to wait until the last to do it, and says it will probably take me 3 weeks for one. But we will see, I will do you something nice before I quit, you can be sure. Mrs. Badger wants me to do coating or suit material in the course of the weaving. Well, we'll see as we weave.

Anyhow Mama is so happy over the prospect of staying here and working at this that I know it can't be wrong to stay in spite of everything that may turn up for me at home. I feel so much better here too, that I think I can really get on my own feet by not having any colds and by soaking up all this California sun instead of Montana frost.

Tell those old busy bodies up there that I have a job with a professional weaver. No more, keep all these details under your hat, tell no one any more unless you fabricate to make it sound big and desirable. Don't tell them I am soiling my hands with housekeeping duties, for god's sake. Puff up a big tale if they nose around, they can never prove it, I mean you'll never have to prove it! Tell Net her life isn't worth a continental if she ever lets a soul know the real truth, base your tales on the fundamental truth that I am working for a professional weaver, but beware of what more you tell anybody.

Hope this finds you well, and warm as can be expected! Love, Susan"

In a letter dated November 23, 1936 from Maggie to Thelma, [*Maggie tells of visiting with various family members and Kansas friends living in the area they are in in California. - mc*]. She states, "We had the most delightful visit at Sylvia's and Grace's. She is a Kansas girl too, also another old friend. In all we had a real old Kansas gathering. Sylvia took us to Forest Lawn Cemetary. Had to walk quite a bit. This trip is hard on me -- too many eats."

In a letter dated December 11, 1936 from Maggie to Thelma, [*Maggie tells of more visits and travels in the California area with friends and family. She tells that Annie is still driving and looking to buy a new car. Apparently Annie loves to visit and be on the go. Maggie states that the weather is mild and*], "The clinging Ivy all over this den is growing now as the new leaves are a light green on the old dark green leaves. Chinese lillies are in bloom in the yard. We have rose boquets all the time, tho it is too cold to go without a fire much of the time.

Today I went with Mrs. B. to weaving school. They have a lovely big new high school there. The grounds are lovely, we weave in the half basement. While there an assembly was called to hear Edward VIII talk over the radio so we weaving ladies went up too.

I am weaving a knitting bag. I wish you would measure the length and width of that Morrison chair and wide enough to go over the sides of the cushion and back pad. O yes, look up all my diamond dyes and send them."

Susan states in a letter to Thelma on January 6, 1937, "Well, I finished the portier at about 7:30. And if I can keep from freezing behind, and roasting before, or visa versa will finish this letter to you.

Was just telling Net she needn't think we are running around in shorts picking bananas! Give her a word cartoon of me as I dash out of there at 7:30 a.m. across the yard to the house to build their kitchen and furnace fires. If I had wanted to, could have given the cartoon in color by telling her to picture a pair of orange pajamas, a green bathrobe and a purple umberella on the dead run in a California downpour! Well, it doesn't happen every morning but you could get the picture frequently.

Mighty glad we have woolen pajamas, hot water bottle and wool blankets and comforts. I build five fires every day - two in the house for Badgers, our kitchen stove, the studio fire, and in the evening the fireplace. It is just now beginning to warm things up here -- my shins are about half baked now. Thought for a while we would have to give up and go to bed to get warm. Now will have to stay up and use up the heat. Should write letters and cards by the dozen, but I don't do anything but weave mostly."

In a letter dated January 6, 1937 Maggie writes to Thelma stating, "Received your letters of January 2. Always glad to get word from home. Hope you have all your snow and cold now - expect the calves will begin to come soon - hard on them. Glad they saved the colt.

Yes, will try to send Gunnar a card. We send so many cards it is hard to keep up our correspondence. Cooler here tonight, will frost. Rains most every day. Lots of snow on Mt. Hamilton and the range east. This would be a warm den if the holes and cracks were closed, tho we make it fine.

I finished the silk strips colored and sewed the last - a big job. All the while I worked on Mrs. B's rags. Now will have more leisure, cut and sewing and coloring for her but go to school twice for weaving and once a week for pottery. Susan takes her weaving here on her things. I like to go - there are 10 or 12 looms, all set to different patterns, some very pretty. My piece is so fine it goes slowly.

Aunt Annie was over today for dinner and New Years too. She is quite a character. I am trying to get her in to weaving but she is so selfish, wants everything her way. Yes, I'd like a goose but will eat it at home. I'll get a hen someday soon and eat it. We had codfish today and I have nearly drank the well dry tonight. Tell Lars that one can get all kinds of drinks, either bottles or barrels, no permit or anything but money, get it and go.

You can send me some money now anytime. Send a check, can have it put in here at the First National Bank and they send for the money for me. I won't know just how much it will take yet, but if you can spare $100.00 O.K. if not, less will help me along. So far I have kept going good on what I had and still have some left. But don't want to be stranded at any time. We burn some coal and don't take long to go. I bot wood and coal. Thot it would see us thru but I think we will have to get more (Just like Oregon).

Sorry Gunnar's ear runs. I think any child should wear a night cap. They get cold in the night.

We gathered oranges and lemons. They gave us some. I want to make marmalade soon. Lots left on trees to waste and poor old man can't sell the prunes - everything tied up with the strike on the coast.

So glad you liked the bag and Net was pleased with her robe. Xmas slipped on us as usual un prepared. We want to make our stay here count and work all the time. I don't go to the shows so I can afford to potter and weave - is very expensive and I like that work - I like that work the best. I think we can get our pottery fired soon. Tomorrow night we go again - our school begins along with the other schools. We haven't much to write so guess I have to close. Love from Ma."

In a letter to Thelma dated January 12, 1937 Maggie [*says Susan is homesick. She states about herself that*] "I don't care much where I am any longer, just so I am busy." [*And busy she is, doing weaving, cutting rags, sewing and all sorts of things to occupy her time and mind. - mc*]

In a letter dated January 22, 1937 from Susan to Thelma states, "Guess I am a poor correspondent, but I'll make up for it all in talking when I get back home again, which pray God is not too long, but we'll hook on behind the first robin that starts north. In about another month I'll keep a close watch on them -- lots of them here in the orchards." [*She further describes the weaving she is doing, the house keeping she does for Mrs. Badger and the cleaning of their own living quarters. Various letters also show that Susan is still deeply interested in the Farmer's Unions and had attended meetings in California while also keeping track of the Farmer's Union activities back home in Montana. - mc She further states*], "Guess if I expect to handle that kid of yours when I get back I'll have to walk several more miles, and do a double dose of setting up excercises! Do send us pictures.

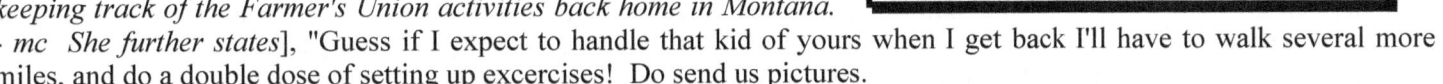
Alvaretta (Hand) & Earl Conklin's first child, Barbara Ann Conklin, born January 1937.

Want to do a letter to Net, so will close this tho haven't really answered your letter, or told you much news either. But what we don't tell now, we are storing up. We travel home nearly every day, one day by way of Salt Lake, next day by way of Oregon, sometimes thru Spokane, and sometimes thru Pocatello. But, we won't really be starting for a while yet, we are freezing to death here, don't want to get into anything like you are having, and are apt to have for a month or so yet. But we won't stay past April, cause we are both anxious to see you all again, when its springtime in the Rockies. Love Susan."

[*In late spring of 1937 Susan and Maggie returned home to Montana. Maggie resumed living at the ranch at Lavon and continued the writings that have allowed us to have this glimpse of how things were. Susan secured a teaching position at Camron, Montana in the fall and spent the following school year there. - mc*]

Cow Puncher

The old timers have most all passed on the long trail. Mud, Isaac, Edinger, and many others I did not know and yesterday, Jimmie Dodd [*d. May 11, 1938*] another of the early days puncher. Butcher, cow trailer and later as a buyer for various cattle firms. He was a colorful character in the Big Hole some 60 years ago. Then at that time there were many lesser punchers that rode with the veterans. They, too, have passed over the long trail, going alone with all their parphanalia, saddles, spurs, and quirt laid away.

Wise River
May 5, 1938

Wise River was an ideal game country and is yet to some extent before too many people came to live in the country. Down the river from Stines an other little creek, Honacker Creek, came out of the high wooded hills. The Wise River bottom as it widened out was too rocky and soil too shallow to make good farms, so most of it was left open or if taken up later, was abandoned. I think Denos lived on Honacker Creek before 1892 and before that a man by the name of the creek. Then opposite this creek or nearly, Vipond Creek came dashing down from the Vipond Park but on that side the soil was gravel and flint and was hard to get a thick and paying crop to grow in the soil. Then, to, the water was too cold for irrigating. John Lawrence's brother, Walter, and family lived there for a few years.

Walter sold the place to Mrs. Staufferson and another man. They lived there some time. Gus died. The partner went to Butte some time before. Then Goldburgs had the place for a time, none seemed to be able to stay on it.

Down river a little ways a Rhudolph Young, a Norwegian, took up a place - he had a family and a good hard working woman. There he built up a nice farm home on a little island, river on one side and slough on the other. He was a hard working man but took demented spells. He never liked for his wife and family to go any place for pleasure and as the children grew older there was more trouble. Horace often got him to help him build. One time he was walling our well when it caved, but never hurt him. That night he left, never said a word. Then later he built the addition on our house. The little place did not support them and he had to work out. Often went to Butte for a time. A brother came to stay once, but he was worse than Rhudolph - in a mad fit he threw all the household goods in the river and left. No one knew where or when he left as his brother and wife and family were in Butte. Being a lonely place neighbors never knew when he left. Finally the boy grew up and went to Butte to find work. The oldest girl married and went to Wyoming. Then Mr. Young died and after the war Frank was not very well but finally grew stronger. He and mother now are in Clear Lake, Calif. Irman worked at the Pump station, married and now lives at the Reservoir near Feely. Ronal, a younger one married, lives at Bradford on the road to Butte at the time of the Wise River flood.

Charley and Dick Trueman took up the place and Mosley but none made a stick of it for any length of time, all going and coming. On the east side of the river the bluff hugs the river till it comes to the Old Clad Hay ranch. Clad only lived there for a short while. The spring of 1894 John Trueman and wife and family moved there from Dewey Flat. The family consisted of Ed (Clara married Abe Dean), Dick, Arthur, Linnie, Elsie and John. This little place cut some hay and in time, with work, was better. Tho none of the boys were good farmers, the first winter the old man and boys cut stulls for Trausk – that's now the saw mill at Divide. This, by the sweat of their brow, gave them rusty bacon, beans, flour and coffee. They wintered and in the spring put in a garden, and had a horse and cow. The old horse had colt after colt; others prospered, so did they. Horace often hired one of the boys. Ed worked for him logging and on the river log drives.

As the Truemans prospered they built more rooms on the house and it was a randivu [*rendezvous*] for all comers and goers. In trading with J. B. Nose (late) they often bot a few delicacies that was not made at home. On this particular time they went to Anaconda and came back with a load of grub. It being late and all tired, they left the load on the wagon. Some time in the night, Old Boon (dog) decided he was hungry and got up on the wagon and found the cake and ate it up. Old Boon was a tried and true friend of old John's. At Dewey's Flat the winter of 1892 and 93, they lived in a little two room house (was formerly a barn) clost to the hill. Many a morning I have seen Old John trek acrost the flat to the back door of the saloon on Front Street for a morning drink. Old Boon clost to his heals. They certainly must have had a hard struggle there, but as soon as the boys could work, times were better then. Old John often got pie eyed. The two older boys sometimes had to tie him up.

Ed [*Trueman*] was a good worker, a dude in appearance - married but soon found out hard work would not put him ahead so he went into the boot legging business, made good, went to Minneapolis in a big ring and did well. He is there now.

Arthur was killed in Triangle Gulch getting out a load of wood. The country was too steep for this rigging and brake stock broke, horses were unable to hold the load back, threw him on a stump and he was killed instantly. Horace and Hoffman found the horses next morning.

The Truemans originated in Missouri. Linnie married Charley Moore. Elise married Hull from Salmon River Country, then Sam Friend. At one time they and all their friends and relatives '22 [*1922*], had small pox on Wise River. They kept it up there for none of the neighbors got it. Even Old John had it.

The Trueman place, being off the main road two or more miles, made it real inconvenient for Elsie when she grew up and wanted to go places and see folks and I have to say it was for Old Riley, the horse that had so many colts, that she rode. Elsie, being quite mindful of the situation, remarked to a neighbor, "When papa jumped this ranch I wish he had jumped on to the road." Just as if the country then had been lousy with jumpable ranches? ?

Dick Trueman and wife, Bell were both young when they got married. The courtship concisting of but one or two trips to French Gulch and the help of a go between, Ida Ordeway. When Dick came back with the news [*that he was getting married*], he went straight to his old tried and true friend in times of need, John Lawrence. Dick, having no means of transportation or money, so he borrowed $25, a team and wagon and John to go along with them to Anaconda. All went well but on the way home after the knot was tied, the wagon axle broke. Roads at that time were only trails and accidents similar often happened. John brot them home to Old John Truemans and the wagon, well all that was just too bad. John L. was better off than they and John had better mend it, so he did. To this union was born Tracy, Wendel, Clova, Frankie and Alice. Tracy, as I have stated, drowned in flood of June 14, '27 [*1927*]. Bell died fall 1907. Dick married an indian and are getting on well.

Charley married Madie McMonigal from Anaconda, but young. They have two children, a girl and a boy.

Mattresses -1938

Alvaretta (Hand) & Earl Conklin's second child, Earl Lincoln Conklin, Jr., born December 1938.

The other day I picked up a Gazzett, a Beloit, Kansas paper dated Nov. 16, 1938. Glancing over the ad I saw where a furniture store advertised all kinds of the latest mattresses. I could not help but go back in my memory to early days on the farm (1874). Did we or any of the country people of that day ever sleep on "Beauty Rests", "Sleep Well", "Simmons" mattresses or even a springbed? The wildest of ideas, never drempt of such a thing. If we could not sleep, it was not the beds fault. We slept on slat beds with either straw or corn husks for mattresses and if the good wife and mother was thrifty, then on top of the fine mattress was a feather bed, goose feathers or even chicken feather beds. My mother even saved the turkey feathers, stripped them and they made a fair feather bed. Feather beds were prized, often handed down and a daughter often got a feather bed when she married, along with other bedding, sheets, blankets. In Kansas blankets were scarce - my mother brot hers with her from Indiana, woven by her - the girls, wool from sheep's backs, carded and spun by the family and finally woven by them. Shortly after we landed, she knew we needed a cow and pig, so she decided to trade a feather bed and some quilts for a cow and pig. I could almost say there was not a mattress in miles in early days. People were poor, come to get rich in early Kansas.

If they did not sleep it was not the bed, but it might be bed bugs, for certain people had them. If they tried to rid them they took the bed out and scalded the ends of the slats and joints of the bed, just heating them up good to hatch again, for in a week here they came again and the process had to be repeated again. Those that got rid of them tried other tactics, carbolic acid and creosote in the cracks and varnished the bed often. They got up nights and hunted them on the bedding, beds and walls after the lights was out a half hour. One place was rid of them this way. For a real mattress, up to 1892, I can say there were none among the laboring class farmers. Very few (in Kansas) 1874 to 1880.

In Indiana before (springs), and about the time of slats, many had corded beds. Thru holes in the sides and ends, a strong cord or rope was drawn forth and back from end and then the sides. They were good until the ropes began to sag, which they mostly did, and then the two occupants spent a miserable night rolling to the middle of the bed.

Speaking of mattresses reminds me of a story Horace loved to tell. Seems he was taking a drummer [*traveling salesman*] - they often hired a man and team to take them to the outlying country stores - that was their means of getting orders and goods for their stores and factories. In their travels, the night overtook them at Laurin on the Ruby River. There was one hotel run by Laurin and wife. They slept quite well, except there seemed to be a hard lump in his pillow. Being young and curious, there was no way to solve the mystery but cut the pillow open. He found a chicken head, well preserved. The good wife in her haste accidentally let it go in with the feathers and never knew her lodgers slept on a chicken head.

'Grinding' Feathers

I have wanted to tell the Montana Farmer readers for a long time how I use feathers. I save all the feathers from turkeys and chickens throughout the year. I dry them and put them away carefully. In the fall I put them through my son's hammermill. They come out so fine one can use them for quilts, sofa pillows and other uses.

I do not think one should mix duck or geese with hen feathers. Turkey feathers make as fine a soft mixture as a chicken.
- Mrs. R. A. Vickers, Lake County

**Montana Farmer
Date unknown
From Maggie's Scrap Book**

John Hay

John Hay, born in New Brunswick, was a cousin of Lucy Robbins and John Lawrence and nephew of Alen Hay. He came to Montana in about 1889, worked at teaming, often spent his leisure time with his relatives. In my big picture of the Big Rock, he and John Lawrence are standing, Horace and Al Griswold are sitting with their feet in the warm spring. He helped work on the road.

January 1939 when I was visiting the Lawrences in Vancouver, B.C. he came to see me twice, to talk over the days he was there and find out what I knew. He was a very good entertainer, each time repeated poems. The Bryant Hotel, a poem, written by a Mr. Carmon, who happened to be in Montana and worked on the grade from the dam up. Horace had the contract to do that work the fall Carmon worked for him (1897-98) and boarded at the Bryant Hotel, which completed the poem. He tells me Carmon just died last fall in New Brunswick. Then he repeated another about a puzzle - was good. He said he saw the stallion that Pa traded for the place "squatters right", Pa got of Griswolds.

The next night he came he repeated a very long poem about the Pope. I never heard anything better. The friend of John's who wrote the poem was a clost friend of some catholic people. He, seeing the influence they lived under, then wrote it.

Roscoe & Verna (Ogilvie) Hand's first child, Virginia Lea Hand, born January 1939.

John said he committed [*to memory*] poems while teaming. When he had an idle moment, he recited. His stay was short in Montana, some over two years. But he tells of his experience there. Having at first lost a saddle horse, so he could get around, he went up to Mrs. Robbins. A real winter was on and he staid for a few days. While there, a man came in late at night, said he was hunting for some horses he had lost. According to the custom of the country, Robbins asked him to put up his horse and stay for supper and the night, which he did. After breakfast he said he was still hunting for the horses. Night came on again and he returned, no horses, tho he was quite sure they were there in the hills. So he partook of Robbins' hospitality again. Being discouraged with his days hunts and the horse wore out, he wanted to trade his three for John's saddle horse. John said from his stories he seemed honest and he really thot he had the horses and felt bad for him, so they traded. That left John afoot. But cousin John had horses, so he borrowed one of his and maybe John L. had seen those horses.

On the way down he stopped at Griswolds. They live on the right hand side of the road just after crossing the big bridge that crossed Wise River. They had a log house there, barns and corrals and on looking at the corrals he spied a bunch of horses in the corrals. Going over, he looked the horses over, yes, there was a white pony, it might be the one the man had described. Throwing the reigns over his borrowed mount, going a little closer, sure enuf. There was the brand just as the stranger had drawn out on a slip of paper. It had just been one among a bunch Griswolds had driven in to look over as they often had to feed the poorer ones.

His pony proved to be a dandy, gentle as a lamb. Shortly afterwards he gave it to Lucy for her very own saddle pony. This much gave him courage as the men all joshed him about his horse trading in Montana and even bet him he would never find a horse. A few days later he borrowed a horse again from Robbins to hunt for the other two horses. This time he went up and over the river to Johnson Creek. This is a large open country mostly higher up, trees fringe the prairie slope. He thot they might be there, so he hunted till horse and man could hardly find their way to the Tong ranch. There finding an always welcome to the weary, he staid over night. Being refreshed by the night rest, he started out again. Hoping against the day before defeat, he started out slowly, trying to conserve strength for both horse and man in case they should sight a bunch of horses. When in the evening he was about to give up hopes, he saw a bunch. By careful maneuvering he drove the horses to Tongs corral and in the bunch were the other two, just as the man described them. Every mark, color and blemish and brand. John said, "Now was ain't I proud. The older men and young could no longer taunt me about my horse trade with which seemed to me as an honest man. Now I had a team broke good and gentle. There was always demand for teamsters but the wagon? I had none. Geo. Vance had a store in the flat, so I'd see him. He says, 'Yes, I'll get you a wagon.' Had no money but with him that was nothing, so I told him when I'd have the money. I went back to help Robbins and not long Vance sent up word the wagon was at Divide. I went down, told Vance I haddent the money yet. He said, 'That's all right, you go get the wagon and go to work, try and not kill yourself if you can.' Now, I was all right, could team as there was plenty to do everywhere."

In about 1891 his father sent for John to come home. Soper, Robbins' partner wanted a team. John said, "I took the team over and helped him a few days to let him see the team was gentle for him. He, being an old fellow, I did not want to sell him something he could not handle."

When getting ready to go, "Soper", said John, "how about the team?" "Well, yes, I want them," but money was scarce and Soper said he would trade him 12 tons of hay for the team. John Lawrence had told him sometime before that Cap Predux was buying teams to haul ore from Quartz Hill to the mill, so if he had horses, he would need hay. Jonh took the 12 tons of hay for the team and went to see John Lawrence. John says, if you sell it to Cap, I'll haul it for $4.00 per ton. So he sold the hay to Cap for $12.00 per ton and in that way got a good price for his team.

The wagon he left with his Uncle Allen Hay. When his uncle's estate was settled later, the wagon was no where to be found. Clad Hay was the scoundrel - that got away with it or maybe two others, at least lay between three, John Lawrence or Walter Lawrence.

When Pa went to New Brunswick in 1910, John Hay was there buying and shipping potatoes. I saw him then. Shortly after that he married and went to Vancouver B.C. where he still lives, a very capable man tho whiskey has done its part to keep a bright mind down.

When in B.C. (1938 & 1939), John Hay tells a story on Pa. This day he and John had been working at the Big Rock, doing road work. It was near quitting time. They had worked hard all day and, for a little diversion, Horace said to John, "Joe Cramer, the Wisdom, Divide stage driver will be along soon, he often has whiskey with him and lets us hold him up and get a drink." So pretty soon here came Joe - out they go with shovel, pick and ax into the middle of the road. Joe, knowing them both well, halted. "No, boys," he says, "I haven't a drop with me this time. Now to make it all right with you, here's 50 cents and you go get a drink." John says he never got a drop for his pains as he was afoot and it was a far walk to Dewey. But Horace had a horse and was going to the flat anyway, so he goes down and got his drink.

John Hay worked for Churchill when he sunk a shaft clost and on the west side of big rock, a short ways from the road. The shaft was down 15 or 20 feet and then turned back to the clift hopping [*hoping*] to catch the spring gulch water. If found, it was to be run in a flume, placed at the outer edge of the grade and run to his ranch, thereby covering more arid, dry land on his place. As they drove the tunnel and timbered, Hay worked the windless on top and time hung heavy on his hand, waiting for Churchill to come with another bucket full of dirt to be lifted. To cause a little excitement below, just as he would hear Churchill coming, he would throw or kick in a little dirt, enuf to excite Churchill. That was always sure to bring forth a string of oaths and Churchill would call him to task for letting the dirt roll back.

One fall while he was in Montana he helped B. B. Lawrence build log dams up Jerry Creek to hold the water to float the logs out they were to get that winter. This creek is small and the logs could be got out of there no other way than building dams and floating (driving) one from the other. Those dams stood, tho gaft, and Horace drove all the logs he got out the two springs (1894 & 1897), so you see, B.B. knew. Having come to Montana from New Brunswick (1879), he had learned the art of dams in his fatherland before coming here. He had gone up the Basin quite early on after he came and took up his ranch, but often came back to Dewey with his young family, to make money to keep going. He and family lived at the flat the first winter I was there but in the spring he moved to Wise River and later back on his ranch where he raised a big family, all girls. Last one was called Nina. One boy [*grandson?*] is on the home place now. Mrs. B.B. is living there too. The first two, Eva and Mable went to school to me at the Flat.

Bean Hole Beans

The secrets of success with bean-hole beans are three, namely, the hole, the beans, and the fire.

A very elementary hole is the bean-hole. In the rough it is only about three feet in depth and in diameter. To get it out of the rough and into a finished condition, requires a stone lining. A large flat rock completely covering the bottom is laid first. Then the side stones are put in; these are partially embedded in the soil. Next, the spaces in between the stone are filled with cement or fire clay. The bean-hole when completed should measure close to 2 1/2 feet in depth and 2 1/2 feet in diameter.

Now the fire for the bean-hole is a very special one. It requires plenty of kindling and plenty of patience. A dry hard wood, split fine, makes the best fuel. The fire is laid, of course, right in the bean-hole and must be built up gradually until it is level with the ground. Then the wood, when the fire reaches ground level, should be heaped up to a height of three feet. One has to be especially careful at this point not to smother the fire, for the bean-hole has a very poor draft - - a necessary feature since you want the wood to burn down to coals, not ashes.

Because it takes nearly an hour and a half for the fire to burn down, utilize it for a wiener or marshmallow roast. When the wood has burned down to a bean-hole full of glowing red coals, the bean pot is ready to be lowered - - ready, that is if the third step has been completed.

The ordinary and anemic little navy bean has no place in this dish for red-blooded people. There are on the market at least two brands of over-size navy beans and these are the beans that should form the heart of the bean-hole bean dish. They usually come in two-pound packages and cost only a few cents more than the regular navy beans. The beans should be soaked in twice their depth of cold water for a period of about twelve hours. At the end of this time the beans will have doubled their size. Add enough water to cover them and a teaspoon of soda; allow the water to come to a boil. Take off the scum that comes to the surface, drain, and rinse the beans several times in cold water. Then cover them with hot water, add a half a pound of good firm salt pork per pound of beans. After the beans and pork have boiled for a couple of minutes, spoon up a few of the beans and blow on them. If the skins curl up, they have been boiled long enough. If not, continue the boiling until they can pass the test. The liquid, next is drained from the beans and saved. The pork is removed and saved, and the beans are put in a Dutch oven (large size holds four pounds). Cover them with sliced pork and garnish with two or three peeled onions, if desired. In a little of the liquid you have saved, dissolve 1/4 of a pound of brown sugar for every pound of beans. Add a teaspoon of mustard (per pound) and salt and pepper with judgment.

The beans themselves are now ready for baking. Put the lid of the Dutch oven on securely. If the beans have cooled slightly put them back on the stove and bring to boiling point. And now the beans are ready for the bean-hole (the hole at this point, you will remember is full of coals). Shovel the coals out of the bean-hole and carefully lower the Dutch oven. When the kettle has been placed on the large flat stone in the bottom of the bean-hole, the coals are raked back over and around it. A large piece of tin or sheet metal is laid over the coals and about eight inches of dirt shoveled in on top. Beans put in at seven or eight in the evening are ready for their ultimate goal (eating) at noon the next day. To attain their best form they should bake twelve to fifteen hours. They are then ready to be brought up.

From The American Home, October 1939
From Maggie's Scrapbook

Bill McClellan told the story on B.B. [*Lawrence*] about the morning he got married (no shoe blackening). Something had to be done. Yes, the best thing, stove blackening would do. So he blacked his shoes with shoe [*stove*] blacken and got married. (I can't vouch for this, I was not there.)

Bean Hole Beans

This clipping [*previous page*] brings to mind many stories Horace told the family about the beans that were cooked in the logging camps of Maine. The cook prepared the beans by parboiling them after they had been soaked in cold water over night. The camp flunky or handy man placed the big iron bean pot in the coal red hole, then carefully drew the coals around the pot and over it, then placed on a thick layer of dirt. Then the cooking took place. After about 12 hours the dirt and coals were raked away and the pot raised up. Each man dipped in the pot with a big spoon and took what he needed. Beans were served from the bean hole. Then, with bisquits and a cup of black coffee, he went to the big table and ate. Such beans a king never ate. They are all thoroughly cooked with the pork mellowed in to all beans. Beans cooked this way, one never tires of.

The hole was dug as soon as camp opened in the fall and used at least twice a week or oftener. The fare there was very plain in those days, which concisted of sow belly (dry salt pork), beans, flour, hogshead black molasses, black coffee. The cook had to roast the green coffee beans in the oven before using. After the roasting, enuf for the meal was ground at a time. Dried fruit and apples, peaches and once in a while rutabagas and potatoes. They could not be kept in quantities as there had not been provided a means of keeping them. No canned vegetables or fruits in those days. The cook baked soda bisquits every meal. All food were bot in large quantities and brot in to camp in the fall. Also, horse feed, hay and grain. When they went logging in this day, they went in the fall and staid there till spring came, then the camp broke up. Then the next job was driving the logs down the rivers.

A letter from the Butte Council of Camp Fire Girls written January 27, 1939 to Miss Susan Hand, Reichle, Montana, states that, "We hope to have a new cabin built near the kitchen for the cook and it would be possible for your Mother to stay there if she came. We would love having her to show the girls about weaving, teaching them to card wool and to develop an appreciation of the art of weaving. We hope to be able to invest in a loom or perhaps get some made. Camp will probably open the ninth of July and run for a period of at least four weeks."

[*A newspaper article found in Maggie Hand's scrap book indicates, Mrs. Margaret Hand [Maggie] as being on staff as a hand craft instructor for the Camp Fire Girls camp. This article is undated but falls among other articles dated 1939. - mc*]

Juice

[*The big undertaking in the area was to get electricity to each home and ranch. Electricity was received with much enthusiasm at the ranch at Lavon. Lars was serving on the Rural Electric Board of Directors and took a very active part in the rural electrification in the area.*

Thelma's diary entries show the excitement and also shows that getting everyone involved in the project was not without its challenges. - mc]

An entry in Thelma's diary dated Friday, March 17, 1939, "Grandma's 70th Birthday. Seems to be in fine health. Sews and is busy at something always. I made her a sponge cake, turned out real good."

Thelma's diary, May 19, 1939 - "The service pole for our electric meter box is staked and signed for - Mr. Rife, Lars and I talked electricity for three hours."

Thelma's diary, May 27, 1939 - "Wire men Davis and Freeman finished up nearly everything today, have a few little things left - payed them $40 have $33.50 left to pay when its passed."

Thelma's diary entry May 29, 1939 - "Mr. Rife was in, we paid him for the wiring material $106.00."

Thelma's diary entry - August 5, 1939 - "Awoke at 4:30 to hear the bus roll up and stop. I knew in a minute it was Aunt Annie here ahead of time. I jumped up, snaped on the lights and ran to meet her. She took a bath, I fed her -

---

ELECTRIFICATION EXTENSION SEEN

176 Miles of Line to Be Installed at $200,000 Cost This Year.

DILLON, March 9. --- (Special) --- Extension of the line of the Jefferson Valley Rural Electrification Cooperative Incorporated through Beaverhead county to Lima has been approved by the federal authorities and construction will start in April, it was announced today by C.E. Blinn, local representative of the organization.

It is indicated the line will be completed this coming summer. Approximately 176 miles of line will be installed at the cost of nearly $200,000.

The line will run from Silver Star up the lower Big Hole valley as far as Melrose and then up the entire Beaverhead valley as far as Lima. The Lima extension was recently approved by the R.E.A.

Bids on the project will be opened in Twin Bridges, Monday, April 3.

Ranchers all along the line will be privileged to use the electrical energy. The consumers will make payments on the total project over a period of 20 years.

**Dillon Tribune
March 9, 1939**

The Dent

June 11, 1939 - News article shows that "Hilary Tate has passed away". [*Mr. Tate was a long time friend of Horace Hand. They had become friends when Horace first came to Glendale. - mc*]

Thelma related a story to me about her father, Horace. Apparently Horace had a dent in his head but would not tell anyone how he had gotten it. Mr. Tate asked Thelma if she knew how her father had gotten this dent. Thelma said he would not tell any of them anything about it. Mr. Tate asked her if she would like to know the story? He then went on to relate that Horace had gotten into a bar room brawl in Glendale in the early days and had been hit on the head with a chair leg, denting his head, and knocking him out cold. Being unable to revive him, his friends took him to an ice house and laid him out with his head on a block of ice. Two days later he came to, apparently not too much the worse for wear but the dent always remained.

then we woke Grandma. She surely is a good scout. Stood the trip fine."

[*Aunt Annie returned home in early September. She, Susan and Maggie did some traveling, going to Glacier Park and other places.*

Early September found war beginning in Europe. This is a cause for concern for the people of the United States. - mc]

Thelma's diary entry - September 1, 1939 – "Left early for Argenta to see Hand Kids as John and Ida are gone. Got into Dillon and heard from the conversation on the street the war in Europe had begun. Something we all feared but hoped sincerely wouldn't happen. The general public all seem to hate it."

Thelma's diary entry - October 5, 1939 – "Electric poles in the air today - a real thrill to see them up."

[*J.B., Net, Susan, Thelma and Lars are all still active in the Farmers Union. Thelma attended the State meeting in Glasgow in October, stopping along the way in Helena to stay with Susan. - mc*]

Thelma's diary entry states, "I was payed $22.00 for my trip to the convention, was enuf to pay all expenses."

Thelma's diary - October 26, 1939 - "Grandma, Gunnar and I went to Dillon on business. Mamma to fix paper with the lawyer Collins in order to probate Pa's will and from there she can divide things the way she wants them after her earthly stay is over. Today she's as smart and spry as lots of women at 50."

Thelma's diary - December 22, 1939 - "Got our xmas tree up early. Gunnar was so interested in getting it up and we have real 110 light bulbs. Oh boy, can't yet get used to this grand juice - and no Delco to carry gas to."

Thelma's diary entry - December 25, 1939 - "Still plenty of snow on the ground to make a white xmas. We put on the noon day xmas dinner. Mrs. Garrison, J.B., Net, Audries came -- Rock and wife were headed for the coast for a vacation. Grandma might have gone but weather seemed to wicked and really believe she wanted to see the electricity on. Net and J. B. gave us their radio and it goes nicely."

Electricity
Dec. 30, 1939

One more day and '39 will be no more, only in memory of those living. After that history will record a meager bit of it. It will never be recorded tho, the struggle of each mortal trying to clothe and feed and shelter his self and dear ones, getting a more comfortable home with appliances long needed so as to take the drudgery out of life.

But the new year when we can write 1940, what will that mean? To many it will lift burdens, with the new step in electricity, to others the same old drag, coil oil lamps, etc. - Maggie

Lanterns, Outdoors

Long years our ancestors had no light other than a candle or a batch of oil in a tin cup with a rag string or twine string for a wick, a button threaded on the string so it could be hung on the edge of the tin cup and not slip in. The end above the button was dipped in the grease and placed on the edge of the tin cup and the end above the button was lit alight when all others failed.

The thrifty household saved their tallow. When enuf was saved, they brot out the candle molds which were made of tin and about 6 were made together. The wick of doubled twine was hung in each candle mold. The melted tallow was poured in gently. When full the mold was placed out in the cold to harden. When

RURAL ELECTRIC LINE ENERGIZED

DILLON, Dec. 20 -----(Special)------
Farm homes along the 30-mile REA line between Melrose and Dillon blazed with light last night as the Vigilante Electric cooperative energized the line for the first time.

Another section, from Dillon to Twin Bridges, will be energized within the next few days, before Christmas, it was stated.

In a few of the ranch homes, difficulty was experienced at first because of improper wiring of the residences, but all will be completely lighted by Christmas, it is expected.

**From Thelma (Hand) Kalsta's Diary
Dillon Tribune
December 20, 1939**

> **ARGENTA SUFFERS
> SERIOUS CONFLAGRATION**
>
> Two houses, one of them an early day structure dating back to the '70's [*1870*], were destroyed when fire broke out in Argenta, historic Beaverhead mining camp, last Sunday night.
>
> The fire broke out in the house occupied by the Miggs Conklin family, when Billy Hand, Argenta youth, in kindling a fire in a stove, poured gasoline from a can which he thought contained kerosene. An explosion resulted and flames were thrown all over the house. Only by breaking a window in the rear was it possible to rescue the Conklin children. All of the house furnishings were burned.
>
> When the fire spread to the adjoining house occupied by George Hartman, the fire became doubly serious when it was learned that a box of dynamite was in the house. This was removed immediately.
>
> Absence of a wind and heroic work by a bucket brigade stopped the spread of flames before they reached the Shafer and French homes.
>
> **Clipping found in Thelma (Hand) Kalsta's Diary
> Source Unknown 4-12-40**

hard they were kept outside to keep form and brot in at a time when needed.

Then the fire place, with its pitch knots, often gave off sufficient light to work by - spin, knit or patch, cook or even do up the supper dishes by. When coil oil came it was a wonderful step forward. Then years passed, coil oil was thot to be a good light with various inventions of better and bigger lights.

Then came gas (natural) or gasoline, tho dangerous. They soon invented lamps. That gave wonderful lights. We all enjoyed their brilliant glow. Electricity, while not so new, it is new to the country folks who now enjoy light, heat and power of the R.E.A. which reaches many country people far and wide thru our country. The light is wonderful, lighting up our once dark room, barns, barnyards and outhouses. But the power helps take the drudgery out of the drug out farm wife by being able to use electric pumps, washers, dish washer, vacuum cleaners, mixers and many, many other appliances. The heat cooks, cleans quickly and thoroughly without lifting wood, cutting, sawing and the many lifts required by the men of the house, then the woman brings it in, feeds the wood stove day in and day out. What more could we ask than an electric cook stove?

Then speed the inventor to invent a cheap, efficient, thorough way of heating our houses by electricity and cut out the drudgery of coal and wood? My plea! - Maggie

[*The New Year of 1940 finds Maggie at the ranch and busy as usual. She is weaving on the big loom and doing other handiwork and work around the house. The biggest change is what the electric "juice" has brought. There are many appliances being purchased for the home, as noted by Thelma in her diary,* "We ordered from J.B. F.U. Trading Co., Butte, a Food Mixer - $15.50, Vacuum sweeper - $42.50 and a 400 chick size brooder." *She also had a washing machine, an electric iron and soon, an electric refrigerator.*

Susan "received the appointment of a school 20 miles north of Joplin" *and bought a new car before she took off for the school. - mc*]

In early **June 5, 1940**, [*Maggie is*] "on the bus headed for Colorado to see Aunt Emma (a trip she talked of for a couple of years), " as per **Thelma's diary notation**. "Aunt Emma is 78 - lives alone, received old age pension."

[*Maggie stayed with Emma for a month, during which they traveled and visited many places in Colorado. Some of Emma's children were close by and they called on them and many of Emma's friends. They saw museums, tourist areas, made baskets and visited about old times. - mc*]

> On April 25, 1940 an Inventory and Appraisement was entered with the District Court of the Fifth Judicial District of the State of Montana, In and For the County of Madison, No. 1383 by the appraisers of the Estate of Horace H. Hand. Maggie E. Hand is shown as the executrix of the estate. The appraisal shows Horace's estate as:
>
> A contract dated March 28, 1933, between said decedent and Maggie E. Hand, his wife, as first parties, and Lars Kalsta and Thelma Kalsta, his wife as second parties, by which the first parties contracted to sell to the second parties, all of the lands and equipment of the first parties, for the sum of $20,000., payable in the amount of $500. for twenty years and until $10,000. is paid. Beginning January 1, 1954, $1,000. per year shall be paid, with interest at 4% per annum. At the time of decedent's death the second parties had paid upon the principal the sum of $3,000., leaving a balance of deferred payments amounting to $17,000. Said contract is appraised at $17,000.
>
> Therefore, the estate appraised at $17,000.

> **Medical Cost**
>
> *The prices of medical treatment might be of interest to some. In mid August, 1940, Thelma was admitted to the St. James Hospital in Butte. She had her tonsils removed. The total of her bill for her hospital stay was $49.50:*
>
> Room, 5 days, $25.00;
> Operating Room, $13.00;
> Laboratory, $10.00;
> Medicines and Dressings, $1.50.
>
> *Thelma was in the hospital the five days and then spent another few days in Butte, staying with Net and J.B., until the doctor released her. - mc*

From **Maggie's diary, dated July 6, 1940** she states: "Knowing Thelma was sick and needed help I decided to leave Monday the 8th on the noon bus for home. Emma and Ester came to the bus to see me off for home. The bus was an hour late. A nice trip, tho would have staid two weeks longer if all had been well at home."

Maggie further notes after she got home: "Thelma drug on sick. Susan came to help, later Julia [*Twiggs*]. All went well. At last about middle of August Thelma was operated on, staid with Nettie for two weeks then first of September she came home yet a sick woman. She soon was able to go and then gradually hit the work. All went well, then they, Lars, Thelma and Gunnar went to Salt Lake in the truck to visit the Pedersons. They had a good visit tho yet Thelma was not well. [*After Lars and Thelma returned from Salt Lake*] I went over to Susan [*at Laurin*]. One week she [*Thelma*] took down. The Barker women came to visit a few days. I was most in so went with Susan. Then Thelma got up and took to flowing. They sent for Nettie. She (Thelma) was too weak from loss of blood to be moved to Butte till Wednesday eve. Went to the hospital, staid 3 days (rest) Crozil and Dr. McGill gave her good advice. She went to Nettie's for a few days and then came home on the bus. To save myself I went over to Susans, rested and played for a time. Tho we came back each weekend and washed. I have not been so well."

[*The fall of 1940 finds Susan teaching at Laurin. Maggie apparently stayed with Susan quite often, visited her other children and was on the ranch fairly regularly.*

During the Christmas school break of 1940, Susan was in Butte and applied for a "new N.Y.A . weaving job". This was a job in Polson teaching Indians how to weave. Susan was very knowledgeable in weaving, having been taught by Maggie and taken various lessons from other weavers such as Mary Atwater. Susan received the job as the teacher of Arts & Craft, resigned her teaching job in Laurin and in early January she and Maggie left for Blue Bay, where they would live and Susan would teach. - mc]

Louise Mae Hand and Carl K. Shafer were married December 1, 1940

In Maggie's diary there is an entry stating that "I was a suprise [*to the people at the Indian Agency*] tho they thot I could stay. Our greeting was none to cordial when we drove up to the main hall. We went in and Susan introduced herself. We then were ushered in to the dirty little guest room filled with W.P.A. sewing. Shortwell [*the person in charge*] set Pete Glover to fixing a shack for us to live in. Danna Perdue was the handy man for the camp. Mrs. Roll was supervisor, June McClosed the director of cooking and sewing, Margie the bookkeeper. Mrs. Lacy was recreation director, a very nice deserving body, with a sick husband and two kiddies at his father's at Moiese. Later [*Mrs. Lacy*] moved her family to a small cabin up the road a ways. Then she had to learn to ride a bycycle to and from camp. Mary and Artell, two Indian women, ran the tanning shop. Mrs. Chandler was the carpenter instructor, a very nice conciderate woman, a school teacher of ours, tho then living at Arlee - on a ranch. There were 35 to 40 Indian girls. The camp was run by several factions - Indian Service at Dixon had the camp here for children since the '30s - they supplied some things. N.Y.A. supplied machines, sheets and paid some wages. The Education Vocation hired Susan."

[*Susan started her classes by teaching the working of the wool, washing, and spinning on Maggie's wheel. Maggie's notes state that*], "in Susan's shop they had three wool cards, a sewing machine, a stove, apple boxes for seats. Susan took her small loom and put it to work." [*Maggie's large loom was sent from the ranch for them to use also. They taught various types of weaving, including making rugs using heavy wool material, using silk to create wall hangings, and the use of linen for scarves and napkins.*

The major challenge was keeping enough material on hand to keep the looms and the girls busy. At first this was a major problem but gradually improved. The next obstacle to overcome was keeping enough students enrolled to keep the school going. The students came from Indian reservations in Montana and other western states. The students would come, stay a while and then leave. It seems some students learned a lot, while others just seemed to put in their time. Maggie apparently helped where she could. She

---

Final Distribution

On December 13, 1940 the Final Report, Petition to Determine Inheritance Tax and Petition for Final Distribution was filed in the estate of Horace H. Hand, Maggie Hand as executrix. It states in part that, the estate consists of a promissory note and escrow agreement made by Lars Kalsta and Thelma Kalsta."

"Said property still stands in the name of said decedent, and will so remain until the purchase price is paid and the deed delivered."

"All Taxes upon said property have been paid, and the same are accounted for in the list of disbursements herewith filed."

"---that no inheritance tax is chargeable against this estate;"

"The heirs of said decedent are the following:
  Maggie E. Hand, your petitioner, widow, Reichle, Montana
  John Hand, son, Dillon, Montana
  Roscoe Hand, son, 827 N. Main St., Helena, Montana
  Nettie Garrison, daughter, 1820 Gaylord St., Butte, Montana
  Thelma Kalsta, daughter, Reichle, Montana
  Susan Hand, daughter, Reichle, Montana
All of said estate, by the terms of said will, is devised and bequeathed to your petitioner.
Exhibit A shows:

RECEIPTS

April 1, 1940, received on Kalsta contract $500.00

DISBURSEMENTS

1938
Oct. 28, Clerk of Court, filing petition for letters   5.00
Dec. 8, Madisonian Publ, Co., publishing notice of
   probate of will, 5.00
Dec. 11, Clerk of Court, admitting will to probate   5.00

1940
Jan. 5, Madisonian Publ., Co., publishing notice to
   creditors, 4.75
May 23, Treasurer, Madison County, 1939 taxes   128.34

SUMMARY

Total receipts
$500.00
Total disbursements
$148.09
Balance cash on hand
$351.91

also planted her flower gardens and enjoyed the area, both winter and summer. She and Susan did quite a bit of traveling, mostly short trips in the general area.

Maggie's notes indicate that Susan did very well with her teaching and enjoyed the job. She received several raises in pay while there.

During the time Maggie and Susan were at Blue Bay, various family members went there to visit and see the area - Thelma, Net, J.B., Gunnar, Rock and Verna. Being fairly close to Hot Springs they went for visits with Seth Halbert's widow, Emma.

Weaving was a great love of Maggie's. In her writings she mentions weaving in various places and with various people, but does not go into depth about the work she did over the years. Weaving was an art she excelled in and continued throughout her life. One person she corresponded with regularly was Mary Atwater. - mc]

Mary Meigs Atwater

[In 1917 Maggie met Mary Meigs Atwater at the fair in Helena. Mary Atwater was considered a "pioneering dean of American weavers". Mary and Maggie apparently formed a lasting friendship and corresponded on a fairly regular basis. Maggie also belonged to the Shuttle-Craft Guild founded by Mary. There are numerous correspondences from Mary to Maggie, general letters and some letters apparently answering Maggie's questions about a weaving pattern or other problems related to weaving. - mc]

From an article in the Woman's Home Companion, January 1949 written about Mary, in part, it states: "Pioneering is in Mary Meigs' blood. Her maternal grandparents left Vermont and went out to Illinois in a covered wagon. Other ancestors fought in the Revolution. Her family tree is studded with doctors and generals and an early president of Yale. When she was a little girl her father had charge of building a canal around the Mississippi River rapids at Keokuk. She spent many pleasant days riding on the Mississippi steamboats, where she made friends with an old ex-salt-water sailor who taught her how to tie knots. As a result her younger sister used to go to school with hair plaited in eight-strand square braids and other unusual arrangements.

She needed all her fighting blood when she wanted to go to art school, around 1900. Art just wasn't considered respectable for a young lady in those days. But Mary succeeded in going to the Institute of American Art in Chicago, where she caused quite a flurry by attending a life class. Later she made two trips to Paris to study. Nevertheless, Mary Atwater still insists, with a twinkle, that her family thwarted her. She says she wanted to go to Massachusetts Institute of Technology and study electrical engineering!

Instead she married an engineer -- Maxwell W. Atwater, who she met on her second trip to Paris. For a few years after their marriage she did a good deal of traveling with him as he went about the western hemisphere making mine inspections. On one of these trips they passed through the wild mining town of Butte and the pretty young brown-haired bride looked out the window and said, "Goodness, I'm glad I don't have to live in that awful place." In 1913 she began calling it home.

In about 1915 she went to live in Basin. Basin, near Butte, was quite a town then. For eighteen hundred inhabitants it had seventeen saloons, nine honky-tonks, and an unknown number of roulette wheels and poker tables. But it didn't offer much outlet for mining engineers' wives who couldn't fill their time with three-room housekeeping. Mary Meigs Atwater looked around for something which would keep not only herself but all the other wives occupied. She thought of weaving.

This was in 1915 and hand weaving, while not exactly a lost art, had certainly been mislaid. Nobody was weaving except a few old women in the southern mountains and a few people generally considered harmless eccentrics. But Mrs. Atwater found a teacher and persuaded him to come and instruct the Basin ladies. Soon they knew as much as he did -- the Honeysuckle and a few other simple patterns. Mrs. Atwater decided that if people were going to weave intricately again she would have to dig out the knowhow herself.

The First World War came along and soldiers with nervous as well as physical disabilities began to fill our hospitals. A few progressive doctors were interested in occupational therapy. Despite the opposition of conservative army surgeons, they succeeded in getting it partially adopted in army hospitals and a call was sent out for volunteers to teach handicrafts. So, she volunteered and till the end of the war did occupational therapy work of great distinction in Pacific Coast army hospitals sharing and teaching her weaving knowledge.

Bed Bug Insecticide

Put 24 ounces of water in each crock. Slowly add 12 ounces of acid.

Put in 1/2 can of Sodium Cyanide in a paper bag and drop in acid mixture.

Note by Thelma (Hand) Kalsta - 1936, "We killed bed bugs in the bunk house this way."

In the early 'twenties she moved to Cambridge, Massachusetts, to be near her son while he went through Harvard. Up to this time she had been plugging quietly away at her hobby. But suddenly people knew about her. From all over the country came letters with questions--from people who had an old loom in the attic or a cherished heirloom counterpane or childish memories of a grandmother who used to weave "coverlids". Her correspondence became so great that she needed help in handling it. To pay for this and because she had now decided that weaving was her profession, in 1923 she organized her Shuttlecraft Guild for answering questions and teaching weaving by correspondence. Soon a monthly bulletin of weaving news was added.

In years of patient research she has resurrected over three hundred old Colonial weaving patterns and put them down in black and white so other weavers can reproduce them. Her **Shuttlecraft Book of American Hand Weaving**, known to modern followers of the craft as the "Weaver's Bible". When she found out all there was to know about Colonial weaves she turned her attention to native American weaving -- Guatemalan, Mexican, Indian and ancient Peruvian -- and those too she has made available to home weavers."

[*Mary lived in Basin, Montana for years and from there did a good deal of traveling, doing research and teaching weaving in various places across the United States and Canada. She eventually moved to Salt Lake City to be near her son in her later years. Upon moving to Salt Lake, her weaving shop on Basin's main street was taken over by a pupil, Mrs. Harriet C. Douglas, who also continued to put out the monthly newsletters. Maggie had many of these newsletters. - mc*]

Bob Hall

When a happy go lucky young fellow, Bob Hall drifted into the Garrison ranch looking for work. When a man is down to one shirt he will work most any place, so with Bob. If the Sunday happened to be a good drying day he could wash it, hang it out to dry and go to bed for a spell. When he attended the dances perchance he could borrow clothes, a shirt, pair of shoes or pants if it so happened the other fellow was stocked up. By some chance he got to the dance with Frankie Beehers, J. B., Bill Garrison and others. Yes, he was always welcome. The money, well if he did not have it, he would get it. He would go, for all the gals in the lower country would be there, the cook, Julia Gransberry, Bob's sweety.

They went to Melrose this time. The dance hall there was the last building on the right hand side of the road going up, tho clost to the old Melrose Hotel bar. All the crowd had a good time, drink was easily gotten, between dances - at that time of the world's affairs women were ashamed to be seen in a saloon. Tho the men could imbibe freely - so they did one and all. Some of the weaker, tender ones such as Frankie Beeher could not carry so much [*hold his alcohol*], so long toward the break of day Frankie slumped over. Word was

**by Bob Hall
Use granted by Garland Hall
From the Thelma (Hand) Kalsta Collection**

quietly passed out to the other ones to hitch up them horses and drive a round clost to the dance hall door. Maggie Bryan was mother of this situation where upon she grabbed poor Frankie up like an infant, stepped out the door and rolled him in the wagon in the hay. By this time the other dancers going to Glen vicinity decided they had better go, seeing the wagon was going that way and away they went.

Bob Hall eventually married and went on to be a very well known Western Artist in the area, doing many pen sketches, illustrations for books and paintings of the western scenes he had grown up with and knew so well.

From newspaper clippings (date and origins unknown) found in Maggie's scrap book, it is stated that Bob Hall was born November 13, 1895. "Always he carried with him a pencil stub, sketching the things he saw and did. Three years wandering in Old Mexico and then in 1916, barely 20, the saddle raised youth hit the Pendleton roundup to try his luck at the game he knew best. After that, a top rodeo rider, matching death against meager prize money and unequalled thrills. Then Bob Hall was married in Butte, and work in a feed store succeeded the glamour of the dust filled rodeo corrals. [*He worked*] various other jobs. Then, 1926 he enrolled in a correspondence school art course and effected a more serious application of his life-long talent."

From Thelma's Diary, September 6, 1941 - *Aunt Annie arrives,* "She's a dandy to be able to make a trip like that - She slept and seemed fine all day."

[*She stayed several days with Thelma and Lars, then left with Net. Aunt Annie went from Net's to stay with Maggie and Susan on Flathead Lake. Maggie and Annie spent time canning, making baskets, weaving and gathering natural material for dyes for their yarns.* Maggie states, "Annie and I walked the beach and brot home currents and alderberries to color [*yarn*] with." *Susan had vacation time coming, so she, Maggie and Annie traveled to Helena, stayed with Rock and Verna, visited with friends in Helena and then went on to Butte to Nettie's. From there they traveled on to the ranch. - mc*]

Maggie (Halbert) Hand and
Annie (Halbert) Briggs about 1940
From the Thelma (Hand) Kalsta Collection

From Thelma's Diary, September 30, 1941 - "Put Aunt Annie on the bus this morning bound for California and home. She's a great old scout - would liked to have her stay longer - She'll be 75 Dec. 7." [*Maggie and Susan returned to Blue Bay a short time later. - mc*]

PEARL HARBOR
DECEMBER 7, 1941

From Thelma's diary, December 7, 1941 - "I turned on the radio about four p.m. and heard about the Japanese attack on Pearl Harbor - called to the men in the yard and they came and listened and have been listening since. They called it a treacherous attack. They made the attack without any notice, while the Japanese envoy was at Washington D.C. pretending to come to an understanding. Well it's awful hard to think of actual war - - always had hopes - - -."

December 25, 1941 - *Susan and Maggie are at the ranch for Christmas.* **Thelma's diary entry states**, "Was a quiet Xmas. Radio is so full of war news it's hard to keep ones mind off it."

[*Following the Christmas holidays, Susan and Maggie returned again to Blue Bay. Maggie described that winter at Blue Bay as a winter to rival anything that the Big Hole Basin had. It was a very snowy and cold winter. They were apparently comfortable, however.*

Alvaretta (Hand) & Earl Conklin's third child, Darlene Conklin, born May 1942.

Susan's job at Blue Bay progressed but there were problems getting enough students, money and materials. On June 29, 1942 the camp at Blue Bay was closed, thus Susan was unemployed. She and Maggie headed back to the ranch at Lavon. - mc] **Maggie's diary states,** "We paid all bills at Polson and left with a clean slate. The trip was fine, no incidents of note on the way. Did not stop at Missoula, by 7 p.m. we were at Nettie's door. Tired as dogs - staid all night and pulled out early for home. We are contented to stay for a while. If the war was over I would take a trip somewhere, as it is I think with all this comotion one is safer at home. The country here is nice with the many spring rains. The hills are green and nice. The garden and crops are late."

From Maggie's Diary - July 4, 1942 - "Nettie, Thelma, Susan and I, Ferdinand, Mary, Julia, Clara, Harold Pederson, (here from Salt Lake), Gunnar, Donald and Caroline Pool - all went up above Brown's Lake for picnic. A safe and sane outing away from the worldly strife."

From Maggie's Diary - July 5, 1942 – "I am weaving linen - table matts and scarves. The Bronson weave. Have more yardage, expect it will take all summer and fall to finish it."

> **August 12, 1942**
> **Weaving Exhibit is Scheduled at Fairgrounds Today**
> An exhibit of old and modern handweaving including colonial coverlets, Lithuanian Shawls and American Linen will be showing from 1 to 5 p.m. Thursday at the School of Fine Arts building at the fairgrounds. The exhibit will be sponsored by the Billings Polytechnic Institute. Modern work in the display is by Miss Susan Hand, teacher of weaving and Mrs. Maggie Hand who reside near Butte.
> **From a handwritten note found in Maggie's Diary.**

From Maggie's Diary - Late August 1942 – "Last Sunday, Net, J.B., Susan, Harold, Gunnar and I and Bill's family all went up to LaMarsh Creek. They went to see the cattle on pasture and we just to be going. We all ate out at the creek, cooked some of the food. That part of the country has a lovely new road. All finished but the oil surface, which will be postponed indefinitely or until this awful "world struggle" is over. At Twin crossing they moved the river over, very few would see the difference. After the hard struggle the freighters had in '94 to '96 or until Gibbonsville went down, now they glide swiftly over these places where a many a team stuck in the mud - if alone perhaps they had to unload and reload or perchance some brother freighter gave him a lift by doubling their team. Those days are only remembered by very few now. The first settlers are the ones that stand the hardships of faraway places. It takes a real pioneer to venture in a new country.

Art and George Reichle are gone. Art to Los Angeles to work in shipyard. George to camp in Utah - Logan. Many have gone and more will."

From Maggie's Diary - September 3, 1942 - "Went to Melrose to visit - staid all night with Mrs. Hoffman - called on Annie Eighorn, Mrs. Swafford, Mrs. Reid and Violet and Mrs. Jones. The town, owing to the war, is somewhat depleted - tho some are coming back for school is soon to open. Slag hauling continues tho expects to quit soon. The town on the whole is battered and worn - 61 years since the RR came in. And today is 50 years since I landed at Divide, September 3rd. An inexperienced teacher. Soon to learn lots as the days rolled by. I stayed the 9 months - went home for the summer with the promise of another term the coming fall. There has, in these 50 years, [been] pleasures in living mingled with hard work and sorrow. Tho on the whole I feel as I did not live or raise in vain."

> **From "John Hand Recalls Lifetime of Mining", Dillon Tribune, 1966, John states:** Spring came, lead price rose to six cents. Pearl Harbor had caused Government to put three cents bonus on all new mined ore, combined price of six cents. This was spring of 1942.
>
> I got a lease from Tony French and started to sample for lead. I had some encouraging assays. Jack Shafer had a truck and we started to ship. Had gotten about five cars out. Jack planned to go to Tacoma, Wash., and work in some of the war production. I said no, I had enough moving around and I was going to stay and starve like a man.
>
> I started to work. The only tools I had were pick, shovel, wheelbarrow, a new pickup truck, a .32 Winchester Rifle. Having lost my compressor, it was a hard start again. I had some luck. Could have been worse.
>
> One month I put out two cars, next got one and got in timber for wood and mine. When cold weather got there, I was under ground. Had a mine car and rails, kept up my one car, then two. I made a deal with Tony French to buy his two claims, pay so much per month, we agreed on. I paid him in a short time. I had gotten a make-shift compressor. Bought a piece of junk for $25 and when gotten in shape was high powered with auto engine. With this I could dig surface deposits very fast. Bill was lots of help, and we shipped very steady.
>
> War time brought problems. Gas was rationed as well as tires, shoes and groceries. Even powder took a special permit. I was issued what was called a P.56. I could buy anything I needed to mine with, but one had to go from town to town and hunt for supplies.
>
> I went to Portland, Ore., but could not get stuff like I wanted. Finally, one day I caught a brand new compressor at Billings. I got it here the next day. I must put this part in. We had come right along. We had to make this last payment on the mine, had several cars of ore on road. I came in for dinner and Mrs. Hand said the check came this morning.
>
> She said, "I don't know how we will make it. The check will finish paying for the mine but only $6 is left for groceries." I said, "I got the deed for the mine. We will manage some way."
>
> She took me to 'the hill and then went to town'. I don't remember how she made it with groceries but we did not go hungry. That deed was the only good piece of paper we ever owned. At that date we owned a mine, and it was producing and still is 23 years later.

Billie Woodward
Sept. 22, '42

Billie Woodward had seen enough of the old west in early days to judge men, know their struggles when trying to make a new home for a wife and family. He did not have to be told anything that was on Charley's mind. Charley Lindlief had come to Montana a young man an industrious Swede from Illinois.

His brother Fred had preceded him a few years and was working for Billie Forrest who owned a cattle, horse, and hay ranch above Divide. When Charley came, Billie Woodward needed just such a man and kept him year after year. A very nice young teacher taught the Divide school then she taught at Glendale and Dewey. Later on Charley was admired by Mary Forrest, tho two now admired Charley. Mary married Fred and Charley married the teacher, Effie Brown.

Charley planned to buy a ranch soon. The new country now was to be home and he must buy a ranch. So they bot the old Corrie ranch on Trapper Creek. All the time Billie kept a fatherly eye on them and their small ranch. Billie knew they needed cattle. The ranges was always good in the surrounding hills. Once, at a chance meeting, they talked as to what Charley was doing. The crops were most always good, the sales were not always so ready, sometimes a hold over with the hay. If he only had some cattle. Billie knew that ready cash for a beginner was hard to get.

Billie says, "Charley do you know of a small bunch of cattle for sale?"

"Yes, when I was down thrashing grain at the Beehers last week I heard of a small bunch for sale. Joe Zeigler down the river a few miles."

"Charley, I am planning to go to California soon for the winter with my folks. I'll leave the money here in the bank at Butte for you to buy those cattle," says Billie.

Billie went to California. Charley went to look at the cattle, then he began to think well now, Billie never told me how much to pay per head. If I pay $80.00 would that be too much? He was at a standstill. What did Billie mean? Then he decided to not buy the cattle. When Billie came back, he went to Charley and says, "How did it come you did not buy those cattle last fall?"

"Well," says Charley "I got to thinking 80 head at about $80.00 maybe you would not like for me to check out that much."

"Well," says Billie, "you need the cattle. You go back and see if Zeigler has the bunch yet and if you can handle them. Buy them at any cost as I first offered you."

Bright and early next morning found Charley and man headed to Zeiglers. The cattle were still for sale with $4.00 for wintering - $84.00 each, cows with calves. The sale was soon closed. Joe said he was not sure as to the number he had for sale, so Charley says, "We can count them right here in the corrals." The three counted them, eighty head. "No," Joe says, "there should be more." So they counted again. The same count. Darkness was falling. Joe still said the count was wrong. Too late to go then, so Joe invited them to stay all night.

After breakfast was over Charley said, "Now we will count them again and you help us." So they counted again.

Again the count was incorrect but said Joe, "You take them at your count." They drove them down the river to cross them on the Pennington bridge as the river was treturous down there and Charley took no chances in drowning a bunch.

Passing Tommie Bird's place, Bird came out to chat with Charley and find out where he had bought the cattle. "Why, I bot the Joe Zeigler bunch."

"How many?" says Bird.

"Well," says Charley, "I bot 80 head and paid for them tho Joe insisted there were more all the time. I felt bad about the count, but we could not count more and we counted them over four times for him and he stood by each count."

"Well," says Bird, "did you not know he could not count?" ---- Charley told me this story last spring at Whitefish - Maggie

[*Susan was accepted as a teacher in Butte in the fall of 1942. She did not take that position, as in early fall 1942, Susan and Maggie moved to San Jose, California. Susan was going to attend San Jose State to get more schooling. Maggie's sister, Annie, was still living there at this time so Annie and Maggie had time together. Susan went to San Jose State the school year of 1942-43. They did as much traveling as the gas rationing would allow and spent much time on arts and crafts. - mc*]

From Maggie's Diary - September 28, 1942 - "My book is nearly full and the summer is nearly done. I have packed and unpacked till I hardly know which way I am going. Today I think I am packing for San Jose, California. Will we get there? I hope so!!

The folks are thrashing the last of the peas. Have had grand weather all fall and part of later summer. Tho it has threatened rain a lot. Gunnar started to school this Sept. and likes it very much. The war still goes on - O God, for what, I hate to think of my boys going or grand child. I hope it is soon over with. I know this is the wish of all mothers and men."

The following are entries from Thelma (Hand) Kalsta's diary:

Thanksgiving 1942 - "Thelma and Gunner went to Net and J.B.'s for dinner. Louise and Carl [*Shafer*] were there - he's working hard in the mines and looks it."

December 1, 1942 - "Gasoline Rationing began -- now it's a very funny feeling to have the wheels knocked out from under you."

Christmas 1942 - "I cooked goose and the trimmings for Aystein, Mr. Leeham, Ole, Andy and us. They seemed to enjoy it.

Funniest Xmas we've seen - you can easily tell there's something wrong with the world as the highway is dead - always before there was strings of cars on holiday."

[*With the progression of the war, the economy continued to improve and the family members prospered despite the hardships of rationing and other war related problems. John's mine was producing, Lars and Thelma's ranch was growing and Susan was doing well in California. Maggie was spending a good deal of time with Susan in California but made visits back to the ranch at Lavon. Net and J.B. were in Butte and doing well. Rock's business was also growing and prospering. The early years of hard times had taught Rock well, along with the teachings of his parents. - mc]*

When asked in an interview with Rock for the Montana Historical Society's Oral History Project, Helena's Business History on March 10, 1987, "How did you learn business then?" He answered:

"Well my old dad taught me. He used to say you gotta learn decypher and the one thing he insisted when I was goin' through public school [*was*] that I knew the times table and I'd come home from school and maybe he'd say how much is eight times eight or six times nine or somethin' like that and the one that used to stick me was nine times seven is sixty-three. I learned that so fast and so good that he saw to it that we learned the times table and then when it come to measurin' and then all the weighin' on grains and things like that. He only had three years of school himself but you couldn't out figure him and he had so many shortcuts of figurin' he was just a jump ahead but he used to say, 'You don't know anything if you can't cypher'. And probably you haven't heard that word cypher, then that's the way those old timers were and when we bought cattle, who would do the weighin' and who would figure it, I'd do it. He'd check alright, he could check in his head a scale full of cattle. You know he would take the weight of the scale off and 'course there's generally the buyer and the seller would each repeat the number of net pounds that you had and then so much a pound, seven cents or whatever it was and he'd have it figured before you'd even start with a pencil."

[*Susan accepts a position of working with sick and disabled children in the Berkley/Oakland area starting in the summer of 1943. There are a few surviving letters from 1943 but no diaries or other information. - mc]*

A post card from Maggie to Thelma, dated May 16, 1943 states,

Dear Thelma:
   This is a very quiet day up here tho the street is plenty noisy. The weather has been quite cool for several days. We went out to see a cacti garden. Many kinds were in bloom along with that the people ran an art shop. They make and bake their own crude wares which sell. Montana needs pottery. Many people could do as well as these people.
   Strawberries have been on the market, now cherries but high. I hope you have help with the garden. I know how busy you all are. Gunner will soon be out of school.
   Haven't seen Annie for over a week now. She keeps busy. The country is lovely now. We haven't had a letter. Hope all is well.
                                                                                                              Love from Ma

---

In a letter from Nettie to Thelma dated August 12, 1943, [*Net talks about correspondence from Susan, which she enclosed for Thelma.*] **She writes**, "Enclosed find a card from Mrs. Gordon and also Mother's ration book. I used her 15 and 16 sugar stamp and took out the 14 and will use it next Monday. I got 10 lb. of sugar and used it all on currant jelly - got such a nice lot - 32 jars - and then put up 11 pt. of pickled beets." [*She goes on about the house cleaning she is doing and waiting for the cleaners to bring back her curtains so she could get them up, etc. - mc*] "Even cleaned the garage," she said. She also conveys her worry about Gunner, stating, "And I have been so worried about him riding on the machinery, especially the buck rakes - do watch him - things happen so fast. Love Net."

In a letter dated October 7, 1943 from Susan to Thelma, [*Susan tells of the trials and tribulations of her job at the Children's Hospital. She seems to be enjoying the job, has a small apartment and talks about various friends. Susan is living in Berkeley, California and Maggie is in Montana. - mc*] **In this letter Susan writes**, "Mama, you can come whenever you want. Please try to come by train and get a berth." [*She also urges Thelma to visit her and go to the doctors in California. Thelma had been suffering from severe "female problems" and Susan urged her to get medical help other than in Butte.*

Susan also had health problems, lots of kidney and bladder infections and sinus problems. Apparently she was getting treatment for these conditions. She wrote in her letters that she was doing better, was getting good medical care and the warmer climate helped her sinus problems but was worried what the rainy season would do to her. A letter dated November 7, 1943 from Susan to Net indicates Susan was planning the holidays in California with friends and co-workers. - mc]

In a letter dated December 20, 1943 to Maggie, [*Susan talked about the conditions there caused by the war*], **stating**, "Yes, I will use the stamps somehow. One thing, we are getting more meat now than formerly for our points. Still I could eat twice what I get, and think I need it." She also goes on to state, "Surely glad that Billy [*Bill Hand*] had his tonsils out, but hope he doesn't get well enuf to get into this mess. War is hell, but you can't tell people." [*Maggie is at the ranch at Lavon. - mc*]

In a letter dated December 29, 1943 from Susan to Thelma,[*she thanked them all for the Christmas gifts and told them about her Christmas*]. "Funny coincidence but where I had dinner the folks had a tree from Kalispell - Flathead National Forest- sent by a ranger friend. I almost felt like shaking limbs with it!

Hope you were all feeling fine by Christmas and able to eat a nice big dinner. Now, I won't be driven to the horse meat market. There is one in Berkeley. People are actually eating horse meat! I simply would be a vegetarian first!

You know, Thelma I'm wondering about Mama coming. She can get a second class pullman for $30+ and about $9 for two nites in a berth. That's a one way ticket. I think I may not stay here another winter anyhow. But she might get a round trip and cash it in in case I decided to stay. Well, I'd like Mama to come if she can stand the trip. It maybe awfully dull here for her with me gone all day. Everyone - almost - works in this apartment house and all are younger people. That's what I've thot of so much. Of course I know she finds things to do but I wouldn't think it too interesting. In San Jose it was quite different and we were right up town. Here we are on a steep hillside and she'd never be able to get out and walk as she did in San Jose where it was level. But I know she dreads the cold weather. I wish I could be in a better place for her tho. I didn't like to take this place because of her but it seemed foolish for me to pay rent and keep up a bigger place for months until she came. Moving is well-nigh an impossibility. One is lucky to have a place at all. Of course it would be nice to have her -for me- but probably not too interesting for her. In San Jose she had Aunt Annie.

Sometimes I think I'd like to move to Los Angeles. If I did that of course it would mean going into a war plant. I believe I could be an electrician - lots of women are and probably dumber and less skillful with their hands. They say it isn't hard. But of course I haven't the guts, much as I dislike this cold foggy place. Love Susan"

In a letter, undated, from Annie to Thelma and Nettie, she states she is doing well except for "an ache in her neck". The letter further reads, "I hear big planes buzzing around. Lots of business out here, all along the Pacific Coast. Everybody that can get loose has come to California and can hardly get a shelter and still they have built - thousands of new houses and still need more. This old war is Hell turned inside out. We don't know what to expect next. There are a lot of dead Japs and a lot more to kill and it takes a lot of our boys to do it."

Chapter XXI

Shattered

****

When Lars and Thelma bought the ranch at Lavon from Maggie and Horace, times were extremely tough. They were in the depths of the depression; there was no money and very little resources to get any cash. Land values were rock bottom and the price that could be gotten for any kind of livestock was also down about as far as it could get. The economy was in shambles throughout the nation and Montana was not untouched.

Toward the end of the 30's, things began to improve and with the start of World War II, the economy took an upswing and people began to prosper. This was true with the various members of the Hand family.

By the early 40's Rock had a business up and running in Helena, and John's mining ventures were finally paying off, due to rich ore deposits and mineral prices going up with the start of the war. Net and J.B. were running the Farmers Union in Butte and apparently doing well. Susan had acquired more education and was working in California. Lars and Thelma were prospering also, making continued improvements to the original ranch and purchasing additional ranch properties. Times had been tough in the beginning for all, but with hard work and the economy improving, they had managed to prosper. Maggie's income remained at $500 a year, the payment agreed to in 1933 when Lars and Thelma purchased the ranch.

The events that took place, for whatever reason, in early 1944 would shatter the family and it would never again be the same.

The information that I have found in research among existing records does not fully explain all that occurred. I visited with various family members, including Susan, Rock, and Thelma, and there is not a clear picture of the events that led up to the happenings. There are no indications of bad feelings in any of the existing letters or diaries prior to 1943. If Maggie kept a diary in 1943 or subsequent years they are missing and are not part of the family records made available to me. What I have gleaned is as follows: - mc]

Thelma's diary entry - January 5, 1944 - "Grandma went in to Butte for a few days."

Thelma's diary entry - January 7, 1944 - "Friday - Just about had supper ready for Andy and I and Net, Grandma [*Maggie*], Grandma Garrison, Mrs. Dingman and daughter came. I made some biscuits, fryed pork - all in terrible hurry. Then Net, Mrs. Dingman and daughter went to Nelson school to F.U. party."

January 8, 1944 - In Maggie's writings *is a hand written page in Maggie's handwriting that states*: "I leave nothing to my daughter Mrs. Kalsta because she has already received more than her share from her father and I."

[*January 10, 1944 - Research at the Madison County Courthouse in Virginia City, Montana revealed that on this date a deed was filed in Virginia City, Madison County, showing a sale of the same land as identified in the escrow agreement signed by Maggie and Horace and Lars and Thelma in 1933. The original agreement was never recorded in the Madison County Clerk and Recorders office. This land was transferred from Maggie Hand to Roscoe K. Hand and Nettie B. Garrison, Bk. 140 of deeds, pg. 518, Madison County, showing Roscoe "Rock" and Nettie paid Maggie $1900.00. The indenture was signed by Maggie, in Helena, Lewis and Clark County, Montana the morning of January 10, 1944 and later filed the same day at the Madison County Clerk and Recorders office. - mc*]

Thelma's diary entry - January 14, 1944 - "Friday - My words would be feeble things to try to explain what happened in this house -- Just after dinner -- Gunnar, Lars and I were here and so help me God will we ever forget. Lars went to Dillon to see Lawyer Collins."

[*The above diary entry refers to Rock and the Madison County Sheriff, Lloyd Brook, coming to the ranch to serve papers on Lars and Thelma for the purpose of evicting them from the ranch for lack of performance as outlined in the original agreement. There was a very heated confrontation between the parties involved. Thelma forcibly removed Rock and the County Sheriff from her house at the point of a butcher knife.*

> **Insurance Document**
> An insurance document, from the Montana Farmers Union Mutual Fire Insurance Co. found in Thelma's records is a Mortgagee Clause with Full Contribution. This document is issued to Lars Kalsta, Reichle, Policy No 5677. It reads:
> Subject to the terms, covenants and conditions set forth in this rider, loss or damage (if any) under this policy on **buildings only** shall be payable as follows:
> FIRSTLY, to Mrs. Maggie E. Hand as 1st Mortgagee.
> Dated: January 18, 1944

Rock claimed that Lars and Thelma had defaulted on their contract with Maggie and thus Maggie had sold the ranch to him and Nettie, as evidenced by the deed for the ranch showing him and Nettie as title holders.

There are many diary entries throughout Thelma's diary as to feelings, withdrawal from friends and family members, for not knowing who was friend or foe. Thelma was ill with female problems at this time. Net and J.B. remained in contact with Lars and Thelma. Thelma wrote that she felt J.B. was very "fair minded" about the situation.

In visiting with various family members and researching writings and documents, as to why this happened and what lead up to these events, I found many different views, but no firm answers. Some felt that the "ranch had been sold too cheaply" and Thelma and Lars should have paid more for it, plus paid interest. Others said they thought Maggie had been "deprived of her home," while still others felt that it was "greed" on Rock and Nettie's part. There were some remarks that Thelma and Lars had "removed Maggie from her rooms" downstairs and had put her upstairs, where there was not enough heat and she had problems getting up and down the stairs. Thelma stated to me that, "Mama always had a good home and a place to live here." Rock stated he had been told that his mother "did not have a home to go to", therefore the contract had been broken. He said, "Nettie started this, dropped it on me and I got stuck with the situation and what else do you do when you find that your Mother has nothing and is not being taken care of properly?" Rock further stated, in a letter to Louise (Hand) Shafer, in 1989 that, "I was against hiring a lawyer and instead getting together and see what we could do for mom." - mc]

A letter dated January 21, 1944 from Aunt Annie to Thelma, "It has been some time since I received your letter. I wrote to Maggie and the family. I got a letter from Nettie and Maggie was up there and not so well." [*The rest of the letter is general chit chat about Annie and her family. - mc*]

The following is some of the correspondence between various parties throughout the following years as events unfolded.

January 22, 1944
Berkeley, California

Dear Thelma,

I've been so stunned I couldn't write. I was in complete and total ignorance. Your first letter and one from Net came Monday. Wednesday or Thursday I received your second letter. No further word from anyone. I've been almost sick with worry of it all. Poor little old Gunnar - I wish he hadn't been there that day. But maybe you couldn't have prevented him knowing about it in some way.

It just seems like a nite-mare to me.

I called Net on Monday nite but she couldn't tell me anything or if there was any chance of settlement now. I certainly wish it could be fixed up out of court. It is going to be so hard on everyone.

I'm not going to worry about my things. They've always been in good care. If need be they could go to Nets, but I would want you to keep some for yourself. But I'm still hoping that something can be done and no change made in your residence.

Mama plans to come down here in February I believe. This isn't going to be easy for me but I certainly don't want to be considered anything but a neutral in all this. Please write me anyhow because I'm awfully anxious over you and especially over how you feel. Do get help somewhere. Nothing is so important as your health.

I'm just too upset to write more - but I want you to know I've been out of it all and intend keeping out. Try to compromise if possible.

Love,
Susan

A letter written January 28, 1944 to Susan from Thelma states,

Dear Susan:

'Take good care of yourself' was Mammas last words as she left January 7 - about 10:30 p.m. It so happens I'm so busy doing that haven't time to answer your letter.

The rattlesnakes are still in their den, but they aren't too bad, they always rattle before they strike. And, Argenta [*brother, John Hand*] had to give up her neutrality seems like they all have had to decide what side to take.

When I went to measure the river I saw a coyote after a chicken. I screamed and shook my apron and the chicken was saved all the agony of death. Then I measured the river there didn't seem to be a ripple here at this point, calmness seems to reighn on these waters. Of course the old addage still hold true "The longer you live the more by Jesus Christ you find out".

Lars and I went to Dillon with the idea in mind "Silence is Golden".

Lars went to Virginia City met a few men who seem to have a trickle of vigilante blood in them yet. He also saw where theres room for one more on boot Hill. Yes, room for Helena's Todajo.

A clear clean conscience seems to still be the most valuable asset I have. It keeps my pulse strong and my eyes clear. Winter evenings are quiet times when folks have a chance to enjoy a home and read a bit - so we dusted off the Bible and read the Crucifixion of Christ - for 20 pieces of silver it was done. After they'd feasted. It is a beautiful story, you should read it. Before I wondered why it was written.

Some recent events made me wonder if I should change my course of study for our Son - but for a while yet I have decided to continue with "Honesty Pays!"

The Japs ran after they bombed Pearl Harbor but they have been paying for it hourly ever since.

Yesterday we and a few other sincere people gathered at our annual R.E.A. meeting - a cooperative meeting based on one of the Golden rules "Do ye unto others as you'd have them do unto ye".

So now I will close without the assistance of any "chop Licking Lawyer" or stool pigeon and still trying to believe what I've been taught, "The truth will out."

Thelma

Letter written February 1, 1944 to Susan from Thelma states,

Dear Susan,

A new month and a new day. The sun is shining and the sky is blue. I tore January off with a song in my heart believing it was ok. Surely would hate to have a snake in the grass, all my life and not know it.

Your neutral, so even what I know would be of personal value to you. I cannot write it. When you get your vacation you come and I'll tell you it all - as honestly as my poor dumb brain can record it.

They wouldn't let me see Grandma - so that might be a clue.

My faith in all things have been well shaken. I yet have reserved faith in your honesty and I hope I can keep it.

Here are things for you to remember. Do your own thinking, don't take orders or suggestions from me or anyone else. Remember what was done was a sneak attack and a sneak on you too.

The only thing that saddens my heart is Grandma's attack on truely her best friends (Gunnar and I). It looks like she had enuf troubles in her life without wanting to kill her best friends, truest she'll ever have.

> Nettie (Hand) & J.B. Garrison adopt a son, Bernard Garrison February 1944

Thelma

> **"J.B." Moves Out**
>
> *The story is told that J. B. Garrison, upon hearing of Rock and Nettie's transaction with Maggie and the move to take over the ranch, moved out of his and Nettie's house to the Finlan Hotel in Butte. He refused to move back home until Nettie removed herself from the legal proceedings. It also appears that he remained friendly towards Lars and Thelma. - mc*

[On **February 2, 1944** *Nettie transferred her interest in the property to Rock that Maggie had transferred to her and Rock on January 10, 1944. This put the title of the original Lavon ranch fully in Rock's name. – Madison County, Bk. 140 of deeds, pg. 560. - mc*]

A letter dated February 4, 1944 from Susan to Thelma states,

Dear Thelma,

If I wrote exactly what I think you probably would misunderstand me. So far I have had nothing to do with the affair so just let it stand that way. I honestly think I'm lucky to be a thousand miles away. I feel no differently toward you or Gunnar. I bought his Valentine candy last month in San Jose before I knew what was coming up so I sent it as I had planned and with no change of heart toward you. How long I can keep a balance depends on my own detachment.

Mama seems well and stood the trip just fine. She didn't run away - I wanted her not knowing what was going on - she came.

I'll burn your note and say nothing. Write anytime you want and to the hospital if you'd rather. Do get medical help. A friend of mine had the same trouble and the operation, is well, working hard and married again this summer. Gunner needs you, so you must do something to get over all that difficulty.

Net will see you I'm sure. She wants to and probably by now has. Now if I keep out of this you can understand I can't do it by taking one side or the other. I'm too far away to help or hinder either side. I think, tho, the sensible thing for all concerned would be to settle the whole thing out of court and as soon as possible. If hatreds enter in you are all lost. But my influence from this distance is too diluted to alter matters.

    With love,
    Susan

A letter dated February 7, 1944 from Susan to Thelma states, "Your note and the registered letter came thru today. She [*Maggie*] seems to feel all right. She stood the trip fine. Has helped me a lot in patching up my clothes and so forth as she always does. We went over to visit my friends the Russells yesterday and came back along the top of the Berkeley hills, it not being much longer that way and much prettier." [*The rest of the letter is general information about Susan's job and what she is doing. - mc*]

Helena, Montana
February 7, 1944

Mr. & Mrs. Lars Kalsta
Reichle, Montana

Dear Thelma and Lars:

    The 15th of this month is the day on which I have demanded that you turn over to me the possession of the ranch property which you now occupy. I now find that Mr. Thomas, my attorney, will be busy in court on that day so we will not be able to get over.

    If you folks are prepared to leave the ranch on that day I wish you would please call me on receipt of this letter, as then I will make arrangeents so that it will not be vacant. My phone number at the garage is 107 and at home is 1955-R.

    Rock

[*Unknown Addressee*]

    Reichle, Montana
    Feb. 11, 1944

    I am thinking of re-financing the place on which I live. Enclosed you will find a map which will fully describe the ranch, and give location. The improvements on the place are:
        10 room 2 story house - 26 yrs. old
        R.E.A. electricity, plumbing
        Horse & cow barn 55x40
        Chicken house, slaughter house, bunk house, machine shed, garage, spud cellar
        Irrigating water out of the Big Hole with ditch in good condition.
        Located on Highway No 91, 7 miles S. of Melrose.
    Outside of the irrigated fields which are shown on the map there is about 200 acres of river bottom pasture-also 880 acres laying on outside of ditch on west side of McCarthy adjoining the ranch. Could you give me an estimate of the loan we could get on this property, length of loan, interest, etc.
    I have lived here eleven years and have all equipment.
    If you can, give me this estimate, then I will know if I can apply for a loan. Thanking you for your consideration.

    Yours truly,
    Lars Kalsta

Thelma's diary entry - February 25, 1944 - "Friday - Rock Hand and the Madison County Sheriff [*Brook*] came just as I was washing dishes -- The sheriff said "This man wants to talk to Lars." I had answered the door so I said, "Come in we are still here." Lars said, "What do you want to say." He said, "Now the month is up and I want to know when you are going to move." Lars answered very calmly, "We will move when the court tells us to." The sheriff asked Lars if he's been sick. Lars told him yes he had ulcers and had been sick. I said, "Effect No. 1 of this sneak attack." Then Rock said something about if we wanted to take this to court and air everything. I said, "So far we haven't done anything wrong and if you want advertising, go to it." The sheriff said "We'd better be going" and they went."

[*On* **February 26, 1944** *Rock filed suit against Lars and Thelma. This suit was filed in Lewis and Clark County. M. J. Thomas of Helena was Rock's attorney and John Collins of Dillon was Lars and Thelma's attorney.*

Rock's Plaintiff's Statement On Pretrial Conference stated that on February 25, 1944 he went to the ranch property to demand that Thelma and Lars turn over the property to him, and that they did foreceably order and threaten him with violence if he did not leave. - mc]

This is a handwritten note to Lars from John Hand written on an Assay Report.

March 14, 1944

Lars, see Mr. Tom Gilbert the lawyer next time you are in town and don't pay him as this is mine. I will settle with him. Bring all those papers with you. I had a long talk with him today.

John Hand

A letter from Maggie to Louise (Hand) Shafer

March 17, 1944

Dear Folks,

We were mighty glad to hear from you. Next time write more. I am sorry that so many of the good young men will have to go *[to war]*. I hope Billie escapes. Too bad he missed out getting to go to school but it is good that he can take a correspondent course. That is better than none. If Carl has to go you go to school too, by all means. You will say too old - no. Did I ever tell you when I was young and out in the prairies we never had more than 3 mo. or 6 mo. *[school]* a year. I see sawed along and at 17 years was not out of the grades. Father moved to town. Mother and a country school teacher we had had wanted me to go to school. So the teacher went with me to get me signed up. I was too bashful to go alone. Just thru pity I think the teacher and P officer thot they would try me in the 8B class. Right there I found out I knew but very little. Finally got acquainted with some good girls. They helped me over many rough spots in my school work. By spring we were promoted to the 9th yr. and yet there were 4 more years staring me in the face if I graduated there. There were no business school or short cuts. Then that spring I was 18, plus 4 years = 22 yrs. when out, not bad. The world then was not going at such a pace and I had nothing else to do. Most all my spare time, thru the year, I helped Mother weave for the public, which kept us busy. One or two summers thru harvest I helped a friend cook on a farm - at $2 per week - a good wage at that time. She often said well, Mag, I never got better help than you and she kept help every summer. So never too late. You are at the right age to go to school and know what you are going for.

That was cute in Darlene. I should have made a white doll. Today I went to see an eye man then went over to the hospital where Susan works. Was all in when I got home. After dinner she went to San Francisco. She will be late coming as she has to see a dentist. I'll have to go back Tuesday to the doctor. Don't ever come to Calif. It is too crowded a place. Stay in Montana - is the best after all. All the money one makes goes here. Everything is high. You know so very few here. Annie may come for a few days and I may go to her to see Ena at Sacramento, our nephew. Nettie sent me a dress - will have to make it soon - for my birthday, got here today and I am 75 today. Glad the folks are all well.

With love from G.ma Hand

[*On **March 22, 1944*** *a motion was filed by Attorney Collins and granted for a change of venue from Lewis and Clark County to Madison County. - mc*]

> **This is a note regarding Maggie taking the river measurements at the ranch at Lavon:**
>
> March 23, 1944
>
> Mr. A. H. Tuttle
> District Engineer
>
> This letter was sent to me. I won't be back to Mont. for two or three mo. My daughter Mrs. Kalsta at the ranch has been measuring for me. Will you please contact her as further service.
>
> Mrs. Maggie Hand
> 1358 Scenic Ave.
> Berkeley, Calif.

> **In a letter from Maggie to Shirley (Hand) Groff, spring of 1944**
>
> "I was glad to get your letter - you now have the joy of spring bursting fourth. It is not so here. One wonders here just where the seasons are. In this section the seasons are much the same. Gardens are so slow. I see tomatoes up a foot high and some not so high. Some put in peas in the fall and now ready to eat. I am lonesome - Annie left yesterday and the days are long tho I find plenty to do. She and I worked together good, we made some sock dolls, I'll have to show you later. Susan went to San Francisco. It is a very busy town. To me it is vicious and don't like to go there but her job calls for her to go twice a week and teach some children in a hospital there. Annie and I went with her once. May 27th we are going to San Jose for two days. The sun shines there and is a much nicer town.
>
> I feed a bunch of birds on the fire escape. They come late and early for bits of bread I put out. I wish I could send you a lot of flowers but this will have to do." [*She had enclosed some pressed flowers - mc*]
>
> How is Barbara, Earl and Darlene. With love to all from Grandma Hand

From Thelma Kalsta's diary - August 1, 1944 - "Ike Dodgson called - told me Maude was in Calif. visiting Grandma."

From Thelma Kalsta's diary - October 3, 1944 - "I went to see Maude Dodgson. She had visited Mamma 2 weeks this summer. Reports her well and of sound mind - so far as she could see. Knew nothing of what she'd done because she never said one word."

> **A letter from Maggie to Shirley (Hand) Groff,**
>
> October 30, 1944
>
> Dear Shirley,
>
> This is quite foggy - most every morning is the same and will be till spring.
>
> Susan and I are going to shop today, mostly window shopping tho, but its nice to do that these times on a weekday when the town is not crowded with people. Berkeley is such a strung out town. I never can go over it all a foot in one day. Susan has two days at home today and tomorrow.
>
> I wish you could see the fall shrubs that are loaded with small red berries, some orange. We have boquets of them now.
>
> You must be quite a cook by now. Grandpa would say "where do you board?" Does Horace cook or is he the dish washer. Did you have a good garden and flowers. I am saving seeds for you to plant next year.
>
> The little pigs are cute. I hope you have good luck with them.
>
> Have you done any knitting or sewing of late. I am glad you have a school and like the teacher. Did your Mom and Dady bring home big red apples? How are they both, well I hope? What do you expect for Xmas? Well I must close - be a good girl.
>
> Love from G.ma
>
> P.S. Take more time when you write and write me a big letter.

A notation in one of Thelma's diary entries states, "Thanksgiving spent at Argenta at Alvarettas and with the rest of the John Hand family."

Other diary notations by Thelma - "Christmas eve - spent at home with neighbors as guests - J. B. called with gifts. Christmas spent in Argenta with John Hand family."

From Thelma Kalsta's diary - December 28, 1944 - "Lars brought me a letter from Mamma that is a good one - Well its too bad she was lead [*led*] into this -- someone should straighten her out -- why should she try to kill Gunnar and I? -- because someone had an idea they could get some money by killing." [*I have never seen the letter this entry refers to. Thelma told me she destroyed the letter. - mc*]

Chapter XXII

Lay It In God's Hand

****

In the spring of 1945 Susan and Maggie returned to Montana from California. Susan started teaching in the Helena school system in the fall of 1945. On October 1, 1945 Rock Hand purchased property in Butte from a Gemma M. Simoni. This home and property, located on Garrison Avenue, became Maggie's home. At this time all of the furniture was removed from the ranch house at Lavon and moved to Maggie's home, as the furniture belonged to Maggie in accordance with Horace and Maggie's escrow agreement with Lars and Thelma. This left no furniture at the house at Lavon, not even a chair to sit on. Thelma and Lars had to start from scratch to refurnish their home, as they had absolutely no furniture left. Thelma told me of the moving van and movers coming to collect the furniture. She had just gotten out of the hospital after having a hysterectomy. - mc]

Nettie (Hand) & J. B. Garrison adopt a daughter, Annette Garrison, July 1945.

Letter to Shirley (Hand) Groff from Maggie dated July 2, 1946.

Dear Shirley,

Was so glad to hear from you and that you plan to come and see me and stay as long as you like. Now that Net & J.B. has taken the trip to the Flathead I don't suppose they will go any place for the Fourth. Also I believe Bill and family & Mother Garrison are coming up the Fourth. The summers are too hot for Mrs. G. Sr. so she came up for the summer.

My how times fly. In the 8th grade next year. I think you have improved your time well. Just now Aunt Annie is tooling away on some Greyhound bus going to Mass. to see Ruby. She will try to go thru the 3 remaining states in the U.S.A. so she will have to say she has gone thru them all. I'll hear from her along the way. I think she left San Jose July 1st in the evening for Los Angles and from there on thru the southern states to Florida and up the coast to Mass. She is tougher than I. I'd hate to have to make that trip.

Now Shirley I'll be looking for you, then too you will want to see the babies at Netties & J.B.

In haste, Love from G.ma. Hand

Carl & Louise (Hand) Shafer's first child, Myrna Carol Shafer, born December 1946.

[Information about Maggie during this time is very limited. I know various family members visited her in Butte. Her health was beginning to fail and by 1947 her health was in a steady decline. - mc]

A letter from Maggie to Horace's niece, Fay Fleming in Houlton, Maine, dated January 27, 1947, reads in part, "I am sorry to have neglected your nice letter. I really haven't any good excuse for not doing things. Life yet is interesting to me and every wakeful minute I can find something to do to help the world along. For years I have had to pause an hour or two and rest my heart.

Horace said grey hair runs in his family. I still have rather dark hair but my hard working days are over. I like to run my own home, so will you. Never give up your own home. I know I am not the best housekeeper in the world but to work at many things we can't always be on a "dress parade". Then sewing keeps me real busy. I have other jobs to branch off on. Now I stay clost to the fire.

We have had a cold snowy weather so far. Susan likes to come over and after missing one or two weekends, then she comes. It is 70 miles over part way a very high mountain meadow. I did not think she would come but she did. Sunday started 4 p.m. to go back in 2 1/2 hours she phones. She had got thru to Helena. I know what a hazard that kind of a road can be and want to know if they are over it. She won't come now for some time.

Nettie and two babies and J.B. were here Sunday for dinner. They are cute, smart kiddies. I think I told you they were adopted. Nettie is 47 last November. J.B. is a few years older. Some friends were shocked at them taking children at that age but she is not afraid. She loves them and will give them a good home and bringing up. The boy will be 3 Feb. 5. The girl is 18 months past. We all think it's wonderful for both mother, father and children and Grandma to sew for.

John was grandpa Christmas day. That makes four grands. Roscoe just got back from a buying trip to the Twin Cities, Chicago, DesMoine, before that to Denver.

I hope to get some snap shots to send you later on. With love and best wishes to you all, Maggie E. Hand."

In a letter to Shirley Hand from Susan Hand and Grandma dated February 8, 1947, Susan states, "You probably know Grandma got home Jan. 28. She has a nice woman with her and things seem o.k. But Grandma got up too much and is not so strong just now. I haven't talked to the doctor but hope to before I leave tonight. I came over in the bus as it was so cold Friday."

Rock and Verna (Ogilvie) Hand's second child, Roger Hand, born February 19, 1947.

[*On* **November 19, 1947** *a judgment on the Kalsta/Hand lawsuit was signed and the judge ordered that action be dismissed at the cost of plaintiff. Rock was charged $33.52.*

In the spring of 1948 Susan accepted a teaching position in Butte. She moved to Butte and lived with Maggie.

On **May 1, 1948** *Rock appealed the case against Kalsta's to the Supreme Court for recovery of costs from Lars and Thelma. - mc*]

> **In a letter from Nettie (Hand) Garrison to John Hand, the letter reads:**
> June 22, 1948
> Dear John:
> Susan is going to Helena today and will talk with Rock. I don't know anything about his offer - and didn't know you were interested.
> I stand where I did in 1933 - the contract is wrong - no able bodied people should get by without reasonable interest on a deal like that. Grandma worked every day - she earned her keep every place she ever stayed. If she had stayed there she would have been dead.
> True, times were hard then - but we all managed to pay interest and principals too.
> I'm only concerned with one thing now. I want Grandma to have enuf to see her thru - Rock has footed the bills - bought the house she lives in and has given her money all along - $500.00 a year doesn't go very far. I have helped some but Rock has done the most.
> I am willing to meet you and the others if you think there is anything we can do. Frankly, I don't believe the contract can be broken. If Lars & Thelma don't agree that the whole thing was a "give-away" there isn't much we can do as I see it.
> Regards,
> Nettie

[*On* **July 3, 1948** *Lars Kalsta paid $12,663.47 to Maggie and the Horace Hand estate. This paid off the ranch.*

On **July 6, 1948**, *Silver Bow, Butte, Montana, Lot 29, Block 4 of the S.C.F. and G.A. Cobban addition to the City of Butte, Montana was conveyed from Roscoe and Verna M. Hand to Susan Hand, pg. 360, Bk 207 (deed book) #164398. This was the home on Garrison Avenue that Rock bought in 1945 that Maggie was living in. - mc*]

Letter from Nettie to Thelma dated July 21, 1948 reads, "Dear Thelma, Mother is very low. We have sent word to the others and feel that you should know. She has had several bad attacks. This morning we had two doctors. We know she cannot last long.

We think you should come to see her. And we think you should come right away. Sincerely, Nettie"

Letter from Susan to Thelma dated July 25, 1948 states, "Bill was here today and Mother asked me after he left if he had delivered the message to you." **Then in letter dated July 27, 1948 states**, "She got thru Sunday and Monday without an attack but yesterday had to have a hypo. If you come you had better call from Melrose -- no use coming if its one of those days she is bad. It comes on very suddenly - yesterday she felt fine in the morning and we were encouraged. I think she'd like to see you. She said, "I sent her word and its funny she doesn't come."

She has been in such an uncertain condition. When John and Ida came she was really too sick to see anyone. After they go she just wilts so those who come often think she's not so sick because she perks up while they are here.

Today she had too many. For the last four days she's had one attack after another and had one or two hypos a day. For a week she was pretty good then Wed. this series hit -- I don't know from hour to hour how she'll be. She's pretty strong in lots of ways yet."

[*Records show that Maggie was in the St. James hospital in Butte in late August, released and readmitted in mid-September, and remained there until her death - mc.*]

Maggie Ellen (Halbert) Hand died October 20, 1948 in Butte, Montana.

HAND FUNERAL AT MELROSE SATURDAY 2 P.M.

Mrs. Maggie Hand, 79, widow of Horace Hand, died Wednesday in a Butte hospital after a long illness. She was the mother of John Hand of Argenta and Mrs. Lars Kalsta, of Reichle. She is also survived by two other daughters and a son who are Mrs. J.B. Garrison and Susan Hand of Butte and Roscoe Hand of Helena. Mrs. Lucy Ann Briggs of San Jose, Calif., is a surviving sister. There are also 10 grandchildren and four great grandchildren. In recent years she has been living in Butte. She was a resident of Montana for more than a half century and had lived much of that time in the Melrose and Wise River communities.

Mrs. Hand, born Maggie Ellen Halbert, in Orangeville, Ind., came to Montana in 1892, first settling in Dewey, where her brother, the late Seth Halbert, was employed as an early day freighter. She was a descendant of Welsh colonists who settled in Virginia and took part in the Revolutionary war. Her father, Enos Halbert, went to California in the gold rush, returned to Indiana and later took part in the Civil war as a Union Army captain.

The family moved to Kansas by covered wagon and settled near Beloit, where Mrs. Hand graduated from the Beloit high school with the class of 1891, and then studied at a normal school to secure a teacher's certificate.

When she first came to Dewey she taught two terms and had 40 pupils in the little log cabin which still stands and which until recent years was used as a school house.

In July of 1894 she was married in Dillon to Horace Hand of Wise River. They developed a ranch in the valley, selling out in 1910. After a trip to Mr. Hand's home in Houlton, Ma., they returned and resumed ranching at Melrose. In 1917 they move to Lavon, near Reichle, where Mrs. Hand resided until 1940. Mr. Hand died in 1936.

She spent some time in San Jose and Berkeley, Calif., before coming to Butte in 1945.

She was a principal instigator in the movement to install a telephone line between Wisdom and Divide. Mrs. Hand was also interested in politics and never missed an opportunity to cast her ballot. She voted from her sick bed in the primary election last July.

Mrs. Hand, during her long period of residence in Montana, won a host of friends. She was known to many for her lovely flower and vegetable gardens and her fine handwork. She possessed and used both a spinning wheel and several hand looms which she used up until her illness overtook her a year ago. She also wrote in longhand a series of stories of early day Montana.

The funeral will be held at Melrose Saturday from the Melrose church and interment made in the Melrose cemetery.

Dillon Tribune
Dillon, Montana
October 22, 1948

The Old Year

What is the old year? 'Tis a book
On which we backward sadly look,
Not willingly quite to see it close,
For leaves of violet and rose
Within its heart are thickly strewn,
Marking love's dawn and golden noon;
And turned down pages, noting days
Dimly recalled through memory's haze;
And tear starred pages, too, that tell
Of starless nights and mournful knell
Of bells tolling through trouble's air
The De Profundis of dispair —
The laugh, the tear, the shine, the shade,
Till 'twixt the covers gently laid;
No uncut leaves, no page unscanned;
Close and lay it in God's hand.

—Clarence Urmy

From Maggie's Scrapbook

**Maggie (Halbert) Hand
1869-1948
From the Susan Hand Collection**

Epilog

The financial records from Rock Hand show that on August 6, 1948 all of Maggie's assets were consolidated. They included $12,663.47 from the Kalsta payment, $202.50 in bonds, and $194.29 cash for a total of $13,060.26. All expenses were paid from these funds.

Records show that Rock was reimbursed for all expenses incurred on the ranch lawsuit, including all travel expenses, court costs and miscellaneous costs in the amount of $598.70. Attorney fees for the ranch litigation were paid to M.J.Thomas of Helena from Maggie's funds in the amount of $2152.00. Rock was also reimbursed for all costs he had incurred for the purchase and improvements of Maggie's home in Butte at 2018 Garrison Avenue in the amount of $2531.02. From 1945 until April, 1948 Rock had also given Maggie money to live on in the amount of $2100.00. This money was also reimbursed to Rock. Rock was reimbursed a total of $5229.72 for all expenses he incurred.

The remaining debt on the house of $1157.37 was paid off at this time. Susan was not reimbursed any cash but the ownership of the house was turned over to her.

The total cost of the ranch lawsuit was $2750.70. The total cost of Maggie's house was $3688.36, which includes interest.

Nettie was reimbursed a total of $1732.90. A notation next to this record indicates this was "for money advanced for taxes and ranch expenses during the years she was teaching."

After Maggie's death all taxes, doctor, pharmacy, and hospital bills, burial expenses, and other expenses were paid in full. - mc

John William Hand
1895-1970

John and Ida made their home in Argenta. He continued in the mining business and had a small ranch there. John had written down various family stories and information, which have been included in this book. From the Dillon Tribune, **"John Hand Recalls Lifetime of Mining", 1966 he states**, "We have shipped 65,000 tons of ore in the last 23 years from this mine. The family, what they have done, and the work they put in, was paid for just the same as anyone else — Friday is pay day. I have one daughter, (Alvarette) the oldest kid, who frame timbered a 200 foot shaft, made perfect fits on all plates. Post guards were 4x6 — 20 wall plates 6x8, post 6x6 — 2 inches in lagging.

John Hand Family Tree Descendent Charts available upon written request to the author.

Next daughter (Louise) drove truck for three years, hauling 16 1/2 miles to railroad at Dillon. My two boys can do any job. They are assayers, surveyors or miners (Bill and Horace). One (Horace) owns Goodall Brothers Assayers Office at Helena.

Bill is here and runs the mine. Shirley has done some bookkeeping. Bill's wife keeps books. My grandson (Earl Conklin) has been at my side since he could toddle. He also can mine, assay, survey and what not.

My wife has the never-ending job of having meals ready. We do not pack a lunch and are always home for noon. We have a modern house and electricity — the only modern house here. We have 60 acres we cut hay on and keep 45 head of cattle as a sideline to pick up feed on patented claims. We have complete assay office at the mine, just for our own use. Our source of finances is derived completely from ore sold."

John and Ida celebrated their 50th Wedding Anniversary at their home in Argenta in April of 1967. Ida passed away December 27, 1967 and John passed away in November 1970. They are both buried at the Mountain View Cemetery, Dillon, Montana.

Nettie Mae (Hand) Garrison
1899 – 1950

Net was bookkeeper-secretary for her husband, John "J. B." Garrison in the Farmers Union Trading Company in Butte from 1935 until 1949. In 1949 J. B. Garrison died of a heart condition, leaving Nettie alone with the two children, Bernard and Annette. Net then taught one quarter in Emerson School in Butte. In November 1949 she became ill and went to Rochester to the Mayo Clinic. She was operated on by Charles Mayo for

Nettie (Hand) Garrison Family Tree Descendent Chart available upon written request to the author.

colon cancer in late November, returned home and was again operated on in Butte by Dr. Kroeze. Her health continued to deteriorate and in May 1950 she went to the Las Encinas, Pasadena, California rest home, where she died June 5, 1950.

Net and J. B. are both buried in Butte.

Roscoe "Rock" K. Hand
1904-1997

Rock and Verna lived in Helena where they made their home since their marriage. Rock had a farm equipment dealership and a hardware store for years, the Rock Hand True Value Hardware being his last store. Verna worked in the businesses with him.

Roscoe K. "Rock" Hand Family Tree Descendent Chart available upon written request to the author.

Rock was a very successful businessman in the Helena area. One of his advertising methods was a radio show that he did each day. This proved to be very popular and I am sure added to his success. Rock also wrote a book entitled **A Lifetime of Nonsense" - A Thousand Jokes & Sayings That can be repeated — In any company**, and belonged to the Toastmasters for thirty-two years. He was a keeper of family records and information. It was through his visits and sharing his records and information that helped in the completion of this book.

In an interview with Rock in 1987 for the **Montana Historical Society's Oral History Project,** when asked what he would have done if he could have gone into any other lines of business other than the farm implement or hardware business, he replied, "I could've bought and sold cattle, we did that at the ranch. But I didn't exactly like that. I've always said I never could see any glory or romance of ridin' around lookin' at the rear end of a bunch of cattle from a saddle horse. We done alot of it, but I didn't like it. You had to feed 'em, you had to put 'em up over night. You'd unhook a tractor and it'd be there the next morning where you unhooked it."

Rock passed away in 1997 in Helena. Verna continued to live in Helena until her death. Both are buried in Helena.

Thelma Victoria (Hand) Kalsta
1909-1994

Thelma and Lars continued to live on the Ranch at Lavon. They saw many seasons come and go on this ranch. With each season there were different activities going on - calving, feeding, planting, haying, moving cattle and Thelma's ever-present job of keeping meals on the table. Thelma always had the meals ready for family, hired hands and anyone else who happened to show up at mealtime. In the summer there

Thelma (Hand) Kalsta Family Tree Descendent Chart available upon written request to the author.

was always the wonderful garden and flowers that she took care of. Continuing in Maggie's footsteps, Thelma also recorded the temperature and measured the precipitation at the ranch for the U.S. Climatic Data Center, as well as measuring the water level of the Big Hole River for many years.

Thelma, over the years, gathered and kept news clippings, and historical photos of Glen, Melrose, and related areas. She also kept family photos and many other historical information items on the family and the area. Many people came to her for information and she was always happy to visit with them and help in any way possible. Access to the information Thelma had collected, her diaries and own personal writings made much of this book possible.

Lars passed away in January 1988. Thelma passed away in October 1994. They are buried at the Melrose Cemetery.

Susan Edith Hand
1911 - 2000

When Nettie died, two children were left without parents. Susan took the children and raised Bernard and Annette to adulthood. We always teased that Aunt Susan was our "Old Maid Aunt" with two kids, which she was.

Susan continued to teach in the Butte school system until she moved to Helena in 1959, moving Bernard and Annette with her. After the children left home, she continued to teach in various schools in Montana. She retired from teaching in 1978, but continued to do tutoring, particularly in the area of reading. Susan was very interested in the methods of teaching reading and did a lot of research in teaching methods. She recrived an award for her efforts in this area.

Susan, too, was a keeper of history. She was interested in all history, but in particular family history. She corresponded with various family members all over the United States and she was the keeper of Maggie's writings, passing them on to me thus making this book possible. She, too, allowed me access to her personal writings and all information she had collected. Susan never married and had no descendants. Susan passed away February 5, 2000 in Helena and is buried in the Melrose Cemetery.

A Family Wish . . .

It was the wish of Susan, Thelma, and Rock that the story of Maggie be told as fully as could be done with the information available. I have tried to do this as accurately and fairly as possible. When writing about someone there will always be questions that remain unanswered. That is true with this story. Many happenings in peoples lives can not be fully explained - why did this happen, when did it happen, how did it happen? Always, there are questions, as with this story. It is with great hope that the reader will enjoy this book for the small glimpse it allows us of the past.

In later years, Thelma and Susan corresponded with one another, talked on the phone some and exchanged photos and some family information. Rock and Thelma corresponded a few times, but never reconciled their differences.

The descendants of Maggie Ellen (Halbert) Hand have grown in numbers over the years. They have spread far and wide. They, too, have raised or are raising families and, in the scheme of things, are probably experiencing the same joys, trials, and tribulations as Maggie did - just different settings. All families seem to experience similarities in life's ebbs and flows. Times may change our circumstances and fortunes but we, as Maggie did, must deal with life as it is handed to us. **And life goes on . . . .**

Appendix A

MAGGIE'S SPELLING

across - acrost, a crost or acrossed
afraid - a fraid
another - a nother
bachelor - batchelor
batching - baching
before - ere
biscuits - bisquites
bless - blezs
boarded - boardered
bought - bot
bouquets - boquets
brought - brot
campaigned - electioneered
Carolina - Carlina
catch - cache
centrally - centerly
chagrined - chargainned
chiseled - chizzeled
cliff - clift
close - clost
coal oil - coil oil
consider - concider
considerate - conciderate
consist - concist
cook - kook
coupe - cupe
crane - crain
crawled - cralled
cucumbers - cuks
did not have - hadden
didn't - din't
dreamt - drempt
embarrassment - barasment
embarrassment - imbarishment
enough - enuf or enuft
entirely - in tirely
etc - &, &, &
every - evry
every day - everday
everybody – everbody
FU – Farmers Union Co-op
fair - fare
flourishing - flurishing
frantically - franticly
get - git
gladiola - glads
going to - gunna
goslings - goslin
gross - grozs
guess - guezs
had not - hadden

hadn't - haddent
heated - het
held - helt
holler - hollow
hollered - hollowed
hollered - yelled
immediately - amediately
inquire - enquire
kitty corner - catacornered
lichens - litchens
mineral - minreral
miss - mizs
molded - moulded
mountain - mt
necessity - needcessity
old - ould
opossum - oposom
ought – aught
papas - pawpaws
paid - payed
perhaps - perhaspe
pestered - pested
picnic - picknick
railroad - R.R.
rebel - rebble
relic - relict
rendezvous - randivu
satisfied - sattisfide
scarce - scarse
scared - scard
shall not - shan't
slaughtered - slattered
they would - they'ed or the'd
this - thizs
though - tho
thought - thot
through - thru
tie - tye
tolerable - tolerble
toll - tole
tying - tieing
uncommon - uncomin
until - til
vegetable - veg
visibility - vizability
we are - we'en
wheezed - wheased
wise - wize
wreck - reck
yell - holler

Appendix B   **Location Map**

Indiana and Kansas

Appendix B   **Location Map**

Montana, California and New Brunswick

Appendix C   **List of Photographs**

PHOTOGRAPHS

Missouri Folding Table Loom	8
Halbert, Francis (Charles)	20
Halbert, Seth	20
Halbert, Enos on Horse - Civil War	35
Halbert, Enos (Capt.) in Civil War	41
Halbert, Maggie Ellen - Child	53
Ad - Coffee Grinder	65
Pony Runabout	72
Halbert, Maggie E. - Young Girl	80
Halbert, Lucy Ann	89
Halbert, Enos	92
Halbert, Susan (Shirley)	92
Halbert Home in Beloit, Kansas	93
Halbert, Maggie - Graduation	94
Hand, Horace - about 1880	101
Narrow Gauge Railroad	103
Hays, Robbins and Lawrences at Wise River	106
Halbert, "Big Al" Seth - Ore Camp to Glendale	111
Halbert, "Big Al" Seth with Freight Outfits	113
Ad - Winchester Repeating Rifle	117
Dewey, Montana	123
Brubaker, Al	126
Cliffs Above Watercress Spring - painting	128
Ad - Bath Tub	138
Dewey, Montana, Main Street	152
Hand, Maggie & Horace - Wedding Picture	157
Ad - COD Store	158
Ad - Shoe Last	160
Ad - Ladies Waists	161
Ad - Sarsaparilla	163
Pettingill, George	165
Hand Home at Wise River Ranch	168
Hand, Byron and John - Children	169
Hand, Byron, Nettie and John	171
Bryant, E. G. Funeral - Dewey, Montana	173
Wise River Ranch	174
Early Day Road near Dewey, Montana	180
Ad - Percale House Dress	185
Hand, Nettie and Roscoe "Rock"	193
Hand, Byron	194
Melrose, Montana	197
Hand Ranch at Melrose, Montana	201
Hand, Nettie, Thelma and Susan - 1913 or 1914	201
Hand, Nettie, Byron, Thelma and Susan - 1916	202
Pushin' it Home	203
Hand, John and Ida (Hartwig)	204
Train at Lavon	208
Lavon Siding	209
Ad - Weavers Delight Loom	210
Hand Home at Lavon - Construction - 1917	211
Hand, Susan and Thelma	211
Delivery Truck for Oregon Feed Store	213
Hand, Nettie, Thelma and Susan in Oregon	213
Hand, Byron in Oregon	214
Hand, Nettie, DAR Costume in Oregon	214
Maxwell Car (The) in Oregon	214
Hand, Byron, Susan, Rock, Maggie and Thelma	215
Ranch House at Lavon	216
Hand, Thelma	219
Cutting Winter Wood at Lavon	220
Hand, Roscoe at Lavon	220
Hand, Byron at Lavon	223
Ad - Agitation Washer	224
Ad - Clothes Wringer	224
Ad - Sad Irons	224
Ad - Wash Board	224
Ad - Wash Boiler	224
Wise River After Flood	225
Railroad Bridge at Lavon - 1927 Flood	226
Kalsta, Lars and Thelma (Hand)	229
Donovan, Mr. and Mrs. Jim	230
Halbert, "Big Al" Seth	231
Hand, Roscoe and Verna (Ogilvie)	233
Hand, Susan - 1933	234
Garrison, J. Bernard and Nettie (Hand)	238
Hand, Susan at Lavon	239
Nakuka and Son	241
Hand, Horace in potato patch	242
Baskets	243
Hand, Maggie With Chickens	248
Building Irrigation Diversion Dam	250
Cutting Hay at Lavon	253
Stacking Hay at Lavon	253
Hand, Horace Hastings - 1936	257
Hall, Bob - Post Card	271
Maggie and Annie	272
Hand, Maggie (Halbert)	286

RECIPES AND POEMS

RECIPES

Mush Scrapple	5
Corn Bread	6
Lye Hominy	10
Chow Chow	22
Corn Meal Crackers	23
Matrimonial Cake	70
Vinegar Pie	76
Pumpkin Pie in a Sack	84
Pumpkin Pie Leather	84
Gingerbread	108
Soft Cookies	175
Carrot Pie	196
Fruit and Nut Confection	212
Home Made Crackers	219
Sweet Beet Pickles	221
Gamers Mocha Cake	244
Hard Soap	246
Rich Shortcake	247
Homemade Wall Cleaner	249
Molasses Pie	254
Green Grape Preserve	255
Bean Hole Beans	265
Bed Bug Insecticide	270

****

POEMS

Lanes of Yesterday by Martha Bell Tumey	
The Sunday Hymns by Louise Gahnett	68
I'm A Stern Old Bachelor, by Clay Brown, W. Va	77
Old Slate (The), 1930, Western Newspaper Union	79
Prophesy, Chambers Journal, Sept., 1895	164
Bryant's Hotel & Toast by John Carmont from Rock Hand	181
Mama's Vaccination, author unknown	191
Garden Card "Just Off The Sunshine Trail" by Thelma Kalsta	236
Song of the Robin (The), by Zula Lloyd Leach	246
By the Road by Fannie Chenoweth	252
Courage by Jane Sayre, from Thelma (Hand) Kalsta's Diary, May 28, 1940, Publication Unknown	258
Old Year (The) by Clarence Urmy	286

All poems are from Maggie's Scrapbook unless otherwise indicated

Appendix E   **Family Tree**

SHIRLEY FAMILY TREE
(Ancestor)

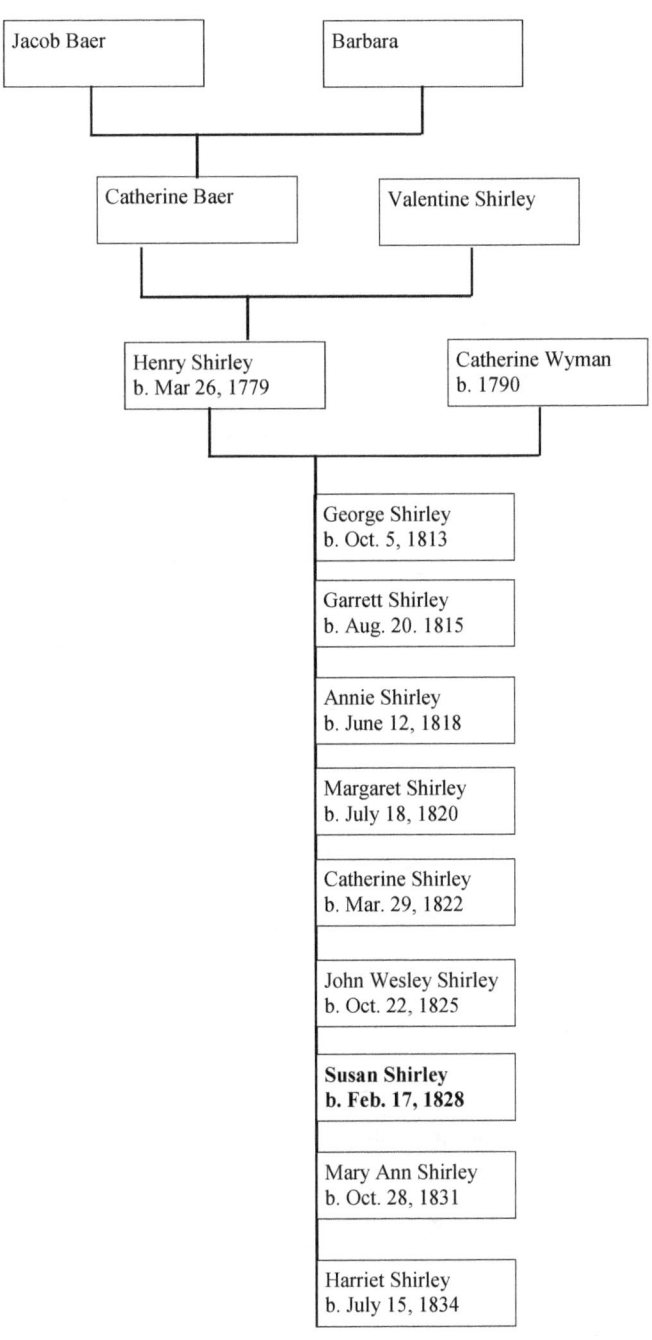

2-26-12

Appendix E   **Family Tree**

HALBERT FAMILY TREE
(Ancestor)

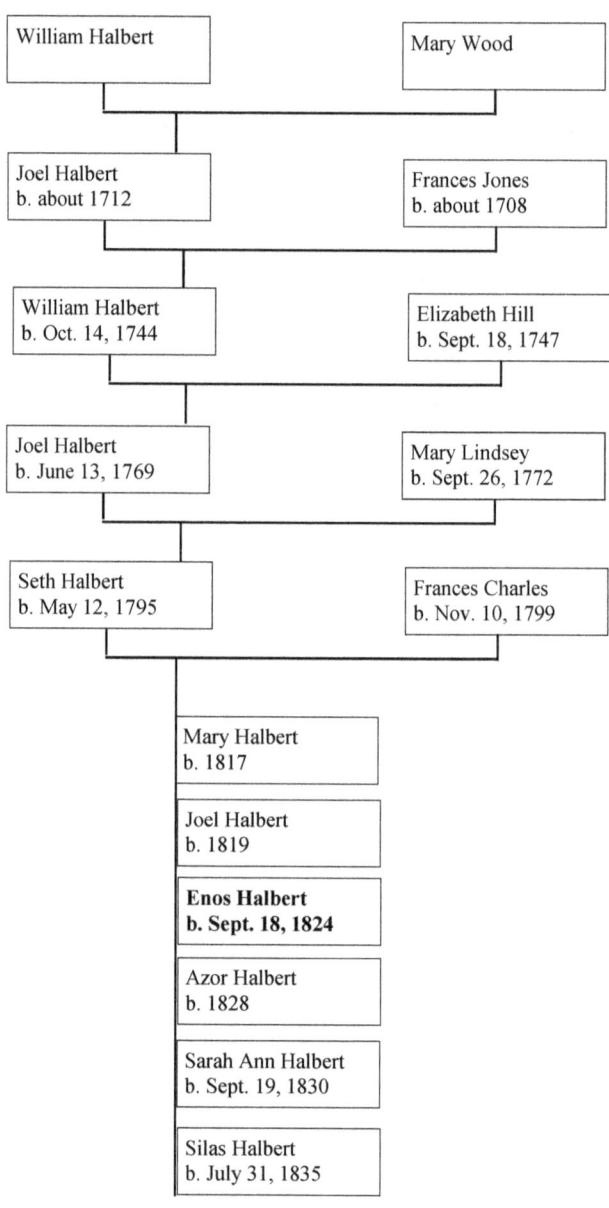

2-26-12

Appendix E   **Family Tree**

ENOS AND SUSAN (SHIRLEY) HALBERT FAMILY TREE
(Descendent)

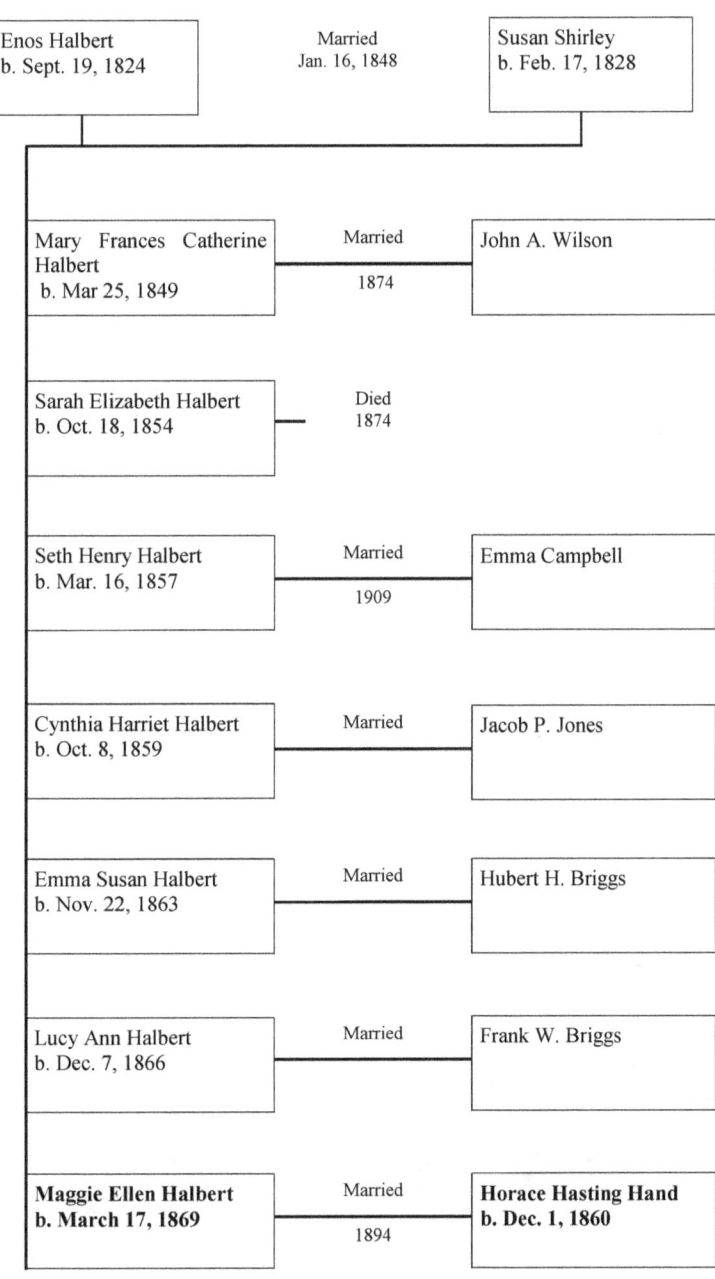

2-26-12

Appendix E   **Family Tree**

HAND FAMILY TREE
(Ancestor)

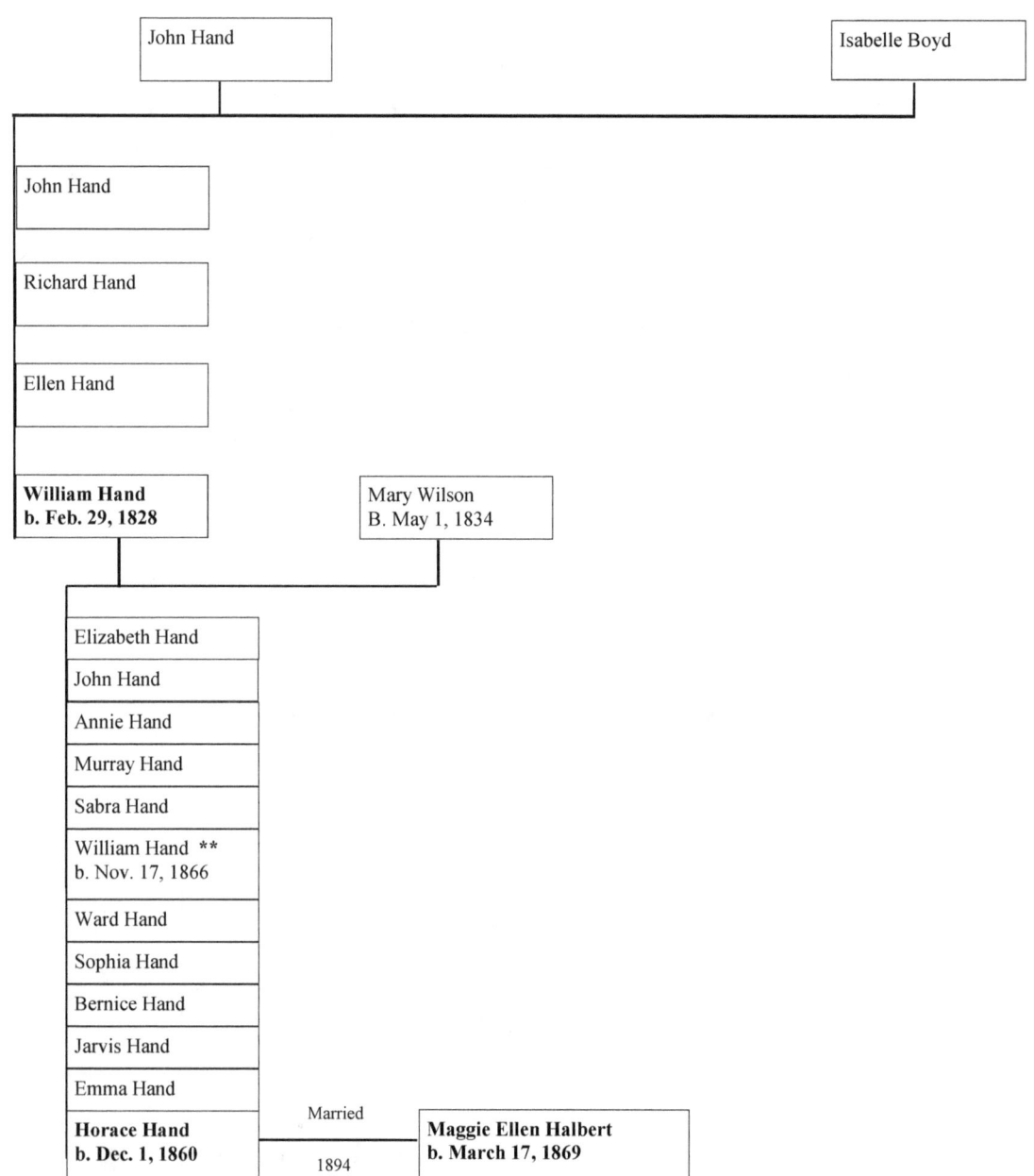

William Hand b. Feb. 29, 1828 — Mary Wilson B. May 1, 1834

Children:
- Elizabeth Hand
- John Hand
- Annie Hand
- Murray Hand
- Sabra Hand
- William Hand ** b. Nov. 17, 1866
- Ward Hand
- Sophia Hand
- Bernice Hand
- Jarvis Hand
- Emma Hand
- **Horace Hand** b. Dec. 1, 1860 — Married 1894 — **Maggie Ellen Halbert** b. March 17, 1869

Parents of William Hand: John Hand & Isabelle Boyd
Siblings of William Hand: John Hand, Richard Hand, Ellen Hand

**William died in 1931 at the Ranch at Lavon of tuberculosis. Buried in Melrose Cemetery in the Hand plot.

2-26-12

Appendix E　　　　　　　　　　　　　　　　　　　　　　　　　　　　　　　　　　　　**Family Tree**

HORACE AND MAGGIE (HALBERT) HAND FAMILY TREE
(DESCENDENT)

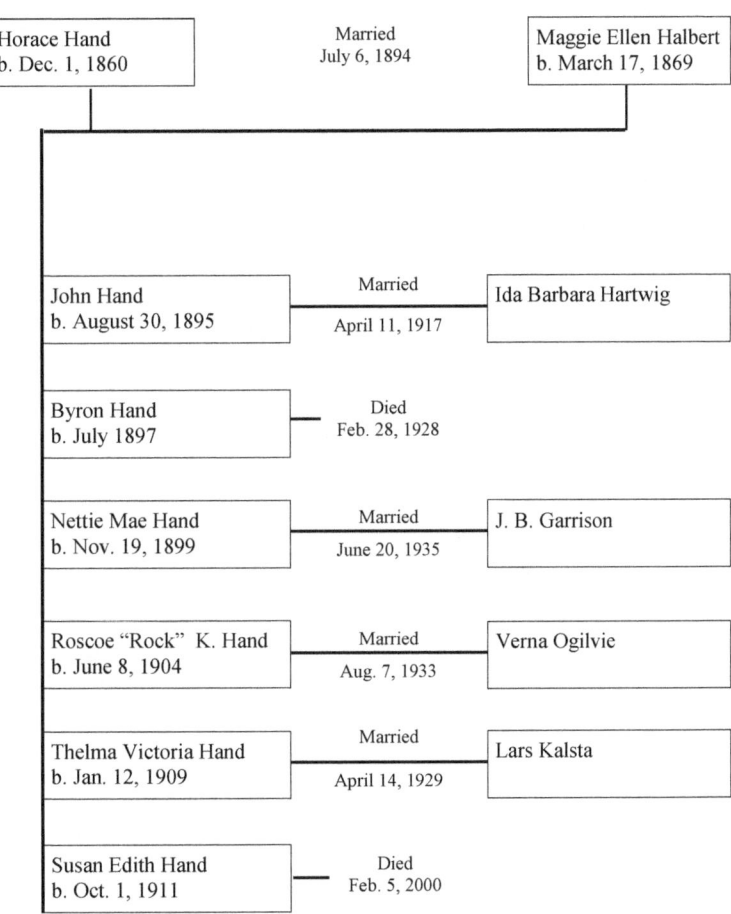

2-26-12

SELECTED REFERENCES

Apportionment of School Money, The Dillon Examiner, Dillon, Montana, December 27, 1893

Argenta Suffers Serious Conflagration, Source Unknown, 4-12-40, found in Thelma (Hand) Kalsta's Diary

Bryant's Hotel and Toast, (John Carmont), A Lifetime of Nonsense With Me & Ed & Ray by Rock Hand, Published by Thurber Printing Company, Helena, Montana, Copyright July 10, 1980

Bureau of Pensions, United States of America, Department of Interior

Byron Hand's Body is Found in River, Dillon Tribune Dillon, Montana, June, 1928

Capt. Halbert Dies, Beloit, Kansas News, Maggie's Scrapbook

Chicken Gulch Sheep and Cattle Fight (The), Spring of 1912, by Rock Hand, Roscoe "Rock" Hand Collection

Clerk and Recorder, Beaverhead County, Dillon, Montana, Book 52, pages 354 and 364

Clerk and Recorder, Beaverhead County, Dillon, Montana, Book 7, page 597.

Clerk and Recorder, Book 112 of Patents, page 227, Virginia City, Madison County, Montana (Byron's Homestead)

Clerk and Recorder, Madison County, Virginia City, Montana

Clerk of Court, Beaverhead County, Dillon, Montana

Clerk of Court, Lewis and Clark County, Helena, Montana

Clerk of Court, Madison County, Virginia City, Montana

Dewey's Flat, Quartz Hill and Vipond Park Mining Districts, Written by Horace Hand for the historical files of the Beaverhead Mining Association

Dewey's Flat Boomed, source and date unknown, Mattie's Scrapbook

Deweys, Dillon Tribune, Dillon, Montana, October 7, 1892

District Court of the Fifth Judicial District of the State of Montana, in and for the County of Madison, in the Matter of the Estate of Byron Hand, April 3, 1930

District Court of the Fifth Judicial District of the State of Montana, In and For the County of Madison, No. 1383 - Horace Hand Estate Appraisal

Divide to Wisdom Stage Line, Early 1900's by Roscoe "Rock" Hand, Roscoe "Rock" Hand Collection

Earl Hand Victim of Sudden Illness, Dillon Tribune, Dillon, Montana, October 1929

Early Mining History of Beaverhead Reviewed, Dillon Tribune, Dillon, Montana, date unknown

Electrification Extension Seen, Dillon Tribune, Dillon, Montana March 9, 1939

Enos Halbert's Pension Records, The National Archives

Forty Niners Bill of Fare - Dillon Examiner, Dillon, Montana August 28, 1895

Genealogy of Valentine Shirley and Related Families, by Henry Shirley Rothrock, copyright 1983

Glen News, Dillon Tribune, Dillon, Montana, Friday, April 13, 1917

Glendale Odd Fellows, Dillon Examiner, Dillon, Montana, Janary 1, 1894

Grinding Feathers, Montana Farmer, date unknown, Maggie's Scrap Book

Halbert-Holbert History, Vol. 1, by Karen R. Moore, copyright 1995

Hand Funeral At Melrose Saturday 2 p.m., Dillon Tribune, Dillon, Montana, October 22, 1948

Hecla Mercantile and Banking, Inc., Melrose, Montana, Silver Bow/Butte Archives Butte, Montana

Helena Temperature Drop, October 28, 1989 - Oct. 28, 1935, Helena Independent, Helena Almanac, Helena, Montana

History of the Thirty-Third Indiana Veteran Volunteer Infantry - Four Years of Civil War - From Sept. 16, 1861 to July 21, 1865, by John R. McBride, Indianapolis, Wm. B. Bruford, Printer and Binder, 1900

Horace Hand Family (The), by Roscoe "Rock" Hand, 1989, Roscoe "Rock" Hand Collection

Horace's Citizenship, Clerk and Recorders Office, Beaverhead County, Dillon, Montana, Book 57, page 517.

John Hand Recalls Lifetime of Mining, Dillon Tribune-Examiner, Dillon, Montana, February 3, 1966, and original,

Myrna Carpita Collection

Journal of Henry S. Reynolds, Massachusetts Audubon Society, August 24, 1973

Kept Corpse Packed in Ice While Bandplayers Learned Funeral Dirge, Anaconda Standard, Date unknown

Lone Pine, Dillon Tribune, Dillon, Montana, Holiday Edition, 1891-92

Maggie Hand Diaries

Maggie Hand Scrapbooks

Mary Carpita Story, by Mary (Zunino) Carpita, James B. Carpita Collection

Mary E. (Raker) Speelman Donovan, Interview by Nettie M. Hand, Melrose, Montana, Susan Hand Collection

Money Orders, Dillon Tribune, Dillon, Montana, November 21, 1892

Montana History, Beaverhead Co., 1885

Nettie (Hand) Diaries

Nicknames, Montana Historical Society's Oral History Project, March 1987, with permission from Montana Historical Society, Helena, Montana

No Trace Is Found Of Young Ranchman, Dillon Tribune, Dillon, Montana, March 9, 1928, Maggie's Scrapbook

Notice of Teacher's Institute, Dillon Tribune, Dillon, Montana, November 18,1892

Old-Time Freighter Crosses The Divide, Dillion Tribune, Dillon, Montana, April 1931, Maggie's Scrapbook

Our Hands, by Faye Thompson Fleming and Vera June Thompson, March 1973

Our Wedding, Dillon Tribune-Examiner, Dillon, Montana April 20, 1967 - By John Hand

Pioneer Rancher Crosses Divide, Dillon Tribune, Dillon, Montana, September 3, 1936, Maggie's Scrapbook

Pony Runabout, American Peoples Encyclopedia, Chicago Spencer Press, Inc., Copyright 1959

Rebecca Jane Bryant's Obituary from the Hazel Madden Records, source and date unknown, Thelma Hand Collection

Review of Damage Done By Flood, Dillon Tribune, Dillon, Montana, June 17, 1927, Maggie's Scrapbook

Rock Creek School by Thelma (Hand) Kalsta, Thelma Hand Collection

Roscoe "Rock" Hand Personal Records, Interviews, Writings and Notes

Roscoe, "Rock" Hand Interview, Montana Historical Society Oral History interview, with permission from Montana Historical Society, Helena, Montana

Rural Electric Line Energized, Dillon Tribune, December 20, 1939, Thelma (Hand) Kalsta Diary

School Monies, Dillon Tribune, Dillon, Montana, December 30, 1892

Sheriff's Office, Madison County, Virginia City, Montana

Some Afterthoughts About Rural School Education by Susan Hand, Susan Hand Collection

State Legislature, Tribune, Dillon, Montana, January 13, 1893

Story Reveals Vipond Had to Use Great Strategy to Obtain Justice in Mexico, Montana Standard, Butte, Montana, date unknown, from Maggie's Scrapbook, Maggie Hand Collection

Susan (Hand) Personal Records, Interviews, Writings and Notes

Susan (Shirley) Halbert Passes, Beloit News, Beloit, Kansas, Susan Hand Collection

Terrific Flood Takes Toll of Four Lives in Wise River Section Early Tuesday Morning When Upper Reservoir Dam Breaks, (Headlines),The Dillon Tribune, Dillon, Montana, June 17, 1927, from Maggie's Scrapbook

Thelma (Hand) Kalsta Diaries, Personal Records, Interviews, Writings and Notes

Time Marches On, by Rock Hand, Helena, Montana, The Madisonian, Virginia City, Mt. December 15, 1983, used by permission from the Madisonian

U.S. Census, 1850, El Dorado Co., California, from Susan Hand Collection

Under Many Tons of Snow, Dillon Examiner, Dillon, Montana, December 6, 1893

When Automobiles Came to Melrose, Montana, by Roscoe "Rock" Hand, from Rock Hand Collection

William Halbert: An Unsung Legend, by Rita Horton McDavid, Anderson, (S.C.) Independent , April 10, 1971

Women's Home Companion, January 1949

INDEX

A

Abling
　Alfred, 77
　Lillie, 77
Accidents, 136
Acker
　Susanna, 4
　William, 4
Adams, Will, Mr. & Mrs., 92
Ahders
　Mrs., 249
　N, Mr. & Mrs., 204
Allen
　B.F., 99
　Mr., 200
Ames
　Claud, 156
　Guy, 123, 147, 156
　Mr. & Mrs., 144
Anderson
　Al, 154
　Clark, 256
　Robert, 3
Anderson County, 3
Anderson District, 17
Annen Store, 130
Argenta, 96, 230, 235, 268
Armstrong, Noah, 96
Atlantus Mine, 96
Atwater
　Mary, 210, 270
　Maxwell W., 270
Austine, Mrs., 71
Automobiles, 199
Avon Mine, 96
Axe, Mrs., 138

B

Badger, Mrs., 259
Barbour, Sam A., 140
Barrett, Bob, 233
Barrows, Willard, 99
Bartleson, W., 198
Bateman, H.K., 156
Bayers, Mr., 234
Bayley
　Della, 73
　Elgan, 73
　Hattie, 73, 80, 85
　Linlie, 73
　Mrs., 71, 72
　Obediah, 72
　Therne, 73
Beattie
　Bob, 142, 150, 184
　Ed, 184
Bedard, Joe, 123
Bedards, 146
Beeher, Frankie, 247
Beehers, 227
Beehrer
　George, 204
　Mr. & Mrs., 204
Bellow, Issac, 126
Bells, 95
Ben-Freighting Dog, 155
Bennet, Eva, 114
Bents, Robert, 85
Bergman, John, 156
Bergstrom,
　Mrs., 140
　Nick, 140
Berry, Elizabeth, 4
Bielenberg, John, 99
Big Al - See Halbert, Al and Seth
Big Hole Battlefield Monument, 180
Big Hole Dam, 167
Bird, Tommy, 256, 274
Biuskirk, 5
Blotcher, 64
　Ella, 80
Boettaker Sr., Mrs., 237
Boetticher, Otto, 256
Boggs
　Etta, 56
　Margaret, 56
Boiler to Gibbonsville, 152
Bolton, 4, 5, 6
　Abanatha, 20, 58
　Fanny, 58
　Rhoda, 20, 21
Bond, 5
　Dr., 111
Bonds, 58
Booker, Bill, 86
Boomer, 167
Bow, 196
Briggs, 64, 80
　Annie, 127, 198, 202, 220, 258, 267, 272 - See Halbert, Annie
　Arta, 220
　Bert, 203

Emma, 198, 202, 220, 231 - See Halbert, Emma
Frank, 77, 79, 90, 259
Harry, 203
Hattie, 77, 79
Herbert, 59, 81, 90
Ken, 220
Lucy, 231
Brodridge, Jack, 104
Brook, Lloyd, 277
Broom Corn, 67
Brown
  Clay, 77
  David, 4
  Effie, 273
  Fanny, 183
  Francis, 243
  Frank, 183
  James, 4
  Jim, 200
  Joe A., 183, 209, 210, 222
  Joe A., Jr., 183
  Joseph A., 196
  May, 183
  Mildred - See Ralston, Mildred
  Tom, 148
Browne, Joe H., 184
Brubaker, Al, 98, 105, 121, 125, 136, 141, 179, 193
Bruce, Mr & Mrs., 137
Bruner, 55
Bruners, 5
Bryan
  Cora, 204
  Eliza, 204
  Frank, Mr. & Mrs., 204
  George, 183
Bryant
  Annie, 108
  E.G., 117, 118, 121, 134, 140, 146, 148, 150, 151, 153, 173
  Jane, 121, 130, 141, 198
  Lillie, 191
  Maude, 108
  Minnie, 108, 121, 146
  Rebecca J. "Jane" (Howard) Woodson, 108
  Sherman, 108, 117, 141
  Tillie, 108
Bryant Hotel, 123, 182
Bulpin, Mr., 139
Butler, Ben, 189, 226
Buyan
  Angela, Miss, 204
  Ann, Miss, 204
  Billie, 248
  Frank, 247
  Joe, 133, 135, 248
  Mary, Miss, 204

C

Calomel, 56
Cambich. - See Kambich
Camelites, 71
Camp Creek Stock Association, 200
Camp Fire Girls, 266
Campbell
  Chester, 231
  Emma, 178, 231
  Mary Emily, 2
  Wallace, 231
Candidates, 135
Carley, Mr., 208, 210
Carmont, John, 182
Carpita, Mary (Zunino), 197
Carr, James, 101
Carruthers, Mr., 210
Carter, Dr., 60
Carver, Eugene, 116
Cashman, Vin, 75, 93
Cattle from the Salmon River Country, 170
Caughey, 80, 87
  Kim, 80
  Mary, 80
  Mrs., 71
  Sam, 80
  Violet, 80
Census, Territory and State of Montana, 95, 119, 194, 231
Chapin
  J., 78
  Win, 75
Chapman, Minnie, 77
Charles, 4, 6
  Francis - See Halbert, Francis
  Samuel, 17
Chenoweth, Fannie, 252
Chicken Business, 239
Chicken Gulch Sheep and Cattle Fight, 200
Childs
  Billie, 69, 90
  Lee, 70
  Mr., 68
  Mrs., 91
Chinaman, 117
Cholera, 56
Christian, Karl, 200
Christmas, 141, 199

Church Suppers
    Box Suppers, 69
    Mush and Milk Suppers, 69
    Neck Tye Suppers, 69
    Oyster Stews, 69
Churchill
    Maggie, 159
    Russel, 159
    Warren, 100, 159, 182
Citizenship, 159
Clark, W.A., 114, 135, 145, 157
Clayton, Mr., 126
Cleopatra Mine, 96
Cleve, 96
Cline
    Al, 98, 136, 137
    Ed, 130, 136
    Mr & Mrs., 136
Coburn, Colonel John, 25, 41
Coles, Mr., 90
Colling, Tillie, 79
Collins
    Allen, 200
    John, 200, 281
Coloma, 15
Concella, Billie, 114
Conklin
    Alvaretta - See Hand, Alvaretta
    Barbara Ann, 261
    Darlene, 272
    Earl Lincoln, Jr., 263
    Earl(Miggs), 249, 254, 268
Connor, Pat, 200
Conway, George B., 96, 256
Copp, 126
Corder, Dad, 227
Corduroy Road, 46
Cosgrove, John, 205
Cotton, Mrs., 80
Coursen
    Christopher E., 91
    Jeff, 91
    Jeffie, 80
    John, 80, 91
    Lizzie, 80, 91
    Mr., 71
    Nora, 91
Coursen's Grove, 80, 91
Cow Puncher, 261
Coward
    Bryant, 5
    J., 5
Cramer
    Ed, 149
    Joe, 265
Crides, Lewis, 90
Crist, Henry, 38
Crosgrove, 5
Cullum, 137
Cummins, John, 242
Cushing, Bill, 230

D

Dahler, Charles L., 96
Darcie, 175
Datenal, 3
Daugherty, A., 198
Davis
    Jack, 107, 136
    Kenneth, 251
Dean
    Abe, 155, 262
    Mrs., 152
Decker, 137
    Mr., 230
Demmins, P., 168
Deno
    Grandma, 144
    Mrs., 104
Denos, 108
Dent, 267
Dentist in Kansas, 88
DeRivers, Louis, 200
Dewey, Dave, 104
Dewey's Flat Mining District, 104
Dickenson, Gale, 249
Dickie, Fred, 142, 144, 145, 152, 153, 185
Ditches, 189
Divide, 146
Divide Cemetery, 143
Dixon, 115
Doblier, D., 243
Dodd, Jimmie, 171, 261
Dodge, F. Mr. & Mrs., 204
Dodgson
    Babe, 144
    George, 97, 170, 256
    Hazel, 121
    Isaac, 97, 98, 118, 121, 179, 256
    Maude, 97, 121, 170, 256
    May, 187, 245
    Millie, 187
    Sherman, 170
    Tice, 97, 98, 170, 173, 193
Dodgson, Sr., Mrs., 130

Dodgsons, 108
Dolman
  Mrs., 141, 143
  Peter, 116
  Tommy, 126
Dolman's store, 123
Donovan
  Jim, 199
  Jim, Mr. & Mrs., 230
  Mary Speelman, 196
  Mrs., 197, 198
Donovan's Parrot, 230
Doolittle, 141
Douglas, Harriet C., 271
Drummy School, 236
Duffy, John, 102
Duncan School, 231
Dunlop, Eugene, 200
Dupee, Mr., 133

E

Earl
  Edith, 207
  Mabel, 207
  Mr., 206, 210
  Mrs., 206, 210
Earl Ranch, 206, 210
Earl's Siding, 207
Edgerton, Sydney, 96
Edgger, Ike, 137
Edison, Dan, 114
Eighorn
  Annie, 273
  George, 256
  Henry, 202
Elder, George, 246
Elgan
  Dela, 80
  Hatie, 80
  Linnlie, 80
  Theme, 80
Eliel, Tyrie and Burfiend Company, 123
Eliel, Lambert, 138
Eliels, 110
Elrod, Mrs., 84
Epworth League, 71
Escrow Agreement, 232
Evans
  John, 105, 131
  Mr., 199

F

Family Wish, 289
Fancett, William, 16
Fassler, Alois, Mr. & Mrs., 204
Fasslet, Florence, 252
Fence posts, 68
Ferdinand Mine, 230
Ferguson, Mr., 121
Ferguson, 242
  Bill, 244
  Charles, 226
  George, 210, 218
  J.C., 256
Fiddler, Mrs., 244
Fisher, 199
Fitchen, Juanita, 204
Fitschen, Gus, Mr. & Mrs., 204
Flannegan, Rean, 185
Fleming
  Bill, 200
  Faye Thompson, 195
Flemming
  Fay, 284
  Si, 250
Flowers, 82
Foley, Frank, 129
Foote, L. R., Mr. & Mrs., 204
Forester, Mrs., 246
Forrest
  George, 145
  Johnnie, 145
  Mary, 145, 273
  Mrs., 145
  William, 145
Fort Bridger, 13
Francis
  Adda, 75
  Etta, 75
Frank, Henry, 167
Franklin Mine, 96
Frassler, Florence, 244
Fremont, John, 99
French Lick, 4
French, Tony, 273
Friend
  Jim, 138
  Sam, 262

G

Gahnett, Louise, 68
Galahan, Tom, 129
Galbraith, 142

George, 105
Mr., 143
Mrs. Scott, 115
Scot, 105, 145
Galholly, Miss, 185
Gallogly, Mary A., 222
Gannon, John, 96
Garnett, Mr., 247
Garrett, Sam, 98
Garrison
   Annette, 284
   Bernard, 279
   Bill, 238
   Eliza, Mrs, 204
   Frankah, 4
   J.B., 233, 234, 236, 275 - See Garrison, J. Bernard
   Jim, 103, 233
   Nettie, 269, 275 - See Hand, Nettie
Garrison, Eliza, 204
Garrison, J. Bernard - See Garrison, J. B.
Garrisons, 227
Garry, Jim, 115
Geering, Mable, 70
Gelhaus
   Joe, 256
   John, 256
Gentle
   Mrs., 98
   Percy, 106
Gentles, 95
Gibbons School, 231
Gibbonsville, 114, 154
Gilbert,
   Deda, 250
   Harry, 107
   Tom, 281
Gist, D, 156
Gleed, Mrs., 240
Glendale, 96, 102
Glover, Pete, 269
Gnose, J.B., 185
Goldburgs, 262
Golden, Mr., 70
Goldsmith mine, 118
Gransberry
   Bud, 219
   F., Mr. & Mrs., 204
Grant
   Mrs. J.W., 204
   Sybil, 204
Grass Valley, California, 15
Green, F.C., Mr & Mrs., 204
Green Mound, 80

Grey Jockey Mine, 118, 125
Grisham
   John, 4
   Martha, 4
Griswold
   Al, 104, 165, 167, 187
   Alvin, 112
   Lew, 104
   Lewis, 112
   Tillie, 104
Griswolds, 101
Gross, Geo., Mr. & Mrs., 204
Ground Hog Mine, 235, 240
Grown, George, 192
Grubb, 65
   Mr., 63
   Mrs., 62

H

Hadden, Hattie, 5
Hagenbarth, 183
Halbert, 2, 12
   Al, 104, 112, 120, 125, 127, 135, 136, 139, 143, 146, 147, 152, 170, 171, 178, 179 - See Halbert, Seth & Big Al
   Al, Mr. & Mrs., 204
   Annie, 52, 53, 62, 69, 75, 76, 81, 82, 88 - See Briggs, Annie
   Arthur, 3, 6
   Azor, 6, 11, 15, 16
   Big Al, 110 - See Halbert, Al & Seth
   Cynthia Harriet, 22
   Elizabeth, 3, 4, 6
   Emma, 56, 69, 75, 76, 77, 79, 80, 81 - See Briggs, Emma
   Emma Susan, 34
   Enos, 1, 3, 5, 6, 8, 9, 14, 15, 16, 18, 20, 23, 25, 26, 27, 29, 32, 34, 35, 37, 40, 50, 52, 59, 60, 65, 71, 85, 90, 91, 92, 94, 198, 202
   Enos, Jr., 55
   Ezra, 5
   Frances, 5, 20
   Francis, 6
   Garrett, 56
   Hattie, 59, 60, 69, 77, 79, - See Jones, Hattie
   Henry, 3
   James, 3, 6
   Joel, 3, 4, 6, 11, 16, 18, 20, 53
   John, 3, 5, 6, 11, 16
   Joshua, 4, 6
   Lucinda, 4, 6

Maggie, 52, 62, 75, 76, 77, 81, 94, 120 - See Hand, Maggie
Martha, 6
Mary, 4, 6, 23, 53
Mary Frances Catherine. 11 - See Wilson, Mary
Micha, 60
Rhoda, 58, 60
Sarah, 6, 23, 59, 60
Sarah Elizabeth, 22, 202
Seth,5, 7, 11, 14, 15, 16, 19, 20, 53, 55, 58, 59, 60, 66, 77, 79, 110, 198, 202 - See Halbert, Al & Big Al
Silas, 5, 6, 11, 20, 21, 23, 60
Susan, 11, 18, 23, 56, 60, 71, 92, 202
Susannah, 6
Walter, 19
Walter P., 16
William, 2, 3, 16
William, Jr., 6
Willie, 55

Hall
  Bob, 271
  Dr., 235
  Mark, 129
Halls, John, 204
Hamby, Ben, 132
Hamples, 200
Hand, 95, 219
  Alvaretta, 249 - See Conklin, Alvaretta
  Alvaretta Pauline Maggie, 212
  Babe, 204
  Byron, 167, 170, 195, 213, 214, 216, 223, 228, 229
  Carl, 95
  Children, 171, 193, 211
  Earl Seth, 223, 230
  Ed, 95
  Hazel, 204
  Horace, 101, 102, 106, 111, 112, 121, 128, 135, 139, 143, 146, 147, 148, 150, 151, 156, 170, 171, 179, 195, 200, 204, 212, 213, 217, 232, 235, 242, 256
  Horace Delos, 237
  Horace, Mr. & Mrs., 204
  Howard, 95
  Ida, 273 - See Hartwig, Ida
  John, 95, 107, 165, 169, 170, 177, 195, 200, 201, 203, 204, 216, 221, 226, 229, 232, 235, 240, 250, 256, 273, 277, 287
  John T., 211
  John William, 164
  Louise, 216, 237 - See Shafer, Louise
  Maggie, 157, 195, 198, 202, 210, 213, 216, 218, 231, 235, 248, 258, 266, 269, 272, 274, 277, 285, 286 - See Halbert, Maggie
  Nettie, 170, 173, 177, 178, 195, 196, 198, 204, 213, 216, 217, 218, 229, 231, 232, 236, 287 - See Garrison, Nettie
  Richard, 95
  Rock, 199, 203, 205, 213, 216, 218, 229, 231, 232, 233, 234, 275, 277 - See Hand, Roscoe
  Roger, 285
  Roscoe, 164, 178, 179, 204, 288 - See Hand, Rock
  Shirley Ann, 234
  Susan, 198, 213, 216, 223, 231, 232, 234, 258, 269, 274, 277, 288
  Thelma, 177, 195, 213, 216, 223, 229, 288 - See Kalsta, Thelma
  Hand, Verna, 244 - See Ogilvie, Verna
  Virginia Lea, 264
  William, 95
  William Murray, 219, 268
  Willie, 161
Hardisty, G.R., 156
Harper, William, 4
Hartman
  Fred, 204
  George, 268
Hartwig
  Fredrick Julius, 228
  Ida, 201,204 - See Hand, Ida
  Isabell, 239
  Jacob, Mrs., 204
  Julius, 204, 256
  Julius, Jr., 228, 235
  Julius, Mr. & Mrs., 204
  Julius, Sr., 237, 249
  Louise, 204 - See Kambich, Lucy
  Pauline, 228, 239
Hartwig Bros., 204
Harvey
  Bill, 212, 250
  Ed, 156
  Herb, 212
  Otto, 202
Harwood, Mrs., 219
Hater, Jennett, 115, 148
Hauser, K., Mr. & Mrs., 204
Hay
  Alen, 97, 108, 179
  Allen, 104
  Bob, 97
  Clad, 97, 108, 262
  Ed, 108
  Henry, 97
  Hugh, 124
  John, 108, 180, 263
  Lillie, 124

Hays, 95
Hecla Consolidated Mining Company, 96
Hecla Mercantile & Banking, Inc. Ledger, 161
Hecla Mine, 96
Heinz, Mrs., 202
Helena Earthquake, 241
Helm, Boone, 196
Herndon, Mr., 230
Hiatt, John D., 94
Higging, 5
Hilbinger, K.N., 156
Hirschy, Mr. & Mrs., 161
Hix, Sam, 7
Hoblet, 5
Hoffman Jr., Mrs., 237
Hoffman, Mrs., 250
Hoffmeister, W.C., 198
Hollinsworth., 154
Hope Guard, 25
Hopkins
  Alfred, 132
  Annie, 132
  Arthur, 132
  Etta, 132, 190
  Harry, 132
  Mark, 132
Horup, Jack, 254
Houghton, Wm., 198
Howard, George, 156
Howe, Mr., 68
Huber Bros., 204
Huber, Mrs. Geo., 246
Huddleson, 5
Hudtloff, Pastor M., 204
Hugh, Mr. & Mrs., 151
Hughes, Cary - See Lewis, Cary
Hull, 262
Humphry, Miss, 138
Hungate, 180
  N.I., 156
Hurtzels, Garrott, 58

I

Innes, Miss, 138
Inventory and Appraisement, 268
Irwin, Joseph L., Rev., 50

J

J. A. Brown, 118
J. P. Lossel Store Co., 137
J. T. Murphy Transportation Company, 102
Jackson
  Andy, 100, 118
  Nancy Catherine (Shirley), 88
Jacobs, Mr. & Mrs., 204
Jay Hawk, 118
Jellison, C.L. Mrs., 205
Jennings, 80
  Bill, 80
  Bob, 80
  Cecil, 80
  Tulip, 156
  Virgil, 105
  Wm., 156
Jewel, George, 110
Johnson, Mrs., 79
Johnston, Alex, 221
Jones
  Arthur, 256
  Mr. & Mrs., 204
  Delbert, Mr & Mrs., 204
  Dr., 143
  Hattie, 198, 202 - See Halbert, Hattie
  Jake, 64, 79
  Joe, 64
  Levi, 82
  Loren, 111
  Maude, 204
  Mr., 64, 68
  Nelson, 64
  Sam, 64
  W.A., 112
  Walter, 189
  White, 64
  Wilber, 64
Josie, 149
Joy, Robert, Mr. & Mrs., 204
Judgment, 285
Juice (Electrification), 266
Junction City, Oregon, 213, 258

K

Kalsta
  Aystein, 258
  Gunnar, 251
  Lars, 228, 229, 232, 275, 277
  Thelma, 231, 232, 268, 275 - See Hand, Thelma
Kambich
  Carl, 218, 249
  Frank, 238, 240
  Joe, 218
  John, 238, 256
  Louise, 228
  Lucy, 238, 240, 243 - See Hartwig, Louise

Keith
   Kato, 242, 246
   Maude, 242, 246
Keith, Mrs. Carrie, 230
Keller,
   Cheo, 153
   Ches, 147
Kennedy
   Annie, 106
   Dave, 106
Kingsberry, Margaret, 62
Kinney's, 147
Kinobby, Professor, 104
Kinsey
   Bill, 94
   Firatie, 94
   Mary, 94
   Mrs., 71, 94
Kitto's, 245
Knippenberg, Henry, 96, 140

L

L. C. Fyhrie, 118
Lacy
   William, 197
   Mr. & Mrs., 204
Ladies Social Club, 204
Lamb, Jimmy, 200
Lane, Rev. Jim, 69
Langley, Floyd, 183
Lanterns, 267
Larson, Miss, 219
Lavon, 206, 216
Lawrence
   B.B., 265
   Eva, 124
   Grandma, 119
   Jennette, 105
   Jessie, 107
   John, 97, 105, 106, 136, 193
   Lucy, 107
   Mable, 124
   May, 124
   Walter, 105, 158
Lawrences, 95
Laybold, Peter, 156
Leach, Zula Lloyd, 246
Lebos, 108
Lee, Light-horse Harry, 3
Legal Tender, 96

Legatte, 180
Leggatt
   Alec, 104
   John, 104
   Rod, 104
Lenkersdorfer, John, Mr. & Mrs., 204
Lester, Mrs., 244
Lewis
   Addison, 191
   Cary, 191
   Ernest, 191
   Frankie, 191, 244
   Glen, 191
   Joe, 191
   Kate, 191, 244
   Louise, 191
   Max, 191
   Maxine, 191
   Merryweather, 191
   Mr., 191
   Mr. & Mrs., 151
   Mrs., 191
   Obe, 170
   Obediah, 191
   Wilfred, 204
Lewis Family, 191
Leybold, Theo., 156
Lillis, Pat, 147
Lindlief
   Charley, 273
   Fred, 273
Lindley
   John 4, 17
   Mary, 4
   Sarah, 4 - See Pyle, Sarah
Lindsey, 4 (*used interchangeably with Lindley*)
Linenweaber, Mr. & Mrs., 254
Linn
   Mr., 91
   Mrs., 91
Linnewealz, Tony, 251
Linnon, Jess, 83
Lion City, 96
Lion Mountain, 96
Lishner, Frank, 246
Lively
   Berl, 256
   Mr. & Mrs., 248
Lone Pine, 104
Lone Pine Mine, 118
Long, Jim, 98, 115, 123, 147
Lossel, George, 147
Lossl, J.P., 256

Lott, Mort, 196
Luban, Dugan, 254
Lyons, Billy, 256

M

Mack
   Frank, 73
   Mr., 70
Maddix, 126
Madison, 185
Maier, A., Mr. & Mrs., 204
Major Jim, 210
Mallon
   Ben, 155, 177, 184, 187, 256
   Millie, 177
Mallow, Hank, 69
Malory, Bill, 237, 245
Marcasau, Mrs., 169
Markley's Grove, 72
Marrow, 227
Marstin
   Mr., 145
   Mrs., 145
Marysville, 15
Mast
   Carl, 256
   Isabell, 235 - See Hartwig, Isabell
Masters, Bud, 231
Mathers, 5
Mathias Creek, 16
Mattresses, 263
Mauz, Thaddous, 204
Maxwell Car, 214
McBride, John R., 25
McCarl, Jno., 156
McCauley
   Marion, 248
   Vince, 199
   Violet, 245, 248
McClellan, Bill, 113, 161, 172, 175
McClellans, 95
McClosed, June, 269
McCrea,
   John, 29
   John, Rev., 50
McDavid, Rita Horton, 3
McDowall, Mr., 70
McElroy, John, 43
McGee, Charlie, 205
McGill, Dr., 236, 239, 246, 269
McGowan, Mrs, 204
McKays, 108

McKinney, Pat, 162, 170
McKinzie, 135, 194, 245
   Earnest, 108, 194
   Jim, 194
   Laura, 194
   Maude, 194
   Mollie, 108
McKinzies, 108
McLaughlin, 202
McLean
   J.W., Mr. & Mrs., 204
   Vincent, 204
McMaster, Dan, 102
McMeekin, Jimmie, 242
McMonigal, Madie, 263
McPherson, 242
   David, 2
   Nathan, 2
McVey, 187
Meade, Mrs., 204
Metlen, David, 102
Mezel
   Elwin, 242
   Mrs., 242
Midnight Mine, 240
Midwives, 148
Miles, Frank, 115
Mill, Emma, 79
Miller
   Dana, 107
   Jessie, 243
   John A., 90
Millard, Joe, 99
Miller, Mrs., 244
Mills - Grist & Saw, 88
Mitchell
   Baling Wire, 118
   Jim "Baling Wire", 122
Mittelmier, Jake, 204
Molleur
   Ailene, 256
   Mrs., 256
Money order, 134
Moor, Linnie, 246
Moore
   Bill, 200
   Charley, 189, 262
Moose Creek, 203
More, Dal, 107
Morrow, Dr., 244
Mudd, Kip, 137
Mueller, Dr., 198, 199
Mulcy, Mr, 190

Mulrany, Dave, 2
Murphy
  John L., 102
  Maggie, 186
Murray, Agnes M., 184
Murry, Frank, 91

N

N. Armstrong & Company, 96
N.Y.A. Weaving Job, 269
Narrow Gauge Railway, 103
Neal, Harry, 154
Neay, Allan, 112
Nester, Ruth Morris, 246
New, Jimmie, 100, 114, 157, 166
New Albany, 17
Nez Perces, 197
Nicknames, 255
Nikel, Ed, Mr. & Mrs., 204
Nobern, Mag, 136
Noblet, 24
Noblit, 5
Nye, Phil Mrs., 237

O

O Lera, Mable, 254
Ogilvie, Verna, 233 - See Hand, Verna
O'Harra, Molly, 186
O'Leary
  Gen, 216
  Miss., 221
Oliver
  Fred, Mr. & Mrs., 204
  Gladys, 204
One Pine Mine, 104
Orange County, 6
Orangeville, 6
Ordeway
  Hide, 158
  Ida, 263
Orem,Con, 102
Orsburn, Mr., 169
Overly
  Flora, 127, 142
  Hank, 127, 142
  Henry, 113, 127, 142
  Lillie, 124, 127, 142
  Mr., 142
  Mrs., 127, 128, 142
Owen, Quitman, 256
Owens
  Llija, 3

  Ralph, 3

P

Padgett, 90
Palmer, Mr., 158
Parsons, 167
Partridge
  Harry, 104
  John, 104
  Nick, 104
Pattengale, George, 112 - See Pettingill, George
Patton, 97
  Ethel, 136, 186
  George, 186
  Hugh, 183, 185
  Maggie, 187
  Mary, 136, 186
  Mrs., 136, 142, 169, 186
  Rose, 136, 186
Pearl Harbor, 272
Pearson, Laura, 75
Pelton, Tom, 185
Pendleton District, 3, 19
Perdue, Danna, 269
Peter, Art, 255
Peterson
  Andrew, 79
  Charley, 66, 75, 78, 79
  David, 75
  Dolph, 131
  Hanna, 75, 79
  John, 78
  Johnnie, 172
  Lesslie, 75
  Mrs. Charley, 77
  Myra, 77, 78, 80
Pettingill, George, 104, 166 - See Pattengale
Pfiefer, Pauline - See Hartwig, Pauline, & Polly
Piano Box, 202
Piccone
  Dan, 228
  Mr. & Mrs., 248
Pickens
  Andrew, 3
  William, 17
Pickett
  A.L., 102
  Laura, 144, 146, 156
  Lou, 144, 146
  Mrs., 120
Pierce, Mrs., 240
Pitcher, 5

Pochantas, 3
Pond and Vance store, 149
Pool, Mac, 243
Potts, Joe, 107
Pourers, L.C., 144
Powell
   Bert, 137
   Jinks, 114
   John W., 114
Powell's Valley, 27
Prairie Wolves, 83
Preacher Honk, 55
Prewett
   Bill, 75
   Oilgal, 75
   Rose, 75
   Tom, 75
   Will, 72
Prickly Pear Post, 238
Prideaux
   Captain, 131, 146
   Harry, 104, 129
   Jim, 104, 129
Prummely, Ruth, 19
Pyle, Sarah, 4 - See Lindley, Sarah

Q

Quartz Hill Mining District, 104
Queens County, 95
Quinine, 60, 179

R

Rain - 1905, 175
Raker, George, 196
Ralston, 137
   Charles, 256
   Charley, 142, 144, 149
   Ed, 144
   Mildred, 144, 243
   Mr & Mrs., 137, 150
   Mrs., 150
   Sis, 144
Rattlesnake Creek, 96
Ray, Andy, 115, 256
Redburn, Mrs., 238
Redfern, Jim, 166
Reichle
   Art, 273
   Ettie, 145
   Frank, 116, 142, 145, 189
   George, 273
Reid
   Clifford, 235
   Lois, 248
   Mary, 248
Reins, Mrs., 67
Reynolds
   Adelia, 206
   Benny, 199
   Ernest, 206
   Henry, 210
   Henry S., 206
   Mrs., 199
   Mrs. Bub, 120
   Vinton, 206
Rhino, John, 156
Rhodes, Sam, 142, 148, 155
Rhoeder, John, 114
Rieber
   Chris, 216
   Elizabeth, 221
   Johnny, 221
   Regina, 250
Rieves, Jim, 90
Rife, Mr. & Mrs., 245
Ritschel,
   Etta, 145, 189
   Frank, 116,129,145,189
Ritter, Dr., 60
Roads, 136
Roads or Trails, 179
Robbins, 97
   John, 107
Robbison, Nade, 93
Robinson, 236
Rock Creek School, 217
Rodgers Gap, 27
Rodgerson, Mr & Mrs., 167
Roe, Ed, 119
Rolk, Mr., 247
Roskie, Dan, 251
Rothrock, Henry Shirley, 1
Rutherford
   Mamie, 76
   Mr., 72

S

Sagebush Tea, 179
Salt Lake, 13
Sassman, 217
Sassman, C., Mr. & Mrs., 204
Schmid, Pat, 204
School Meetings, 106
School Monies, 136, 151

School Outing, 125
Schools, 74
Schuler, Harriet, 243
Schultz Brothers, 200
Schultz, Boby, 147

Scott, 5
   Laura Tolman, 96
Seaman
   Mrs., 71
   Rev., 70, 73
Seylers, 200
Shafer
   Carl, 269
   Jack, 240, 273
   Louise, 269 - See Hand, Louise
   Myrna Carol, 284
Shafer Mine, 240
Sharkey, Clark, Miss, 156
Sheelar, Mrs., 244
Sherman, General W.L., 25
Shirley, 1, 12
   Betsy, 2, 56
   Catherine, 1
   Cliff, 62
   Dell, 62
   Francis, 62, 87
   Garrett, 1, 62
   George, 2, 10, 24, 54
   Harriet, 1
   Henry, 1, 4, 5, 62
   Henry Wilson, 2
   Jacob, 4
   Jane, 62
   Kate, 62
   LeRoy O'Blenis, 2
   Lizzie, 57
   Mag, 62
   Margaret, 1
   Maria Lavinia Elizabeth, 2
   Samuel Albert, 2
   Susan, 1, 5 - See Halbert, Susan
   Valentine, 1, 4
   William Crawford, 2
Shirts, Mr., 71
Shirtz, Reverent, 55
Shultz, Bobby, 123
Sidenstickers, 200
Silver Bow Bill, 137
Simoni, Gemma M., 284
Sinnbaugh, John, 175
Slate, George, 254
Slater, 199

Smail, Billie, 126, 148
Smith
   Don, 251
   Dr., 67
   Jack, 200, 246, 256
   Pat, 200, 219, 237
   Pearl I, 218
Smock, Mrs., 145
Snodgrass, Mrs., 241, 247
Snow Slide, 140
Soap Gulch, 103
Solomon, 63
Some Afterthoughts About Rural School Education, 216
Soper, 97
Sopher, 192
Speakman
   Annie, 75
   Eddie, 78
   Emma, 75
   Henry, 75
Speelman
   Eddie, 77
   James, 196
   Jim, 198
Sperrier
   Hank, 176
   Wolf, 177
Spinal Meningitis, 230
Spritzer, Peter, 204
Spur, Billy, 96
Spurr, Billie, 104
Squires
   Geneveve, 236
   Mr., 238
Stackhouse, 5
   Abling, 76
   Alfred, 55, 58, 73, 76
   Azor, 74, 76
   Drew, 73
   Fanny, 74, 76, 79
   George, 67, 74, 78
   Henry, 58, 64, 67, 68, 70, 73, 74, 78
   Hude, 74
   Jennie, 74
   Jess, 74
   John, 73
   Lillie, 76
   Lucy, 73
   Mary, 73
   Milton, 73
   Nancy, 73
   Polly, 74

Stanford, 73
Tom, 67, 74
Stages, 153, 179
Stanley, Mrs., 244
Staufferson
   Gus, 114, 262
   Mrs., 262
Stine, Asbury, 187
Stockdale, Mr., 200
Stone, 196
   A.P., 139
   Al, 135
Storm, Joe, 131, 222
Streb
   Albert, 243
   Bertha, 198
   Patsy, 200
   Ralph, 237, 256
Streb Brothers, 199
Street, Jimmie, 5
Strowbridge, Clarence, 137
Stuart, Granville, 96
Stubs, Govenor, 87
Summers, Matt, 205
Sutherland, 147
Swafford, Jess, 235
Swamp Creek, 154

T

Tate
   Frank, 199, 210, 256
   Frank P., 156
   Nina, 210
Teachers, 74
Teacher's Certificate, 141
Teachers Institute, 133
Teaslie, Wash, 67
Teasly, Nash, 74
Terry
   Grace, 156
   Luella, 156
Thirty Third Indiana, 25
Thomas
   M.J., 281
   R.Z., 105
   Tom, 123, 137
Thompson
   Anna, 75
   Annie Speakman, 75
   Boice, 96
   Homer, 75
   Hugh, 158, 226

   Joe, 75
   Mrs. Joe, 75
   Vera June, 195
   William, 96
   Wm., 102
Todd, Winnie, 169
Todoviche, 242
Tolivers, 5, 6
Toll bridge, 183
Tolviers, 4
Tong
   Babe, 118
   Bud, 118
   Effie, 118
   George, 118
   Georgia, 118
   Georgie, 137
   Gladys, 118
   Mr., 100
   Mrs., 118
Townsend, Dr., 164
Tradgett, Rev., 238
Trapper City, 96
Trapper Lode, 96
Tristler, Logan, 94
True Fissure Mine, 96
Trueman, 108
   Alice, 263
   Arthur, 262
   Bell, 263
   Charley, 124, 262
   Clara, 262
   Clova, 263
   Dick, 193, 262, 263
   Ed, 262
   Elsie, 124, 262
   Frankie, 263
   John, 124, 192, 262
   John B., Jr., 193
   Linnie, 124, 262
   Maude, 193
   Mrs., 160
   Mrs. J. B., 148
   Tracy, 226, 263
   Wendel, 263
Truth Seeker, 71, 91
Twiggs, Julia, 268

U

Ureka Chapel, 72
Urmy, Clarence, 286
Ustead, 234

V

Vance
- Ed, 121
- Ethel, 124
- G.R., 156
- George, 123, 135, 136, 139, 256
- Mary, 239
- Oscar, 145
- Pete, 79
- Peter, 77
- Roy, 124

Vance and Pond General Store, 123
Vanoy, 200
Vanvincent, Joseph, 144
VanWart
- Bertha, 108, 242, 257
- G., Mrs., 204
- Gilbert, 108

Vaughn
- Fred, 144
- Norman, 144

Veach, Mr., 60
Verbance, 245
Vermont Mine, 230
Vigilantes, 197
Vincennes, 12
- Big bridge swing out, 62
- Emigrant Corral, 61
- Ferry boat, 12
- Wagon Train, 12

Vineyard, George, 192
Vipond
- Billy,(Billie), 98, 131, 183, 222
- John, 222
- William, 118

Vipond District, 98
Vipond Park Mining District, 104

W

Waddle, Absalom, 48
Wakes, 240
Wample, Joe, 204
Wanderlick, Louis, 256
Wanderlie Ditch, 179
Wanzer, 68
Wanzers, 64
Wanzer's Grove, 72
Waran, 55
Warefield, 93
Warner, Fred D., 90
Water Company, 116
Waters, Ernest & Jack, 204
Waters, John, Mr. & Mrs., 204
Webbe, Charles H., 101
Welborn, Sarah, 19
Wells
- Jimmie, 164
- Roy, 168

Wesley Chapel, 6, 54
West Baden, 4
Widger, Wm., 198
Wilber, Judge, 189
Wild Man of Wise River - See Pettingill
Wilkie, Mr. & Mrs., 167
Williams
- Maggie Hater, 115, 149
- Mrs., 240
- Tommy, 213

Williamson, E.B., 198
Willis Station, 206
Willoby, Mrs., 138
Wilnot
- Ed, 161
- Fred, 161

Wilshire
- Henry, 57, 60
- Mr., 57
- Tom, 57, 58, 61, 87

Wilson
- Eliza, 161
- Elizabeth, 2
- Enos, 66, 220
- Fred, 107, 161, 170
- John, 61, 64, 69, 70, 195
- John A., 59
- Margaret, 95
- Mary, 5, 64, 66, 71, 85, 95, 161, 198, 202, 220
- Mary (Mrs. J.A.), 231
- Nathanial, 5

Wilsons, 95
Wines
- Enos, 81, 91
- Mrs., 71
- Winnie, 70, 80

Winters, 167
Wise River, 225, 262
Wise River Dam, 225
Woodard,Mr., 80
Woods
- Charles, 256
- Fred, 176
- Pete, 123

Woodward ditch, 179
Woodward, Billie, 114, 273
Wooley, Joseph F., 90

Wornell, Pres, 28
Wyman, Catherine - See Shirley, Catherine

Y

Yellowstone Park, 252
Young
   Frank, 262
   Irman, 262
   Rhudolph, 262
   Ronal, 262

Z

Zabel, Ernest, 204
Zeigler, Joe, 191, 274
Zerr, Miss, 204
Zimmerman, Tommy, 249

www.ingramcontent.com/pod-product-compliance
Lightning Source LLC
Chambersburg PA
CBHW080408300426
44113CB00015B/2437